Flash MX Acti

The Designer's Edge

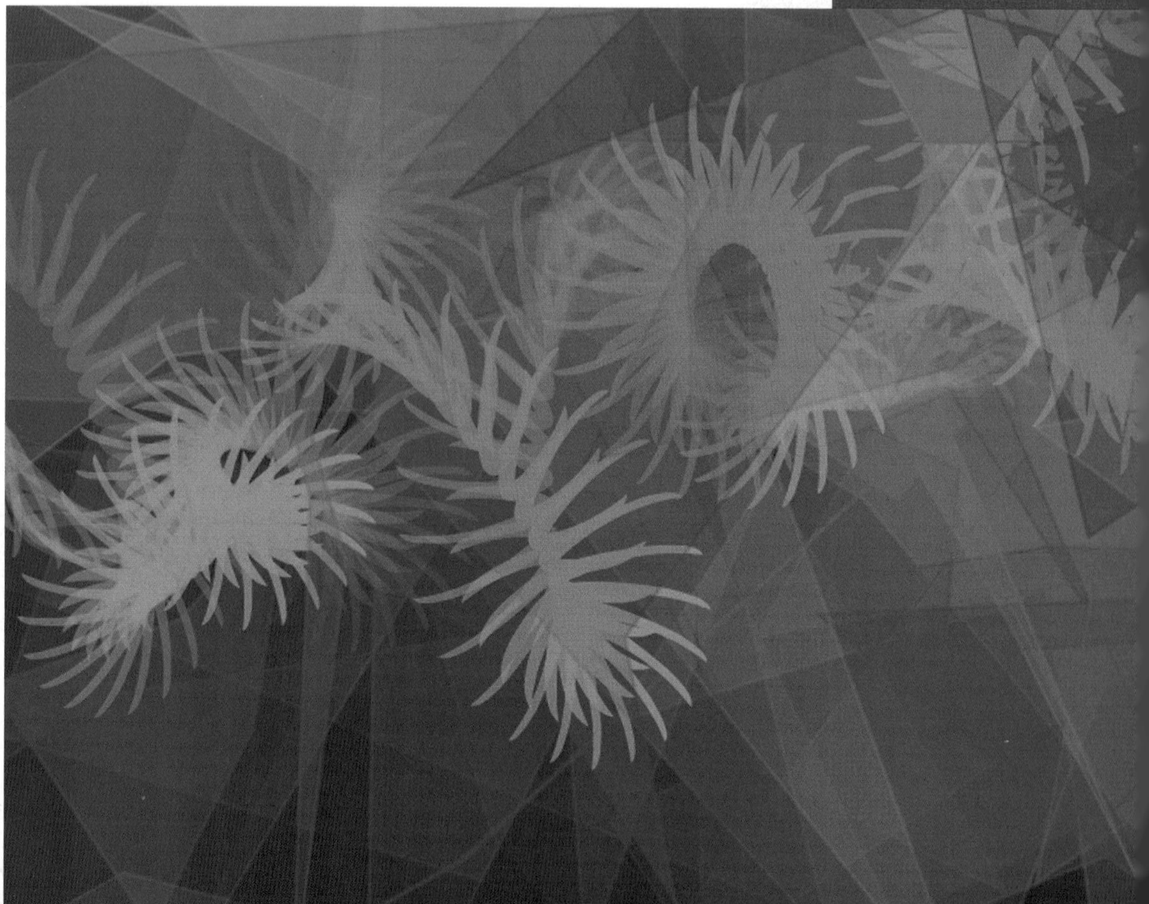

Flash™ MX ActionScript

The Designer's Edge™

J. Scott Hamlin

Jennifer S. Hall

SYBEX®

San Francisco • London

Associate Publisher: Dan Brodnitz
Acquisitions Editor: Mariann Barsolo
Developmental Editor: James A. Compton
Production Editor: Dennis Fitzgerald
Editor: Marilyn Smith
Technical Editor: Scott Balay
Book Design and Composition: Mark Ong, Side By Side Studios
Graphic Illustrator: J. Scott Hamlin
Proofreaders: Dave Nash, Laurie O'Connell, Nancy Riddiough
Indexer: Jack Lewis
Cover Designer: John Nedwidek, Emdesign
Cover Illustrator/Photographer: J. Scott Hamlin

Library of Congress Card Number: 2002108068
ISBN: 0-7821-4121-8

Manufactured in the United States of America
10 9 8 7 6 5 4 3 2 1

Acknowledgments

It was a great pleasure to work with Jennifer on this book. Jennifer is the uncommon programmer, who (gasp) actually has a life apart from bits and bytes. Jennifer was a kick to work with, while being a real professional throughout the entire project. Thank you Jennifer. I couldn't have asked for a better coauthor.

Thanks also to Mariann Barsolo for being such a trooper. Mariann really came through for us on some critical parts of our vision and helped us navigate the bumpy spots. She even put up with my incessant, tiresome need to talk things out to their *n*th degree with remarkable grace (I hope you were playing solitaire or something while I was blabbering away, Mariann). Seriously, thank you Mariann!! Thanks also to Daniel Gray for referring me to Mariann.

Thanks also to Scott Balay who did an excellent job, as usual, tech editing the book. Thanks for not pulling punches, Mr. Jive Ninja sir! Speaking of great editing, I'd also like to thank Dennis Fitzgerald, Marilyn Smith, and Jim Compton for their fine work in editing the book.

This book was easily the most all-consuming book I've ever worked on. Our schedule gave us more time than most books in this genre, and we ended up taking almost a month longer than planned (despite cutting a chapter or two). Through it all, Staci, my wife and best friend, was tirelessly supportive (as always). In addition my son, Aidan, and daughter, Audrey, provided numerous playful breaks that helped me maintain my sanity and perspective. Not one of you reading this can know how outstandingly blessed I am to have a wife like Staci and kids like Aidan and Audrey. It is no joke when I tell you that I am the richest man I know (and it has nothing whatsoever to do with my bank account, I can *assure* you).

Finally, out of sheer humble recognition of the raw facts, I am, as always, compelled to acknowledge the source. It is fully by the grace of God that I came to be capable of producing this book. For my part, it is He who should be given all credit, not me.

—Scott Hamlin

I would love to thank Scott Hamlin, so I will. Thank you Scott for being kind and patient, and for providing me with opportunities. I love working with you.

Thank you Cliff Hall and Susie Hall for being the greatest parents and always being supportive of my exploits, even the crazy ones.

Thank you Betty for being the best sister. I'm so glad you're my sister.

Thank you great friends for the encouragement and constant support.

Thanks Mariann Barsolo for helping us do this book.

—Jennifer Hall

About the Authors

Scott Hamlin

Scott Hamlin is the director of Eyeland Studio (www.eyeland.com and www.swiftlab.com). Eyeland Studio is a web-content design studio specializing in Flash game production and original content design. Eyeland Studio's client list includes Wrigley, Scholastic, Basic Fun, Nokia, Procter & Gamble, Sun Microsystems, MTV Europe, and Nabisco. Eyeland Studio produces several products sold over the Web and on CD-ROM. Eyewire.com, one of the world's largest stock imagery companies, carries Eyeland Studio's products. Eyeland Studio is also the creator of SwiftLab (www.swiftlab.com).

Scott is also the author/coauthor of numerous books, including *Flash 5 Magic* and *Flash 4 Magic*. He also writes for *Computer Arts Special* magazine and *AV Video and Multimedia Producer* magazine, and he writes a bi-monthly column called Flash Talk at www.graphics.com.

Jennifer Hall

Jennifer Hall produces multimedia training for JPMorganChase. She also teaches Flash and Director for Multimedia Enterprise. She has been a contributing author for *Flash 5 Magic* and technical editor for *Flash MX Magic, Drag, Slide, and Fade,* among other books. Jennifer has worked with leading multimedia companies including Top Drawer (Human Code (Sapient)), Cortex Interactive, and Eyeland Studio; and for clients including Disney, Prentice-Hall, Nokia, Lycos UK, Wrigley, and Holt, Rinehart and Winston. In her spare time, Jennifer eats, reads, runs, sits, rock climbs, dances, loves, and lives. Visit her at www.jennifershall.com.

Contents

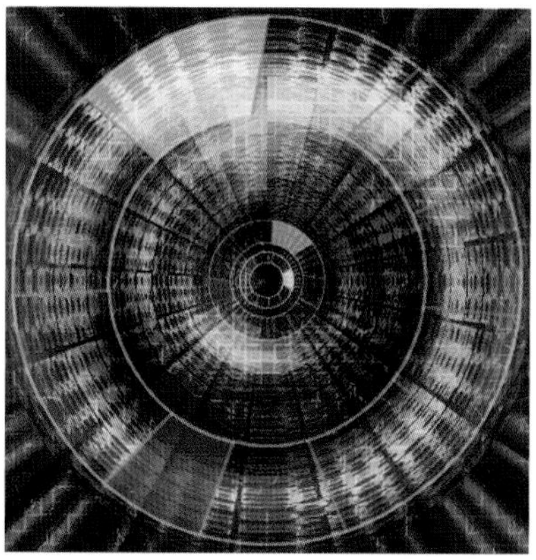

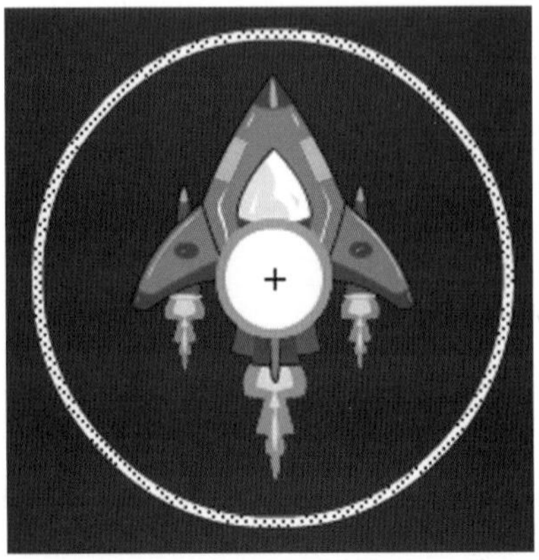

Introduction

Some designers and non-programmers might need to ask, "What exactly is ActionScript?" In very simple terms, ActionScript is a language that you can use to tell the Flash Player what to do with your movie. The Flash Player is the application or browser plug-in that displays the output of Macromedia Flash; in other words, it plays the `.swf` file.

The Flash Player is like a person who speaks only one language—let's say Swahili (if you're new to ActionScript, you may feel like it's Swahili). If you try to speak Spanish in order to talk to this person who speaks only Swahili, you're not likely to be understood. You're going to need to learn Swahili.

Now let's say that you know a little Swahili (your parents lost you for a few months when they went on safari). You might intend to say, "Give me a few sticks of that gum." But since you know only a little of the language, your Swahili-speaking associate might understand you to say, "Give me a swift kick in the bum." He would give you a quizzical look, shrug his shoulders, and .... You would realize there was a communication breakdown after you felt a particularly rude sensation on your backside.

Fortunately, you don't actually need to learn Swahili to issue commands to the Flash Player; you only need to learn ActionScript. However, you do need to learn it well enough to avoid rude sensations on your backside (which would probably come from your boss or client).

ActionScript can be daunting for those who do not have a programming background. If you're a designer with little or no programming experience, learning ActionScript can be difficult. You not only need to learn the specific syntax and structure of ActionScript, but how to devise programming solutions for your own applications. However, the rewards of using ActionScript to make your Flash movies are well worth the effort of learning it.

If you have some programming experience but have never worked with ActionScript, you'll most likely be productive with Flash scripting very quickly. You already understand the basic programming tools and processes.

Whether or not you have programming experience, this book will teach you how to reap the benefits of Flash ActionScript. By following the step-by-step instructions that walk you through producing working movies, you won't be just reading about ActionScript—you'll be applying it and seeing the results.

The Problem with Most ActionScript Books

The problem with most books on programming is that they are typically written by programmers, who are more adept at writing a program than they are at explaining how the program works. And they may be even more at a loss to explain to newcomers how the language itself works. Experienced programmers typically add comments to their code—short explanations of what a single instruction or block of code does. Books written by programmers are often merely an extension of these comments. They tell you the end result of the code, but not how the code actually works.

When programmers run into a programming concept that's difficult to explain, they tend to sort of skip over it; they make cognitive leaps when they are attempting to explain their code. These cognitive leaps are where books on scripting let down readers with little or no programming experience. Without the benefit of a programming background, you just can't understand how the script works.

Why We Think We Have the Solution

While there have been a growing number of ActionScript books out there, they have all been in one of two categories. They are either written by programmers or they are written by designers who only recently took up programming. So you either get a book that's essentially for experienced programmers or a book in which it's clear that the authors are a bit out of their realm.

This book was not written by a programmer, and this book was not written by a designer. This book was written by *both* a programmer and a designer. Jennifer Hall is the programmer, and she began the writing process by creating the examples and writing the first draft. She passed these drafts on to Scott Hamlin, the designer. Scott augmented the chapters, filling in gaps and adding explanations for the code. We think you'll find the results show that two heads really are better than one. You get the expertise of professional programmer combined with the sensibilities and needs of a designer.

This book takes a "don't tell me—*show* me" approach. Along with providing detailed explanations, we illustrate many programming concepts, so that designers—who tend to think more visually—can traverse those cognitive gaps you'll find in most programming books.

How to Use This Book

This book covers many basic topics, such as programming buttons or simple animations with ActionScript, and then moves steadily forward to more advanced ActionScript that professional Flash designers need to stay competitive. In the later chapters, this book covers topics such as designing math-based animations, drawing graphics dynamically, and creating components—because most designers can't make a living by merely programming buttons.

Throughout this book, you'll try out scripting examples (using `.fla` files from the Sybex website). You'll add ActionScript code, following step-by-step instructions. At each step, we'll explain how the code works in detail. Often, you'll then improve on the code by editing and adding to it. This is how most experienced programmers work—step by step—and it's an excellent way to learn ActionScript.

This book takes a progressive approach to teaching you how to program with ActionScript. For instance, in Chapter 2, "Flash Communication," you'll learn how Flash handles communication between objects by working through examples that you'll program yourself. We'll explain the ActionScript and concepts behind the code in detail. Then, in later chapters, it will be assumed that you're already familiar with those concepts. Each chapter builds on the previous chapter's information to introduce new concepts. This is true even of the later chapters. For instance, the trigonometric functions that you will learn about in Chapter 7,

"ActionScript Trigonometry," will be used in different ways in Chapter 8, "Games: Responding to Events," and Chapter 9, "Drawing with ActionScript." Therefore, we recommend that you work through this book from the beginning to the end.

We have made every attempt to use concepts you've learned in different ways so that you can gain confidence in applying them. For instance, you'll learn about functions and `for` loops early in the book, and then you'll use them repeatedly throughout the remainder of the book.

We also often show you several ways to program something. For example, in Chapter 3, you'll learn different ways to program buttons, leading up to the method we believe is the most efficient. By learning various approaches, you'll understand why one approach is better than another. This will also allow you to choose which method you would like to use in the future.

In the step-by-step instructions, we show you precisely which code to enter and where to enter it, both in the text and in screenshots of how your program should look at that step. In the text, the code is presented as you should type it in yourself. However, in some cases, the length of the code line is longer than will physically fit within this book's margins. In those cases, you'll see a small, red continuation arrow at the end of the line, like this:

```
createRectButton("ContactButton", "CONTACT", 75, 30, 100, 50, ▶
MenuComp.buttonColor, level++);
```

This means that you should enter the code on one line.

In addition to screenshots showing you the code for each step of building the script, most of the chapters also feature diagrams that help to visually explain points about the ActionScript. Most of these figures are self-explanatory (at least in the context of the discussion at hand). Additionally, some of the figures feature icons that provide a visual clue to which action or object is being discussed.

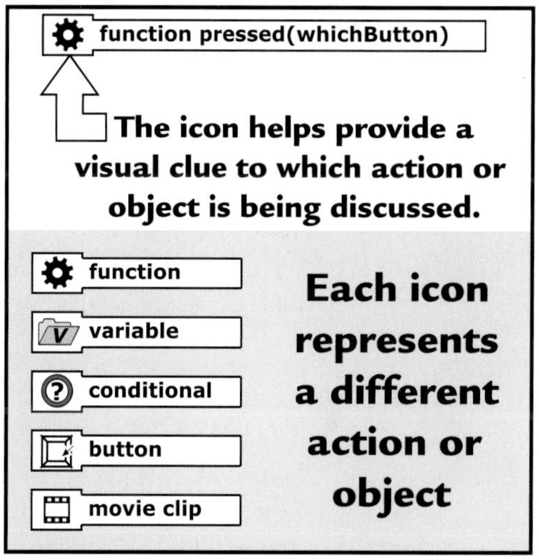

Have fun and experiment with the examples in each chapter. In some cases, we'll suggest other features you might add, but you can continue to work on any of the examples to make them better. We recommend that you go beyond working through this book and start applying what you learn to your own Flash projects. One of the best ways to learn to program with ActionScript is to just do it. The more you practice writing, editing, and troubleshooting ActionScript, the more confidence you'll gain.

How to Work with the Web Files

To work through this book's tutorial examples, you'll use .fla files available from the Sybex website, www.sybex.com. (Navigate to the catalog page for this book, click the Download link, and follow the instructions that appear.)

Each time we instruct you to open a new file, you'll see a symbol like the one in the margin here, as a reminder that it's from the Web. WWW.

For each example, you'll find two files: one whose name includes _Start and one whose name includes _Final. The _Start file is the one you'll work with. (Actually, you'll first be instructed to save it as _Modified and make your changes to that version, so that you'll have the original version if anything goes wrong.) The _Start file includes all the elements of the sample program, except the code you'll add in the steps of the tutorial. The _Final file is the completed example; you can use this to check your work against ours.

Fundamental ActionScript

No matter what you may have heard, most of the basic programming concepts are not really difficult to understand, but they do require a different, more abstract, way of thinking.

For instance, consider the simple programming concept of a variable. This is a "container" you designate for a specific piece of information that may change. Suppose your movie clip has a bouncing ball. You might create *ballXPos* and *ballYPos* variables to keep track of its *x* and *y* coordinates; the specific values of these variables will change, but what they represent—the *x* position and the *y* position—do not. What might not be so easy to understand about variables is that they have *scope*; that is, the variable you've created may exist—have meaning—only in certain parts of the movie.

NOTE In this book, we've used a special italic "program" font for program words that are defined by the user. When you write a script, you give your variables (meaningful) names, such as *ballYPos* and *ballXPos*. For the program words that are built into Flash ActionScript, we use a nonitalic "program" font. For example, `stop()` is the ActionScript action for stopping at a Flash frame.

Programming concepts become less mysterious and confusing when you actually start using them. Learning a new language is often a function of familiarity. The more you become familiar with something, the more you understand it. However, we won't leave learning ActionScript entirely to familiarity. We will thoroughly explain each programming concept when it is introduced, and then you'll become familiar with the language by using it over and over again. To help you get started, here is a preview of the most important concepts: objects, object-oriented programming, properties, and methods.

Objects and Object-Oriented Programming

The term *object* gets thrown around quite a bit, causing quite a bit of confusion (as well as bruises—when you throw objects around, someone is bound to get hurt) to non-programmers. The term has different but overlapping meanings, which can be difficult even for programmers to keep straight. An object can be something visible on the stage, or a piece of code, or an abstract idea, or all of those things. There are graphical objects on the stage, user-defined objects, and built-in objects in ActionScript.

Probably the easiest type of object to understand is a graphical object. Any drawing, text, or other item on the stage is a graphical object. A bitmap image of a monkey eating a banana is a graphical object. A graphic symbol of a static spaceship is a graphical object. An animation showing steam rising off of a pie is a graphical object. A text field is also a graphical object. The most important thing for new ActionScript programmers to understand is that a graphical object does not consist only of the image you see; it also includes instructions for Flash about how to display that image. These instructions are in the form of properties and, in some cases, methods.

Built-in objects are essentially encapsulated pieces of ActionScript that Macromedia has decided will likely be used frequently by most users. For example, you'll be using the `Date` object, the `Sound` object, and the `Color` object in this book. Like graphical objects, these objects contain properties and methods that are related to their specific functionality.

User-defined objects are a way to carry around information that is linked together in some way. For instance, let's say you had a toggle button (on/off), and you wanted to know whether it was on and at what time it had been turned on. You could create an object that would hold this information for you in one place.

Object-Oriented Programming

Magical, mysterious object-oriented programming, or OOP, is simply a way of thinking about how to structure your code. Object-oriented programming is the idea that an object knows about only itself, and only needs to do things that relate to itself.

For example, consider the stop button for a music player. The stop button stops the music. It also handles the graphics for the stop button's down and rollover states and the change in the mouse cursor. This is all done by the stop button, and no other part of the program needs to know about what is happening. The fast-forward and the rewind buttons operate completely independently of the stop button. These buttons do not need to know that the stop button has been rolled over or has been pressed.

All ActionScript in Flash is inherently object oriented because everything is taking care of itself. There is no overlap unless you specifically create it. Even the ActionScript that is attached to frame 1 and available throughout the whole movie is inherently object oriented. It is attached to a specific frame, which is an object—a frame object. It just so happens that any code in frame 1 can be available to other frames also.

OOP is based on the idea of reusable code. Because each object is separate, it can easily be lifted from one project and used in another project. More important, objects can be reused in your movie as often as needed.

NOTE The concept of OOP also involves a specific way of structuring code. However, this is not important for your coding with ActionScript in this book.

Properties and Methods

Properties are a natural extension of the concept of objects. If you draw a box, its properties include height, width, line weight (stroke), and so on. There are built-in standard properties for all graphical objects.

Methods are actions that you want to do to a specific object. They are attached to a specific type of object. For instance, in the `Sound` object, you have a `play()` method, which is not available to a `TextField` object. This makes sense—you want the sound to play, but what would a text field do when told to play? Flash provides built-in methods for commonly used actions, and you can also create your own methods.

One More Thing Before You Begin...

Don't be afraid to supplement this book with the information Flash MX itself provides about ActionScript. It has several built-in features, such as the Reference panel and the Show Code Hints buttons, that give you quick access to information about specific actions. Don't think for a moment that you're somehow cheating or that you're not a "real" programmer if you use these features. Professional programmers use programming reference guides all of the time. Macromedia has just made it easier for them and you to access the information you need.

Have fun and experiment with the examples in each chapter. In some cases we will suggest other features you might add, but don't limit yourself to our suggestions. You can always make something better.

And finally, we'd love to hear from you. Let us know what you like about this book, and what you don't like (any mistakes, for example), by going to `www.sybex.com` and clicking the Contact Sybex link.

—Scott and Jennifer

CHAPTER one

ActionScript for Non-Programmers

For many of us, *making the transition from user to programmer—from working "manually" with an application program's interface to building scripts that automate complex operations—can be an intimidating prospect.* Coding, *the common name for writing scripts in a programming language, seems to imply a set of cryptic, inflexible rules that may take ages to learn.*

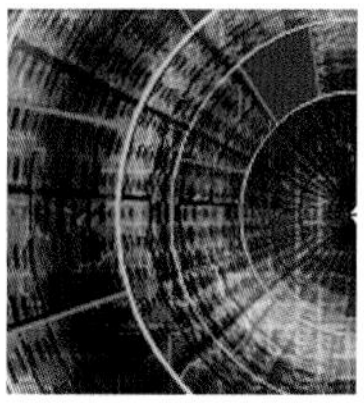

It's true that there is a lot to learn, and your scripts do need to follow the rules in order to work. But Flash MX provides an interface to ActionScript that does some of the work of creating scripts for you. Learning to write Flash MX scripts will be much less intimidating once you become familiar with the ActionScript environment and its core mode of operation. You'll gain this familiarity as you work through the examples in this book.

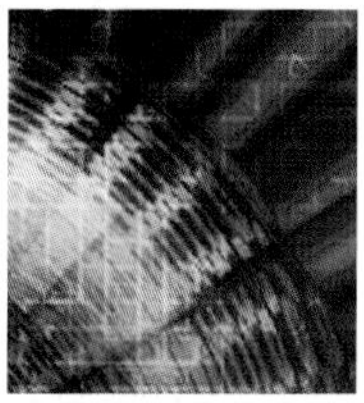

The most important tool that Flash MX provides for working with ActionScript is the Actions panel. It is your interface for creating simple to complex scripts. It allows you to drag and drop commonly used code lines into your script, as well as to enter code directly. In this chapter, you'll become familiar with the Actions panel and learn how to use its many useful and timesaving features. You'll learn how to take advantage of features like the Actions toolbox, the Reference panel, auto-formatting, code hints, and the View Line Numbers option. You'll also begin to learn some nuts and bolts about how ActionScript works.

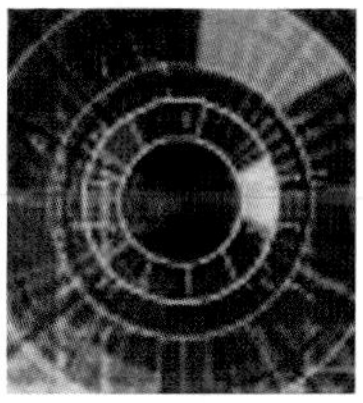

Getting Comfortable with the Actions Panel

For many designers, the Actions panel can be somewhat intimidating. It's not as scary as it seems—even when you're working in the dreaded Expert mode. In this book, you'll be spending all of your time in Expert mode. Most of the coding in this book is infeasible (or awkward at best) in Normal mode.

The main difference between Expert and Normal mode is that in Expert mode, you can type in the code directly, as well as drag it from the Actions toolbox. In Normal mode, you can only drag and drop code from the Actions toolbox; you cannot enter code manually.

In many ways, this book is about making anyone who is not experienced with programming comfortable in Expert mode. You'll start to see the blank, white space in the Actions panel as a doorway to endless possibilities, rather than as a members-only door accessible only to a select few.

Adding ActionScript in the Actions Panel

This is a book in which you'll learn by doing. Throughout this book, you'll be building scripts, testing the results, and analyzing what the elements of each script do. By following the examples here, and by continuing to practice on your own, you'll develop firsthand knowledge of how ActionScript works. In this first example, however, you'll just start exploring the Actions panel. In the second half of the chapter, you'll try your hand at scripting.

1. Open the File

WWW.

Begin by opening the file named Chapter1_Start.fla in Flash MX (1.1). If you haven't already downloaded this book's sample movie clips from the Web, see the Introduction for a complete

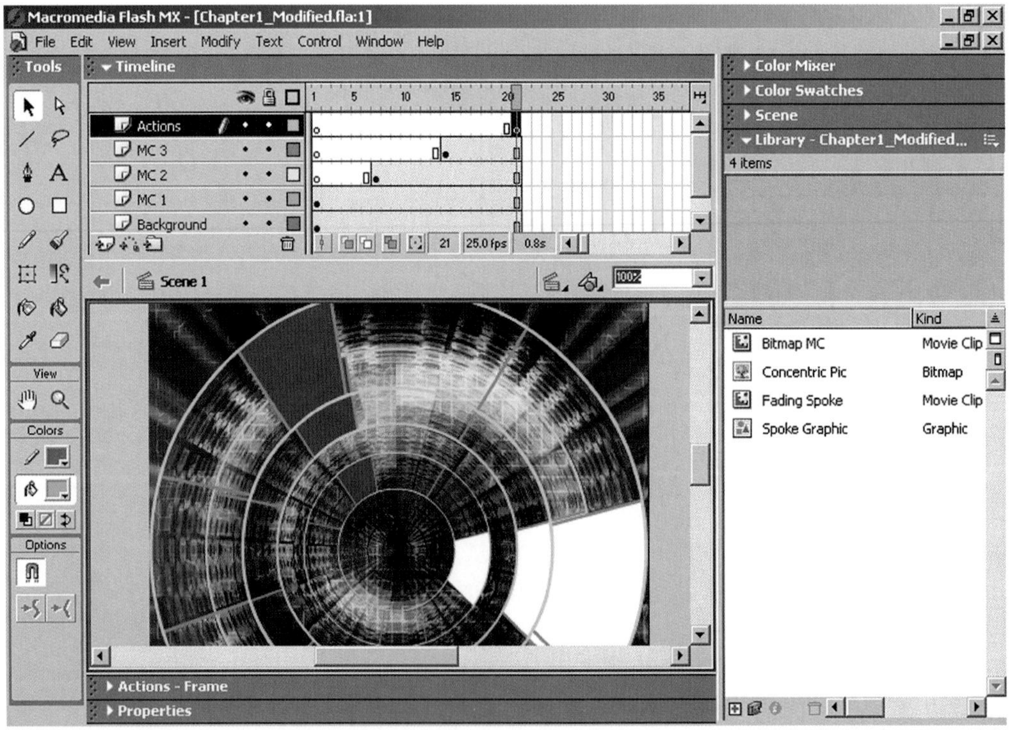

1.1: The Chapter1_Start.fla *file in Flash MX*

description. Save the file to your local hard drive with the name Chapter1_Modified.fla. (To see a finished version of this movie, open Chapter1_Final.fla.)

Going from the bottom to the top of the timeline, you can see that the Chapter1_Start.fla file has five layers: Background, MC1, MC2, MC3, and Actions. The MC1, MC2, and MC3 layers contain the same movie clip, named Fading Spoke. The Fading Spoke movie clip fades a graphic symbol named Spoke Graphic from 100% alpha to 0% alpha.

2. Test the Movie

Test the movie before you enter any code. Press Cmd/Ctrl+Enter or choose Control ➢ Test Movie to see what the animation does.

Each instance of the animation goes through the alpha fade transition. The movie clips appear on the timeline in a staggered manner. The instance of the Fading Spoke movie clip on the MC1 layer is always visible, but the instance on the MC2 layer is visible only from frame 7 through frame 21, and the instance on layer MC3 shows up on frame 14 and plays through to frame 21.

You will see why we constructed the file this way in a moment. Now let's get ready to enter some simple ActionScript. Whenever you want to write or edit ActionScript, you will need to access the Actions panel. By default, the Actions panel is nested below the stage in Flash MX.

3. Toggle the Actions Panel

Close the Test Movie window and then open the Actions panel. To open the Actions panel, press F9 (1.2). This keystroke toggles the Actions panel between open or expanded and closed or minimized.

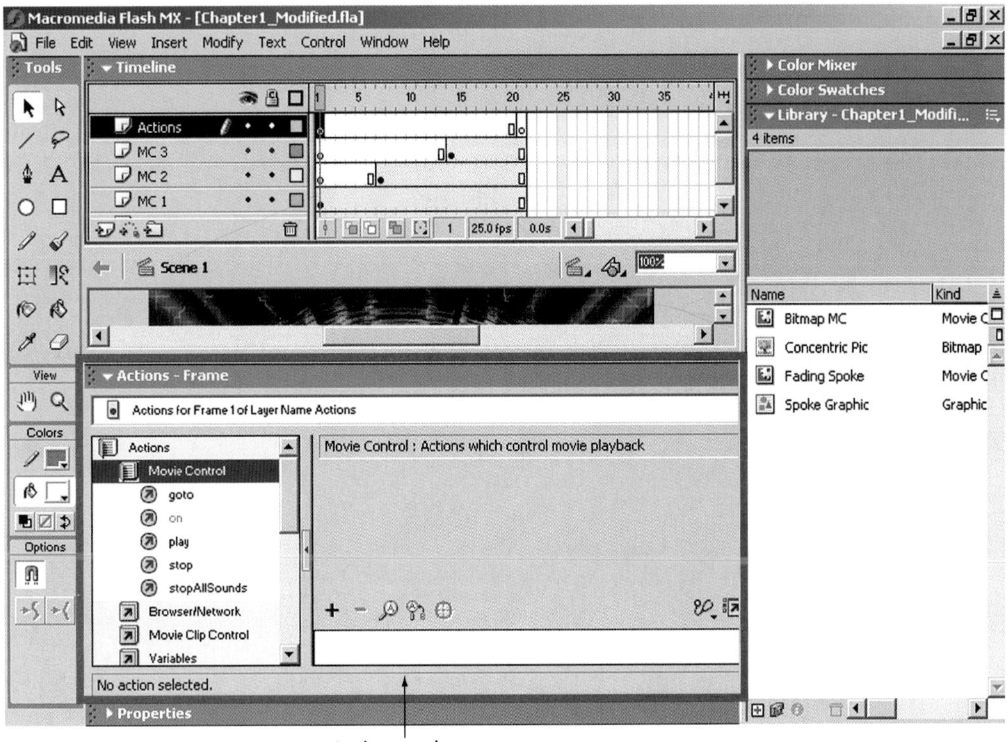

1.2: The F9 key toggles the Actions panel.

Notice that when you open the Actions panel, it partly obscures the stage; this makes the ability to toggle the panel on and off quite useful. You can toggle it on and off by choosing Window ➢ Actions.

The first time you open the Actions panel, it will be in Normal mode (as in 1.2). You will not be using the Normal mode in this book. Go directly to Expert mode.

4. Select Expert Mode

Click anywhere within the Actions panel to make sure it is selected, and then press Cmd+Shift+E (Mac) / Ctrl+Shift+E (Win) to go to Expert mode. (Using the keyboard shortcut for switching to Expert mode will have no effect if the Actions panel is not selected.) When you switch to Expert mode, you'll see that the white area on the right side of the Actions panel (called the *script window*) takes up much more space than it did in Normal mode.

On the left side of the Actions panel, you see the Actions toolbox (1.3). It contains a list of actions, organized in folders of categories—such as Operators, Functions, Constants, Properties, and so on. You can use the Actions toolbox to select actions. You won't be using the Actions toolbox for most of the examples in this book, because it's generally quicker to type commands than to work through the categories to select them. However, the toolbox can be useful until you're familiar with ActionScript syntax or if you need a reminder of which ActionScript commands are available. So let's take a few minutes to explore some of the useful aspects of the Actions toolbox.

5. Expand Categories in the Actions Toolbox

Select frame 21 of the Actions layer. Click the Actions folder in the Actions toolbox to expand the category. You'll now see a list of subcategories such as Movie Control, Browser/Network, Movie Clip Control, and so on. Click the Movie Control folder to expand the Movie Control subcategory, and you'll see a list of actions for controlling a movie.

6. Double-click the Stop Action

Double-click the stop action in the Actions toolbox (1.4). Flash will add the following line to the script window on the right:

```
stop();
```

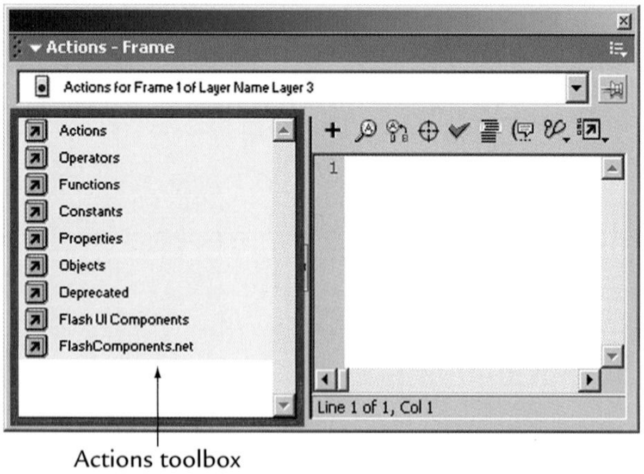

1.3: The Actions toolbox organizes actions in categories.

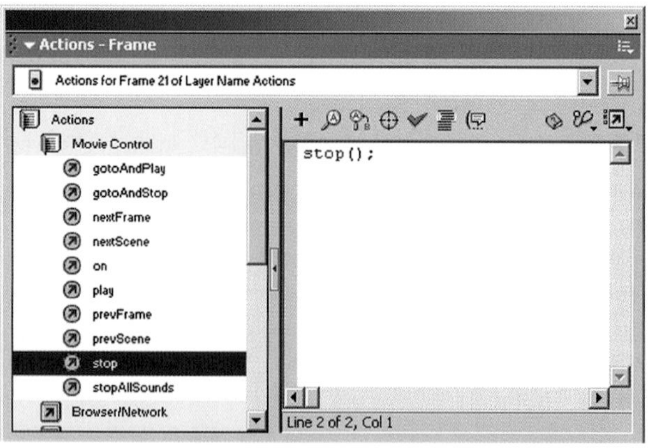

1.4: Double-click the stop action in the Actions toolbox to add it to the script window.

7. Test the Movie

Now press Cmd/Ctrl+Enter to test your movie again. You'll notice that the spokes stagger onto the stage, but once they get there, they each cycle through the fade at a different time and keep repeating. That's because even though you've told the main timeline to stop in frame 21, each Spokes Fade movie clip timeline continues to cycle through the frames within each movie clip. Each animation started on a different frame of the main timeline, so even though they are all the same movie clip, they are going through their fading cycle at different times.

On the positive side, the value of using the Actions toolbox for entering ActionScript in the Actions panel is that you are assured of getting the syntax correct. The downside is that it would be very taxing on your time to need to hunt down the actions all the time. Usually, you'll want to use the Actions toolbox to enter code only if you're having trouble recalling the syntax of a certain line of ActionScript.

Getting Quick Information about Actions

A particularly useful aspect of the Actions toolbox is that it can give you some quick information about actions. Let's look at an action that's not as obvious as the `stop()` action (in terms of what it does or what it is used for) to demonstrate this feature:

1. Close the Test Movie window, and then click the Movie Control folder in the Actions toolbox to minimize it.
2. Click the Conditions/Loops folder.
3. Roll the cursor over the `default` action. Don't click; just place the cursor over the action and hold it there. After a second or two, you'll see some pop-up text explaining what the `default` action is used for (1.5). In this particular case, unless you know about `switch` statements, the explanation only brings up more questions.

Flash MX provides information about ActionScript and specific actions in several ways. Later in this chapter, you'll use the Reference panel, code hints, and syntax coloring, all of which provide different kinds of information. While you're learning how to use ActionScript, these features will be invaluable. First, however, let's finish looking at the Actions toolbox.

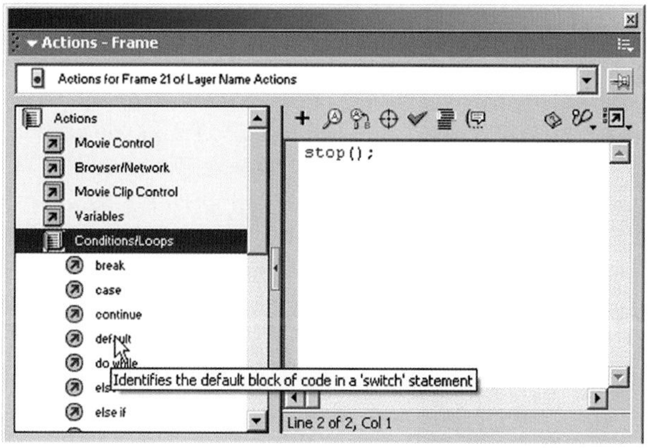

1.5: Roll your mouse over an action to get a brief explanation of what it does.

Resizing and Closing the Actions Toolbox

If you plan to use the Actions toolbox regularly, you can minimize how much space it takes up. Hold your mouse over the gray bar that separates the Actions toolbox from the script window. Don't place it over the button with the left-pointing arrow (that's the minimize/maximize button, as you'll see in a moment). When you see the cursor change to two lines with arrows pointing left and right, you can click and drag to resize the window. Drag the bar to the left to make the Actions toolbox smaller (1.6).

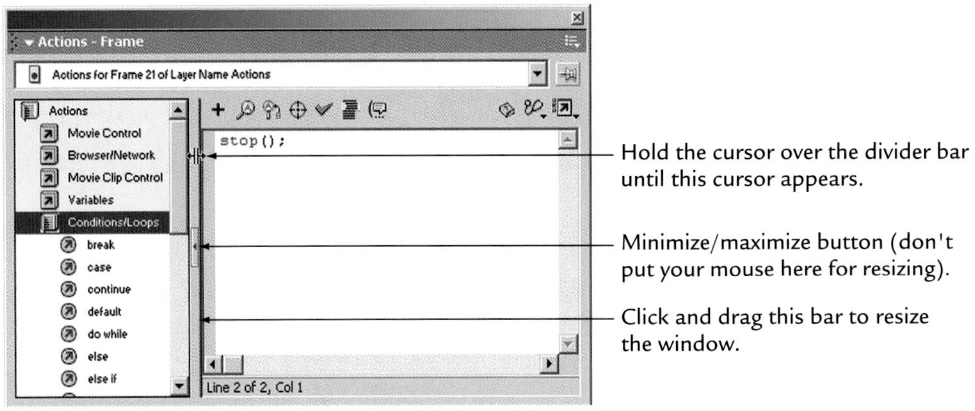

1.6: Resizing the Actions toolbox

NOTE Resizing the Actions toolbox is temporary. If you minimize and then maximize the Action toolbox, Flash does not remember the position of the resized Actions toolbox. Similarly, Flash will not remember the position of the Actions toolbox if you close and reopen Flash. However, minimizing the Actions toolbox is retained.

While the Actions toolbox has its uses, it will often be more trouble than it's worth. As you become more proficient with ActionScript, the space that it takes up will probably be more valuable to you than using it to enter actions or to find information about actions. Fortunately, you can close, or minimize, the Actions toolbox. To minimize the Actions toolbox, just click the small button in the middle of the bar that separates the Action toolbox from the script window (1.6).

When the Actions toolbox is not minimized, the arrow on this button will point left. When the Actions toolbox is minimized, the arrow will point right (1.7). You can expand the Actions toolbox by clicking the button again. You're going to leave the Actions toolbox minimized from now on.

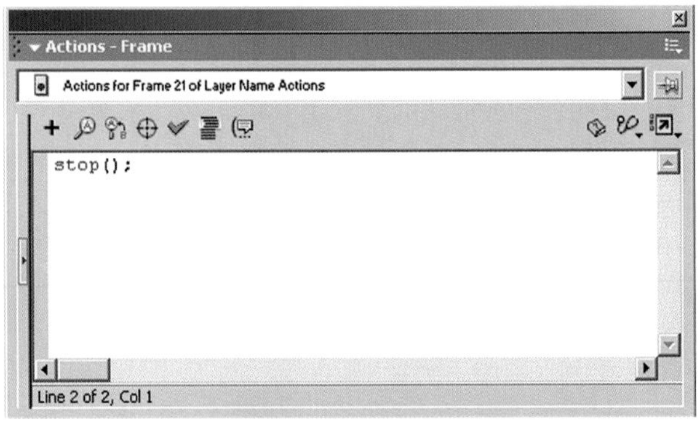

1.7: Minimizing the Actions toolbox

Writing a Simple Script

At this point, this chapter's example consists of three instances of the Fading Spoke clip, each fading at different times. Now you'll make it more interesting by adding some code. What this simple demonstration program does, however, is not as important as what it can show you about the Flash MX interface to ActionScript. You'll use these few lines of code to become more familiar with the Actions panel. In particular, you'll explore two more features that provide information: the Reference panel and code hints.

In the first exercise, you applied some simple ActionScript to a keyframe on the timeline (by double-clicking the stop action in the Actions toolbox). In this exercise, you'll also use another way of applying ActionScript.

Keyframes on a timeline (both on the main timeline or on a timeline within a movie clip) are one of three places that you can assign ActionScript. The other places that you can apply ActionScript are directly on movie clips or buttons. As you will see in this exercise, when you apply ActionScript to a movie clip, you can control how that movie clip behaves programmatically.

Beginning the Script

In this example, you're going to write a relatively simple script that will control the Fading Spoke movie clips in two ways. First, the code will scale the movie clip instances, and then it will randomly rotate the movie clip instances. You will use the same script for all three instances of the Fading Spoke movie clip.

1. Select the Movie Clip

Move to frame 1 on the main timeline and select the Fading Spoke movie clip instance on the MC1 layer. You will apply ActionScript to this movie clip.

2. Assign ActionScript to Movie Clip

If the Actions panel is not open, press F9 to open it. Notice that the Actions panel is now labeled Actions - Movie Clip (1.8). This is an affirmation that you're now assigning Action-Script to a movie clip, rather than to a keyframe.

NOTE If the Actions panel is labeled Actions - Frame, you will be assigning the ActionScript to the keyframe on frame 1 on the MC1 layer, not the movie clip on frame 1. Make sure the Actions panel says Actions - Movie Clip before continuing with the exercise.

Enter the following code in the Actions panel:

```
onClipEvent() {
```

This is the first line of your code. Before you finish entering the code, let's look at a few useful features in the Actions panel.

Using the Actions Panel for Reference

If you are wondering what `onClipEvent()` does, Flash MX offers an easy way to find out. The Reference panel, accessed by clicking the Reference button in the Actions panel, lets you look up what a particular action does.

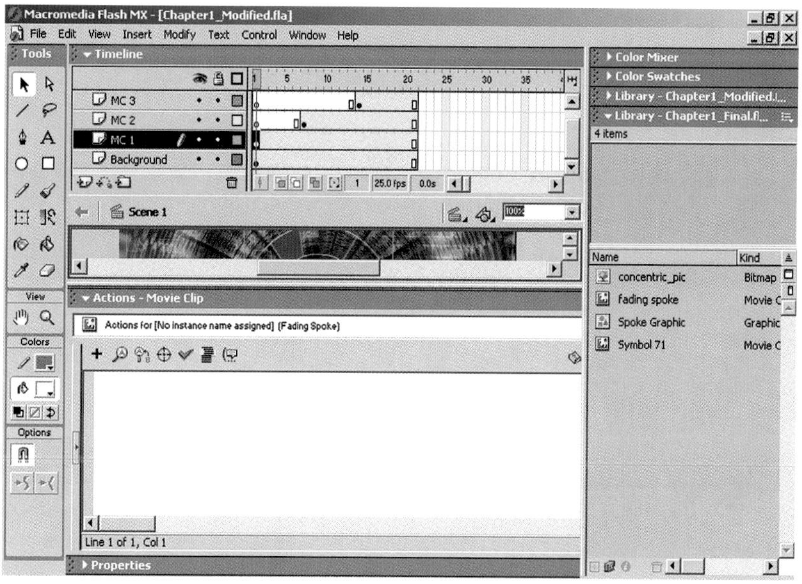

1.8: Make sure you that you are assigning the code to the movie clip instead of the keyframe.

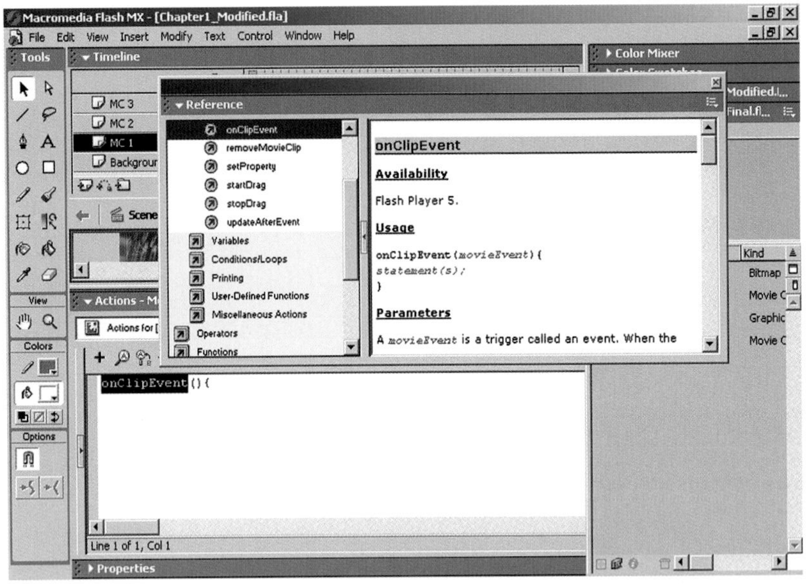

1.9: When you click the Reference button with ActionScript code selected in the Actions panel, Flash MX displays the Reference panel entry for that command or other keyword.

1. Use the Reference Panel

Use your mouse to drag over just the text `onClipEvent()` (don't select the parentheses and the open bracket).

Click the Reference button, which is the button with a little blue book icon on the right side of the Actions panel toolbar panel (see the sidebar "Un-nesting the Actions Panel"). When you click the Reference button with an ActionScript keyword selected, Flash will open the Reference panel with that code already selected (1.9).

The left side of the Reference panel works similarly to the Actions toolbox in the Actions panel. You can select any action to get detailed information about it. The right panel displays information about that action.

You might have noticed that Flash MX does not come with an ActionScript reference guide. Now you know why: Flash MX has the reference guide built into it. In this example, you can see that the Reference panel displays a lot of information about `onClipEvent()`. If you scan through the information to the end, you'll notice some cross-linked topics that take you to information about related actions.

The Reference panel is particularly useful when you need information about various parameters for a specific action. For example, in this case, you'll be using the `load` parameter for the `onClipEvent()` action. Scroll down in the Reference panel until you see the `load` parameter and read up on what it does. But don't type `load` into the `onClipEvent()` action just yet. When you're finished, close the Reference panel.

Un-nesting the Actions Panel

At this point, you may run into a problem with the new Flash MX interface layout. Macromedia's redesign of the Flash interface in Flash MX is largely a substantial improvement for workflow and usability, but there are a few hitches here and there.

One problem crops up if you're working in 800×600 or 640×480 screen resolution. When working in lower screen resolutions, some useful tools in the Actions panel might become hidden. For instance, the screenshot below shows Flash MX at a screen resolution of 800×600. The illustration points out where some of the tools are hidden.

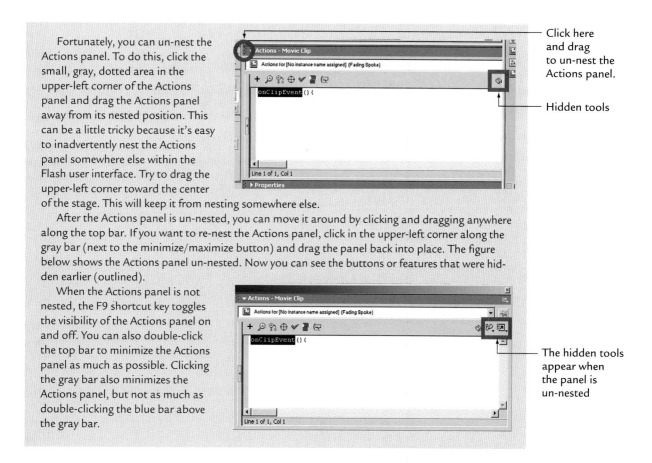

Fortunately, you can un-nest the Actions panel. To do this, click the small, gray, dotted area in the upper-left corner of the Actions panel and drag the Actions panel away from its nested position. This can be a little tricky because it's easy to inadvertently nest the Actions panel somewhere else within the Flash user interface. Try to drag the upper-left corner toward the center of the stage. This will keep it from nesting somewhere else.

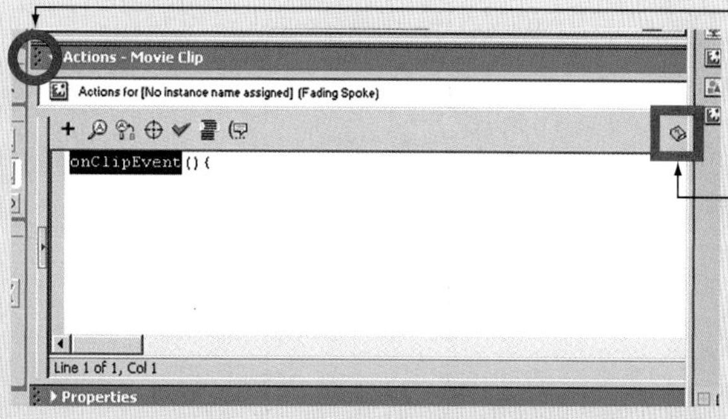

After the Actions panel is un-nested, you can move it around by clicking and dragging anywhere along the top bar. If you want to re-nest the Actions panel, click in the upper-left corner along the gray bar (next to the minimize/maximize button) and drag the panel back into place. The figure below shows the Actions panel un-nested. Now you can see the buttons or features that were hidden earlier (outlined).

When the Actions panel is not nested, the F9 shortcut key toggles the visibility of the Actions panel on and off. You can also double-click the top bar to minimize the Actions panel as much as possible. Clicking the gray bar also minimizes the Actions panel, but not as much as double-clicking the blue bar above the gray bar.

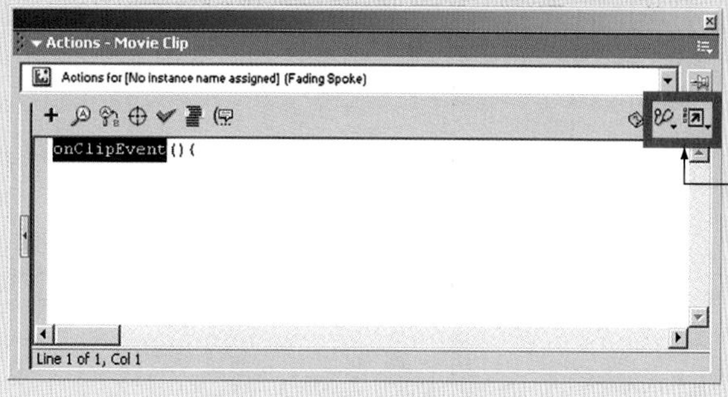

2. View Code Hints

Now let's look at another useful feature in the Actions panel—code hints. Clicking the Show Code Hint button in the Actions panel toolbar produces a hint pop-up window, whose contents depend on the location of your cursor when you click the button. The Show Code Hint button is particularly useful if you need to know what parameters an action supports.

1. Place your mouse cursor between the opening and closing parentheses in the line of code in the Actions panel:

   `onClipEvent(){`

2. Click the Show Code Hint button in the Actions panel toolbar (1.10). In this case, the code hints show the various parameters available for the `onClipEvent()` action.
3. Double-click the `load` parameter to select it.

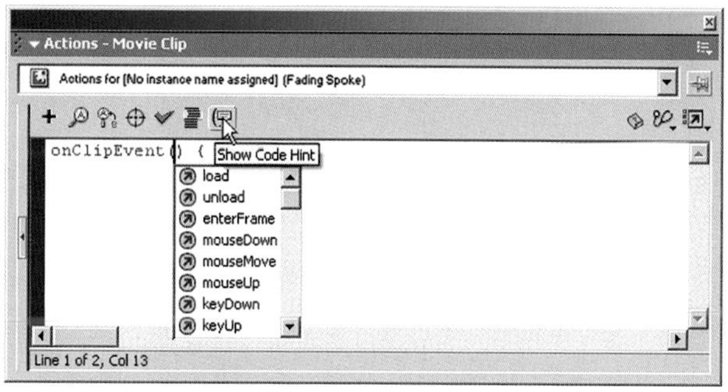

1.10: Click the Show Code Hint button to see code hints.

4. In some cases, clicking the Show Code Hint button will show you a series of hints. For instance, type the following in the Actions panel:

```
do {
}
for () {
}
```

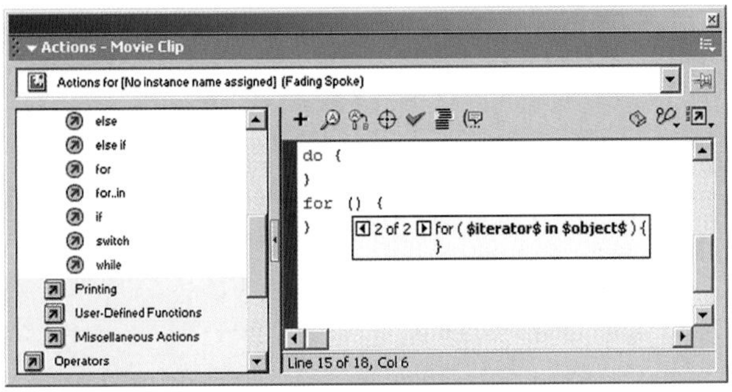

1.11: Some actions have more than one hint associated with them.

5. Place your cursor between the parentheses after `for` and click the Show Code Hint button. The hint pop-up window will feature left- and right-pointing buttons that allow you to cycle through two hints for the `for()` action (1.11).
6. Delete the `do/for` code, leaving only the `onClipEvent(load) {` line of code.
7. Code hints don't always provide useful information. For example, type `getTimer()`, place your cursor between the parentheses, and click the Show Code Hint button. Flash will just repeat the action—`getTimer()`—in the pop-up hint window.
8. Delete the line `getTimer()`.

NOTE Usually, you will not see any hints if you click the Show Code Hints button when the cursor is anywhere outside the parentheses that go with an action that has parameters.

Completing the Script

Now that you have explored some of Flash's features for getting information—the Reference panel and code hints—let's return to the sample script.

1. Finish the Code

Complete the code by adding the following ActionScript after the `onClipEvent(load)` line (1.12):

```
    _xscale = _yscale = 1;
    _rotation = Math.random()*360;
    var scale = 1;
}
onClipEvent(enterFrame){
    scale += 5;
    if (scale > 100){
        scale = 1;
        _rotation = Math.random()*360;
    }
    _xscale = _yscale = scale;
}
```

Within the `onClipEvent(load)` event handler, you're setting the scale of the movie clips in both directions (`_xscale` and `_yscale`) to 1%. You're also setting the rotation of the movie clip (`_rotation`) to a random rotation. This is done only once to set up the movie clips so they start out looking the way you want them to (scaled and rotated).

The `onClipEvent(enterFrame)` event is where the actual work takes place. You increase the scale in both directions by 5%, and then you check if you've scaled past 100%. If you have, you want to start over, so you set the scale back to 1%. For additional flair, each time you start the scaling over, you randomly rotate the movie clip again.

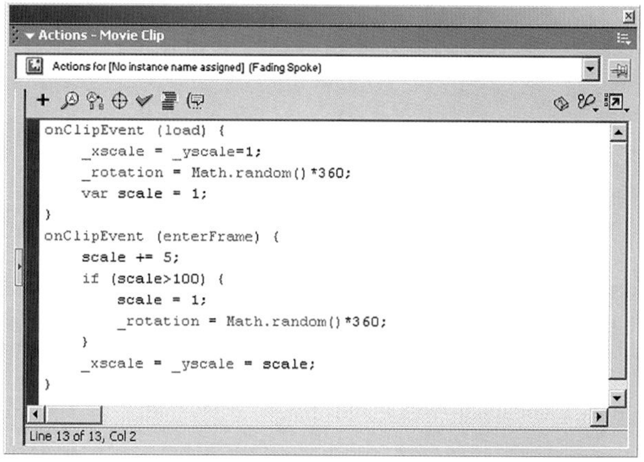

1.12: Complete the ActionScript for the Fading Spoke movie clip instance.

2. Test the Script

Press Cmd/Ctrl+Enter to test your movie. Notice the outer two spokes look the same, but the inner spoke grows more and rotates each time it starts at the beginning again. You'll learn more about the `onClipEvent(load)` and `onClipEvent(enterFrame)` event handlers that make this happen at the end of this chapter and in the following chapters.

Using Other Actions Panel Features

Now that you have all of your code, let's look at a few more features available in the Actions panel. You'll learn about line numbering, syntax coloring, and other Preferences settings, as well as the Find and Replace function.

Adding Line Numbers in the Actions Panel

Line numbers make it easier to refer to specific lines in the script. Click the View Options button in the Actions panel toolbar (the button on the far right side) and select View Line Numbers. This will add numbers before every line in your script. (1.13)

Line numbers are useful for several reasons:

- They make it easier for you to stay oriented when you're dealing with a very long script.
- They are helpful when you're debugging code. As you'll see later in this book, Flash lets you know which line in the script contains a problem.
- Line numbers make it easier to collaborate with other programmers and designers because you can reference the lines in the script using the numbers.

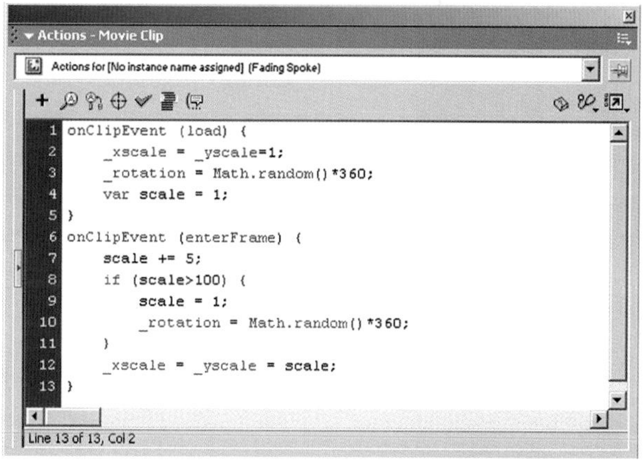

1.13: Adding line numbers to the Actions panel

In our example, you should have 13 lines of code, including the close bracket on the last line. The line `onClipEvent(load) {` should be on line 1, and the line `onClipEvent(enterFrame){` should be on line 6.

Setting Syntax Coloring

Look carefully at the script in the Actions panel and notice that some of the script is colored dark blue and some of it is colored black. Flash MX automatically colors actions for you as you write your script. If you prefer, you can specify colors used for syntax coloring.

To see the Syntax Coloring options, open the Actions panel options menu (click the drop-down button in the top-right corner of gray bar that contains the label Actions - Movie Clip) and select Preferences (1.14). This opens the Preferences dialog box to the ActionScript Editor tab.

> **NOTE** Notice that the top two choices on the Actions panel options menu are Normal Mode and Expert Mode. You can use these menu choices to switch between Actions panel modes.

There are six options for Syntax Coloring (1.15). Two of the options are Foreground and Background. The foreground color is the color that you will see for everything in your script that is not a keyword, identifier, comment, or string. The background color is the color of the script window.

Notice that the default color for keywords and identifiers is the same (or very similar). Let's change that. Click the small color swatch next to the Keywords option and change the color to bright red (hex value #FF0000). Next click the small color swatch next to the Identifiers option and change the color to dark green (hex value #009900) (1.16). Click the OK button to apply the changes.

Look at your script in the Actions panel (1.17), and you'll see that two instances of `onClipEvent()` and `if` have changed to red. Red is the color that you specified for keywords, so Flash MX recognizes these words or actions in the script as keywords. Other actions have

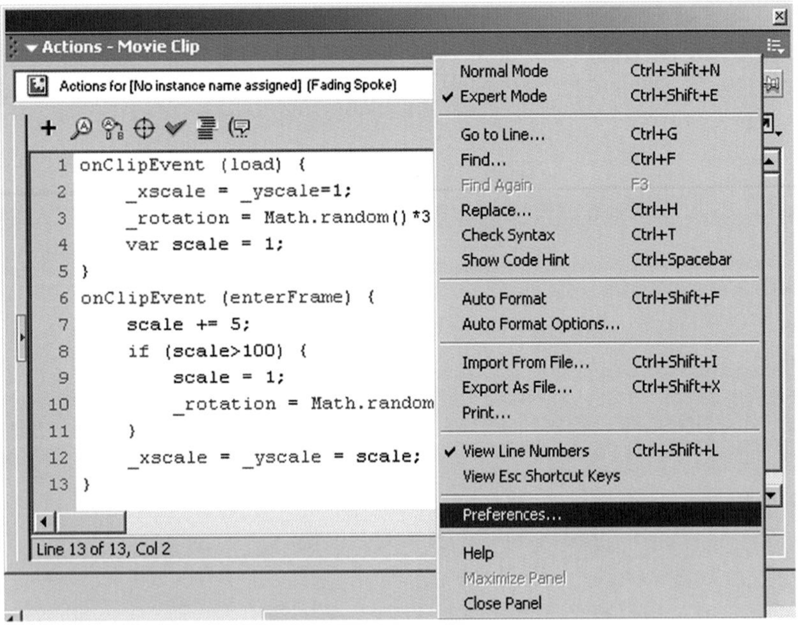

1.14: Select Preferences from the Actions panel options menu.

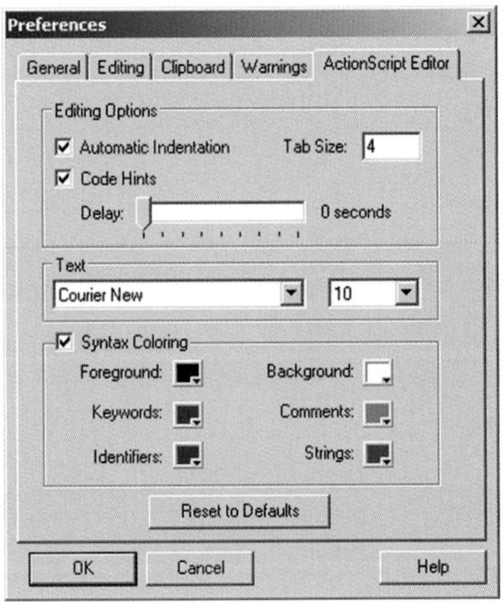

1.15: The Syntax Coloring default settings

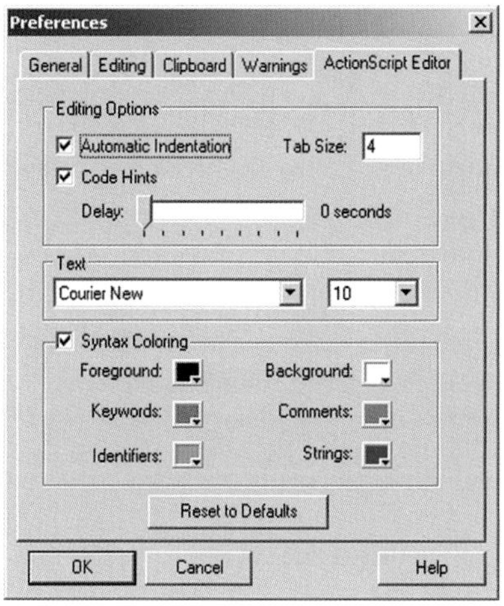

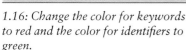

1.16: Change the color for keywords to red and the color for identifiers to green.

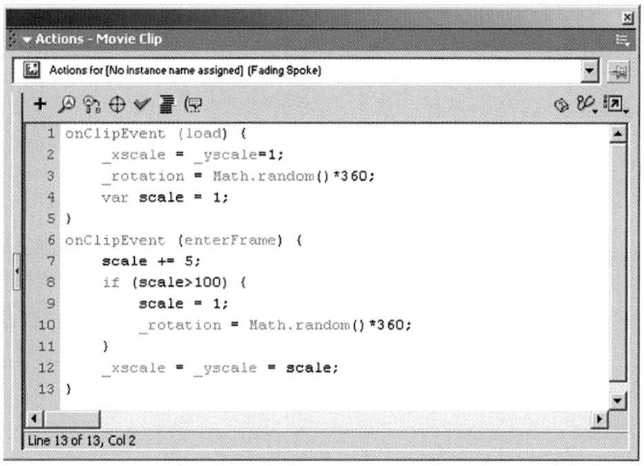

1.17: Flash MX changed the colors of portions of the script according to the Preferences dialog box settings.

been changed to green, including `load`, `_xscale`, `_yscale`, `random()`, and so on. Green is the color that you specified for identifiers, so Flash MX recognizes these words or actions in the script as identifiers.

Automatic syntax coloring is useful for several reasons. First, syntax coloring lets you know which parts of the script are keywords, identifiers, comments, or strings. Because you can look through your script according to the colors, you can easily find items. For example, if you want to be able to identify strings in large blocks of scripts, you could change the colors for strings to stand out more so they are easier to hunt down.

Another useful aspect of automatic syntax coloring is that it lets you know if you've gotten the spelling and capitalization right. If actions in your script change color as you enter each line, you know you've written it correctly. Conversely, if they don't change color when they should, you know something is wrong. For instance, say you want to add a comment to your script. If the comment doesn't change colors, you have a visual clue that your comment isn't written properly. (You'll learn about strings and comments in later chapters.)

In this book, you'll be using the default colors. Open the Preferences dialog box again and select Reset to Defaults to return to the default Syntax Coloring settings.

NOTE You may find it helpful to temporarily change the syntax coloring colors to check a script. Just open the Preferences dialog box and set the Syntax Coloring options on the ActionScript Editor tab as you want. When you're finished, revert to the defaults by clicking the Reset to Defaults button in the Preferences dialog box.

Setting Other Actions Panel Preferences

Select Preferences from the Actions panel options menu to open the Preferences dialog box to the ActionScript Editor tab again (1.15). Along with the Syntax Coloring options discussed in the previous section, there are several other useful options for working with the Actions panel.

The Automatic Indentation option refers to the format of your scripts. You might have noticed that Flash automatically indented your code for you, because this option is selected by default. You can change the Tab Size setting (from the default of four spaces) for a smaller or larger indentation.

NOTE Indenting your script makes it easier to read and navigate through your code. Indenting is also standard programming convention. For example, code that follows an open curly bracket ({) is indented until the closing curly bracket (}). This shows you at a glance that the indented code is linked together or on the same level.

The Text options let you change the font and font size for the code in the Actions panel. This can be useful for those late nights when your eyes are getting tired. Also, as you learned earlier, Flash can get a little cramped in smaller screen resolutions. If you want to be able to see the Actions panel and more of your stage contents, you might opt to work at a higher screen resolution (if your video card supports it) so that you can see more. The ability to increase the size of the font for the script can come in handy in that case.

In this book, the examples use the default indentation and font settings, but you may set them according to your own preferences.

Using Find and Replace

There are two more useful features in the Actions panel that should be introduced here: the Find and Replace functions. As you would expect, these options allow you to locate certain code elements and replace them if you desire.

To see how the Find function works, click the Find button (the second one on the left, with the magnifying glass icon) in the Actions panel toolbar to open the Find dialog box. Enter **_rotation** in the Find What field, and then click the Find Next button. The first instance of `_rotation` in the Actions panel will be selected (1.18). If you click the Find Next button again, the next instance of `_rotation` will be selected.

The Find feature is useful when you need to locate a particular item within a big block of code. However, if you want to also fix or change what you're looking for, the Replace feature might be a godsend. Close the Find dialog box and click the Replace button (to the right of the Find button) to open the Replace dialog box. Enter **_rotation** in the Find What field and **_height** in the Replace With field. Now click the Replace All button. Flash will very quickly replace all of the instances of `_rotation` with `_height` (1.19).

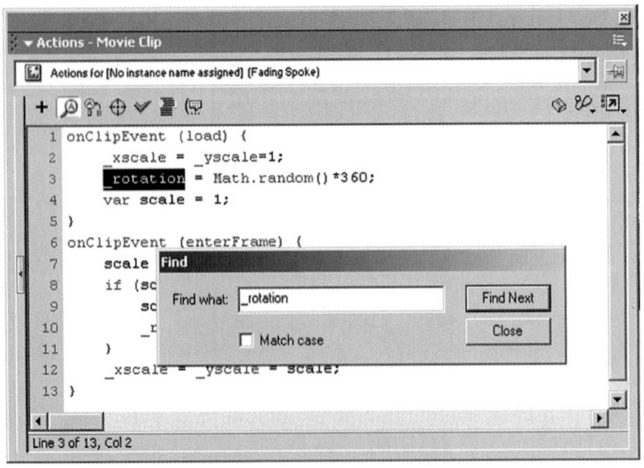

1.18: Use the Find feature to find the first instance of the `_rotation` *property.*

The Find Next and Replace buttons in the Replace dialog box allow you to choose when you want to replace instances. You can click Find Next to jump to the next instance of the script snippet. Then click Replace if you determine that you want to replace the instance, or click the Find Next button again to skip it and move onto the next instance.

The Replace feature is useful for several reasons. First, it makes it easier to correct mistakes. For example, let's say you have determined that there is a bug in your latest creation and the reason is that

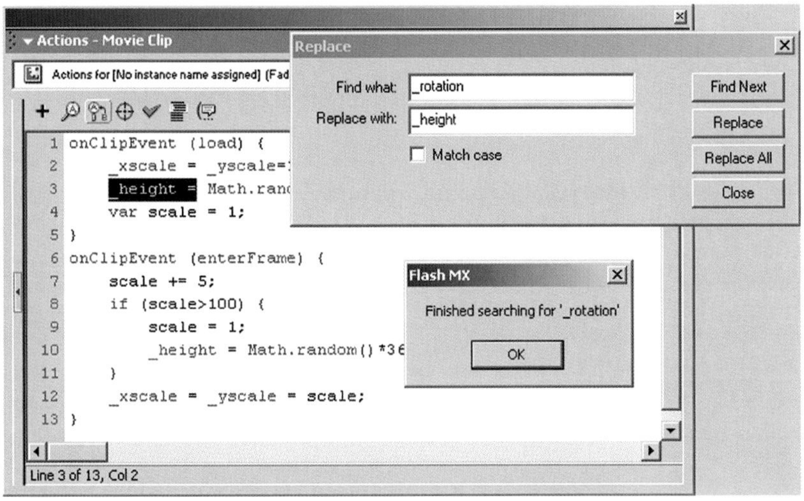

1.19: Use the Replace feature to swap the instances of `_rotation` *with* `_height`.

you've typed an arbitrary variable that you created using two spellings. For instance, sometimes you typed *`MyVariable`* and other times you typed *`MyVariables`*. You can correct the problem quickly and easily by using the Replace feature.

Another slick thing you can do is use the Replace feature to experiment with scripts you've downloaded over the Internet. For example, you could replace a property with another property and see how it affects the code. That is, in fact, what you did when you replaced `_rotation` with `_height`.

As you become more experienced writing scripts, you'll see how useful the Find and Replace functions can be. For now, close the Replace dialog box and press Cmd/Ctrl+Z (Edit ➢ Undo) to undo the Replace results.

Creating Two Movie Clips

Now that you're familiar with the Actions panel, let's copy the code you've been working on from one movie clip to another. Having two movie clips that use the same code will make it a little easier to learn about how the code works.

1. Copy the Code

The first task is to duplicate the existing code. You'll copy and paste the code on one layer onto another layer.

1. Select the Fading Spoke movie clip that has the ActionScript, and then select the Actions panel.
2. In the Actions panel, press Cmd/Ctrl+A to select all the contents. Then press Cmd/Ctrl+C to copy the code.
3. With the Actions panel still open, select frame 7 on the MC2 layer in the main timeline. Notice that the Actions panel has the label Actions – Frame in the upper left.
4. Click the instance of the Fading Spoke movie clip that's on frame 7 of the MC2 layer. The Actions panel's label now has the label Actions – Movie Clip.

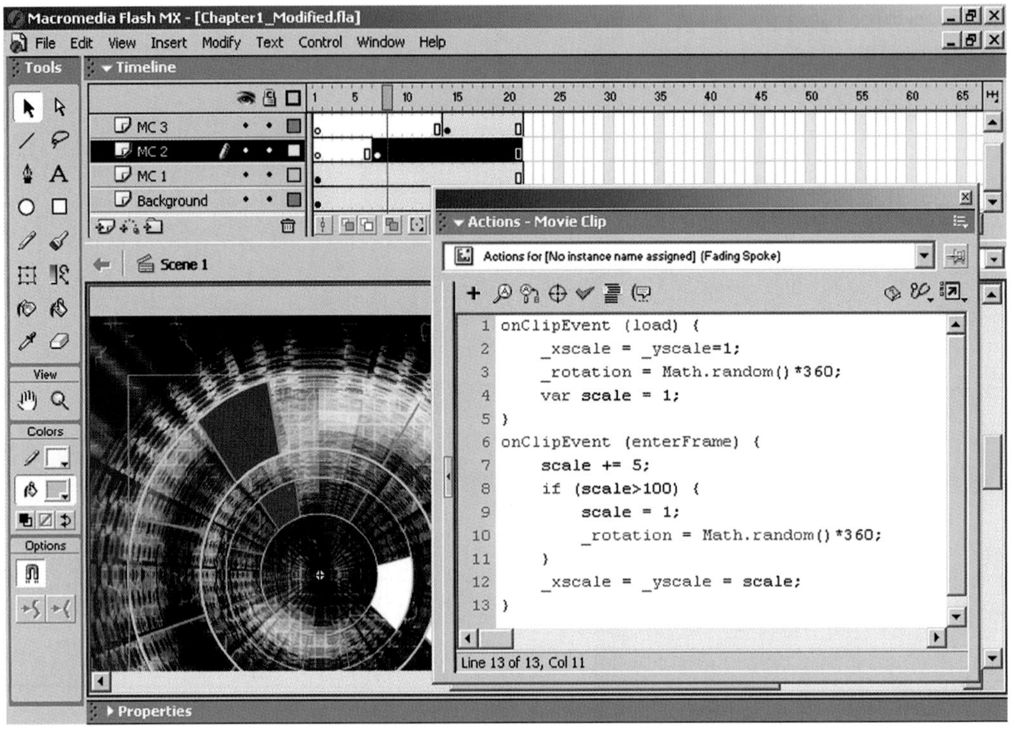

1.20: Copy the code from the Fading Spoke movie clip instance on the MC1 layer to the Fading Spoke movie clip instance on the MC2 layer.

5. Click in the Actions panel and press Cmd/Ctrl+V to paste in the code (1.20).

   You've just copied and pasted the code from one movie clip to another. When the movie runs the code, both movie clips will run independently of one another. In other words, the code that is assigned to the Fading Spoke movie clip on the MC1 layer will run independently of the code that is assigned to the instance of the Fading Spoke movie clip that's on the MC2 layer.
6. Paste the code onto the Fading Spoke movie clip instance that is on the MC3 layer (which becomes visible on frame 14).

NOTE When you copy and paste code, or when you write new code that you're not sure about, try clicking the Auto Format button on the Actions panel toolbar (the button to the right of the button with a check mark). If your code is not syntactically correct, Flash will display a dialog box with an error message that says, "This script contains syntax errors, so it cannot be Auto Formatted. Fix the errors and try again." This is an easy way to check your code and make sure you haven't missed something like a closing bracket or a semicolon at the end of a line.

---

7. Press Cmd/Ctrl+Enter to test the movie (1.21).

Now the movie clips rotate randomly, and their sizes incrementally increase, creating a more interesting effect. However, notice that the Fading Spoke animations are concentrated in the center of the stage. They do not take up the whole stage area. Let's fix this.

2. Fix the Scaling

To adjust the animation size, you'll edit the code in the movie clip instances. After you make these changes, each movie clip will have slightly different code.

1. Close the Test Movie window.
2. Select the Fading Spoke movie clip instance that appears on frame 7 of the MC2 layer and locate the following line of code:

```
if (scale > 100){
```

3. Change `100` to `175`, so that the code now looks like this (1.22):

```
if (scale > 175){
```

4. Select the Fading Spoke movie clip instance that appears on frame 14 of the MC3 layer and edit the same line of code (1.23). Change `100` to `250`.
5. Press Cmd/Ctrl+Enter to test the movie (1.24). Now the Fading Spoke movie clip instances fill the pages as they animate.
6. Close the Test movie window.

1.21: The Fading Spoke movie clips are a little too small for the stage size.

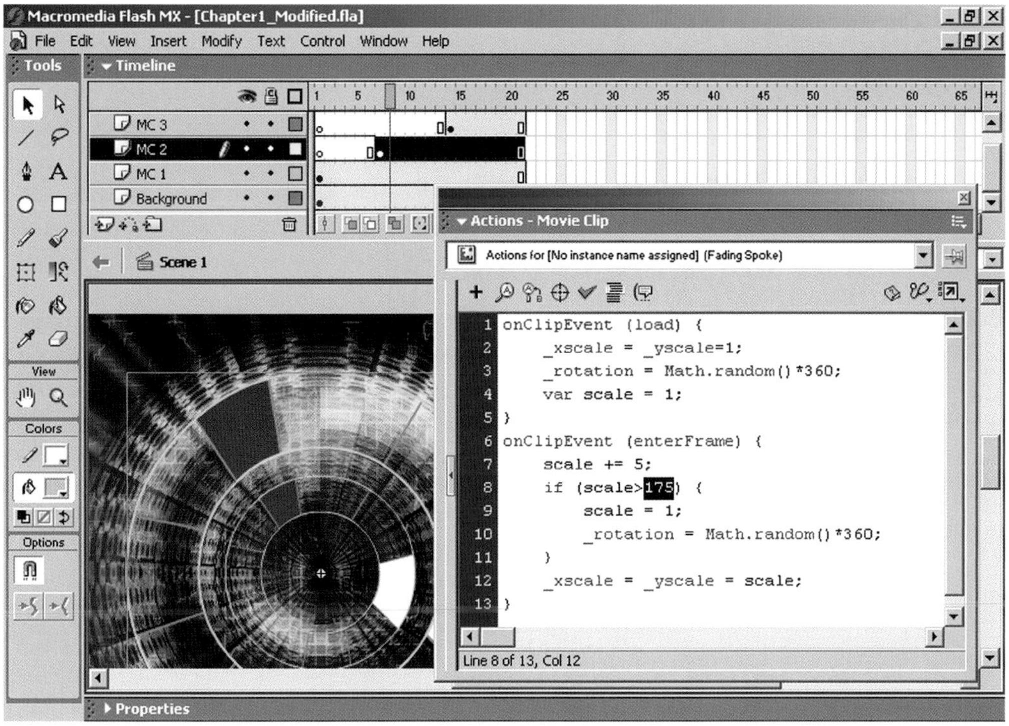

1.22: On the MC2 layer, increase the number from `100` to `175` within the `if` statement.

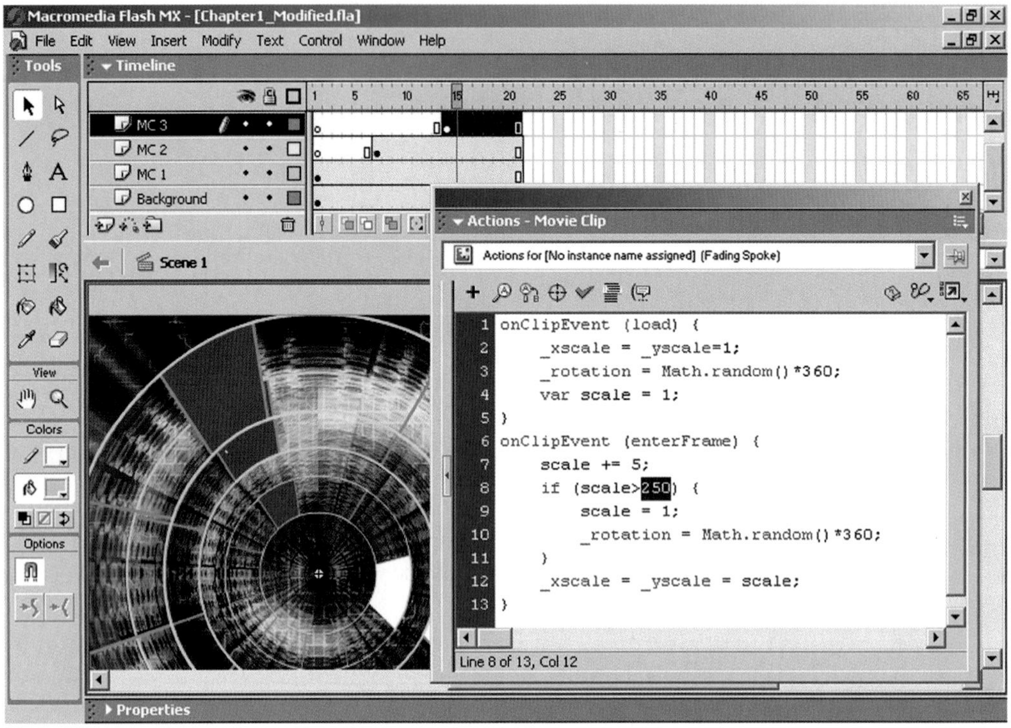

1.23: On the MC3 layer, increase the number from `100` *to* `250` *within the* `if` *statement.*

The main point of this example is to demonstrate how each movie clip uses its own code (it doesn't matter whether it's the same code or different code). This is a simple example of so-called object-oriented code in Flash. Each object acts independently of the other, and the code on each object executes independently of the code on the other objects.

Now let's take a closer look at what the code is doing in this example. There are two main sections of the code: the `onClipEvent(load)` section and the `onClipEvent(enterFrame)` section. The curly brackets after each `onClipEvent()` is where the real action takes place. Curly brackets are used in Flash to designate the beginning and ending of chunks of code. These cannot be used arbitrarily.

The `onClipEvent(load)` is executed when the movie clip is first drawn on the stage, and it is executed only once. Within the `onClipEvent(load)` is the initialization code. Since it only happens once when the movie clip is being loaded, this is where you put anything that needs a value to start with. It is also where you set how you want the movie clip to look when the user first sees it. In this example, you set the scaling of the movie clip to 1%. You also rotate the movie clip about itself by some random amount. This is how the user will first see the Fading Spoke movie clip: very small and rotated.

The `onClipEvent(enterFrame)` code is executed at the frame rate. In this case, the frame rate is 25 frames per second (fps), so this code will be executed 25 times per second. The `onClipEvent(enterFrame)` is where the actual work takes place, because it is repeated over and over. In this example, you tell the Fading Spoke to get bigger, but only up to a certain point. When that certain point has been reached, you reset the Fading Spoke to very small (1%) again, and then rotate it in some other direction.

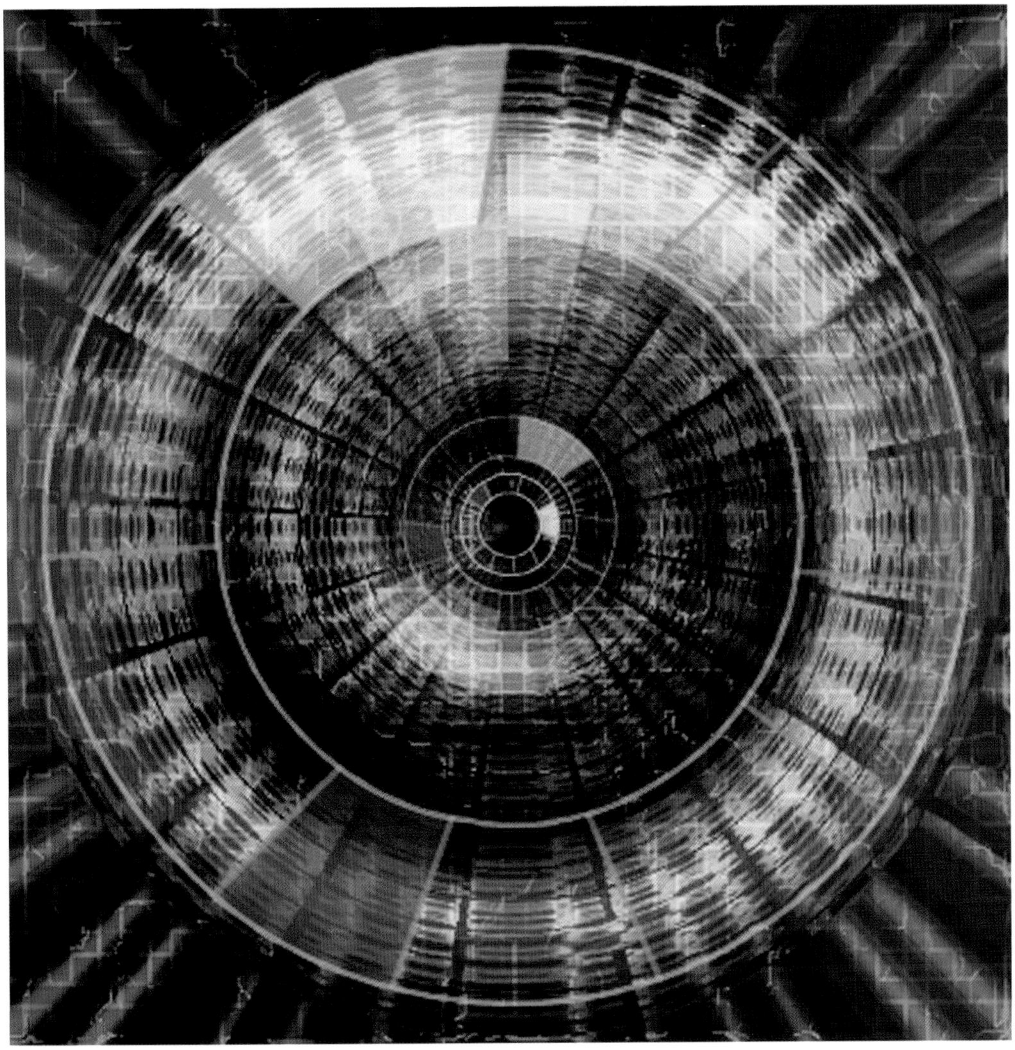

1.24: The Fading Spoke movie clips instances now scale upward enough to fill the stage.

Conclusion

Flash MX has several built-in features that give you quick access to information on actions. Don't think for a moment that you're somehow cheating or that you're in some way less of a programmer if you use the Reference panel or Show Code Hint button, or even if you select actions from the Actions toolbox. Professional programmers use programming reference guides all of the time. Macromedia has just made it easier for them and you to access the information you need.

Now that you've explored the Actions panel and its tools, you're ready to put ActionScript to use. In the next chapter, you'll learn more about Flash MX's features for controlling movie clips.

CHAPTER two

Flash Communication

In Flash, objects such as movie clips

can contain movie clips, which, in turn, can contain more movie clips. Each of these movie clips has its own timeline. In fact, buttons can contain movie clips that contain movie clips that contain buttons, and so on. Additionally, you can load external movies into Flash, and there can be multiple scenes within a movie. You can even load resources from the library or external sources, and they will be placed on the stage when you export your Flash movies. All of these objects can, and often need to be, communicated with in your scripts.

For example, you often need to control a movie clip based on an event controlled by another object such as a button. You might need to send a command to a movie clip that is nested several layers down within a movie clip to another movie clip that is nested several layers down within an entirely separate movie clip. At another time, you might need to communicate from an object in one movie to an object within a movie that has been loaded externally.

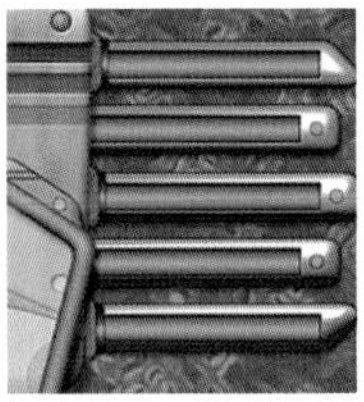

As you can see, just describing communication in general terms can get complicated. Fortunately, handling communications is actually much easier than it seems—most of the time. This chapter will clarify how Flash's communication system works. You'll look at communication on the main timeline, between different movie clips, between levels of loaded movies, and between attached movies.

Getting Oriented

The first exercise in this chapter shows how ActionScript handles communication within a hierarchy of multiple movie clips. You'll learn how to communicate with multiple layers of movie clips and from within a layered movie clip to the main timeline.

The basic concept to understand for communication is the way that movie clips are referenced within each other. Understanding these references will eliminate many communication problems and make much of your coding a breeze.

1. Open the File

WWW. Open Chapter2_A_Start.fla (2.1). Save it to your local hard drive as Chapter2_A_Modified.fla. (For the final version, see Chapter2_A_Final.fla.) (If you haven't already downloaded this book's sample movie clips from the Web, see the Introduction for a complete description.)

Take a moment to get oriented with the file. It has two movie clips on the main timeline, and each of those movie clips has a movie clip nested within it.

There are 15 frames of animation on the main timeline. There is a `stop()` action on the first frame of the main timeline, so the remaining frames on the main timeline do not immediately play when you view the movie. The main timeline movie has a graphical yellow label that says A1-Main Timeline.

There are two movie clips on the main timeline: one with a graphical blue label that says B1-Movie Clip and with a red label that says C1-Movie Clip. Like the main timeline, the B1 and C1 movie clips each have 15 frames of animation, with a `stop()` action on the first frame.

Finally, the B1 and C1 movie clips have movie clips nested within them. The B1 movie clip contains a movie clip graphically labeled B2-Movie Clip in green, and the C1 movie clip contains a movie clip graphically labeled C2-Movie Clip in purple. Once again, the B2 and C2 movie clips each have 15 frames of animation, with a `stop()` action on the first frame.

Notice that the B1 and C1 movie clips are entirely surrounded by the black area, which signifies the *scope* for the main timeline. This means that the B1 and C1 movie clips are under the main timeline's control. In other words, if you want to access the B1 or C1 movie clip, you must go through the main timeline.

Similarly, the B2 movie clip (which is a darker gray than the B1 movie clip) is within, or under, the B1 movie clip, just as the C2 movie clip is within the C1 movie clip. There is a simple hierarchy in this example: The B2 and C2 movie clips are nested within the B1 and C1 movie clips, respectively, and all of the movie clips are contained within the overall timeline, which is labeled A1 (2.2).

Next notice that there are five sets of five colored buttons. The largest set of colored buttons is on the main timeline. Each of the movie clips also contains a set of colored buttons. The buttons are color-coded and labeled to correspond with the main timeline or one of the movie clips. For example, there is a yellow button labeled A1 in each of the five sets of colored buttons.

In this example, you will program the buttons so that no matter which button with the same label you click, it will always result in the same action. For example, clicking any yellow A1 button will play the animation on the main timeline, and clicking any blue B1 button will play the animation on the B1 move clip's timeline. As you work through the example, you'll learn how to route commands to the correct movie clip in the Flash hierarchy.

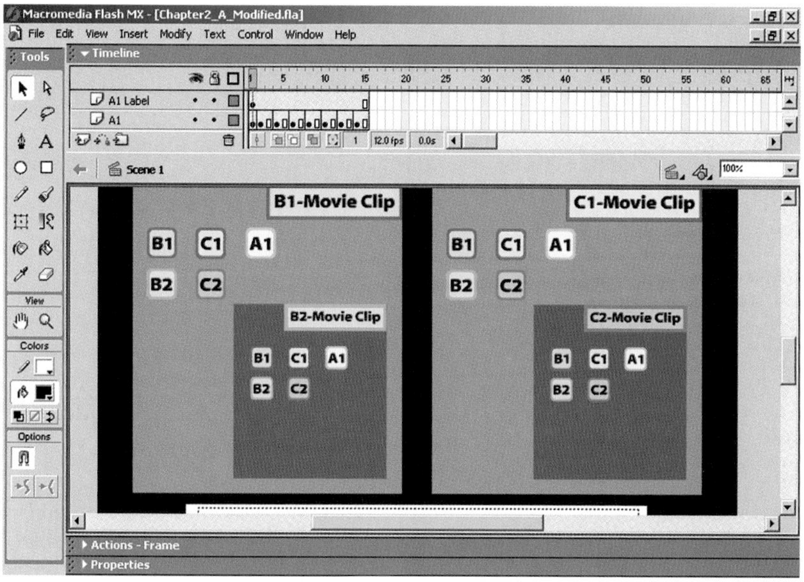

2.1: *The* Chapter2_A_Modified.fla *file*

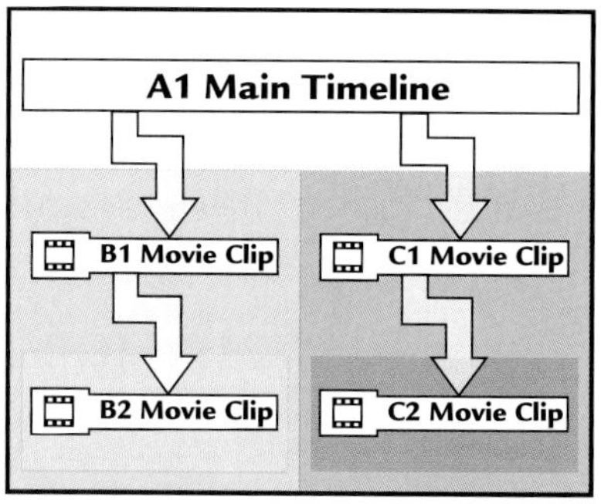

2.2: *The* Chapter2_A_Modified.fla *file hierarchy*

To avoid unnecessary repetition, most of the buttons in this example already have the code assigned to them. You'll add the code to only a few buttons.

Before you start, notice that there is also a text field set on top of a white rectangle at the bottom of the file. Later, you'll add code that will use this text field to display the ActionScript you are using to route the command to the correct movie clip. The text field will give you visual feedback on how the button works and what the button is doing.

2. Review the ActionScript Attached to the A1 Button

Select the A1 button on the main timeline. Open the Actions panel and look at the ActionScript that is attached to this button (2.3).

```
on(release){
   play();
   var pathtext = "play()";
}
```

The first line of code, `on(release)`, is an event handler, similar to the `onClipEvent()` event handler you learned about in Chapter 1, "ActionScript for Non-Programmers." In this case, however, `on(release)` is triggered by a different event. This code is assigned to a button, so the `on(release)` event occurs when the user clicks and then releases the mouse on that button.

There are two simple lines of code in the `on(release)` event handler. The first line contains one of the most basic ActionScript commands in Flash: `play()`. Obviously, this command tells something to play. In this case, the `play()` command is sent to the main timeline, not to the button. The code is assigned to, or *attached to*, the button, but the command is being sent to the main timeline.

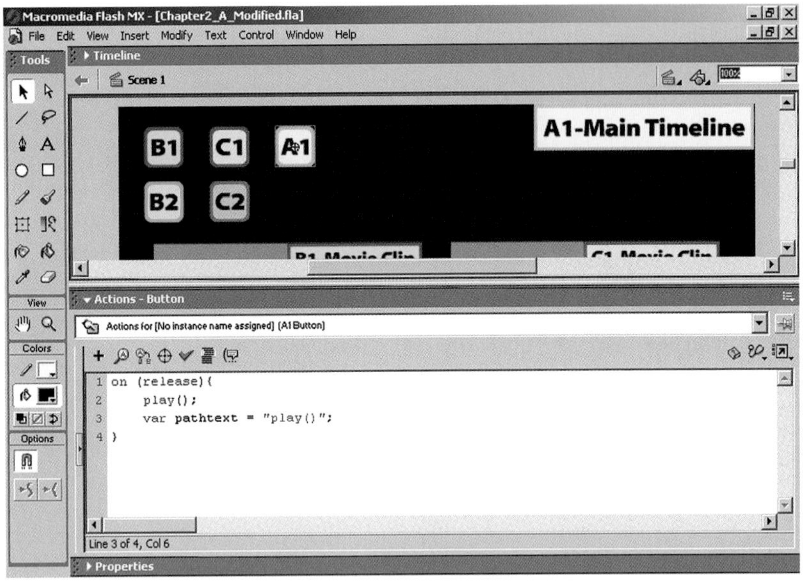

2.3: *The code preassigned to the A1 button on the main timeline*

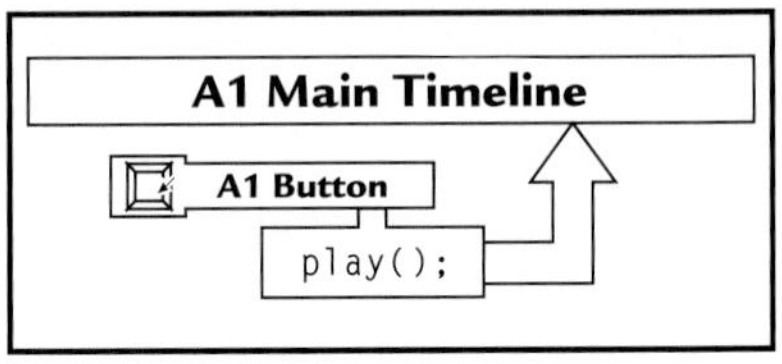

2.4: *The* `play()` *command on the A1 button on the main timeline is routed to the main timeline.*

When you have a button with a `play()` command on it, that command is sent to the timeline that the button is placed on, whether it is the main timeline or a movie clip timeline. In this case, the button is on the main timeline. Therefore, the `play()` command that is on the button tells the main timeline to play. There is nothing special required for the proper communication to take place between the button and the main timeline—the `play()` command takes care of it (2.4).

NOTE Buttons don't have a timeline like the main timeline or a movie clip's timeline, which is a sequential timeline. Buttons have four built-in keyframes, which you'll learn more about in later chapters. A `play()` command refers to a sequential timeline. The sequential timeline that buttons access is the timeline on which they are sitting.

The second line in the `on(release)` event handler is a feature that you wouldn't include in a real-world script. It's included in this example for learning purposes. This line of code uses the text field mentioned in step 1 to provide visual feedback on the ActionScript that each button is issuing. Let's take a look at the text field's properties to see how this works.

3. Open the Properties Panel

Click the text field that is set above the white rectangle toward the bottom of the stage area and press Cmd/Ctrl+F3 to toggle open the Properties panel (2.5).

Notice that the text field's type is set to Dynamic Text and that it has been assigned the variable name *`pathtext`*. This means that the content displayed in the field can vary, depending on the current value of the *`pathtext`* variable.

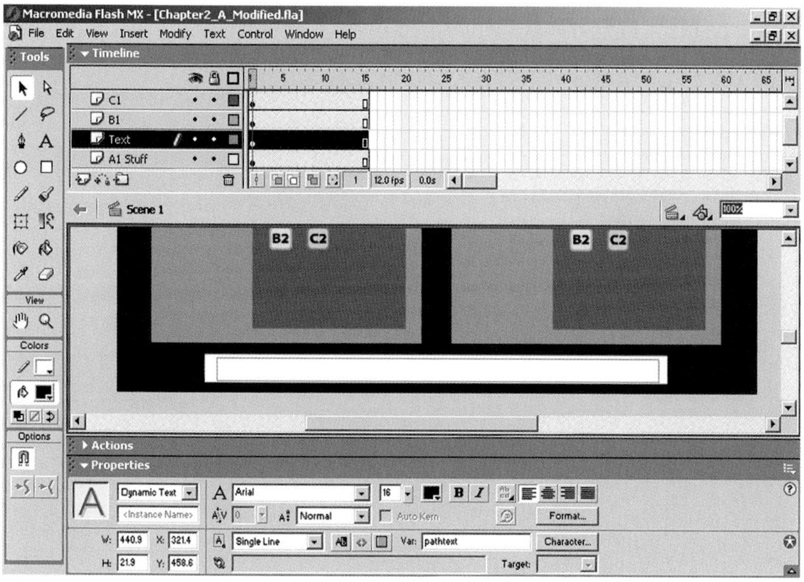

2.5: The Properties panel with information about the text field

---

NOTE What's a variable? If you're not already familiar with this basic programming concept, you soon will be. Later in this chapter, you'll take a detailed look at the role of variables in ActionScript and the rules for using them. For now, the essential thing to understand is that a variable provides a way of containing information (a value). A script can use a variable's value later, without knowing what that value is. The variable's role in the program (in this case, identifying the text to be displayed in the box) doesn't change, even if its value (the particular text to be displayed) does change.

A dynamic text field can display changing content. This means that what is displayed in the text field can change, and it can quite literally display the value of a variable (the variable named `pathtext`). So the text field will display whatever value you assign to the `pathtext` variable, and you can dynamically change the value of the `pathtext` variable.

So what does this tell us about Flash communication? The second line in the `on(release)` handler for the A1 button on the main timeline sets a value for the `pathtext` variable:

```
var pathtext = "play()";
```

In essence, this sets the `pathtext` variable to the characters that are set between the quotation marks. Because the `pathtext` variable is the variable name associated with the text at the bottom of the screen, whatever is in the `pathtext` variable is also displayed in the text field.

Therefore, when someone clicks the A1 button on the main timeline, the text field will display `play()`. The `pathtext` variable matches the `play()` command used in the previous line. In this way, the second line in the A1 button's `on(release)` handler provides a simple method of informing the user which ActionScript is being issued when the A1 button on the main timeline is clicked.

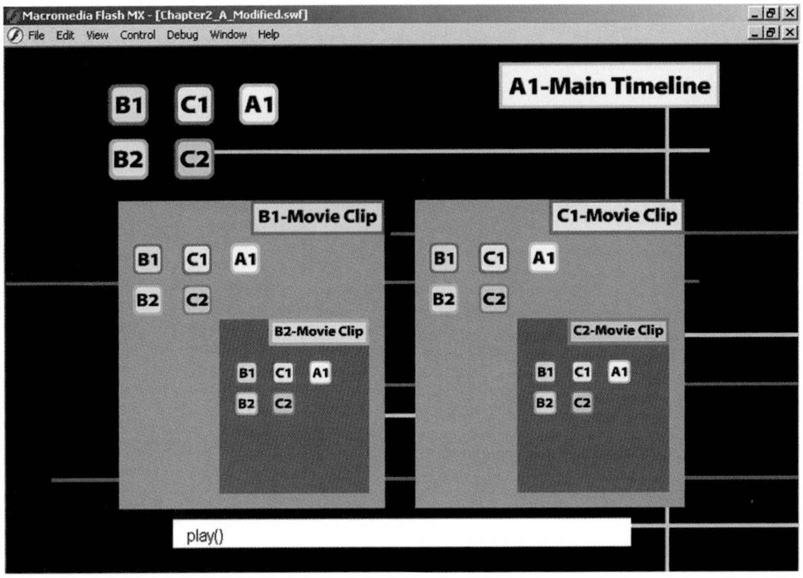

2.6: Test the movie and click the A1 button on the main timeline.

Notice that once again there is nothing special in the code that tells Flash how to send the "`play()`" value to the *`pathtext`* variable. All that is needed to dynamically change the value of the *`pathtext`* variable is to specify the variable and set it equal to a value.

4. Test the Movie

Press Cmd/Ctrl+Enter to test the movie. Click the A1 button on the main timeline and observe the results (2.6).

When you click the A1 button on the main timeline, two things happen:

- The frames of animation on the main timeline play.
- The text field displays the text `play()`.

Close the Test Movie window when you're finished testing.

You've seen that when you apply code directly to a button, the code refers to whatever timeline the button is sitting on (in this case, the main timeline). But what happens when you apply code to a movie clip? The following steps will show that the code affects that movie clip.

5. Add ActionScript to the B1 Button

Select the blue B1 button on the main timeline. Press Cmd/Ctrl+F3 to toggle the Properties panel closed, and then press F9 to toggle the Actions panel open.

Add the following lines in the Actions window (2.7):

```
on(release){
   B1.play();
   var pathtext = "B1.play()";
}
```

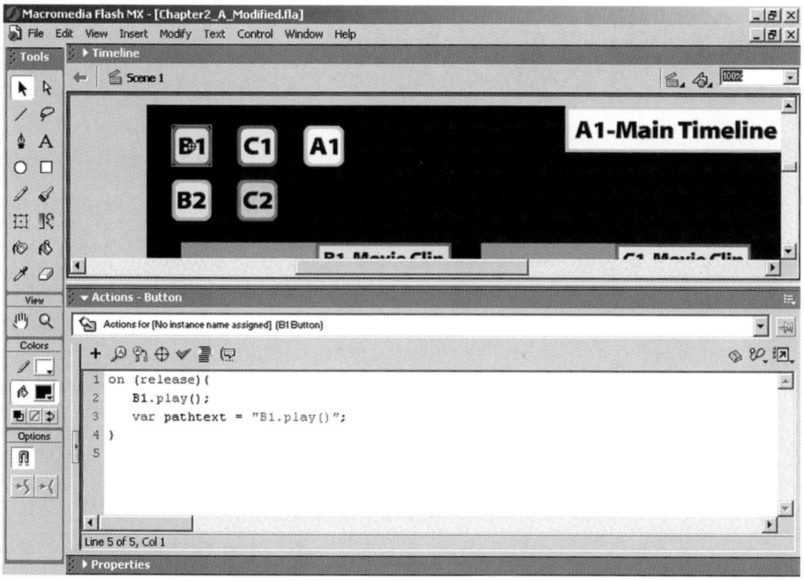

2.7: Apply code to the B1 button on the main timeline.

Notice that this code within the event handler is slightly different from the code used on the A1 button. In this case, the `play()` command has something added to it. When the user clicks the B1 button, you want the B1 movie clip to play. Revising the `play()` command to `B1.play()` lets Flash know that the B1 movie clip, rather than the main timeline or any of the other movie clips, should receive the `play()` command.

6. Add an Instance Name

Select the B1 movie clip (the light rectangle on the left with the blue B1 label). Press F9 to toggle off the Actions panel, and then Cmd/Ctrl+F3 to toggle on the Properties panel. Enter **B1** in the Instance Name field (2.8).

If you look in the Movie Clips folder in the library (press Cmd/Ctrl+L to open the library), you'll see that the B1 movie clip is actually named B1. However, since you can have any number of instances of the B1 movie clip on the stage, Flash needs something more specific to determine which movie clip should get the `play()` command. An *instance name* provides this specific information.

NOTE An *instance* is any and all symbols—an object, a movie clip, a button, or a graphic—that are placed on the stage. You can place a movie clip on the stage many times, and each time is a different instance of the movie clip. This is another benefit of object-oriented thinking.

In order to send commands to a movie clip in Flash, you must give the movie clip an instance name. Movie clips are kind of like those cookie-cutter houses in subdivisions. There can be many instances of the same house on the same street. The instance name is like a unique address for one of the houses. Putting the `B1` before the `play()` command is like addressing a package to that address (2.9).

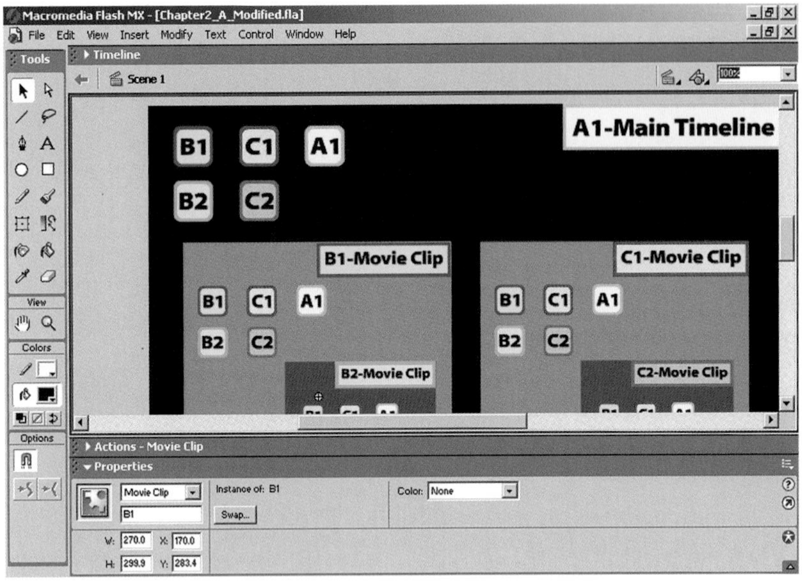

2.8: *Select the B1 movie clip instance and give it the instance name B1.*

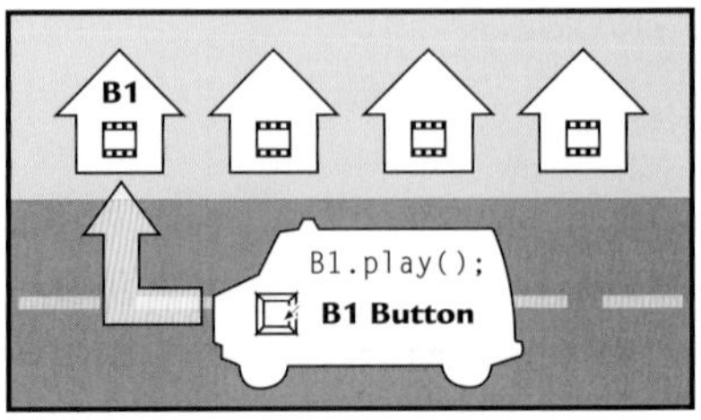

2.9: *The instance name is like the address for a house. It is what Flash uses to deliver commands to the correct destination.*

Now you know how to send commands from a button on the main timeline to a movie clip: You need to add an instance name to the `play()` command. This identifies the correct movie clip, so that ActionScript will correctly understand what to do and where to do it.

So how do you send a command from a button on the main timeline to a movie clip that's nested within another movie clip? At this point, it should not be too hard to guess, but let's take a look at one of the buttons to see.

7. Review the ActionScript Attached to the B2 Button

Select the B2 button on the main timeline. Press Cmd/Ctrl+F3 to toggle the Properties panel closed, and then press F9 to toggle the Actions panel. Now look at the preassigned code (2.10):

```
on(release){
   B1.B2.play();
   var pathtext = "B1.B2.play()";
}
```

This is similar to the code assigned to the B1 button on the main timeline, but in this case, the `play()` command is routed through the B1 instance of the B1 movie clip down to the B2 instance of the B2 movie clip (the B2 movie clip has already been given the instance name B2). Each reference to the instance name, as well as the actual command, `play()`, is separated by a dot, or period (2.11).

Notice that in the `B1.B2.play()` command, `B1` is placed before `B2`. If the order were reversed (`B2` before `B1`), Flash would try to send the `play()` command to a movie clip instance named B1 nested within a movie clip instance named B2. Of course, in this example, that would not work.

With nested movie clips, you can go down many levels. The basic approach to sending or routing a command still applies: Just reference each of the clip's instance names, separated

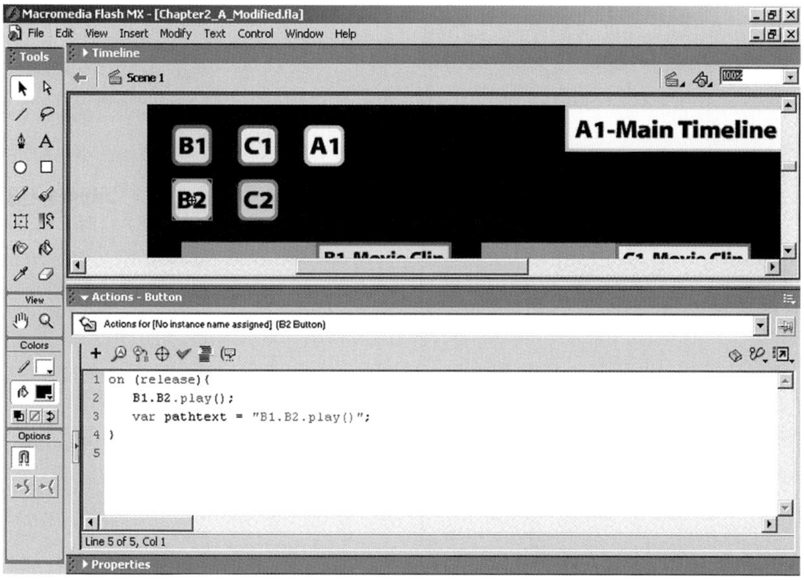

2.10: Look at the code assigned to the B2 button on the main timeline.

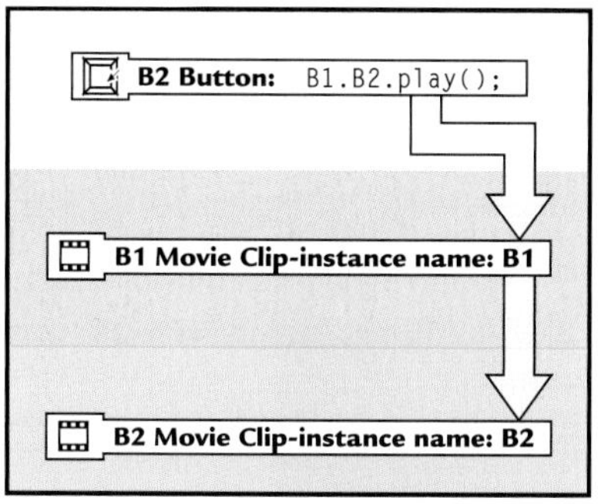

2.11: The `play()` *command is routed down through the B1 movie clip to the B2 movie clip.*

by a dot. For example, if you had a B3 movie clip nested within the B2 movie clip, the `play()` command from a button on the main timeline would need to be as follows:

```
B1.B2.B3.play();
```

It is quite common to nest movie clips within each other. One example is an animation for a spaceship that has different reactions based on what the user is doing. In this case, one movie clip would contain all of the spaceship's reactions, which each would be in another movie clip nested within that one.

Not all commands need to be routed from the main timeline down to a movie clip. In fact, often you'll want one movie clip to communicate with another movie clip. Let's look at a few examples of communicating between movie clips.

8. Edit the C1 Movie Clip

Select the C1 movie clip and press Cmd/Ctrl+E to edit it. Now click the A1 button within the C1 movie clip. Open the Actions panel to see the ActionScript attached to the A1 button that is in the C1 movie clip (2.12):

```
on(release){
   _root.play();
   _root.pathtext = "_root.play()";
}
```

Flash's ActionScript refers to the main timeline as `_root`. By adding `_root` before the command, you're telling Flash that the command should be routed all the way back up to the main timeline (2.13). Therefore, the A1 button in the C1 movie clip issues the `play()` command to the main timeline.

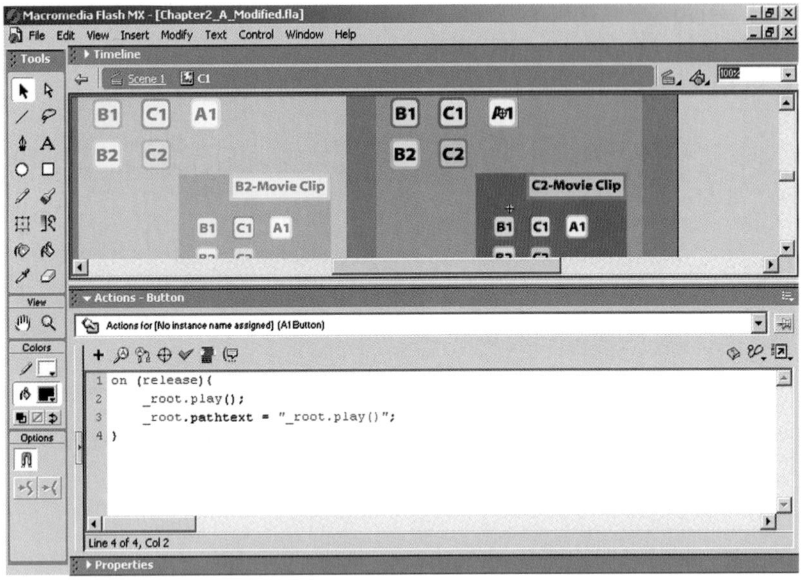

2.12: Edit the C1 movie clip and look at the code assigned to the A1 button in the C1 movie clip.

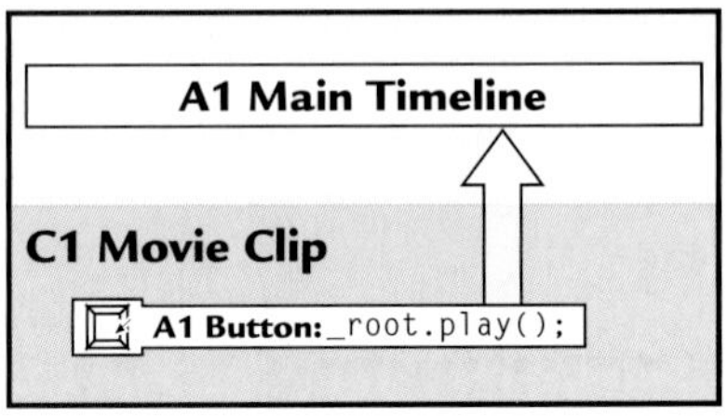

2.13: The `_root` *keyword tells Flash to route the command to the main timeline.*

> **NOTE** `_root` is a keyword, or a reserved word, that Flash has designated to mean the main timeline. You cannot use it in any other way. Internally, Flash refers to the main timeline as `_level0`, and you will see this when you have Flash display the internal names of things. You could have also written `_level0.play()` instead of `_root.play()`, but this is considered obsolete ("deprecated" in programmer's jargon).

Earlier, you saw how to route commands from the main timeline down through movie clips. Here, you've seen that to get commands back up to the main timeline, you simply need to follow the referencing rules you've learned. You can also continue this routing from the main timeline by going back down to a movie clip or through a series of nested movie clips. Let's look at an example.

9. Review the ActionScript Attached to the B2 Button

Select the B2 button within the C1 movie clip. Look at the ActionScript attached to the B2 button in the Actions panel (2.14).

```
on(release){
    _root.B1.B2.play();
    _root.pathtext = "_root.B1.B2.play()";
}
```

The line with the `play()` command starts with `_root`, so the first thing that happens is that the command is routed up to the main timeline. Then the command is routed down through the B1 movie clip to the B2 movie clip. As you can see, you can route the command

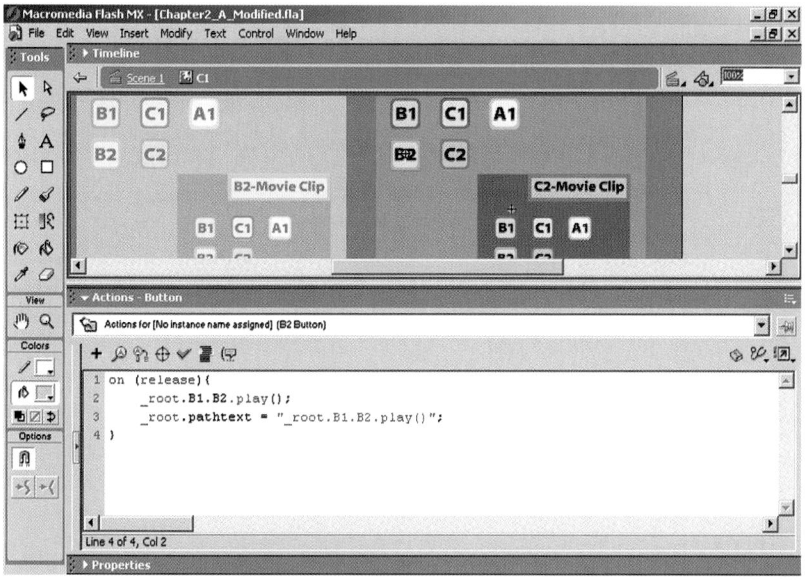

2.14: Look at the ActionScript assigned to the B2 button within the C1 movie clip.

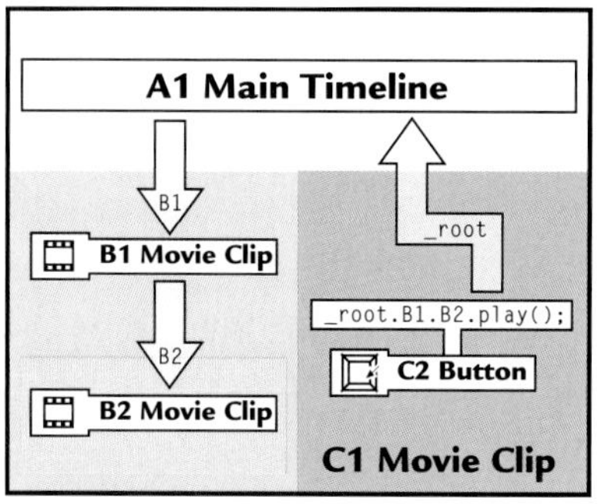

2.15: The `_root` *keyword allows you to start from the main timeline and work down through a series of movie clips by referencing the instance names.*

directly up to the main timeline, and then down to another movie clip, through the host movie clip.

The `_root` keyword allows you to skip up to the main timeline, no matter how far down the button is nested within movie clips (2.15). If you needed to work your way up through a series of movie clips and then back down through another series of movie clips, the `play()` command might become prohibitively long.

The `_root` keyword helps keep the code manageable when you're routing commands from movie clip to movie clip. However, there are times when it can be useful to send a command up through the chain of movie clips, rather than jumping straight to the main timeline, as you'll learn in the next section.

10. Review the ActionScript Attached to the C1 Button

Open the C2 movie clip and look at the code attached to the C1 button (2.16).

```
on(release){
   _parent.play();
   _root.pathtext = "_parent.play()";
}
```

`_parent` is another keyword that refers to the timeline on which the current movie clip is sitting. In this case, the C2 movie clip is nested within the C1 movie clip, or sitting on the C1 movie clip's timeline, so the C1 movie clip is the *parent* of the C2 movie clip.

Using the `_parent` keyword is a great way to create ActionScript that is versatile. With this syntax, ActionScript does not need to know the instance name of the parent movie clip. Therefore, this action will work even if you put this button into another movie clip. For example, you could have a movie clip that contains a button that always tells its parent movie clip to do something. You could place this movie clip with its button into any number of other movie clips, and the same code would work in the same way in every instance.

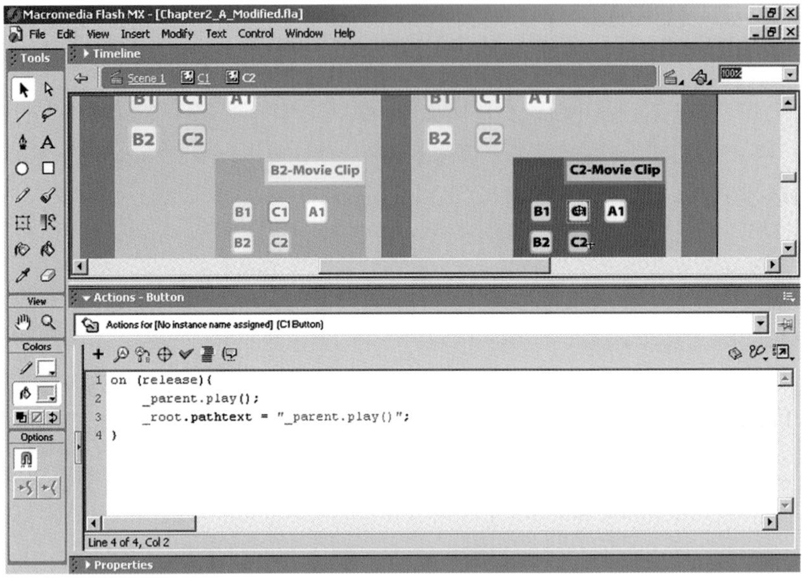

2.16: View the ActionScript assigned to the C1 button in the C2 movie clip.

In the case of the movie clips B1 and C1, the parent is the main timeline. Therefore, you can use the `_parent` keyword to refer to the main timeline.

NOTE Remember that no matter how deep you are in movie clips, you can always refer to the main timeline simply with `_root`. However, `_parent` only refers to the parent movie clip for a movie clip—which may or may not be the main timeline.

11. Test the Movie

Press Cmd/Ctrl+Enter to test the movie. Select each button in each of the different movie clips. Notice what is displayed in the text box at the bottom. This will help you understand how the buttons and movie clips communicate with each other.

The principles that you have looked at so far apply to all Flash communication. The basic rules don't change, no matter how the movie clip is placed on the timeline— permanently placed, dynamically placed, or set on a different scene. Let's look at some of the different ways that you can place movie clips with ActionScript and how communication works in these various scenarios.

Placing Movie Clips with ActionScript

Flash offers several options for integrating movie clips into a Flash movie beyond movie clips that you, as the Flash designer or programmer, place on a stage. Movie clips can be integrated into Flash movies with the following commands:

`duplicateMovieClip()` This command works as its name suggests: It duplicates a movie that is already on the stage. You can't use `duplicateMovieClip()` if the movie is not already on the stage. If there is ActionScript attached to a movie when you use `duplicateMovieClip()`, that code will be duplicated along with the movie clip. To remove movie clips that have been placed with `duplicateMovieClip()`, you must use `removeMovieClip()`.

`attachMovie()` This command is used to duplicate a movie clip from the library. The movie clip must have a name given to it using Flash's Linkage properties, as you will see in this chapter. To remove movie clips that have been placed with `attachMovie()`, you can use either `removeMovieClip()` or `unloadMovie()`.

`loadMovie()` This command is used to load an existing and external `.swf` file. To remove movie clips that have been placed with `loadMovie()`, you must use `unloadMovie()`.

`createEmptyMovieClip()` This command is new to Flash MX and is used to create an empty movie clip. This technique is mainly used with the new Flash drawing tools, which are covered in Chapter 9, "Drawing with ActionScript." To remove movie clips that have been placed with `createEmptyMovieClip()`, you must use `removeMovieClip()`. You won't be using this command in this chapter.

All four of these commands can be used on the main timeline or from within a movie clip. Now you'll learn about the unique characteristics of each option (except `createEmptyMovieClip()`) and see how they fit into Flash's communication scheme.

Duplicating Movie Clips

Duplicating movie clips is a valuable capability for a variety of applications, such as games and dynamically generated interfaces. For example, for a game, you might want to have a bunch of bad guys who all behave the same way. Often, it wouldn't be very feasible to place the bad guys on the stage manually. What would happen, for instance, if a bad guy got blown up and you wanted another bad guy to take his place? You could use `duplicateMovieClip()` to dynamically generate another one. In fact, you could use `duplicateMovieClip()` to create five bad guys for game level 1, 10 bad guys for game level 2, and so on (2.17).

NOTE *Dynamically generated* movie clips are those that are generated after the movie starts playing. They are not brought into existence until the code is executed and the code determines that the movie clip is needed.

Another useful application for `duplicateMovieClip()` is to create a dynamically generated menu bar. For example, you might want to make it easier to modify a site's navigation bar by getting each button's name and associated URL from a text file. That way, you could just edit the text file to update the menu bar, rather than needing to edit the Flash movie every time you wanted to make a change. In this scenario, you could use `duplicateMovieClip()` to duplicate movie clips that contain buttons depending on how many items are specified in the text file for the navigation bar (2.18).

Of course, these are only a few examples. The ability to dynamically generate duplicates of a movie clip is invaluable, and you'll be using the capability in several examples throughout the book. For now, let's explore how you can communicate with movie clips generated by `duplicateMovieClip()`.

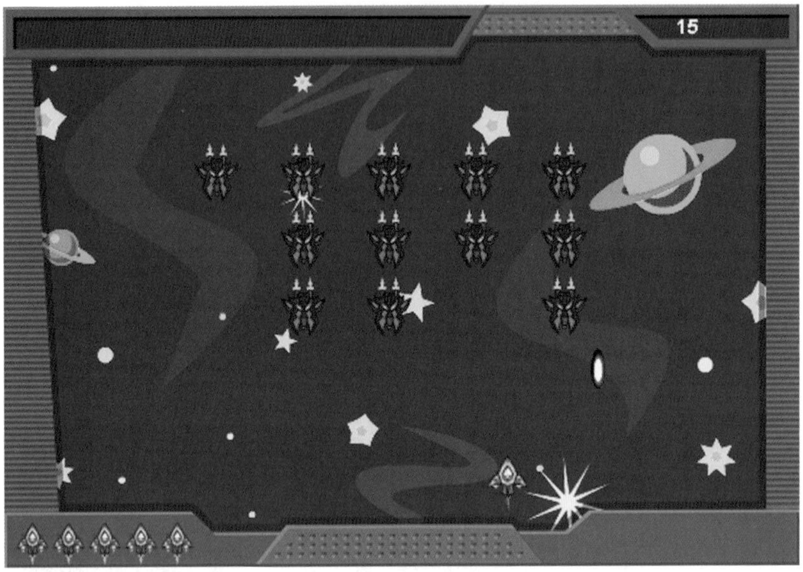

2.17: All of the red spaceships in the Invasion of the Galactic Goobers game from Eyeland Studio are dynamically generated using `duplicateMovieClip()`.

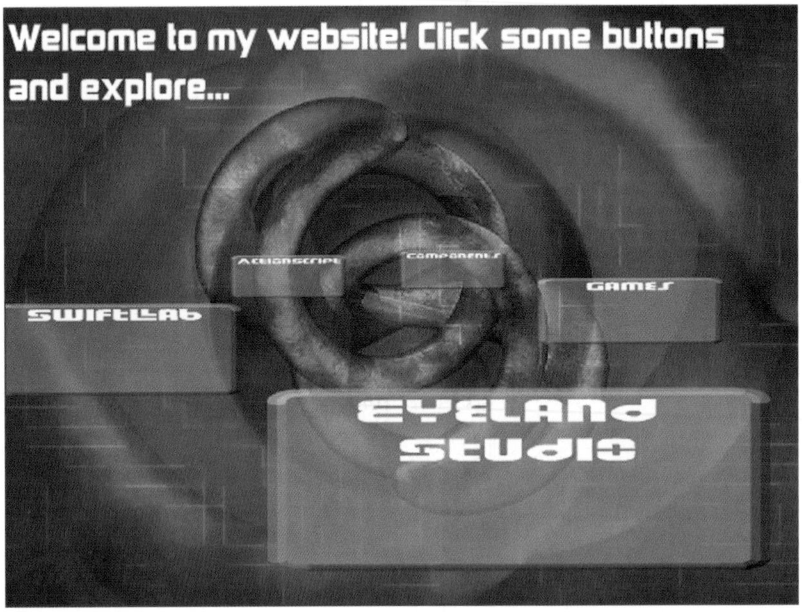

2.18: All of the buttons in this rotating menu from SwiftLab are dynamically generated using `duplicateMovieClip()`.

1. Open the File

WWW.

Open Chapter2_B_Start.fla. Save the file to your local hard drive and name it Chapter2_B _Modified.fla. (To see the finished version, open Chapter2_B_Final.fla.)

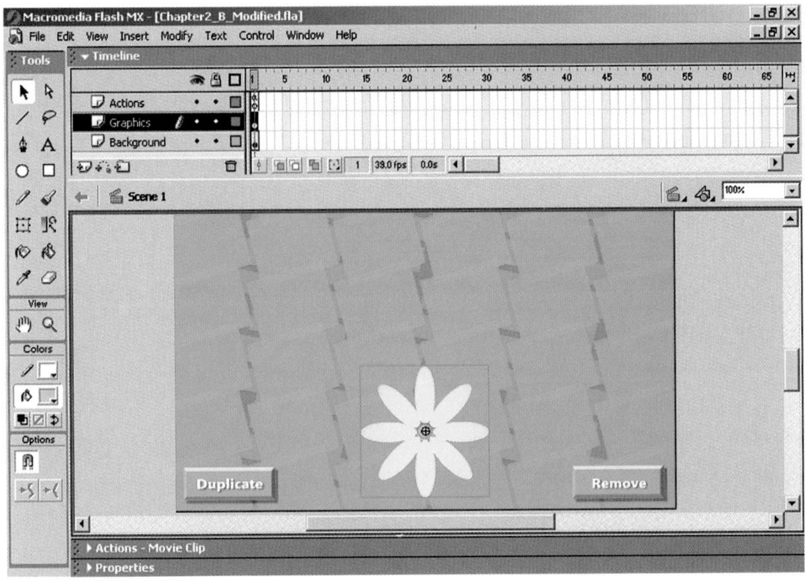

2.19: *The* Chapter 2_B_Modified.fla *file*

Notice that there are two buttons (Duplicate and Remove) and one Flower movie clip already on the main timeline (2.19). Test the movie and observe that the Flower movie clip plays (rotates and fades out), but the buttons don't work.

You will be writing code to duplicate and remove the Flower movie clip. Once you create duplicates of the movie clip, you'll need to be able to communicate with the duplicates in order to issue the command to remove them.

2. Review the ActionScript in Frame 1

Look at the ActionScript attached to frame 1 on the Actions layer. It begins like this:

```
// number of duplicate movie clips on the stage (also used
// for keeping the depths of the duplicates different)
```

The first two lines of code are called a *comment*. Whenever you see a line in a script that starts with two backslash characters (//), you know it is a comment. Comments are not executable code. They are for you, the human being, not Flash, the machine. Comments help you to stay oriented in the code and to explain what is happening in the code.

It's good programming practice to enhance your code with detailed comments. Comments make it easier for you to understand your code (which you'll appreciate if you look at it a year or so after you wrote it), as well as easier for other programmers to navigate through your code. You'll use comments throughout this book.

NOTE We won't talk about the remaining comments in the examples, because they're self-explanatory. Just remember that you add them to help orient yourself and others with the code.

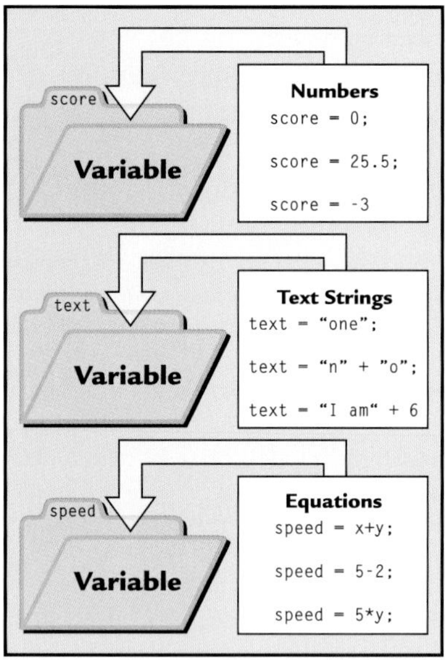

2.20: Variables are like folders where you can keep data in the form of numbers, strings, or results of calculations.

In this same ActionScript, you also see the definition of a variable named `num_movie_clips` set to 0.

```
var num_movie_clips = 0;
```

In this example, the `num_movie_clips` variable will be used to put each movie clip on a separate *level*. When Flash duplicates movies, the movies are placed on specific levels that can be numbered and tracked. If you tell a duplicate movie clip to occupy the same level as another duplicate movie clip, the new duplicate will replace the old duplicate, and you'll have only one duplicate of the movie clip.

Now that you've seen a few examples of variables in use, let's take a closer look at what variables are and how to use them in ActionScript.

Variables are containers that hold information. You can think of variables as virtual manila folders that can be any color or size. The folder is the name of the variable, in this case, `num_movie_clips` (2.20).

Variables can have almost any name. You could just have easily named the variable in this example `George` or `Fred`, and it would work. (Of course, names like those would not give you much idea what information the variable represented; using meaningful names is another way of documenting what your script does, along with adding comments.)

The important thing for the variable is the value. In this example, the variable `num_movie_clips` is set equal to 0. You will use this variable later in the code.

NOTE Variable names cannot start with a number; they must start with a letter or an underscore (_). They can have only letters, numbers, or underscores—no punctuation. Variable names are not case sensitive.

Notice the keyword `var` in front of the variable `num_movie_clips`. This specifically defines the variable the first time it is used. In Flash, it isn't necessary to use the keyword `var` for declaring a variable, but it's a nice habit to get into, because seeing `var` makes it easier to understand what the code is doing.

All variables exist for the duration of the movie by default. In some cases, you might want to use a variable for only a short time, as would be the case for a temporary variable. In this case, you don't need the variable to exist for the whole movie. You can limit the scope or duration of a variable, so that the variable has meaning only within a particular function or operation in a program, by using the `var` keyword and declaring it "locally" inside that function. For example, consider this `on(release)` event handler for a button:

```
on(release){
var myName = "jennifer";
gotoAndStop(myName);}
```

In this case the variable, `myName`, exists only while the actions within the braces are being performed, and then it is no longer available. In other words, if you wrote some ActionScript outside the braces and tried to get the value of the `myName` variable, you wouldn't get anything, because that variable would no longer exist.

NOTE Using the `var` keyword is a good way to keep your code optimized and efficient, especially when you choose to limit how long it has value or its scope. If you will need the variable only for a short time and/or in a limited context, using `var` will limit the scope of the variable. As a result, Flash won't need to keep track of the variable when it isn't needed, and your movie will run more smoothly and efficiently. The examples in this book will use `var` to define all variables, so that Flash will take care of the scope of each variable on its own.

3. Name the Instance myMovie

Select the Flower movie clip, open the Properties panel, and give it the instance name **myMovie** (2.21). You're going to add the code to duplicate a movie clip to the Duplicate button. The Flower clip needs an instance name, because this code must refer to a specific movie clip, or Flash won't know which movie clip to duplicate.

4. Assign ActionScript to the Duplicate Button

Attach the following code to the Duplicate button (2.22).

```
on(release){
   // keep track of how many movie clips are duplicated
   num_movie_clips++;
   // duplicate the movie clip
   myMovie.duplicateMovieClip("myMovie" + num_movie_clips, ►
num_movie_clips);
   // position the movie clip
   _root["myMovie" + num_movie_clips]._x = Math.random() * 550;
   _root["myMovie" + num_movie_clips]._y = Math.random() * 350;
}
```

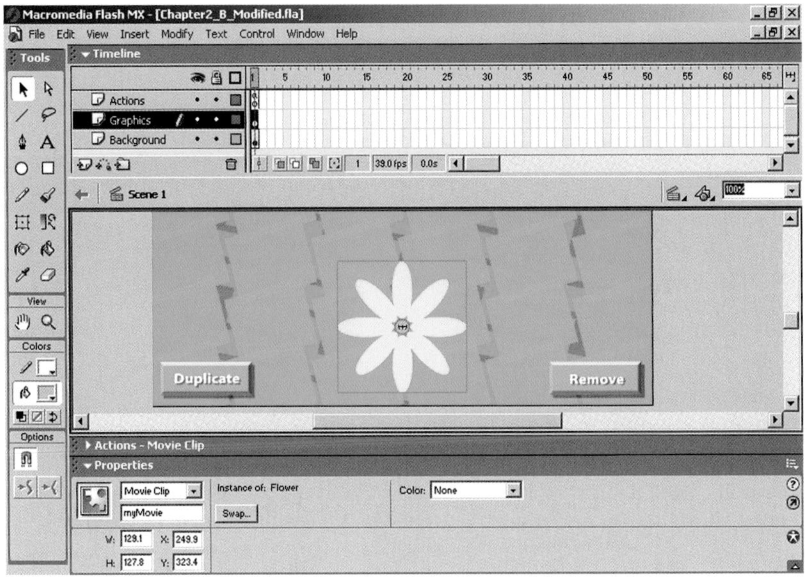

2.21: Give the Flower movie clip an instance name.

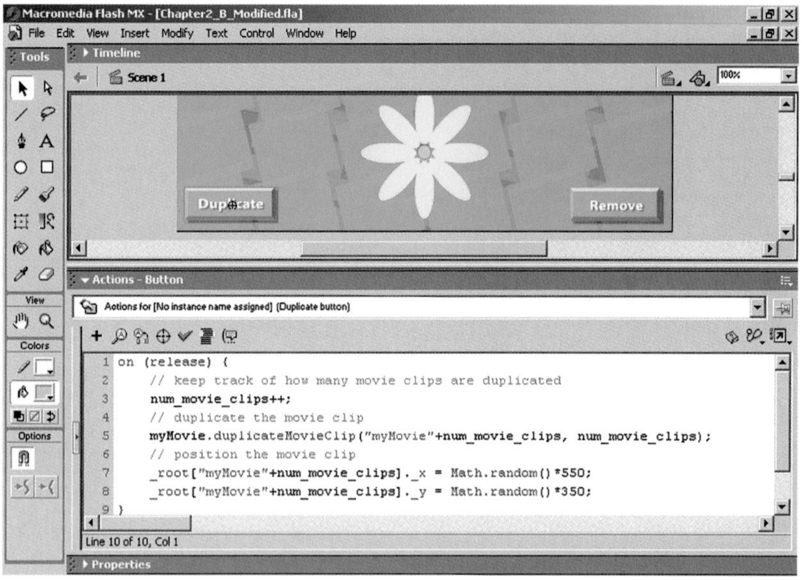

2.22: *Assign the code to the Duplicate button.*

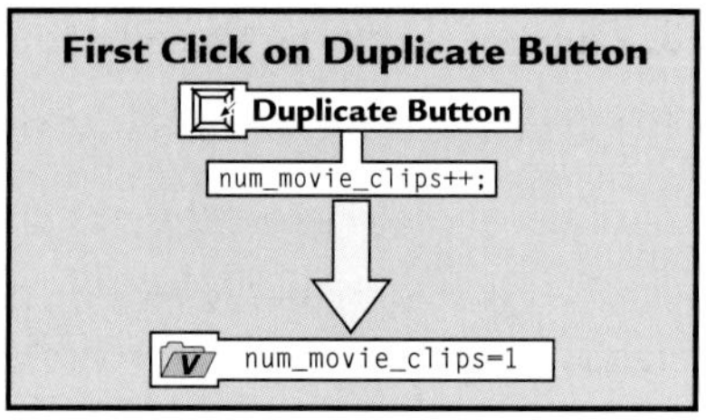

2.23: *The first click on the Duplicate button increases the value of the* `num_movie_clips` *variable by one.*

The first line within the event handler increments the `num_movie_clips` variable by one.

```
num_movie_clips++;
```

The ++ at the end of the line is called an *operator*. Operators are used in programming languages to perform common tasks, such as addition (+), subtraction (-), checking if equal (==), and, in this case, incrementing by one (++). Here, you want to take the value of the `num_movie_clips` variable and increase it by one each time the event handler executes. This is the same thing as saying:

```
num_movie_clips = num_movie_clips + 1.
```

Operators are very important in ActionScript. In fact, you've already been using another common operator: the equal sign (=). Other common operators include the following:

<	Less than
>	Greater than
*	Multiply
/	Divide
<=	Less than or equal to
>=	Greater than or equal to
--	Decrement by one

You will use many operators in the examples throughout this book.

In the current example, you increment `num_movie_clips` because you will use this variable to set each duplicate movie clip on a separate level. So, the first time someone clicks the Duplicate button, the first line in the script takes the value of the `num_movie_clips` variable, which is set to 0 when the movie first starts, and increases it by one. This means that after the first click on the Duplicate button, the `num_movie_clips` variable will equal 1 (2.23).

5. Duplicate the myMovie Movie Clip

The next line in the script is where you duplicate the myMovie movie clip:

```
myMovie.duplicateMovieClip("myMovie" + num_movie_clips, num_movie_clips);
```

Notice that this line in the script starts off with `myMovie`. By now, you should understand this reference. The `myMovie` portion of this statement tells Flash where to send the `duplicateMovieClip()` command—basically, which movie to duplicate. `myMovie` is a direct reference to the instance name you added to the Flower movie clip in the previous step.

The `duplicateMovieClip()` command works for any movie clip, even if it's embedded in another movie. Any movie clip can take advantage of this method and be duplicated. If the movie is embedded in another movie, the levels are within that movie clip. In this case, the levels are on the main timeline. If you were to put this within a movie clip, the levels would be for the timeline within the movie clip, not the main timeline.

Now notice that `duplicateMovieClip()` is followed by items in parentheses, which are called *arguments*. The `duplicateMovieClip()` method takes two arguments: The first argument is the name of the new movie clip, and the second argument is the depth, or level. Each argument is separated by a comma. So, the first argument is `"myMovie" + num_movie_clips`, and the second argument is `num_movie_clips`.

It's standard practice to name the new movie clip with the same name as the original plus the level number. In this case, the first argument has the instance name of the Flower movie clip, myMovie, as a string set within quotation marks. This string is concatenated with the value of the *`num_movie_clips`* variable. After the first click, the value of the *`num_movie_clips`* variable is 1. Therefore, in this case, the name of the new movie clip is myMovie1.

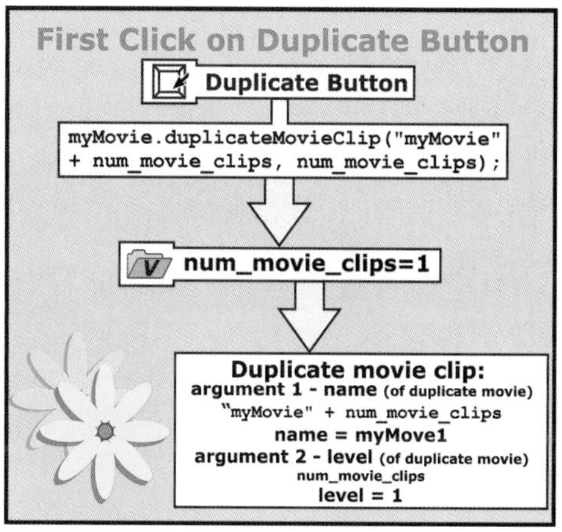

2.24: The name argument for the `duplicateMovieClip()` *command resolves to myMovie1, and the level argument resolves to 1.*

NOTE The term *concatenate* is used commonly in programming. It means that something is combined or appended to something else. For example, if you take "`Word`" and add 1 to it to make "`Word1`", you have concatenated the string "`Word`" with the number 1.

The second argument is the depth, or level, number that the duplicate movie clip is placed on. This argument simply uses the current value of the *`num_movie_clips`* variable. So, after the first click, the duplicate movie clip is placed on level 1. Remember that each duplicated movie clip needs to be placed on a separate level (2.24).

NOTE Do not confuse the levels/depths for movie clips created by `duplicateMovieClip()` with the layers on the timeline. There is no conflict between the layers in the timeline and this level 1. User-placed movie clips and movie clips placed by ActionScript will not conflict.

Finally, the third and fourth lines in the script add a bit of interest.

```
_root["myMovie" + num_movie_clips]._x = Math.random() * 550;
_root["myMovie" + num_movie_clips]._y = Math.random() * 350;
```

This code randomly places the new movie clip somewhere on the stage area. This ActionScript uses Flash MX functions and properties, as well as a bit of ActionScript trickery.

You are setting the *x* and *y* position of the movie clip using the properties `_x` and `_y`. These represent the clip's position on the stage along the horizontal axis (*x*) and vertical axis (*y*). You'll learn more about these properties in Chapter 3, "Cursor Interactions."

The `Math.random()` function returns a number between 0 and 0.9999 (which you can think of as 1). This will not help in the placement of the movie clip, because the result would be either 0 or 1, which isn't very random. To use the results from the `Math.random()` function to place the movie clips, you need to multiply it by a number. In this case, for the *x*-axis, you multiply it by 550, so the results will be numbers between 0 and 550.

NOTE It's important to know that the lowest number for the `Math.random()` function returns is 0, not 1. So if you want a number between 1 and 550, you need to use `Math.random() * 549 + 1`. You'll learn more about `Math.random()` and other useful functions in Chapter 4, "Used and Reused ActionScript."

In order to access the duplicated movie clip, you need to do a little trick. You know that the movie is named myMovie1, so you could simply write:

```
myMovie1._x = Math.random() * 550;
```

The problem with this is that the next time you duplicate a movie clip it will be named myMovie2. The solution is to make the ActionScript generic enough to handle this, by using `"myMovie" + num_movie_clips` to get the name of the current movie. Notice that the name starts with a ", which is why you cannot simply say this:

```
"myMovie" + num_movie_clips._x = Math.random() * 550;
```

Flash will return an error on the above statement because you are starting out with a string, `"myMovie"`, and trying set it equal to something. You can set variables equal to strings like `"myMovie"`, but you cannot set strings equal to anything but themselves.

If you write the following:

```
("myMovie" + num_movie_clips)._x = Math.random() * 550;
```

Flash won't return an error, but it also won't set the `_x` property to anything different. This is because Flash doesn't know what to do with the string at the beginning of the statement.

What you need to do is force Flash to evaluate `("myMovie" + num_movie_clips)` so that it will know that it is equal to myMovie1. In this example, you did this by using `_root[]`:

```
_root["myMovie" + num_movie_clips]._x = Math.random()*550;
```

The `_root[]` forces Flash to evaluate what is in the square brackets.

NOTE In this case, `_level0[]` would also work. Other keywords that can be used to force the evaluation are `_parent[]`, `this[]`, or a specific name of a movie, as in `sampleMovie[]`. For this particular case, you have the choice of `_root[]` or `_level0[]`. Remember that it's the square brackets that force the evaluation. Also, the `eval()` function, `eval("myMovie" + num_movie_clips)`, does the same thing.

6. Test the Movie and the Duplicate Button

Test the movie and click the Duplicate button several times. Notice that each time you release the Duplicate button, a new Flower movie pops up on the stage in a new place (2.25). Each one is a completely separate movie clip.

Now close the Test Movie window. It's time to enter the ActionScript to remove the movie clips.

7. Attach ActionScript to the Remove Button

Attach the following code to the Remove button (2.26).

```
on(release){
   // remove the last movie clip
   _root["myMovie" + num_movie_clips].removeMovieClip();
   // keep track of the number of duplicate movie clips
   num_movie_clips--;
}
```

2.25: Clicking the Duplicate button generates duplicates of the Flower movie clip.

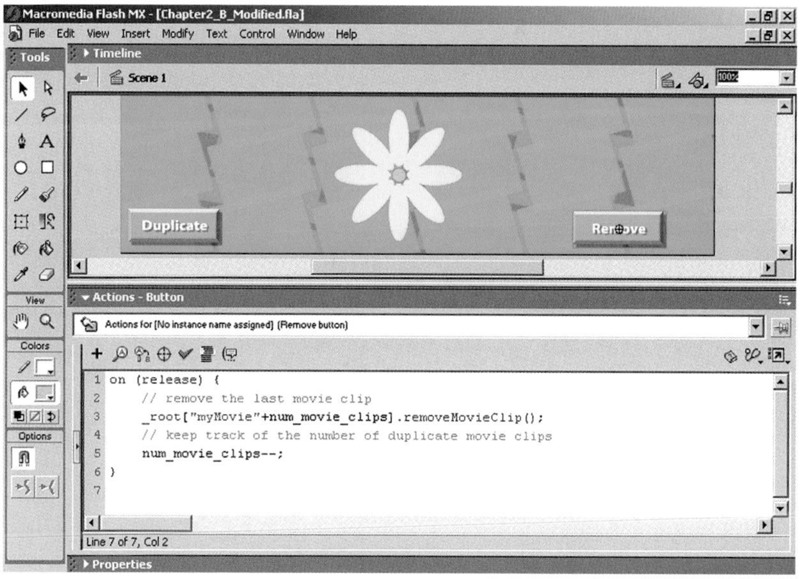

2.26: Add the script to the Remove button.

The first line of the code starts off with `_root["myMovie" + num_movie_clips]`. This portion of the `removeMovieClip()` line is what Flash uses to identify which movie clip to remove—which duplicate movie clip will receive the `removeMovieClip()` command.

By now it shouldn't be too hard to see how it works. The string `"myMovie"` is once again concatenated with the *`num_movie_clips`* variable. In this case, the idea is that the resulting number will result in targeting the last duplicate movie clip that was created. For instance, if you have clicked the Duplicate button five times, the *`num_movie_clips`* variable will equal 5, and the fifth duplicate will be named myMovie5.

If, at this point, you click the Remove button, the *`num_movie_clips`* variable will still be equal to 5. So the first line in this `on(release)` handler will resolve as follows:

```
myMovie5.removeMovieClip();
```

Therefore, this code always ends up removing the last movie clip that was created with the `duplicateMovieClip()` code attached to the Duplicate button.

Notice that `removeMovieClip()` does not need any arguments. It is a method of a particular movie clip, so when you call `removieMovieClip()`, you are essentially telling the movie clip to remove itself.

The second line in the script uses the `--` operator to decrement (subtract one) from the *`num_movie_clips`* variable, so that there is an accurate count of how many duplicates remain on the stage.

This example shows that communicating with duplicated movie clips is similar to communicating with movie clips on the stage. You still need to refer to the instance name of the movie clip when you issue a command to the movie clip. The main difference is that you need to create a variable to keep track of the number of movies created with the `duplicateMovieClip()` method. Then you can use that variable to generate the instance names that you need to be able to issue commands such as `removeMovieClip()` by concatenating the value with the base name for the duplicates.

If you had duplicated movie clips named mySecondMovie within the myMovie movie clip, the `removeMovieClip()` ActionScript would look like this:

```
_root.myMovie5.mySecondMovie1.removeMovieClip();
```

This is a simplified version that does not have variables for the levels.

8. Test the Movie

Test the movie. Notice that each time a movie is duplicated, it starts spinning and the fade starts. No matter how many duplicate clips you have out there, they are all doing their own thing, fading and rotating independently of each other. Click the Duplicate button and notice where the newest movie clip is positioned. Next click the Remove button and notice that the most recent movie clip is removed. When you are through testing, close the Test Movie window.

Attaching Movie Clips

Flash's `attachMovie()` method works basically the same as `duplicateMovieClip()`, but it adds a clip from the library rather than duplicating a clip that is on the stage. To learn about `attachMovie()`, you will replace `duplicateMovieClip()` with `attachMovie()` in the script you just tested.

1. Open the File

Save the file you worked with in the previous example (**Chapter2_B_Modified.fla**, or **Chapter2_B_Final.fla** if you prefer) as **Chapter2_C_Modified.fla.** (To see the completed version, open **Chapter2_C_Final.fla.**)

2. Export the Clip for ActionScript

Press Cmd/Ctrl+L to open the library. Cmd+Click (Mac) or right-click (Win) on the Flower movie clip and select Linkage from the pop-up menu. In the Linkage Properties dialog box that appears, click the Export for ActionScript check box. Leave the Export in First Frame check box selected. Type **AttachTest** in the Identifier field (2.27).

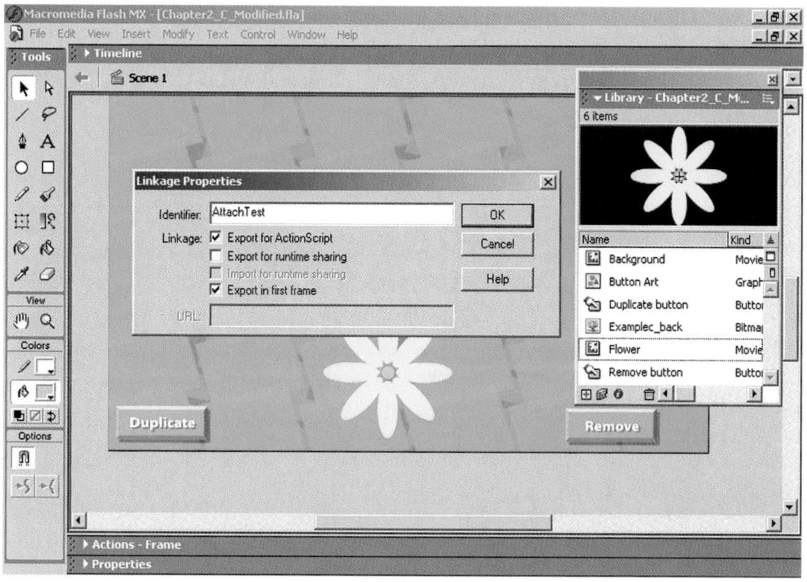

2.27: Give the Flower movie clip the identifier AttachTest.

By setting the Linkage to Export for ActionScript, you are telling Flash to export this symbol when the movie is run, even if the movie clip isn't on the stage. As with all movie clips that you want to control with ActionScript, the movie clip needs an instance name or identifier, which is AttachTest in this example. Scroll to the right in the library, and you'll see that the Linkage column reports that the Flower movie clip will be exported and AttachTest is its identifier (2.28).

3. Insert the *attachMovie()* Code

Open the Actions panel to see the ActionScript attached to the Duplicate button. Replace the line that has `duplicateMovieClip()` with the following (2.29):

```
_root.attachMovie("AttachTest", "myMovie" + num_movie_clips, ►
num_movie_clips);
```

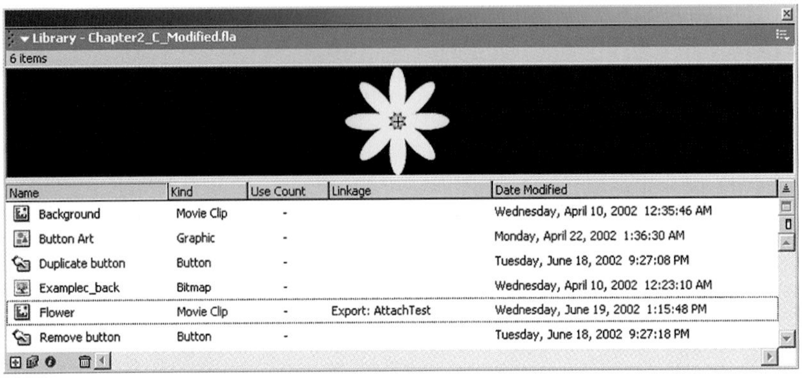

2.28: *The Linkage column shows that the Flower movie clip will be exported and has been given the identifier AttachTest.*

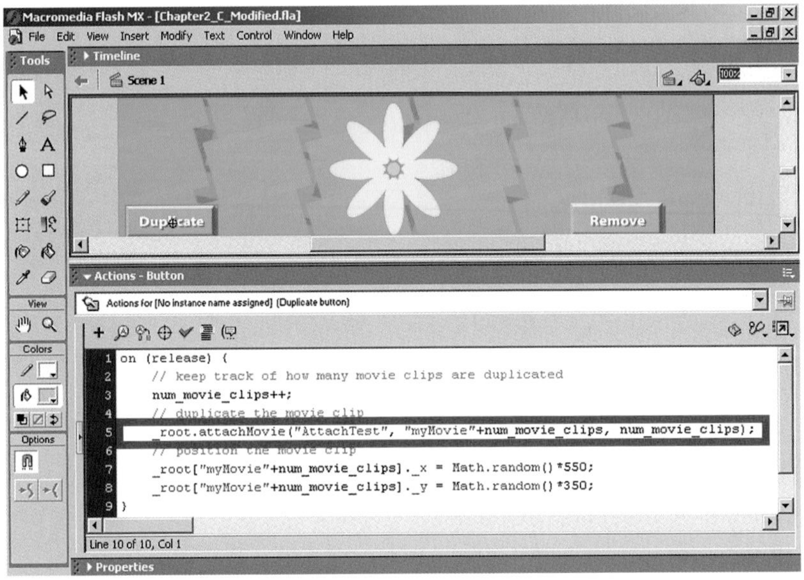

2.29: *Replace the* `duplicateMovieClip()` *code with* `attachMovie()` *code.*

The main difference between `duplicateMovieClip()` and `attachMovie()` is that `attachMovie()` takes one more argument than `duplicateMovieClip()`. Its first argument is the name of the movie to attach, or duplicate, which is AttachTest in this example. The other two arguments are the same as those for `duplicateMovieClip()`—the name of the new movie clip and the depth or level.

Essentially, you are duplicating the same movie clip, but it's being duplicated from the movie clip that is in the library, not from the movie clip on the stage.

4. Test the Movie

Test the movie. Click the Duplicate button a few times. Notice that the movie clip duplicates, but the duplicates no longer rotate or fade as they did when you used `duplicateMovieClip()`.

This is because the movie clip in the library—the one that was duplicated—does not have the code that is assigned to the Flower movie clip instance (myMovie) on the stage. If you want the duplicates that are created with the `attachMovie()` code to rotate and fade, you need to add to the library a movie clip that has the ActionScript attached to the myMovie instance, and then attach that clip instead. You'll do that next.

While you're still in test mode, click the Remove button a few times. You'll see that the Remove button works just fine. This is because `removeMovieClip()` works with movie clips added with `attachMovie()` or `duplicateMovieClip()`. Close the Test Movie window when you're finished.

5. Change the Movie Clip Instance

Select the myMovie movie clip on the stage and press F8 to open the Convert to Symbol dialog box. Enter **Flower Holder** in the Name field, select Movie Clip as its behavior, and click the OK button (2.30).

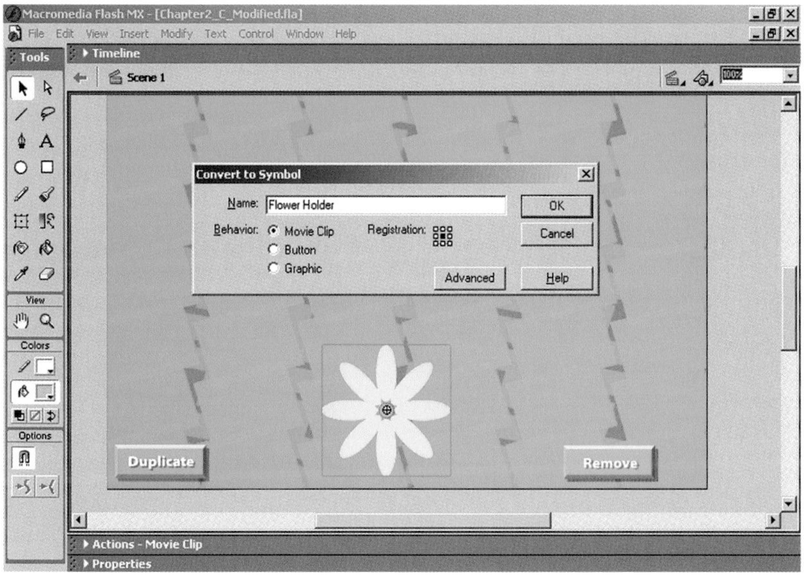

2.30: Turn the Flower movie clip instance on the stage into a movie clip named Flower Holder.

You've just created a movie clip that contains the movie clip instance that is on the stage. This means that the code that goes with that instance is also attached to the new movie clip, Flower Holder.

6. Unlink the Old Movie Clip and Link the New Movie Clip

Press Cmd/Ctrl+L to open the library. Cmd+Click (Mac) or right-click (Win) on the Flower movie clip and select Linkage from the pop-up menu. In the Linkage Properties dialog box, remove the check in the Export for ActionScript check box, and click OK.

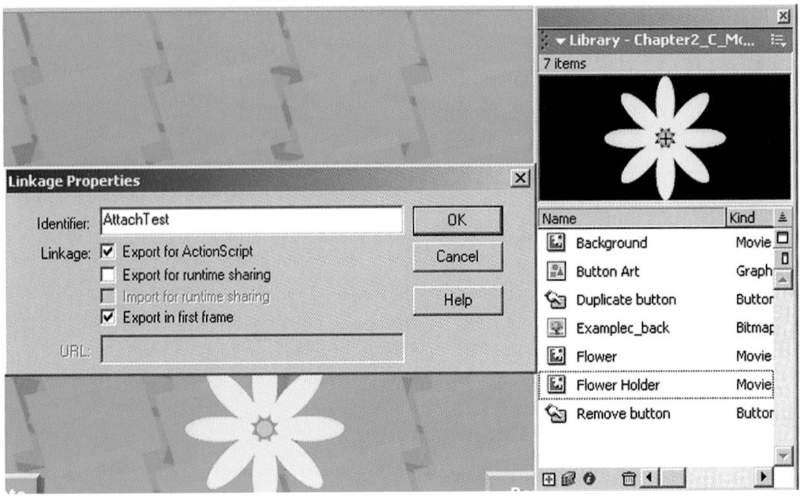

2.31: Set the Flower Holder movie clip to Export for ActionScript and give it the identifier AttachTest.

Next select the Flower Holder movie clip in the library, open its Linkage Properties dialog box, select the Export for ActionScript option, name it **AttachTest**, and click the OK button (2.31).

7. Test the Movie

Test the movie. You'll see that it behaves just the same as in the first example when you used `duplicateMovieClip()`, because the attached movie clip has the same ActionScript as the movie clip on the stage. Because the duplication is coming from the Flower Holder movie clip that is in the library, you no longer need the Flower Holder instance on the stage. This is the great thing about using `attachMovie()`. Close the Test Movie window when you're finished testing the movie.

Loading Movies

Flash movies can also be loaded into Flash using the `loadMovie()` command. This command actually loads an external `.swf` file that is already created. Because the `.swf` file is external, loading a movie is a way to update a Flash movie without going into the base movie; you can just change the external `.swf` file that is loaded.

There are some unique aspects to communicating with loaded movies as opposed to communicating with normal movie clips. However, much of what you've already learned applies to communicating with loaded movies. Let's look at an example to see the differences.

1. Open the *Load1.fla* File

WWW.

Open **Load1.fla** and save it to your local hard drive (2.32). This is the file for one of the two movies that you will load into a third movie. Test the movie.

This movie is composed of a simple tweening animation, two buttons, and a Movie 1 title. The two buttons are for starting and stopping Movie 2. Movie 2 is the other movie that

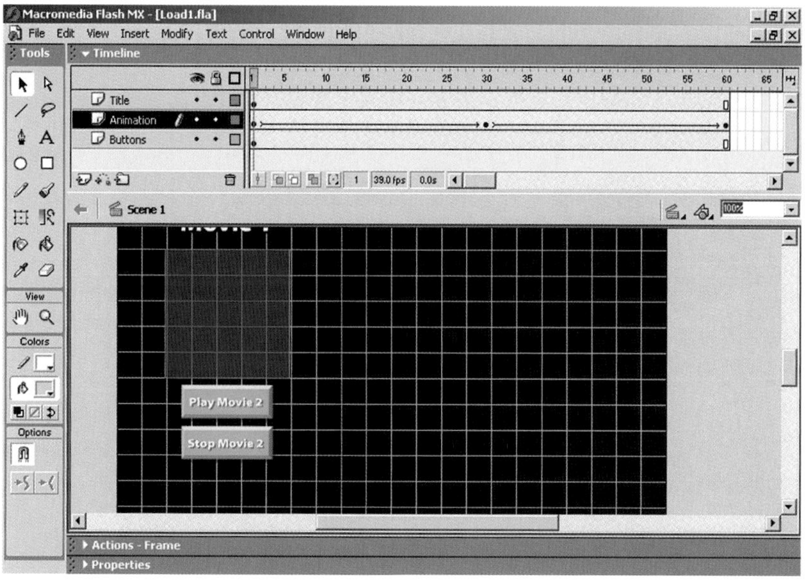

2.32: *The* Load1.fla *file*

is being loaded with `loadMovie()`. This means the buttons will need to communicate with a separate movie.

2. Review the ActionScript Attached to the Play Movie 2 Button

Look at the ActionScript attached to the Play Movie 2 button.

```
on(release){
   _level2.play();
}
```

This ActionScript tells whatever movie is in level 2 to play. At this point, you don't have a movie in level 2, so this button won't work. However, as you can see by the `_level2.play()` command, to communicate with loaded movies, you need to reference their level, rather than their instance name or identifier.

3. Open the *Load2.fla* File

Close Load1.fla. Open Load2.fla and save it to your local hard drive in the same directory in which you saved the Load1.fla file (2.33). This is the second movie you're going to load. Test the movie. WWW.

This movie contains an animation similar to the animation in the Load1.fla file, but the title says Movie 2 and the buttons are for playing and stopping Movie 1.

In this example, you'll load the Load1 and Load2 movies into a third movie using the `loadMovie()` command. The `loadMovie()` command needs .swf movies to work with. Fortunately, when you test movies, Flash automatically creates or exports the movies to the .swf format.

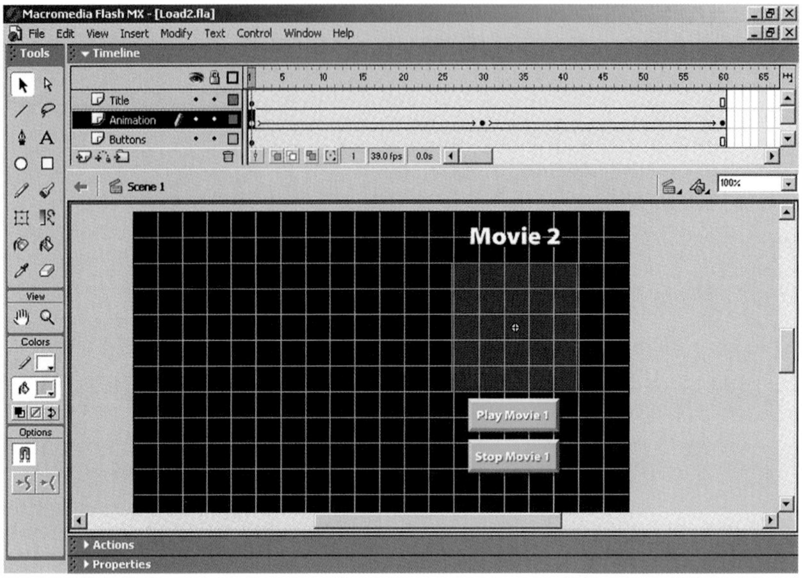

2.33: The Load2.fla *file*

4. Open the *Chapter2_D_Start.fla* File

WWW. Close Load2.fla. Open Chapter2_D_Start.fla and save it to your local hard drive as Chapter2_D_Modified.fla in the same directory in which you saved the Load1 and Load2 files. (To see the finished version, open Chapter2_D_Final.fla.)

The Chapter2_D_Modified.fla movie contains four buttons for playing and stopping Movie 1 and Movie 2 (as well as some background art). In this example, you'll attach ActionScript to each of these buttons, so it will do exactly what it says—play or stop the specified loaded movie.

5. Attach ActionScript to Frame 1

Attach the following ActionScript to frame 1 of the Actions layer (2.34).

```
// load the two animation movie clips
loadMovie("Load1.swf", "");
```

Here, you're using the `loadMovie()` global function, which takes two arguments: the name of the `.swf` file to load and the target (the name of a movie clip or the name of a level) to put it in. In this case, the second argument appears as two quotation marks with nothing between them, which the `loadMovie()` function interprets as `_root` (the default target).

NOTE There is also a `loadMovie()` method that is a method of the MovieClip object. The `loadMovie()` method and the `loadMovie()` function do essentially the same thing, but the `loadMovie()` method needs to be called from a movie clip, and it does not have a level parameter. The `loadMovie()` method replaces the movie clip that uses the method with the newly loaded movie. So, if you had a movie clip named Flower and you said, `Flower.loadMovie("Load1.swf");`, the Flower movie clip would become the Load1 movie.

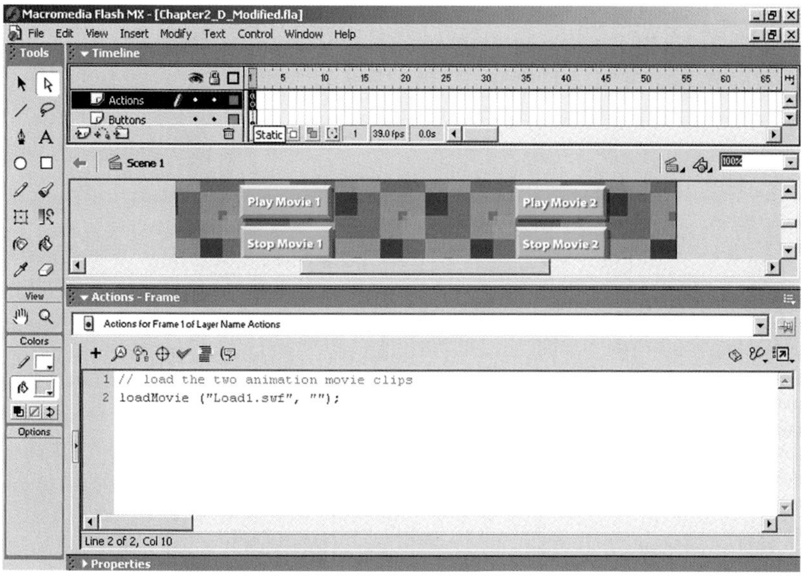

2.34: *Assign the code to the first frame.*

6. Test the Movie

Test this movie. You'll see that the Load1 movie has loaded, and the animation is playing. But notice that the buttons that were in the main timeline from the Chapter2_D_Modified file are gone.

The buttons that you're seeing are the buttons that are within Movie 1 (Load1.swf). This is because you loaded the movie into the `_root` timeline; whatever else was there has been replaced. In some cases, you might want this to happen. For instance, you could have a slide show broken down into smaller sections and load each one into the `_root` timeline as needed. However, in this case, it is not what you want.

The `loadMovie()` function's second argument is always the target. You could create an empty movie clip, place it on the main timeline, give it an instance name, and use the instance name as the second argument. This would load the movie into the empty movie clip and not affect the `_root` timeline. Loading a movie into a movie clip allows you to place a loaded movie more precisely, and it also means that you can animate or apply scripting to the movie clip that contains the loaded movie. You could also use the `loadMovie()` method attached to the empty movie clip to achieve the same results.

However, for now, let's take a simpler approach. You'll use another global function called `loadMovieNum()`. Close the Test Movie window, and let's continue.

7. Modify the *loadMovie()* Code

Modify the `loadMovie()` ActionScript in frame 1 to look like this (2.35):

```
loadMovieNum("Load1.swf", 1);
```

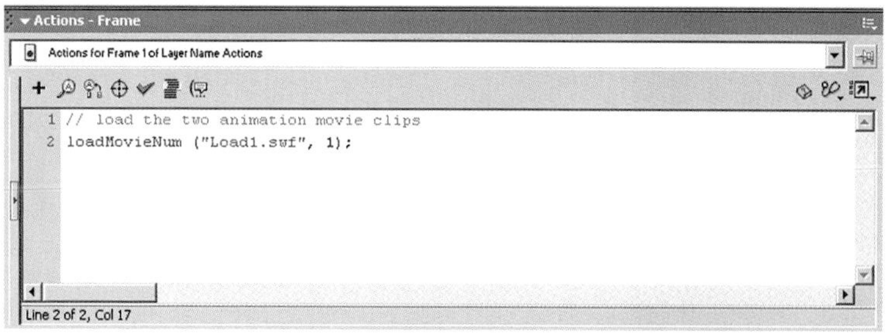

2.35: *Modify the code on the Actions layer.*

Like the `loadMovie()` function, the `loadMovieNum()` function also takes two arguments. The difference is that the second argument is the number of the level in which to load the movie. This example loads the same movie (Load1) into level 1. (Level 0 is the `_root` timeline.)

8. Test the Movie

Test the movie. Now Movie 1 (Load1) loads into the host Flash movie without replacing the original buttons on the main timeline of the host movie. As you might have guessed, using `loadMovieNum()` also helps to facilitate communication with the loaded movies by referring to what level the loaded movies are on.

How does Flash know where to place Movie 1 (Load1) and Movie 2 (Load2)? In this case, if you look at the **Load1.fla** file, you'll notice that the stage size is the same size as the movie it is getting loaded into (**Chapter2_D_Modified.fla**), and that the art in **Load1.fla** is all to the left side of the stage. When you load a movie to a level, it loads in the exact center of the main timeline and overlaps anything that is already on the main timeline. You can see the existing buttons in the `_root` timeline because the **Load1.fla** file doesn't have anything on its timeline to hide them. If you put a background image in either Movie 1 (Load1) or Movie 2 (Load2), the background image would cover the buttons and the background from the host movie.

Close the Test Movie window. Now let's load the other movie.

9. Add ActionScript to Frame 1

Put the following ActionScript in frame 1, below the line you entered previously (2.36).

```
loadMovieNum("Load2.swf", 2);
```

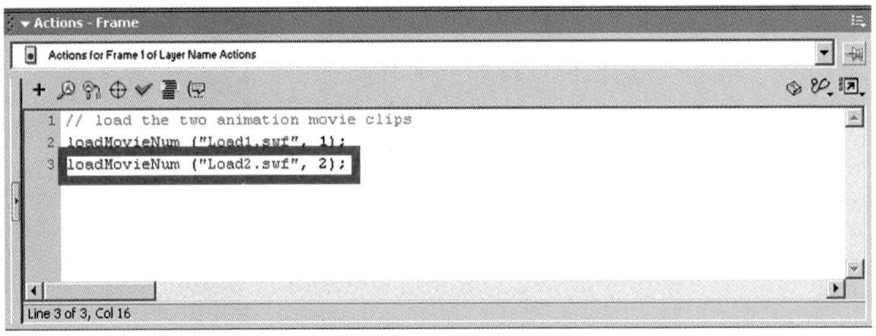

2.36: Add the second `loadMovieNum()` *action.*

Notice that this line is similar to the line you entered earlier. You are loading the **Load2.swf** file (Movie2) and putting it on a different level (level 2).

> **NOTE** Although you added the second `loadMovieNum()` command beneath the first one in this example, this wasn't really necessary. Because these are separate commands and they have no dependency on each other, it doesn't matter which one comes first.

10. Test the Movie

Test your movie. Now you see both movies running at the same time. However, you really have three movies running simultaneously—the two loaded movies and the main, or host, movie.

If you test the buttons that come with the loaded movies, they will work, because the code for controlling the movies has already been assigned. Don't worry—the actions used on those buttons are the same actions you're about to enter for the buttons in the host movie.

The buttons in the loaded movies work because you loaded them in the expected levels. If you had loaded the movies into level 3 and 4, the buttons would not have worked, because they would be referring to something in two levels that don't exist.

Close the Test Movie window. Now let's look at how easy it is to communicate with these loaded movies.

11. Attach ActionScript to the Play Movie 1 and Play Movie 2 Buttons

Attach the following code to the Play Movie 1 Button (2.37).

```
on(release){
   _level1.play();
}
```

Attach the same code to the Play Movie 2 button, except change the level number reference.

```
on(release){
   _level2.play();
}
```

As you can see, this script is very simple. To issue a command to a loaded movie, you just need to point the command to the level on which the movie is loaded. Here, you just tell whatever movie is in level 1 to play. Since Movie 1 (Load1) is loaded into level 1, this script tells Movie 1 to play. You did the same thing for the Play Movie 2 button.

Only one movie can occupy a level at a time (as you saw when you loaded Movie 1 into the `_root` layer). These levels are the same levels used in `duplicateMovieClip()` and `attachMovie()` commands, so if you loaded a movie into level 2 and also attached a movie into level 2, these movies would conflict. In that case, only the last movie would appear on level 2.

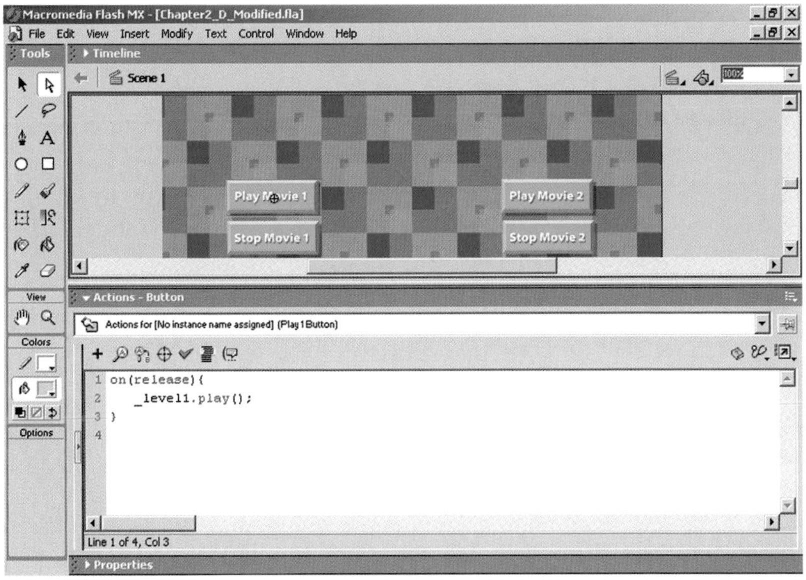

2.37: Add the script to the Play Movie 1 button.

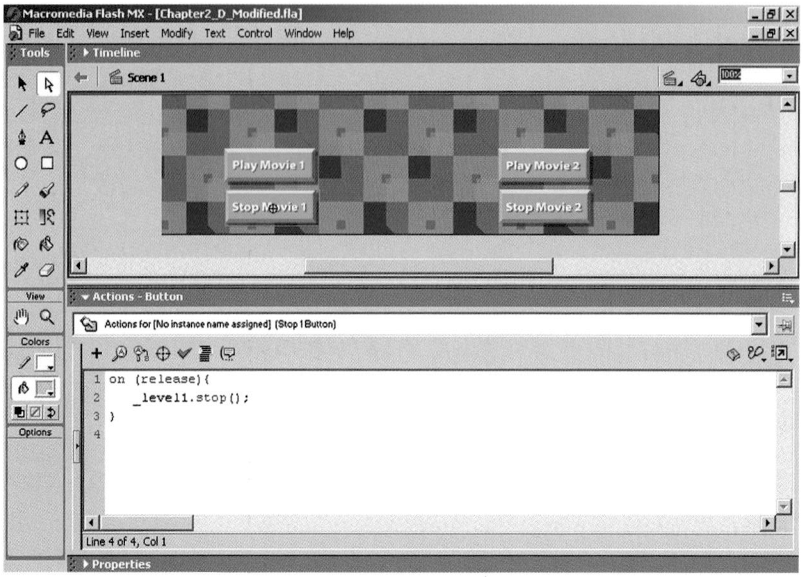

2.38: Add the script to the Stop Movie 1 button.

12. Attach ActionScript to the Stop Movie 1 and Stop Movie 2 Buttons

Attach the following code to the Stop Movie 1 button (2.38).

```
on (release){
    _level1.stop();
}
```

Attach the following code to the Stop Movie 2 button.

```
on (release){
    _level2.stop();
}
```

13. Test the Movie

Test your movie. Now all of the buttons work. Close the Test Movie window.

In this example, you've seen that communication with loaded movies is very simple and consistent. For example, the buttons within the loaded movies also refer simply to `_level1` and `_level2`, and yet they work just as well as the buttons in the main movie. Working with `loadMovie()` can be challenging when you're coordinating between the various Flash files for the various movies, so it's nice that the communication between the movies is simplified.

Unloading Movies

There are two options for unloading movies that have been loaded using the `loadMovie()` function: `unloadMovie()` or `unloadMovieNum()`. When you are using `unloadMovie()`, you need to reference a target. In this case, the target is the path. For example, to unload a movie placed with `loadMovie()` on level 2, the ActionScript would be as follows:

```
unloadMovie("_level2");
```

Notice that the level is in quotation marks.

The `unloadMovieNum()` function references a level number to remove a movie. For example, to unload Movie 1 on level 1, the ActionScript would be as follows:

```
unloadMovieNum(1);
```

There is a bit of a drawback to using these methods. You cannot refer to the movie by name; you must refer to the level. Remember that the code to play the loaded movie was `_level1.play()`, not `movie1.play()`.

For more "idiot-proof" ActionScript that is forgiving even if you load in different levels, I suggest using the `loadMovie()` method on an empty movie clip. The movie clip would have nothing in it, and you could load it into any level. When you wanted to play the loaded movie, since it is loaded into a movie clip, you could simply tell the movie clip to play using its instance name, which would, in turn, play the loaded movie. This way, it wouldn't matter on which level the movie was loaded.

Communication between Scenes

Flash allows you to place movies on different scenes. Scenes are a way of organizing your movie. Sometimes it's easier to have the parts of a Flash movie in different sections. For instance the preloader could go on the first scene, the main movie on the second scene, and the farewell screen on the third scene.

When you move from scene to scene, movie clips can essentially go away, which can make communication difficult. When you want to communicate between movie clips on different scenes, you need to go to a little extra trouble. Let's look at an example.

1. Open the File

Open Chapter2_E_Start.fla and save it to you local hard drive as Chapter2_E_Modified.fla (2.39). (To see the finished version, open Chapter2_E_Final.fla.) WWW.

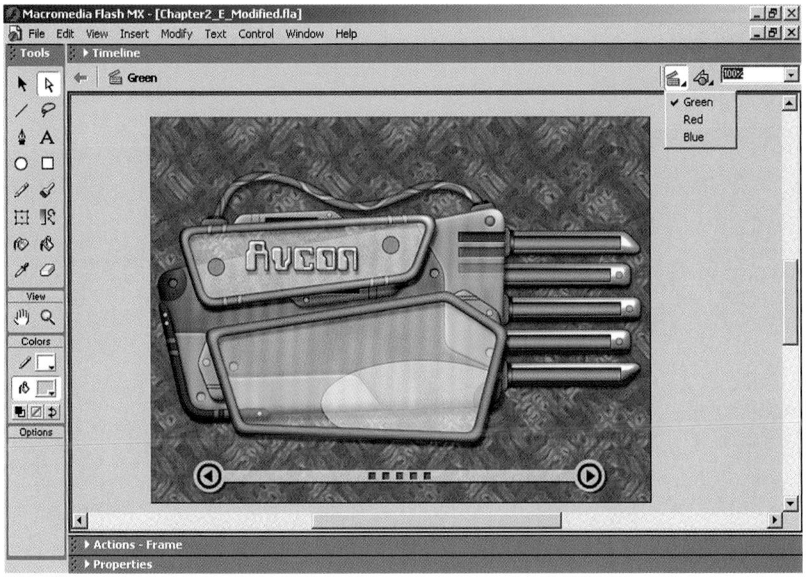

2.39: The Chapter2_E_Modified.fla *file*

This Flash file has three scenes. Each scene has a movie clip placed on the stage and a simple button bar with forward and backward buttons. Each scene is also labeled Begin in the first frame. Each movie clip has three frames with different art in each frame.

2. Test the Movie

Test the movie. You get the rollover effect for the buttons, but nothing else. That's because you haven't programmed anything in yet.

Also, notice that the Output panel has two warning messages in it about duplicate labels (2.40). Even though the scenes have different names, the example uses the same label (Begin) for the first frame of each scene. Flash doesn't like this, and it will definitely cause problems. It's best to give each label a different name, even in separate scenes.

Close the Test Movie window. Next you'll fix the label problem and then add some code.

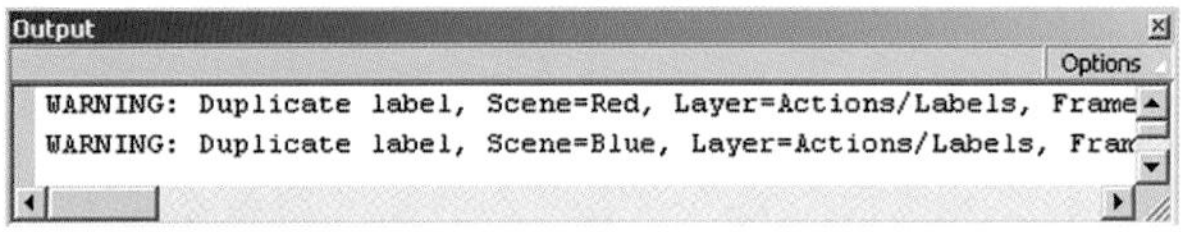

2.40: The Output panel produces two warnings about duplicate labels.

3. Name Each Scene's Label

Go to each scene, open its Properties panel, and rename the Begin label to **BeginGreen**, **BeginRed**, and **BeginBlue**, respectively (2.41). If you want, you can add some frames to the Actions/Labels layer, so that you can see the new frame labels better. This will not affect the movie, because there is a `stop()` action on the first frame of every scene.

Adding the unique labels will help you to avoid duplicate label warning messages and other problems.

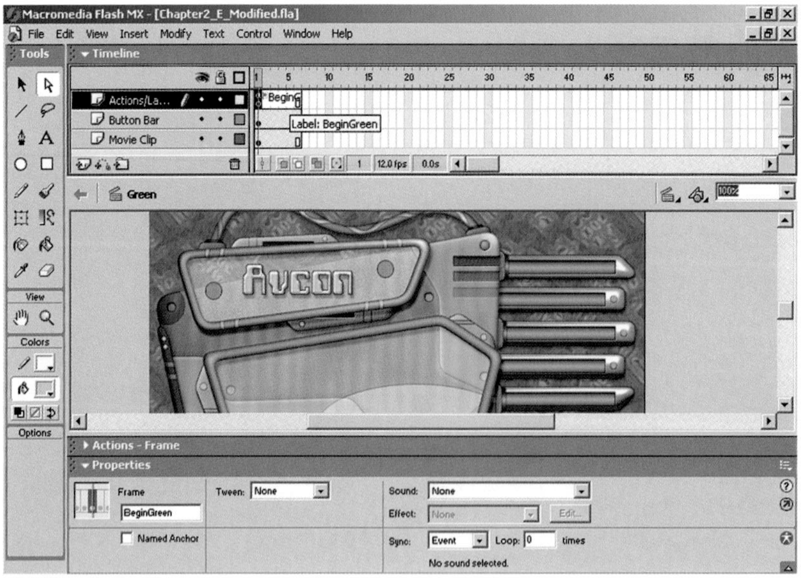

2.41: Rename the frame labels for the first frame of each of the scenes.

Now you're ready to add some ActionScript. You're going to program this example so that every time you click the forward or backward button, it will not only go to the next or previous scene, but it will also tell the movie clip in the next or previous scene to display a random frame from the movie clip that is in that scene.

You could just have each movie clip display a random frame every time the scene is displayed by attaching a random script to each movie clip in each scene. However, to demonstrate how to communicate between scenes, you'll use the buttons to handle the random code.

Typically, you would program the buttons to change scenes with code something like this:

```
gotoAndStop("Red", 1);
```

However, that only takes you to the next scene; it doesn't let you communicate with the movie clip in the next scene. To establish communication, you need something a bit more robust, as you'll see in the next step.

4. Attach Code to Frame 1 of the Green Scene

Attach the following ActionScript to frame 1 of the Green scene above the `stop()` action (2.42).

```
Label1 = "BeginGreen";
Label2 = "BeginRed";
Label3 = "BeginBlue";
LabelNumber = 1;
```

This will initialize variables that have the frame 1 labels for each of the scenes. The *LabelNumber* variable sets the number of the scene that you are in (the Green scene is scene 1). This way, you can say `gotoAndStop(Label3)`, and Flash will go to the BeginBlue frame, because the variable *Label3* is equal to `"BeginBlue"`.

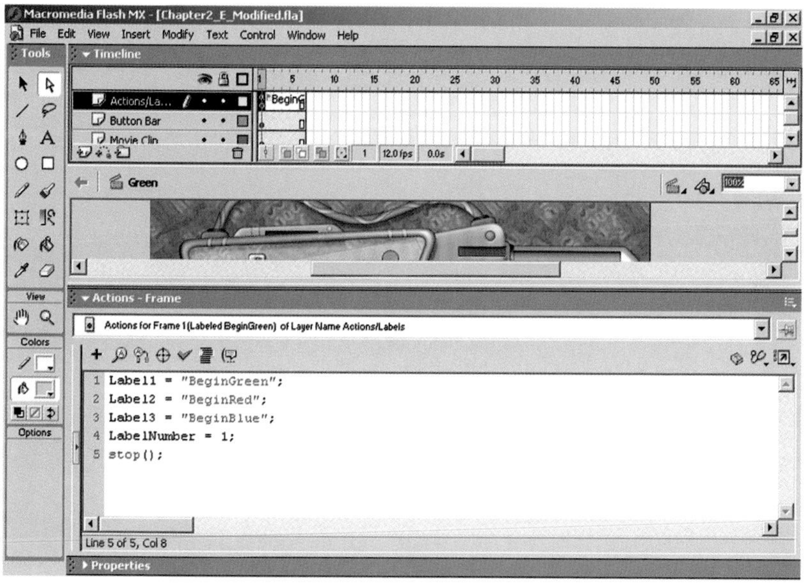

2.42: Add code to frame 1 of the Green scene.

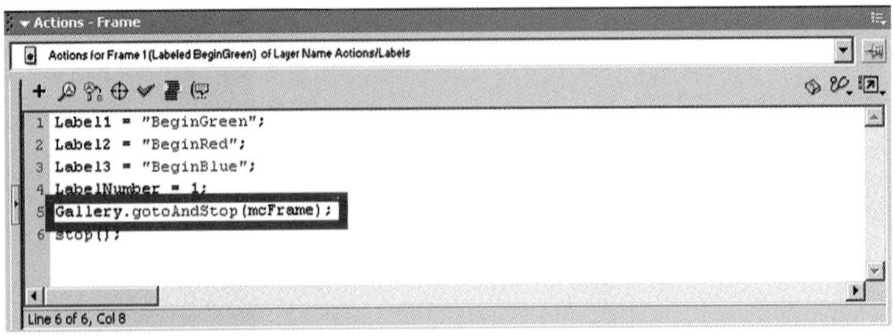

2.43: Assign each movie clip on each scene the instance name Gallery and apply the code to frame 1 of each of the scenes.

5. Name the Scene's Movie Clips

Select the movie clip in the Green scene, open the Properties panel, and give it the instance name **Gallery**. Go to the Red scene and name that movie clip **Gallery**. Now go to the Blue scene and name that movie clip **Gallery** also.

Attach the following ActionScript to each scene at frame 1 before the `stop()` action (2.43).

```
Gallery.gotoAndStop(mcFrame);
```

Each frame now has something that communicates with its respective movie clip. All of the movie clips have the instance name Gallery. It doesn't matter that they all have the same instance name, because when you go from one scene to the next, the movie clip from the previous scene goes away.

The code you just added tells the movie clip Gallery to go to the frame *`mcFrame`*. You cannot apply a command like `Gallery.gotoAndStop(1)` to a button on scene 1 (Green) and have it directly communicate with the Gallery movie clip on scene 2 (Red). However, you can have a variable that exists between scenes and use the variable as the communication link. In this example, the variable is *`mcFrame`*, which you'll define in the next step.

6. Attach ActionScript to the Next Button

Attach the following ActionScript to the next button (the circle with a right-pointing arrow) on the Green scene (2.44).

```
on(release) {
    _root.mcFrame = Math.round(Math.random() * 2 + 1);
    _root.LabelNumber++;
    if (_root.LabelNumber > 3){
        _root.LabelNumber = 1;
    }
    _root.gotoAndStop(_root["Label" + _root.LabelNumber]);
}
```

There's a lot happening here, so let's go through it line by line. The first line after the `on(release)` event handler is:

```
_root.mcFrame = Math.round(Math.random() * 3);
```

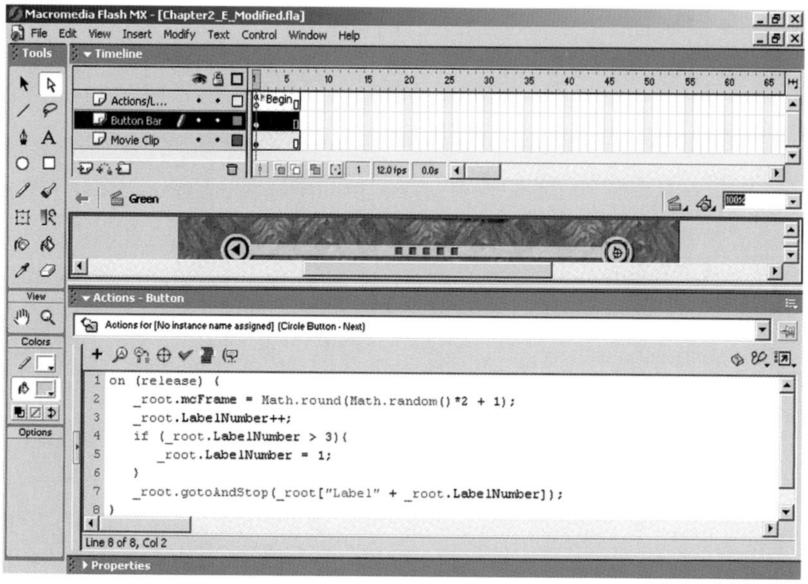

2.44: Apply the script to the next button in the Green scene.

This script is where you establish the value of the *mcFrame* variable. You're going to put the buttons into a movie clip, so you need to use `_root` to reference any variables that are on the main timeline.

In Flash, a variable is instantiated the first time it is used, so in this case, `_root.mcFrame` does not exist until you press a button. Also remember that the *mcFrame* variable you referred to in the previous ActionScript is the same thing as `_root.mcFrame` here.

This first line sets the variable *mcFrame* to a random number between 1 and 3. As explained earlier in this chapter, the `Math.random()` method returns a number between 0 and 0.999. In this case, you want a number between 1 and 3, so you multiply the results from `Math.random()` by 2, which will give you number between 0 and 1.999, and then you add 1 to the results, which will give you a number between 1 and 2.999, but it will be a decimal, or fractional, number. Frame numbers are whole numbers (like 1, 2, and 3) not decimal numbers (like 1.34 and 2.56). So you need to round the fractional number using the `Math.round()` method. This method will take whatever number is returned by the `Math.random()` method and round it to the nearest integer.

As mentioned previously, each movie clip actually has three frames of different graphics. You want to be able to access each of these, and you want to have them accessed randomly. In other words, each time you go to a different scene, you randomly show a different graphic from within the movie clip.

The next line is:

```
_root.LabelNumber++;
```

This code increments the *LabelNumber* variable (on the `_root` timeline). The ++ operator function means *LabelNumber* = *LabelNumber* + 1. When the user clicks the next button on the Green scene, the *LabelNumber* variable is changed to 2, so the code will be able to see that you're on the second scene.

The next two lines are:

```
if (_root.LabelNumber > 3){
_root.LabelNumber = 1;}
```

These lines use an `if` statement, or condition, to decide if this ActionScript needs to be executed. You'll learn about `if` conditions in Chapter 4. For this example, you just need to know that this `if` condition checks if the *LabelNumber* value is higher than 3. If the *LabelNumber* value is higher than 3, then the next line is executed; if it is not, the script skips the section that is within the curly braces `{}`. The line within the `if` statement (or curly braces) simply resets the *LabelNumber* variable back to 1. This line won't be executed if the value of the *LabelNumber* variable is less than 3. These two lines ensure that the *LabelNumber* variable value never gets above 3, which is the last scene. It's important that these two lines come *after* the code that increments the *LabelNumber* variable.

Finally, the last line is:

```
_root.gotoAndStop(_root["Label" + _root.LabelNumber]);
```

This tells the main timeline to go to the appropriate label. Remember that you named the first frame of each scene BeginRed, BeginGreen, and BeginBlue. Also recall that you put the names of these frames in the variables *Label1*, *Label2*, and *Label3*. In the above ActionScript, you are saying go to *Label2*, which is equal to BeginRed and found only in the Red scene. So you go to the next scene.

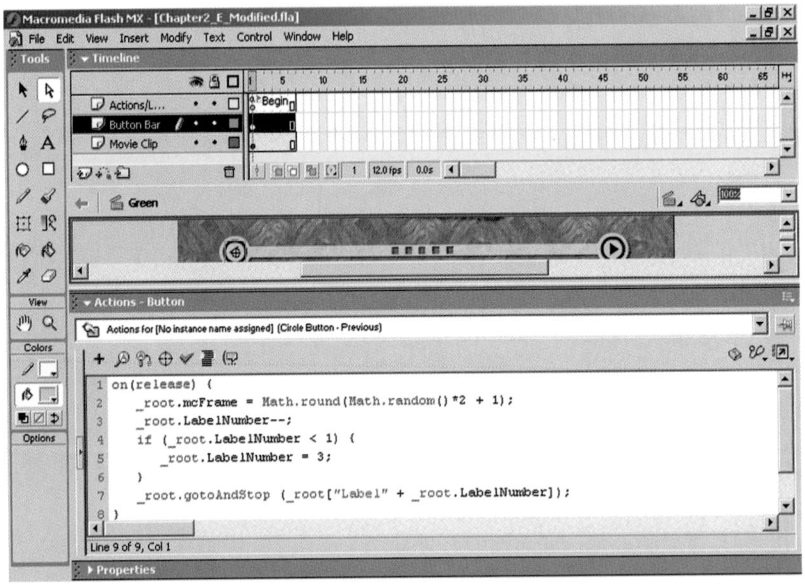

2.45: Apply the script to the previous button in the Green scene.

7. Attach ActionScript to the Previous Button

Attach the following ActionScript to the previous button (the circle with a left-pointing arrow) on the Green scene (2.45).

```
on(release) {
```

```
        _root.mcFrame = Math.round(Math.random() * 2 + 1);
        _root.LabelNumber--;
        if (_root.LabelNumber < 1) {
            _root.LabelNumber = 3;
        }
        _root.gotoAndStop (_root["Label" + _root.LabelNumber]);
    }
```

This code is similar to the code that you attached to the next button. In fact, it works pretty much the same, except for a couple of differences:

- The *LabelNumber* value is decremented (`_root.LabelNumber--`) by one each time the previous button is clicked.
- The `if` statement keeps the *LabelNumber* variable from going below 1. If it drops below 1, it is reset to 3.

The code you've just entered for both buttons on the Green scene will actually work on any scene. You don't want to reenter all of that code again for each of the buttons on each scene. Fortunately, there's an easier way.

8. Create a Button Bar Movie Clip

Select the two buttons and the white bar graphic on the Green Scene and press F8 to open the Convert to Symbol dialog box. Enter **Button Bar** in the Name field, choose Movie Clip for the behavior, and click the OK button (2.46).

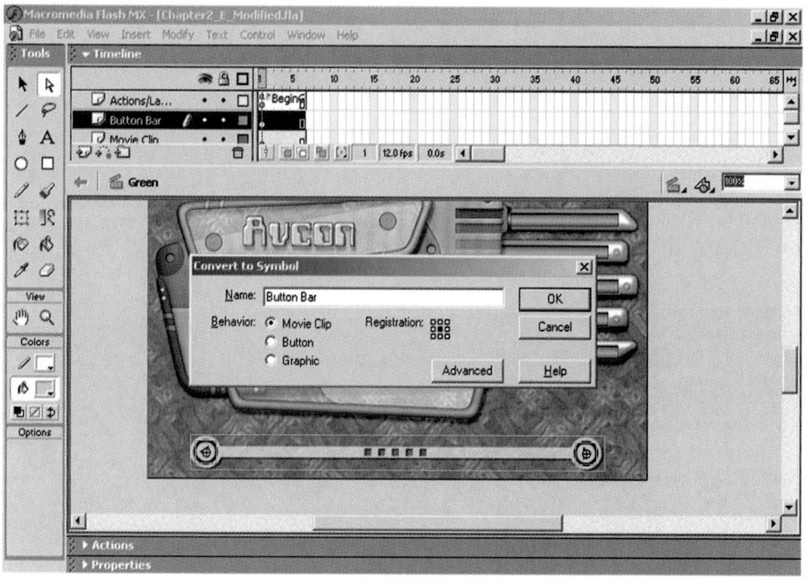

2.46: Make a movie clip name Button Bar out of the buttons and the white bar artwork.

9. Copy the Button Bar Movie Clip

Follow these steps to replace the buttons on each scene with the Button Bar movie clip:

1. Select the Button Bar movie clip on the Green scene and press Cmd/Ctrl+C to copy it.
2. Go the Red scene and delete the buttons and the white bar artwork.
3. Select the first frame of the Button Bar layer and press Cmd+Shift+V (Mac)/ Ctrl+Shift+V (Win) to paste in place. This will paste the Button Bar movie clip into the Red scene in the same location that it is on the Green scene.
4. Go the Blue scene and delete the buttons and the white bar artwork.
5. Select the first frame of the Button Bar layer and press Cmd+Shift+V (Mac)/ Ctrl+Shift+V (Win) to paste in place.

Now you have the same Button Bar movie clip in all three scenes. It's time to test the movie and see if it works.

10. Test the Movie

Test the movie. Notice that you're using the same Button Bar movie clip for all of the scenes, and it works. This saved some time.

Also notice that each time you go to a new scene, you get a new graphic in the movie clip. This proves you are communicating with a movie clip on the next scene. Even though you gave the movie clips on each scene the same name, you cannot communicate with a movie clip that is in a scene that is not currently displayed. So you used the `mcFrame` variable instead. This variable is helpful because it is on the `_root` timeline, so it's always available.

Debugging Communication and Scenes

Debugging is the process of finding out why your Flash movie doesn't behave in the way you expected or wanted it to. Debugging can often be intimidating if you're not an experienced programmer. Debugging will be covered in detail in Chapter 11, "Troubleshooting." But since the most common problems with ActionScript tend to involve communications issues, let's take a look at some easy solutions.

As you've seen in this chapter, you'll use instance names for movie clips, identifiers for `attachMovieClip()`, and variable names in a lot of your scripts. Effective communication in Flash hinges on whether or not these instance names, identifiers, and variables have been spelled correctly. If you're trying to send a `play()` command to a movie clip with an instance name of myMovie and you inadvertently write something like `mymovi.play()`, your `play()` command won't be sent to the correct movie (in fact, it probably won't go to any movie at all). One of the most common and easy debugging techniques is to go through and make sure all of your references to instance names, identifiers, and variables are spelled correctly.

Also, it's a good idea to be careful when naming scenes, labels, movie clips, and functions. If any of them have the same name, the results are interesting and usually not what you want. Also be aware that scene names are case sensitive—"red" is not the same as "Red."

Another point to keep in mind is that scenes can be accessed only from the main timeline. You could not have the Button Bar movie clip tell the movie to go to scene Green. It would not work, no matter how you spelled it. A trick to get scenes to advance from a movie clip is to put a label on the last frame of the scene you are in. Then you can call this label from your movie clip with the `gotoAndPlay(label)` command. When Flash hits the last frame of the scene, it will advance to the next scene.

Conclusion

In this chapter, you've learned how to handle Flash's various levels of communication. You now know how to communicate with the main timeline, no matter how deeply embedded the command is in a movie clip, by using the keyword `_root` in front of a command or to access a variable. You also learned how to communicate with movie clips, wherever they are located, by using the instance name and the path. Another approach covered here allows you to write reusable ActionScript: By using the keyword `_parent`, you can access the timeline the movie clip is sitting on, whether it's the main timeline or the timeline of a movie clip nested several layers deep.

You used the various techniques for communicating with movie clips to create a movie clip on the stage dynamically, using the `duplicateMovieClip()`, `attachMovie()`, and `loadMovie()` commands. Although each of these commands is used in a slightly different way, they all use the same communication structure as regularly placed movie clips. Finally, you learned how to use scenes to organize your movies and how to communicate between scenes.

The concepts and tools covered in this chapter are fundamental to creating animation in Flash. Once you understand Flash communication, you can move onto other basic programming techniques, such as using and creating buttons, which is the topic of the next chapter.

CHAPTER three

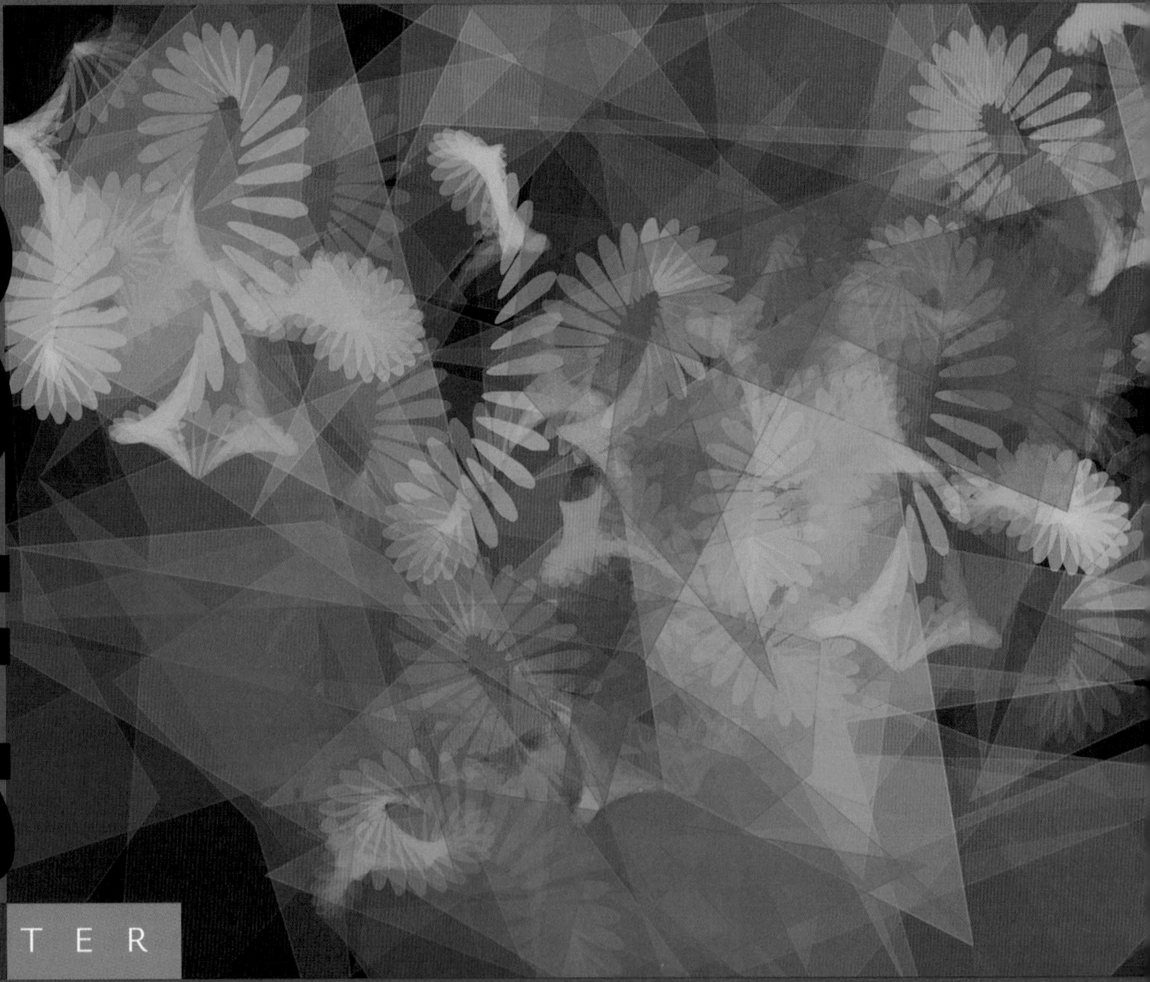

Cursor Interactions

The cursor or mouse *is the main means by which people interact with a Flash movie. Clicking buttons, in particular, is the most common trigger for event handlers. This means that, for a designer, buttons are one of the keys to implementing interactivity.*

Buttons in Flash now have some built-in behavior. They handle functionality such as cursor changes, rollover changes, and key-down changes inherently—*that is, without any additional programming. They also have event handlers to capture just about anything you would normally do with a button. However, Flash MX has added a lot more functionality for buttons to give you more control. You can now control buttons' properties and methods. Also, Flash MX has opened the door to making movie clips act like buttons, which makes it easier to create more interesting animated buttons.*

This chapter provides a deeper look at some of the ways to use and create buttons, as well as ways to use their properties and methods. You'll also learn about using movie clips as buttons and mouse interaction.

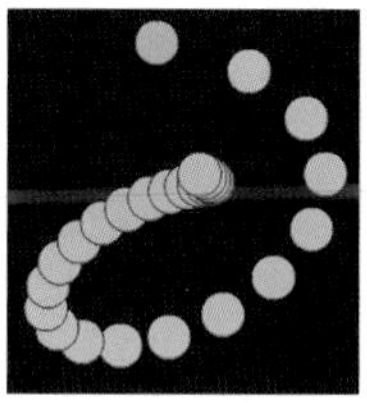

Programming Buttons

In Flash MX, all buttons are now Button objects. Flash MX has added to buttons almost all the same properties that are available for movie clips, so you can control both elements in much the same way. This provides a good opportunity to use code for controlling properties. That's what you'll do in the following examples.

Changing a Button's Properties

To get started, you'll change a single property of a button, to make it appear to become transparent when you roll the mouse over it. You'll open the sample file, give the button an instance name, change the property that controls transparency, and, finally, test the movie.

1. Open the File

Open the Chapter3_A_Start.fla file. Save the file to your local hard drive with the name Chapter3_A_Modified.fla. (To see a finished version of this movie, open Chapter3_A_Final.fla.)

2. Give the Button an Instance Name

Select the button that is already on the stage, open the Properties panel, and give it the instance name **NewButton** (3.1).

You'll be using instance names for the buttons so that you can route commands to the buttons, as you learned in Chapter 2, "Flash Communication."

> **NOTE** Flash 5 (and earlier) users might recognize that this is a new capability in Flash MX. Previous versions of Flash had no option for giving a button an instance name.

3. Change the Button's Transparency

Attach the following ActionScript to the NewButton button (3.2).

```
on(rollOver) {
   NewButton._alpha = 50;
}
on(rollOut) {
   NewButton._alpha = 100;
}
```

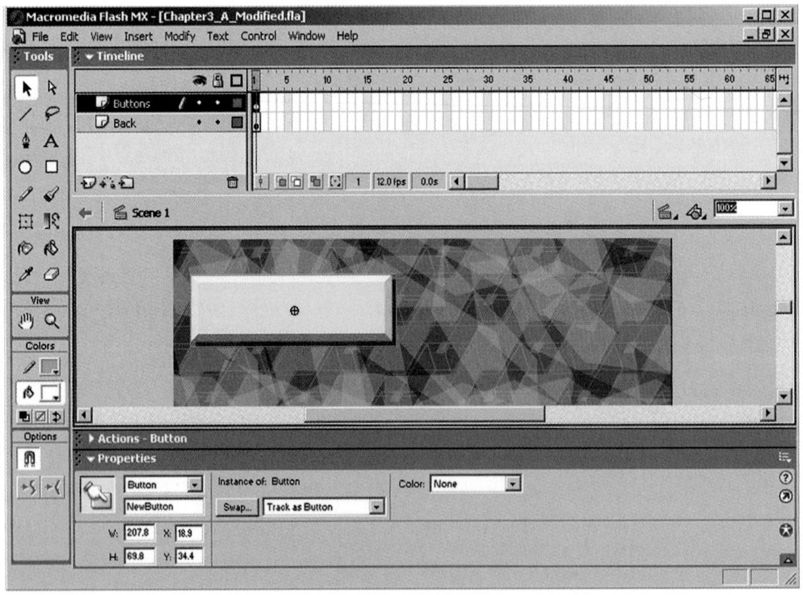

3.1: Add the instance name NewButton to the button that is already on the stage.

This script changes the `_alpha` property, or transparency, of the button to 50% when someone rolls the cursor over the button. The `_alpha` property reverts to 100% (fully opaque) when the cursor rolls off the button.

Note that this is the sort of change you could have made by putting artwork that was 50% opaque in the Over state of the button. However, using the button's Over state takes more time and resources. You get a small file-size savings when you create the effect with code, rather than using the graphical interface, and it's quicker and easier to implement and change. For instance, if you wanted to change the `_alpha` to 80%, you would just go in and change `50` to `80`.

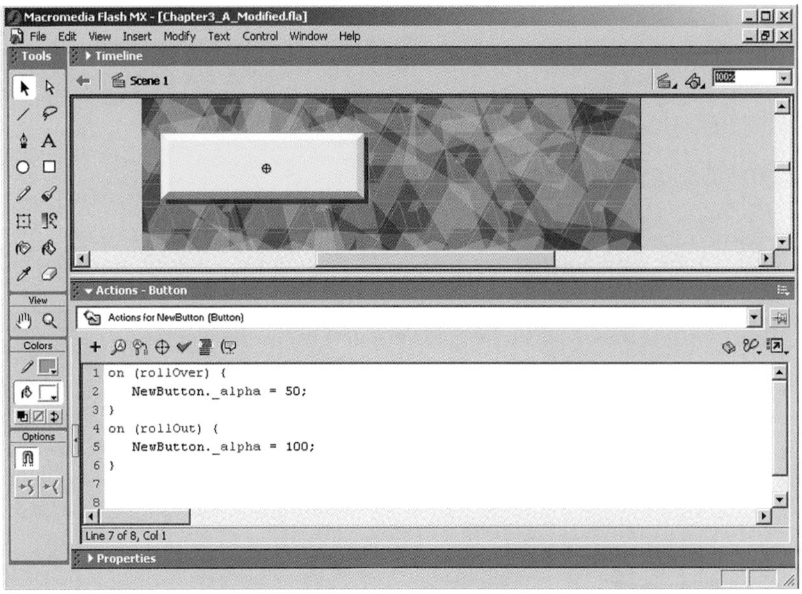

3.2: Add the script to the button.

This code changes the `_alpha` property of the button. *Properties* are characteristics of an object that can be manipulated with ActionScript. By adjusting properties, you can control characteristics of an object, such as its opacity, position, height, width, and so on.

Properties can be compared to human characteristics (3.3). For example, your hair color could be a property of the object You. Let's say you wanted to write code to change your `_haircolor` property when the `Mid_Life_Crisis()` event is triggered, and then revert back to the default blonde for `_haircolor` when the event `Come_To_Your_Senses()` is triggered. The event handlers for such a sequence might look something like this:

```
On(Mid_Life_Crisis) {
   You._haircolor = red;
}
on(Come_To_Your_Senses) {
   You._haircolor = blonde;
}
```

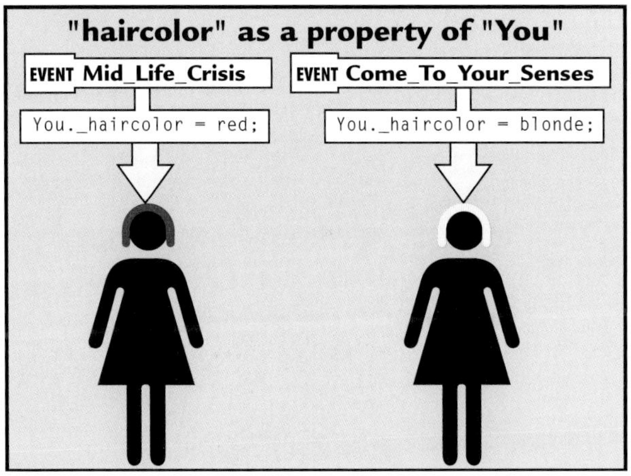

3.3: Properties of a Flash object are similar to characteristics of a human.

Note that properties are not arbitrary. Just as you cannot arbitrarily decide to have wings so that you can fly, you cannot arbitrarily define a property for a button to have it turn into an audio clip. A button's properties in ActionScript are appropriate to the ways buttons function in Flash MX. Any given object has a limited number of properties, and they can be manipulated in only specific ways.

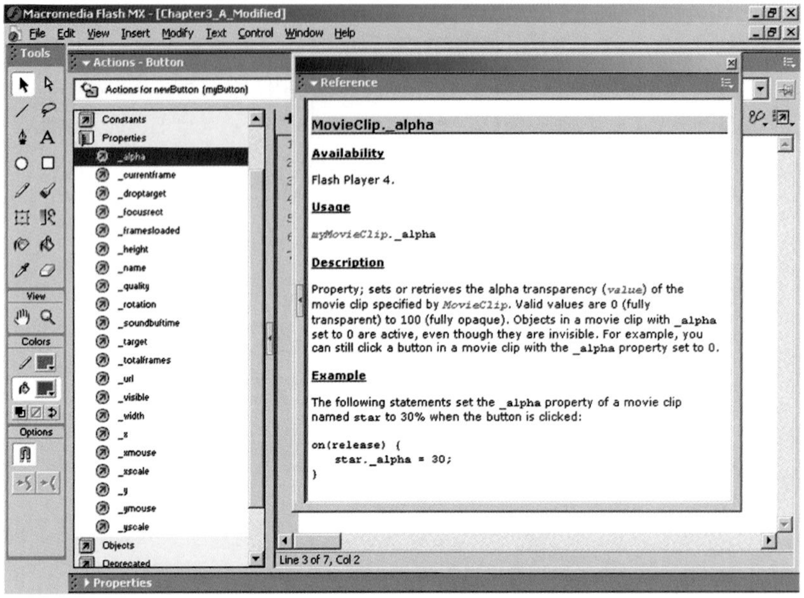

3.4: You can use the Actions toolbox to get quick information on properties.

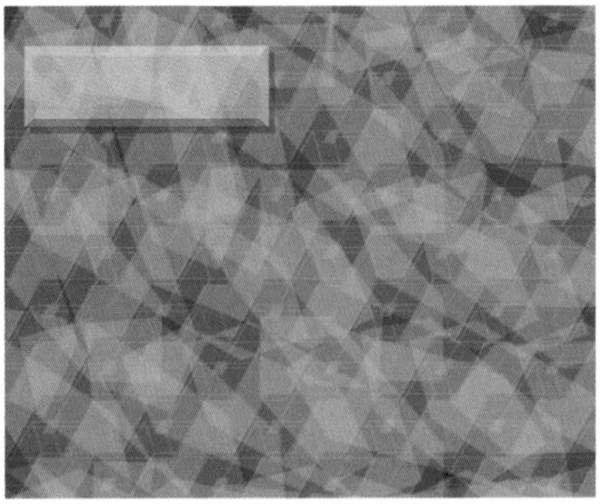

3.5: The button becomes 50% opaque on rollover.

You can see a list of an object's available properties by opening the Actions toolbox and expanding the Properties tab. Option+click (Mac) or right-click (Win) the name of the property and select View Reference to get a full explanation of the property, as well as information about how to manipulate it properly (3.4).

4. Test and Watch

To test the movie, roll your mouse in and out of the button. Notice that it turns 50% opaque when you roll over it (3.5). When you roll off, it becomes fully opaque again.

5. Move a Button

Now you're going to work with some ActionScript to become familiar with how items move along the *x* and *y* coordinates in Flash.

If you're still testing, close the Flash Player window. Now add the following ActionScript to the NewButton button (3.6) and test it.

```
on(press){
   NewButton._x += 3;
   NewButton._y += 3;
}
on(release, releaseOutside){
   NewButton._x -= 3;
   NewButton._y -= 3;
}
```

This code uses a couple of new properties: _x and _y. The _x property is the *x* coordinate of the object on the stage. In other words, it's the position on the stage along the horizontal axis (*x*). The _y property is the *y* coordinate of the object on the stage, or the position on the stage along the vertical axis (*y*). These are very useful properties, and you'll be taking advantage of them frequently throughout the book.

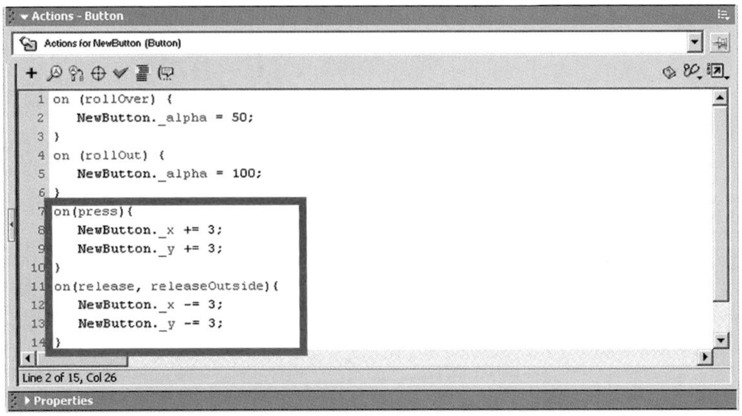

3.6: Add more script to the button.

In Flash's coordinate system, positive *x* values move to the right, and positive *y* values move downward (3.7). To some, this might seem counterintuitive, particularly the way the *y* coordinates work. In regular mathematics, positive *y* values move upward. However, in Flash they move downward.

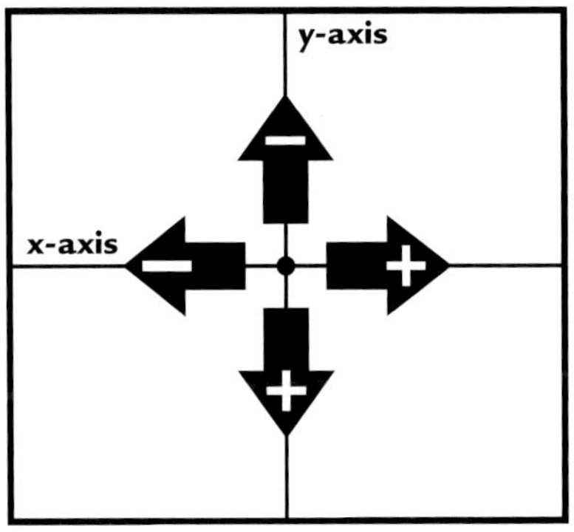

3.7: In the Flash coordinate system, the x *direction is horizontal, and* y *is vertical. Positive numbers for* x *go to the right, and positive numbers for* y *go down.*

Since the _x and _y properties can manipulate the position of an object, they are commonly used to animate objects with ActionScript. You can easily animate an object with ActionScript by scripting changes to these values. For now, however, you're just moving the button slightly.

The script you've applied to the button moves the button 3 pixels to the right (*x*) and 3 pixels down (*y*) when the user presses the button, and then moves the button back when the button is released. Once again, you've used code to create an effect that you could have produced by adding a graphic to the Over state of the button—a graphic that was positioned 3 pixels down and to the right of the artwork in the Up state. However, using code is easier and more versatile. If you want to make changes, it's easier to change the ActionScript for the _alpha and the _x and _y. All the button state properties are stored in one place, on one frame. Using the "old" approach would still require editing the Over state on one frame and the Down state on another.

To understand how this code works, let's look at the Info panel. Click the button to select it and press Cmd+Option+I (Mac) / Ctrl+Alt+I (Win) to open the Info panel (3.8). Notice that the Info panel reports that the position of the button is 18.9 on the *x*-axis and 34.4 on the *y*-axis.

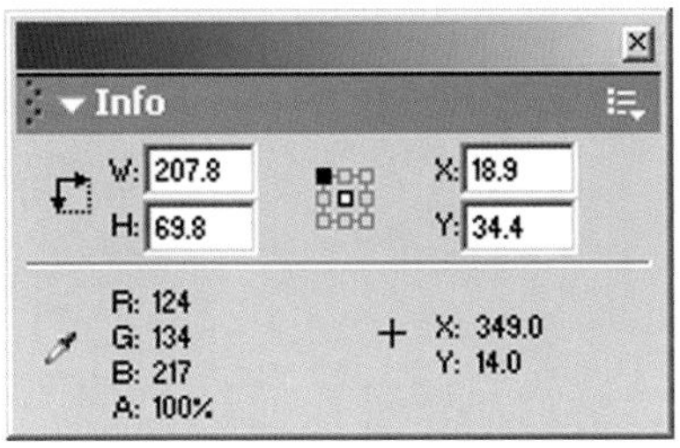

3.8: The Info panel shows that the x *and* y *coordinates for the button are based on the upper-left corner.*

Notice the little grid of tiny squares to the left of the *x* and *y* coordinate field in the Info panel. The upper-left square is filled or black, which indicates that the *x* and *y* coordinates (18.9, 34.4) refer to the upper-left corner of the button image (not to its center or any other point). This location is known as the button's *registration point*. You can use the Info panel and its registration-point grid to verify that your code is placing objects on the Flash stage exactly where you intend.

This code relies on the fact that when the movie is playing, Flash knows the *x* and *y* coordinates of the button object. So the code adds 3 pixels to both of these values to reposition the button when you press it and subtracts those same 3 pixels when you release it.

The key to how these lines of code work is found in the operators. The lines of code in the `on(press)` handler use the += operator:

```
NewButton._x += 3;
```

The += operator takes the current value of the specified property (in this case, `_x`) and adds the specified value to it. The += operator is shorthand for a traditional addition assignment; the same line could be written like this:

```
NewButton._x = NewButton._x + 3;
```

The -= operator does the opposite of the += operator. It takes the current value of the specified property (in this case, `_y`) and subtracts the specified value from it. So the script line that uses -= could instead be written using a subtraction symbol:

```
NewButton._x = _NewButton.x - 3;
```

Before you do anything with the button, its `_x` property is 18.9 and its `_y` property is 34.4. When someone presses down on the button, the code adds three to each using the += operator. The value of `_x` becomes 21.9, and `_y` becomes 37.4. When the button is released, the -= code lines subtract three from both, so the property values end up back where they started.

Working with Groups of Buttons and Functions

What do you do if you have a group or collection of buttons and you want them all to do the same thing? You could manually duplicate or copy and paste one button several times, and then put some text for each button on a separate layer above the buttons graphic, within the button itself. However, if you decide to change the transparency or the amount of change to the `_x` and `_y` properties during the `on(Press)` event, you would need to go back and edit each button. Fortunately, ActionScript provides more flexible alternatives. This section looks at a few ways to handle this common scenario, starting with the basic tool called *functions*.

1. Add Functions

To begin this example, you need to create some functions. Insert a new layer named Actions. Attach the following ActionScript in frame 1 of the Actions layer (3.9).

```
// function to handle the rolling over any button
function rolledOver(whichButton){
   // whichbutton is the button that got rolled over
   whichButton._alpha = 50;
}
// function to handle the rolling out of any button
function rolledOut(whichButton){
   // whichbutton is the button that got rolledOut over
   whichButton._alpha = 100;
}
// function to handle the press of any button
function pressed(whichButton){
   // whichbutton is the button that got pressed over
   whichButton._x += 3;
   whichButton._y += 3;
}
```

```
// function to handle the mouse release of any button
function released(whichButton){
   // whichbutton is the button that got released over
   whichButton._x -= 3;
   whichButton._y -= 3;
}
```

You will be using functions extensively throughout this book, so let's take a moment to talk about them. Functions are containers for ActionScript. They are used to keep code for related actions together. Functions are also commonly used when the actions they contain are going to be employed repeatedly by a variety of objects. If you want to make some ActionScript accessible to a variety of objects, you will typically use a function.

In general, you can think of a function as a sort of engine or battery (3.10). When you need power, you call on the function. One function can power many objects. When any given object needs power, it just makes a call to the function.

The battery analogy is helpful in terms of understanding that you can empower a series of similar objects from a remote source. However, a function can also take information in the form of an argument, process the information, and then return the information in its processed form. For example, functions can be like a microwave oven. If you put a TV dinner in the microwave oven, it gets cooked; when it's done, you can take out your hot dinner. A function can take something, manipulate it, and then give it back in its changed form. You'll be using functions that work in this way throughout this book.

In this example, you have created four functions. The actions within the functions should look very familiar because they actually do the same thing as the ActionScript that you applied directly to the button in the first example. The main difference is that these actions will be contained within functions and refer to `whichButton` instead of `NewButton`. Instead of having the same actions in many different places, as you would if the actions were applied to a series of buttons, you will create functions that contain the same actions and call them when you need them.

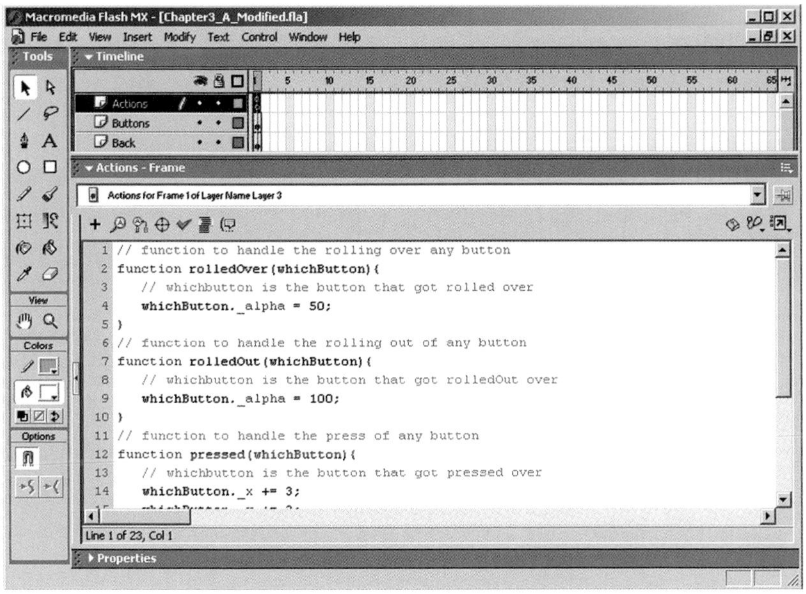

3.9: *Add a layer named Actions and add the code to the first frame.*

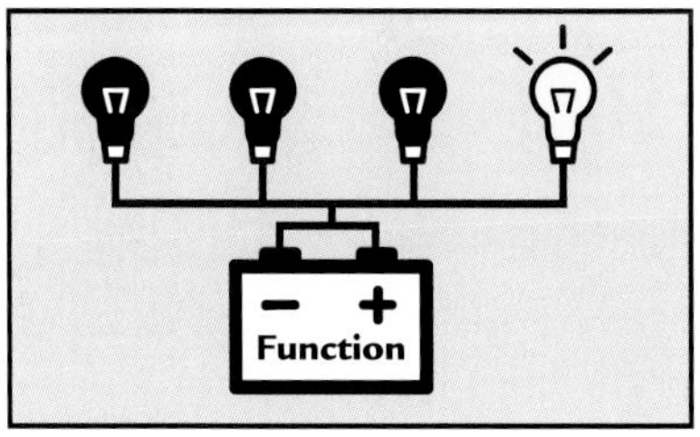

3.10: *Functions are like a battery that can be used to supply power to any number of objects.*

Functions and Arguments

Functions can take as many *arguments* as you want. When you define a function, you include a variable for each item of information the function needs in order to operate. For instance, a function that has five arguments would look like this:

```
function myFive(a, b, c, d, e){
}
```

Notice that each argument is separated by a comma, and the arguments are all within the parentheses. To call the sample function, you would write:

```
myFive(1, 3, 5, 8, 9);
```

This line calls the function called `myFive()` and sets values for each of the arguments. (Calling the same function to do its operation somewhere else in your ActionScript, you might assign the arguments different values.) Functions do not need to have arguments. If you don't need to have information passed to a function, simply leave the parentheses empty in both the function definition and the function call. In other words, the function definition would look like this:

```
function myFive(){
}
```

The function call could look like this:

```
myFive();
```

Functions can both take in information and return information. Each of the functions has an argument named `whichButton`, which is a variable within the function. In a moment, you'll add code to the buttons that will make a call to these functions, and that call will pass in a value for the `whichButton` argument. The `whichButton` argument will then be passed down into the code contained within the function.

Notice that each function uses the same `whichButton` argument. Flash doesn't get confused with the different instances of the `whichButton` argument, because these arguments exist only within each function. The idea or principle that an argument or a variable exists—has meaning—within certain programmatic boundaries is called *scope*. So it can be said that the scope of each `whichButton` argument exists only within each function.

Flash executes each function only when the function is called, and it never executes more than one function at the same time. So as it's working through the functions, at any given moment, Flash sees only one instance of the `whichButton` argument (3.11). For instance, when Flash is executing the second function—`rolledOut()`—Flash is unaware of the `whichButton` argument in the previous `rolledOver()` function or the subsequent `pressed()` function.

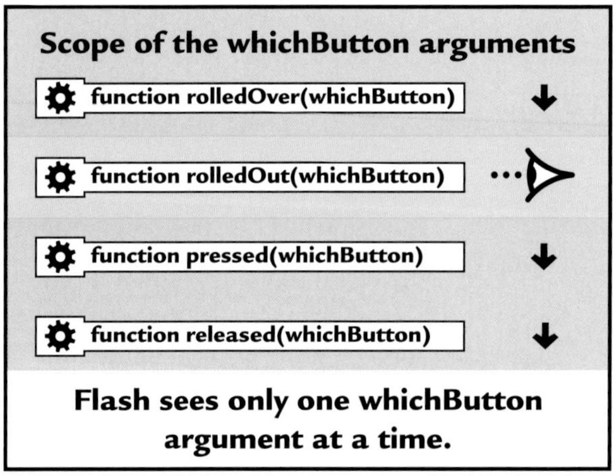

3.11: Flash works through each function sequentially, so it sees only one `whichButton` *argument at a time.*

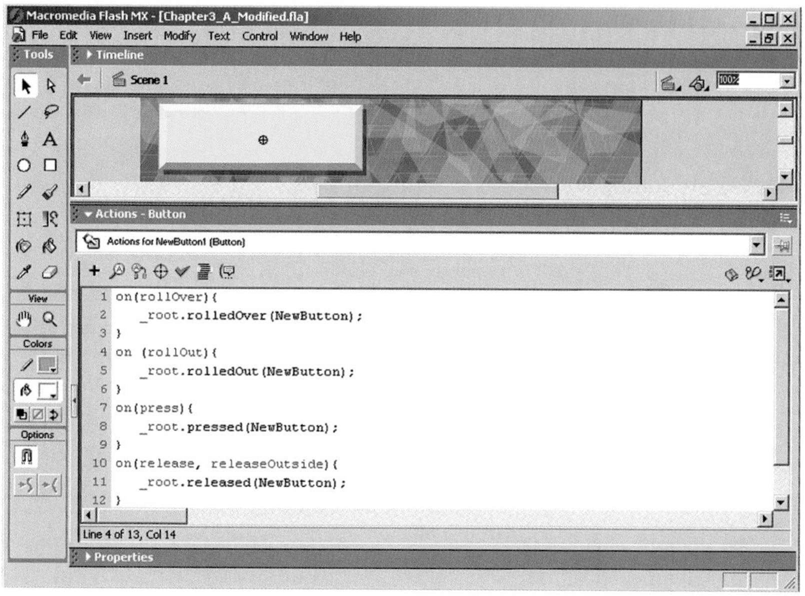

3.12: Replace the code on the button.

2. Call the Functions

Each of these functions will be called from the appropriate event handler on the button. Replace the ActionScript that is attached to the NewButton with the following (3.12):

```
on(rollOver){
   _root.rolledOver(NewButton);
}
on(rollOut){
   _root.rolledOut(NewButton);
}
on(press){
   _root.pressed(NewButton);
}
on(release, releaseOutside){
   _root.released(NewButton);
}
```

Each event handler (*rollOver*, *rollOut*, *press*, and *release*) contains a function call. Each function call passes the argument `NewButton` to its function. The `NewButton` argument is the name of the button instance. Therefore, every time one of the functions is called, the argument `NewButton` replaces the *whichButton* argument. Each function then feeds the `NewButton` argument into the code contained within function.

For instance, when a user rolls over the button, the `on(rollOver)` event is triggered (3.13). Then a call is made to the *rolledOver()* function, and the argument `NewButton` is passed into *rolledOver()*. At that point, *whichButton* is equivalent to `NewButton`. So the code inside the function becomes:

```
NewButton._alpha = 50;
```

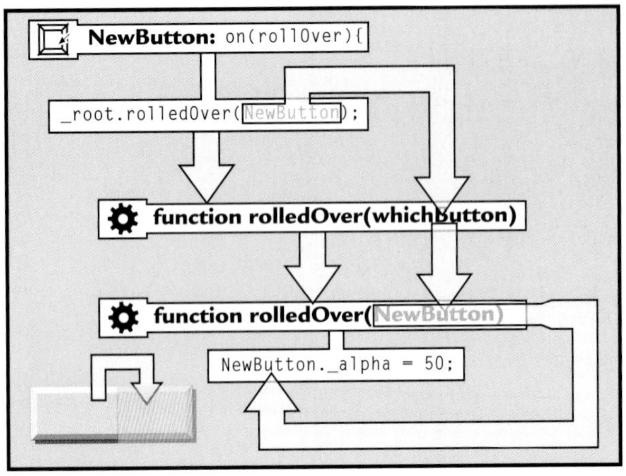

3.13: The `on(rollOver)` *event handler feeds the* `NewButton` *argument into the* `rolledOver()` *function.*

That line of code should look familiar. It is the same line that you originally had assigned to the button. In fact, the results are the same as before. The button becomes 50% opaque when a user rolls the cursor over the button. Remember that the main reason you're doing it this way is so that you can easily duplicate buttons and be able to change their reactions quickly and easily.

Each of the other event handlers works with its respective functions in the same way. Each one passes the `NewButton` instance name to the function's argument, which, in turn, feeds that argument into the code within the function (3.13).

3. Test and Watch Again

Test the movie. Nothing should change. The button should behave exactly as before. Right now, there's little apparent advantage to reworking the code. Let's add some buttons and take advantage of this new approach.

4. Copy the Button

Copy the button on the stage four more times. The instance name for each button needs to be different. Give the first copy the instance name **NewButton1**, the second copy the instance name **NewButton2**, and so on (3.14). Edit the code assigned to each button copy to pass its respective instance name. For example, the code on the first button copy (NewButton1) should look like this:

```
on(rollOver){
   _root.rolledOver(NewButton1);
}
on(rollOut){
   _root.rolledOut(NewButton1);
}
on(press){
   _root.pressed(NewButton1);
}
on(release, releaseOutside){
   _root.released(NewButton1);
}
```

5. Test the Movie

After you've made the copies, renamed their respective instances, and edited the ActionScript on each copy, test the movie again.

Notice that each button works independently of the others (3.15). Now if you want to change the `_alpha` to 30 for each button when the rollover event takes place, all you need to do is edit the `rolledOver()` function. If the ActionScript were still assigned directly to the

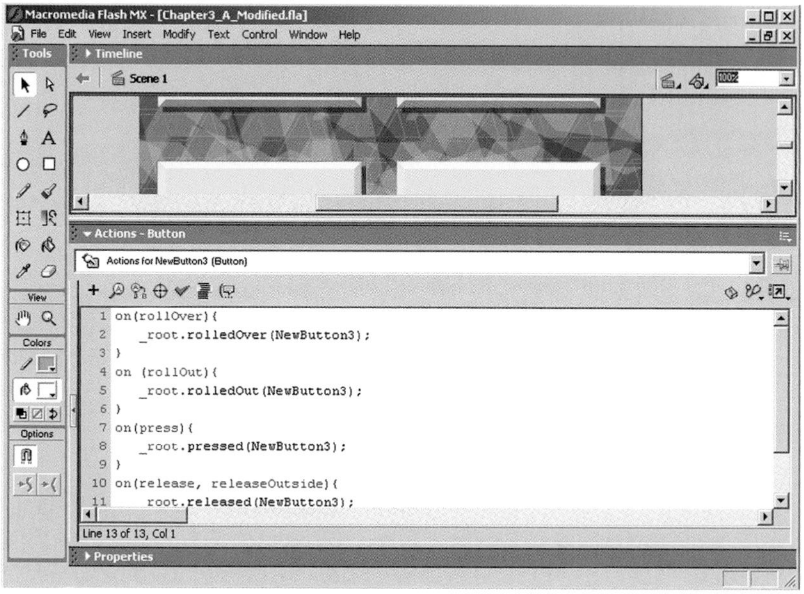

3.14: The third copy of NewButton

buttons (as in the original example), you would need to make the change to the code assigned to each button.

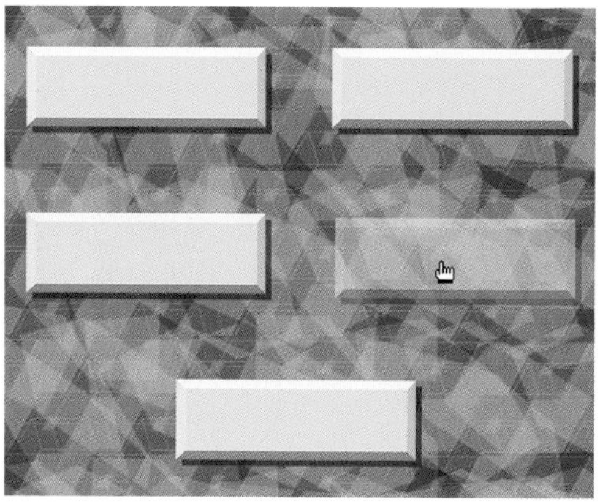

3.15: Each button works independently of the others.

Turning Buttons into Movie Clips

Our new approach is more efficient, but there is one more step you can take to improve it. Wasn't it a little tedious editing the function calls in each of the buttons to reference each button's unique instance name? You cannot access the name of the button dynamically; in other words, when the program is running, there is no way to access the name of the button as you can with a movie clip (`_name`). But if you turn them into movie clips, you can use the keyword `this` to make the code even more efficient.

The keyword `this` is used within movie clips to reference the clip itself. When the program is running, the keyword `this` will contain the name and the path of the movie clip to which it is attached.

In buttons, the keyword `this` references the timeline the button is sitting on, which won't work for our purposes because it's `_root` for all of them. In many cases, you can write ActionScript that doesn't need the specific instance name of the movie clip where the ActionScript resides. The keyword `this` includes not just the instance name of the move clip, but also the whole path, so you don't need to worry about adding `_root` in front. The keyword `this` takes care of everything for you.

Let's try out the button-as-movie-clip approach. You just need to convert one of the existing buttons to a movie clip, edit its ActionScript to use `this`, and then duplicate the modified button (movie clip).

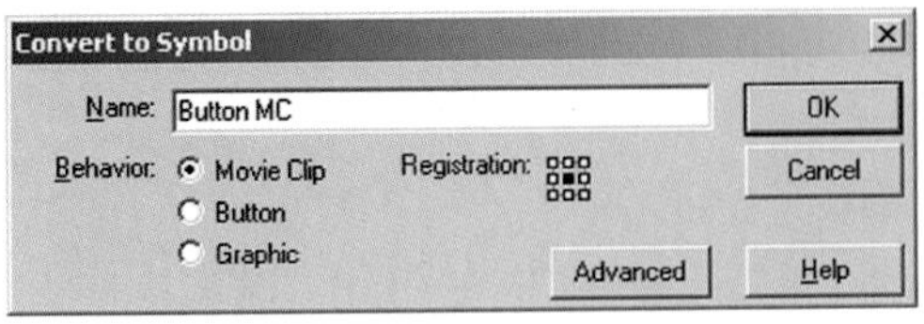

3.16: Convert the button to a movie clip.

1. Convert a Button to a Movie Clip

Delete all of the buttons from the stage except NewButton1. Select that button and choose Convert to Symbol. For its Behavior, select Movie Clip and name it **Button MC** (3.16).

Now the button is contained within a movie clip. More important, the ActionScript that is attached to the button is inside the movie clip.

2. Edit the ActionScript

Edit the Button MC movie clip. Change the ActionScript that is attached to the NewButton1 button inside this movie clip so that each reference to the button name (`NewButton1`) uses the keyword `this` instead (3.17). The ActionScript should look like this:

```
on(rollOver){
   _root.rolledOver(this);
}
on(rollOut){
   _root.rolledOut(this);
}
on(press){
   _root.pressed(this);
}
on(release, releaseOutside){
   _root.released(this);
}
```

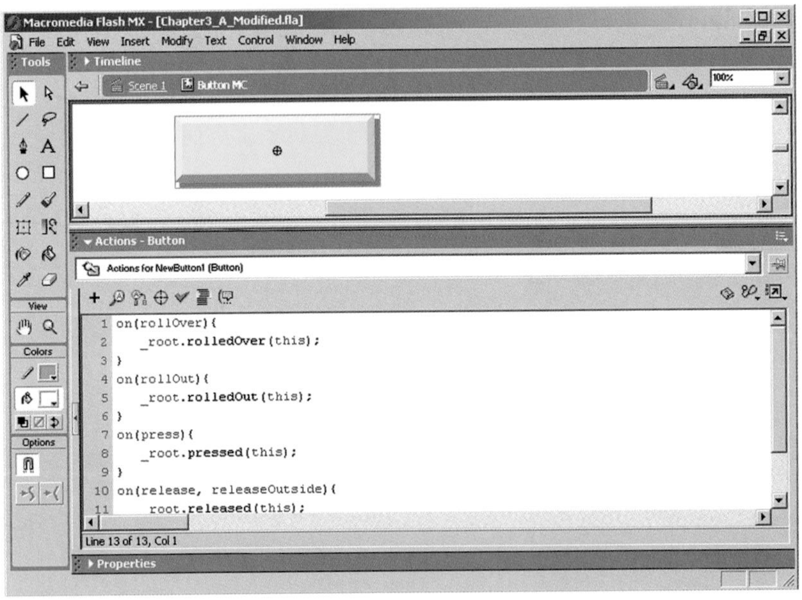

3.17: Change all of the button calls on the code for the button within the newly created Button MC movie clip to `this`.

3. Duplicate and Test

Return to the main timeline, duplicate Button MC four more times, and then test the movie (3.18).

The buttons should work exactly as they did before. Using the keyword `this` takes care of everything. All you needed to do was put the button inside a movie clip.

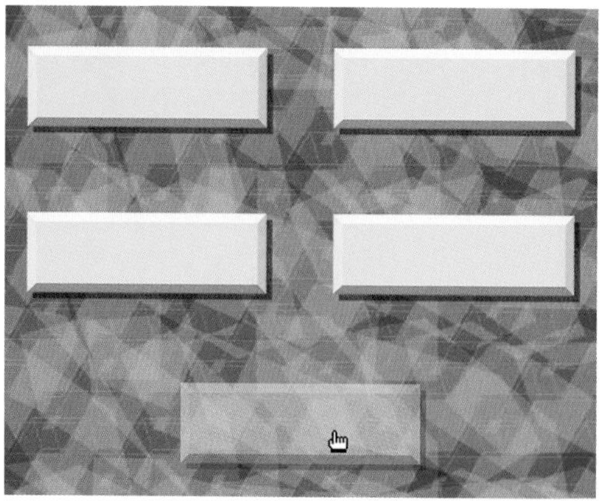

3.18: Make several copies of the Button MC movie clip and test the movie.

Working with More Buttons

Flash MX actually allows you to go one step further than the previous example. In Flash MX, you no longer need to assign any code to the button in order to use the button capabilities. You can simply write ActionScript in frames and use it from there. This is very handy for using the same ActionScript over and over again.

1. Open the File

Open **Chapter3_B_Start.fla.** Save the file to your local hard drive as **Chapter3_B_Modified.fla.** (To see the finished project, open **Chapter3_B_Final.fla.**) WWW.

This file already has two buttons placed on the stage. The buttons have instance names assigned to them: Button1 and Button2, respectively. These buttons are not contained within movie clips as in the previous example.

2. Look at the Code

Look at the ActionScript assigned to the Actions layer on frame 1 (3.19).

```
// function to handle the rolling over any button
function rolledOver(){
   this._alpha = 50;
}
// function to handle the rolling out of any button
function rolledOut(){
   this._alpha = 100;
}
// function to handle the press of any button
function pressed(){
   this._x += 1;
   this._y += 1;
}
// function to handle the mouse release of any button
function released(){
   this._x -= 1;
   this._y -= 1;
}
```

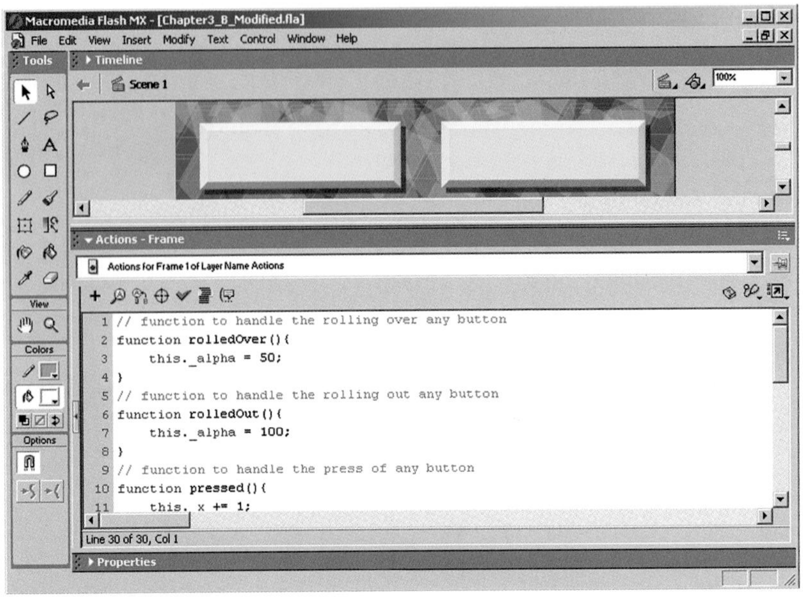

3.19: The code assigned to frame 1 of the Actions layer

This code should look very familiar. It's similar to the code you just used in the previous example.

The difference is that each of the functions no longer has the `whichButton` argument. For this example, you won't need to pass an argument into these functions. Also notice that now you're using the keyword `this` in place of the instance names for the buttons (or the argument for the function that you used to insert the instance name for the buttons).

Flash MX now allows you to create functions that are directly attached to the button event. In the previous example, you called the functions when a given event occurred. In this example, you'll be attaching the functions directly to the button event itself. Let's enter the code and then talk about how it works.

3. Attach the Functions

Add the following code in frame 1 at the bottom (3.20).

```
// attach above functions to Button1
Button1.onRollOver = rolledOver;
Button1.onRollOut = rolledOut;
Button1.onPress = pressed;
Button1.onRelease = released;
```

This code uses the new Flash MX methods `onRollOver`, `onRollOut`, `onPress`, and `onRelease`. A *method* is a function that is available only to a certain object or certain types of objects. By contrast, `on(RollOver)`, `on(RollOut)`, `on(Press)`, and `on(Release)` are not methods—they are *events*.

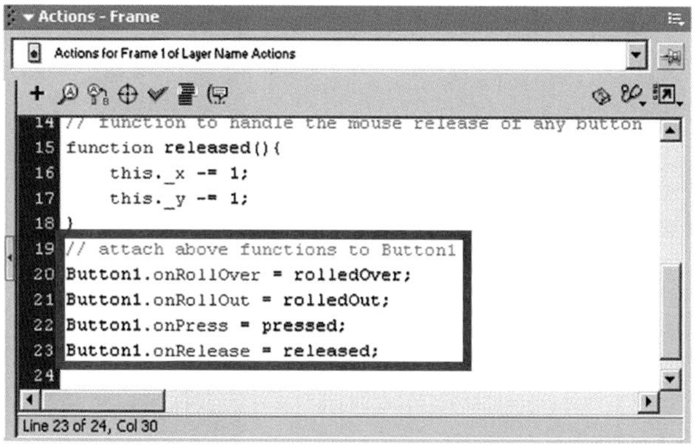

3.20: Add the new function code below the existing code on the first frame of the Actions layer.

NOTE You can see the difference between a method and an event just by the fact that methods have parentheses to take arguments; events do not take arguments. The event is the keyword `on`, and within the parentheses is the trigger by which the event will be called. In this case, you call these actions "methods" because they are essentially an added functionality that is built into buttons in Flash MX. Methods, in general, are not new to Flash, but these particular methods are new to Flash MX.

These new methods allow you to place the event handlers within the function code. The advantage is that all the code is in one place, and you do not need to make separate adjustments to the code for all of the objects.

Each line you just added works by referencing the button's instance name with the respective event handler method. For instance, consider this code fragment:

```
Button1.onRollOver
```

Here, `onRollOver` is the method, and it's attached to the Button1 instance. So this portion of the code watches for the rollover. When a rollover occurs, the code makes a function call to the `rolledOver()` function:

```
Button1.onRollOver = rolledOver;
```

Each line works in the same way.

Now let's add the code for the other buttons to show that this approach can be used to implement more than one button.

4. Apply to Multiple Buttons and Test

Add the following code in frame 1 at the bottom (3.21).

```
// attach above functions to Button2
Button2.onRollOver = rolledOver;
Button2.onRollOut = rolledOut;
Button2.onPress = pressed;
Button2.onRelease = released;
```

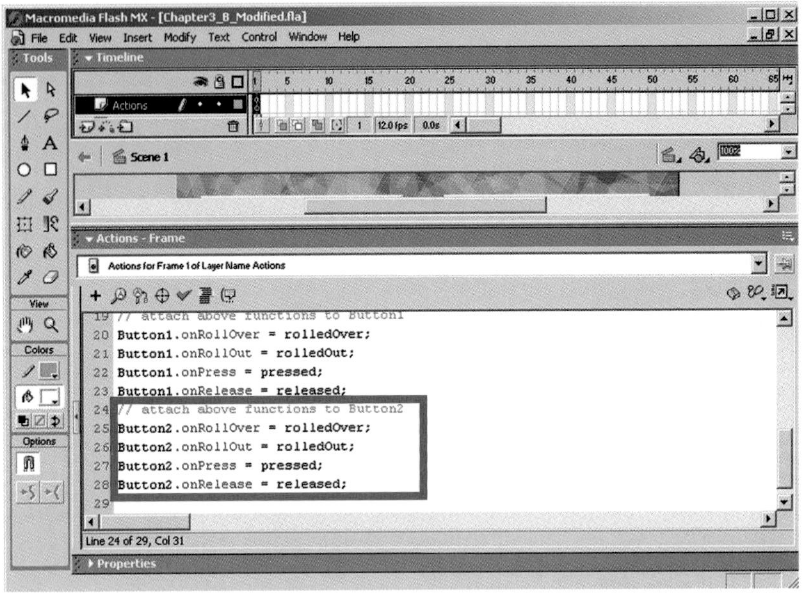

3.21: Apply the code for Button2 to frame 1 of the Actions layer.

Test your movie. Once again, the buttons work the same as in the last few examples. The difference is that now you need to go to only one place if you want to make any changes to the code. You don't need to look for code assigned to a button and relate it to code assigned to a keyframe on the timeline. Your code is all in one place, making it easier to edit and troubleshoot.

Earlier, in the "Turning Buttons into Movie Clips" section, you converted a button into a movie clip. Using movie clips with buttons has been made easier with Flash MX. Now let's further explore how you can use a movie clip as a button.

Using Movie Clips As Buttons

Sometimes you want to use a movie clip with a button to get a nice, fluid animated rollover effect. Without using ActionScript, you can put animations in any state of the button. For example, imagine a button that gradually grows larger when you roll over it. This is easy enough to create with a standard Flash button. You would simply add, to the Over state of the button, an animation of the button growing larger. However, when you rolled the cursor off the button, it would snap back to the original size. If you wanted to have the button shrink back down using a fluid animated transition, you would need to use a movie clip. Our next example does just that.

1. Open the File

WWW.

Start with the same file you have open, or open **Chapter3_C_Start.fla** (3.22). Save the file to your local hard drive as **Chapter3_C_Modified.fla**. (The finished version is in **Chapter3_C_Final.fla**.)

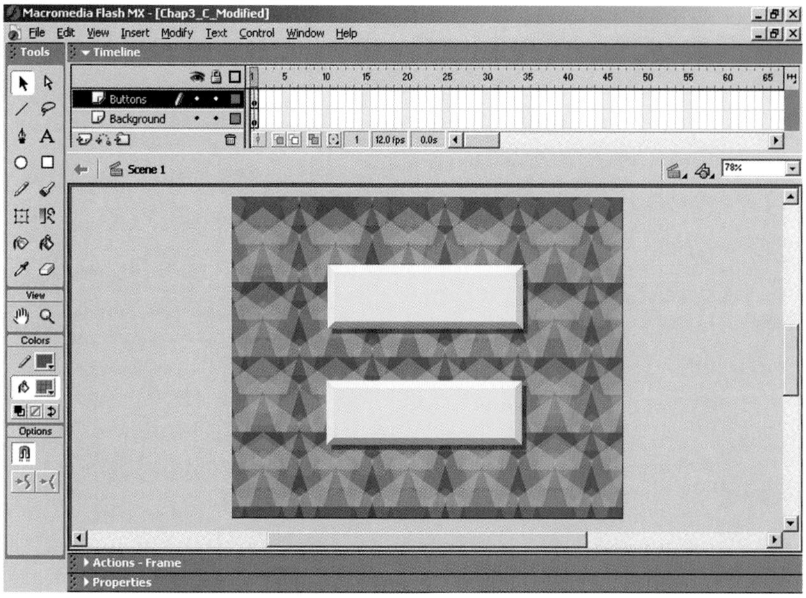

3.22: *The* Chapter3_C_Modified.fla *file*

This file looks similar to the file you just worked with. However, the two buttons on the stage are actually movie clips that contain animation. They are two instances of the same movie clip.

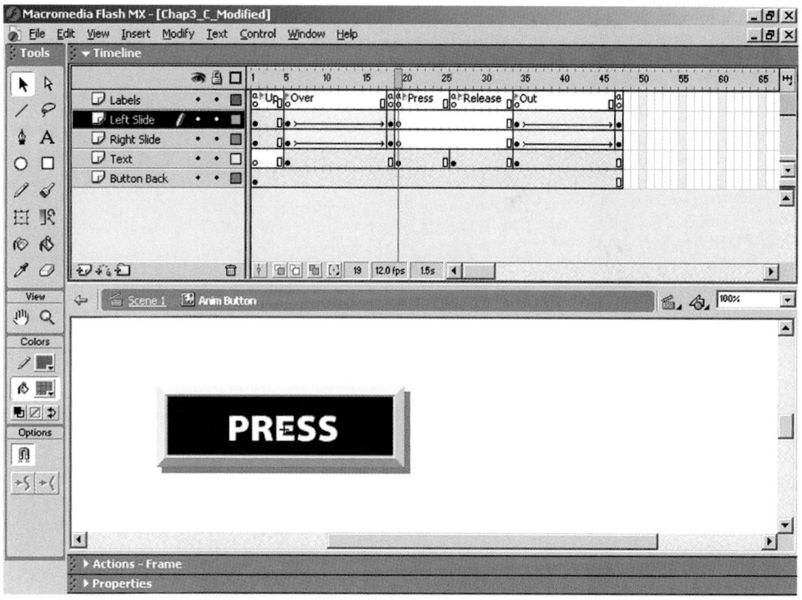

3.23: *Inspect the timeline.*

2. Deconstruct a Movie Clip

Select one of the Anim Button movie clips on the stage and press Cmd/Ctrl+E to edit it. Now you can see how this movie clip is constructed (3.23).

First, notice that the clip consists of several layers. The actual motion within this movie clip is on the Right Slide and Left Slide layers. Simple rectangles on each of these layers have a shape tween applied to them, so that the top of the button appears to slide away to reveal a black screen below. There is also a Labels layer (3.24), which contains labels for each of the events (Over, Press, Release, and Out). For the code, this is the important layer.

If you click frame 1 of the Labels layer and open the Properties panel, you'll see that the frame label Up has been assigned to the frame. Then if you open the Actions panel while you have frame 1 selected, you'll also see that there is a `stop()` action applied to frame 1.

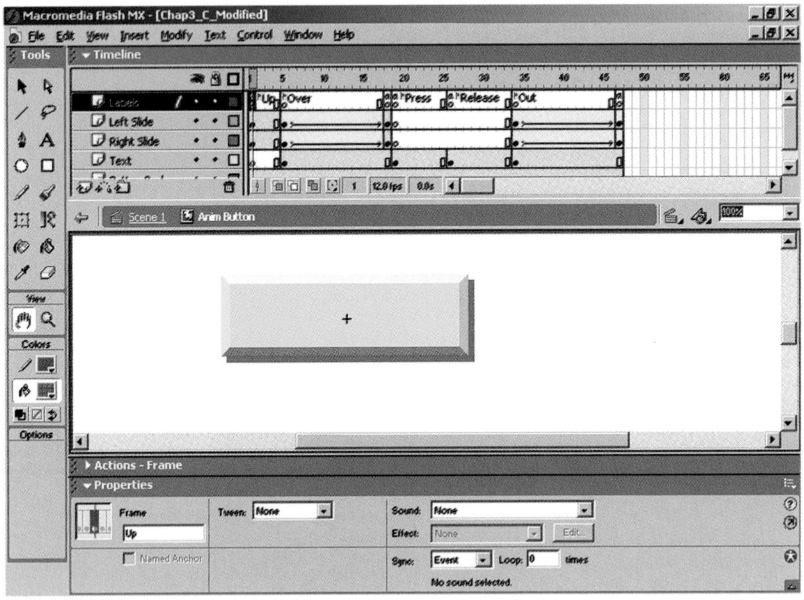

3.24: Several of the frames have labels assigned to them.

The Labels layer has several other frames with labels and `stop()` actions applied to them. There are frame labels named Up, Over, Press, Release, and Out. Several of the other keyframes also have `stop()` actions assigned to them to stop the playback of the movie clip at certain points. Finally, there is an action assigned to the last frame that tells the movie to go back to the Up frame label. Now let's apply some code to control this movie clip as if it were a button.

3. Attach ActionScript

Return to the main timeline and attach the following code to both Anim Button movie clips (3.25).

```
onClipEvent(load){
   this.onRollOver = function (){
      this.gotoAndPlay("Over");
   }
   this.onRollOut = function (){
      this.gotoAndPlay("Out");
   }
   this.onPress = function (){
      this.gotoAndPlay("Press");
   }
   this.onRelease = function (){
      this.gotoAndPlay("Release");
   }
}
```

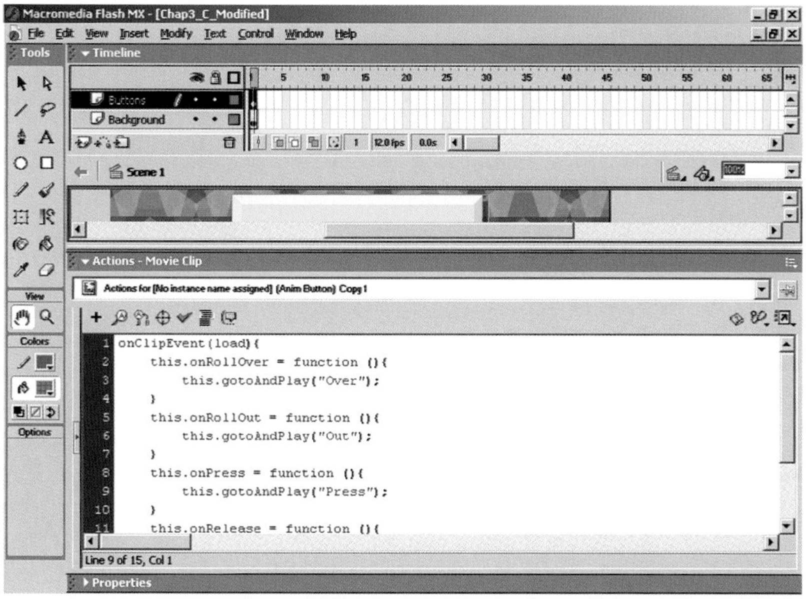

3.25: Apply the code to each of the movie clips to make them behave like buttons.

This code uses the same methods as in the previous example with buttons. This time, however, the methods are attached directly to the movie clip, which is new to Flash MX. The first line in each event uses the keyword `this` to tell Flash that the methods (`onRollOver`, `onRollOut`, and so on) should be tied to the movie clip that this code is assigned to.

So, for example, when a user rolls over one of the Anim Button movie clips, the `onRollOver` method is triggered. This causes its associated function to execute. In the case of the `onRollOver` method, the function contains the following statement:

```
this.gotoAndPlay("Over");
```

This line tells the movie clip to go to the frame labeled Over and play. The rest of the ActionScript works in the same way. You have defined all of these methods at the loading of the Anim Button movie clip—`onClipEvent(load)`—and so they are available for the life of the movie clip.

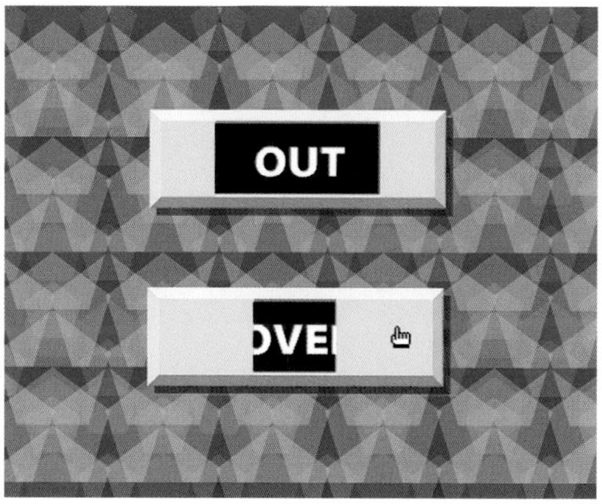

3.26: Notice that the movie clips behave like buttons; the cursor changes to the familiar "selection" symbol.

4. Test the Movie

Test the movie by rolling your cursor over the movie clips as well as clicking and releasing them. Notice that the mouse cursor changes as if this movie clip were a button (3.26), even though it is not. That's because you are using methods that act like buttons.

NOTE To create the same effect in Flash 5, you would need to use an invisible button to control a movie clip. Invisible buttons have nothing in the Up, Over, and Down states. You could control the movie clip by using the invisible button's event handlers to control the movie clip.

Although buttons are one of the most common ways you interact with the cursor, they are not the only way. So far, you've seen functions and methods in the discussion of buttons and movie clips that behave like buttons, but the scripts haven't been very complex.

Now let's look at other ways you can interact with the mouse and try out some more substantial code in the process. In the following section, you'll look at some relatively simple code that you can use to change the mouse cursor.

Programming Custom Mouse Cursors

In many cases, you will want your Flash animation to display a specialized mouse cursor or a couple of specialized cursors. Controlling the mouse cursor image is fairly straightforward, but you need to use a movie clip to replace the default cursor. Let's go through an example to demonstrate how this works.

1. Open the File

WWW. Open **Chapter3_D_Start.fla**. Save the file to your local hard drive as **Chapter3_D_Modified.fla**. (The finished version is in **Chapter3_D_Final.fla**.)

This movie contains the movie clip that you'll use for a mouse cursor. The clip is named Cursor. You might want to use a cursor like this for an interactive game, for example.

2. Attach ActionScript Code

Attach the following ActionScript to the Cursor movie clip that is on the stage. (3.27).

```
onClipEvent(load){
   Mouse.hide();
}
onClipEvent(enterFrame){
   this._x = _root._xmouse;
   this._y = _root._ymouse;
}
```

First, this code hides the default mouse cursor within the `onClipEvent(load)` movie clip event. You do this by using the `Mouse` object's built-in `hide()` method, which makes the default mouse cursor invisible.

Next the code uses the `onClipEvent(enterFrame)` event to tell the movie clip to follow the mouse. As you learned in Chapter 1, "ActionScript for Non-Programmers," the `onClipEvent(enterFrame)` event occurs every time a frame is displayed. In other words, the event repeats at the movie's frame rate—12 times per second if the frame rate is set to 12fps.

The code works by setting the *_x* and *_y* properties of the movie clip equal to the *x* and *y* coordinates of the mouse position. For instance, consider the following line:

```
this._x = _root._xmouse;
```

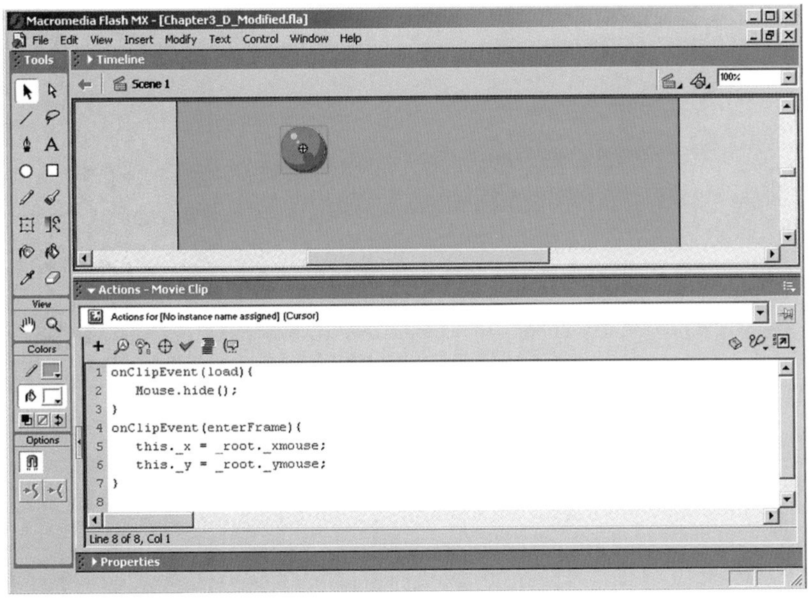

3.27: Apply ActionScript to the Cursor movie clip.

First, the code uses the keyword `this` to reference the movie clip it is attached to, setting the _x property. Then the code is sent to the main timeline (`_root`) to get the `_xmouse` property. The `_xmouse` property accesses the *x* coordinate of the mouse cursor (the cursor's physical position as reported to Flash via the mouse driver software and the operating system).

In short, this code sets the *x* coordinate of the movie clip to the *x* coordinate of the cursor position. The next line works the same way for the *y* coordinate of the movie clip using the `_ymouse` property. Once again, the `onClipEvent(enterFrame)` event happens several times a second (this example is set to 12fps). So Flash is essentially updating the position of the Cursor movie clip constantly.

3. Test the Movie

Test the movie clip. Move your cursor around and notice that the movie clip follows your mouse. Notice that when you move your mouse faster, it will not follow your cursor as fluidly. You can increase the frame rate of the movie to help Flash be more responsive.

NOTE Even though Flash is not case-sensitive in many cases, you will notice that in order for Flash to recognize the `onClipEvent()` command, the capitalization needs to be exact. As a general rule, you will want to make sure you use correct capitalization for all built-in items.

This will work for any movie clip—even a movie clip with animation in it. Now let's try another example that is a little more complicated, using a movie clip that contains some animation. This is a movie clip in the **Chapter3_D_Modified.fla** file named Mallet_Clip, which shows a smashing mallet.

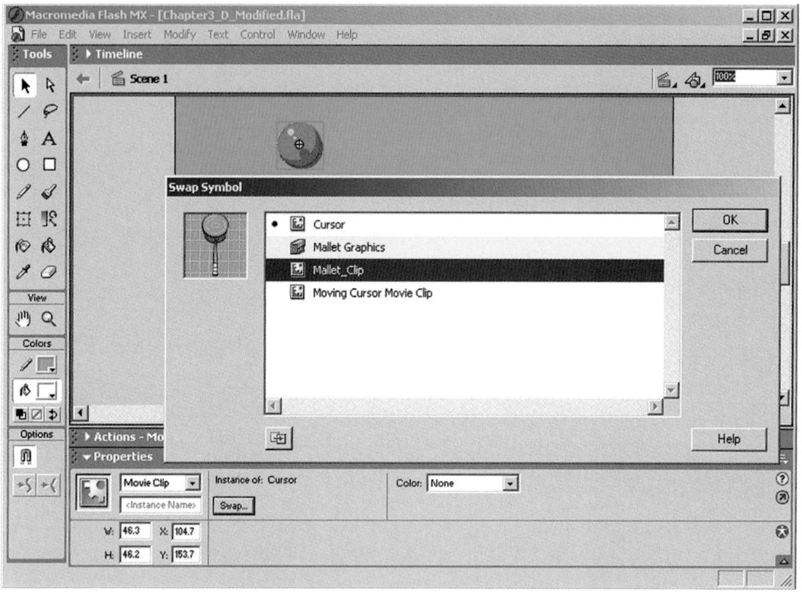

3.28: Click the Swap button on the Properties panel and use the Swap Symbol dialog box to swap the Mallet_Clip movie clip in place of the Cursor movie clip.

4. Swap Cursors and Test

Close the Test Movie window. Select the Cursor movie clip instance and open the Properties panel. Click the Swap button and, in the Swap Symbol dialog box, select the Mallet_Clip movie clip to replace the Cursor movie clip (3.28). Click the OK button to close the Swap Symbol dialog box, and then test the movie.

Notice that swapping the movie clips doesn't remove the code that you added earlier. The Mallet_Clip movie clip follows the mouse, just as the Cursor movie clip did. In this case, however, the Mallet_Clip movie clip cycles through its animation repeatedly. That's not quite what you want. Let's make the mallet hit only when the user clicks the mouse button.

5. Edit the Mallet_Clip Movie Clip

Edit the Mallet_Clip movie clip and add a layer at the top called Actions. Put a `stop()` command in frame 1 of the Actions layer:

```
stop();
```

Add a keyframe at frame 2 and label it **Swing**. Add a keyframe in the last frame (frame 10) and insert this line:

```
gotoAndStop(1);
```

This will keep the mallet in the upright position (frame 1) until the swing is triggered (frame 2). At the end of the swing, the animation goes back and waits in the upright position again.

Now let's add some code to trigger the swing (3.29).

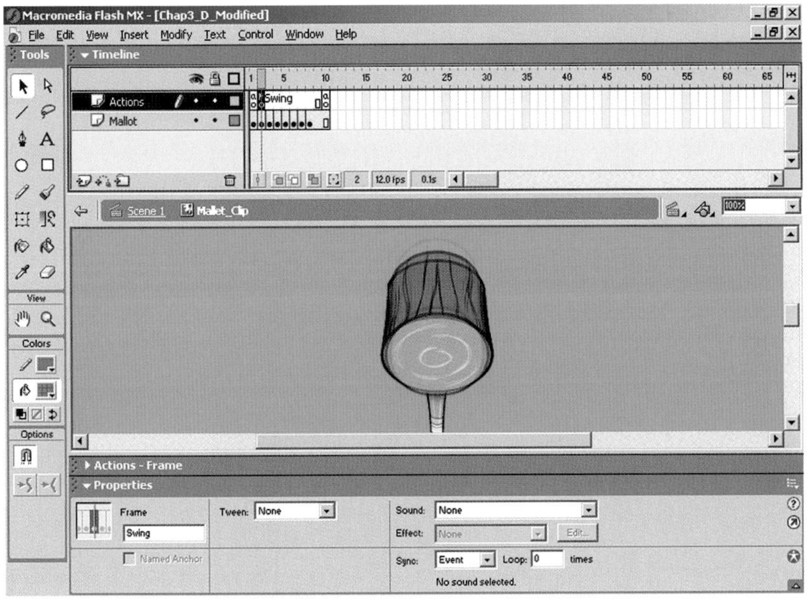

3.29: Add animation controls to the Mallet_Clip movie clip.

6. Add Code to Trigger the Swing

Return to the main timeline and add the following code to Mallet_Clip within the `onClipEvent(load)` event handler.

```
this.onMouseDown = function(){
   this.gotoAndPlay("Swing");
};
```

So all of the code attached to the Mallet_Clip should look like this:

```
onClipEvent(load) {
   Mouse.hide();
   this.onMouseDown = function() {
      this.gotoAndPlay("Swing");
   };
}
onClipEvent(enterFrame) {
   this._x = _root._xmouse;
   this._y = _root._ymouse;
}
```

By now, this code should not be difficult for you to understand. Once again, the code uses the keyword `this` to refer to the movie clip that it is assigned to. In this case, you're using the `onMouseDown` method, which checks for a mouse-down event. The `onMouseDown` method is not concerned with whether you've actually clicked on the movie clip, just with whether the mouse is down in general.

If the mouse is down, the function's code is executed and the Mallet_Clip movie clip is told to go to the frame labeled Swing and play.

3.30: The sample script can be used in games like Eyeland Studio's Mole's Revenge.

7. Test the Movie

Test the movie. Now the Mallet_Clip movie clip follows the mouse around, and the mallet does its little animation only when you press down the mouse button. These kinds of mouse animations are great for games. In fact, this script is part of a game from Eyeland Studio (eyeland.com) called Mole's Revenge (3.30), in which this mallet is used to whack away at poor, hapless moles (although as the name suggests, they get to hit back).

Programming Repetition

The next example starts where the last one left off. It uses a movie clip containing the same basic ActionScript that you looked at in the previous example. The mouse cursor is hidden, and a movie clip is set to follow the mouse around. The difference is that this time, you will add a trail effect to the movie clip cursor. This involves duplicating the clip, which requires ActionScript to repeat some of the code. So, in this example, you'll use another fundamental programming tool—the `for` loop, which allows you to control repetition.

Programming a Basic Animated Mouse Effect

In this first section of the mouse movement, you will use a basic graphic of a blue ball. It creates a simple trailing mouse.

1. Open the File

WWW. Open Chapter3_E_Start.fla. Save the file to your local hard drive as Chapter3_E_Modified.fla. (The finished version is in Chapter3_E_Final.fla.)

The BlueBall clip already has the ActionScript attached to it to make it follow the cursor around. Now you'll add an animated trail effect. In order to create a trail, you need to duplicate a movie clip that will follow the mouse around at different increments.

Rather than duplicate the BlueBall movie clip that is currently on the stage, you will duplicate the BlueBall clip that is in the library, using the `attachMovie()` method (which was introduced in Chapter 2). The main reason you don't want to duplicate the BlueBall clip on the stage is that it already has code attached to it. Every duplicate would get the same code, and you would not have a trail. By using the BlueBall clip from the library, you get a fresh copy that doesn't have any code attached to it.

The linkage of the BlueBall movie clip has already been set using Export for ActionScript, and it has been given the identifier Cursor1.

2. Add the Actions

Add a layer named Actions above the Cursor layer and place the following ActionScript in frame 1 of the Actions layer (3.31).

```
duplicateNumber = 27;
for (var trailCount = 1; trailCount <= duplicateNumber; trailCount++){
   attachMovie("Cursor1", "trail" + trailCount, trailCount);
}
stop();
```

The first line of the code establishes a variable named *`duplicateNumber`* and sets it equal to 27. This will be the number of duplicated movie clips that will follow the cursor around to create the trail. The next line of code introduces something new: a `for` loop.

A `for` loop is useful for executing an ActionScript command or series of commands multiple times. In this case, you need to dynamically generate 27 duplicates of the BlueBall movie clip. So you use the `for` loop for the repetitive process.

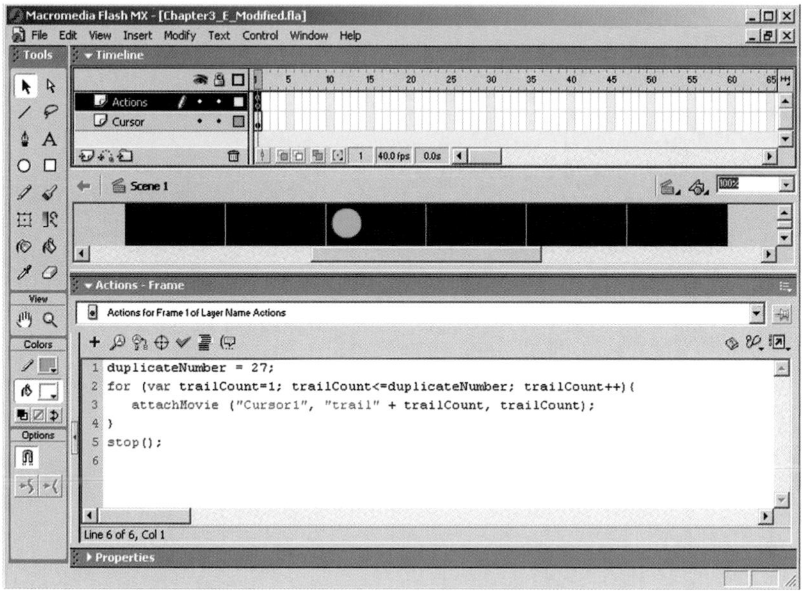

3.31: Add a layer named Actions and apply the code to it.

The framework of a `for` loop has three parts: the initialization (`trailCount = 1`), the condition (`trailCount <= duplicateNumber`), and the next, or update, statement (`trailCount++`). Together, these elements control the repetition of the instructions within the loop.

Initialization The first section of the `for` loop performs what is called *initialization.* The `for` loop begins by creating a variable called *`trailCount`* and setting it to 1. The initialization gives the `for` loop a starting place. Then, as the loop is repeated, this section is ignored (otherwise, the *`trailCount`* variable would be repeatedly set back to 1).

Condition The next section of a `for` loop is called the *condition.* As the name suggests, this defines a test that must be met for the instructions in the loop to keep repeating. In this example, the `for` loop sets the condition `trailCount <= duplicateNumber`. The variable *`duplicateNumber`* is set to 27, so this means that the `for` loop will continue operating until the variable *`trailCount`* is equal to 28. As long as it is less than or equal to 27, the `for` loop will continue operating.

Update The last section of a `for` loop is the *update* section. Typically, using the `++` operator, this increments the variable referenced in the initialization and condition sections. In this case, the *`trailCount`* variable is incremented by one in the update section of the `for` loop. The update occurs after the code within the `for` loop is executed, but before the `for` loop repeats.

Notice that there is some code within the `for` loop. You'll see what this code does in a moment; for now, just note that every time Flash runs through the `for` loop, this bit of code is executed. First, let's summarize how the `for` loop works.

When the `for` loop begins, *`trailCount`* is set to 1. Then the loop checks to see if *`trailCount`* is less than *`duplicateNumber`*. Since 1 is less than 27, the code within the `for` loop is executed. Finally, the update section of the `for` loop increments the *`trailCount`* variable by one. So the *`trailCount`* variable is set to 2 at the end of one cycle through the `for` loop (3.32).

After the code within the `for` loop is executed, you start the process all over again (3.33). This time, the initialization section of the `for` loop is ignored, and the `for` loop immediately checks to see if *`trailCount`* is less than *`duplicateNumber`*. Since 2 is less than 27, the loop continues. The code within the `for` loop is executed again, and the `for` loop increments the *`trailCount`* variable. So the *`trailCount`* variable is set to 3 at the end of the second cycle, and

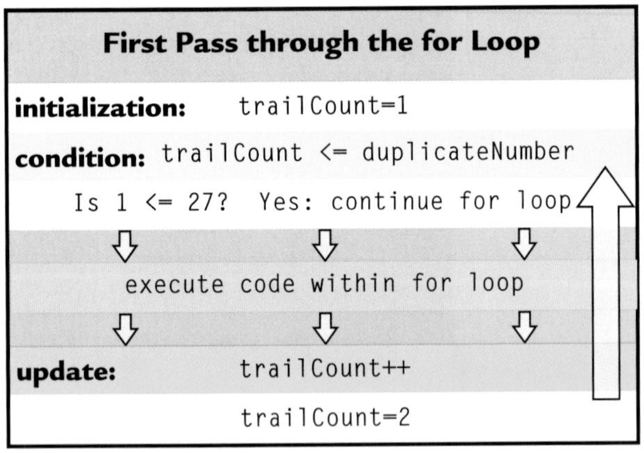

3.32: The first pass through the `for` *loop*

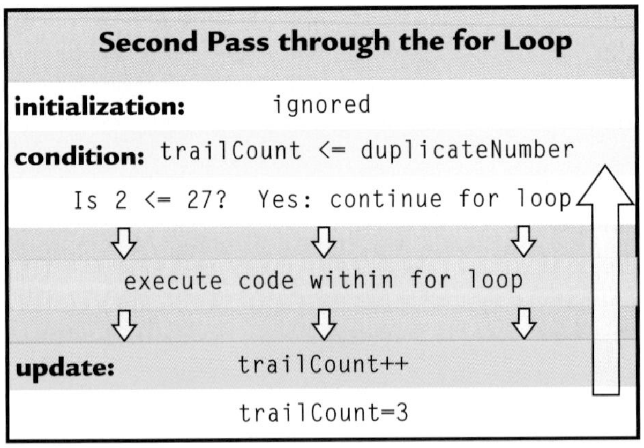

3.33: The second pass through the `for` *loop*

the cycle is repeated over and over until *trailCount* is equal to 28. At that point, the `for` loop stops executing.

Now that you understand how the `for` loop operates, let's look at the code within the loop:

```
attachMovie("Cursor1", "trail" + trailCount, trailCount);
```

This code uses the `attachMovie()` method, covered in Chapter 2. Here is a quick refresher. Within the parentheses, there are three arguments associated with the `attachMovie()` method. The first argument, *Cursor1*, references the identifier. Recall that you gave the BlueBall movie clip the identifier Cursor1, so the first section tells the `attachMovie()` action to make a copy of the BlueBall movie clip.

In Chapter 2, you learned how instances of a movie clip created by `attachMovie()` need a unique name and to be placed on a unique level. That is what the next two arguments of the `attachMovie()` method do. The second argument gives the new instance of the BlueBall movie clip a name by concatenating trail with the value of the *trailCount* variable. The third argument sets the new instance of the BlueBall movie clip on a level equal to the value of the *trailCount* variable.

The value of the *trailCount* variable is 1 when the code is executed in the first pass through the `for` loop. (Remember that it's incremented to 2 only after the code is executed.) So the first instance of the BlueBall movie clip created by the `attachMovie()` action is given the name trail1, and it's set on level 1. On the second pass through the `for` loop, the second instance of the BlueBall movie clip is given the name trail2, and it's set on level 2, and so on.

Finally, you put a `stop()` command at the end because you don't want the main timeline to loop; you want this ActionScript to execute only once. After the `for` loop has created 27 copies of the BlueBall movie clip, you don't want it to repeatedly create 27 more copies.

If you test this now, you will notice very little difference, but you will have the appearance of two blue balls on the stage—one you can drag around and one that sits still. Actually, the ball that sits still contains all 27 trail*N* movie clips stacked on top of each other. If you need proof that all 27 really are there, while you are in test mode, select Debug ➢ List Objects (Cmd/Ctrl+L) (3.34). The Output panel will display a list of all the objects that are currently running.

Next you want to create two variables to contain the position of each of the duplicated movies. These variables need to have a starting value that will not be used except to initialize the variables.

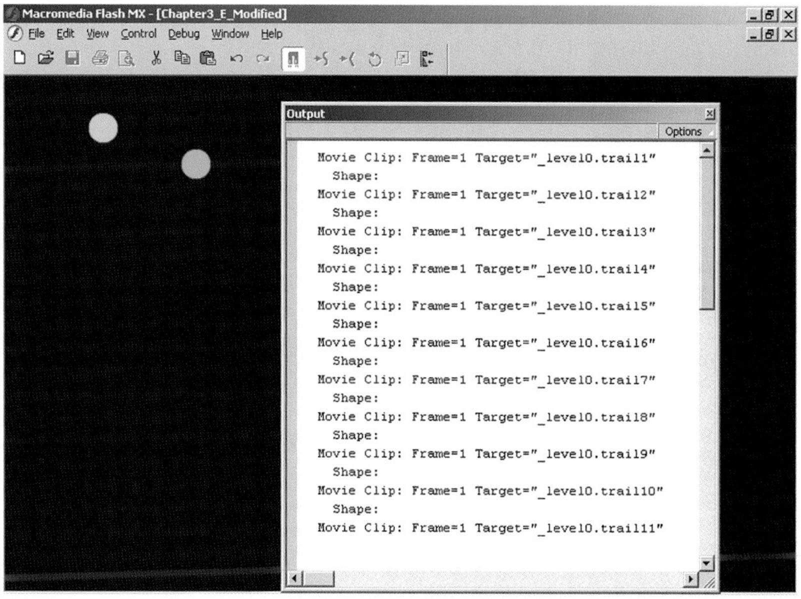

3.34: The Output panel shows that 27 copies of the BlueBall movie clip have been generated when you test the movie at this point.

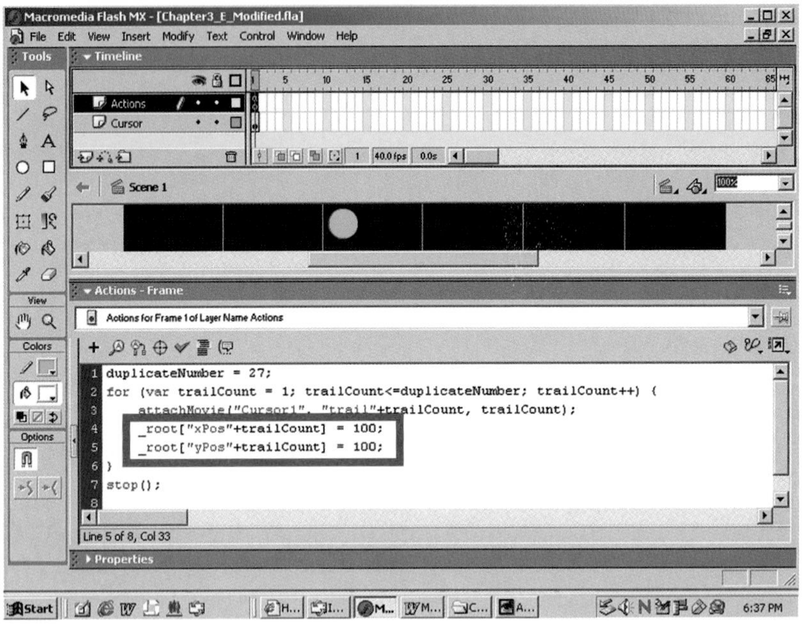

3.35: Add the code that will store the position of the copies of the movie clip in a preselected place.

3. Position the Duplicates

Insert the following code within the curly brackets of the `for` loop, after the `attachMovie()` code (3.35).

```
_root["xPos" + trailCount] = 100;
_root["yPos" + trailCount] = 100;
```

This is a way of keeping track of where each movie clip is. These statements create two variables, *xPosNN* and *yPosNN*, for each movie clip—one variable to contain the *x* position and the other to contain the *y* position. To each variable name, the code appends the current value of *trailCount*. So for the movie clip trail3, there will be a variable *xPos3* that contains its *x* position and a variable *yPos3* that contains its *y* position.

Here, you are creating the variable "xPos" + trailCount. In order for Flash to interpret "xPos" + trailCount and make it *xPos3*, you need to put the _root[...] around it, so you get _root["xPos" + trailCount], which gives you *XPos3* on the _root level. The [...] is used for evaluation and cannot stand alone, so you couldn't say ["xPos" + trailCount]; you need to put a timeline in front of it. So you are setting each *xPosNN* and *yPosNN* for each trail*N* movie clip to 100. Remember that the starting number of these two variables will not be used.

If you test this now, you still won't see any difference. So let's move the trails with the mouse.

4. Move the Trails

Select the MovingCursor instance on the stage. Attach the following ActionScript to the MovingCursor instance of the BlueBall movie clip within the `onClipEvent(enterFrame)` section and below the existing code (3.36).

```
_root.xPos0 = _x;
_root.yPos0 = _y;
```

```
// loop through each of the trailing movie clips
for (var trailCount = 1; trailCount <= _root.duplicateNumber; ▶
trailCount++){
//compute each movie clip based on the next one's position, add this
//position to the next one's position and divide by two;
//this way, each new instance is closer to the previous
   _root["xPos" + trailCount] = (_root["xPos" + (trailCount - 1)] + ▶
   _root["xPos" + trailCount]) / 2;
   _root["yPos" + trailCount] = (_root["yPos" + (trailCount - 1)] + ▶
   _root["yPos" + trailCount]) / 2;
   _root["trail" + trailCount]._x = _root["xPos" + trailCount];
   _root["trail" + trailCount]._y = _root["yPos" + trailCount];
}
```

At first glance, this code might appear intimidating. However, if you look at the code carefully, you'll see that it is composed of elements that should be familiar by now—in particular, a `for` loop and several references to the variables. When you break it down, it's much simpler than it appears.

The first two lines are very simple; they set the variables *xPos0* and *yPos0* equal to where this movie clip is, which is also where the cursor is. You don't have a trail0 movie clip, but essentially it is the BlueBall movie clip that is being moved around. So the variables *xPos0* and *yPos0* represent the position of movie clip 0, which is really the main BlueBall movie clip.

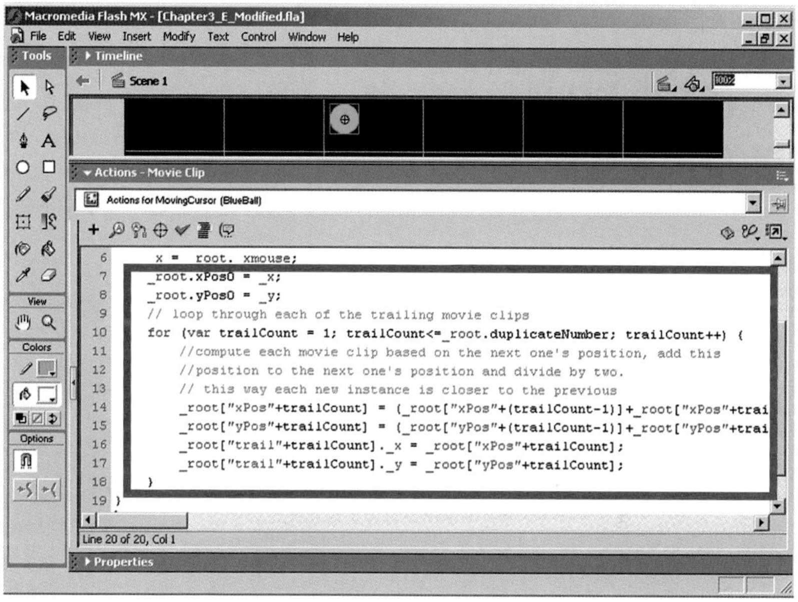

3.36: Add the code that will be used to animate all of the BlueBall movie clip instances to the clip instance that is on the stage.

The next line is the same `for` loop you used earlier. The loop itself works the same as before, but it contains different code. This time, the code needs to loop through each trail*N* movie clip (created in the `for` loop discussed earlier) and move each trail*N* movie clip based on where the user has moved the cursor. In other words, the code will reposition each of the duplicate movie clips based on the values of the *xPos0* and *yPos0* variables. Let's walk through the code to see how this is accomplished.

The code calculates the new position for each trail movie clip and updates the *xPosNN* and *yPosNN* variables, where the *NN* is the *trailCount* number. The *x* and the *y* positions are calculated using the same formula. Here is the code for calculating *xPosNN*:

```
_root["xPos" + trailCount] = (_root["xPos" + (trailCount - 1)] + ▶
_root["xPos" + trailCount]) / 2;
```

First, notice that although this line is fairly long, it really is composed of multiple references to the same string ("*xPos*") and the variable (*trailCount*). The easiest way to understand how this works is to plug in values for the *trailCount* variable. Again, this code is contained within the for loop. On the first pass of the for loop, *trailCount* is equal to 1. So let's plug that value into the code:

```
_root["xPos" + 1] = (_root["xPos" + (1 - 1)] + _root["xPos" + 1]) / 2;
```

That simplifies things significantly. You can easily simplify things further by making the concatenations and simple calculations within the parentheses. If you do that, the above line reads like this:

```
_root.xPos1 = (_root.xpos0 + _root.xPos1) / 2;
```

Now the code is far less intimidating. To understand it, all you need to do is plug in some values. Recall that *xPos0* is wherever the mouse happens to be (which is also where the MovingCursor instance is located). Before this calculation is performed, let's say the mouse's current *x* coordinate is 100. This means that *xPos0* = 100. *xPos1* is wherever the trail1 movie clip is located. In fact, let's say its *x* coordinate is at 50. This means that *xPos1* = 50. So let's plug these numbers into the formula:

```
_root.xPos1 = (100 + 50 / 2);
```

The result of this calculation is that *xPos1* = 75. So the code that looked a little scary earlier really just resolves down to a simple calculation. This code moves the *x* coordinate of the trail1 movie clip 25 pixels, or half the distance closer to the MovingCursor instance (3.37). The code for calculating the *yPosNN* values works in the same way.

Once you have calculated the new position, the code sets the trail*N* movie clip to its new position. So you set the *x* position and *y* position of that copy of the movie equal to the appropriate *xPosNN* and *yPosNN* variables. Let's continue looking at what would happen during the first pass of the for loop for the *x* coordinate. The code looks like this:

```
_root["trail" + trailCount]._x = _root["xPos" + trailCount];
```

Again, this can be simplified by plugging in the value of the *trailCount* variable, which is still 1:

```
_root["trail" + 1]._x = _root["xPos" + 1];
```

This translates to the following:

```
_root.trail1._x = _root.xPos1;
```

This line of code sets the _x property of the trail1 movie clip to the value of the *xPos1* variable, which, in the example, is 75. Again, the code works the same for the *y* coordinate.

To review, the for loop works through each instance of the trail*N* movie clip instances. Each time the position of the trail*N* movie clip is compared to the previous trail*N* movie clip (the one closer to the MovingCursor movie clip), and a calculation is performed that cuts the distance between the two in half. Then the code repositions each instance of the trail*N* movie clip as it works through the for loop.

Note that the first for loop on frame 1 of the main timeline, which creates all the instances of the BlueBall movie clip with the attachMovie() method, works only once. In other words, that for loop creates the instances of the movie clips and then never runs again. This for loop runs repeatedly because it is within the onClipEvent(enterFrame) event handler. So this code is constantly positioning and repositioning the instances of the BlueBall movie clips (or the trail*N* movie clips) based on the mouse movement.

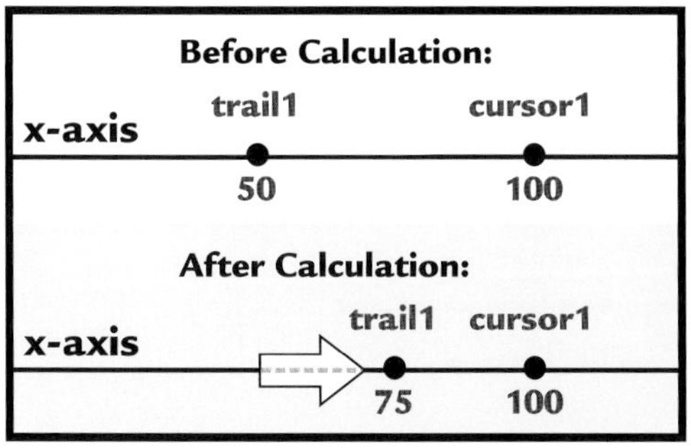

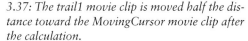

3.37: The trail1 movie clip is moved half the distance toward the MovingCursor movie clip after the calculation.

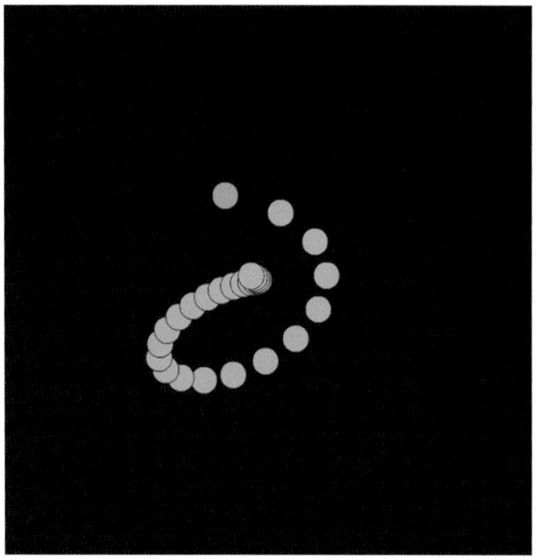

3.38: The BlueBall movie clip instances continually follow the Cursor1 movie clip.

5. Test the Movie

When you test the movie, you will see the duplicates of the BlueBall movie clip continually follow the MovingCursor instance (3.38), which is attached to the mouse movements. If you hold the mouse still, all of the instances of the BlueBall movie clip will eventually congregate under the MovingCursor instance.

This is pretty slick, but let's add a little more depth. You can have the trail*N* movie clips gradually fade out by changing the `_alpha` property.

6. Fade the Trail

On frame 1, add the following code at the bottom of the `for` loop, but still within the `for` loop (3.39).

```
// fade out
_root["trail" + trailCount]._alpha = 100 - 100 / duplicateNumber * ▶
trailCount;
```

Once again, the easiest way to understand how this line of code works is to plug values into the variables. Let's start with *`trailCount`* equal to 1 (remember the *`duplicateNumber`* variable is set to 27). When you do that, this code looks like this:

```
_root.trail1._alpha = 100 - 100 / 27 * 1;
```

So the `_alpha` property of the trail1 movie clip is set to 96. (The `_alpha` property takes only integers, so 96.3 gets rounded to 96.)

As the *`trailCount`* variable moves higher, the `_alpha` property value gets smaller. For instance, on the tenth pass through the `for` loop, the *`trailCount`* variable is equal to 10 and the `_alpha` for trail10 is set to 63.

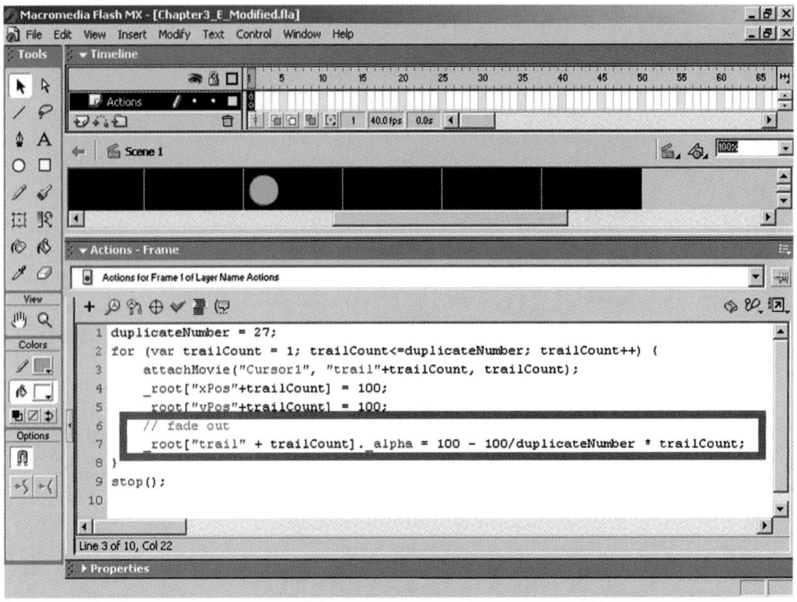

*3.39: Add the code to make the trail*N *or BlueBall movie clip instances fade out sequentially.*

NOTE Flash performs basic calculations just the way you were taught: multiplication and division are performed before addition and subtraction; otherwise, operations are carried out from left to right. For example, in the calculation 100 - 100 / 27 * 10, the 100 / 27 is figured first to get 3.7, which is multiplied by 10 (10 * 3.7 = 37), and then 37 is subtracted from 100.

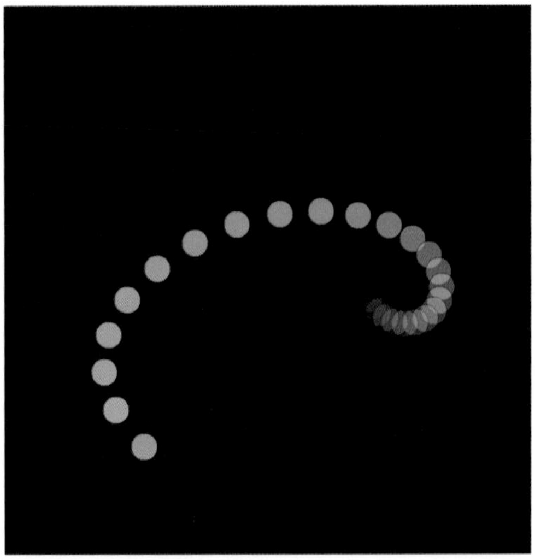

3.40: The BlueBall movie clip instance fades out sequentially down the line.

7. Test the Movie

Test the movie again. Now the animated mouse effect is looking pretty slick (3.40).

You can make it look even better by using a more interesting movie clip. Fortunately, it's very easy to swap in a new movie clip.

Getting a Better Animated Mouse Effect

The better the graphics, the better the mouse effect. Now you'll use a better graphic with animation to create this mouse trail.

1. Swap the Movie Clip

Select the BlueBall movie clip on the stage. Open the Properties panel and swap the BlueBall movie clip with the Spiral movie clip (3.41). (This is another movie clip in the Chapter3_E_Modified.fla file.)

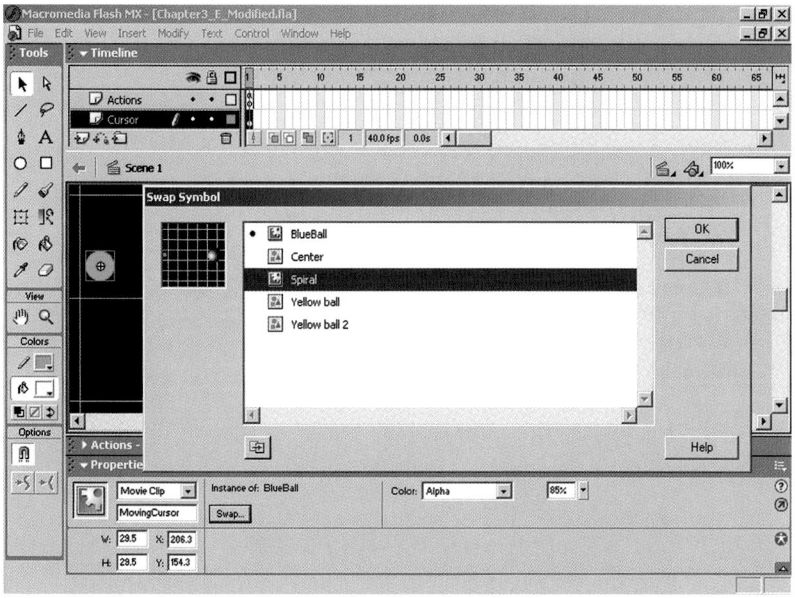

3.41: *Swap the Spiral movie clip with the BlueBall movie clip.*

The only other update is to tell Flash which movie clip it should be duplicating in the `attachMovie()` statement, which is in the `for` loop on the first frame. Linkage properties for the Spiral movie clip have already been set using the Export for Action-Script command, setting it to the identifier Cursor2.

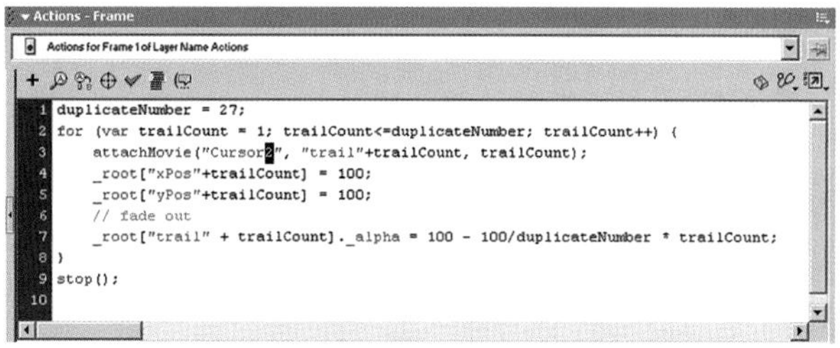

3.42: *Update the* `attachMovie()` *action to refer to Cursor2 instead of Cursor1.*

2. Edit the MovingCursor ActionScript

Edit the ActionScript code attached to frame 1 by changing Cursor1 in the `attachMovie()` statement to Cursor2 (3.42). You should have the following code:

```
duplicateNumber = 27;
for (var trailCount = 1; trailCount <= duplicateNumber; trailCount++) {
   attachMovie("Cursor2", "trail" + trailCount, trailCount);
   _root["xPos" + trailCount] = 100;
   _root["yPos" + trailCount] = 100;
   // fade out
   _root["trail" + trailCount]._alpha = 100 - 100/duplicateNumber * ▶
trailCount;
}
stop();
```

Now let's add one more effect—rotation.

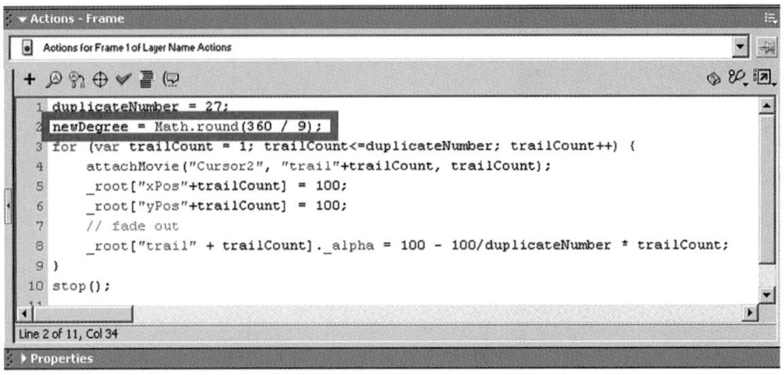

3.43: Add the `newDegree` *variable line to the top of the ActionScript on frame 1.*

3. Add a New Variable

Edit the ActionScript attached to frame 1 to add the following line at the top (3.43):

```
newDegree = Math.round(360 / 9);
```

This statement assigns a variable, *newDegree*, to the integer 40. You could have easily said this:

```
newDegree = 40;
```

However, this form would not have helped you to understand where the value came from. By looking at `360 / 9`, you know that you are taking the maximum number of degrees in a rotation (360) and dividing it by 9. We picked 9 to make an even rotation of the 27 attached Spiral movie clips. This way, there will be three complete rotations of the Spiral clip.

4. Rotate Cursor Trails

Now add the following ActionScript within the `for` loop at the bottom (3.44).

```
_root["trail" + trailCount]._rotation = 360 - (trailCount * newDegree);
```

To understand how this works, let's plug in values for the variables once again. If the *trailCount* variable is equal to 1 and *newDegree* is equal to 40, the code looks like this:

```
_root.trail1._rotation = 360 - (1 * 40);
```

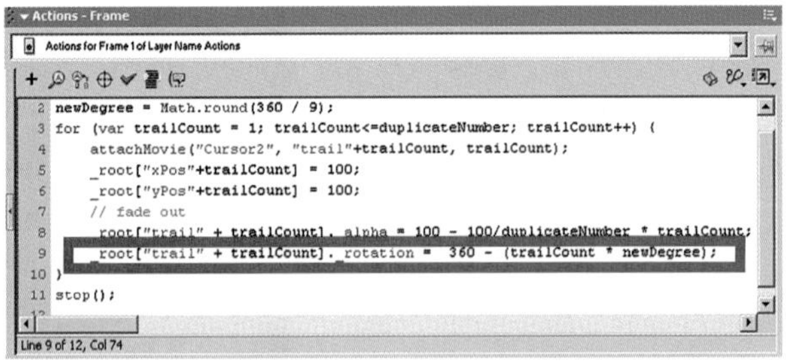

3.44: Add the code that rotates the Spiral movie clip instances within the `for` *loop on frame 1.*

This would set the `_rotation` property of the trail1 movie clip to 320. Therefore, this code rotates each trail*N* movie clip by 40 degrees from the last one, producing three full circles over the 27 instances. The code relies on the fact that the registration point for the Spiral movie clip is the center of the white ball within the clip, not the center of the clip itself.

5. Test the Movie

Test this modified version. You'll appreciate the effects your ActionScripting has achieved (3.45).

3.45: Final cursor modifications

Conclusion

In this chapter, you have learned the basics of interactions with the mouse and been introduced to some valuable new features in ActionScript along the way. You looked at several ways to empower buttons in Flash with ActionScript and also saw how movie clips can now do almost anything a button can do—and sometimes more efficiently than a button. You also got an introduction to methods.

Buttons are the main resource for navigation and interactivity, so it's important to know the different ways to set up and to use them. Each of the examples in this chapter has strengths and drawbacks. The decision on which method to use is based on the goals of the final product and your preferences as the programmer.

The cursor or mouse is also very useful in creating interactivity or just plain "Wow!" power. These examples have some creativity, but their main purpose is to provide you with an introduction to the basics of cursor manipulation.

In the next chapter, you will learn about many of Flash's more commonly used built-in methods and objects, such as the `random()`and `getTimer()` functions. These tools will allow you to create increasingly interesting and valuable scripts.

CHAPTER four

Used and Reused ActionScript

Creating code that you *(and other programmers) can reuse in other projects will save you a lot of time and effort. You can build a library of ActionScript, and then simply reuse the code in your collection, rather than needing to rewrite it for each new project.*

Flash MX provides many built-in ActionScript functions and objects with methods. You can use these functions and methods to create reusable code. This chapter explains how to program some common tasks, including determining how much of the movie has been loaded (to create a preloader), generating a random number, discovering the stage size, and keeping track of time.

Coding Flash Preloaders

If you are using a lot of graphics in your Flash movie, it might take a while to load the whole Flash file. Preloaders provide viewers with something to look at while they're waiting for a movie to download.

Preloaders can be just a "Please wait while loading" message, a simple repeated graphic, or some form of progress bar. In the examples in this chapter, you'll create preloaders that show a progress bar. With Flash MX, there are a couple of ways to create a preloader, as you'll see in the following examples.

NOTE In previous versions of Flash, you needed to resort to placing all of the symbols that were to be used in the Flash movie in a preloader scene before the rest of the movie. All of the symbols were hidden behind some graphics, or otherwise displayed in some artful manner. Typically, you would distribute the symbols on different frames, so that the preloader wouldn't get bogged down at any one place. Essentially, you were forcing the symbol to load by placing it on the stage, whether you needed it or not. The method was tedious, awkward, and inefficient. Fortunately, Flash MX offers more elegant solutions.

Using the *_framesloaded* and *_totalframes* Properties

One useful technique is to use the `_framesloaded` and `_totalframes` properties to test how much of a movie has loaded. In the example here, you'll use these as properties of the main timeline, which means you'll be testing to see if the entire movie is loaded before Flash allows the movie to proceed. However, you can also use `_framesloaded` and `_totalframes` as properties of a movie clip, which allows you to test when a specific movie clip has loaded.

1. Open the File

WWW. Open **Chapter4_A_Start.fla** (4.1). Save it to your local hard drive as **Chapter4_A_Modified.fla.** (For the final version, see **Chapter4_A_Final.fla.**)

This file is the similar to the last example (**Chapter2_E_Final**) presented in Chapter 2, "Flash Communication." However, this version of the file has an additional scene called PreLoader. The PreLoader scene has two layers: Actions and Progress.

The Progress layer contains a movie clip, Progress MC (with the instance name ProgressBar), which will be used to show the movie-loading progress. It is 100 frames long, which corresponds to 100%. In other words, you'll program the preloader so that the loading rate will

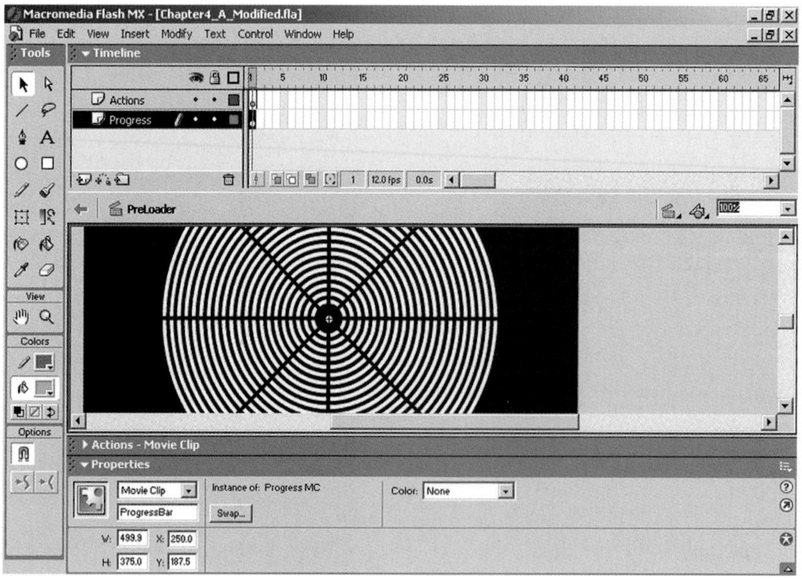

4.1: Notice that the **Chapter4_A_Modified.fla** *file already has the Progress MC movie clip instance name set to ProgressBar.*

correspond to the playing of the Progress MC movie clip. For instance, when 30% of the movie has been loaded, the viewer should be viewing frame 30 of the Progress MC movie clip.

You need to stay in the PreLoader scene until all of the frames are loaded from the rest of the movie.

2. Add a Test to Control the Preloader

Put the following code in frame 1 of the Actions layer (4.2).

```
if (_totalframes > 0) {
   if (_framesloaded == _totalframes){
      // finished loading
      gotoAndPlay("Green", 1);
   }else {
      var progress = Math.round(100 * (_framesloaded / _totalframes));
      ProgressBar.gotoAndStop(progress);
   }
}
```

This code starts off with a conditional: an `if` statement. Conditionals are a relatively easy programming concept. Like a doorman at an exclusive nightclub who decides which customers look rich or beautiful enough to enter, a conditional statement defines a specific condition that must be met in order for a set of instructions to be executed.

In this first example, the condition is that the value of the `_totalframes` property must be greater than 0 before Flash will be allowed to execute the rest of the script. The second test is whether `_totalframes` and `_framesloaded` have the same value. These two built-in properties of the main timeline are essentially channels of communication between Action-Script and the Flash player, asking specific questions about the movie's status: "How many frames have been loaded?" (4.3) and "How many total frames are in this movie?"

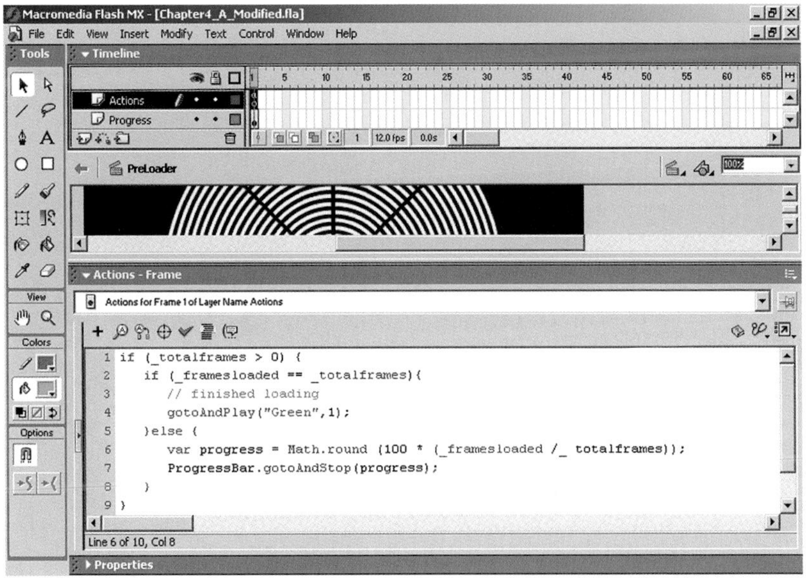

4.2: Add the code that controls the preloader to the first frame on the Actions layer.

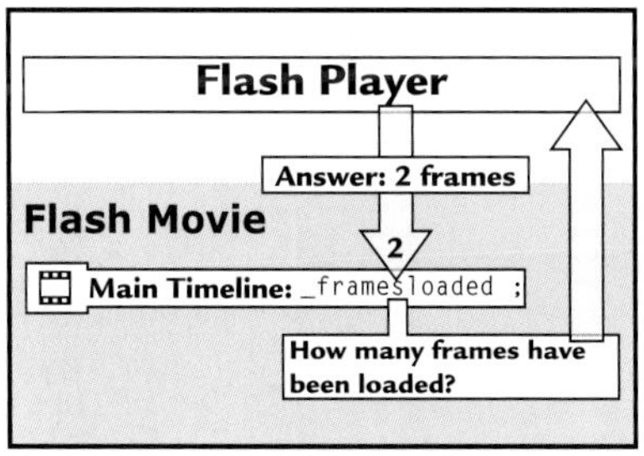

4.3: The `_framesloaded` property essentially asks the Flash Player how many frames have been loaded, and the Flash Player responds with a number.

The first `if` statement checks to see if enough of the movie has been loaded for the Flash Player to determine how many frames have been loaded. If the movie isn't quite ready to start playing, or if there is some other reason why the Flash Player cannot give a value for the `_totalframes` property, the rest of the script won't be executed.

> **NOTE** Actually, the Flash Player gets the value for `_totalframes` pretty quickly. However, the rest of the script needs for there to be a value for the `_totalframes` property, so the initial conditional simply ensures that this value exists before the code is executed.

Next the script has another conditional. This one is an `if/else` conditional, which provides an alternative action if the first condition is not met. In this example, the `if` statement checks to see if the value of the `_framesloaded` property is equal to the value of the `_totalframes` property.

Logically, if the values of these two properties are the same, then the entire movie has been loaded. So the code within this `if` statement tells the movie to go ahead and play the next scene. However, if the two properties are not equal, the code moves onto the `else` statement, which is where the code that powers the preload animation is located.

The line that controls the *`progress`* animation uses something you have not seen before: the `Math` method `round()`. Don't be intimidated by the word *Math*. This code is fairly easy to understand. First, let's look within the inner parentheses. Here, the code is making a simple calculation:

```
_framesloaded / _totalframes
```

The code is dividing the value of `_framesloaded` by the value of `_totalframes`. This will give you a percentage of the frames that are loaded. However, you need this in a whole number, so you multiply the result by 100, because it is a percentage:

```
(100 * (_framesloaded / _totalframes))
```

For instance, let's say you have 220 total frames, so the value of `_totalframes` would be 220. Now let's say that at a given moment that this script executes, the value of the `_framesloaded` property is 147. In that case, the calculation would look like this:

```
100 * (147 / 220)
```

The result of this calculation is 66.81. Since you'll need to use this value to communicate a frame number for the progress animation to go to, and you probably don't have a frame 66.81, you need to round this number to a whole number. That's what the `Math` method `round()` does: It rounds the decimal to the closest integer, which would be 67 in this example.

Taking the example further, the line would now read:

```
var progress = 67;
```

The variable named *`progress`* now has a value of 67.

> **NOTE** Many preloader animations are not 100 frames long. You can easily change the ActionScript in this example to work with any preloader movie by simply replacing the `100` in the line `var progress = Math.round (100 * (_framesloaded / _totalframes));` with `ProgressBar._totalframes`. This would accommodate a preloader animation of any size.

The next line of code uses the *progress* variable to tell the ProgressBar movie clip which frame to go to.

```
ProgressBar.gotoAndStop(progress);
```

In this example, this would be:

```
ProgressBar.gotoAndStop(67);
```

This tells the movie clip instance that has the instance name ProgressBar to go to frame 67 and stop.

Now that you've entered the code to control the preloader, you need to create a loop so that this code is executed over and over again until the file is loaded.

3. Create a Loop to Repeat the Test

Add nine frames to the movie. Insert a keyframe in frame 10 of the Action layer and enter the following ActionScript (4.4).

```
gotoAndPlay(1);
```

This code creates a simple loop. The frame rate of this movie is 12fps. With the code you added on frame 10, you've created a loop that will execute the code on frame 1 approximately once per second.

When you test the movie (4.5), you probably won't see the PreLoader scene. If your computer is really slow or bogged down with other programs, you might see the PreLoader scene for a fraction of a second. This is because the Flash movie is already on your local system, so there's no real delay in loading it. Therefore, the value for the `_framesloaded` property equals the value for the `_totalframes` property almost immediately, which means that Flash jumps right to the Green scene.

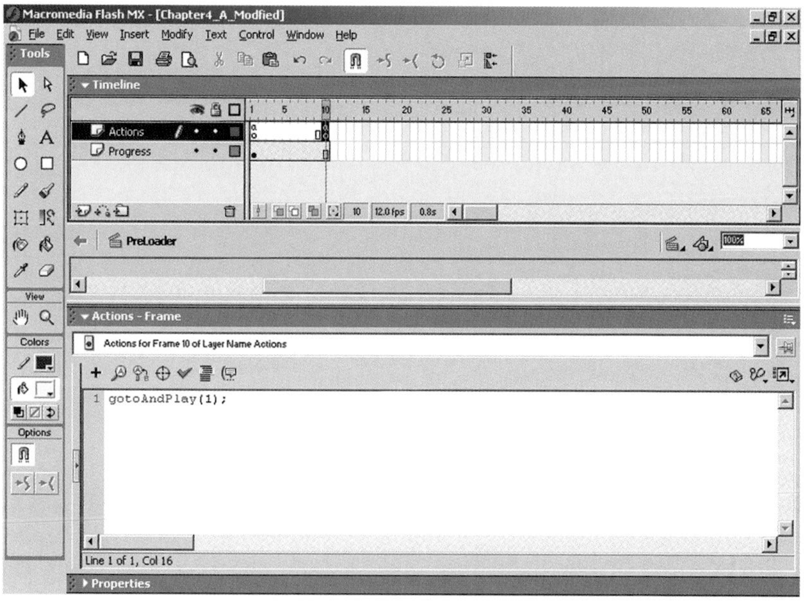

4.4: Add nine frames to the movie, add a keyframe on frame 10 of the Actions layer, and then add a `gotoAndPlay()` *command to the new keyframe.*

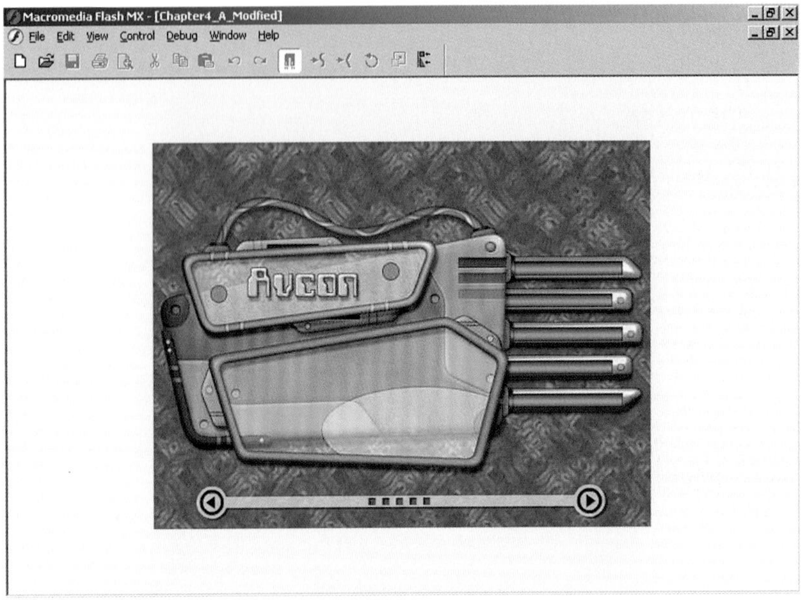

4.5: When you test the movie, it will probably jump right to the Green scene.

When you're working with preloaders, you need a way to emulate how your movie will appear on the Web. Conveniently, Flash provides a Debug menu from within the testing environment for testing how the Flash movie will load over different Internet connections.

4. Select a Connection Speed

With the movie still in the testing environment, select Debug ➢ 28.8 (2.3 KB/s) from the Debug menu (4.6). This is the slowest connection speed commonly used today, so it's a "worst-case scenario" for your movie. (If you close the Test Movie window, the Debug option will not be available on the menu.) Now press Cmd/Ctrl+Enter to restart the test movie.

Now you can see the Flash movie as it will look when it is downloaded over the Internet using a slow 28.8Kbps modem. You should see the PreLoader animation play as the movie loads (4.7). At 28.8Kbps, the preloader should be visible for about 30 seconds before the movie goes through to the Green scene.

5. Use the Bandwidth Profiler

Flash's Debug option is great, but you can get even more information about what's happening by using the Bandwidth Profiler. Select View ➢ Bandwidth Profiler or press Cmd/Ctrl+B. Now select Debug ➢ 28.8 (2.3Kb/s) again and press Cmd/Ctrl+Enter to restart the test movie (4.8).

Watch the Bandwidth Profiler as the movie plays (4.9). The playback head is shown over a green bar that indicates how much of the movie has been loaded. Notice three sections of the Bandwidth Profiler:

- The Movie section lists useful information such as the size of the movie (in kilobytes and bytes).
- The Settings section displays the current bandwidth settings of the test.
- The State section displays information about the current state of the loading process.

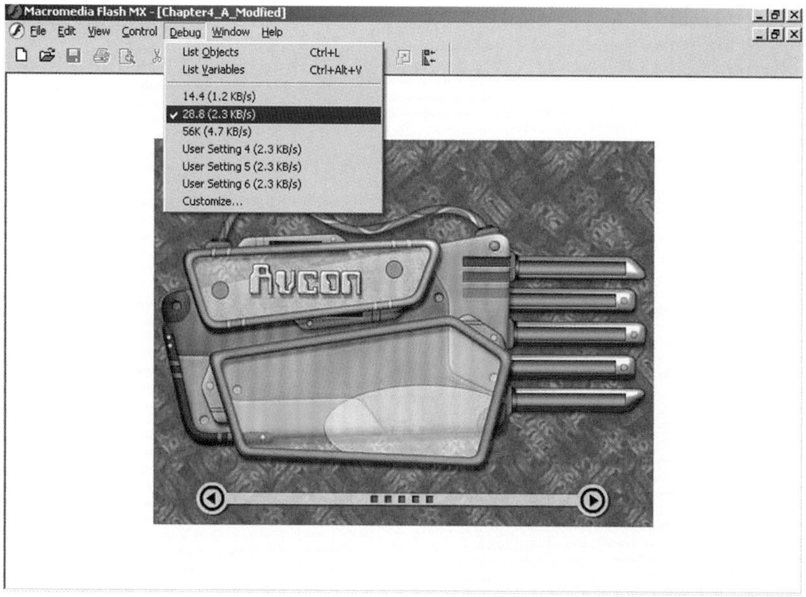

4.6: Select 28.8 (2.3Kb/s) from the Debug menu.

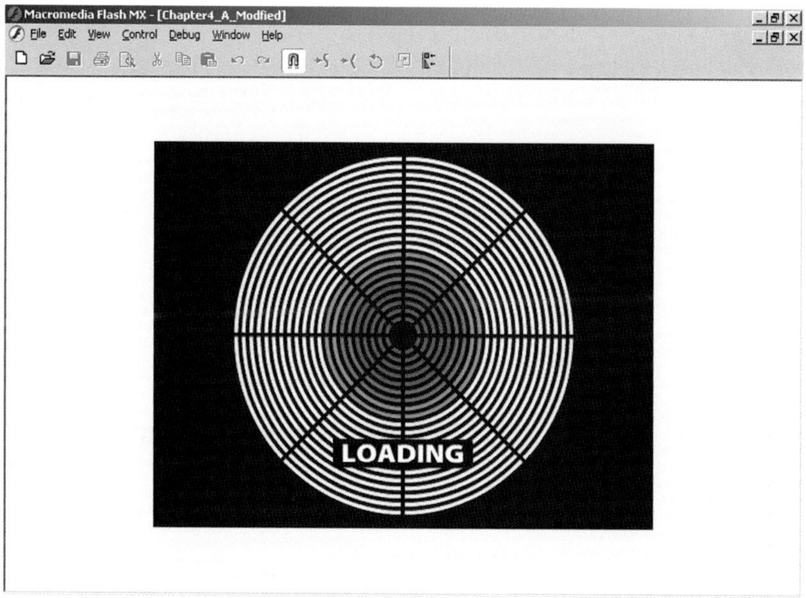

4.7: Debugging for a slow connection speed should allow you to see the preloader in action.

The Movie and Settings sections are useful, but the State section is the most relevant for testing a preloader. While the test movie is playing, the State section shows you the current frame, the amount of data a given frame contains (in kilobytes), and the percentage of the total that is loaded. All of this information gives you a very clear picture of what's going on while your movie is loading.

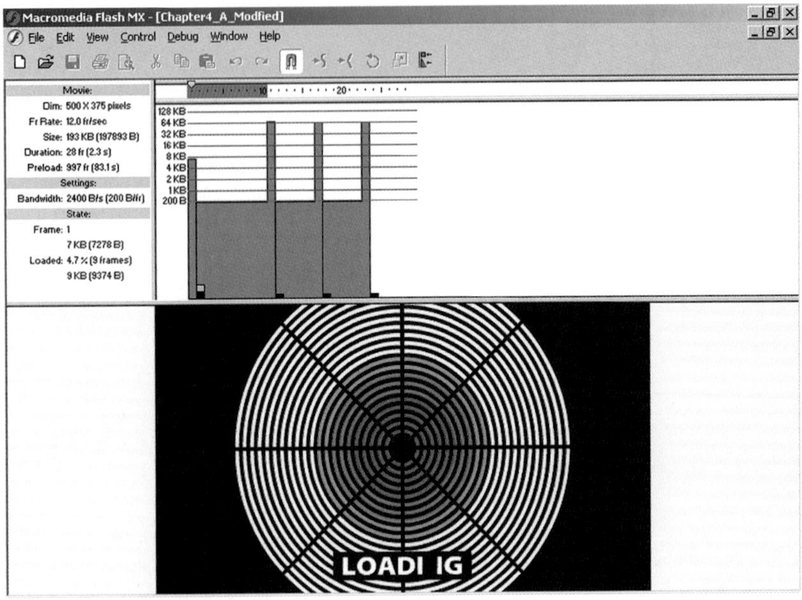

4.8: *Turn on the Bandwidth Profiler, reselect 28.8 (2.3 KB/s) from the Debug menu, and retest the movie.*

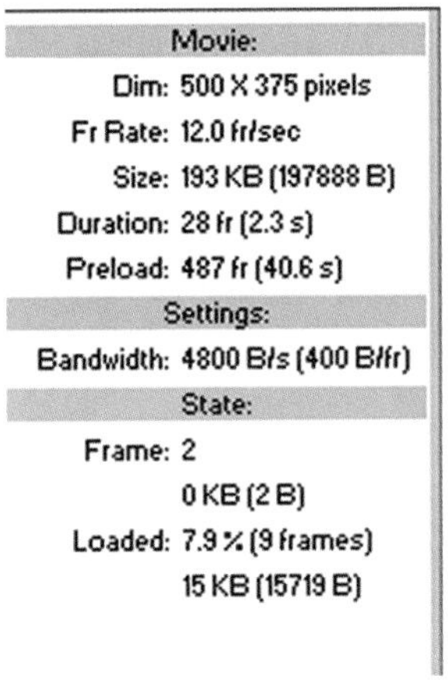

4.9: *The Movie, Setting, and State sections of the Bandwidth Profiler provide dynamic information about the movie.*

Now let's take a look at another way you can code the preloader. This time, you'll be able to have just one frame in the PreLoader scene.

6. Decrease the Number of Frames, Move the Code, and Test

Close the Test Movie window. In the PreLoader scene, decrease the number of frames to only one frame on all layers (by pressing Shift+F5). Delete the existing ActionScript that is in the Actions layer and replace it with a `stop()` command.

```
stop();
```

Attach the following code to the ProgressBar movie clip (4.10).

```
onClipEvent(enterFrame) {
   if (_root._totalframes > 0) {
      if (_root._framesloaded == _root._totalframes) {
         // finished loading
         _root.play();
      } else {
         var progress = Math.round(100 * (_root._framesloaded / ►
_root._totalframes));
         gotoAndStop(progress);
      }
   }
}
```

This code is almost identical to the ActionScript you entered in the previous example. One of the key differences is that now the code is within an `onClipEvent(enterFrame)` event

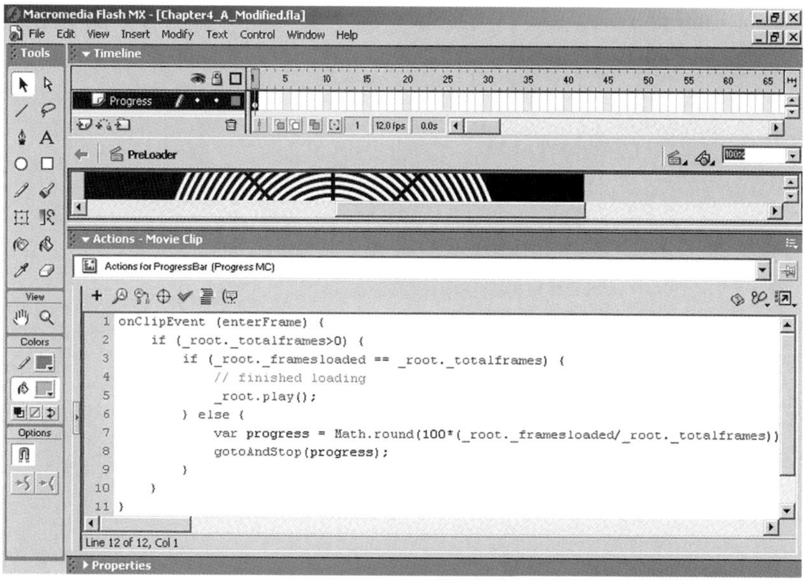

4.10: Replace the code on frame 1 on the Actions layer with code on the ProgressBar movie clip.

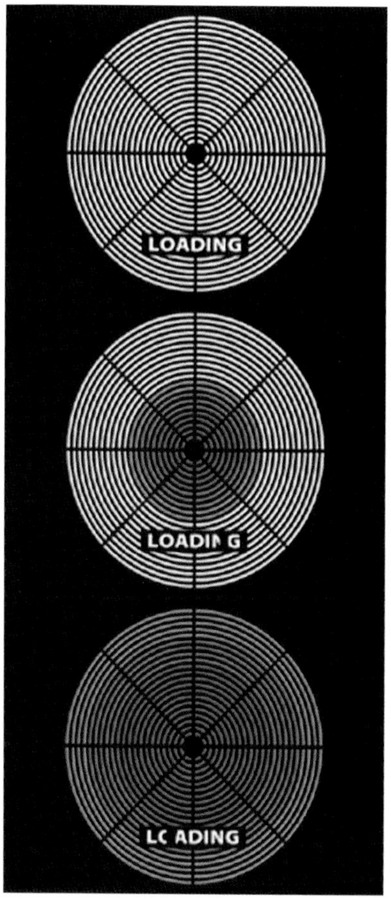

4.11: Using the `_framesloaded/_totalframes` method of coding the preloader results in three distinct jumps for the ProgressBar movie clip.

handler. Previously, the code was being executed once every 10 frames, which was roughly once a second. Now the code is executed much more frequently (12 times a second because of the frame rate of 12fps).

Also, the code uses `_root` in front of all of the references to `_framesloaded` and `_totalframes`. The `_root` tells Flash that you want the `_framesloaded` and `_totalframes` property values to come from the main timeline. Otherwise, Flash would assume `_framesloaded` and `_totalframes` were property values for the ProgressBar movie clip, which is not what you want.

Another difference is how the code continues on to play the rest of the movie when it has finished loading. As discussed in Chapter 2, you cannot reference scenes from within a movie clip. However, since you've removed all of the extra frames, you simply need to issue a `play()` command to the main timeline, which will send the movie to the next scene.

Test the movie with the Bandwidth Profiler still visible. Notice that the preloader works essentially the same as it did in step 5. You might notice that the preload animation appears to be a bit more responsive, since the code is executed every frame instead of about once per second.

By now, you have probably noticed a problem with this approach to coding the preloader. Specifically, the preloader shows progress in only three distinct intervals (4.11). This is because this code is based on the contents in each of the frames within the movie. Aside from the PreLoader scene, you have three scenes, each with one frame. Each of the frames in each of the scenes has a lot of data (three bitmap images in each scene). So the `_framesloaded` / `_totalframes` method results in displaying the progress animation in three surges as it loads each of these three frames. If the data or resources were spread out over more frames, this method would work more smoothly, but as it is, this example exposes a shortcoming of this approach to coding a preloader.

In order to have the preloader animation play smoothly, you need to employ a different approach to coding the preloader, as you'll see in the next example.

Using the *getBytesTotal()* and *getBytesLoaded()* Methods

Another approach you can use for preloader scripts is to use two built-in ActionScript methods: `getBytesTotal()` and `getBytesLoaded()`. As discussed in Chapter 3, "Cursor Interactions," a method is a function that is available only to a certain object or types of objects. In this case, all movie clips can use the `getBytesTotal()` and `getBytesLoaded()` methods, but no other type of object can. These methods are available for only movie clips and the main movie timeline.

The `getBytesLoaded()` method returns the number of bytes loaded of a specific movie clip. The `getBytesTotal()` method returns the total number of bytes of a specific movie clip. All you need to do to change the ActionScript from the previous example is replace the `_root._totalframes` with `_root.getBytesTotal()` and the `_root._framesloaded` with `_root.getBytesLoaded()`.

NOTE Notice that properties, such as `_totalframes`, have an underscore in front of them. Methods, such as `getBytesTotal()`, have parentheses at the end.

1. Replace the Properties with Methods and Test

Change the ActionScript attached to the ProgressBar movie clip to the following (4.12).

```
onClipEvent(enterFrame) {
   if (_root.getBytesTotal() > 0) {
      if (_root.getBytesLoaded() == _root.getBytesTotal()) {
         // finished loading
         _root.play();
      } else {
         var progress = Math.round(100 * (_root.getBytesLoaded() / ►
         _root.getBytesTotal()));
         gotoAndStop(progress);
      }
   }
}
```

Test the movie. You'll notice that the progress bar now increments steadily as the program loads (4.13). This is because you're no longer comparing just the frames. Instead, the code is making its calculation based on the percentage of bytes of data that has been loaded compared to the total number of bytes for the movie.

This is a much more meaningful way of displaying the loading information to the user. Long pauses can lead a viewer to assume that the connection is bad or that there is something wrong with your movie. A preloading animation or progress bar that runs smoothly lets the users know things are working properly, and it allows them to gauge how much longer the movie will take to load.

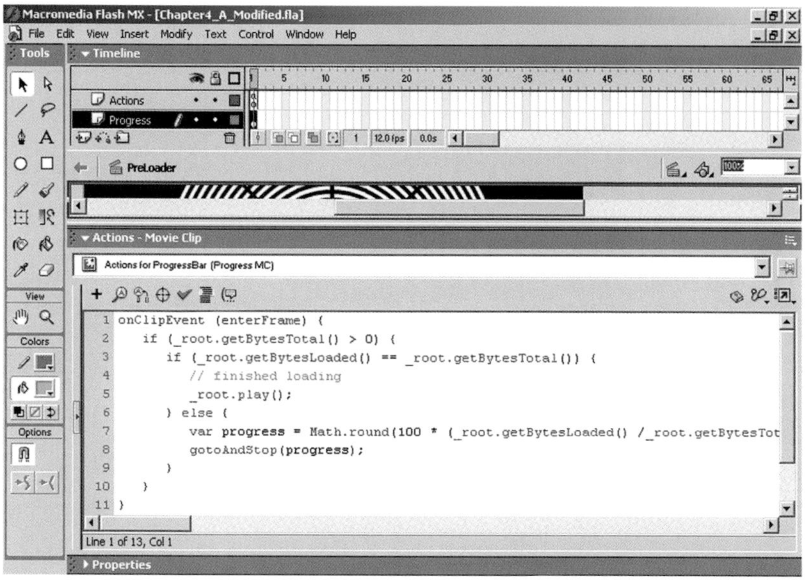

4.12: Replace the code on the ProgressBar movie clip with code that uses the `getBytes` *methods of controlling the preloader.*

However, even though everything works beautifully, the code is a little inefficient. Each time you use `getBytesTotal()`, the program needs to calculate the total number of bytes for the whole movie. This is another difference between using a property and using a method. The property already has the value, so all you need to do is access it. The method must actually do something to get the value. The total number of bytes is not changing, so it's a bit inefficient to force Flash to make the calculation each time you use the `getBytesTotal()` method. You can make things more efficient by using the `getBytesTotal()` method once, and then using a variable to store the information.

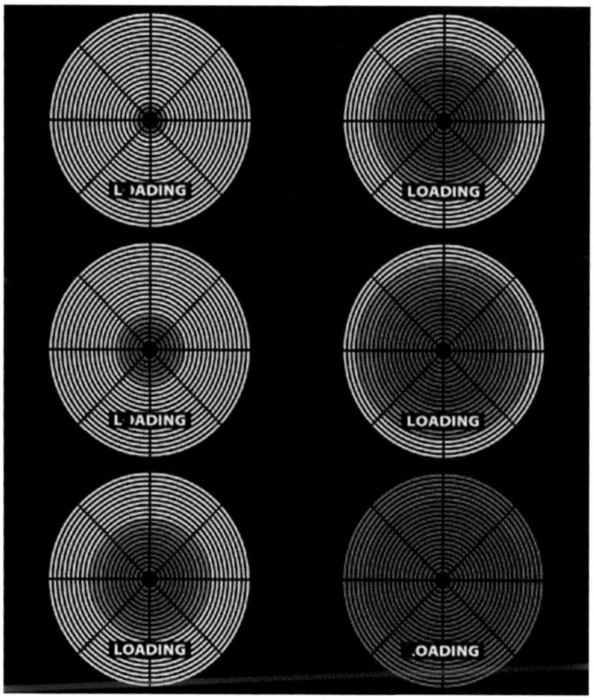

4.13: The ProgressBar animation moves along more smoothly using the `getBytes` *methods.*

2. Load the Bytes Value into a Variable

Add the following ActionScript to the movie clip above all the rest of the ActionScript (4.14).

```
onClipEvent(load){
   var myTotal = _root.getBytesTotal();
}
```

This code loads the total number of bytes into a variable called `myTotal`. Next you need to use the variable instead of calling `getBytesTotal()` each time.

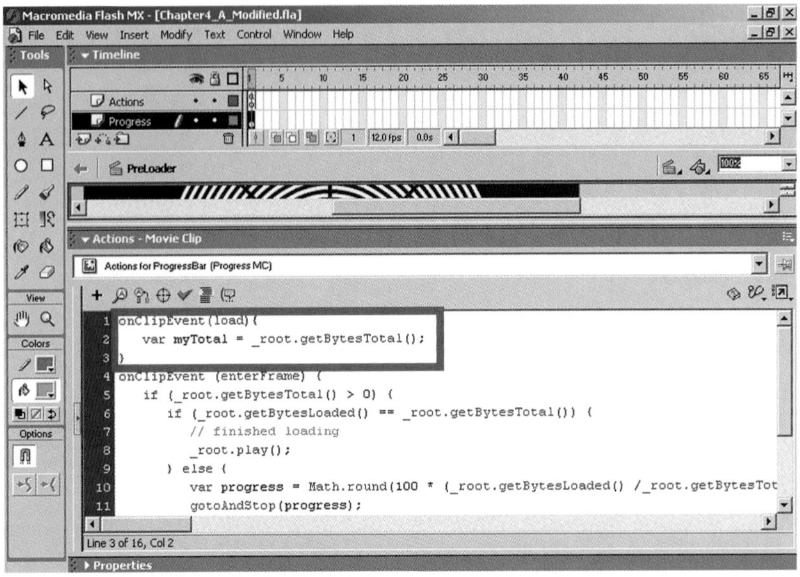

4.14: Add the `onClipEvent(load)` *event handler to the code attached to the ProgressBar movie clip above the existing code.*

3. Replace the Method with the Variable and Test

Replace each occurrence of `_root.getBytesTotal()` in the `enterFrame` event with `myTotal` (4.15). Your ActionScript should look like this:

```
onClipEvent(load) {
    var myTotal = _root.getBytesTotal();
}
onClipEvent(enterFrame) {
    if (myTotal > 0) {
        if (_root.getBytesLoaded() == myTotal) {
            // finished loading
            _root.play();
        } else {
            var progress = Math.round(100 * (_root.getBytesLoaded() / ►
            myTotal));
            gotoAndStop(progress);
        }
    }
}
```

Test the revised script. Notice that nothing has visibly changed. If you were to run the inefficient code on a very slow machine, you might notice a difference between the two, but the idea here is to make sure that the ActionScript is as efficient as possible and not doing extra steps.

Some form of preloader is used in almost every Flash movie. Sounds are also commonly used, and some Flash movies use dates. Each of these has its own object, and you'll explore their uses in the next section.

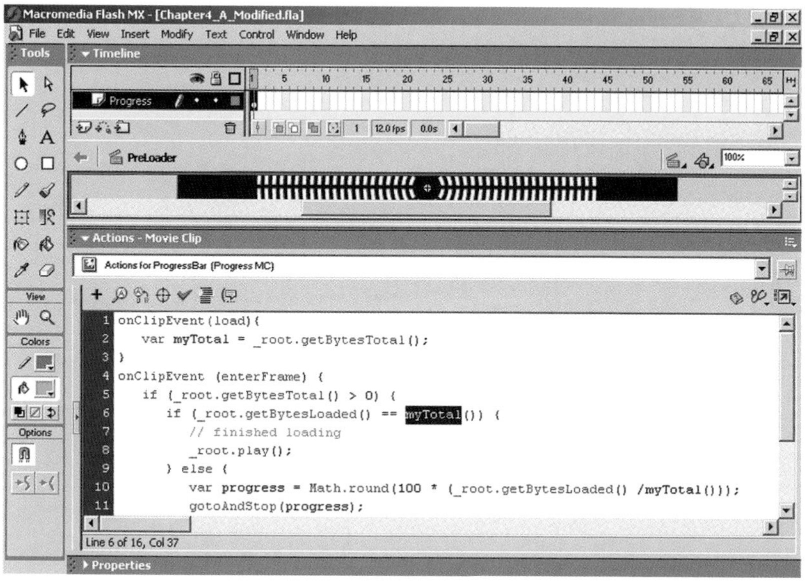

4.15: Replace each instance of `_root.getBytesTotal()` *in the code with* `myTotal`.

Using the *Date* and *Sound* Objects to Code a Clock

The `Date` and `Sound` objects were first introduced in Flash 5 and continue to be very useful for Flash MX projects. The `Date` object is built into Flash. It works through the Flash Player to get the current time on your system clock. The `Sound` object is also built into Flash, and it allows you to play the sounds. You can play and stop a sound on command, as well as control volume and panning.

Let's see how these objects work by creating a clock that chimes on the hour and the quarter hour.

Creating a Clock with the *Date* Object

The `Date` object has methods that allow you to find out what time or date it is. In this example, you'll use the `Date` object and its methods to create a clock with working hour, minute, and second hands.

1. Open the File

Open the **Chapter4_B_Start.fla** file (4.16). Save the file to your local hard drive as **Chapter4_B_Modified.fla**. (For the finished version, see **Chapter4_B_Final.fla**.) WWW.

This file contains a cartoon clock, complete with an hour, minute, and second hands. All of the hands are within the Clock movie clip.

Each hand is a movie clip that rotates around the face of the clock. The second hand and minute hand movie clips have 61 frames. Each one goes from frame 1 to frame 61. Note that each frame corresponds to a minute or second, except it's off by one. For example, for the minute 15, you would need to go to frame 16. The hour hand movie clip is similar,

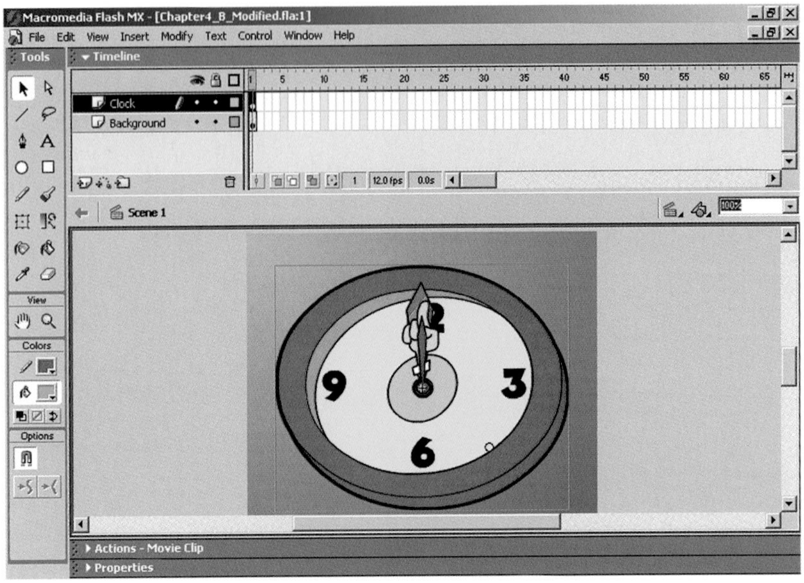

4.16: In the Chapter4_B_Modified.fla *file, the hands for the cartoon clock are in the Clock movie clip.*

except it contains 13 frames, so for 6 o'clock, it would need to go to frame 7. This is because there is no frame 0, but there is a time when the second and minute are equal to 0.

2. Get the Current Time

Attach the following ActionScript to the Clock movie clip (4.17).

```
onClipEvent(load) {
   // get the current time
   currentTime = new Date();
   myHour = currentTime.getHours();
   myMin = currentTime.getMinutes();
   mySec = currentTime.getSeconds();
}
```

The first task is to get the current time, so the code reads the current time when the Clock movie clip is loaded, in the `onClipEvent(load)` event.

In order to use the `Date` object, you need to create an instance of the `Date` object. This is called *instantiating* the object. The keyword `new` says that an instance of the `Date` object needs to be created. The keyword `new` is used for any object that needs to be instantiated.

There are certain objects—such as `Date` object, `Array` object, and `Sound` objects—that cannot exist unless they are instantiated using the keyword `new`. This is in contrast to `MovieClip` objects, for instance, which exist without being instantiated because they are effectively constructed as a graphical movie clip. The `Date` object needs to be created with ActionScript. In order to create an object that is not graphical, you use the word `new`, followed by the name of the object you want to create. You also need to give this instance a name, so you use a variable.

```
currentTime = new Date();
```

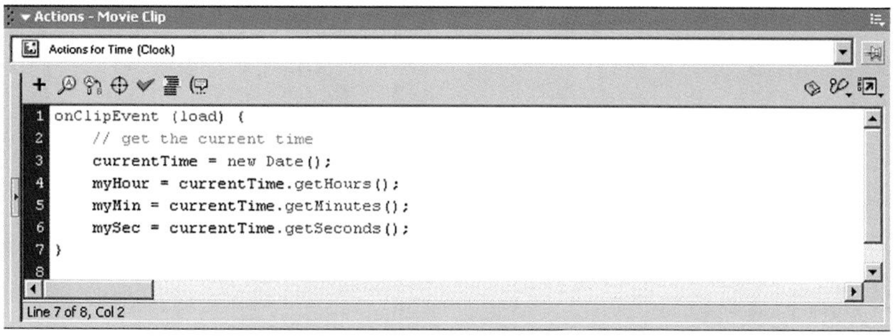

4.17: Attach the `onClipEvent(load)` *code to the Clock movie clip.*

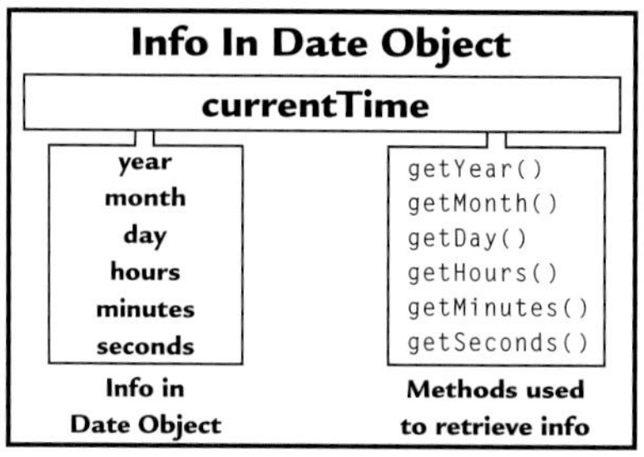

4.18: The `currentTime` `Date` *object stores many time-related data items (more than are shown here). You can retrieve the data with the* `get` *methods.*

The variable *`currentTime`* is now a `Date` object (4.18). It is easy to confuse the *`currentTime`* `Date` object with a typical variable; that is, it doesn't look very different from how a variable is set up. If you like, you can think of *`currentTime`* as a sort of super variable. The *`currentTime`* `Date` object doesn't contain a simple value—it's a conglomerate or concatenation of values for the date and time.

Next the script uses the `getHours()`, `getMinutes()`, and `getSeconds()` methods of the `Date` object to get the hour, minute, and second, respectively, and stores each piece of information in a variable:

```
myHour = currentTime.getHours();
myMin = currentTime.getMinutes();
mySec = currentTime.getSeconds();
```

Without establishing the *`currentTime`* as a `Date` object, you wouldn't be able to use these methods. The *`currentTime`* `Date` object doesn't get updated automatically. It becomes a frame of reference for starting the clock. In other words, you'll find out what time it is, then set the hands of the clock according to the *`currentTime`*, and then start running the clock from there.

NOTE Notice that you retrieve `Date` object data using methods, not properties. You can tell because of the parentheses at the end. This means, for example, upon calling `getHours()`, the machine accesses the *`currentTime`* `Date` object and does some calculations. The `Date` object only has methods; it does not have properties.

Each of these methods returns the appropriate information, so you need a variable to hold the information. For example, consider the following code:

```
mySec = currentTime.getSeconds();
```

This retrieves the seconds information from the *`currentTime`* `Date` object and stores it in the *`mySec`* variable. The script creates three variables from the *`currentTime`* `Date` object to use for the clock.

Next let's start to use the time information by making the second hand go to the appropriate place.

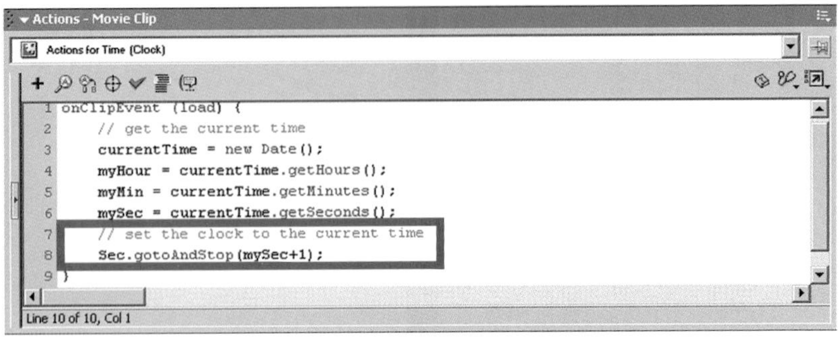
Actions - Movie Clip
Actions for Time (Clock)
onClipEvent (load) {
// get the current time
currentTime = new Date();
myHour = currentTime.getHours();
myMin = currentTime.getMinutes();
mySec = currentTime.getSeconds();
// set the clock to the current time
Sec.gotoAndStop(mySec+1);
}
Line 10 of 10, Col 1

4.19: Add the code that controls the second hand to the clock movie clip.

9
3
6

4.20: The second hand is positioned according to the time on the system clock, but it does not move.

3. Add Code to Control the Second Hand and Test

Add the following code below the previous lines but still within the curly braces of the `onClipEvent(load)` handler (4.19).

```
// set the clock to the current time
Sec.gotoAndStop(mySec + 1);
```

The instance of the second hand movie clip is already named Sec, so this code simply tells the Sec movie clip to go to the frame that is equal to `mySec + 1`. Remember that the seconds are off by one in the movie clip, so to display the correct time, the code needs to add one to the value of the *`mySec`* variable.

Test the movie. Notice that the second hand jumps to a position but does not move after that (4.20). Now let's get the second hand to move.

4. Add Code to Move the Second Hand and Test

Add the following ActionScript to the Clock movie clip below the code you entered in the previous step (4.21). Enter the code after the `onClipEvent(load)` code.

```
onClipEvent(enterFrame) {
   //need to get new Date object with the new current time
   currentTime  = new Date();
   mySec = currentTime.getSeconds();
   Sec.gotoAndStop(mySec + 1);
}
```

In the `onClipEvent(enterFrame)` event handler, you're going to check the time for each change—in this case, 12 times per second. Remember that the `Date` object from the `onClipEvent(load)` code captures the time, but it doesn't update the *`currentTime`* `Date` object. In order to have a real clock, you need to update the *`currentTime`* `Date` object. The only way to update the time is to create a new `Date` object.

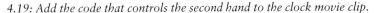

The code to move the second hand creates a new `Date` object and gives it the same name as it has in the `onClipEvent(load)` section for the sake of simplicity. So 12 times per second the code creates a new `Date` object with the new time in it. Notice that the next two lines of

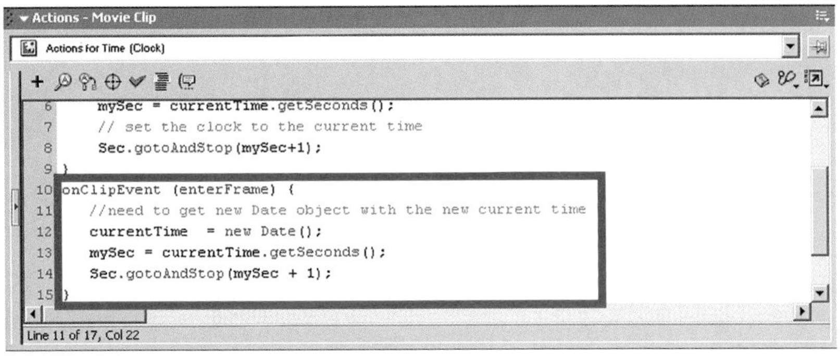
Actions - Movie Clip
Actions for Time (Clock)
mySec = currentTime.getSeconds();
// set the clock to the current time
Sec.gotoAndStop(mySec+1);
}
onClipEvent (enterFrame) {
//need to get new Date object with the new current time
currentTime = new Date();
mySec = currentTime.getSeconds();
Sec.gotoAndStop(mySec + 1);
}
Line 11 of 17, Col 22

4.21: Add the code that will move the second hand below the `onClipEvent(load)` *event handler section.*

4.22: Now the second hand moves around the clock.

code are identical to the ActionScript in the `onClipEvent(load)` section. The only difference is that now the code is contained within an `onClipEvent(enterFrame)` event handler, so the code is executed more frequently.

Now test the movie again. The second hand should move around the clock (4.22). Let's work on the minute hand next.

5. Add Code to Position the Minute Hand

Add the following code to the Clock movie clip within the `onClipEvent(load)` section (4.23), at the bottom (below the code you entered in step 3).

```
function setMinute(someDate) {
   myMin = someDate.getMinutes();
   Min.gotoAndStop(myMin + 1);
}
setMinute (currentTime);
```

This code creates a function called *`setMinute()`* within the Clock movie clip. The function has an argument called *`someDate`*, which will be used to set the correct time for the minute hand. Any time the code needs to update the minute hand, it will simply call this function. You'll see how this is accomplished in the next step.

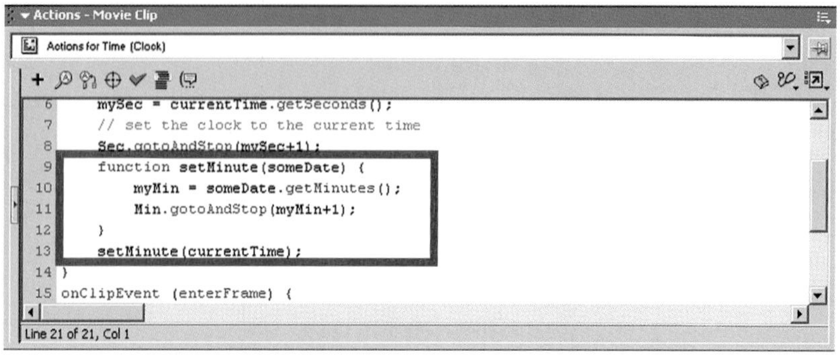
Actions - Movie Clip
Actions for Time (Clock)
mySec = currentTime.getSeconds();
// set the clock to the current time
Sec.gotoAndStop(mySec+1);
function setMinute(someDate) {
myMin = someDate.getMinutes();
Min.gotoAndStop(myMin+1);
}
setMinute(currentTime);
}
onClipEvent (enterFrame) {
Line 21 of 21, Col 1

4.23: Add the code that positions the minute hand in the `onClipEvent(load)` *event handler.*

NOTE It is common to place functions that will be used by only a specific movie clip in the `load` section of the movie clip. You could have easily placed this function on the main timeline and then used `_root` when you called it.

Within the function, there is a call to the `getMinutes()` method. The code uses the `getMinutes()` method to update the *myMin* variable, which, in turn, is used to position the Min movie clip (the minute hand). As with the seconds code earlier, the code adds one to the value of the *myMin* variable so that it will display the correct frame in the Min movie clip.

After the function is created, you must call it and send it the *currentTime* object. If you test the code now, you'll see that the minute hand starts at the correct place. However, if you wait more than 60 seconds, the minute hand won't update. You'll fix that in the next step.

6. Add the *setMinute()* Function Call and Test

Add the following ActionScript at the bottom of the `onClipEvent(enterFrame)` section (4.24).

```
setMinute(currentTime);
```

The code simply calls the *setMinute()* function with the *currentTime* `Date` object as the argument. Remember that the *currentTime* `Date` object is being continuously updated, so this code works virtually the same as the code that was used to control the second hand.

Now test the movie. Wait up to 60 seconds, and you'll see that the minute hand moves.

Let's code the hour hand now (and it's about time, wouldn't you say?). The script follows the same pattern as for the minute hand, creating a function in the `onClipEvent(load)` section and then calling it in the `onClipEvent(enterFrame)` section.

7. Add Code to Control the Hour Hand

Add the following ActionScript to the bottom of the `onClipEvent(load)` section (4.25).

```
function setHour(someDate) {
   myHour = someDate.getHours();
   if (myHour > 12){
      myHour -= 12;
   }
```

```
    Hour.gotoAndStop(myHour + 1);
}
setHour(currentTime);
```

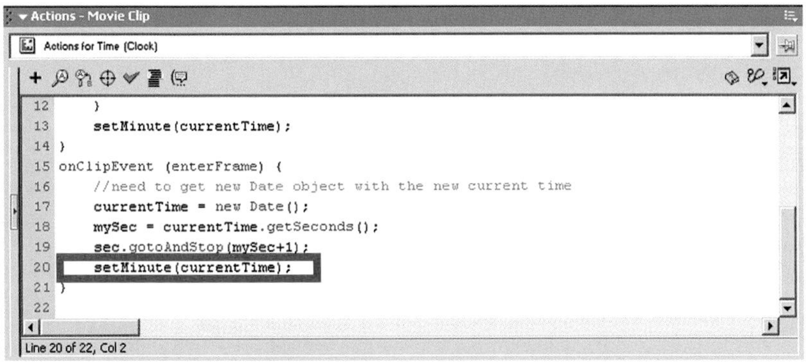
Actions - Movie Clip
Actions for Time (Clock)
}
setMinute(currentTime);
}
onClipEvent (enterFrame) {
//need to get new Date object with the new current time
currentTime = new Date();
mySec = currentTime.getSeconds();
sec.gotoAndStop(mySec+1);
setMinute(currentTime);
}
Line 20 of 22, Col 2

4.24: Add the `setMinute(currentTime);` *code to the bottom of the* `onClipEvent(enterFrame)` *section.*

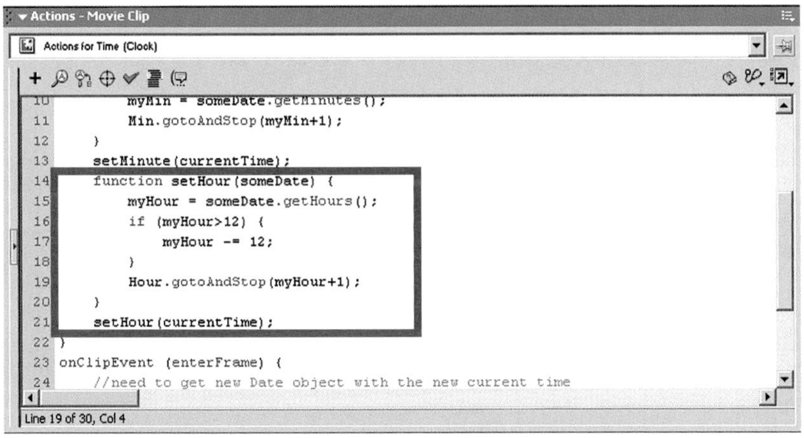
Actions - Movie Clip
Actions for Time (Clock)
Min.gotoAndStop(myMin+1);
}
setMinute(currentTime);
function setHour(someDate) {
myHour = someDate.getHours();
if (myHour>12) {
myHour -= 12;
}
Hour.gotoAndStop(myHour+1);
}
setHour(currentTime);
}
onClipEvent (enterFrame) {
//need to get new Date object with the new current time
Line 19 of 30, Col 4

4.25: Add the code that controls the hour hand to the bottom of the `onClipEvent(load)` *section.*

The main difference between the `setHour()` function and the `setMinute()` function is that when the code is calculating hours, it sometimes needs to subtract 12 from the returned value of `getHours()`. The `getHours()` method returns the time for a 24-hour clock, but you are displaying a 12-hour clock. So if the `myHour` value is greater than 12, the code subtracts 12. The `-=` operator essentially means `myHour = myHour – 12`.

8. Add the *setHour()* Function Call and Test

Now add the call to the `setHour()` function at the bottom of the `onClipEvent(enterFrame)` section (4.26).

```
setHour(currentTime);
```

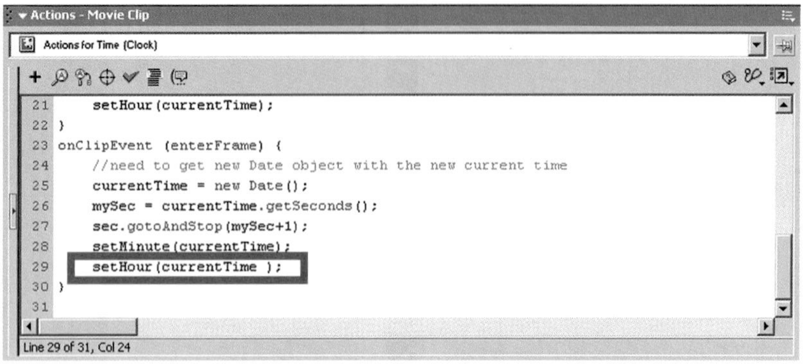
Actions - Movie Clip
Actions for Time (Clock)
setHour(currentTime);
}
onClipEvent (enterFrame) {
//need to get new Date object with the new current time
currentTime = new Date();
mySec = currentTime.getSeconds();
sec.gotoAndStop(mySec+1);
setMinute(currentTime);
setHour(currentTime);
}
Line 29 of 31, Col 24

4.26: Add the `setHour(currentTime);` *code to the bottom of the* `onClipEvent(enterFrame)` *section.*

12
9
3
6

4.27: Now all of the hands on the clock work.

Test the movie. The hour should be set to the correct hour. If you have the patience to watch it, you should see that it will change to the correct hour after 60 minutes (4.27).

At this point, you have a working clock. Next you want to check how it works to see if you can optimize your code. Let's add a `trace()` function so that you can see what's happening in the `enterFrame` section of the code.

9. Add a *trace()* Function to Check How the Code Works and Test

In the `onClipEvent(enterFrame)` section, locate this line:

```
mySec = currentTime.getSeconds();
```

Add the following ActionScript directly below that line (4.28).

```
trace(mySec);
```

`trace()` is a built-in function, and it's the easiest debugging tool to use. It takes whatever you put in the parentheses and displays it to the Output panel. In this case, it's the value of a variable, `trace(mySec)`. This could be text, such as `trace("setting the hour now")`, or both, as in `trace("the second is " + mysec)`. (Notice that you use the + sign to append one item to another.)

NOTE **The `trace()` function will display output to the Output panel only if you don't have it omitted in the Publish Settings dialog box. You can omit all `trace()` statements by going to the Publish Settings Flash tab and selecting Omit Trace Actions in the Options section.**

Test the movie and watch the Output panel, where you'll see the seconds output. Notice that the same number appears 12 times before it displays the next number (4.29). This is inefficient because it is 11 times more than you need. In this case, you could simply change the frame rate to 1 and be done with it, but that's a stopgap solution. If you later decide to add animation to the hands or face of the clock, it's not very likely that you'll want

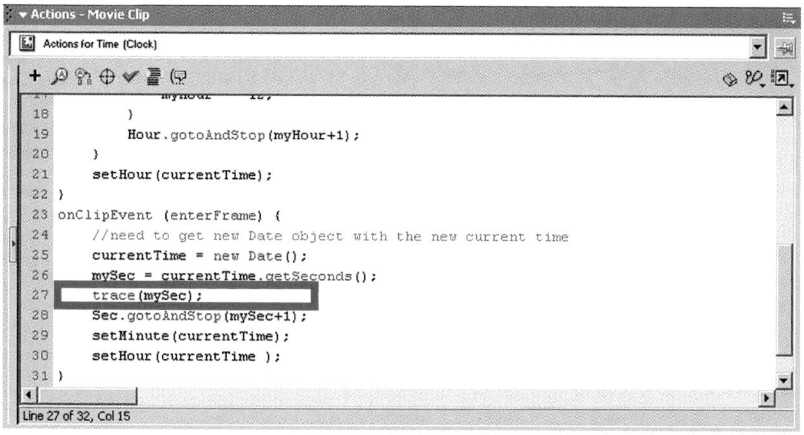

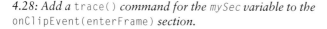

4.28: Add a `trace()` *command for the* `mySec` *variable to the* `onClipEvent(enterFrame)` *section.*

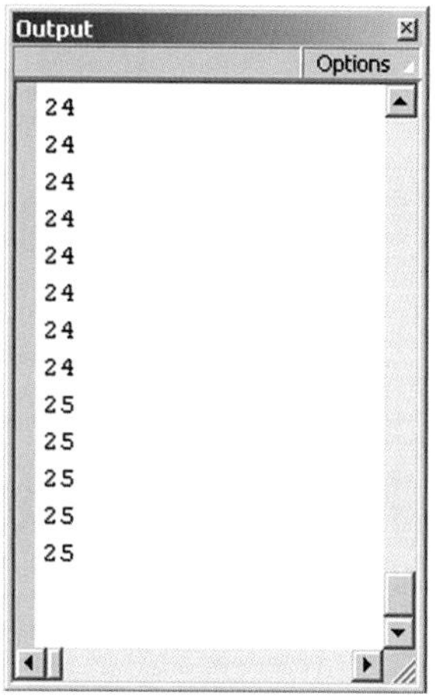

4.29: The Output panel shows that the `mySec` *variable is updated 12 times, which is 11 times too many.*

the animations running at 1fps. So let's change the code so that it executes all the ActionScript only when you need it and at 12fps.

10. Add Code to Compare Seconds and Test

In the beginning of the `onClipEvent(enterFrame)` section, the first line is as follows:

```
currentTime = new Date();
```

Add the following code as the second line of code in this section, directly below the above line. Also, add a closing curly brace (`}`) at the end of all the code in the `enterFrame` section (4.30). You want all of the remaining ActionScript within this conditional statement.

```
// update the second hand only if a new second
if (currentTime.getSeconds() != mySec) {
```

This code compares the current second that is in the value of the seconds in the *`currentTime`* `Date` object to the value of the *`mySec`* variable. The `if` statement allows the rest of the code to execute only if the values are different.

Test the movie and watch the output in the Output panel. You'll see that the second is displayed only once. So, instead of updating the second hand 12 times per second, now the code is updating it only once per second.

The code is now more efficient as far as the second hand is concerned, but it's still setting the minute and hour every second. For computers that can make a large number of calculations within a second, it probably doesn't cause much of a problem to calculate and set the minute and the hour every second. However, it's sloppy coding. Your code needs to reset the *`setMinute`* variable only when seconds start over at 0. Similarly, the code needs to reset the *`setHour`* variable only when minutes start over at 0. Let's adjust the code to do this.

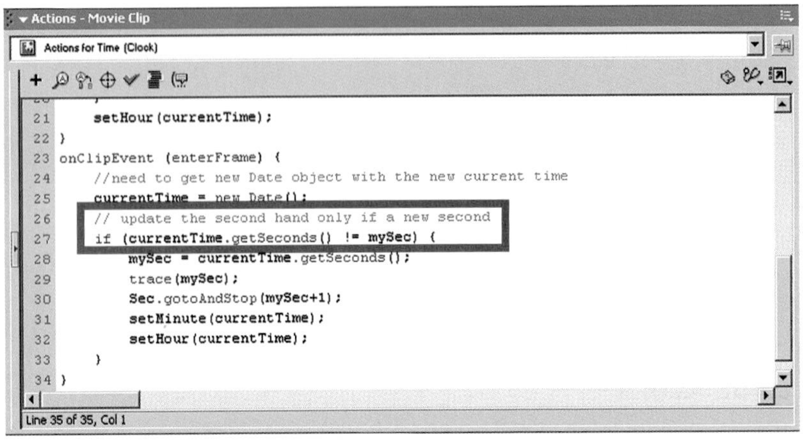
Actions - Movie Clip
Actions for Time (Clock)
setHour(currentTime);
}
onClipEvent (enterFrame) {
//need to get new Date object with the new current time
currentTime = new Date();
// update the second hand only if a new second
if (currentTime.getSeconds() != mySec) {
mySec = currentTime.getSeconds();
trace(mySec);
Sec.gotoAndStop(mySec+1);
setMinute(currentTime);
setHour(currentTime);
}
}
Line 35 of 35, Col 1

4.30: Add code just below the first line in the `onClipEvent(enterFrame)` *section.*

11. Add Code to Check the Second and Minutes

Delete the `trace()` statement. Add the test for the second and the minute in the `onClipEvent(enterFrame)` section just below the line `Sec.gotoAndStop (mySec + 1);`. The code should look like this (4.31):

```
if (mySec == 0){
   setMinute(currentTime);
   if (myMin == 0){
      setHour(currentTime);
   }
}
```

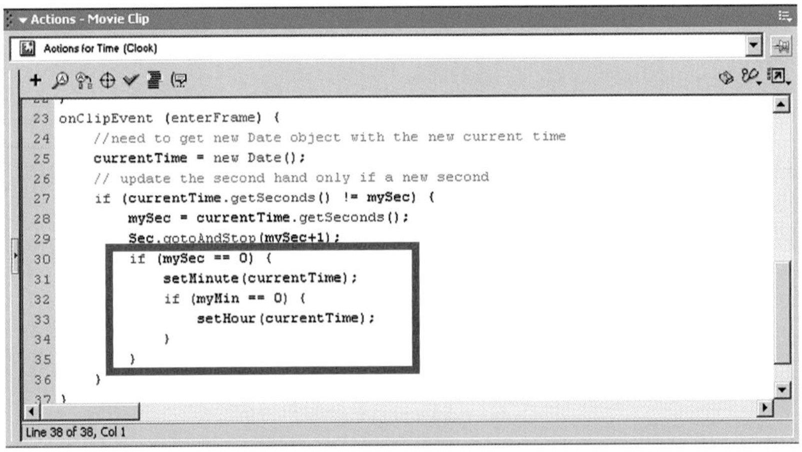
Actions - Movie Clip
Actions for Time (Clock)
onClipEvent (enterFrame) {
//need to get new Date object with the new current time
currentTime = new Date();
// update the second hand only if a new second
if (currentTime.getSeconds() != mySec) {
mySec = currentTime.getSeconds();
Sec.gotoAndStop(mySec+1);
if (mySec == 0) {
setMinute(currentTime);
if (myMin == 0) {
setHour(currentTime);
}
}
}
Line 38 of 38, Col 1

4.31: Add an `if` *statement to the* `onClipEvent(enterFrame)` *code.*

The code uses an `if` statement inside another `if` statement. The code checks to see if the `mySec` variable is equal to 0. If so, it calls the `setMinute()` function using the `currentTime` `Date` object as the argument, and then it checks to see if the `myMin` variable is equal to 0. If the `myMin` variable is equal to 0, the code calls the `setHour()` function using the `currentTime` `Date` object.

Notice that you want to set the hour hand only if the minutes are at 0 *and* the seconds are at 0, too. If you didn't check for the seconds first, the code would set the hour every second when the minute is set to 0. In other words, the hour would be reset 60 times when the minute variable was equal to 0. You wouldn't be able to see anything different, but it would be another small inefficiency within the code.

If you test the clock now, you won't see a visible difference, but the computer will not be executing unnecessary ActionScript.

Adding Sound to the Clock

Now that you've gained some experience with the `Date` object, let's look at the `Sound` object. What is a clock without a little sound? Answer: a less annoying clock. Still, let's get the clock to chime on the hour and to chime the number of hours.

The `Sound` object is similar to the `Date` object in that it needs to be instantiated. Unlike the `Date` object, the `Sound` object does have properties. The `Sound` object has two properties: *duration* (how long the sound is) and *position* (where in the sound it is currently playing). With the `Sound` object, you can play and stop a sound on command, which means that the sound does not need to be on the timeline. You'll be pulling the sound from the library as needed.

In order to use the `Sound` object, you must set the linkage for the audio file. This is the same as setting the linkage for a movie clip, as you did in Chapter 2 when you used `attachMovie()`, except that the linkage is for a sound file. This enables the sound to be used directly from the library without placing it on the timeline. It also gives you a lot more control over the sound.

1. Add the Chime Sound

Select the Chime sound in the library and open the Linkage Properties dialog box. Select the Export for ActionScript option and enter **Hour** in the Identifier field (4.32).

The Chime sound is now ready to be used with the `Sound` object. First, you need to initialize a variable to contain the `Sound` object so you can use it, and you also need to tell it which sound to use.

2. Add Code to Set Up the Chime Sound

In the `onClipEvent(load)` section of your Clock code, locate this line:

```
mySec = currentTime.getSeconds();
```

Add the following ActionScript below the `mySec` variable definition (4.33).

```
hourSound = new Sound();
hourSound.attachSound("Hour");
```

The first line creates a variable called `hourSound` that is of the `Sound` object type, so `hourSound` can use any of the methods and properties that belong to the `Sound` object. The second line assigns the actual sound to the `hourSound` object by referencing the identifier attached to the Chime sound, `"Hour"`. Note that this doesn't play the sound. This code only sets up the sound so that it can be played. Now let's write some code to play the sound.

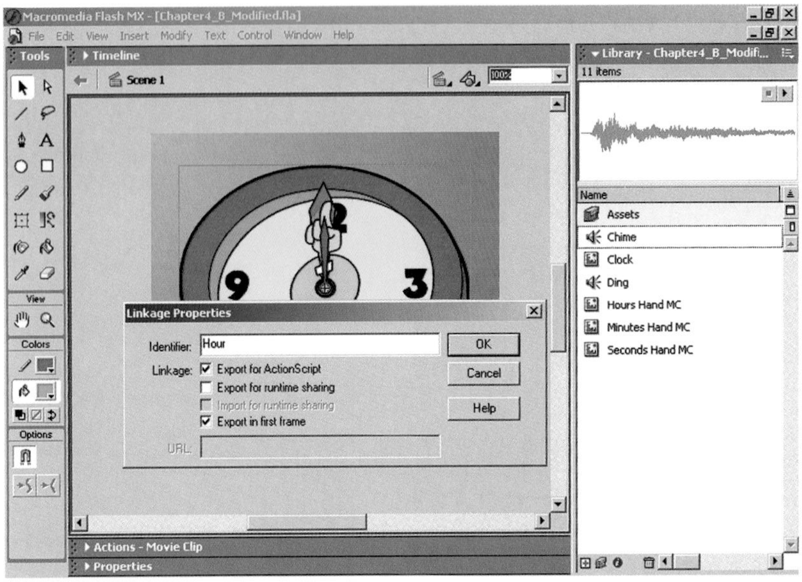

4.32: *Set the Linkage properties for the Chime sound file in the library.*

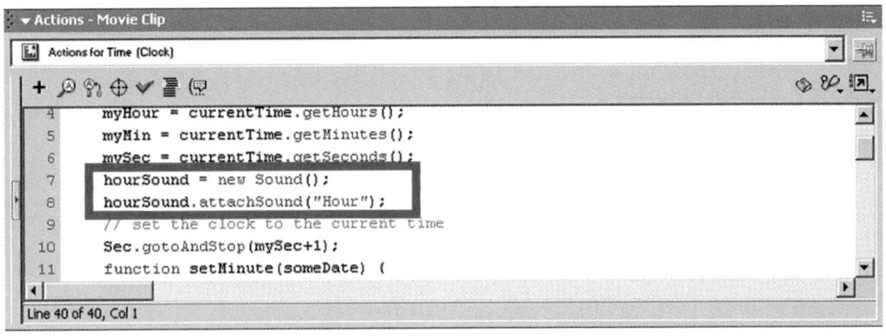

4.33: *Add code to the* `onClipEvent(load)` *section to set up the Chime sound.*

3. Add Code to Play the Chime Sound and Test

Add the following ActionScript in the *`setHour()`* function (4.34).

```
// time to chime
hourSound.start(0, myHour);
```

Because you placed this code within the *`setHour()`* function, the sound will play each time you call that function. The code references the *`hourSound`* variable (which contains the `Sound` object) using the `start()` method.

The `start()` method tells the sound to play. The `start()` method takes two arguments. The first argument specifies how many seconds into the sound file you want to start playing. For example, you could start playing in the middle of a sound. In this example, you want to start at the beginning, so the seconds offset is 0.

The second `start()` method argument establishes how many times to loop the sound. By placing the *`myHour`* variable within the second argument, the code is telling the sound to loop according to the value of the *`myHour`* variable. For example, if it is 7 o'clock, the value of

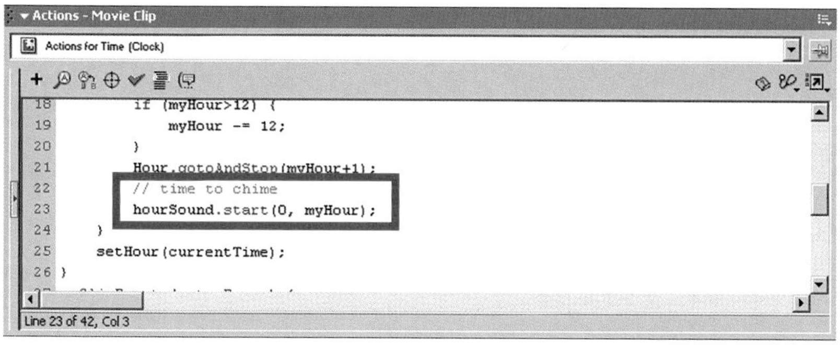

4.34: Add code to the `onClipEvent(load)` *event handler to set up the Chime sound.*

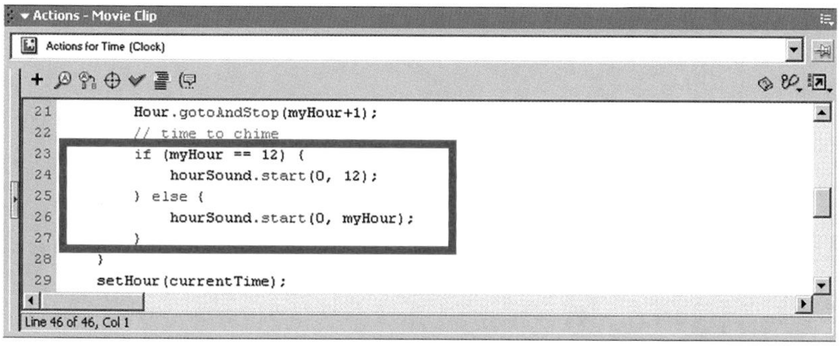

4.35: Replace the code from the previous step with the `if/else` *statement.*

the *`myHour`* variable will be 7, and the `start()` method for the *`hourSound`* variable will instruct the `Sound` object to loop the Chime sound seven times.

When you test the movie, you'll hear the clock chime right away. It will chime according to whatever hour it is on your computer's system clock. It will also chime each time the hour changes.

What happens when the clock is at 12? At 12 o'clock, the *`myHour`* variable will be equal to 0. As a result, the *`myHour`* variable would be fed into the second argument of the *`hourSound`* `start()` method and, instead of looping the sound 12 times, the sound won't play at all. To fix this, you need to add a special case just for 12 o'clock.

4. Add an *if/else* Statement to Handle 12 o'clock

Replace the ActionScript you entered in the previous step:

```
hourSound.start(0, myHour);
```

with the following code (4.35).

```
if (myHour == 12){
   hourSound.start(0, 12);
} else {
   hourSound.start(0, myHour);
}
```

This is another `if/else` conditional statement. If the *myHour* variable equals 12, the code calls the `start()` method of the *hourSound* variable using 12, rather than the *myHour* variable, as the second argument. Otherwise, the code uses the original call to the `start()` method of the *hourSound* variable, using the *myHour* variable as the value for the second argument. Thus, this code treats 12 o'clock as special, and the clock will chime 12 times; otherwise, it will chime the number that is in the *myHour* variable. Now when the clock strikes 12, you'll hear 12 chimes.

Now let's handle the sound for the minutes. You'll write the code so that the minute's sound will play every 15 minutes, rather than every minute. At 15 minutes past the hour, it will ding once; at 30 minutes, it will ding twice; and at 45 minutes, it will ding three times.

5. Add the Ding Sound

Select the Ding sound in the library and open the Linkage Properties dialog box. Select Export for ActionScript and enter **Minute** in the Identifier field (4.36).

The Ding sound is now ready to be used with the `Sound` object.

6. Add Code to Set Up the Ding Sound

Add the following ActionScript in the `onClipEvent(load)` section, directly below the code that you used to set up the *hourSound* variable (4.37).

```
minSound = new Sound();
minSound.attachSound("Minute");
```

This will create a variable of the `Sound` object called *minSound*, and then attach the Ding sound to it by referencing the Minute identifier that you entered for the Ding sound in the previous step. Now let's write the code that will play the sound.

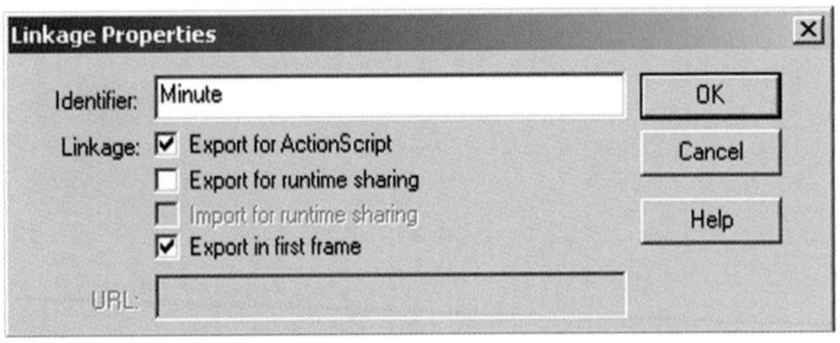

4.36: Set the Linkage options for the Ding sound file.

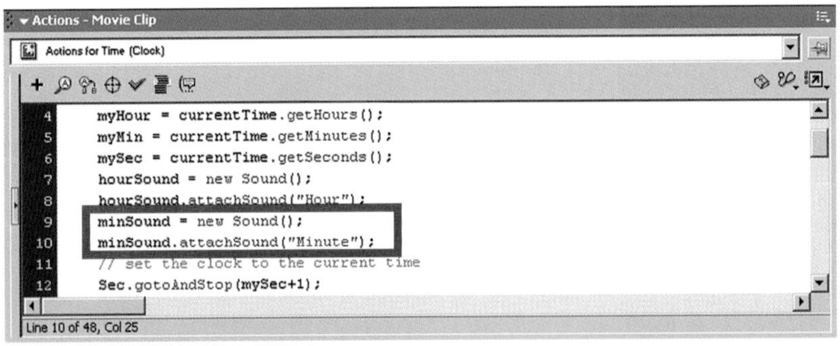

4.37: Add code to the `onClipEvent(load)` *section to set up the Ding sound.*

7. Add Code to Control the Ding Sound and Test

In the `onClipEvent(enterFrame)` section, locate this line in the *`setMinute()`* function:

```
Min.gotoAndStop(myMin + 1);
```

After this line, add the following lines (4.38).

```
if (myMin == 15) {
   minSound.start(0, 1);
} else if (myMin == 30) {
   minSound.start(0, 2);
} else if (myMin == 45) {
   minSound.start(0, 3);
}
```

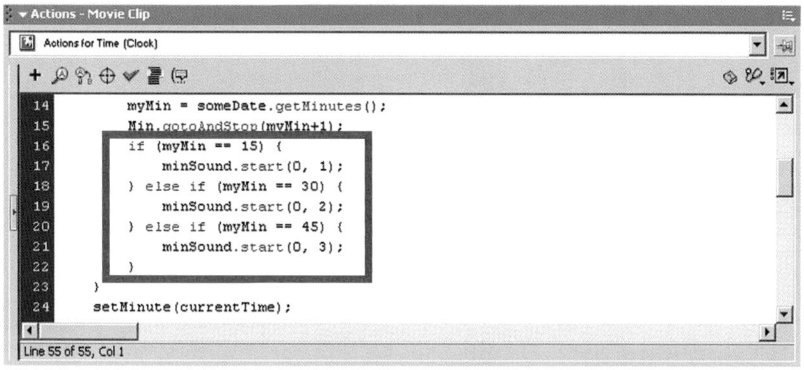

4.38: Add code to the `onClipEvent(enterFrame)` *section to control the Ding sound.*

This code establishes a three-part conditional. This is very similar to all of the other conditionals you have seen so far, except that it uses two `else if` statements within the `if` statement to establish three specific conditions.

This code checks if the *`myMin`* variable is equal to 15, 30, or 45. If it is equal to 15, the *`minSound`* variable is called with `1` as the second argument for the `start()` method. If it is equal to 30, the *`minSound`* variable is called with `2` as the second argument for the `start()` method. If it is equal to 45, the *`minSound`* variable is called with `3` as the second argument for the `start()` method.

You could have written the above ActionScript as follows:

```
if (myMin == 15) {
  minSound.start(0, 1);
}
if (myMin == 30) {
  minSound.start(0, 2);
}
if (myMin == 45) {
  minSound.start(0, 3);
}
```

This code would work the same as the code you entered, and you would hear no difference when the movie plays. However, this approach is relatively inefficient. If you use `if` statements for each call to the *minSound* variable, the code must check each `if` statement every time.

For instance, let's say the time on the system clock is 1:15. This would mean that the `if` statement that checks to see if the *myMin* variable is set to 15 would execute its code and make a call to the *minSound* variable using the `start()` method to play the sound. Well, if the *myMin* variable is equal to 15, then it certainly can't be equal to 30 or 45. Nevertheless, if you use `if` statements instead of `if/else` for each line, the code will still need to check to see if the *myMin* variable is set to 30 or 45.

Using the `if/else if` conditional approach is more efficient. When *myMin* is equal to 15, the code checks the first `if` statement and plays the sound; it doesn't go on to the check the other `else if` statements. The `else if` statements are executed only if the *myMin* variable is not equal to 15. The last `else if` statement is checked only if the *myMin* variable is not equal to 15 or 30.

Test the movie after you have entered the code. You now have a working clock that chimes and dings at certain times. Now let's explore some other Flash MX built-in features: the `GetTimer()` function and the `Stage` object.

Using the *GetTimer()* Function and the *Stage* Object to Code a Game

Another useful feature for working with time in Flash is the `GetTimer()` function. The `GetTimer()` function simply gets the number of milliseconds that have elapsed since the movie started playing. You can use this information to implement time-based effects.

In the next example, you'll use the `GetTimer()` function to create a timer for a game that is similar to Atari's Asteroids game. Objects will be flying around, and you'll program them so that when an object moves off the stage, it will wrap around to the other side. The `Stage` object is the key to implementing this capability. The `Stage` object is new to Flash MX and allows the programmer to determine the size of the stage dynamically.

1. Open the File

WWW. Open **Chapter4_C_Start.fla**. Save the file to your local hard drive as **Chapter4_C_Modified.fla** (4.39). (For the finished version, see **Chapter4_C_Final.fla.**)

This sample file has a movie clip called SatelliteOne on the stage. This is the movie clip that will be moved around the stage. The example also has a movie clip called Timer, which will show the time left for the movie. When the time runs out, it will go to the GameOver scene. On the GameOver scene, there is a button that will take the player back to the Game scene.

Let's start by adding some code to get the satellite moving.

2. Add Code to Calculate a Place for SatelliteOne Movie Clip and Test

Attach the following ActionScript to the SatelliteOne movie clip (4.40).

```
onClipEvent(load) {
   _x = Math.random() * Stage.width;
   _y = Math.random() * Stage.height;
   var xspeed = Math.random() * 5 + 1;
```

```
   var yspeed = Math.random() * 5 + 1;
}
onClipEvent(enterFrame) {
   // Propulsion
   _x += xspeed;
   _y += yspeed;
}
```

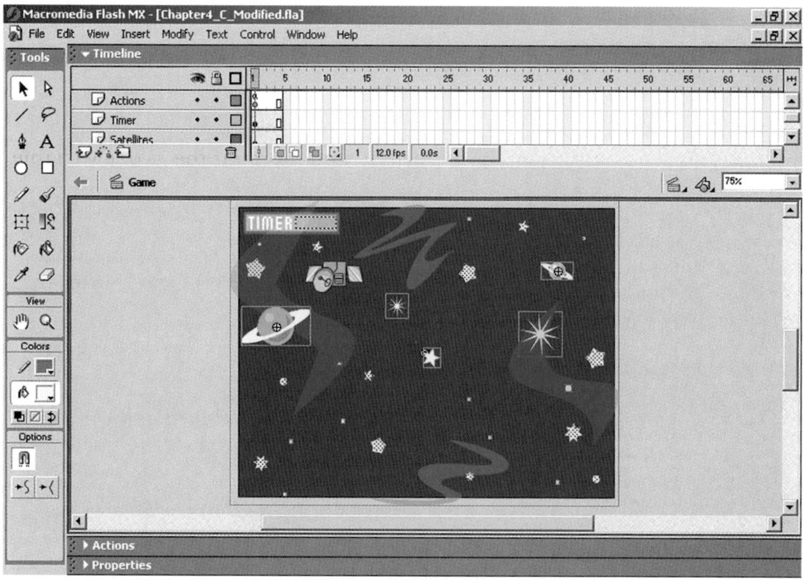

4.39: The Chapter4_C_Modified.fla *file contains a Satellite movie clip and a Timer movie clip.*

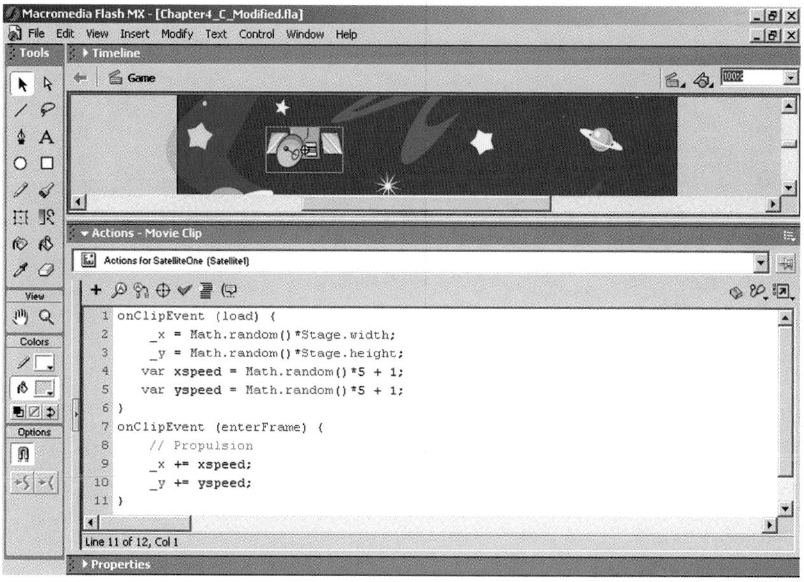

4.40: Attach the code to the SatelliteOne movie clip.

Test the movie. Notice that the SatelliteOne movie clip appears somewhere on the stage and moves from upper left to lower right and off.

This code first calculates a random place for the SatelliteOne movie clip to start out within the `onClipEvent(load)` event handler. For instance, the first line reads:

```
_x = Math.random() * Stage.width;
```

This code uses the `Stage` object. Notice that you do not need a constructor for this object, because it exists automatically as soon as the movie starts. `Stage.width` is the width of the stage, and `Stage.height` is the height of the stage.

NOTE In previous versions of Flash, programmers needed to specify the stage size, or use a movie clip that covered the whole stage and get that movie clip's dimensions. Using Flash MX's new `Stage` object is a lot easier.

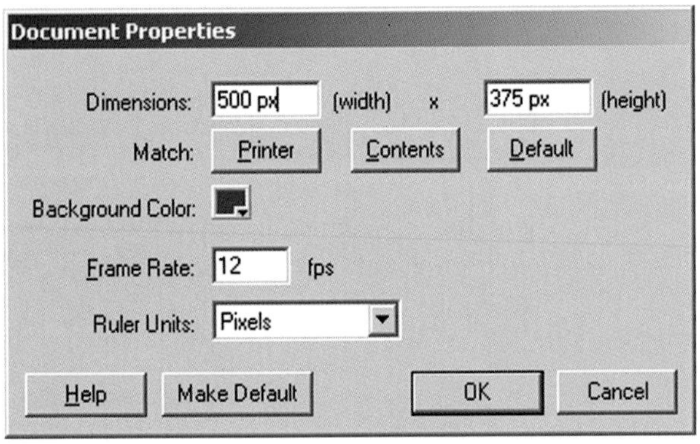

4.41: The Document Properties dialog box shows that the stage is set to 500 pixels wide and 375 pixels high.

By now, you should be familiar with the `_x` property, which is the *x* coordinate of the object on the stage. The code calculates the *x* coordinate for the host movie clip (the SatelliteOne movie clip) by placing the `Stage.width` object within a `Math.random()` function. By checking the Document Properties dialog box for this Flash movie (4.41), you can see that the stage size for this movie is 500 pixels wide, so the *x* coordinate will be a random number between 0 and 499.999. The *y* coordinate is calculated in the same way using the `Stage.height` object.

Next, within the `onClipEvent(load)` event handler, the code randomly determines how fast the SatelliteOne movie clip should move over the stage. For example, let's look at the following line:

```
var xspeed = Math.random() * 5 + 1;
```

This code establishes a variable named *`xspeed`*. The `Math.random()` function is multiplied by 5 which returns a number between 0 and 4, and then 1 is added to it. Therefore, the value of *`xspeed`* will be a random number between 1 and 5. The *`yspeed`* variable is calculated in the same way.

If your code did not add one to the results of the `Math.random()` function, you would sometimes get a value of 0 for *`xspeed`* and *`yspeed`*. This would mean that the SatelliteOne movie clip wouldn't move in the *x* and/or *y* direction. That would be fine if one variable were 0 and the other were not, but if both variables were 0, the SatelliteOne movie clip would not move at all, it would just sit there.

Finally, in the `onClipEvent(enterFrame)` section, you actually move the SatelliteOne movie clip using the *`xpseed`* and *`yspeed`* variables. For example, let's look at this first line of code within the `onClipEvent(enterFrame)` event handler:

```
_x += xspeed;
```

This line of code is very simple. The key to how it works is in the operator +=. Let's plug in an arbitrary value. Say that the *x* position of the SatelliteOne movie clip is 200 and the value of the `xspeed` variable is 4. The += operator takes the current value of the `_x` property and adds the value of the `xspeed` variable to it. In other words, using the += operator is like saying `_x = _x + xspeed` or `_x = 200 + 4`. So during the first pass of the `onClipEvent(enterFrame)` event handler, the *x* coordinate is updated to 204. During the next pass, the *x* coordinate is updated to 208, and so on (4.42).

Now let's make a few more copies of the SatelliteOne movie clip.

3. Enter Code to Duplicate the SatelliteOne Movie Clip and Test

Enter the following ActionScript on frame 1 of the Actions layer above the `stop()` command (4.43).

```
var numberOfSatellites = 5;
for (var level = 1; level <= numberOfSatellites; level++){
   SatelliteOne.duplicateMovieClip("Satellite" + level, level);
}
```

This code should look somewhat familiar because it uses a `for` loop to create duplicates of the movie clip, similarly to how you created duplicates for the mouse trail effect in Chapter 3 (**Chapter3_E_Final.fla**).

First, the code establishes a variable called `numberOfSatellites` and sets its value to 5. Next the code contains a `for` loop that creates a variable named `level` and sets the value of `level` to 1 within the initialization section. In the condition section of the `for` loop, the value of `level` is compared to the `numberOfSatellites` variable, and the `for` loop continues until the value of `level` is greater than the value of `numberOfSatellites`. As usual, the next

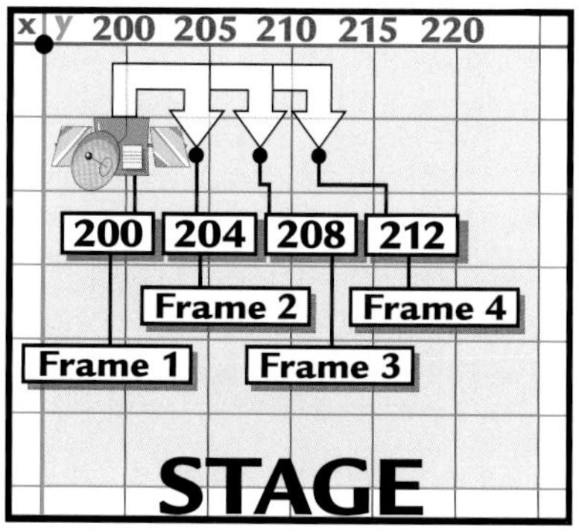

4.42: The value of the `xspeed` *variable is added to the current position of the SatelliteOne movie clip each time the* `onClipEvent(enterFrame)` *event occurs.*

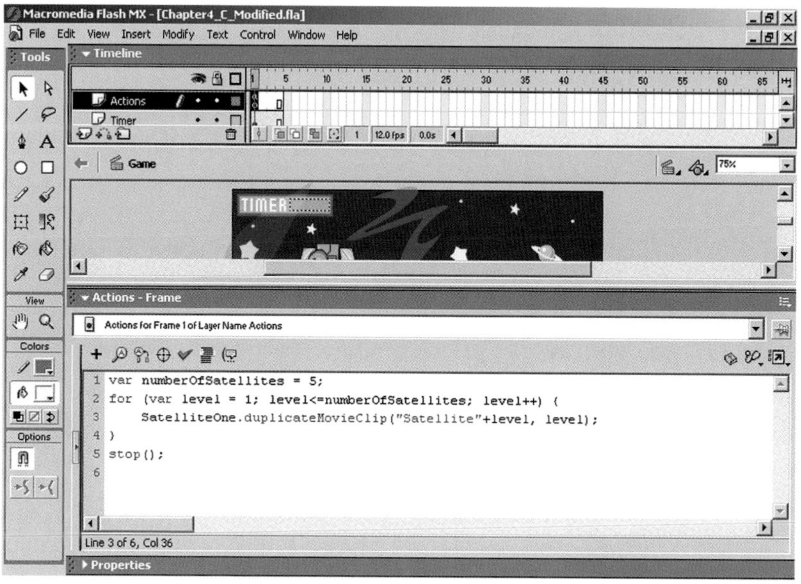

4.43: Enter code that will create five duplicates of the SatelliteOne movie clip to frame 1 on the Actions layer.

section of the `for` loop increments the value of the variable established in the initialization phase. In this case, it increments the `level` variable, with the ++ operator.

Within the `for` loop is the code that duplicates the movie clip. The code specifies the SatelliteOne movie clip instance and gives each duplicate a name by concatenating the value of the `level` variable to the `"Satellite"` string. The `level` variable is also used to establish on which level each duplicate is placed. So the first duplicate is called Satellite1 and set on level 1, the next duplicate is Satellite2 and set on level 2, and so on.

Test the movie. Notice that there are actually six copies of the SatelliteOne movie clip moving on the stage (five plus the original). Each new Satellite*N* movie clip has the same ActionScript attached to it, which causes it to move. Each moves at a slightly different speed and in a slightly different direction. But notice that they are all moving down and to the right—in the positive direction for both the *x* and *y* directions. That's not very interesting. Let's revise the code so that some duplicates move in the negative direction.

4. Randomly Choose Between Positive and Negative Speed and Test

On the SatelliteOne movie clip, change the original calculations of `xspeed` and `yspeed` to the following.

```
// get direction and speed in x direction
if (Math.round(Math.random()) == 0) {
   var xspeed = Math.random() * 5 + 1;
} else {
   var xspeed = -(Math.random() * 5 + 1);
}
// direction and speed in y direction
if (Math.round(Math.random()) == 0) {
   var yspeed = Math.random() * 5 + 1;
} else {
   var yspeed = -(Math.random() * 5 + 1);
}
```

This code uses the result from `Math.round(Math.random())` in the `if` statement. This works because Flash does the calculation in the parentheses first, executing code from the innermost parentheses and working outward. First, Flash calculates `Math.random()`, then it rounds it to the nearest integer, so it would be either a 0 or a 1, and then it compares the result to 0. Remember that `Math.random()` will return a number from 0 to 0.999, so when you round it, the results will be only a 0 or a 1. If `Math.round(Math.random())` is a 0, the movie clip will go in the positive direction; otherwise, it will move in the negative direction by adding a negative operator in front of the `(Math.random() * 5 + 1)` code.

The code works the same for both the *x* and the *y* directions. Note that in the negative section, you need to include `Math.random() * 5 + 1` in parentheses, because you want the result to be negative, not just `Math.random() * 5`. If you wrote `-Math.random() * 5 + 1`, the results would be:

$-0 + 1 = 1$

$-1 + 1 = 0$

$-2 + 1 = -1$

...

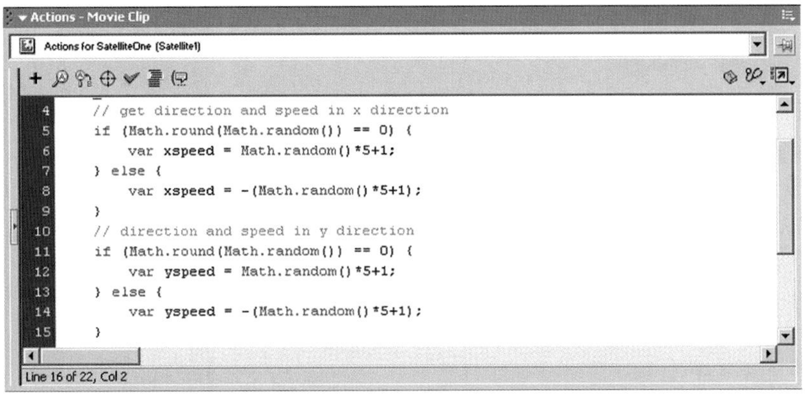
Actions - Movie Clip
Actions for SatelliteOne (Satellite1)
// get direction and speed in x direction
if (Math.round(Math.random()) == 0) {
var xspeed = Math.random()*5+1;
} else {
var xspeed = -(Math.random()*5+1);
}
// direction and speed in y direction
if (Math.round(Math.random()) == 0) {
var yspeed = Math.random()*5+1;
} else {
var yspeed = -(Math.random()*5+1);
}
Line 16 of 22, Col 2

4.44: Replace the original two lines of code for calculating the `xspeed` *and* `yspeed` *with code to calculate directions in both the positive and negative directions.*

By placing the `Math.random()` function within parentheses, you get:

$-(0 + 1) = -1$

$-(1 + 1) = -2$

$-(2 + 1) = -3$

...

Now test the results again. You'll see that the satellites move in different directions, which is much more interesting. But notice what happens to the Satellite*N* movie clips once they get to the end of the stage—they keep going. Let's fix this so that the movie clips loop back around when they go off the stage (4.44).

5. Add Code to Find the Movie Clip's Location on the Stage and Test

Add the following ActionScript to the SatelliteOne movie clip in the `onClipEvent(enterFrame)` event handler, below the code you added in earlier steps (4.45).

```
// Screen wrap
var satelliteBounds = this.getBounds(_root);
if (satelliteBounds.yMax < 0) {
   _y = Stage.height;
} else if (satelliteBounds.yMin > Stage.height) {
   _y = 0;
}
// check x boundary
if (satelliteBounds.xMax < 0) {
   _x = Stage.width;
} else if (satelliteBounds.xMin > Stage.width) {
   _x = 0;
}
```

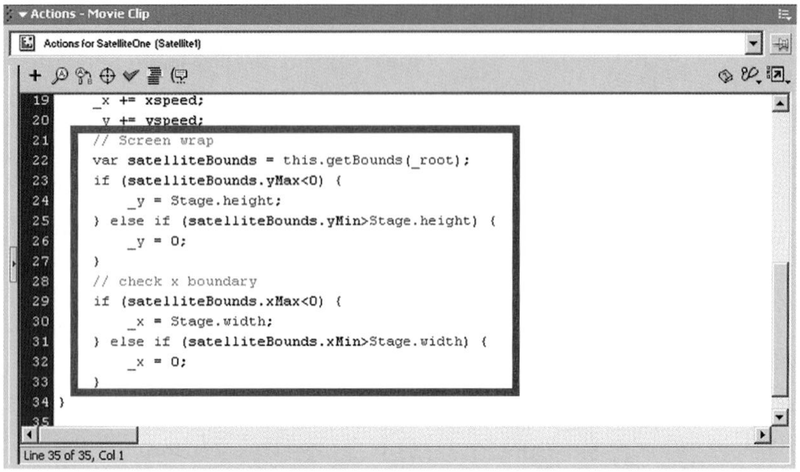
Actions - Movie Clip
Actions for SatelliteOne (Satellite1)
_x += xspeed;
_y += yspeed;
// Screen wrap
var satelliteBounds = this.getBounds(_root);
if (satelliteBounds.yMax<0) {
_y = Stage.height;
} else if (satelliteBounds.yMin>Stage.height) {
_y = 0;
}
// check x boundary
if (satelliteBounds.xMax<0) {
_x = Stage.width;
} else if (satelliteBounds.xMin>Stage.width) {
_x = 0;
}
}
Line 35 of 35, Col 1

4.45: Add code to the `onClipEvent(enterFrame)` *handler to make the satellites wrap around to the other side of the stage when they go off the stage.*

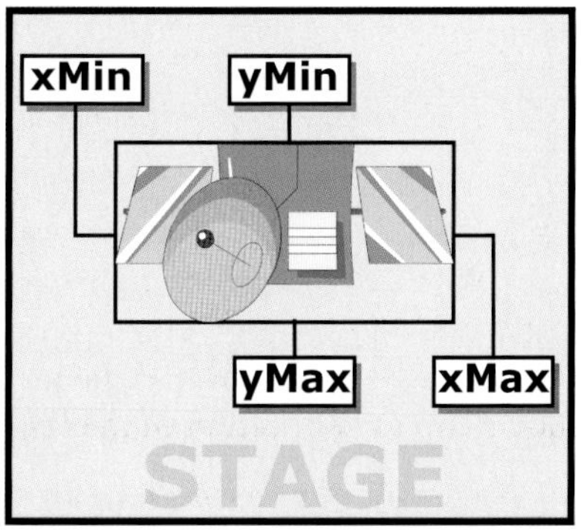
xMin
yMin
yMax
xMax
STAGE

4.46: The `getBounds()` *method provides the* `xMin`*,* `xMax`*,* `yMin`*, and* `yMax` *values of the SatelliteOne movie clip.*

First, the code needs to find out where the SatelliteOne movie clip is on the stage. To do this, the code uses the bounding box of the SatelliteOne movie clip:

```
this.getBounds(_root);
```

The `getBounds()` method returns the *xMin*, *xMax*, *yMin*, and *yMax* values in a variable *satelliteBounds*. The *satelliteBounds* variable is another one of those super variables, which has four values connected to one name. The *xMin* is the left side of the SatelliteOne movie clip, the *xMax* is the right side, the *yMin* is the top, and the *yMax* is the bottom (4.46).

Each of the values for these variables refers to the location on the main stage. The values are for the main stage because the code passed in `_root` as the argument for the `getBounds()` method. If the argument for the `getBounds()` method were left blank, the returned *x* and *y* bounds would be for the SatelliteOne movie clip within itself. Those values would never change, because the SatelliteOne movie clip is not moving within itself; it's moving on the main stage. Thus, it's important to place `_root` as the argument for the `getBounds()` method.

After the code gets the edges, or bounds, of the SatelliteOne movie clip, it needs to compare those values to the edges of the stage. For instance, if the right edge of the SatelliteOne movie clip (*xMax*) is less than the value for the left edge of the stage (0), it would mean that the SatelliteOne movie clip is completely off the stage on the left side. At that point, the code will set the SatelliteOne movie clip position to the right side of the stage (`Stage.width`). That is what the following code does (4.47):

```
if (satelliteBounds.xMax < 0) {
    _x = Stage.width;
}
```

This code uses an `if` statement and checks to see if the *xMax* property of the *satelliteBounds* object is less than 0. If it is, the code simply repositions the `_x` property of the SatelliteOne movie clip to the value of the `Stage.width` object.

The rest of the code works in essentially the same way. If the left side of the SatelliteOne movie clip (`xMin`) is greater than the right side of the stage (`Stage.width`), the SatelliteOne movie clip is completely off the right side of the stage, so the code sets the SatelliteOne movie clip to the left side of the stage (0).

```
} else if (satelliteBounds.xMin > Stage.width) {
   _x = 0;
}
```

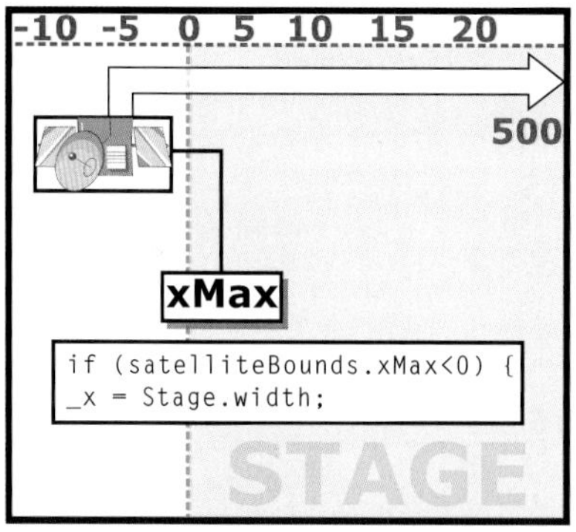

4.47: When the right side of the SatelliteOne movie clip goes off the left side of the stage, the code repositions the SatelliteOne movie clip on the right side of the stage.

So to continue (even though you probably already understand the rest of what is going on), if the bottom of the SatelliteOne movie clip (`yMax`) is less than the top of the stage (0), the code sets the SatelliteOne movie clip to the bottom of the stage (`Stage.height`).

```
if (satelliteBounds.yMax < 0) {
   _y = Stage.height;
}
```

Finally, if the top of the SatelliteOne movie clip (`yMin`) is greater than the bottom of the stage (`Stage.height`), the code sets the SatelliteOne movie clip to the top of the stage (0).

```
} else if (satelliteBounds.yMin > Stage.height) {
   _y = 0;
}
```

When you test the movie, you might notice a slightly odd behavior of the SatelliteOne movie clips. In Flash's Test Movie window, you can actually view more than the stage size that is specified for the movie (4.48). The code can behave as if the stage size were larger than the value specified in your Document Settings dialog box. If you view the actual output file for the Flash movie (the .swf file) in the Flash player, you'll see the movie with the correct stage size dimensions (4.49).

At this point, the movie should have six copies of the SatelliteOne movie clip moving in all directions, and they should wrap around when they move off the stage. Now let's use a timer to move to the end of the game.

6. Add the *getTimer()* Function

Attach the following ActionScript to the Timer movie clip (4.50).

```
onClipEvent(load){
   // game time in milliseconds
   var gameTime = 10 * 1000;
   var startTime = getTimer();
   TimerDisplay.text = gameTime / 1000;
}
```

This code uses the global function called `getTimer()`, which returns how long the movie has been running in milliseconds. This code sets the game time to 10 seconds, so the

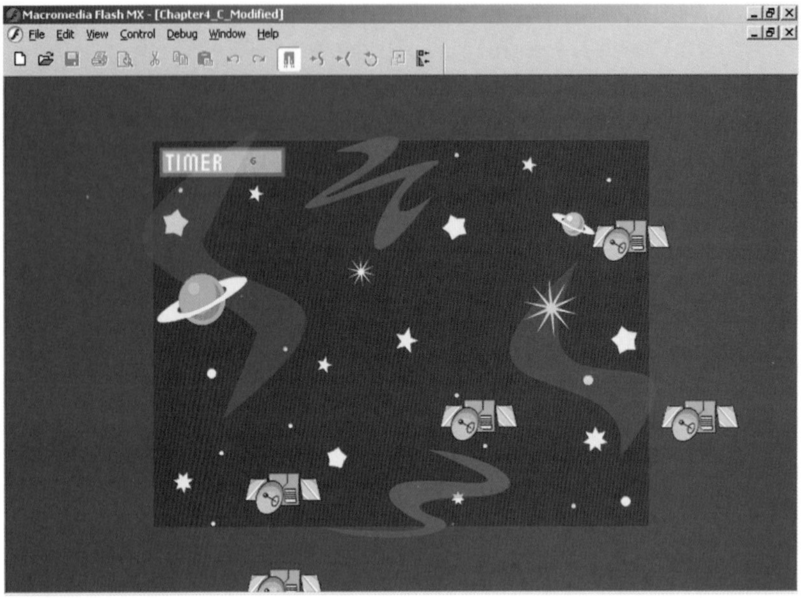

4.48: When you test the movie, the SatelliteOne movie clips don't wrap around properly.

4.49: The SatelliteOne movie clips wrap properly in the Flash Player or when viewed in a browser.

SatelliteOne movie clips will animate for 10 seconds, and then the movie will go to the GameOver scene. Obviously, this is not long enough for a real game, but using smaller values like this is good for testing purposes while you're writing the code—you wouldn't want to wait 3 minutes to see if the code works.

The first line within the `onClipEvent(load)` event handler creates a variable named *`gameTime`* and sets it equal to 10 times 1000. The code multiplies 10 times 1000 to set the *`gameTime`* variable's value in milliseconds, because `getTimer()` works in milliseconds. You could have just as easily written the line like this:

```
var gameTime = 10000;
```

However, writing the code as 10 times 1000 makes it a little easier to edit and to understand at a glance. If you know you want the game time to last for 1 minute, you could simply change the 10 to 60.

In the next line, the code gets the time you started this game, using `getTimer()` for this information.

```
var startTime = getTimer();
```

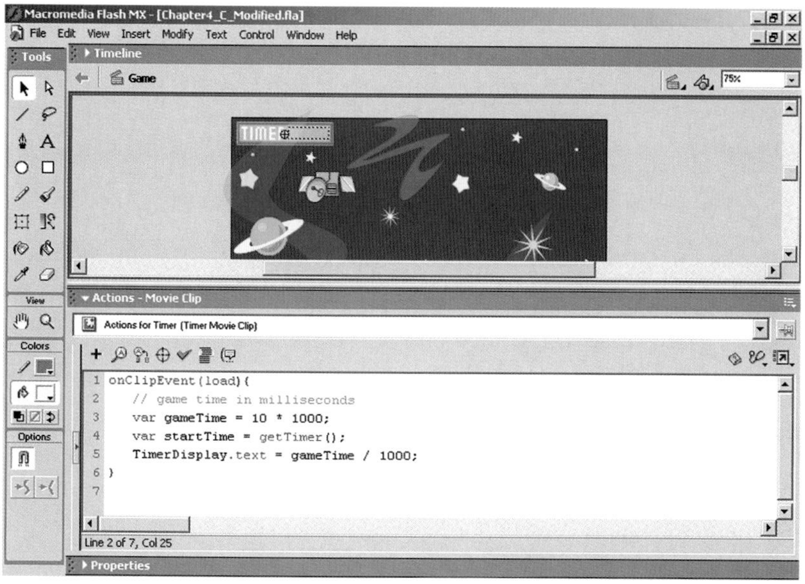

4.50: Add the `onClipEvent(load)` *code to the Timer movie clip.*

The value that the `getTimer()` function comes up with is placed in the *`startTime`* variable. The actual number that is in the *`startTime`* variable depends on how fast the code executes on whatever system it's running on. However, you don't need to be concerned with the actual value, because the *`startTime`* variable becomes a frame of reference. Whatever number it contains, you can essentially think of the *`startTime`* value as 0, because it is the starting point from which the code will begin counting.

The last line in the `onClipEvent(load)` event handler displays the number of seconds for the countdown. The display is inside the Timer movie clip. It is a dynamic text field called TimerDisplay. This is the instance name of the text field, not the variable name. When your text field has an instance name, you can take advantage of the new `TextField` object.

NOTE The new `TextField` object allows you to perform dynamic changes to the text such as change the color, the transparency, the position, and many other characteristics of the text on the fly. You'll be looking at many of the advantages of the new `TextField` object in later chapters. In this case, you could use the variable name to reference the dynamic text field, and the code would work virtually the same.

The code sets the `text` property of the TimerDisplay `TextField` object equal to *`gameTime`* in seconds by dividing the value of the *`gameTime`* variable by 1000. You want the display to show only seconds, not milliseconds.

```
TimerDisplay.text = gameTime / 1000;
```

These three lines of code establish the `gameTime` and `startTime` variables, and set the text in the Timer movie clip with a value that corresponds to the time in the `gameTime` variable in seconds.

If you test the movie now, you'll see that the timer displays 10 and then does nothing more. Let's add the code to make the timer count down.

7. Add Code to Update the Timer and Test

Add the following ActionScript below the `onClipEvent(load)` attached to the Timer movie clip (4.51).

```
onClipEvent(enterFrame){
   var timePlayed = getTimer() - startTime;
   var newTime = Math.round((gameTime - timePlayed) / 1000);
   if (newTime != TimerDisplay.text){
      TimerDisplay.text = newTime;
   }
}
```

Let's look at the first line of code:

```
var timePlayed = getTimer() - startTime;
```

The objective is to update the display in the Timer movie clip at least every second. First, the code computes how long the game has been playing by subtracting the value of the `startTime` variable from the current time. The code gets the current time by using the `getTimer()` function. The results of this calculation are saved in a variable called `timePlayed`.

The next line of code computes the new time that will be displayed in the Timer movie clip:

```
var newTime = Math.round((gameTime - timePlayed) / 1000);
```

The objective is to have the display count down. This code creates a variable named `newTime`. Then the code subtracts the value of the `timePlayed` variable from the `gameTime` variable. The results are then divided by 1000 and rounded to the nearest number, so the results are in even seconds.

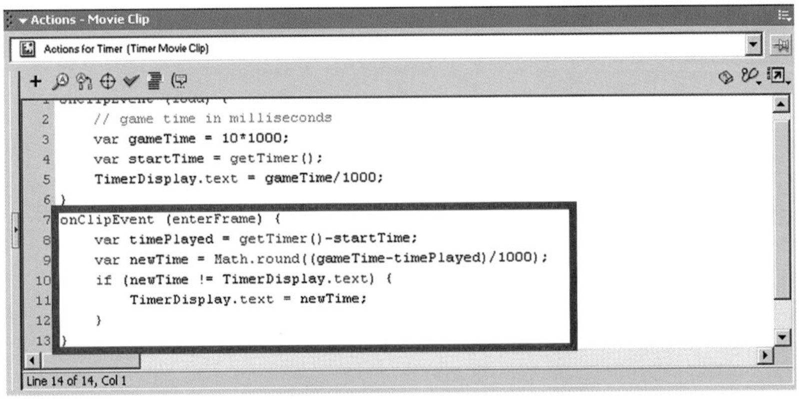

4.51: Add the `onClipEvent(enterFrame)` *code to the Timer movie clip.*

The last line of this code uses the `newTime` variable to update the `TimerDisplay.text` object.

```
if (newTime != TimerDisplay.text){
   TimerDisplay.text = newTime;
}
```

This code uses an `if` statement. It compares the value of the `newTime` variable with the current value of the `TimerDisplay.text` object. If the value of the `newTime` variable is different, the `TimerDisplay.text` object is updated using the value of the `newTime` variable.

When you test the movie, notice the timer ticking. If you watch for more than 10 seconds, you'll see the display show negative numbers. Now let's add some code that tells the game what to do when the timer reaches 0.

8. Add Code to End the Game and Test

Add the following ActionScript at the end of the `onClipEvent(enterFrame)` section (4.52).

```
if (newTime == 0){
   _root.play();
}
```

This code is very simple. If the `newTime` variable is equal to 0, the code sends a `play()` command to the main timeline. Note that you cannot write something like this

```
gotoAndStop("GameOver",1)
```

Remember that you cannot access scenes in movie clips, so the code simply tells the main timeline to play, and it jumps ahead to the GameOver scene.

Test the movie. You'll see that at the end of 10 seconds, when the display is 0, the movie jumps to the GameOver section. The GameOver scene has a Play Again button, which will take you back to the beginning. However, you have a small problem. You still have all those SatelliteOne movie clips floating around, even in the GameOver scene. When you use `duplicateMovieClip()` to create a movie clip, the duplicates stick around until you tell them to disappear. Let's do a little cleanup.

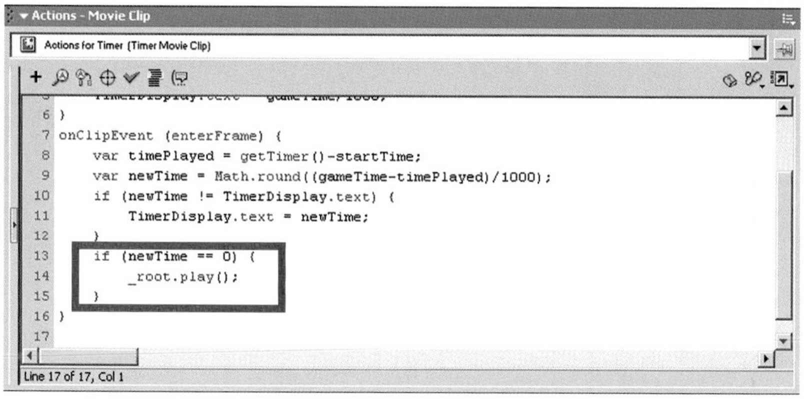
Actions - Movie Clip
Actions for Timer (Timer Movie Clip)
6 }
7 onClipEvent (enterFrame) {
8 var timePlayed = getTimer()-startTime;
9 var newTime = Math.round((gameTime-timePlayed)/1000);
10 if (newTime != TimerDisplay.text) {
11 TimerDisplay.text = newTime;
12 }
13 if (newTime == 0) {
14 _root.play();
15 }
16 }
17
Line 17 of 17, Col 1

4.52: Add code to go the GameOver scene when the `newTime` *variable reaches 0.*

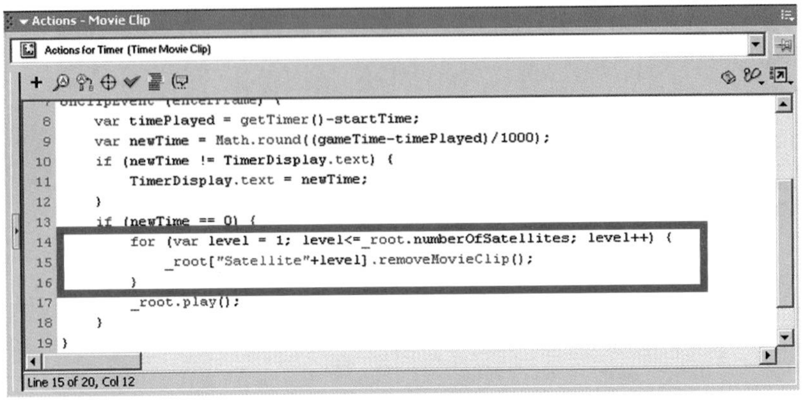

4.53: Add code to remove the duplicates before going to the GameOver scene.

9. Add Code to Remove Duplicates and Test

Insert the following ActionScript below the test for `newTime == 0`, but before the `_root.play()` command (4.53).

```
for (var level = 1; level <= _root.numberOfSatellites;level++){
    _root["Satellite" + level].removeMovieClip();
}
```

This is almost identical to the ActionScript that you used to duplicate the SatelliteOne movie clips, but there are a couple of differences. One difference is that the variable *`numberOfSatellites`* has a value only in the main timeline, so the code uses `_root` to reference it. Also, instead of duplicating the movie clips, the code is removing them based on the name you gave each duplicate. This makes it easy to quickly remove all of the duplicate SatelliteOne movie clips.

What about the original satellite, SatelliteOne? You're not removing it in the above ActionScript. Because the original SatelliteOne movie clip is only on the Game scene, it's left behind when the code moves onto the GameOver scene. (Movie clips created with `duplicateMovieClip()` and `attachMovie()` exist across all scenes.)

Next let's look at a different way to power the timer. In the example in the following section, you'll use a new feature in Flash MX that allows you to call a function periodically.

Using the *setInterval()* Function to Call a Function Periodically

Flash MX now includes the `setInterval()` function, which does something at a preset interval. To demonstrate its usefulness, let's use this for the end-of-game code you added in the previous section. You will tell the `setInterval()` function to execute the end-of-game sequence at 10 seconds.

1. Open the File

WWW. Open Chapter4_D_Start.fla. Save the file to your local hard drive as Chapter4_D_Modified.fla. (For the finished version, see Chapter4_D_Final.fla.)

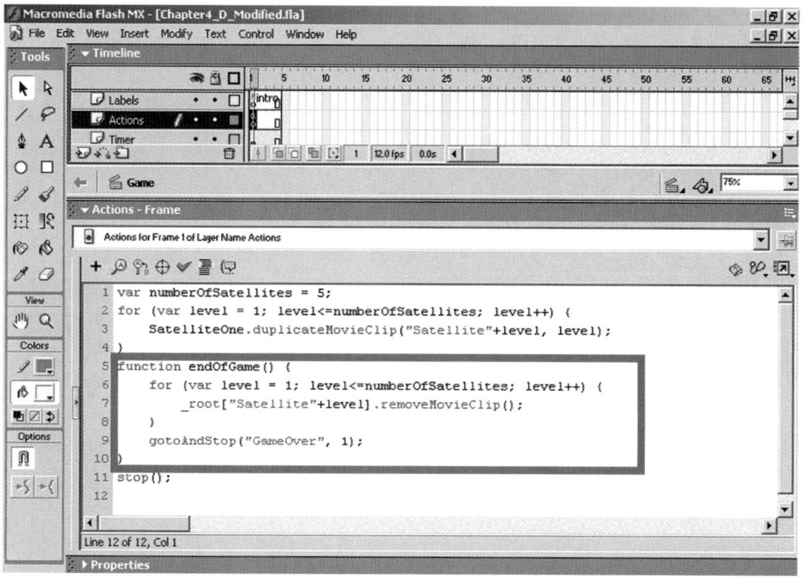

4.54: *Add the* `endOfGame()` *function to frame 1 on the Actions layer.*

This is the same file as your finished version of the previous example (Chapter4_C_Final). You're going to replace the end-of-game ActionScript that is attached to the Timer movie clip with code that uses `setInterval()`. First, you need to remove some of the ActionScript that is attached to the Timer movie clip.

2. Delete the End-of-Game Code Attached to the Timer Movie Clip

Delete the following ActionScript that is attached to the Timer movie clip.

```
if (newTime == 0){
   for (var level = 1; level <= _root.numberOfSatellites;level++){
      _root["satellite" + level].removeMovieClip();
   }
   _root.play();
}
```

In the next step, you'll create a function that replaces this functionality you just deleted.

3. Add the *endOfGame()* Function

On frame 1 of the Actions layer, before the `stop()` command, add the following ActionScript (4.54).

```
function endOfGame(){
   for (var level = 1; level <= numberOfSatellites;level++){
      _root["Satellite" + level].removeMovieClip();
   }
   gotoAndStop("GameOver", 1);
}
```

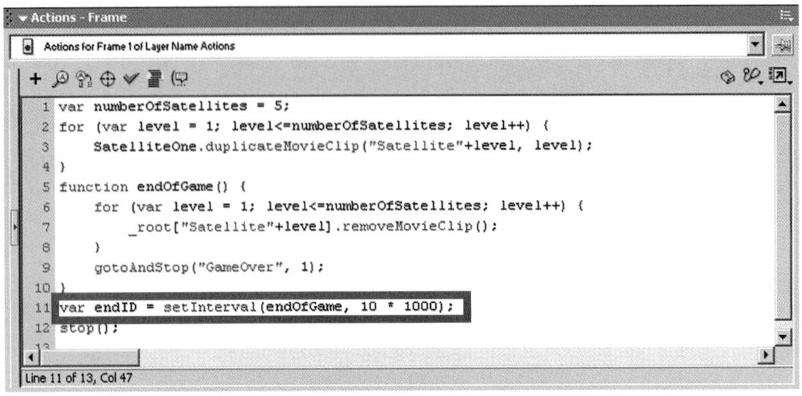
Actions - Frame
Actions for Frame 1 of Layer Name Actions
var numberOfSatellites = 5;
for (var level = 1; level<=numberOfSatellites; level++) {
SatelliteOne.duplicateMovieClip("Satellite"+level, level);
}
function endOfGame() {
for (var level = 1; level<=numberOfSatellites; level++) {
_root["Satellite"+level].removeMovieClip();
}
gotoAndStop("GameOver", 1);
}
var endID = setInterval(endOfGame, 10 * 1000);
stop();
Line 11 of 13, Col 47

4.55: Add the endID variable frame 1 on the Actions layer.

This code creates the *endOfGame()* function, which the `setInterval()` function will execute. Notice that the function definition contains almost the same code that you deleted from the Timer movie clip in the previous step, with a few differences:

- The *numberOfSatellites* does not need `_root` in front of it, because this function and the variable are both on the main timeline.
- This code does not need to check if the *newTime* is equal to 0; the `setInterval` function will take care of that.
- The `gotoAndStop()` command is on the main timeline, so now the code can access the GameOver scene.

4. Add Code to Create the *endID* Variable

Add the following ActionScript directly above the `stop()` command on frame 1 in the Actions layer (4.55).

```
var endID = setInterval(endOfGame, 10 * 1000);
```

This code creates a variable named *endID*. The value of the *endID* variable is calculated with the new `setInterval()` function. The `setInterval()` function requires two arguments: the name of the function to be called and the interval at which to call it. This example has `setInterval()` calling the function *endOfGame()* every 10 seconds.

If you left the code as it is now, the *endOfGame()* function would be called every 10 seconds, even after the user was sent to the GameOver scene. Therefore, you need to stop the `setInterval()` function, which is the purpose of the `clearInterval()` function. The `clearInterval()` function needs the ID of the specific interval to stop. This ID is returned when you call `setInterval()`. Each time you call `setInterval()`, a unique ID is returned. This way you can stop any particular function you have loaded into the `setInterval()` function. That is what the variable *endID* contains and why you need it.

You want to call the *endOfGame()* function once and then not again unless the game is played again. To do this, you'll call `clearInterval()` in the *endOfGame()* function itself.

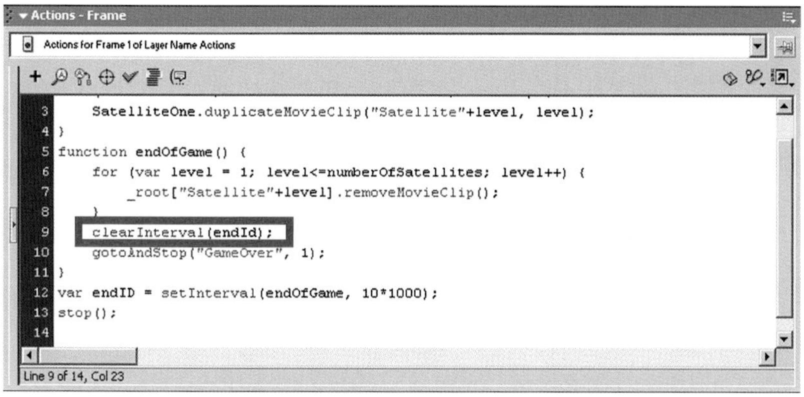
Actions - Frame
Actions for Frame 1 of Layer Name Actions
SatelliteOne.duplicateMovieClip("Satellite"+level, level);
}
function endOfGame() {
for (var level = 1; level<=numberOfSatellites; level++) {
_root["Satellite"+level].removeMovieClip();
}
clearInterval(endId);
gotoAndStop("GameOver", 1);
}
var endID = setInterval(endOfGame, 10*1000);
stop();
Line 9 of 14, Col 23

4.56: Add the `clearInterval()` *function to frame 1 on the Actions layer.*

5. Add the *clearInterval()* Function

Add the following ActionScript to the *`endOfGame()`* function, before the `gotoAndStop()` action (4.56).

```
clearInterval(endId);
```

The `clearInterval()` function takes one argument: the interval ID to cancel. Now let's change the code for the timer and use a `setInterval()` call to change the display.

6. Change the Timer Code to Use *setInterval()*

Delete all the ActionScript that is attached to the Timer clip and replace it with the following (4.57).

```
onClipEvent(load){
   // game time in milliseconds
   var gameTime = 10;
   TimerDisplay.text = gameTime;
   function timeLeft(){
      gameTime--;
      TimerDisplay.text = gameTime;
   }
   var timeID = setInterval(timeLeft, 1 * 1000);
}
```

Once again, you're going to call the *`timeLeft()`* function from within the Timer movie clip, so you place it in the `onClipEvent(load)` section. The first line in the `onClipEvent(load)` event handler still defines the *`gameTime`* variable. However, the `setInterval()` function takes care of calculating everything in milliseconds.

For this version, you'll use the *`gameTime`* variable to do two things: contain the total amount of the game and contain the time left of the game. This means that you will use the

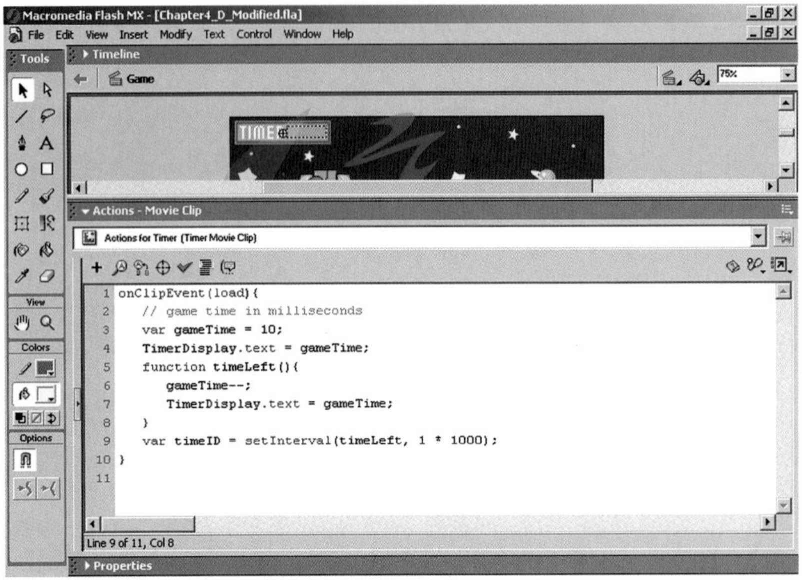

4.57: Replace the code on the Timer movie clip.

variable to count down also, instead of using the `newTime` variable as you did in the previous example.

Next the `TimerDisplay.text` object is instantiated with the value of the `gameTime` variable, as before. You then display the current time left using a function called `timeLeft()`.

Then you create the function that the `setInterval()` function will call every second. This function, `timeLeft()`, first decreases the `gameTime` by one and then displays it in the TimerDisplay text field. Since you are going to be calling this function only once a second, you don't need to do any checking. You know you're going to be here only if it's a new second.

Finally, you set the `setInterval()` function to call the `timeLeft()` function every second. Remember that it's in milliseconds, so 1 second is 1 * 1000, and you need to get an interval ID so you can tell it to stop.

When do you tell it to stop? Let's do that in the `endOfGame()` function also.

7. Add Code to Stop the *setInterval()* Function Call

Add the following ActionScript in the `endOfGame()` function below the other `clearInterval()` function call on frame 1 of the Actions layer (4.58).

```
clearInterval(Timer.timeID);
```

This will stop the `setInterval()` call. Notice that in order to access the variable, you need to tell it which movie clip to find it in.

Test this and see how clean this version is. It's a lot simpler to let Flash do the testing for the time instead of programming it in. And you don't need to worry about efficiency.

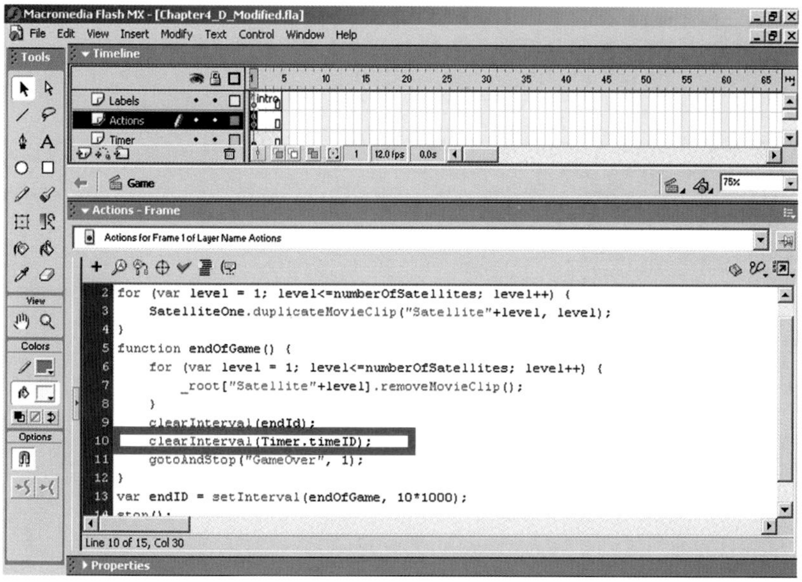

4.58: Add the code to frame 1 of the Actions layer.

Conclusion

You've now learned a lot about many different Flash MX built-in methods and functions. First, you learned how to code a preloader using the `_framesloaded` and `_totalframes` properties, which create a jumpy preloader. Then you saw how using the `getBytesTotal()` and `getBytesLoaded()` methods creates a smooth preloader.

Next you learned about the `Date` and `Sound` objects by programming a clock. Each of these objects has many other uses, and you barely touched the surface of each. However, you did get an idea of how the `Date` and `Sound` objects work.

Then you learned about using the `getBounds()` method of a movie clip in combination with the `Stage` object. This approach allows you to test to see if a movie clip had moved off the screen, and then to move it back on again.

Finally, you learned two ways to keep track of time. The `getTimer()` function provides you with the length of time the Flash movie has been playing. The `setInterval()` and `clearInterval()` functions allow you to call a function at a specific interval, and then to stop calling the function when it isn't needed.

The functions and methods covered in this chapter are just a few of the many that you'll work with as you gain Flash expertise. However, they are very necessary ones, and the examples in this chapter have given you a good idea of how to use them.

CHAPTER five

Coded Animation Techniques

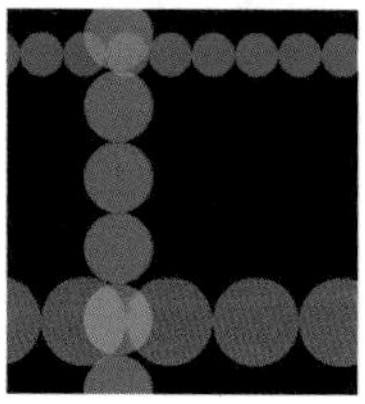

Motion tweens, shape tweens, *and basic keyframe animations have their place in Flash, but as a Flash designer, you'll want to round out your animation toolbox by learning to use ActionScript to create your animations. Many animation effects that are relatively easy to generate with ActionScript can be prohibitive, if not impossible, with Flash's basic animation features.*

In previous chapters, you've learned how to create some simple animations by controlling the `_x` *and* `_y` *properties of a movie clip with ActionScript. In this chapter, you'll learn some techniques that expand on that basic approach, as well as some other techniques, such as animating zooms, rotation, and color shifts with ActionScript. You'll also continue working with functions—both global functions and those that are built into movie clips.*

Animating Marching Circles

Using a single graphic to create animation is a great way to keep your Flash movie small but still interesting. The animation effect you'll create in this example demonstrates how to create a simple animation using a single graphic and ActionScript. The movie will start with a shape—a circle, in this case—and duplicate it, placing the copies side by side and then moving them across the stage. This is a versatile animation that can look very different each time you use it.

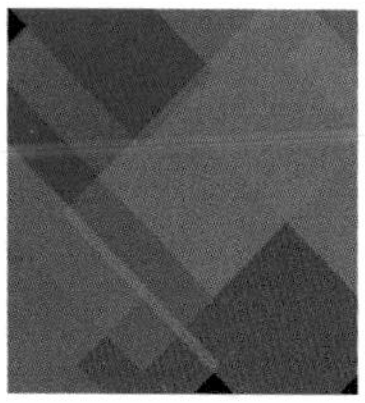

WWW.

1. Open the File

Open Chapter5_A_Start.fla. Save the file to your local hard drive as Chapter5_A_Modified.fla. (To see the finished version, open Chapter5_A_Final.fla.)

Notice that there are three movie clips in the library: Empty MC, Circle MC, and Diamond MC. The Circle MC and Diamond MC movie clips have a linkage property already defined and are named Circle and Diamond, respectively. In this example, you'll be using only the Empty MC and the Circle MC movie clips. The Diamond MC movie clip is provided for your extra amusement, so you can see how easy it is to change the look by swapping graphics.

There is one layer named Shapes. On the Shapes layer is an instance of Empty MC. You'll be using only the Empty MC movie clip on the stage. You'll use ActionScript to change its behavior, beginning with presenting a moving string of circles. The Empty MC movie clip does not need to have an instance name.

2. Attach Initialization Code

Flash represents movie clips with no graphical content in the first frame as a small, white dot on the stage, which is how the Empty MC movie clip appears. Select the white dot and apply the following ActionScript to the Empty MC movie clip (5.1).

```
onClipEvent(load) {
   // settings
   var radius = 40;
   var alpha = 60;
   var direction = "horizontal";
   var speed = 5;
}
```

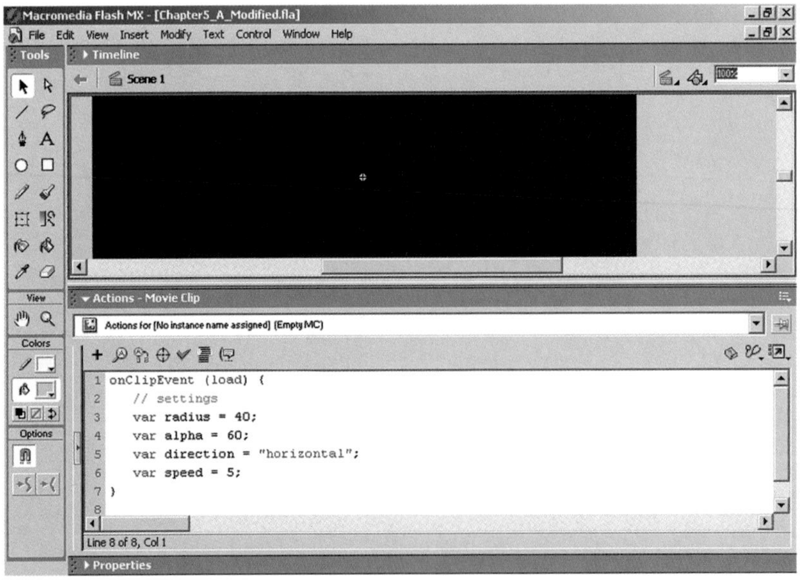

5.1: Apply the `onClipEvent(load)` *code to the Empty MC movie clip that is on the stage.*

This code defines some variables within the `onClipEvent(load)` event handler. The variables establish some of the settings for the animation effects: The radius of each circle will be 40 pixels, the alpha transparency will be 60, the direction of movement will be on the horizontal plane, and the speed of movement will be 5 pixels per frame.

Next you'll attach the Circle MC movie clip and duplicate it the necessary number of times.

3. Attach the Circle Movie Clip and Test

Add the following ActionScript to the bottom of the ActionScript attached to the Empty MC movie clip (5.2). Make sure it is within the `onClipEvent(load)` section.

```
if (direction == "horizontal") {
   //start off first graphic at 0
   _x = 0;
   // how many circles to create
   var num = Math.ceil(Stage.width / radius) + 2;
   for (var j = 0; j < num; j++) {
      attachMovie("Circle", "Circle" + j, j);
      // setting both the height and width of this circle
      // to the radius
      this["Circle" + j]._width = this["Circle" + j]._height = radius;
      this["Circle" + j]._alpha = alpha;
      // placing this circle next to last circle
      this["Circle" + j]._x = j*radius - radius;
      this["Circle" + j]._y = 0;
   }
}
```

This section of the code is contained within an `if` statement that checks the direction. For now, you're entering the code for only the horizontal direction, which you set as the value of the *`direction`* variable in the previous step. Later, you'll enter the code for the vertical

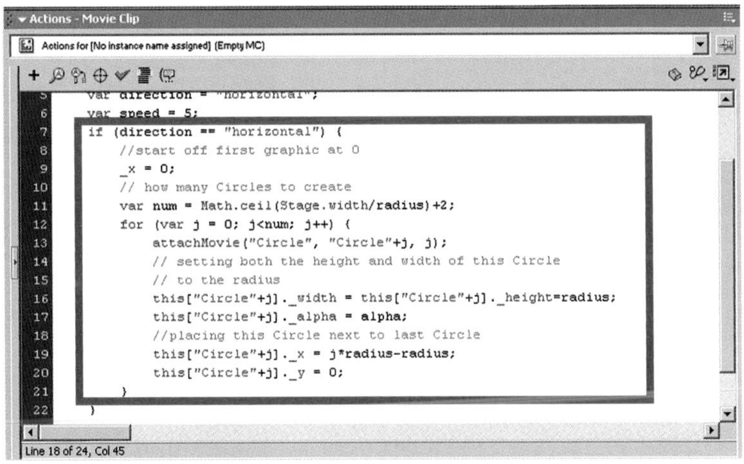

5.2: Add the code that creates the duplicates of the Circle MC to the bottom of the `onClipEvent(load)` *event handler.*

direction, which is very similar. Remember that all of this is happening within the Empty MC movie clip.

The first line in the `if` statement is simple:

```
_x = 0;
```

This sets the *x* position of this Empty MC movie clip to the farthest left point, which is 0 in the *x*-axis. Subsequent lines of code will create duplicates of the Circle MC movie clip using the `attachMovie()` method. The code will position the duplicates to the right of each other. So this code merely starts the duplicates at the left of the stage.

The next line of code within the `if` statement determines how many duplicates of the circle to create, based on the width of the stage and the value of the *`radius`* variable:

```
var num = Math.ceil(Stage.width / radius) + 2;
```

To determine the necessary number of duplicates, you divide the width of the stage by the radius of the circle (5.3). In this example, the width of the stage is 550. You set the value of the *`radius`* variable to 40 in the previous step. Therefore, the code performs the calculation 550 / 40, which equals 13.75.

This line of code assigns a value to the *`num`* variable, which the code will later use in duplicating the Circle MC movie clip. The number 13.75 isn't much use to the code, since it cannot create 13.75 duplicates (or at least you wouldn't want it to). This is what the `Math` method `ceil()` is used for. `Math.ceil()` rounds the number up to the next highest integer, turning 13.75 into 14 in this example. After the code executes the `Math.ceil()` method, it adds 2 to the results, so that there is some overlap at both ends of the stage. The code ends up with 16 as the value for the *`num`* variable.

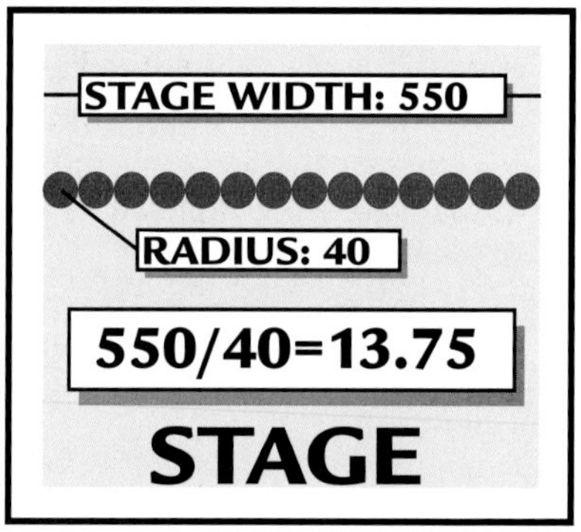

5.3: The code determines the number of duplicates of the Circle MC movie clip required for the animation effect by dividing the width of the stage by the value of the `radius` variable.

NOTE Note that if the code had something like `Math.ceil(13.1)` you would still end up with the number 14. `Math.ceil()` always rounds the number up to the next higher whole number, unlike `Math.round()`, which rounds the number to the nearest whole number. It's easy to remember this difference if you know that `ceil` is short for "ceiling." As you might expect, there is also a `Math.floor()` method, which rounds its argument down to the next lower whole number. For example, `Math.floor(13.75)` would return 13.

Once the code has a value for the *`num`* variable, it moves onto making duplicates of the Circle MC movie clip using a `for` loop and the `attachMovie()` method:

```
for (var j = 0; j < num; j++) {
   attachMovie("Circle", "Circle" + j, j);
```

First, the `for` loop establishes the arbitrary variable *`j`* in the initialization phase and sets its value to 0. In the condition phase of the `for` loop, the value of the variable *`j`* is compared to the value of the *`num`* variable. If the *`j`* variable is less than the *`num`* variable, the code within the for loop is executed, and then the value of the j variable is incremented by one using the ++ operator.

NOTE This for loop looks a little different from the for loops you've seen in previous chapters. This for loop is more compact, mainly because it uses the variable name j rather than a more descriptive variable name (such as MovieCopy).

The code attaches the Circle MC movie clip using the attachMovie() method (referencing the linkage name Circle), gives it a new name based on the string "Circle" and the current value of the j variable ("Circle" + j), and then puts it on a new level based on the value of the j variable. Remember that when attaching movie clips to movie clips, the levels are within the movie clip you are attaching to (the Empty MC movie clip in this example), not on the main timeline. Since the value of the num variable is 16, the for loop generates 16 copies of Circle MC within the Empty MC movie clip.

The next thing the code needs to do is size the Circle MC duplicates. Earlier, you created a variable named radius and set it to 40. Now you need to use that variable to actually set the radius of each duplicate. That is what the next line in the code does:

```
this["Circle" + j]._width = this["Circle" + j]._height = radius;
```

This code accomplishes the same thing as the following:

```
this["Circle" + j]._width = radius;
this["Circle" + j]._height = radius;
```

It just takes less space. In fact you could write something like a = b = c = d = e = 0 to assign the variables a, b, c, d, and e equal to 0.

You've set the _width and _height properties for the newly created duplicate of the Circle MC movie clip to the value of the radius variable (40). Therefore, during the first pass through the for loop, the Circle0 movie clip's _width and _height properties are each set to 40.

The next line in the for loop works in the same way to set the _alpha property of the newly created duplicate movie clip to the value of the alpha variable:

```
this["Circle" + j]._alpha = alpha;
```

Earlier, you set the value of the alpha variable to 60 in the onClipEvent(load) handler. So during the first pass through the for loop, the Circle0 movie clip's _alpha property is set to 60.

Finally, the code places the newly generated Circle*NN* movie clips at the end of the line of circles generated by the for loop:

```
this["Circle" + j]._x = j * radius - radius;
```

During the first pass through the for loop, this code sets the _x property for the Circle0 movie clip. The position of the _x property is calculated as follows:

```
j * radius - radius;
```

Let's plug in some values to see how this works. During the first pass through the for loop, the value of the j variable is 0 and the value of the radius value is 40. Therefore, the calculation during the first pass through the for loop is 0 * 40 – 40. Flash performs multiplication and division before addition and subtraction, so first 0 is multiplied by 40 and then

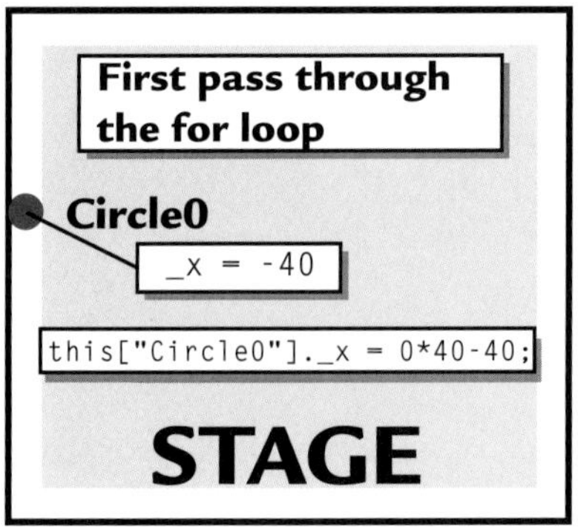

5.4: *The first pass through the* `for` *loop resolves to –40 for the* `_x` *property of the Circle0 movie clip.*

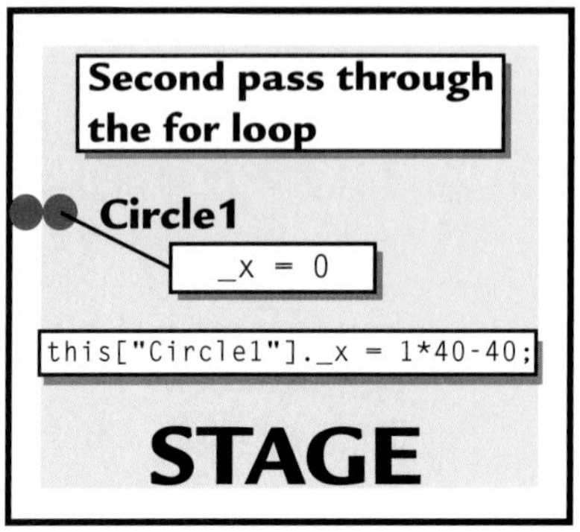

5.5: *The second pass through the* `for` *loop resolves to 0 for the* `_x` *property of the Circle1 movie clip.*

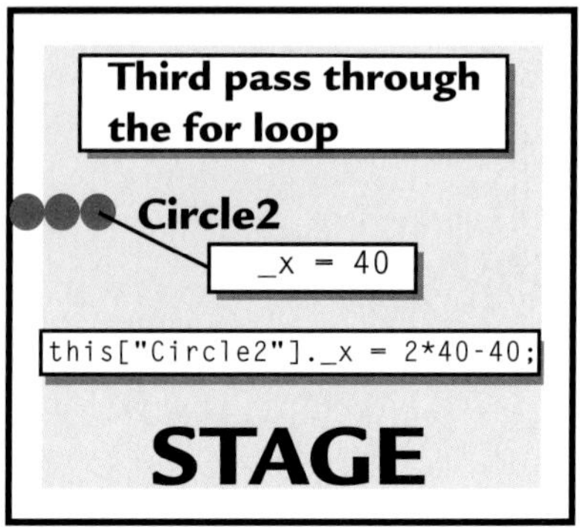

5.6: *The third pass through the* `for` *loop resolves to 40 for the* `_x` *property of the Circle2 movie clip.*

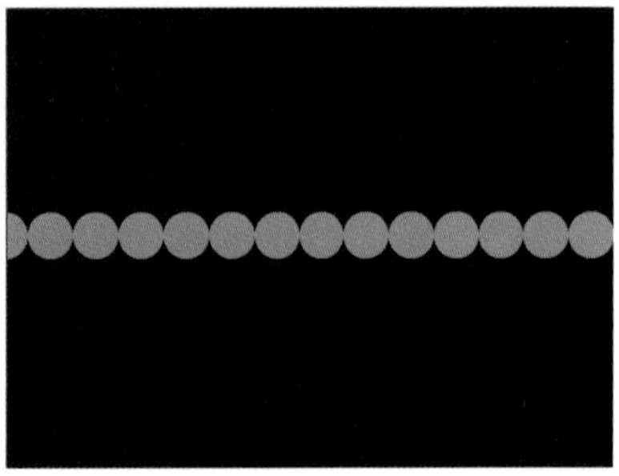

5.7: *The duplicates of the Circle MC movie clip line up end to end horizontally.*

the results are subtracted by 40. Therefore, the `_x` property for Circle0 is set to –40 on the first pass (5.4).

On the second pass (5.5), the value for the `j` variable is 1. The calculation is 1 * 40 – 40 = 0, so the `_x` property for the Circle1 movie clip is set to 0. On the third pass (5.6), the value for the `j` variable is 2. The calculation is 2 * 40 – 40 = 40, so the `_x` property for the Circle2 movie clip is set to 40 (5.6).

The `for` loop continues placing the duplicate movie clips using this formula as long as the value of the `j` variable is less than the value of the `num` variable, which is 16. That means that the last time the `for` loop executes, the variable `j` will be equal to 15. Therefore, on the last pass through the `for` loop, the calculation is 15 * 40 – 40 = 560, and the `_x` property for the Circle15 movie clip is set to 560.

Recall that the stage is 550 pixels wide. Thus, this code generates a series of duplicates of the Circle MC movie clip within the Empty MC movie clip. The first duplicate is positioned at –40, and the last duplicate is positioned at 560, which means that the circles cover the entire width of the stage, overlapping on both sides.

The last line within the `for` loop sets the _y property for each of the Circle movie clips at 0.

When you test this movie clip (5.7), you'll see a horizontal line of gray circles across the stage. The circles appear to be gray because the stage is black and the alpha setting is 60%. Now let's add color to the circles.

4. Add Color Variables to the Circles

Add the following ActionScript to the `onClipEvent(load)` section, below the `speed = 5;` line of code and above the `if()` statement (5.8).

```
var red = 255;
var green = 100;
var blue = 255;
```

These are the RGB values that the code will use to dynamically recolor the Circle*NN* movie clips. The actual circle graphic is white. The color tinting will work for any color. In

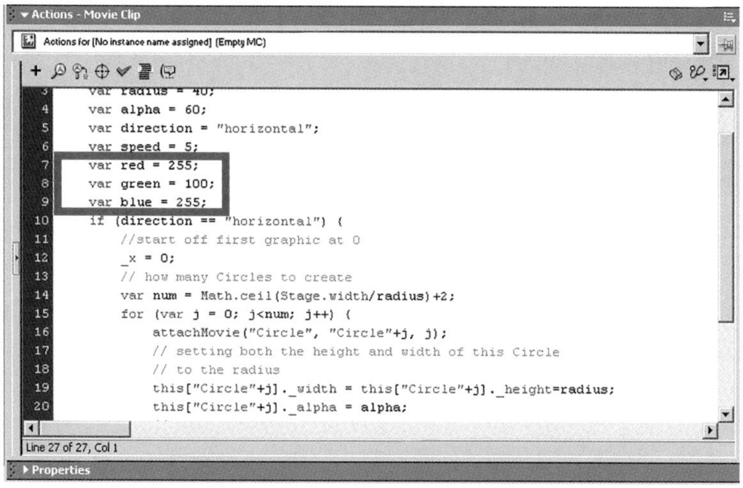

5.8: Add color variables to the `onClipEvent(load)` *section.*

other words, the base color can be any color, and the code will recolor the shape according to the RGB values you specify. This works for any graphic, even if the graphic is multicolored.

5. Add the Color Object to the Circle MC Clip and Test

Add the following ActionScript at the bottom of the `onClipEvent(load)` section, right after the end of the `for` loop and just above the last curly brace (`}`) (5.9).

```
var col = new Color(this);
col.setRGB(red << 16 | green << 8 | blue);
```

First, the code creates an instance of the `Color` object called with the variable name *`col`* using the keyword `new`. You need to target the object (graphic) you wish to color. In this case, the target is the Empty MC movie clip, so you use the keyword `this`.

Then you actually set the RGB of the `Color` object *`col`* to the RGB values you entered earlier. This code involves working with binary numbers.

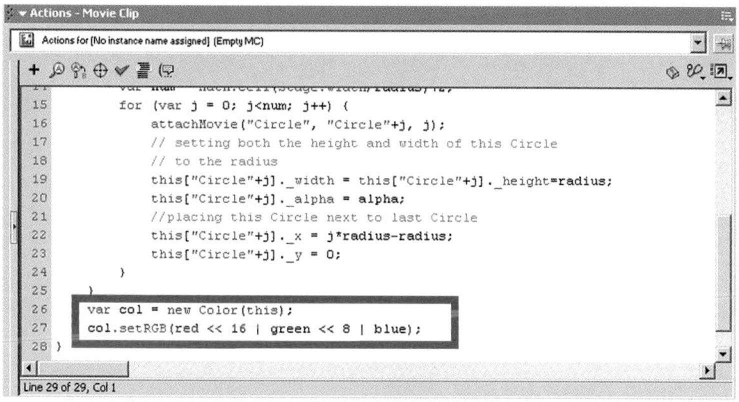

5.9: Add the `Color` *object code to the bottom of the* `onClipEvent(load)` *code.*

Color Values in Binary Numbers

The `setRGB()` method needs the RGB values in the form of a single 24-bit binary number, in which the first 8 bits represent the red value (in this example 255, or 11111111 in binary), the middle 8 bits represent green (100, or 01100100), and the last 8 bits represent blue (255 again):

111111110110010011111111

When the individual 8-bit values for the colors are represented in 24 bits, they all have their leftmost 16 bits set to 16 zeros:

000000000000000011111111
000000000000000001100100
000000000000000011111111

In order to get one 24-bit number that represents the three colors, you need to shift two of the 8-bit blocks that actually have information in them into their appropriate positions, and then combine all three of the numbers into one value. The standard RGB definition means that the red value is in the first 8 bits, the green value takes the next 8 bits, and the blue value takes the last 8 bits. That's what the following formula in the code does:

```
red << 16 | green << 8 | blue
```

This formula uses two operators specific to working with bits. The `<<` symbol, called the *bitwise left shift*, takes the variable on its left and shifts it leftward in bits by the number of bit positions specified on its right. The expression `red << 16` takes the value of the *red* variable:

000000000000000011111111

and shifts it over 16 bits:

111111110000000000000000

The expression `green << 8` shifts the value of the *green* variable by 8 bits. You can leave the value of the *blue* variable alone, since it needs to be in the last 8-bit place, according to the standard RGB definition.

After shifting the red and green values into their correct positions, the binary values look like this:

111111110000000000000000 (red)
000000000110010000000000 (green)
000000000000000011111111 (blue)

Combining the three 24-bit numbers is the work of the | symbol, known as the *bitwise OR* operator. The bitwise OR operator compares two binary numbers, bit position by bit position. If either one of them is a 1, then the output is a 1 in that position. If both are 0, then the output is a 0 in that position; otherwise, it will be a 1. In other words for one bit, using the bitwise OR operator, you get the following:

0 | 0 = 0
0 | 1 = 1
1 | 0 = 1
1 | 1 = 1

When you bitwise OR the three numbers for the color values together, you get the following:

111111110110010011111111

This is the same as 16,737,535 in decimal.

> Many programmers find it convenient to represent the long binary numbers used for RGB values in *hexadecimal* (base-16), or *hex*, numbering, which uses the numerals 0 through 9 and the letters A through F. The advantage of using 16 digits is that any number 0 through 255 (the range of values for an individual color) can be represented with two hexadecimal digits. The number 111111110110010011111111 would be written in hex as FF64FF, which may be more readable and is acceptable to the `setRGB()` method.

Test the movie. Notice that all of the circles now appear purple (5.10). However, the circles still don't move, so it's not very interesting. Now let's add some movement.

6. Move the Circles and Test

Add the following ActionScript to the Empty MC movie clip on the stage, below the `onClipEvent(load)` code that you already assigned to the Empty MC movie clip (5.11).

```
onClipEvent(enterFrame) {
   if (direction == "horizontal") {
      _x += speed;
      if (_x >= radius) {
         _x = 0;
      }
   }
}
```

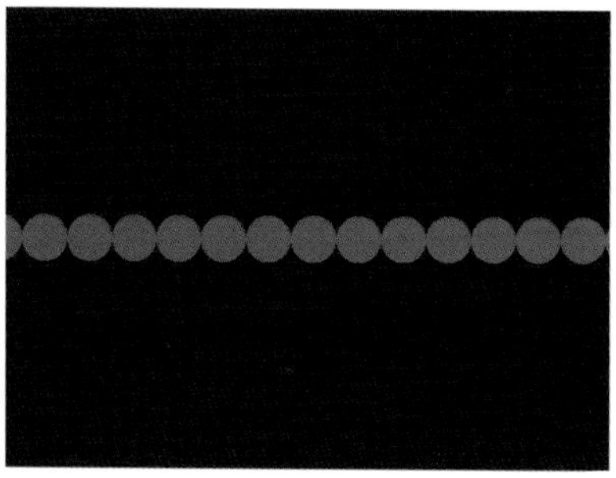

5.10: You've created a row of circles and added color, but you still need to add motion.

All of the movement for the Empty MC movie clip is accomplished by the code within the `onClipEvent(enterFrame)` event handler. First, the `if` statement checks if the *`direction`* variable is set to horizontal (which it always is at this point). If so, it moves the *x* position using the `_x` property of the Empty MC movie clip by adding the value of the *`speed`* variable to it with the += operator. The *`speed`* variable is set to 5, so the Empty MC movie clip moves 5 pixels to the right every time the `onClipEvent(enterFrame)` code is executed.

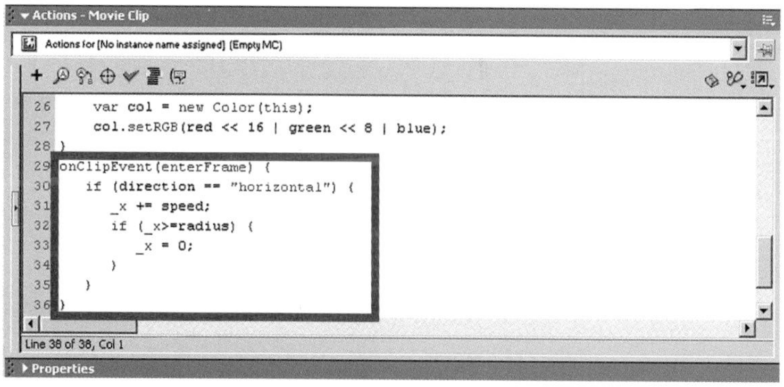

5.11: Apply the code to move the Empty MC movie clip.

Next, another `if` statement within the first `if` statement checks to see if the value of the `_x` property is greater than the value of the *`radius`* variable (which is 40). If the value of the `_x` property is greater than 40, this means you've moved the Empty MC movie clip the distance of one circle, so the code resets the `_x` property to 0.

Test the movie again. Notice that the line of circles appears to march across the stage. This is an illusion. What is actually happening is that all of the circles are grouped in one movie clip, Empty MC. All of the Circle*NN* movie clips are embedded within the Empty MC, so they move whenever the Empty MC moves. It's the instance of the Empty MC movie clip that is moving across the stage. As soon as it has moved the distance equal to the radius of one circle (40 pixels), it is shifted back to the starting point.

The code sets the Empty MC movie clip's _x position to 0 to begin with, and then moves the Empty MC movie clip to the right 5 pixels at a time, until the _x property reaches 40. Then the code resets the _x position to 0. The Circle0 movie clip, which is the first duplicate in the line of duplicates Circle0 to Circle15, is positioned at –40 within the Empty MC movie clip. This means that the Circle0 movie clip is positioned off the left side of the stage when the Empty MC movie clip begins animating (5.12). As the Empty MC movie clip moves to the right, the Circle0 movie clip moves onto the stage. The result is the illusion that there is an endless stream of circles coming from the left and animating off to the right.

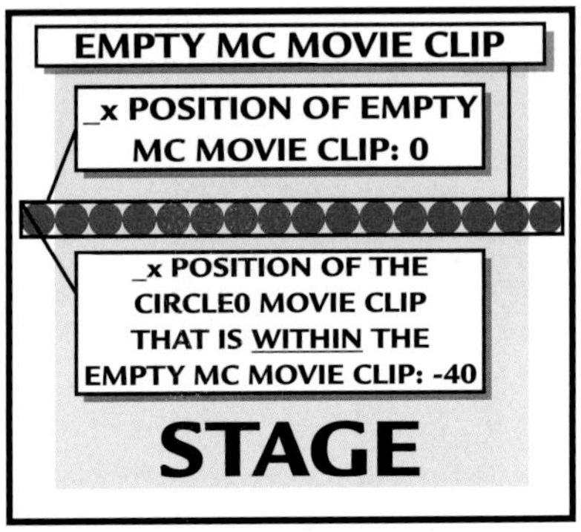

5.12: The _x position of the Circle0 movie clip relative to the Empty MC clip

Now let's add code to create the same animation effect moving vertically.

7. Create Vertical Circles

Add the following ActionScript within the `onClipEvent(load)` section, directly above the `var col = new Color(this);` line (5.13):

```
else if (direction == "vertical") {
   this._y = 0;
   var num = Math.ceil(Stage.height / radius) + 2;
   for (var j = 0; j < num; j++) {
      this.attachMovie("Circle", "Circle" + j, j);
      this["Circle" + j]._width = this["Circle" + j]._height = radius;
      this["Circle" + j]._alpha = alpha;
      this["Circle" + j]._x = 0;
      this["Circle" + j]._y = j * radius - radius;
   }
}
```

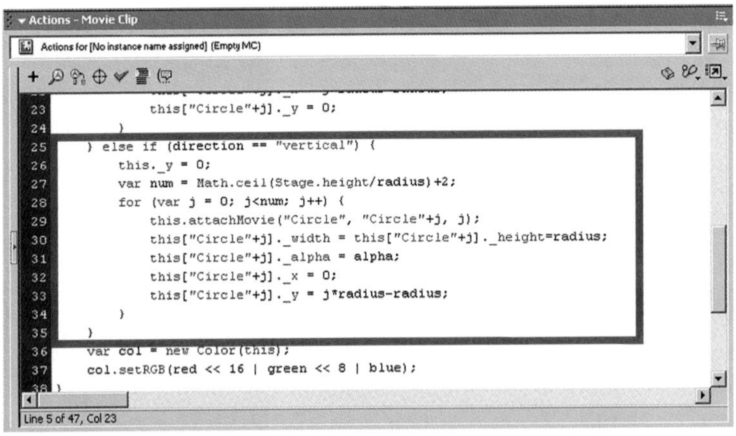

5.13: Add the code to create vertical duplicates of the Circle MC movie clip.

This code works the same as the code for the horizontal direction, except that it creates duplicates positioned vertically. To accomplish this, it uses the `Stage.height` property instead of the `Stage.width` property, and positions the duplicates according to the `_y` property instead of the `_x` property.

8. Move the Vertical Circles

Add the following ActionScript in the `onClipEvent(enterFrame)` section for the Empty MC movie clip, directly above the last curly brace (5.14):

```
else {
    _y += speed;
    if (_y >= radius) {
        _y = 0;
    }
}
```

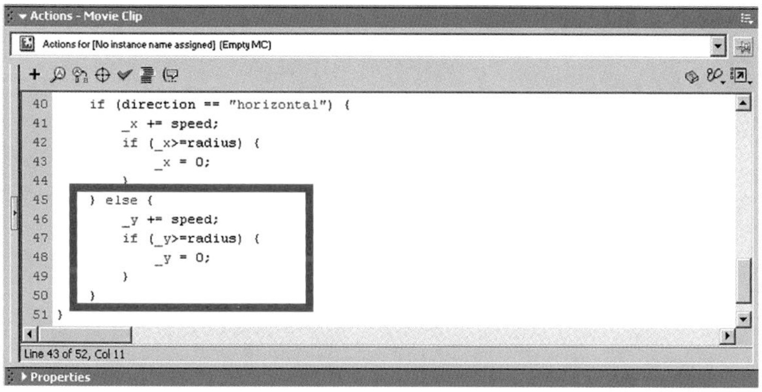

5.14: Add the code to power the vertical animation.

This code also does the same thing as the code for moving in the horizontal direction, except that it updates the `_y` property to move the movie clip in the vertical direction.

Now you have horizontal and vertical movement in your animation. Let's make things a little more interesting by changing some of the variables.

9. Copy the Movie Clip, Change Some Variables, and Test

Copy the Empty MC instance on the stage and paste it three more times. Adjust the variables in the settings section (in the `onClipEvent(load)` section, denoted by the `settings` comment) on each of the copies, so that some of them animate vertically and some animate horizontally. Also try changing the *`radius`*, *`alpha`*, *`speed`*, *`red`*, *`green`*, and *`blue`* variables. Test the movie (5.15).

Now try placing the movie clips close to each other and moving some copies around on the stage so that there is some distance between them. Add more copies if you like (5.16). Exact positioning is not important. Have a little fun with it. You could even use the Diamond-linked graphic instead of the Circle graphic. Test the movie to see the effects of your changes.

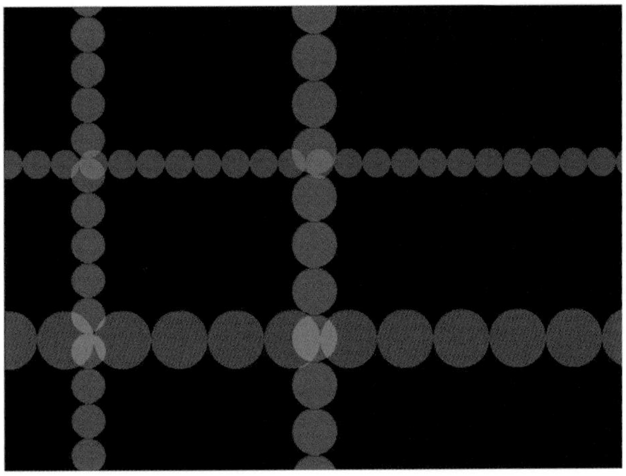

5.15: Create several duplicates of the movie clip and adjust the variables.

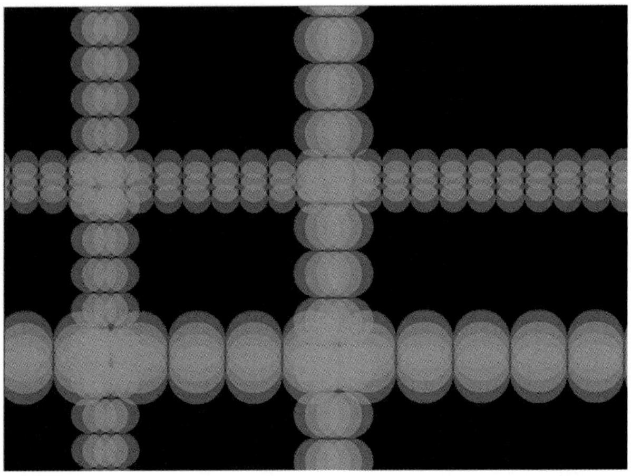

5.16: This is example was created by creating four duplicates of the movies, each with similar settings in the variables.

Enlarging a Diamond

Up to this point in this book, you have frequently manipulated the `_x` and `_y` properties to create animation. Now let's look at some other properties that you can manipulate to generate animation: the `_xscale`, `_yscale`, and `_visibility` properties. In this example, you will scale a graphic using ActionScript. In the process, you'll create your first method and also use the `setInterval()` function to help scale the movie clip.

1. Open the File

WWW.

Open Chapter5_B_Start.fla. Save the file to your local hard drive as Chapter5_B_Modified.fla. (To see the finished version, open Chapter5_B_Final.fla.)

This file is almost exactly the same as the file you began with in the previous example. There are the same three movie clips in the library: Empty MC, Circle MC, and Diamond MC. The Circle MC and Diamond MC movie clip have a linkage property already defined and are named Circle and Diamond, respectively. There is one layer, Scale, which contains an instance of the Empty MC movie clip. As in the previous example, you will be applying ActionScript to the Empty MC clip.

2. Attach Initialization Code

Attach the following ActionScript to the Empty MC movie clip that is on the stage (5.17).

```
onClipEvent(load) {
   // init our variables
   var diamondTime = 2 * 1000;
   var scaleType = "grow";
   var scaleIncrement = 100;
   var alpha = 70;
   var red = 0;
   var green = 0;
   var blue = 200;
}
```

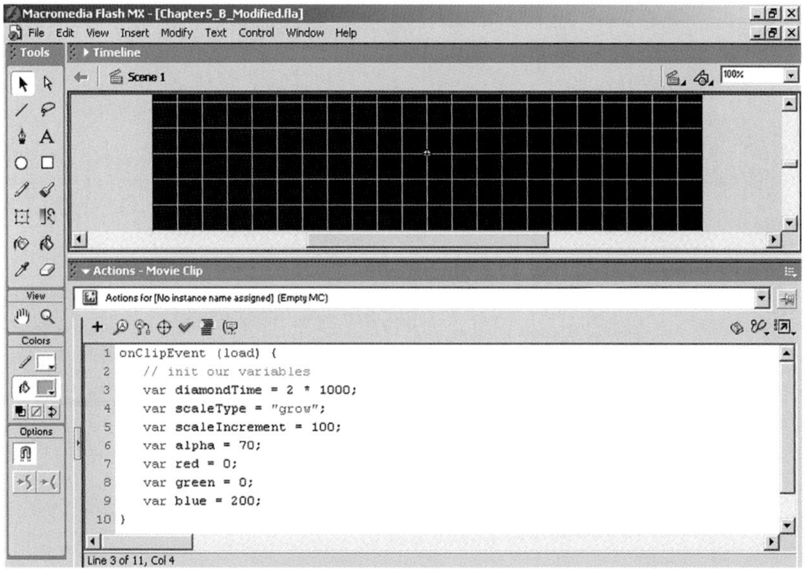

5.17: Initialize some variables within the `onClipEvent(load)` *event handler.*

This code, once again, takes advantage of the `onClipEvent(load)` handler to set up some variables. The *diamondTime* variable is used to set the frequency of how often you'll do the scaling. The *scaleType* variable will be used to determine whether to grow or shrink the movie clip that the code will later generate inside the Empty MC movie clip. The *scaleIncrement* variable is how fast the scaling animation will play. The *alpha* variable will be used in conjunction with the `_alpha` property. Finally, the *red*, *green*, and *blue* variables are the settings for the `Color` object.

Next you will attach the Diamond MC movie clip and set the color. (5.18).

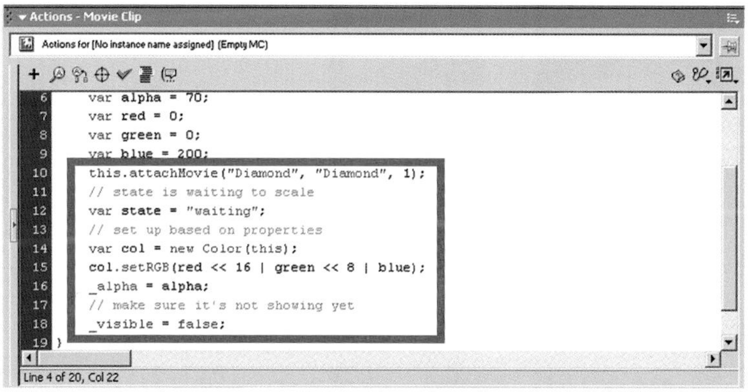

5.18: Add code to the `onClipEvent(load)` *event handler that creates an instance of the Diamond MC clip within the Empty MC clip and sets up the color, alpha, and visibility.*

3. Attach the Diamond Movie Clip and Add Color

Add the following ActionScript within the `onClipEvent(load)` event handler, below the code from the previous step (above the last brace).

```
this.attachMovie("Diamond", "Diamond", 1);
// state is waiting to scale
var state = "waiting";
// set up based on properties
var col = new Color(this);
```

continues

```
col.setRGB(red << 16 | green << 8 | blue);
_alpha = alpha;
// make sure it's not showing yet
_visible = false;
```

The first line of code uses the `attachMovie()` method to dynamically generate an instance of the Diamond MC movie clip within the Empty MC movie clip. Unlike the previous example, you're not creating a string of circles. You need only one diamond, so the `attachMovie()` code is much simpler. The code references the identifier for the Diamond MC clip (Diamond), gives it an instance name (also Diamond), and sets the instance of the Diamond MC clip on level 1.

Then you set a variable called *`state`*. This will be used to determine if the diamond is currently scaling or waiting to start scaling. This is important because you want a pause—a waiting time—between each time the diamond scales, and you don't want to start the waiting time while the diamond is still scaling. So the state of the Diamond movie clip starts off as waiting. You cannot just say this:

```
var state = waiting;
```

So you use a string for the *`state`* variable and that works just as well:

```
var state = "waiting";
```

Next the code sets the color of the diamond to the colors you selected using the `Color` object. This `Color` object code works the same as the code you used in the previous example. The code then sets the `_alpha` property to the *`alpha`* variable. Finally, the code sets this movie clip to be invisible by setting the `_visible` property to `false`. The `_visible` property has only two settings: `true`, which means it will be visible, or `false`, which means it will not be visible.

The frequency of the scaling animation will be triggered according to the *`diamondTime`* variable that you created in the previous step. You'll use the `setInterval()` global function, as you did at the end of Chapter 3, "Cursor Interactions," so that the code can control the timing from within the movie clip. Recall that `setInterval()` will make a call to a function at the specified interval. However in order to attach `setInterval()` to this movie clip, you'll need to use a slightly different form of the `setInterval()` function, which requires a method that belongs to the movie that it is attached to. You have worked with Flash's built-in methods in previous examples, but you have not yet created your own method. Next you'll create a method that the `setInterval()` can call in order to start the scaling.

4. Create a Method

Add the following ActionScript within the `onClipEvent(load)` event handler, below the code from the previous step (above the last brace) (5.19).

```
// method for the movie clip
doScale = function () {
   _visible = true;
   _x = Math.random()*Stage.width;
   _y = Math.random()*Stage.height;
   state = "scaling";
   clearInterval(scaleId);
};
```

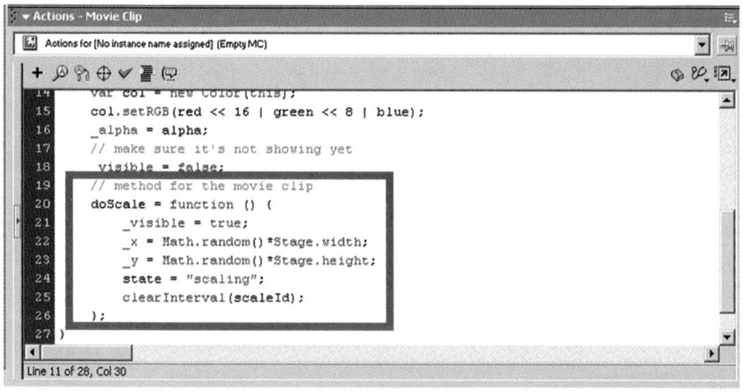

5.19: Create a method called `doScale()` *within the* `OnClipEvent(load)` *event handler.*

The name of the method is *`doScale()`*. It is assigned to a function that has no name. At the end of the function's closing curly brace, there is a semicolon. The method you've written does not take any arguments.

NOTE You can also create methods that take arguments. For example, you could write the first line like this: `doScale = function (myArg, my2arg){`. In this case, the function would take two arguments.

Within the method, the code sets the `_visible` property to `true`, which makes the Diamond MC movie clip visible. Next the code randomly positions the movie clip on the stage using the `Math.random()` function with the `Stage` object `width` and `height` properties. Since the width of the stage is 550, the `_x` property value will be a random number between 0 and 550. The random position for the *y* coordinate works in the same way.

Next the code sets the *`state`* variable to "`scaling`". Now you will be scaling the diamond. So far, you've set the *`state`* variable to its two different states (waiting and scaling); later, you'll write code that uses this variable.

Finally, you stop testing for the interval with the following line:

```
clearInterval(scaleId);
```

The `setInterval()` function is designed to make repeated calls to a function or a method at regular intervals. However, in this case, you're using `setInterval()` to take advantage of the fact that it will count down for you (so you don't need to use the `GetTimer()` function). Therefore, once the *`doScale()`* method has been called with the `setInterval()` function, you need to stop the `setInterval()` function from making another call to the *`doScale()`* method. This is accomplished by using the `clearInterval()` function with the *`scaleId`* variable. Remember that in order to stop the interval from continuing, you need an ID for it, which is what the *`scaleID`* variable will hold.

NOTE Although it may appear that you've called the `clearInterval()` function before you called the `setInterval()` function, you haven't actually called the `clearInterval()` function. It will be called when the *`doScale()`* method is called. Functions need to be defined before they are called. In this case, this is not a problem because the call to the *`doScale()`* method doesn't come until a specific interval. However, in many cases, you need to make sure of the order of your functions and your calls to your functions.

The last thing to do in the `onClipEvent(load)` section is to start the countdown before scaling with the `setInterval()` function.

5. Set the Interval

Add the following ActionScript within the `onClipEvent(load)` event handler, below the code from the previous step (above the last brace) (5.20).

```
scaleId = setInterval(this, "doScale", diamondTime);
```

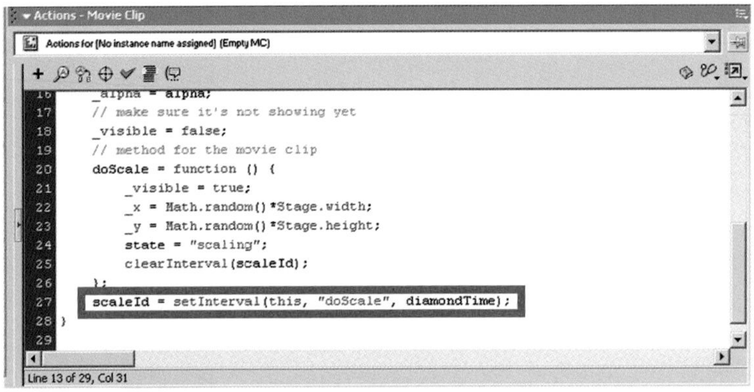

5.20: Add the `setInterval` *code to the bottom of the* `OnClipEvent(load)` *event handler.*

This line of code uses the `setInterval()` function to call the *`doScale()`* method after an interval has passed. In order to attach the `setInterval()` function to a movie clip instead of the main timeline, the first argument references the Empty MC movie clip using the keyword `this`. The second argument is the name of the method, and it must be in quotation marks. The third argument is the length of time to wait, which is determined by the *`diamondTime`* variable. The variable *`scaleId`* is set to equal the return value from the `setInterval()` function.

Now let's add the code that actually performs the scaling animation. You've set up everything in the `onClipEvent(load)` section of the code, and you're ready to move onto the `onClipEvent(enterFrame)` section.

6. Scale the Movie Clip

Add the following ActionScript below the code you've already entered (5.21).

```
onClipEvent(enterFrame) {
   // is ready to scale
```

```
        if (state == "scaling") {
            // growing
            _xscale += scaleIncrement;
            _yscale += scaleIncrement;
        }
    }
```

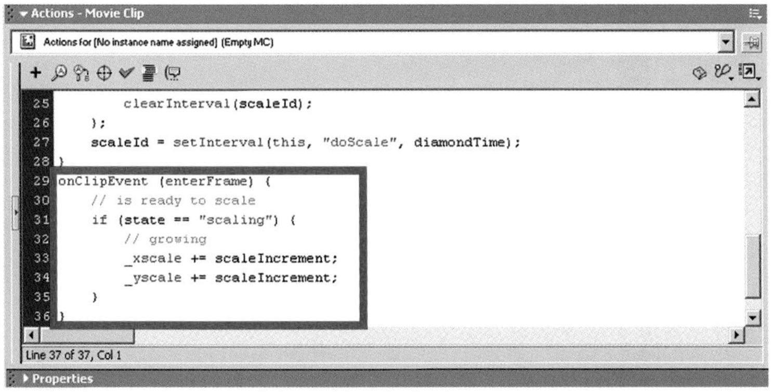

5.21: Write an `onClipEvent(enterFrame)` *event handler that generates the scaling animation.*

This code is contained within an `onClipEvent(enterFrame)` event handler, so as usual, the code within the handler will be executed on every frame. The frame rate for this example file is 39fps, so the code within the `onClipEvent(enterFrame)` event handler will execute 39 times per second.

NOTE In practice, sometimes the CPU cannot actually execute at the frame rate specified. This may be because of other tasks or because there is too much to do within the Flash movie itself.

The `if` statement checks to see if the *state* variable is equal to the string "`scaling`". You set the *state* variable to the string "`scaling`" in the *doScale()* method, so when the *state* is equal to "`scaling`", this code will move onto the two lines within the `if` statement.

The next two lines generate the scaling animation using the `_xscale` and `_yscale` properties. These properties are similar to the `_x` and `_y` properties, but they affect the dimensions of the movie clip, rather than its position on the stage.

The `_xscale` and `_yscale` properties are a percentage value, not a pixel value like the `_width` and `_height` properties. So for the `_xscale` and `_yscale` property, 100 is equal to not scaled at all. Earlier in the code, you set the value of the *scaleIncrement* variable to 100. Each line of code uses the += operator. Therefore, each line of code takes the current value of the `_xscale` and `_yscale` properties and adds 100 to it on every frame (5.22). Using these properties is similar to scaling the graphic using the Free Transform tool to drag the graphic larger or smaller. Because you are setting both the `_xscale` and `_yscale` properties, the ratio will remain the same; in other words, the height and width will remain proportional to each other.

The result is that the size of the movie clip increased by 100 percent high and wide on every frame. If you wanted to make the movie clip grow at a slower rate, you would make

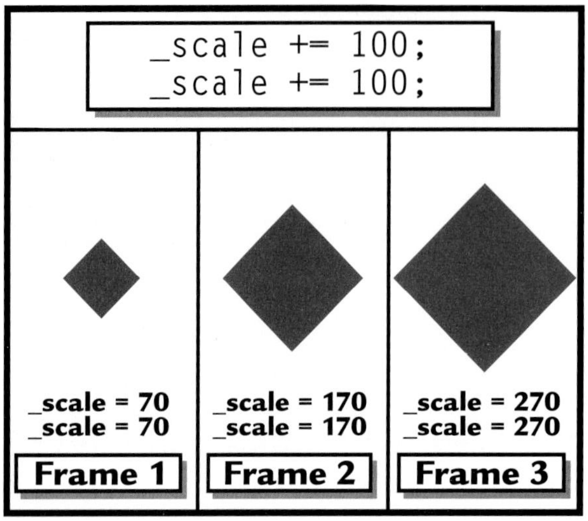

5.22: The code increases the `_xscale` and `_yscale` properties of the movie clip by 100 on each frame.

the value of the *scaleIncrement* variable smaller. Conversely, if you wanted the scaling animation to grow faster, you would make the value of the *scaleIncrement* variable larger.

With the code as it is at this point, the movie clip will continue to scale infinitely. Now let's add some code that imposes some limitations on how much the movie clip will scale.

7. Limit Scaling and Test

Add the following ActionScript to the `onClipEvent(enterFrame)` event handler. Place this code within the `if` statement, below the `_yscale += scaleIncrement;` line of code and above the closing brace for the `if` statement.

```
// limit the scaling animation and reset variables
if (_height > Stage.height * 2 || _width > Stage.width * 2) {
   scaleId = setInterval(this, "doScale", diamondTime);
   _visible = false;
   _xscale = _yscale = 100;
   state = "waiting";
}
```

This `if` statement checks if either the `_height` or `_width` property of the movie clip is two times as big as either the height or width of the stage. The `||` is a logical OR operator (which is different from the `|` bitwise OR used in the `setRGB()` method). The logical OR operator tells the `if` statement that only one of the conditions—the expression on the left of the operator or the one on its right—needs to be true for the instructions within the `if` block to be executed. If the height of the movie clip is bigger than the stage height *or* the width of the movie clip is bigger than the stage width, then the code within the `if` statement is executed.

The first line of code within the `if` statement restarts the `setInterval()` function (5.23). If the movie clip is scaling, then the `clearInterval()` function will have already-cleared the previous instance of the `setInterval()` function. The `setInterval()` function inside this `if` statement starts it again. The `setInterval()` function is the same as the `setInterval()` function you looked at earlier.

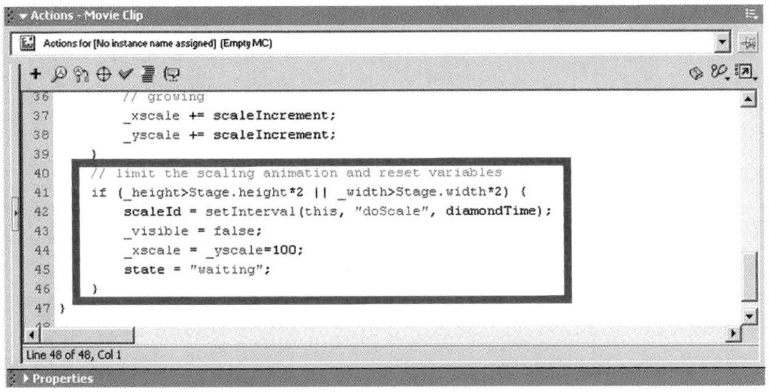

5.23: *Add code to the end of the* `onClipEvent(enterFrame)` *event handler to limit the scaling animation, reset the* `setInterval()` *function, and reset several variables.*

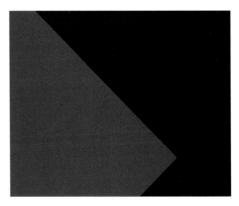

5.24: *Test the movie and notice that the Diamond grows every two seconds.*

Then you hide the movie clip and reset the scale of the movie clip to its original size. By setting the `_xscale` and the `_yscale` properties to 100 (100%), you return the movie clip to its original size.

Finally, you set the *`state`* variable back to `"waiting"`, so that none of code within the `enterFrame` event handler ActionScript will be executed.

Test the movie (5.24). Notice that every 2 seconds, a semitransparent, blue diamond pops up in random places and grows bigger. However, the animation always grows; it never gets smaller. Now let's add some code to make the shape start out big and then shrink.

8. Add Code to Check If the Diamond Should Shrink

Add the following ActionScript within the `onClipEvent(load)` code, after the `_visible = false;` line of code and before the *`doScale()`* method (5.25).

```
// if shrinking, start big
if (scaleType == "shrink") {
   _xscale = _yscale = Stage.width * 2;
}
```

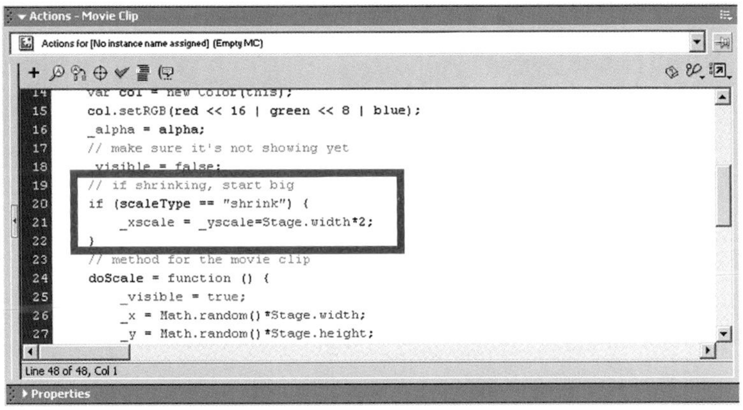

5.25: *Add code to the* `onClipEvent(load)` *handler to check if the movie clip will shrink instead of grow.*

The `if` statement checks to see if the *`scaleType`* variable is set to "`shrink`". If so, the `_xscale` and `_yscale` properties of the movie clip are set to two times the size of the stage width using the `Stage.width` property. The stage is 550 pixels wide in this example, so the movie clip will be set to 1100 pixels high and wide. Now let's add the code that will perform the shrinking animation.

9. Add Code to Start Shrinking the Movie Clip

Add the following ActionScript in the `onClipEvent(enterFrame)` section, directly below the line `if (state == "scaling") {`. The code for enlarging the diamond will now be below this ActionScript (within the `else` statement), and you will need to add a closed curly brace (`}`) at the end of that code due to the `if` statement that checks for *`scaleType`* (5.26).

```
// if shrinking
if (scaleType == "shrink") {
   _xscale -= scaleIncrement;
   _yscale -= scaleIncrement;
   // check if small enough
   if (_height < 10 || _width < 10) {
      scaleId = setInterval(this, "doScale", diamondTime);
      _visible = false;
      _xscale = _yscale = Stage.width;
      state = "waiting";
   }
} else {
```

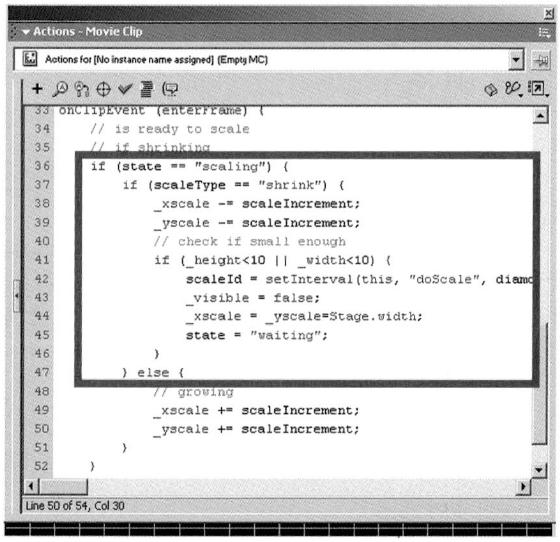

5.26: Add code to the `onClipEvent(enterFrame)` *handler that will shrink the movie clip.*

If the *`scaleType`* variable is set to "`shrink`", the code within the `if` statement is executed. Otherwise, the code within the `else` statement is executed (the code that scales up the movie clip). The next two lines of code decrement the `_xscale` and `_yscale` properties by the value of the *`scaleIncrement`* variable. This will make the movie clip shrink.

The next `if` statement checks the `_height` or `_width` property of the movie clip to see if it has scaled down to 10 pixels. If it has, the code restarts the `setInterval()` function, sets the visibility of the movie clip to invisible, sets the size of the movie clip to the original size (using the `_xscale` and `_yscale` properties), and, finally, sets the *`state`* variable to "`waiting`".

10. Copy the Movie Clip and Test

Copy the Empty MC movie clip and paste it a couple of times on the stage. It doesn't matter where you put the movie clips, because they are randomly placed by the code. Again, have fun changing the initial settings. Try changing the color, the *`diamondTime`* variable, and make sure one of the diamonds is shrinking. Test the movie to observe the results (5.27).

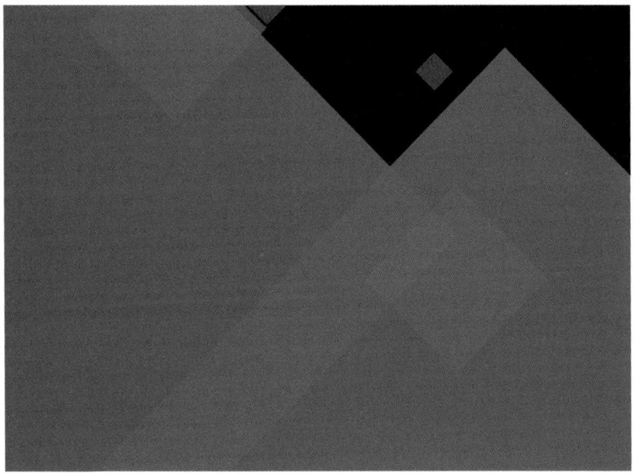

5.27: *Make several copies of the Empty MC movie clip and try adjusting the settings.*

Working with Angles and Rotation

It's great to move objects across the stage, but you can produce even more interesting motion effects using ActionScript. In this example, you'll work with the rotation of an object, spinning it across the stage at different angles. This will involve figuring out the angle you want an object to move across the stage, without using trigonometry.

1. Open the File

Open Chapter5_C_Start.fla. Save the file to your local hard drive as Chapter5_C_Modified.fla. (To see the finished version, open Chapter5_C_Final.fla.) WWW.

Like the previous sample files, this file contains the Empty MC, Circle MC, and Diamond MC movie clips. Additionally, this file includes a new movie clip, named Crooked Circle MC, in the library. The difference between the Circle MC clip and the Crooked Circle MC clip is the registration point. The registration point of the Crooked Circle MC is in the upper-left corner, rather than in the center. The Circle MC, Diamond MC, and Crooked Circle MC movie clips have a linkage property already defined and are named Circle, Diamond, and Crooked, respectively.

There is one layer, named Movement. On the Movement layer, there is once again an instance of the Empty MC clip. As in the previous examples, you will be attaching ActionScript to the Empty MC clip.

2. Add Initialization Code

Attach the following ActionScript to the Empty MC movie clip that is on the stage (5.28).

```
onClipEvent(load) {
   // initialize the properties
   var alpha = 60;
   var rotateIncrement = 5;
```

continues

```
        var moveIncrement = 3;
        var radius = 100;
        // angle must be greater than 0 and less than 91
        var angle = 60;
        // the direction of movement
        var horMovement = "left";
        var verMovement = "up";
    }
```

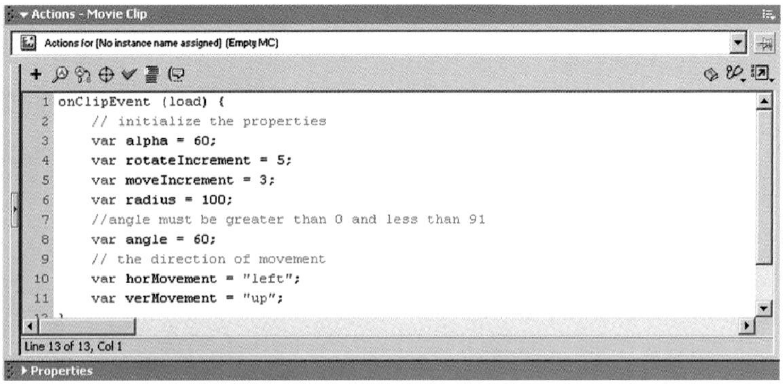

5.28: Apply the `onClipEvent(load)` *handler code to the Empty MC clip that is positioned on the stage.*

As usual, this code in the `onClipEvent(load)` event handler initializes some variables. The *`alpha`* variable is for the `_alpha` property, and the *`rotateIncrement`* variable is for the `_rotation` property. The code will use the *`rotateIncrement`* variable to determine how fast the graphic will rotate about itself. If the value of the *`rotateIncrement`* variable is a negative number, the rotation will be in the counter-clockwise direction.

The *`moveIncrement`* variable is how many pixels in each direction the movement is based on; this will change depending on the angle. The *`radius`* variable is used to determine how big the graphic is. The *`angle`* variable is used to determine an angle between 0 and 91. If the angle is 45, the movement will be equal in the x and y directions. If the *`angle`* is less than 45, the movement will be more in the y direction; if the *`angle`* is greater than 45, the movement will be more in the x direction.

The last two variables determine whether the movement will be up, down, left, right, or not all at. The *`horMovement`* variable will move the graphic along the horizontal plane, toward the right (`horMovement = "right"`), toward the left (`horMovement = "left"`), or not at all (`horMovement = "none"`). The *`verMovement`* variable will move the graphic along the vertical plane, up (`verMovement = "up"`), down (`verMovement = "down"`), or not at all (`verMovement = "none"`). Note that this is a combination of movements. If you choose left and up, the graphic will move from right to left and from bottom to top at an angle. You can also choose none for each, and the graphic will either do no vertical movement and go straight across, or do no horizontal movement and go straight up or down.

Next let's add some code for setting the colors.

3. Add Code to Set the Colors

Add the following ActionScript below the code from the previous step. Add the code within the `onClipEvent(load)` event handler, placing it above the last closing brace (5.29).

```
//color
var red = 0;
var green = 0;
var blue = 200;
// recolor movie clip based on properties
var col = new Color(this);
col.setRGB(red << 16 | green << 8 | blue);
```

This code works the same as the color variables and `Color` object code you used in the previous two examples. Now let's attach the movie clip and set up the movie based on the settings you've made.

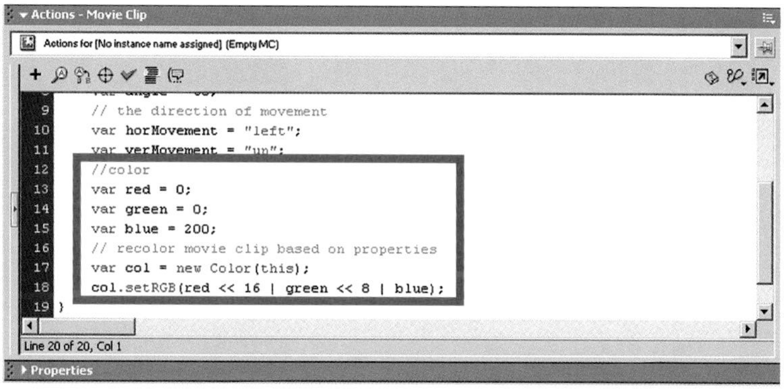

5.29: Add the code for setting the color to the `onClipEvent(load)` *event handler.*

4. Attach the Graphic Movie Clip

Add the following ActionScript below the code from the previous step, within the `onClipEvent(load)` event handler (above the last closing brace) (5.30).

```
// attach the graphic movie clip
this.attachMovie("Diamond", "Diamond", 1);
_alpha = alpha;
_width = _height = radius;
// compute angle
var xRatio = angle / 90;
var yRatio = 1 - xRatio;
```

Once again, the code uses the `attachMovie()` method to create an instance of the Diamond MC movie clip by referencing the Diamond linkage identifier. The `_alpha` property is set to the *`alpha`* variable. The `_width` and `_height` properties of the graphic are set to the *`radius`* variable. Finally, the code computes the ratio of movement in the *x*-axis and *y*-axis based on the *`angle`* variable.

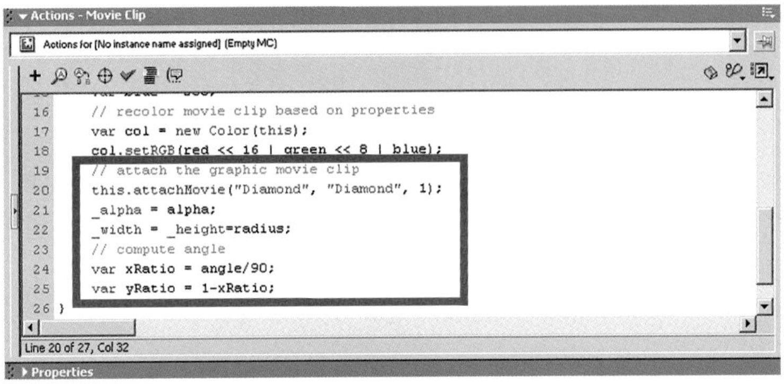

5.30: Add the `attachMovie()` *code and the code for computing the angle to the* `onClipEvent(load)` *event handler.*

You divide the `angle` variable by 90, because that is a square angle (a 90- degree angle is a square angle). This results in a value for the `xRatio` variable that is a number less than 1. Then you subtract the `xRatio` value from 1 to get the `yRatio` value. The `xRatio` value will be used to compute the movement in the *x* direction, and the `yRatio` value will be used to compute the movement in the *y* direction. This is the distance along the *x*-axis compared to the distance along the *y*-axis to travel. The ratio is the comparison.

This code generates the movie clip and establishes some variables. Now let's write some code to actually generate the movement.

5. Rotate the Movie Clip

Add the following ActionScript below the `onClipEvent(load)` code, placing it below the last closing brace for the `onClipEvent(load)` event handler (5.31).

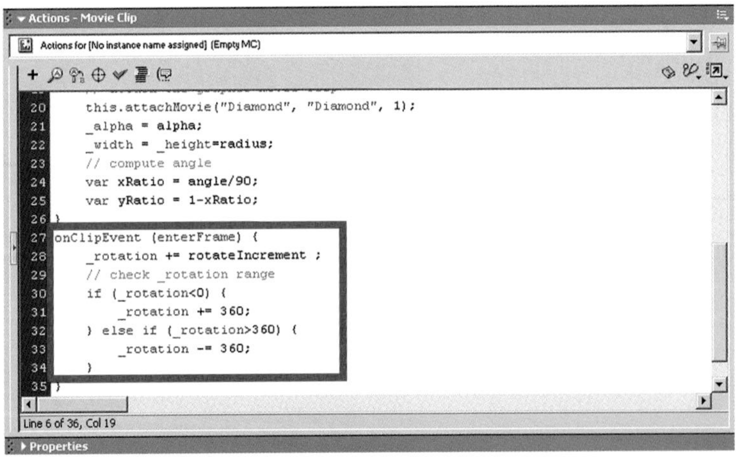

5.31: Begin the `onClipEvent(enterFrame)` *event handler with code that rotates the movie clip.*

```
onClipEvent(enterFrame) {
   _rotation += rotateIncrement;
   // check _rotation range
```

```
    if (_rotation < 0) {
        _rotation += 360;
    } else if (_rotation > 360) {
        _rotation -= 360;
    }
}
```

This code uses the onClipEvent(enterFrame) event handler to create the movement. First, the code rotates the graphic by taking the value of the *rotateIncrement* variable and adding it to _rotation. You set the *rotateIncrement* variable equal to 5 within the onClipEvent(load) event handler, so this code takes the current value of the _rotation property and adds five to it on every frame (5.32).

The if/else if statement keeps the value of the _rotation property between 0 and 360. If _rotation is less than 0, you add 360 to the value of the _rotation property. If _rotation is greater than 360, you subtract 360 from it. This way, the _rotation value is always within the 0 to 360 range.

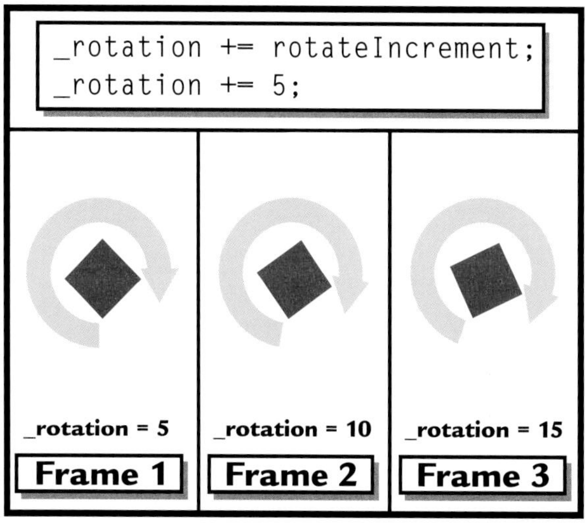

5.32: The value of the rotateIncrement variable is added to the _rotation property on every frame.

NOTE You can make the object rotate in the counter-clockwise direction by using a negative value for the *rotateIncrement* variable. This would subtract the number from the _rotation property, and the movie clip would rotate in the other direction. Checking the boundaries of the _rotation property is not necessary. It works fine, even if the _rotate property is over 360 or a negative number. This code performs the check only for learning purposes and to demonstrate good practice.

Now let's add the movement in the *x* and *y* directions.

6. Move the Movie Clip

Add the following ActionScript below the code you entered in the previous step but still within the onClipEvent(enterFrame) section (5.33).

```
//move in horizontal direction
if (horMovement == "right") {
    _x += moveIncrement * xRatio;
} else if (horMovement == "left") {
    _x -= moveIncrement * xRatio;
}
// move in vertical direction
if (verMovement == "up") {
    _y -= moveIncrement * yRatio;
} else if (verMovement == "down") {
    _y += moveIncrement * yRatio;
}
```

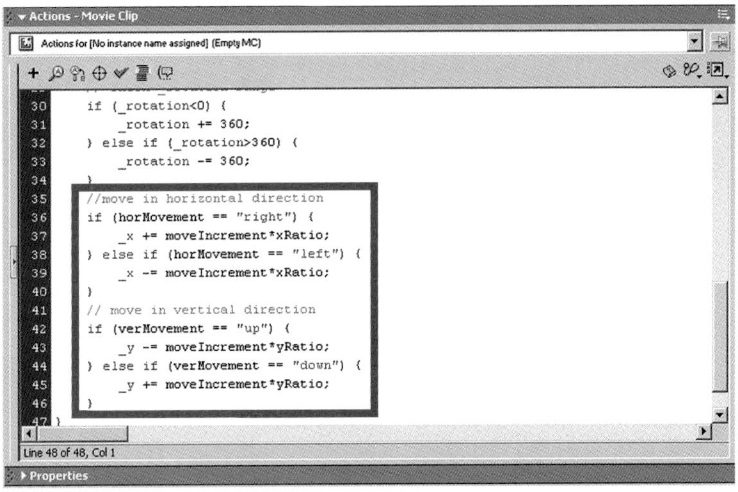

5.33: Add code to the `onClipEvent(enterFrame)` *event handler that moves the movie clip in the* x *and* y *directions, depending on the value of the* `horMovement` *and* `verMovement` *variables.*

This code contains two `if/else if` statements. The first `if/else if` statement checks for horizontal movement (right or left), based on the value of the *`horMovement`* variable. The second `if/else if` statement checks for vertical movement (up or down), based on the value of the *`verMovement`* variable.

If the value of the *`horMovement`* variable is "`right`", the result of the calculation (`moveIncrement * xRatio`) is added to the value of the `_x` property, which moves the movie clip right. If the value of the *`horMovement`* variable is "`left`", the result of the calculation (`moveIncrement * xRatio`) is subtracted from to the `_x` property, which moves the movie clip left. If the value of the *`horMovement`* is "`none`", then there is no movement in the horizontal direction, because there is no ActionScript that deals with this case. The second `if/else if` statement works in a similar manner, using the *`verMovement`*, *`yRatio`*, and `_y` values to move the movie clip downward or upward (or not move it in the vertical direction if the value of *`verMovement`* is "`none`").

Notice that all of the calculations that move the `_x` properties are the same (`moveIncrement * xRatio`). Similarly, the calculations that move the `_y` properties are the same (`moveIncrement * yRatio`). You set the value of the *`moveIncrement`* variable to 3 in the `onClipEvent(load)` event handler, so the calculation is three times the value of the *`xRatio`* variable or three times the value of the *`yRatio`* variable.

Now let's look at how the values for the *`xRatio`* and *`yRatio`* variables were calculated, and then plug them into the calculation to see how they work. Here is the code that calculates the value of the *`xRatio`* and *`yRatio`* variables:

```
var xRatio = angle / 90;
var yRatio = 1 - xRatio;
```

You set the value of the *`angle`* variable to 60 in the `onClipEvent(load)` event handler, so the *`xRatio`* variable is 60 divided by 90, which is 0.67 (60 / 90 = 0.67). The value of the *`yRatio`* variable is the result of 1 minus the value of the *`xRatio`* variable, so *`yRatio`* equals 0.33 (1 – 0.67 = 0.33).

Now that you have values for the `xRatio` and the `yRatio` variables, you can see how they work in the sample code. Earlier, you set the value of the `horMovement` variable to "`left`" and the value of the `verMovement` variable to "`up`" within the `onClipEvent(load)` event handler. Therefore, in this example, the `_x` calculation code is as follows:

```
_x += moveIncrement * xRatio;
```

Plugging in the numbers, you get the following calculation:

```
_x += 3 * 0.67
```

The result is that the `_x` property of the movie clip is increased by 2.01, moving the movie clip approximately 2 pixels on every frame.

The `_y` property is calculated in the same way:

```
_y += moveIncrement * yRatio;
```

And again, plugging in the numbers, you get the following:

```
_y -=3 * 0.33
```

Therefore, for this example, the `_y` property of the movie clip is decreased by 0.99, moving the movie clip approximately 1 pixel on every frame.

So, when this code executes, the movie clip will move to the right and upward at a rate of approximately 2 pixels to the right and 1 pixel up per frame. The code you added in the previous step will also be rotating the movie clip.

Now let's complete the `onClipEvent(enterframe)` code by adding ActionScript to wrap the movie clip around the stage if it goes off the stage.

7. Wrap the Movie Clip Around the Stage and Test

Add the following ActionScript at the bottom of the previous code and within the `onClipEvent(enterFrame)` section (5.34).

```
// check boundary
if (_x < 0) {
   _x = Stage.width;
} else if (_x > Stage.width) {
   _x = 0;
}
if (_y < 0) {
   _y = Stage.height;
} else if (_y > Stage.height) {
   _y = 0;
}
```

This code is similar to the code that you used in Chapter 4, "Used and Reused ActionScript," to wrap the satellites when they reached the end of the stage (**Chapter4_C_Final.fla**). However, in this case, you're not using the `getBounds()` method values for the movie clip (`xMax`, `xMin`, `yMax`, and `yMin`). Instead, this code simply compares the value of the `_x` and `_y` properties to see if they are off the stage, using the center of the movie clip for comparison (with the `getBounds()` variables, the edges of the movie clip are used for comparison).

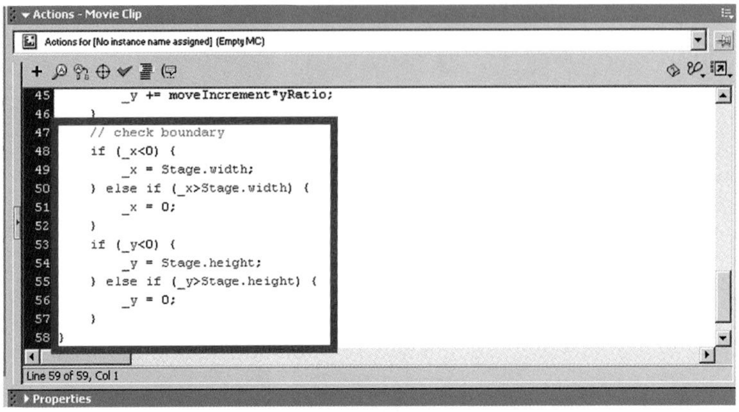

5.34: Add code to the `onClipEvent(enterFrame)` *event handler that wraps the movie clip around to the opposite side of the stage when it goes off any side of the stage.*

For instance, the first `if` statement checks to see if the `_x` property is less than 0. If so, the value of the `_x` property is set to the value of the width of the stage using the `Stage.width` property. The result is that if the movie clip goes off the left edge of the stage, the movie clip will be repositioned to the right edge of the stage.

Test the movie. Notice that the diamond spins and moves at an angle across the stage towards the left and up. Also notice that the movie clip wraps around to the other side of the stage when it goes off the stage. Let's add a couple more instances of this movie clip.

8. Copy the Movie Clip and Test

Copy the Empty MC movie clip on the stage and paste it a couple more times. Change the settings so that you can see the variety that can be created (5.35). Also try changing the movie clip that is being attached from the Diamond MC clip to the Crooked Circle MC clip, using the Crooked linked name.

When you test this, notice that the instance with the Crooked Circle MC clip attached to it doesn't look like it's going in a straight line. It follows a more wavy path. In reality, the Crooked Circle MC clip is rotating around the upper-left corner of the circle rather than the center. This produces the wavy appearance.

So far in this chapter, you've learned how to manipulate the `_x` and `_y` properties, the `_xscale` and `_yscale` properties, and the `_rotation` property to generate animation. As you saw in this last example, you can even combine properties to scale, rotate, and move movie clips. All of these animation effects could have been very roughly emulated with tweens, but they would have been far less customizable and significantly more tedious to implement. Now let's look at one more animation effect you can accomplish with ActionScript: changing colors.

Changing Colors

You can use color changes to produce eye-catching animations. Using ActionScript, you can create a color shift in any range—in the red, green, or blue spectrum, or across all the color ranges. In this example, you'll create a simple animation that changes color.

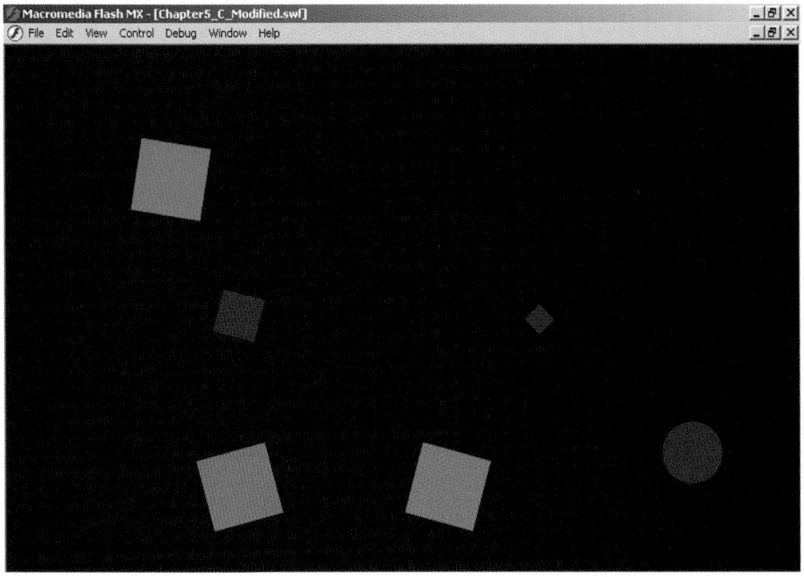

5.35: Duplicate the Empty MC movie clip several times, try various settings, and observe the results.

1. Open the File

Open **Chapter5_D_Start.fla**. Save the file to your local hard drive as **Chapter5_D_Modified.fla**. (To see the finished version, open **Chapter5_D_Final.fla**.)

WWW.

This file is set up like the others you've used in this chapter, with the Empty MC, Circle MC, and Diamond MC clips in the library. The Circle MC and Diamond MC movie clips have a linkage property already defined and are named Circle and Diamond, respectively. There is one layer, named Color, which has an instance of the Empty MC clip, to which you'll attach ActionScript.

2. Add Initialization Code

Attach the following ActionScript to the Empty MC movie clip that is on the stage (5.36).

```
onClipEvent(load) {
   // init our variables
   var alpha = 80;
   var radius = 155;
   var red = 30;
   var green = 5;
   var blue = 200;
   // what color range to change
   var changeRed = true;
   var changeBlue = true;
   var changeGreen = false;
   //what direction in the color range
   var forwardRed = true;
   var forwardBlue = false;
   var forwardGreen = true;
}
```

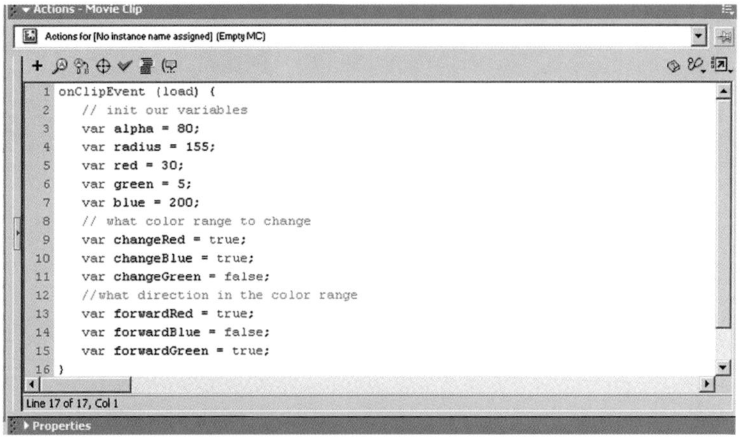

5.36: Initiate the `color` *and* `alpha` *variables within the* `onClipEvent(load)` *event handler.*

As in the previous examples, this code initializes an *alpha* variable, *radius* variable, and three color variables (*red*, *blue*, and *green*).

The next three variables—*changeRed*, *changeBlue*, and *changeGreen*—are used to determine whether to change the color of the object in that range. In this case, *changeRed* and *changeBlue* are set to `true`, and *changeGreen* is set to `false`. So the object will change in the red and blue range, but not in the green range.

The other three variables—*forwardRed*, *forwardBlue*, and *forwardGreen*—determine the direction to start changing the color. If the *forward* variables are set to `true`, you'll change that color range moving up through the colors; otherwise, the color range will move down.

How these variables are used will become more clear when you look at the rest of the code. Now let's add the `Color` object and `attachMovie()` code.

3. Attach the Movie

Add the following ActionScript below the code you entered in the previous steps, within the `onClipEvent(load)` section (5.37).

```
// set up based on properties
var col = new Color(this);
col.setRGB(red << 16 | green << 8 | blue);
// attach the movie clip
this.attachMovie("Diamond", "Diamond", 1);
_alpha = alpha;
_width = _height = radius;
```

At this point, this code should look very familiar. The code uses the `Color` object to set the color of the movie clip, as in previous examples. Next the code uses the `attachMovie()` method to create an instance of the Diamond MC movie clip referencing the linkage identifier, Diamond. Then the code sets the `_alpha` property according to the value of the *alpha* variable. Finally, the dimensions of the movie clip are set according to the value of the *radius* variable.

That completes the setup. Now let's add the animation effect.

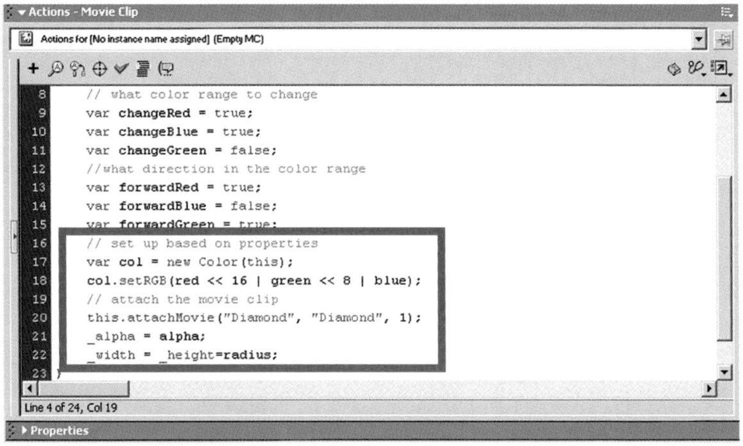

5.37: Complete the `onClipEvent(load)` *event handler with the* `Color` *object and* `attachMovie()` *code, as well as the code that sets the* `_alpha`, `_width`, *and* `_height` *properties.*

4. Add Code to Handle the Blue Color Shift

Add the following ActionScript below the code you added in the previous step. (5.38).

```
onClipEvent(enterFrame) {
   // change the blue color
   if (changeBlue) {
      // change in the forward direction
      if (forwardBlue) {
         if (blue < 255) {
            blue++;
         } else {
            forwardBlue = false;
         }
      //backward change in color
      } else {
         if (blue > 0) {
            blue--;
         } else {
            forwardBlue = true;
         }
      }
   }
}
```

This first portion of the code handles only the blue color shift. Notice the code is composed of an `if/else` statement that contains nested `if/else` statements within the parent `if/else` statement, all contained within one `if` statement. The first `if` statement checks to see if the *`changeBlue`* variable is set to `true` (5.39).

Another way you could have written this is `if (changeBlue == true)`. However, you can write the code more compactly because of how Flash works. Fundamentally, the conditional

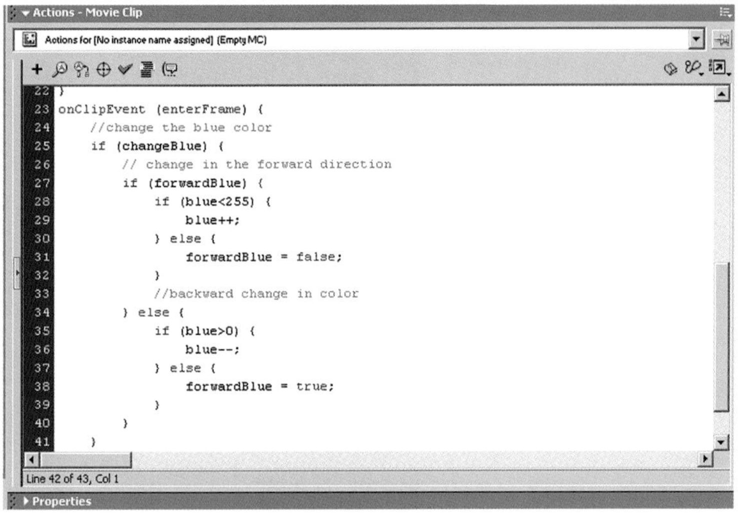

5.38: Begin the `onClipEvent(enterFrame)` *portion of the code with the code that controls the blue color shift.*

tests for something that is `true`. So the variable *`changeBlue`* is already set to `true` when you create the variable. You do not need to go to the trouble of writing `if (changeBlue == true)` because Flash already knows that the value of *`changeBlue`* is `true`.

If the *`changeBlue`* variable is `true`, the code checks to see if the *`forwardBlue`* variable is also `true`. If so, the code checks to see if the value of the *`blue`* variable is less than 255, and then increments it by one if this is the case. If the value of the *`blue`* variable is greater then 255, then the value of the *`forwardBlue`* variable is set to `false`.

If the value of the *`forwardBlue`* variable is set to `false`, then on the next frame, the code within the `else` statement (the `else` statement beneath the `//backward change in color` comment) will execute. If the *`forwardBlue`* variable is set to `false`, then the code checks to see if the value of the *`blue`* variable is greater than 0. If so, the code decrements the value of the *`blue`* variable by one using the `--` operator (`blue--`). If the value of the *`blue`* variable drops below 0, the code sets the value of the *`forwardBlue`* variable back to `true` within the nested `else` statement.

The net effect is that if the *`changeBlue`* variable is set to `true`, then this code cycles the value of the *`blue`* variable back and forth between 0 and 255. In other words, the color of the movie clip will change over time.

Now let's add the rest of the ActionScript for the other two colors.

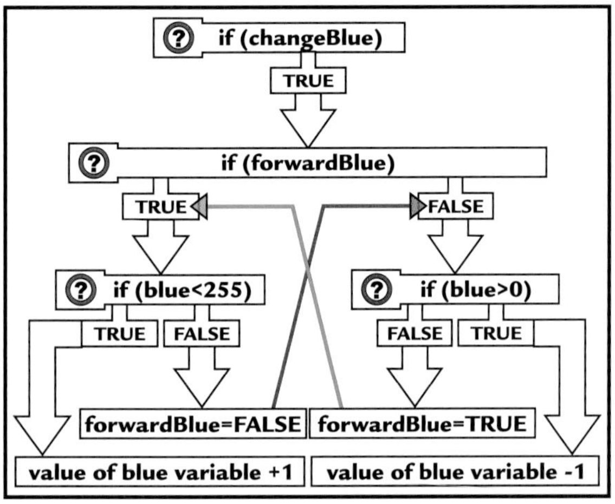

5.39: A flowchart for the `changeBlue` `if` *statement*

5. Add Code to Handle the Red and Green Color Shifts

Add the following ActionScript below the code you entered in the previous example and within the `onClipEvent(enterFrame)` section (5.40).

```
// check for red
if (changeRed) {
   if (forwardRed) {
      if (Red < 255) {
         Red++;
      } else {
         forwardRed = false;
      }
```

```
      // backward red
      } else {
         if (Red > 0) {
            Red--;
         } else {
            forwardRed = true;
         }
      }
   }
   // check for green
   if (changeGreen) {
      if (forwardGreen) {
         if (Green < 255) {
            Green++;
         } else {
            forwardGreen = false;
         }
      // backward green
      } else {
         if (Green > 0) {
            Green--;
         } else {
            forwardGreen = true;
         }
      }
   }
```

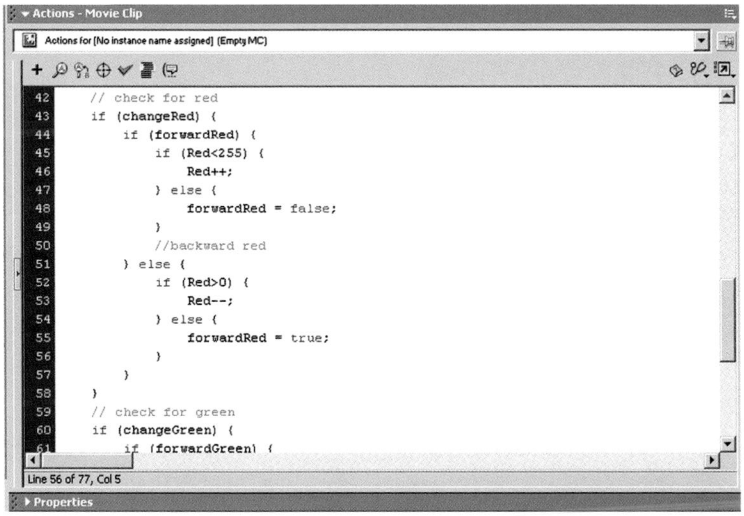

5.40: Add the code for the red and green color controls to the `onClipEvent(enterFrame)` *event handler code.*

This code works the same as the code that increments and decrements the value of the `blue` variable, except that it affects the values of the `red` and `green` variables (between 0 and 255).

Now all you need to do is add the `Color` object code, so that the color of the movie clip will actually change according to the new values of the `blue`, `red`, and `green` variables.

6. Add Code to Change the Color and Test

Finally, to actually change the color, add the last line of ActionScript within the `onClipEvent(enterFrame)` section (5.41).

```
col.setRGB(red << 16 | green << 8 | blue);
```

This will set the movie clip to the appropriate changing color.

Test the movie and watch the changing colors.

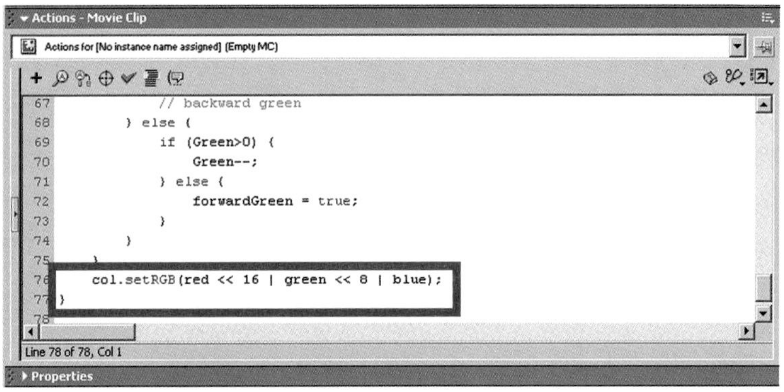

5.41: Complete the `onClipEvent(enterFrame)` *event handler code with the* `Color` *object code that actually changes the color of the movie clip according to the values of the* `blue`, `red`, *and* `green` *variables.*

7. Copy the Movie Clip and Test

Copy the Empty MC movie clip on the stage and paste it several times. Arrange the movie clips so that some of them overlap, and then change the settings. Test the movie, and you'll see interesting results (5.42).

Conclusion

You have experimented with many types of animations—all relatively simple examples. While these animations use some calculations, they mainly involve manipulation of the various properties of movie clips.

Each animation effect, by itself, might not be very visually compelling, but you can combine the effects to achieve more interesting results. For an example of all of the effects combined together, see **Chapter5_E_Final.fla**.

One of the great things about creating the animations this way is that they can easily be used as background animations. As long as the layer the movie clips are placed on is below

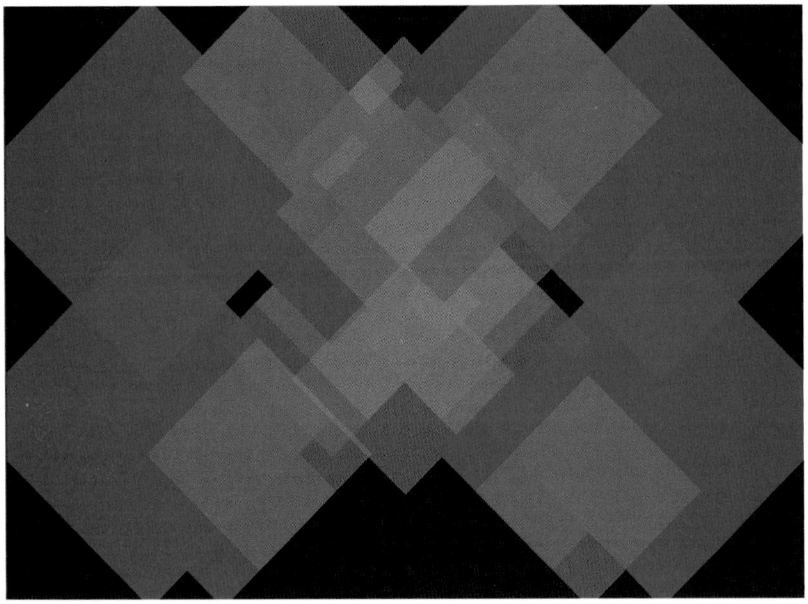

5.42: Try making several copies, changing the variables, and arranging the copies around the stage to make interesting patterns.

any other graphic, they will be in the background, even with the `attachMovie()` call. The only problem with creating animations this way is that if you later find a problem with your code or need to make a change, you need to alter the code in each movie clip duplicate that is on the stage. In Chapter 7, "ActionScript Math," you'll learn how to solve this problem by keeping the ActionScript in one place.

Now you've learned how to use conditional statements, functions, methods, and many built-in features of ActionScript. In the next chapter, you'll build on that knowledge by adding arrays and prototyping to your ActionScript bag of tricks.

CHAPTER six

Working with Text

Flash movies often display text—*in the form of titles, instructions, or simply as a part of a graphic design. Also, reading user input is frequently one of the most useful tasks that Flash can perform. Many websites need to collect information from visitors and process it through a database for some purpose. Flash is an excellent tool for creating a user-friendly "front end" to a database-driven web application.*

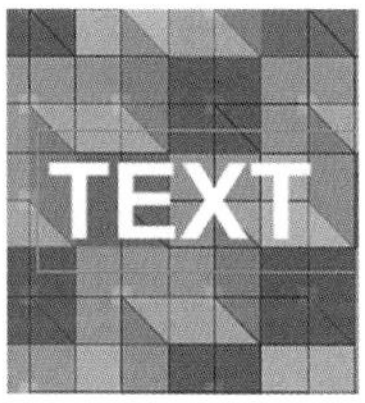
TEXT

In this chapter, you'll learn about Flash MX's new `TextField` *object and how you can use simple text to create dynamic text changes. You'll also learn about user-input and dynamic text fields. Along the way, you'll be introduced to several very powerful ActionScript tools—user-defined objects and arrays—and learn how to extend built-in objects.*

OBJECT

Working with the *TextField* Object

The `TextField` object was introduced in Flash MX to provide a way for ActionScript to dynamically control text. This object allows you to manipulate text in any way that you choose. You can set or change any text property dynamically, including the position, rotation, and scaling. You can also change the font type and size, the text color, and most of the other properties available in the Properties panel.

The examples in this section demonstrate using the `TextField` object for a very simple form of animation—fading text in and out by controlling its `_alpha` property. Along the way, you'll continue to use techniques you've worked with in earlier chapters, such as defining functions.

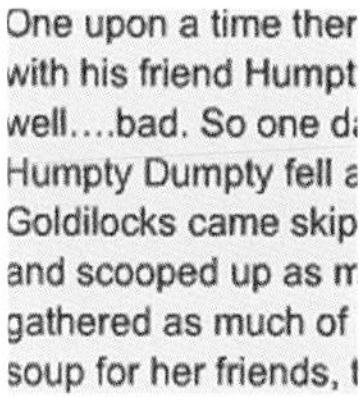
One upon a time ther
with his friend Humpt
well....bad. So one d
Humpty Dumpty fell
Goldilocks came skip
and scooped up as m
gathered as much of
soup for her friends,

NOTE In previous Flash versions, you needed to put the text in a movie clip and then manipulate that movie clip to create many of the effects you'll learn about here. In Flash MX, you can do more with the `TextField` object than with text in a movie clip, and you don't need to place the text in a movie clip.

1. Open the File

WWW. Open **Chapter6_A_Start.fla**. Save it to your local hard drive as **Chapter6_A_Modified.fla** (6.1). (For the final version, see **Chapter6_A_Final.fla.**)

This Flash movie has four layers: Actions, Text1, Text2, and Background. The Actions layer is empty. The Text1 and Text2 layers have a text field placed on them.

In this example, you'll manipulate the appearance of the text in the text fields—specifically, its opacity—using the `TextField` object. You won't change the actual text that is displayed in the text fields.

Open the Properties panel for each of the text fields. Notice that both are dynamic text fields. The `TextField` object works with only the dynamic or input text types. It does not work with static text. Also, in order to manipulate the text using the properties of the `TextField` object, the font must to be embedded.

A text field needs to have an instance name if you plan on using the `TextField` object. The text fields in this example already have instance names assigned to them. The text field on the left ("TEXT") has the name FadingText1, and the text field on the right ("OBJECT") has the name FadingText2. The ability to assign an instance name to a dynamic text field is new to Flash MX. (If you're experienced with earlier versions of Flash, that difference should be a clue that you can now do more with a text field.) Now that you can have an instance name, you can use the instance name in ActionScript to change it on-the-fly.

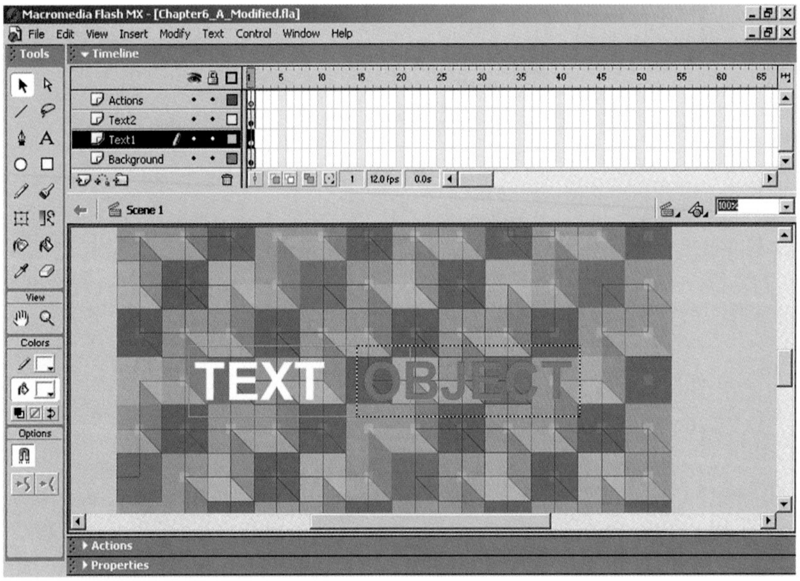

6.1: The Chapter6_A_Modified.fla *file contains two text fields, each on a separate layer.*

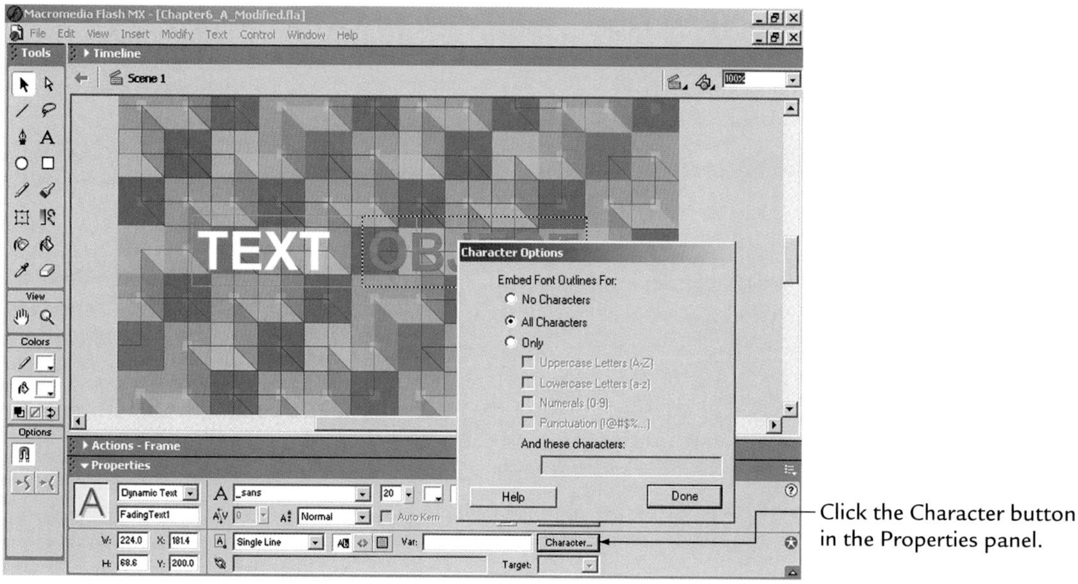

6.2: You can embed fonts in Flash using the Character Options dialog box.

Neither text field has a variable name. Text fields do not need to have a variable name in order to use the methods and properties of the `TextField` object.

Unlike a movie clip or a button, the `TextField` object cannot have ActionScript directly attached to it. Also, as mentioned earlier, the font must be embedded. To embed the font, select the Character button in the Properties panel to open the Character Options dialog box. You'll notice that all of the text is already embedded for both of these text boxes (6.2).

Let's have the text fade by using the `_alpha` property of the `TextField` object.

2. Add Code to Fade the Text

Place the following ActionScript on frame 1 of the Actions layer (6.3).

```
// initialize variables for 1st text
var alpha = 100;
FadingText1._alpha = alpha;
var alphaChange = 5;
// function for FadingText1
function changeText() {
   alpha -= alphaChange;
   FadingText1._alpha = alpha;
}
setInterval(changeText, 50);
```

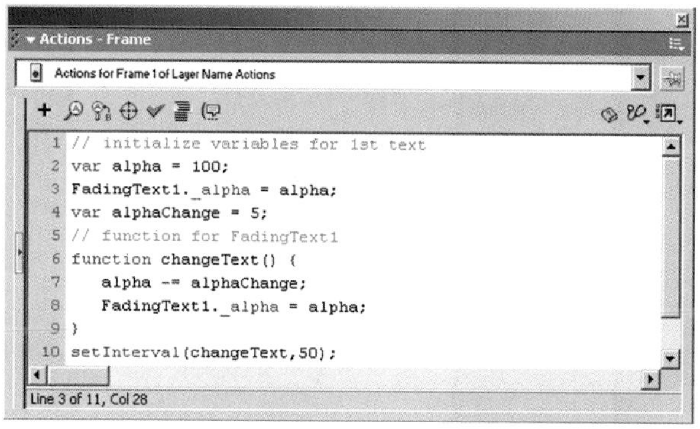

6.3: Add the code shown here to frame 1 of the Actions layer.

This code will affect only the dynamic text field with the instance name FadingText1. The first line in this script establishes a variable named *`alpha`* and sets it to 100. A value of 100 for the alpha (transparency) is fully opaque. The next line of code sets the `_alpha` property of the text field with the instance name FadingText1 to the value of the *alpha* variable. Notice that you reference a `TextField` object's `_alpha` property in the same way as you reference this property for a movie clip. Also notice that you didn't need to use the `new` keyword to start using the FadingText1's `TextField` object. This is because it's a graphical object; in other words, the `TextField` object already exists, like the `MovieClip` and `Button` objects.

The third line in the script initializes a variable named *alphaChange* and sets its value to 5. The *alphaChange* variable will be used to dictate how much the `_alpha` property will change at each interval.

Next the code creates a function named *changeText()*. The *changeText()* function will do the work of changing the `_alpha` property of the text field with the instance name FadingText1. Within the function *changeText()*, the variable *alpha* is decremented by the value of the *alphaChange* variable. The next line within the function updates the `_alpha` property of FadingText1 to the new value of the *alpha* variable.

Finally, the code calls the *changeText()* function every 50 milliseconds, or 20 times per second, using the `setInterval()` function.

3. Test the Movie

Test the movie and notice that the word *TEXT* fades out until you can no longer see it. The word *OBJECT* stays the same, because it's a different `TextField` object. This demonstrates how you can create different looks for different text using the `TextField` object.

> **NOTE** You could achieve this same effect with a simple text field by tweening the alpha across frames. However, if you need to change the text in the text field after it has been tweened, it can get a little tricky, especially if you have multiple keyframes within your tween.

Now let's add some boundaries within the code, so that the `_alpha` property of FadingText1 will not go below 0. Let's write some code so that it will fade to 0% and then go back up to 100% opacity. In other words, the text field will cycle between 100% opacity and 0% opacity (6.4).

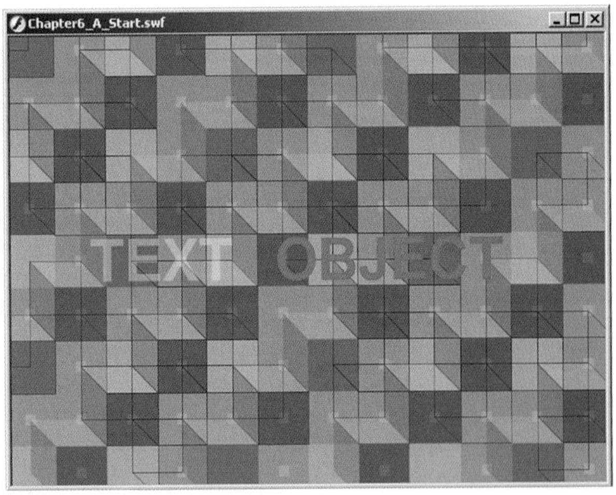

6.4: The word TEXT *fades until it is invisible.*

4. Add Boundaries for the *alpha* Variable and Test

Add the following line below the `var alpha = 100;` line of code (6.5).

```
var direction = "decrease";
```

And then change the function to look like the following code (6.5).

```
function changeText() {
   // do 1st one
   if (direction == "increase") {
      alpha += alphaChange;
      if (alpha > 100) {
         alpha = 100;
         direction = "decrease";
      }
   // decrease 1st one
   } else {
      alpha -= alphaChange;
      if (alpha < 0) {
         alpha = 0;
         direction = "increase";
      }
   }
   FadingText1._alpha = alpha;
}
```

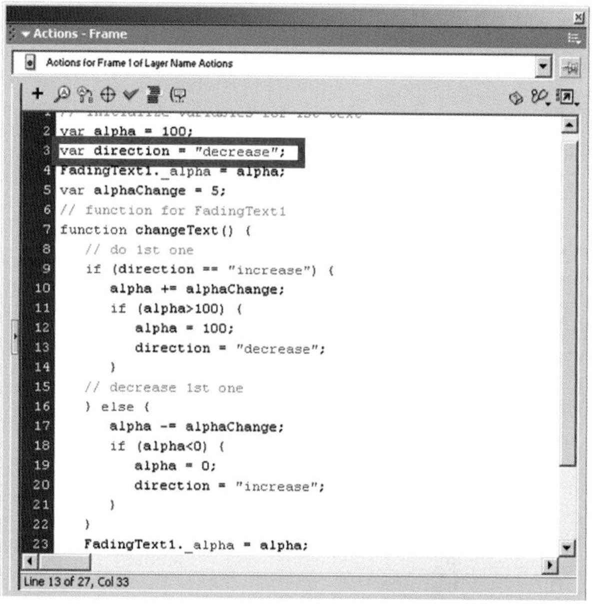

6.5: Add code to make the `_alpha` *property of the FadingText1 text field cycle between 100% and 0% opacity.*

In the initialization section, you added a variable named *`direction`* and set it to "`decrease`". This will determine which way to change the `_alpha` property when the code is first executed.

You've changed the *`changeText()`* function considerably, but at this point in the book, it should not be difficult to understand. First, the code uses an `if/else` conditional to check which direction to change the `_alpha` property, either to increase it or decrease it.

If the value of the *`direction`* variable is set to "`increase`", then the value of the *`alpha`* variable is incremented by the value of the *`alphaChange`* variable every time the function *`changeText()`* is called. If the value of the *`direction`* variable is set to "`decrease`", the value of the *`alpha`* variable is decremented by the value of the *`alphaChange`* variable every time the *`changeText()`* function is called.

After the *`alpha`* variable is incremented or decremented, the code uses a pair of `if` statements to check if the value of the *`alpha`* variable is over 100 or under 0, respectively. If the value of the *`alpha`* variable is greater than 100, the code resets the value of the *`alpha`* variable to 100 and sets the *`direction`* variable to "`decrease`". If the value of the *`alpha`* variable is less than 0, the code resets the value of the *`alpha`* variable to 0 and sets the *`direction`* variable to "`increase`". This is how the *`changeText()`* function cycles the `_alpha` property of the text field FadingText1 back and forth between 100% and 0%.

Test this movie. Notice that the word *TEXT* fades out until you can no longer see it, and then brightens until it is fully visible again. The word *OBJECT* still does nothing. Let's add some code to make this text behave the same way as *TEXT* behaves.

5. Change FadingText2 and Test

Add the following ActionScript at the very bottom, within the `changeText()` function (6.6).

```
FadingText2._alpha = alpha;
```

Test this version of the movie. Now both words fade and brighten at the same time.

You can use all of the script that you originally entered for the FadingText1 text field simply by referencing the same `alpha` variable. However, what if you want the text fields to change at different rates and in different directions? For that effect, you'll need some way to keep the variables and value information separate for each text field.

6. Create Separate Text Variables

Delete all of the code and add the following code (6.7).

```
// initialize variables for FadingText1
var alpha1 = 100;
var direction1 = "decrease";
var alphaChange1 = 5;
FadingText1._alpha = alpha1;
// initialize variables for FadingText2
var alpha2 = 0;
var direction2 = "increase";
var alphaChange2 = 5;
FadingText2._alpha = alpha2;
```

This code basically initializes two sets of variables: one set for the FadingText1 text field and another set for the FadingText2 text field. These variables are essentially the same as the

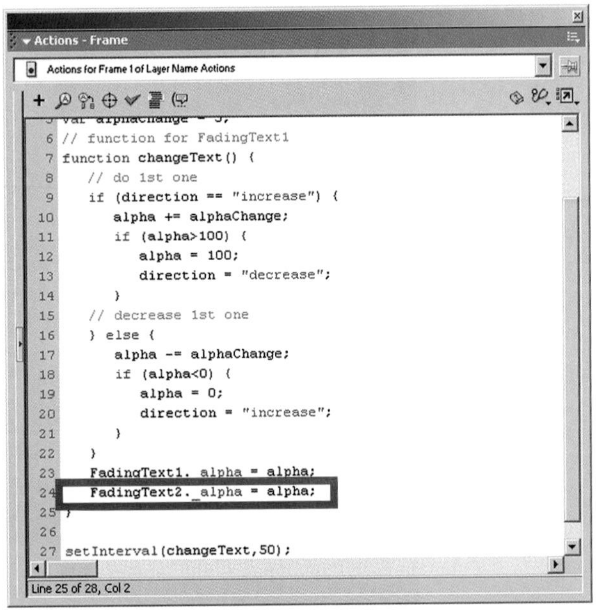

6.6: *Add code to manipulate the* `_alpha` *property of the FadingText2 text field.*

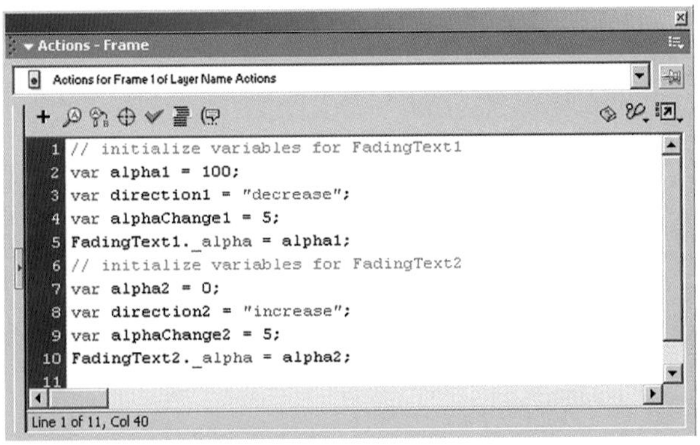

6.7: *Initialize variables for the FadingText1 and FadingText2 text fields.*

original variables, except that the first set of variables are all appended with a `1` (`alpha1`, `direction1`, and `alphaChange1`) for the FadingText1 text field, and the second set of variables are all appended with a `2` for the FadingText2 text field. The main difference between the two sets of variables is in the values for the `alphaN` and `directionN` variables. For FadingText1, the `alpha1` variable is set to 100 and the `direction1` variable is set to "`decrease`". For FadingText2, the `alpha2` variable is set to 0 and the `direction2` variable is set to "`increase`". In other words, the `alphaN` and `directionN` variables are opposite for each text field.

Now let's change the function code.

7. Change the *ChangeText()* Function and Test

Add the following ActionScript after the code you entered in the previous step (6.8).

```
// function for FadingText1
function changeFirstText() {
   // do 1st one
   if (direction1 == "increase") {
      alpha1 += alphaChange1;
      if (alpha1 > 100) {
         alpha1 = 100;
         direction1 = "decrease";
      }
   // decrease 1st one
   } else {
      alpha1 -= alphaChange1;
      if (alpha1 < 0) {
         alpha1 = 0;
         direction1 = "increase";
      }
   }
   FadingText1._alpha = alpha1;
}
// function for FadingText2
function changeSecondText() {
   // do the second alpha
   if (direction2 == "increase") {
      alpha2 += alphaChange2;
      if (alpha2 > 100) {
         alpha2 = 100;
         direction2 = "decrease";
      }
   // decrease 2nd one
   } else {
      alpha2 -= alphaChange2;
      if (alpha2 < 0) {
         alpha2 = 0;
         direction2 = "increase";
      }
   }
```

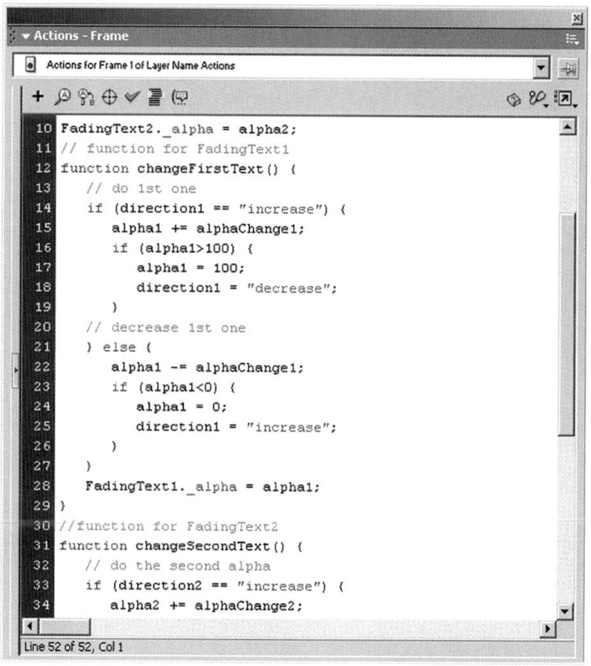

6.8: Write functions to animate each of the text fields.

continues

```
    FadingText2._alpha = alpha2;
}
// call the functions at slightly offset intervals
setInterval(changeFirstText, 50);
setInterval(changeSecondText, 75);
```

That's a lot of ActionScript, but notice that it's very repetitious. You've written two functions that do the same thing as the original function. The *changeFirstText()* function handles FadingText1 using its respective variables, and the *changeSecondText()* function handles FadingText2 using its respective variables. The main difference is that there are now two `setInterval()` functions, one for each function. Notice that the timing is slightly different. The `setInterval()` function that calls the *changeFirstText()* function is set to repeat every 50 milliseconds. The `setInterval()` function that calls the *changeSecondText()* function is set to repeat every 75 milliseconds.

Test the movie. Notice that each text field animates in the opposite direction and at a slightly different rate.

Now let's use another one of the `TextField` object's properties—the `textColor` property. As you would expect, this property controls the color of the text associated with the `TextField` object.

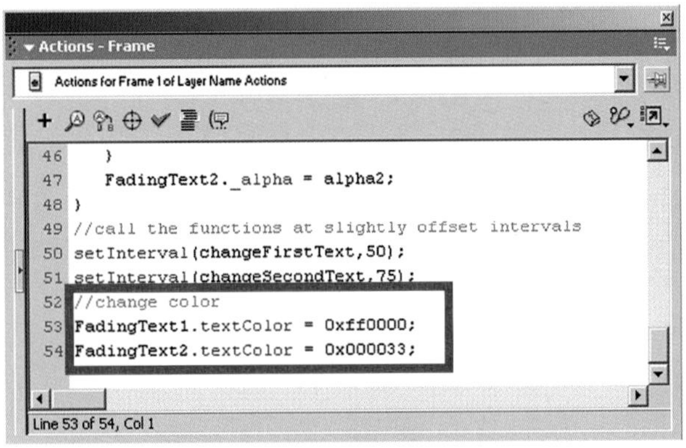

6.9: Change the color of the text fields.

8. Change the Text Color and Test

At the bottom of the ActionScript you entered in the previous step, add the following code (6.9).

```
// change color
FadingText1.textColor = 0xff0000;
FadingText2.textColor = 0x000033;
```

The code uses the `textColor` property of the `TextField` to set the FadingText1 and FadingText2 text to different colors than the text is actually.

Test this version of the movie. You'll notice that the text is now a different color than it was originally. This demonstrates how you can easily change the color of text dynamically.

NOTE Changing the color of text dynamically using the `TextField` object's `textColor` property is a new capability in Flash MX. You could do this in earlier versions by placing the text in a movie clip. In this case, you would need two movie clips, because you want each text field to act differently. In Flash MX, you can now animate any number of properties for a text field, without needing to put the text in movie clips.

This example works fine. The problem is that the code and the variable names are repetitive, which can be quite confusing. Whenever you see repetitive code, you should try to figure out a way to get rid of some of the repetition. In the next section, you'll see how you can create user-defined objects and extend existing objects to avoid repetition and organize your variables.

Creating User-Defined Objects and Extending Existing Objects

In Chapter 4, "Used and Reused ActionScript," you learned how the `Date` object actually stores several pieces of information, which you can extract by using the `get...` methods. You can generate this same level of functionality by creating your own object or by extending an existing object. Both of these techniques help you to organize your variable information.

In the previous example, you needed to keep all of the variables for each of the `TextField` objects separate from one another. This can be accomplished by creating a special object using the generic `Object` object. Unlike the `Date` object, which contains only time-related information, an object that you create can contain exactly what you want. Similarly, you can extend the existing `TextField` object by adding properties to it.

First, let's rewrite the previous example so that the variables related to the two text fields (FadingText1 and FadingText2) are stored in two different objects. You'll use a user-defined object, the `Object` object, to hold all the variables for each of the text fields.

1. Open the File

Open **Chapter6_B_Start.fla** (6.10). Save it to your local hard drive as **Chapter6_B_Modified.fla.** (For the final version, see **Chapter6_B_Final.fla.**) WWW.

This Flash movie starts with the same setup as the previous example.

In the previous example, you used a number at the end of the variable names to distinguish which variable went to which text field. In this case, you're going to create an object that will do that for you.

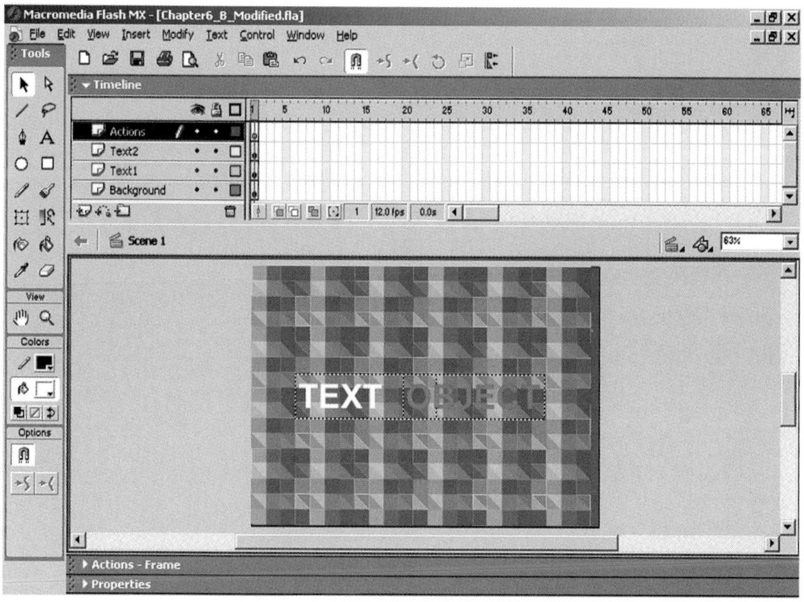

6.10: The **Chapter6_B_Modified.fla** *file has the same setup as the previous example (except for the different background, which is just to help visually distinguish it from the previous example).*

2. Create an Object

Attach the following ActionScript to the frame 1 of the Actions layer (6.11).

```
// init
var TextObj1 = new Object();
TextObj1.alpha = 90;
TextObj1.alphaDir = "decrease";
TextObj1.alphaChange = 5;
TextObj1.Text = FadingText1;
```

As you can see, creating your own object is actually very straightforward. The first line of code creates the object using the generic `Object` object.

To create a new object, you simply give the object a name, which is *`TextObj1`* in this example, and set it equal to `new Object()`. As in examples in previous chapters, the keyword `new` creates a new instance of an object. In this case, you're creating a new instance of type `Object`, named *`TextObj1`*. This is the object that will contain all the information for the FadingText1 text field.

The information that is in the *`TextObj1`* object is called its properties. The rest of the code creates the properties for the *`TextObj1`* object (6.12). As you create each of the properties, you also give it a value. The code adds a series of properties to the *`TextObj1`* object by naming the object, giving the property a name, and then giving the property a value. For instance, the code `TextObj1.alpha = 90` creates a property of the *`TextObj1`* object called *`alpha`* and sets its value to 90. So all you need to do to add properties to the user-defined object is write the object's name, followed by a dot, the name of the property, an equal sign, and the value of the property.

NOTE The `Object` object is very flexible—you can add new properties at any time in the ActionScript, not just at the beginning when the object is created. Some languages are stricter and require you to define all the properties you're going to use when you create the object.

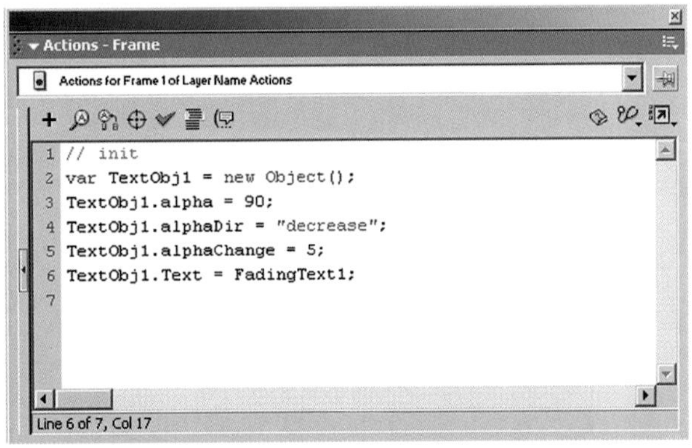

6.11: Create an object called `TextObj1` and the variables for the `TextObj1` object.

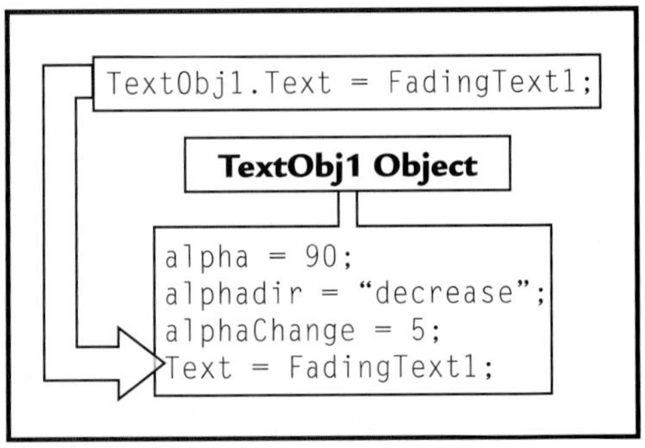

6.12: You can add properties to a user-created object by referencing the object, giving the property a name, and then giving the property a value.

This code creates four properties of the *TextObj1* object: `TextObj1.alpha` to contain the `_alpha` property setting for the FadingText1 text field, `TextObj1.alphaDir` to contain the direction that the `_alpha` property is to be changed, `TextObj1.alphaChange` to determine how large the change will be, and `TextObj1.Text` to contain the instance name of the actual text field, so you can reference it.

Now let's create a function to change the `_alpha` property using this new *TextObj1* object. In fact, as you'll soon see, you'll be able to use your function with any object that has the same properties as the *TextObj1* object.

3. Add a Function

Add the following ActionScript below the code you entered in the previous step (6.13).

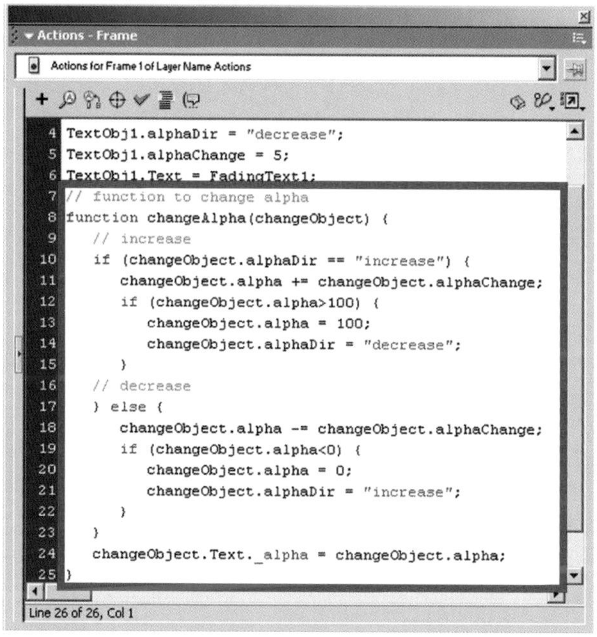

6.13: Add the function code that will change the alpha of the text field.

```
// function to change alpha
function changeAlpha(changeObject) {
   // increase
   if (changeObject.alphaDir == "increase") {
      changeObject.alpha += changeObject.alphaChange;
      if (changeObject.alpha > 100) {
         changeObject.alpha = 100;
         changeObject.alphaDir = "decrease";
      }
   // decrease
   } else {
```

continues

```
            changeObject.alpha -= changeObject.alphaChange;
            if (changeObject.alpha < 0) {
               changeObject.alpha = 0;
               changeObject.alphaDir = "increase";
            }
         }
         changeObject.Text._alpha = changeObject.alpha;
      }
```

This function does the same thing as the corresponding functions in the previous example. While the code might look a little different from the functions in the previous example, they are actually structured the same way.

The `changeAlpha()` function uses an argument called `changeObject`. The `changeObject` argument will contain the same type of information as `TextObj1`. Even though the `changeObject` is a complex variable, with multiple variables and values contained within it, it's still passed in as an argument, just like any other variable.

The first thing the code within the `changeAlpha()` function does is determine in which direction this object changes the `_alpha` property. An `if` statement tests the `changeObject` variable's `alphaDir` property (`changeObject.alphaDir`). If `alphaDir` is equal to "`increase`", the `alpha` property (`changeObject.alpha`) is increased using the `alphaChange` property (`changeObject.alphaChange`).

Next, the code checks for the limits. If the `alpha` property is greater than 100, the top limit, then the direction is reversed. The code also does the same thing for decreasing the `_alpha` property.

Finally, set the text to the new `alpha` setting:

```
changeObject.Text._alpha = changeObject.alpha;
```

You now need to actually call the `changeAlpha()` function in order for this code to work. That's the job of the `setInterval()` function, which you'll add next.

4. Add the *setInterval()* Function and Test

Add the following ActionScript below the code you added in the previous step (6.14).

```
setInterval(changeAlpha, 50, TextObj1);
```

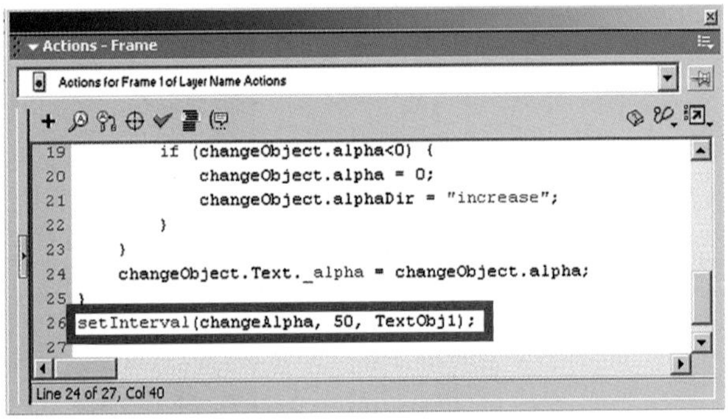

6.14: *Add the* `setInterval()` *function to call the* `changeAlpha()` *function every 50 milliseconds.*

This `setInterval()` function is a little different from the previous `setInterval()` functions you've looked at so far in this book. It contains one extra argument. As usual, the first argument makes the function call (*changeAlpha*), and the second argument specifies the interval time (50 milliseconds), but what does the third argument do?

The `setInterval()` function is defined by Flash so that anything after the interval argument is considered an argument that needs to be passed to the function that is being called. The third argument sends the *TextObj1* object to the function *changeAlpha()*. So, as far as the code is concerned, the following line from the *changeAlpha()* function:

```
if (changeObject.alphaDir == "increase")
```

becomes:

```
if (TextObj1.alphaDir == "increase")
```

NOTE In this case, the *changeAlpha()* function needs only one argument. However, if it needed more, you would just add as many arguments as necessary after the `setInterval()` function's interval argument.

Test the movie. Notice that the word *TEXT* fades and reappears, just as in the previous example. So far, your user-created object hasn't made a big difference, but it will. Now let's apply the same effect to the FadingText2 text field.

5. Add Code for the Second Text Field and Test

Insert the following ActionScript after the `TextObj1.Text = FadingText1;` line of code, before the *changeAlpha()* function (6.15).

```
TextObj2 = new Object();
TextObj2.alpha = 90;
TextObj2.alphaDir = "decrease";
TextObj2.alphaChange = 5;
TextObj2.Text = FadingText2;
```

And add the following at the bottom, below the `setInterval(changeAlpha, 50, TextObj1);` line (6.16).

```
setInterval(changeAlpha, 75, TextObj2);
```

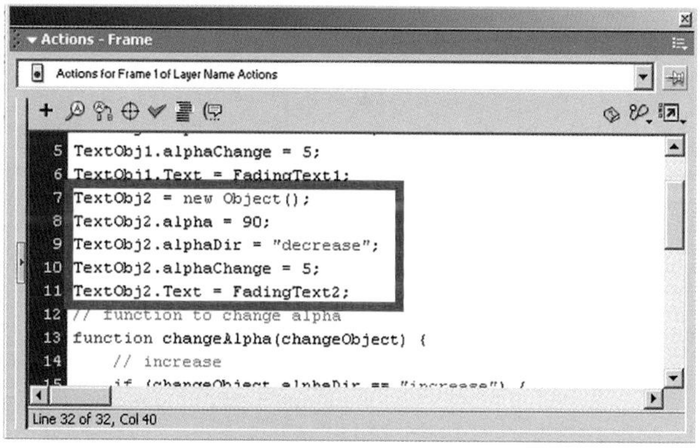

6.15: Create another object.

This code creates another user-defined object for the other text field, FadingText2. You have created an object called *TextObj2* with the same properties as *TextObj1*. Notice that you don't need to create a function for the *TextObj2* object. Instead, you take advantage of the *changeAlpha()* function that you've already written. The `setInterval()` function sends in the *TextObj2* object, argument rather than the *TextObj1* object argument.

Test the movie. You'll see that the text fields fade and reappear in the same way as they did in the previous example. In this case, however, you used less code to accomplish the same effect. You were able to use one function, rather than writing two functions for the different text fields.

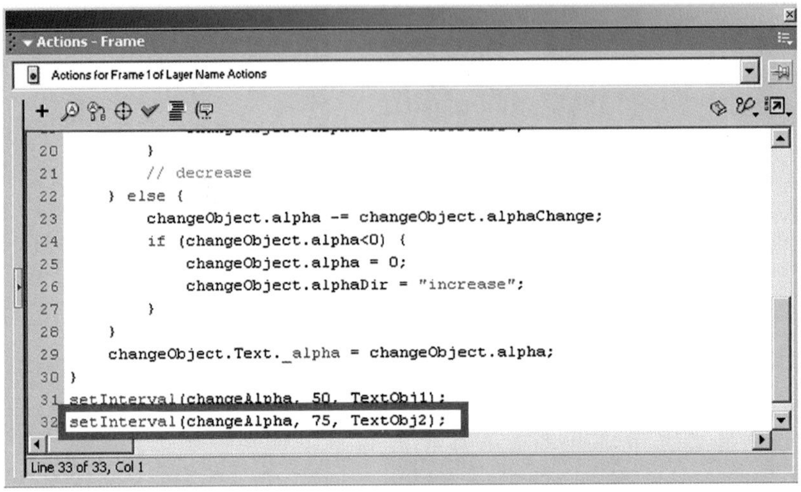

6.16: Add a `setInterval()` *function call to use the new object with the* `changeAlpha()` *function.*

As you've seen, user-defined objects are very useful for holding information that needs to be kept together. An `Object` object is a great empty container. However, rather than starting with an empty object, there is a simpler way. In this case, you already have a container that can be added to—the `TextField` object.

You can add properties to the `TextField` object in the same way you added properties to your *`TextObj1`* and *`TextObj2`* user-defined objects. Using this technique, you *extend* the existing object to give the built-in object added functionality. Let's extend the `TextField` objects, FadingText1 and FadingText2, to see how it works.

6. Extend the *TextField* Object

Change the initialization section of the code to the following (6.17)

```
// init
FadingText1.alpha = 90;
FadingText1.alphaDir = "decrease";
FadingText1.alphaChange = 5;
FadingText2.alpha = 90;
FadingText2.alphaDir = "decrease";
FadingText2.alphaChange = 5;
```

You've made a couple of changes to the previous code. Instead of creating an `Object` object, you're using the existing `TextField` objects, FadingText1 and FadingText2.

You create a property by giving it a value. So the first time Flash sees `FadingText1.alpha` here, it makes room for the property in the `TextField` object and also gets a value for the property (in this case, 90). You create the three properties that you need for both `TextField` objects. You don't need the `Text` property, because you're using the `TextField` object itself.

That was really easy. Now let's pass the `TextField` object to the *`changeAlpha()`* function.

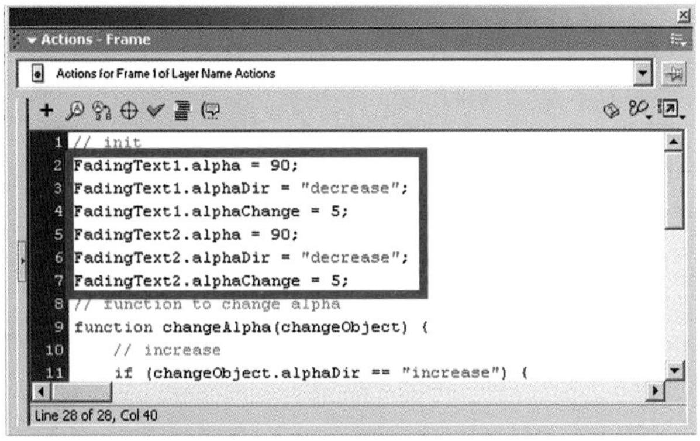

6.17: *Change the code to extend the* `TextField` *object.*

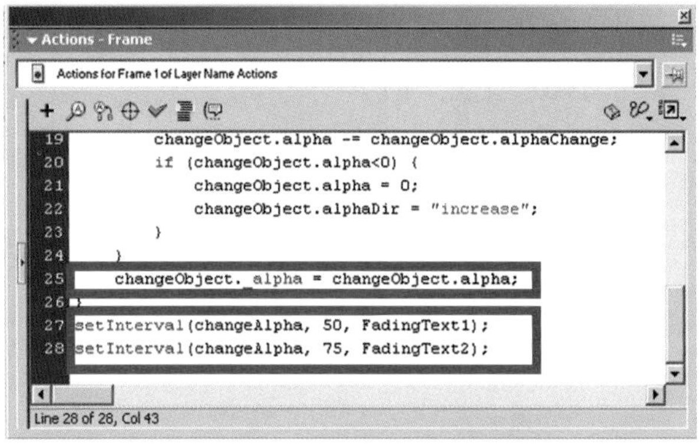

6.18: *Make these changes to use the* `TextField` *object.*

7. Pass the *TextField* Object to the Function and Test

Within the *`changeAlpha()`* function, change the last line to the following (6.18):

```
changeObject._alpha = changeObject.alpha;
```

Then change the `setInterval()` functions to pass the actual `TextField` objects (6.18):

```
setInterval(changeAlpha, 50, FadingText1);
setInterval(changeAlpha, 75, FadingText2);
```

Because you no longer have a `Text` property and you're passing the actual `TextField` object into the *`changeAlpha()`* function, the line that changes the `_alpha` property needs to use the `_alpha` property of the passed-in `TextField` object. You then need to change the passed-in objects from the user-defined objects that you created to the `TextField` objects that you've extended. Again, these are simple changes.

Test this version. Notice you have the same results as with the previous versions. The differences are that you have fewer lines of code than with the first example, and it's less confusing than the second example.

You can extend any of the built-in objects within Flash in the same way. Here, you added properties to a built-in object. You can also add methods to built-in objects, as you'll learn in the next section.

So far, you've worked with dynamically changing the *look* of a piece of text. But Flash also offers the ability to capture what the user enters in a text field, called input text, and use it in your movie. In the next section, you'll learn how to capture user input text and redisplay it in another context.

Using Text Fields and Arrays

Flash offers three types of text fields: Static, Dynamic, and Input. For text that always remains the same, you use static text fields. Dynamic text fields are used to display changing text; in other words, text that is not going to be the same each time you run the program. You use input text fields to accept information entered by the user.

You've used dynamic text in the previous examples in this chapter, but not really in the way dynamic text is meant to be used. Its use was simply a requirement for using the

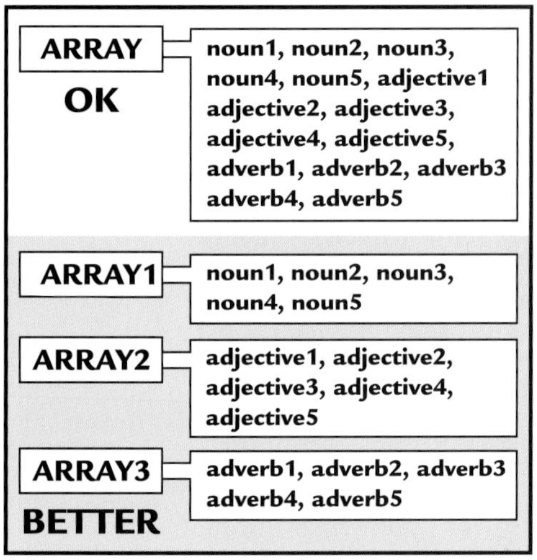

6.19: Arrays can contain different types of information, but it's often easier to read your code when the information types are separated into different arrays.

`TextField` object. However, you've seen how dynamic text is actually used in earlier chapters, such as for the TimerDisplay field in Chapter 4's game example (Chapter4_C_Final.fla).

Both dynamic and input text fields can have changing information in them driven by ActionScript. The main difference between input and dynamic text fields is that the user can enter information into an input text field. The user can select the information from a dynamic text field and copy it, but not enter in information in the field.

In this example, you'll use input text fields in a script that creates a story by capturing words entered by the user. The story will be different each time because the words will be rearranged each time you read the story. You'll manage the words used in the story by employing another very useful ActionScript tool: arrays.

Arrays offer a way to store information and keep it linked together, similar to a user-defined object. Arrays are like lists; they can have anything in them and can be very long. In this example, you'll be working with a list of nouns, adjectives, and adverbs. The list of nouns, adjectives, and adverbs will be integrated within a silly story.

It's possible for an array to contain different types of information, just like a list. So, in the example, you could use one big long list and just figure out where the nouns, adjectives, and adverbs are. For instance, you could construct the array so that the nouns were the first five entries, the adjectives were the next five entries, and the adverbs were the last five entries. However, it's just as easy to create three different arrays (lists), which will help organize your code and make it easier to read for you, the programmer (6.19).

Although this example may seem a little frivolous, it demonstrates how to read user input and store it in arrays. Let's get started.

1. Open the File

WWW. Open Chapter6_C_Start.fla. Save it to your local hard drive as Chapter6_C_Modified.fla. (For the final version, see Chapter6_C_Final.fla.)

There is a lot to this sample file that has already been preconstructed. The movie has three scenes: the Intro scene, the Entry scene, and the Story scene. The Intro scene (6.20) is where you read the original, unaltered story. There is a button on the lower-right side of the screen labeled CONTINUE, which has already been programmed. You won't need to do anything in the Intro scene.

The Entry scene (6.21) is where the user enters in the nouns, adjectives, and adverbs. This scene has 10 layers: Prototypes, Functions, Actions, Buttons, Adverbs, Adjectives, Nouns, Title, Text Back, and Backdrop. You'll only need to be concerned with the Nouns, Adjectives, and Adverbs layers for now. Later, you'll add ActionScript to the Prototypes, Functions, and Actions layers. The other layers are for graphics.

Each of the Nouns, Adjectives, and Adverbs layers contains five input text fields with the instance names, Noun1, Noun2, and so on. The Buttons layer has a button labeled FINISHED, which will be used to advance to the Story scene.

The Story scene (6.22) is where the words entered in the Entry scene are displayed in order to make the silly story even sillier. The Story scene has eight layers: Functions, Actions,

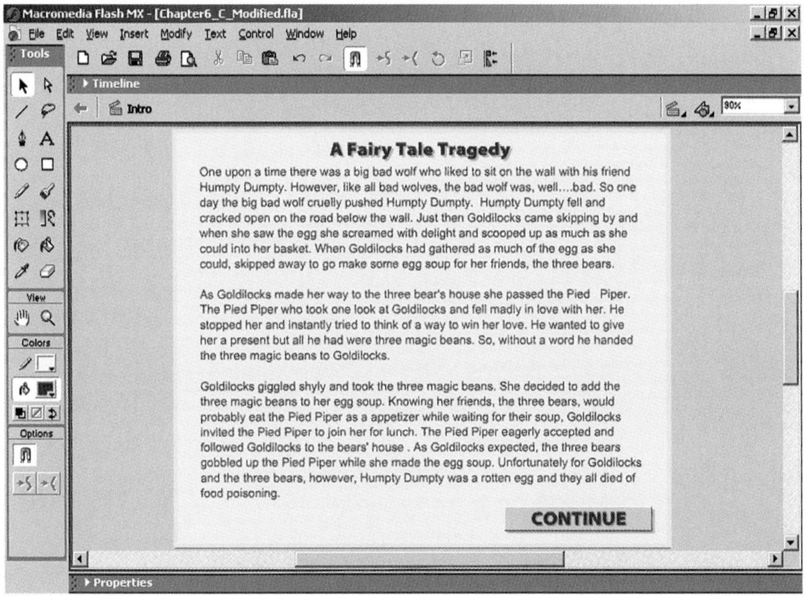
Macromedia Flash MX - [Chapter6_C_Modified.fla]
File Edit View Insert Modify Text Control Window Help
Tools
Timeline
Intro
A Fairy Tale Tragedy
One upon a time there was a big bad wolf who liked to sit on the wall with his friend Humpty Dumpty. However, like all bad wolves, the bad wolf was, well....bad. So one day the big bad wolf cruelly pushed Humpty Dumpty. Humpty Dumpty fell and cracked open on the road below the wall. Just then Goldilocks came skipping by and when she saw the egg she screamed with delight and scooped up as much as she could into her basket. When Goldilocks had gathered as much of the egg as she could, skipped away to go make some egg soup for her friends, the three bears.
As Goldilocks made her way to the three bear's house she passed the Pied Piper. The Pied Piper who took one look at Goldilocks and fell madly in love with her. He stopped her and instantly tried to think of a way to win her love. He wanted to give her a present but all he had were three magic beans. So, without a word he handed the three magic beans to Goldilocks.
Goldilocks giggled shyly and took the three magic beans. She decided to add the three magic beans to her egg soup. Knowing her friends, the three bears, would probably eat the Pied Piper as a appetizer while waiting for their soup, Goldilocks invited the Pied Piper to join her for lunch. The Pied Piper eagerly accepted and followed Goldilocks to the bears' house . As Goldilocks expected, the three bears gobbled up the Pied Piper while she made the egg soup. Unfortunately for Goldilocks and the three bears, however, Humpty Dumpty was a rotten egg and they all died of food poisoning.
CONTINUE
Properties

6.20: The Intro scene lets the viewer read the unaltered story. You can ignore this scene for the purposes of this example.

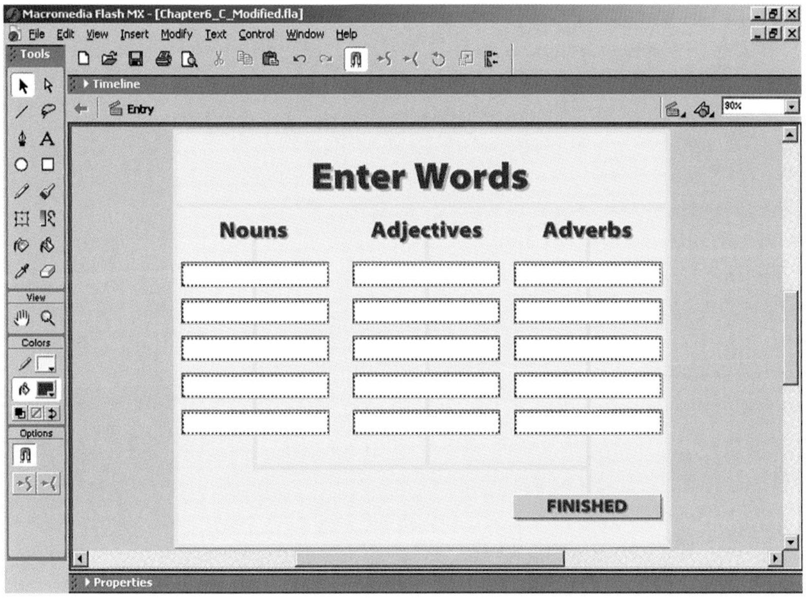
Macromedia Flash MX - [Chapter6_C_Modified.fla]
File Edit View Insert Modify Text Control Window Help
Tools
Timeline
Entry
Enter Words
Nouns
Adjectives
Adverbs
FINISHED
Properties

6.21: The Entry scene contains text fields to let the user enter nouns, adjectives, and verbs that will be displayed on the Story scene.

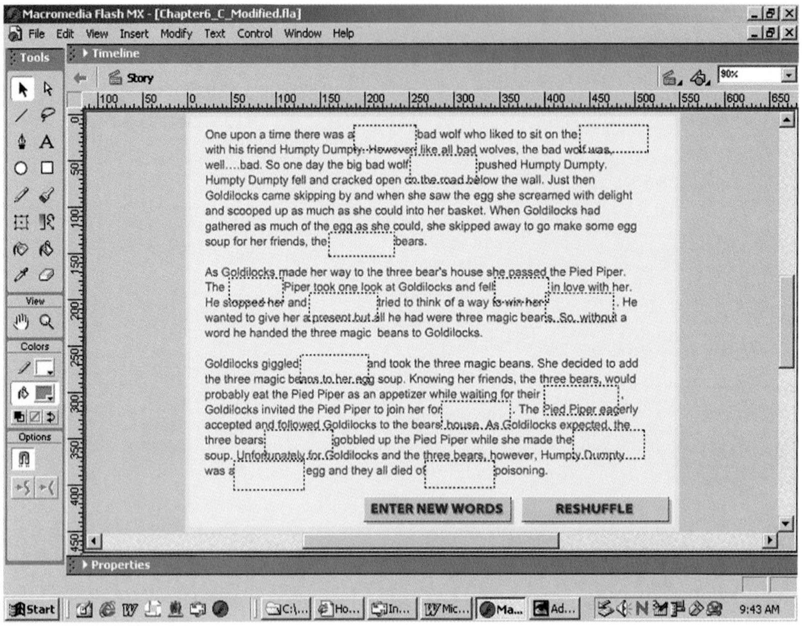

6.22: *The Story scene contains text fields that will display what the user entered, in random order.*

Button, Adverbs, Adjectives, Nouns, Story, and Background. The important layers, again, are the Nouns, Adjectives, and Adverbs layers. Each of these layers has some dynamic text fields named Noun1, Noun2, and so on. These will be related to the words that are entered during the Entry scene. The Story layer has the story on it with spaces in the text for the user-entered words. The Button layer contains two self-explanatory buttons labeled ENTER NEW WORDS and RESHUFFLE.

Let's begin with the Entry scene. Virtually every input form expects users to press Tab after filling in each field to move to the next field. The default tabbing order is based on the order in which the text fields were created. This can produce random results. You can specify how you want the user to tab through the text fields using the `tabIndex` property of the `TextField` object. You can use the `tabIndex` property to establish a specific order for the user to tab through the text fields on your input form. For this example, the order will be all the nouns first, then the adjectives, and then the adverbs. (In a real-world input form, the tab order would simply be the top-to-bottom sequence in which users should fill in the fields.)

2. Set the Tab Order

In the Entry scene, in frame 1 of the Actions layer, add the following ActionScript before the `stop()` (6.23).

```
// set tabbing in appropriate order
var tabCount = 1;
// loop through nouns first
for (var i = 1; i < 6; i++){
   _root["Noun" + i].tabIndex = tabCount;
   tabCount++;
}
```

```
// loop through adjectives
for (var i = 1; i < 6; i++){
    _root["Adj" + i].tabIndex = tabCount;
    tabCount++;
}
// loop through adverbs
for (var i = 1; i < 6; i++){
    _root["Adv" + i].tabIndex = tabCount;
    tabCount++;
}
```

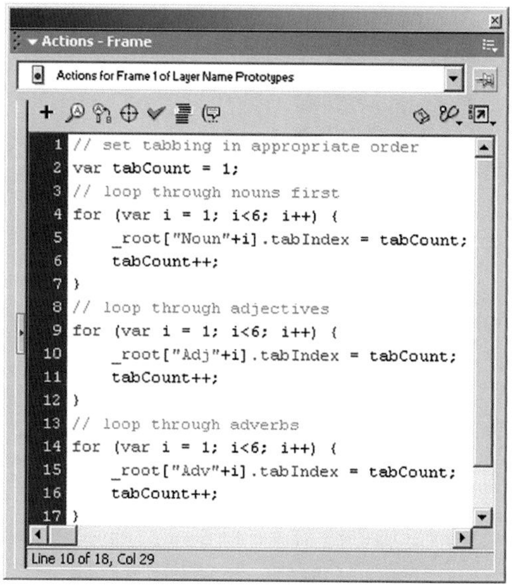

6.23: Add code to control the order in which the user will be able to tab through the text fields.

First, the code sets a variable called *`tabCount`* to 1. The *`tabCount`* variable will be continuously incremented. It will be used for the `tabIndex` value and will make sure that none of the nouns, adjectives, and adverbs have the same `tabIndex`. (If text fields have the same `tabIndex` property, Flash goes to the first text field that has that `tabIndex` when the user presses Tab.)

Notice that the code is a series of three `for` loops, starting with a `for` loop to go through the text fields for the nouns, then a `for` loop to go through the text fields for the adjectives, and finally a `for` loop to go through the text fields for the adverbs. Each of the `for` loops works in essentially the same way, and they run in sequence. In other words, all of the `tabIndex` properties are set for all of the noun text fields before the code moves on to set the `tabIndex` properties for all of the adjective text fields. Let's look at the code for the first `for` loop:

```
for (var i = 1; i < 6; i++){
    _root["Noun"+i].tabIndex = tabCount;
    tabCount++;
}
```

First, a variable named *`i`* is set to 1 in the initialization argument of the `for` loop. Next the conditional section checks if the *`i`* variable is less than 6 (because there are five text fields for each word type). The update section of the `for` loop's arguments increments the variable set in the initialization stage. The line within the `for` loop does all the real work. It uses the value of the *`i`* variable and concatenates it to the string "`Noun`", and then it sets the `tabIndex` property of the referenced text field to the value of the *`tabCount`* variable. The last line increments the *`tabCount`* variable. So the first time through the `for` loop, the *`i`* variable is set to 1 and the *`tabCount`* variable is set to 1. The first line within the `for` loop resolves to the following:

```
Noun1.tabIndex = 1;
```

The result is that the `tabIndex` property for the Noun1 text field is set to 1.

In the second pass through the `for` loop, the `tabIndex` property for the Noun2 text field is set to 2, and so on. When all of the `tabIndex` properties for the noun text fields are done (and the *`i`* variable is greater than 5), the next `for` loop kicks in. At that point, the *`tabCount`* variable is set to 6 and the *`i`* variable is reset to 1. So the Adj1 text field's `tabIndex` property will be set to 6, and the `for` loop will work through the adjective text fields. When you run the movie, you click the top-left text field, and then tab through the text fields in each column sequentially.

Now let's add the code that will capture the user entries and load them into arrays.

3. Create Arrays

Add the following ActionScript in frame 1 of the Functions layer in the Entry scene (6.24).

```
function getEntries() {
   // create arrays to hold user answers
   nounArray = new Array(5);
   adjArray = new Array(5);
   advArray = new Array(5);
   // loop through and grab user answer and put into array
   for (var i = 0; i < nounArray.length; i++) {
      nounArray[i] = _root["Noun" + (i + 1)].text;
      adjArray[i] = _root["Adj" + (i + 1)].text;
      advArray[i] = _root["Adv" + (i + 1)].text;
   }
}
```

The first three lines of code in the `getEntries()` function create three arrays using the `new` keyword and the `Array` object. In this case, the new arrays are set to be five items long by placing 5 in the `Array` argument. This means the arrays will initially be created with five blank spaces, ready to contain five items of information.

NOTE Have you noticed how the names of the functions try to describe what is going on? Also notice that you put the ActionScript on the Functions layer and not on the Actions layer. It would work the same in either layer. When you have a lot of code, it's nice to keep things as descriptive and organized as possible, so when you're looking for a particular line of code, you can easily find it. In this case, all of the functions will go on the Functions layer. The only ActionScript that will go on the Actions layer is calls to these functions and other short lines of code.

Notice that you did not use the `var` keyword in front of the arrays when you created them. This is because you want these arrays to be available everywhere, not just within this function. This is a very good example of the scope of a variable. If you put the word `var` in front of these variables, this would signal to Flash that these variables need to exist only for this function—the *scope* of the arrays would be for the `getEntry()` function only. For example, the `i` variable in the `for` loops exists only for the `for` loop, because it is defined as `var i`.

This is the first time you have defined a variable in a function but want that variable to be used outside the function. In the previous examples, you have defined the variables on the main timeline, and then they were available to the whole movie, even when the keyword `var` was used in front of them. So if you want a variable to be available everywhere, and you're not defining that variable on the main timeline, be careful that you don't use the `var` keyword.

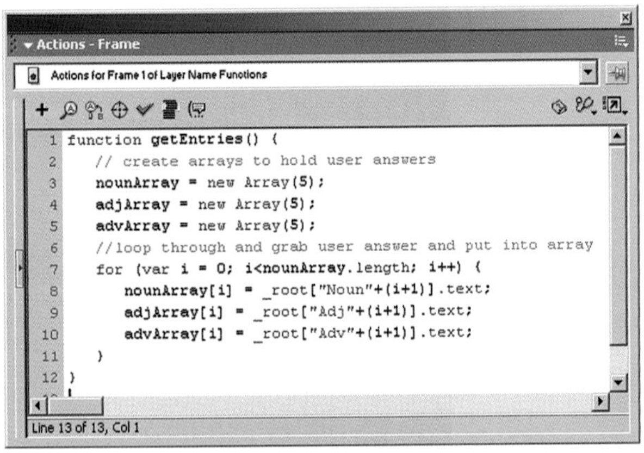

6.24: Create a function that pulls the entries from the text fields and uses them to generate arrays for the nouns, adjectives, and adverbs.

Note that you don't need to specify how big the array should be when you initially create an array. You could easily have written the following:

```
nounArray = new Array();
```

This code would work just fine. Flash will dynamically add more items to an array if your code specifies more items for the array than it already has. For instance, the *nounArray* array that is created in this ActionScript is set to five spaces, or items. However, you can add more items to the array simply by putting something in the sixth place, seventh place, and so on. Flash creates more space within an array if you add items to the array. However, in this example, the code uses the specified length of each of the arrays to load the arrays with information, as you will see in a moment.

Information within an array is accessed like this:

```
nounArray[1]
```

This will access the item that is in place 1. However, in arrays, place 1 is not the first place. Arrays start with 0, so to access the first place of an array, you write:

```
nounArray[0]
```

This is commonly referred to as *zero-indexing* (6.25).

Next you use a `for` loop to load each of the arrays with the information entered by the user. The condition section of the `for` loop uses the length of the *nounArray* to determine when to stop (`nounArray.length`). The `Array` object property `length` returns the number of items in the array. Using a variable is much more flexible than using a literal number. This code will still work if *nounArray* grows to contain 10 words. If you had written `5` instead, the `for` loop would quit after more than five entries.

Notice that the code references *nounArray*'s `length` property only for the conditional section of the `for` loop. This is fine for the example, because each of your arrays has the same length. Therefore, this code works properly only if each array is the same length (or contains the same number of items).

Also notice that you don't need to use the `_root[…]` syntax here to load the arrays, because the names of the arrays are constant. The scope of these arrays is essentially global. The `_root[…]` syntax is used on the text field side because the name of the text field changes.

The code loops through each of the text fields and puts the information into the appropriate spot in the array. It doesn't matter if the user enters anything in the text fields or not. If there is nothing entered in a given text field, the array would simply get an empty string ("").

Let's walk through the `for` loop to see how it works. On the first pass through the `for` loop, the value for *i* is 0. The first line within the `for` loop is as follows:

```
nounArray[i] = _root["Noun" + (i + 1)].text;
```

This resolves to:

```
nounArray[0] = _root["Noun1"].text;
```

or:

```
nounArray[0] = _root.Noun1.text;
```

This code tells Flash to look at the text field named "`Noun1`" on the main timeline and place its contents in the 0 position of the

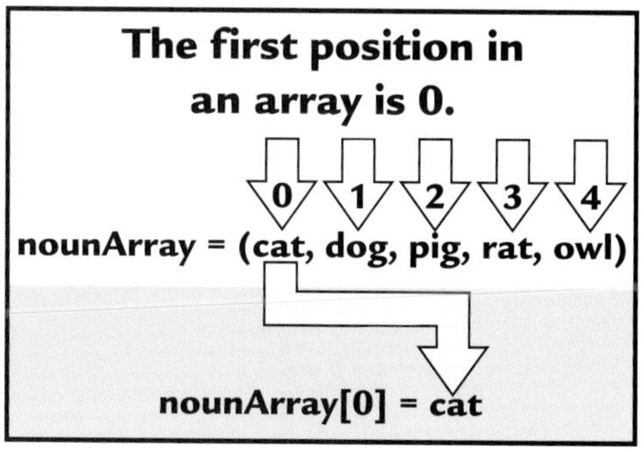

6.25: Arrays in Flash are zero-indexed. The first position in the array is referenced as 0.

array named *nounArray*. The variable *i* used in the text field name has the 1 added to it because the arrays start at 0 and the text fields start at 1.

> **NOTE** The value of this variable *i* is not at all related to the value of the *i* variable used in the `tabIndex` code. This is because the scope of the variable *i* is limited to the `for` loop by the `var` keyword in front of the *i* when it is defined. The *i* variables for each `for` loop have limited scope. As far as Flash is concerned, they do not exist past the end of the `for` loop.

The next line within the `for` loop is:

```
adjArray[i] = _root["Adj" + (i + 1)].text;
```

This does the same thing for the *adjArray* array. The code looks at the text field name "`Adj1`" and places the contents in the 0 position of the adjective array.

This process is repeated five times. Is this right? If the conditional of the `for` loop is set to `i < nounArray.length`, which means that it is *i* < 5, won't the `for` loop cycle only four times? No, because *i* starts off at 0. So the `for` loop will execute five times and set all of the five positions in each of the arrays to the five values of each of the five text fields.

Next let's add some code to the FINISHED button so that it calls the `getEntries()` function that you just created.

4. Add Code to the Finished Button and Test

Attach the following ActionScript to the button labeled FINISHED (6.26).

```
on(release){
   getEntries();
   gotoAndStop("Story", 1);
}
```

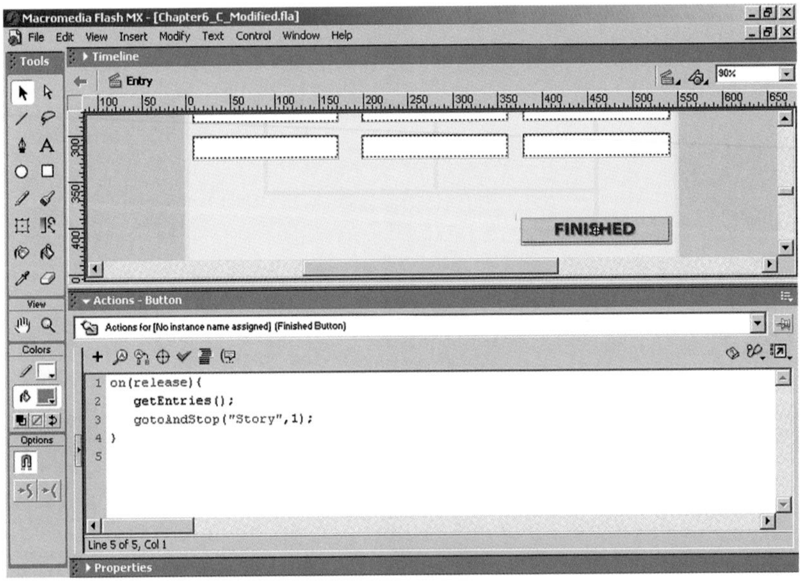

6.26: Add code to the button labeled FINISHED that calls the `getEntries()` function and sends the movie to the Story scene.

First, this code calls the `getEntries()` function you created in the previous step. When the `getEntries()` function executes, all of the user inputs are placed into arrays, so you can use the information later in the story. The code on the FINISHED button also sends the viewer to the Story scene.

Test the movie. Notice that you can click a text field and then tab through the text fields. The tabbing order goes down each column from left to right. You can also press Shift+Tab to go back through the text fields. After you click the FINISHED button, you move to the Story scene, but all you see is the story with holes in it. You'll write some code to plug these holes in the next step. Close the Test Movie window.

5. Load Story Words in the Story Scene and Test

Add the following ActionScript to frame 1 of the Functions layer in the Story scene (6.27):

```
function loadWords() {
   // load words from arrays
   for (var i = 0; i < nounArray.length; i++) {
      _root["Noun" + (i + 1)].text = nounArray[i];
      _root["Adj" + (i + 1)].text = adjArray[i];
      _root["Adv" + (i + 1)].text = advArray[i];
   }
}
```

Also, add the call to `loadWords()` function in frame 1 of the Actions layer before the `stop()` action in the Story scene (6.27).

```
loadWords();
```

In the Story scene, the story has holes within it. At each hole, there is a dynamic text field. If you select one of the text fields, you'll see that it has an instance name of the same style as the input text fields used on the previous scene.

The function called `loadWords()` loops through the different arrays and transfers the contents of the arrays into the text fields on the stage. Once again, the arrays go from 0 to 4. However, the text fields go from 1 to 5, so you need to add a 1 to the *i* variable when referencing the text field.

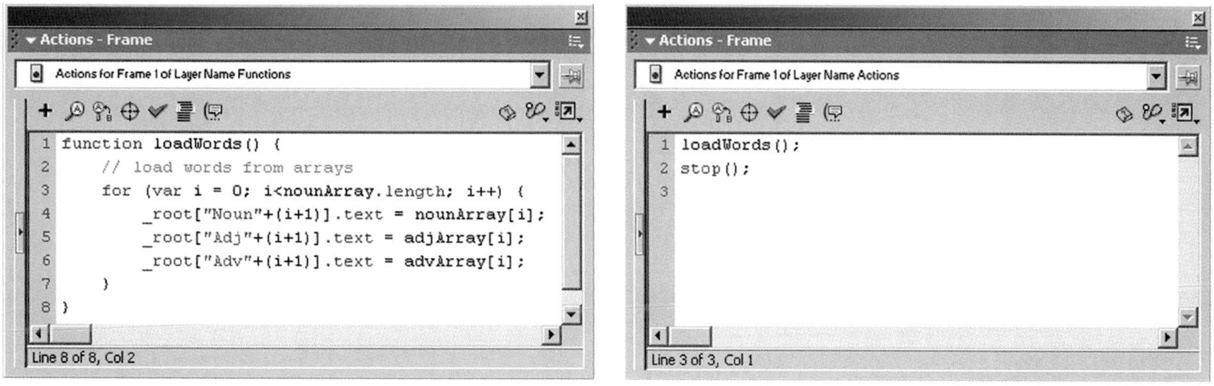

6.27: Write a function that pulls the words from the arrays and places the words in the text fields on the Story scene.

The code within the `for` loop is similar to the code that you wrote to place the contents of the text fields into the arrays, but this time the process is reversed. Let's look at an example:

```
_root["Noun" + (i + 1)].text = nounArray[i];
```

On the first pass through the `for` loop, the value of the *i* variable is 0. So this line of code resolves to the following:

```
_root.Noun1.text = nounArray[0];
```

This code take the contents that are in the 0 position in the *nounArray* array and places them in the text field that has the instance name Noun1.

In this example, the arrays act as a temporary storage receptacle for the contents of each of the text fields. The first function you entered, `getEntries()`, populates the arrays from the input text fields. The second function, `loadWords()`, takes the contents of the arrays to populate the text fields on the Story scene.

Lastly, the code calls the function on the Actions layer. This may seem a little odd. Why make the `loadWords()` into a function at all? Soon you'll see how this function is used to redisplay the words after some shuffling.

Test the movie. Enter some words, and then click the FINISHED button (6.28).

You'll see that the story now actually has words in it (6.29).

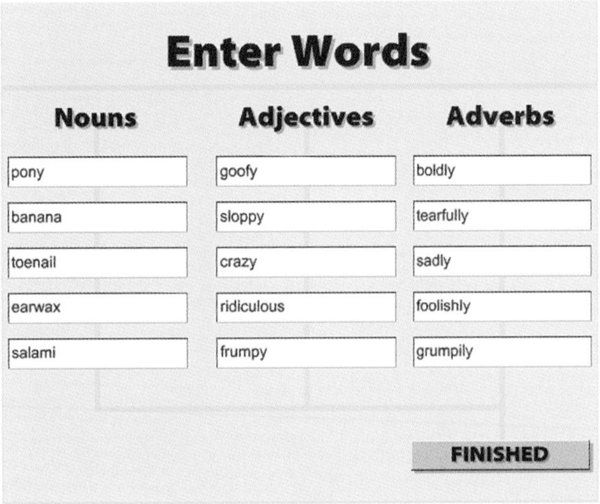
Enter Words
Nouns
Adjectives
Adverbs
pony
goofy
boldly
banana
sloppy
tearfully
toenail
crazy
sadly
earwax
ridiculous
foolishly
salami
frumpy
grumpily
FINISHED

6.28: Type words in the text fields and click the FINISHED button.

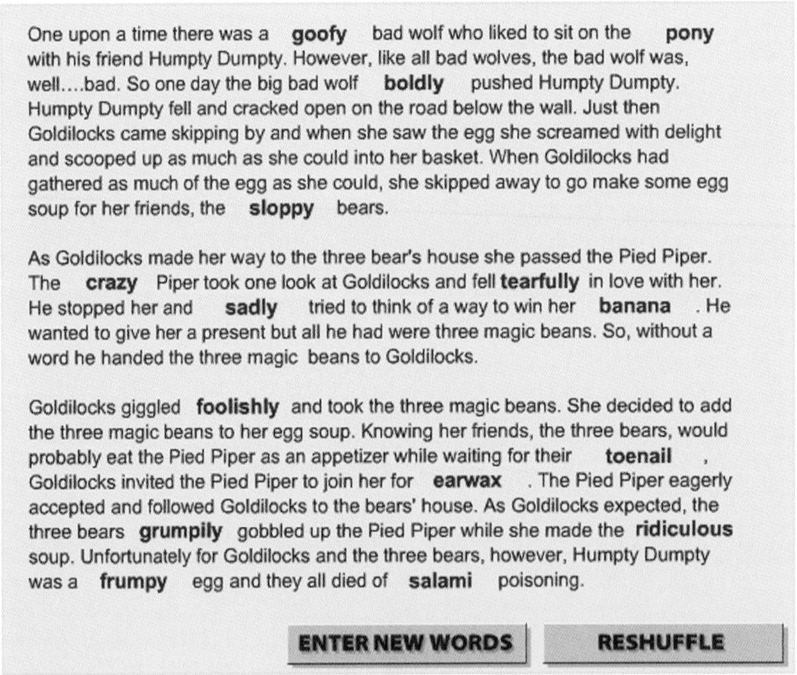
One upon a time there was a goofy bad wolf who liked to sit on the pony with his friend Humpty Dumpty. However, like all bad wolves, the bad wolf was, well....bad. So one day the big bad wolf boldly pushed Humpty Dumpty. Humpty Dumpty fell and cracked open on the road below the wall. Just then Goldilocks came skipping by and when she saw the egg she screamed with delight and scooped up as much as she could into her basket. When Goldilocks had gathered as much of the egg as she could, she skipped away to go make some egg soup for her friends, the sloppy bears.
As Goldilocks made her way to the three bear's house she passed the Pied Piper. The crazy Piper took one look at Goldilocks and fell tearfully in love with her. He stopped her and sadly tried to think of a way to win her banana . He wanted to give her a present but all he had were three magic beans. So, without a word he handed the three magic beans to Goldilocks.
Goldilocks giggled foolishly and took the three magic beans. She decided to add the three magic beans to her egg soup. Knowing her friends, the three bears, would probably eat the Pied Piper as an appetizer while waiting for their toenail , Goldilocks invited the Pied Piper to join her for earwax . The Pied Piper eagerly accepted and followed Goldilocks to the bears' house. As Goldilocks expected, the three bears grumpily gobbled up the Pied Piper while she made the ridiculous soup. Unfortunately for Goldilocks and the three bears, however, Humpty Dumpty was a frumpy egg and they all died of salami poisoning.
ENTER NEW WORDS
RESHUFFLE

6.29: The words will be mixed into the story.

Now let's add some randomness to the story. Let's have the arrays be rearranged after the user enters the words. Then each time the user clicks the RESHUFFLE button, the words will be rearranged and displayed in a different order.

6. Create a Prototype to Copy an Array Object

Add the following ActionScript to frame 1 of the Prototypes layer of the Entry scene (6.30).

```
// extends the Array object
// copies one array into another
// usage - newArray.copy(oldArray)
Array.prototype.copy = function(oldArray) {
   for(var j = 0; j < oldArray.length; j++) {
      this[j] = oldArray[j];
   }
};
```

This code is essentially used to copy one array into another. You might think you could simply write something like the following:

```
adjArray = nounArray;
```

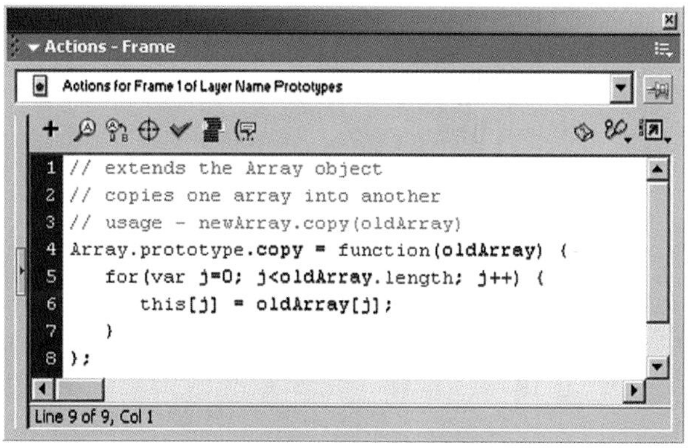

6.30: Add code that will be used to copy one array into another.

Unfortunately, this doesn't work. If you were dealing with normal variables, you could create a completely new variable in this way. Changes in one of the variables would not affect the other variable. However, array variables are more complex. The above statement makes `adjArray` equal to `nounArray`, so they actually become the same array. If you changed something in the `nounArray` array, it would also change in the `adjArray` array. However, in this example (and typically when you copy an array), you want two distinct array variables, not merely two array variables that effectively refer to the same array.

To handle the array-copy operation, you used *prototyping* to create a method for a built-in object. Prototyping is similar to what you did earlier in the chapter, when you extended the properties of the `TextField` object, but you add methods rather than properties. You can add methods to any type of built-in object by using prototyping. This comes in very handy when you want to do something over and over again to a built-in object, such as these arrays.

NOTE *Prototype* is really just a fancy word for defining a function. It can be used to define properties when you get into object-oriented programming (OOP). However, for now, you're using simply using it to define a function and how many arguments it will take.

To create a prototype, you use the keyword `prototype` after the object you want to extend, and you then you add the name of the new method after that.

```
Array.prototype.copy = function (oldArray){
      ..
};
```

This says that you want to add a method called *copy()* to the `Array` object. You're also saying the *copy()* method will execute the following function. Notice this function does not have a name after the keyword `function`. That is because when creating methods, the method name comes before the function name. In this case, the method *copy()* takes an argument, which is the array to copy, *oldArray*. *oldArray* must also be an `Array` object; otherwise, this method won't work.

Within the method there is a `for` loop that loops through the length of the *oldArray* array and uses the keyword `this` to reference the array that this method is being called from. In other words, if you called the *copy()* method from the *nounArray* like this:

```
nounArray.copy(someArray);
```

The keyword `this` would represent the *nounArray* array. So each time through the `for` loop, the `this` array gets a value from the *oldArray* array and places it in the same place or index. This will copy the array.

Next you'll create another prototype to randomize an array.

7. Create a Prototype to Randomize an Array Object

Attach the following ActionScript in frame 1 of the Prototypes layer (6.31), below the code you added in the previous step.

```
// extends the Array object
// randomizes the array
// usage - myArray.Randomize()
Array.prototype.Randomize = function() {
   // new place holder array
   var tempArray = new Array(this.length);
   tempArray.copy(this);
   // go through array of numbers and pick each one only once
   for (var i = 0; i < this.length; i++) {
      var ranIndex = Math.floor(Math.random() * tempArray.length);
      this[i] = tempArray [ranIndex];
      // remove letter used so it's not used again
      tempArray.splice(ranIndex, 1);
   }
};
```

This code, again, uses prototyping to make another method of the `Array` object. This method doesn't take any arguments and is called *Randomize()*.

First, the code creates a temporary array, *tempArray*, of the same length as the `this` array. (Remember that the keyword `this` is the array that called the *Randomize()* method.) The *tempArray* array will be used to make sure no values are repeated. Each time a value is used, it's deleted from the *tempArray* array. After creating the new *tempArray* array, everything from the `this` array is copied into the *tempArray* array, using the *copy()* method that you created in the previous step. For example, if *nounArray* called the *Randomize()* method, and *nounArray* contained this:

```
NounArray = ["sun", "moon", "dog", "cat", "chicken"]
```

tempArray would contain the same items in the exact same order.

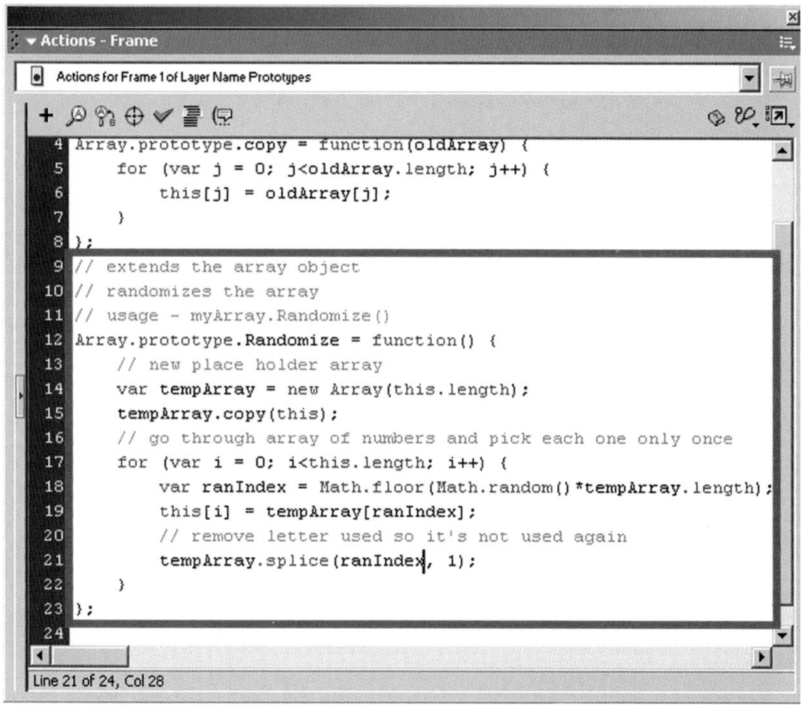
Actions - Frame
Actions for Frame 1 of Layer Name Prototypes
Array.prototype.copy = function(oldArray) {
for (var j = 0; j<oldArray.length; j++) {
this[j] = oldArray[j];
}
};
// extends the array object
// randomizes the array
// usage - myArray.Randomize()
Array.prototype.Randomize = function() {
// new place holder array
var tempArray = new Array(this.length);
tempArray.copy(this);
// go through array of numbers and pick each one only once
for (var i = 0; i<this.length; i++) {
var ranIndex = Math.floor(Math.random()*tempArray.length);
this[i] = tempArray[ranIndex];
// remove letter used so it's not used again
tempArray.splice(ranIndex, 1);
}
};
Line 21 of 24, Col 28

6.31: Add code to randomize the array.

Next is the code that actually does the randomization. The idea is to randomly select a value from the *tempArray* array, put it in a new place in the `this` array, and then delete it from the *tempArray* array, so it cannot be selected again. This means that the *tempArray* array is going to gradually get smaller until there is nothing in it, and the `this` array is gradually going to change, starting from the first index.

The first line in the `for` loop gets a random number based on the length of *tempArray*. Since this length is going to be changing, this is the perfect way to make sure the number that comes out of the `Math.random()` method is a valid number. Remember that the `Math.random()` method returns a number between 0 and 0.9999, so in order to use this as an array index into the *tempArray* array, you need to multiply it by the length of *tempArray*.

```
Math.random() * tempArray.length;
```

However, this returns a decimal number (between 0 and 4.999, in the first loop's case), but you need an integer. Also remember that the `Array` object is zero-indexed, so only 0 through 4 are possible. If you used `Math.round()`, you could possibly get the number 5, which is not valid. Instead, you use the `Math.floor()` method. This drops all the decimal numbers to leave just an integer.

```
var ranIndex = Math.floor(Math.random() * tempArray.length);
```

The integer result is stored in the *ranIndex* variable. Next, the item that is in the place *ranIndex* of the *tempArray* array is moved to the *i* place of the `this` array. Then the item that is in the *ranIndex* place of the *tempArray* array is removed using the `splice()` method. This `splice()` method of the `Array` object removes items from an array based on the starting point, which is the first argument, and the number of items to remove, which is the second argument. In this case, you want to remove only one item, so the second argument is 1.

Let's walk through this for the first loop, with `i = 0`. The *tempArray* array and the `this` array contain the exact same thing:

```
["sun", "moon", "dog", "cat", "chicken"]
```

ranIndex is calculated based on the length of *tempArray*, which is 5. `Math.floor(Math.random() * tempArray.length)` will return a number from 0 to 4. In this case, let's say it returns a value of 3. So *ranIndex* is equal to 3. Then the next line:

```
this[i] = tempArray [ranIndex];
```

resolves to:

```
this[0] = tempArray[3];
```

and the `this` array would look like this:

```
["cat", "moon", "dog", "cat", "chicken"]
```

Notice that there are now two instances of cat in the array, but that will be fixed by the end, because each item in the `this` array is going to get a new value.

Finally the `splice()` method is used:

```
tempArray.splice(ranIndex, 1);
```

which would be:

```
tempArray.splice(3, 1);
```

which is telling the *tempArray* array to remove one item starting at the third place. This is not just telling it to create an empty space; it's also telling the array to close up all holes. So before the `splice()` call, *tempArray* looks like this:

```
["sun", "moon", "dog", "cat", "chicken"]
```

After the `splice()` call, *tempArray* looks like this:

```
["sun", "moon", "dog", "chicken"]
```

Now the *tempArray* has only four items in it, which is what the random selection is based on.

You've created a *Randomize()* method for the arrays. Now let's use it.

8. Randomize the Arrays and Test

Add the following ActionScript in the Functions layer of the Entry scene (6.32).

```
// randomizes arrays
function randomizeArrays() {
   nounArray.Randomize();
   adjArray.Randomize();
   advArray.Randomize();
}
```

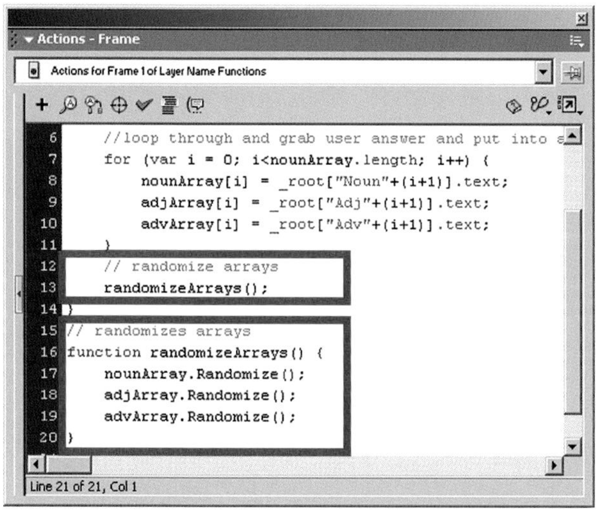

6.32: Add the `randomizeArrays()` *function to the Functions layer.*

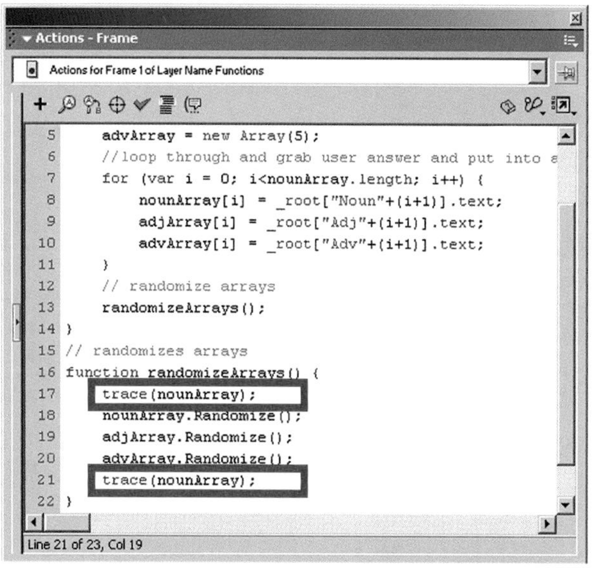

6.33: Add two `trace()` *commands to the* `randomizeArrays()` *function.*

Also, insert the following in the `getEntries()` function at the bottom (6.32).

```
// randomize arrays
randomizeArrays();
```

The first bit of code creates a function called `randomizeArrays()` to randomize each of the arrays. In this function, each of the arrays—`nounArray`, `adjArray`, and `advArray`—is randomized using the `Randomize()` method that you created in the previous step.

Then, within the `getEntries()` function, after the arrays have been loaded, you call the `randomizeArrays()` function, so that the arrays will start out randomized.

Test this version. Notice that the order in which you enter the words is not the same order that they appear in. It is now important to fill in all the words; otherwise, there is a possibility of getting a blank in the story spot. Later you'll add code to make sure that the script doesn't continue if any text fields are blank.

Before continuing with the randomizing, let's take a look at the randomized arrays at this point. You can do this with a simple `trace()` statement.

9. Trace the Arrays

In the `randomizeArrays()` function, put the following ActionScript at the start of the function (6.33), within the function.

```
trace(nounArray);
```

Then put the same line at the bottom of the function, but also within the function (6.33).

This way, you can see what the `nounArray` array looks like before and after the `Randomize()` method is called.

Test the movie and look at the output in the Output panel (6.34). This shows the items of the `nounArray` array before randomization on the first line, and after randomization on the second line. Notice that each item of the `nounArray` array is separated by a comma. This is just the Output panel's way of displaying an array.

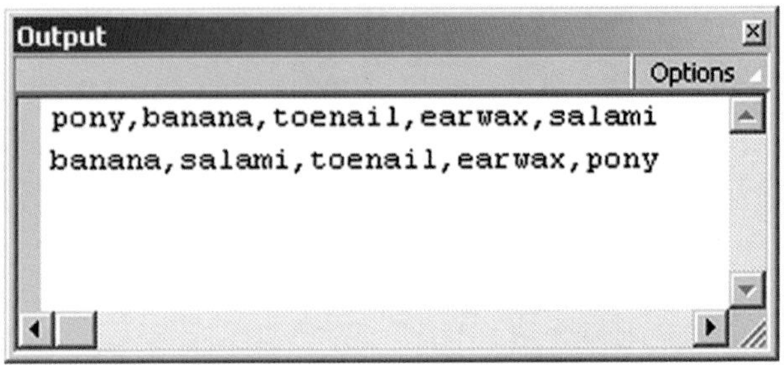

6.34: The Output panel shows the array before and after randomization.

10. Randomize the Story and Test

You can take the `trace()` statements out. Switch to the Story scene and place the following ActionScript on the RESHUFFLE button (6.35).

```
on(release){
   randomizeArrays();
   loadWords();
}
```

Here, you're calling the `randomizeArrays()` function that you created in step 8. The call to the `randomizeArrays()` function will take the arrays and randomize them again. Notice that the `randomizeArrays()` function is in the previous scene. The code works because the scope of a function is not limited to one scene. However, you do need to make sure the function has been loaded.

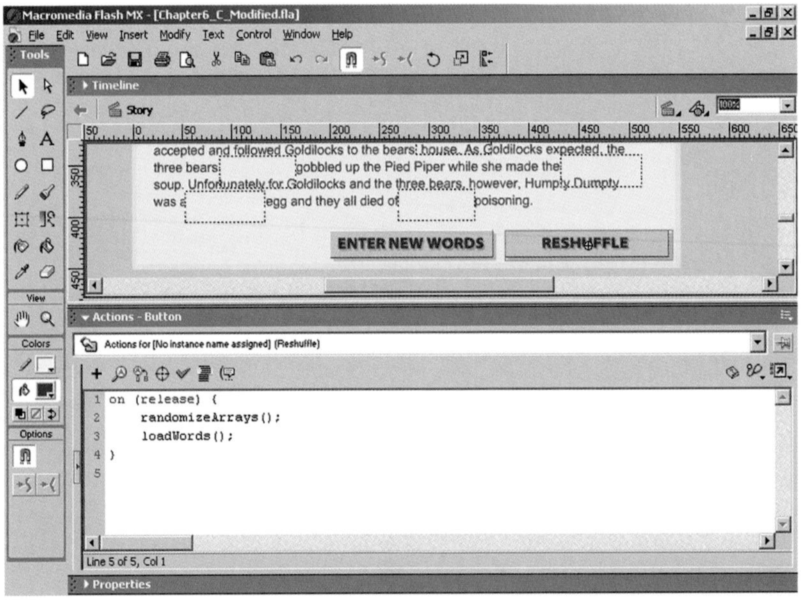

6.35: Add calls to the `randomizeArrays()` and `loadWords()` functions to the RESHUFFLE button.

NOTE A safe bet for ensuring the functions you need are loaded is to make sure they are in the previous or the current scene. In other words, you should never try to call a function from an upcoming scene. Putting all of your functions in the first scene would also avoid any problems. But here, all the functions are on the scenes they are related to, which make things simple.

Next, the code calls the `loadWords()` function. This is the reason you put the code for loading words into a function—each time the user clicks the RESHUFFLE button, you can simply call the `loadWords()` function to redisplay the words.

Test this version. You'll see that each time you select the RESHUFFLE button, the words are reordered.

Now you need to make sure the user enters something in every entry spot. Otherwise, you would get empty spaces for some of the words in the story, and it would make even less sense.

11. Add the Warning Movie Clip

Drag the Warning MC movie clip from the library onto the Buttons layer of the Entry scene. Center it on the stage and give it the instance name **Warning**. Attach the following Action-Script to the movie clip (6.36).

```
onClipEvent(load){
   _visible = false;
}
```

This movie clip will be used to warn users that they need to enter all the words. Setting the visibility of the movie clip to `false` will make sure it's not visible to the user until some ActionScript tells it to be visible. This will be when the user doesn't enter all of the words.

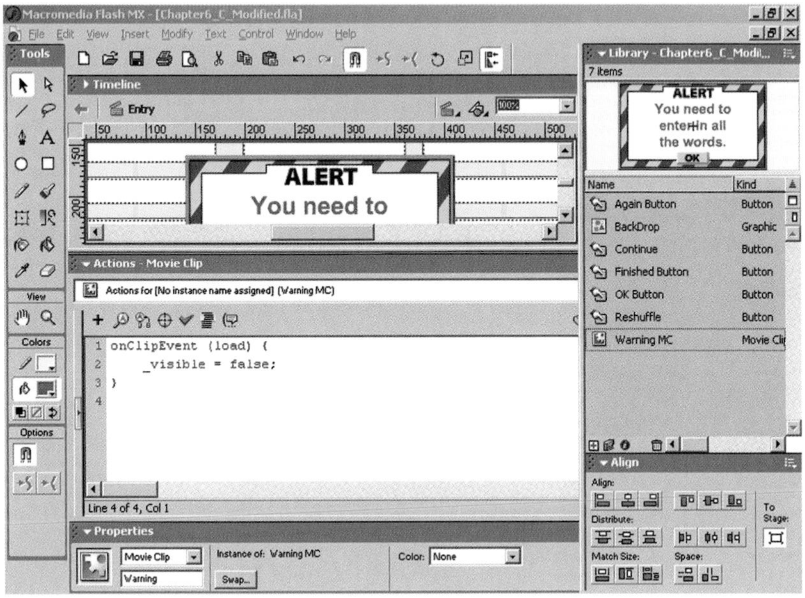

6.36: Place the Warning MC movie clip on the stage and assign code to it to make it invisible.

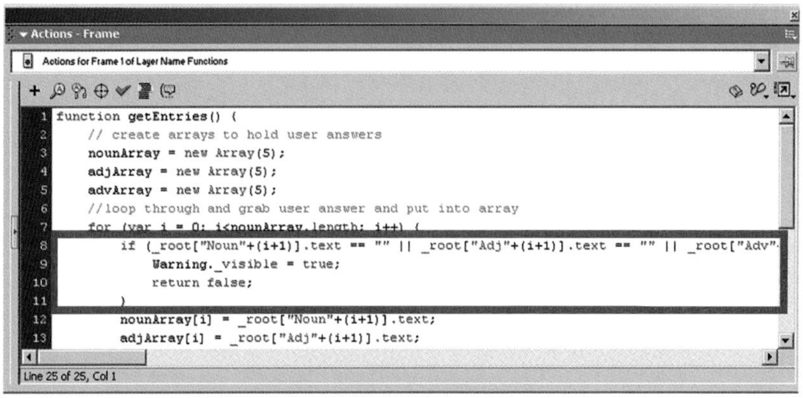

6.37: Add code to check that words have been entered in all the text fields.

Within the Warning MC movie clip is a button that already has ActionScript attached to it. When the user clicks the button, the Warning MC movie clip will become invisible again.

Now let's add code to check the user entries to make sure there is something in all of the text fields.

12. Add Code to Check Entries

Add the following ActionScript as the first line within the `getEntries()` function within the `for` loop (6.37).

```
if (_root["Noun"+(i+1)].text == "" || _root["Adj"+(i+1)].text == "" || ▶
_root["Adv"+(i+1)].text == ""){
   Warning._visible = true;
   return false;
}
```

This will check for each text field to make sure there is something in it. If there is nothing in it, the text field is equal to "", an empty string. The `||` is an OR test, so if any one of the text fields is empty, you want to make the Warning MC movie clip visible.

Then you need to make sure that the movie doesn't go to the next scene. The `return false` line is used to send a message back to where `getEntries()` was called. It essentially stops the rest of the `getEntries()` function and leaves. So even if the `for` loop were only in the first iteration, and you found an empty string, everything else would be skipped over and not done.

If you tested this now, the movie would just jump to the Story scene, even if something were empty. Let's add the code to make sure this doesn't happen.

13. Add Code to Continue

Add the following ActionScript to the bottom of the `getEntries()` function (6.38).

```
return true;
```

If the function made it to the last line of code, that means all of the entries have something in them. Therefore, this code will to send a message to the FINISHED button that it's okay to continue.

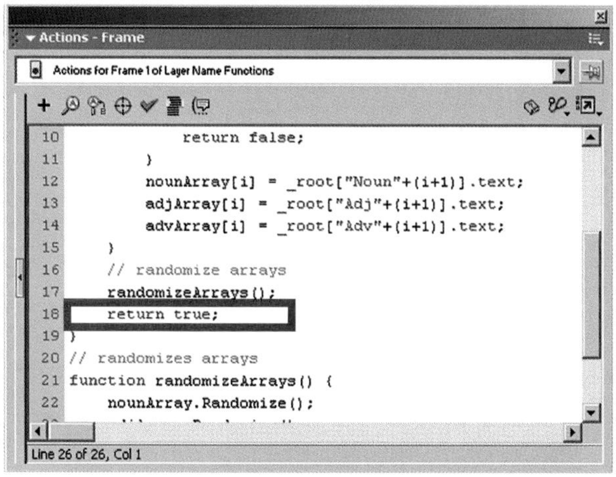

6.38: *Place the* `return true;` *line at the bottom of the* `getEntries()` *function.*

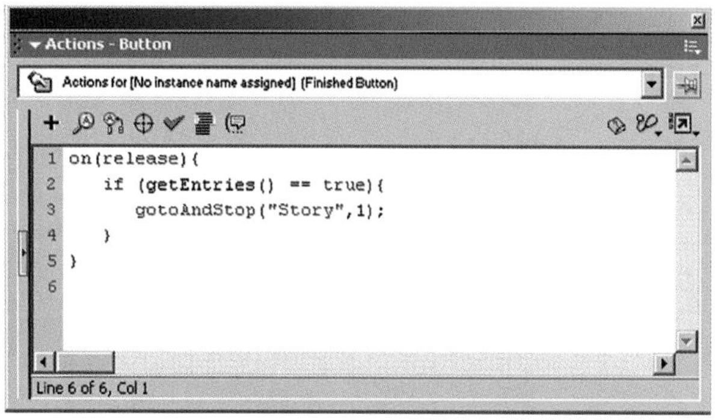

6.39: *Change the FINISHED button code.*

14. Add Code to the Finished Button to Complete the Check

Change the ActionScript attached to the FINISHED button at the bottom of the Entry scene to be the following (6.39).

```
on(release){
   if (getEntries() == true){
      gotoAndStop("Story", 1);
   }
}
```

The code on the FINISHED button checks if the `getEntries()` function returns `true`. Then, and only then, will the movie advance to the Story scene.

Test this movie. Notice that you cannot advance until all of the entries are filled in. If something is left blank, the Warning movie pops up.

Conclusion

In this chapter, you've learned a lot about text fields, new objects, arrays, and even how to make the built-in objects more powerful. Text is an essential part of design, so it is really nice that Macromedia has given programmers more control over text fields with the `TextField` object.

You also learned an approach to populating text fields dynamically by using arrays. Arrays are useful for a wide number of other applications. For example, you can use arrays to store numbers such as scores for a multiplayer game or prices for various products in an e-commerce store.

Two other techniques you learned here demonstrated how you can add to built-in objects. You can extend objects by adding to their properties, and you can use prototyping to add to an object's methods. The ability to add to built-in objects helps you to avoid repetition and keep your code organized.

CHAPTER seven

ActionScript Trigonometry

So far, you've been animating *objects in straight lines. Now you're ready to start working with more interesting paths.*

In order to move an object in a circular motion programmatically, you need to employ trigonometry. Trigonometry is used to move an object in circles, turn a dial, rotate a ship to fire in any direction, or make waves. Once you understand a few things about trigonometry and how Flash uses those principles, you'll see that moving in a circular direction is not that much more difficult than animating objects in straight paths.

This chapter shows you how to use trigonometry to create animations with circular and wave motion. You'll learn how the formulas in the code actually work using a variety of examples.

Trigonometry and ActionScript

Let's begin with a refresher on basic trigonometry as it relates to how you'll use Action-Script's built-in math functions to animate circular motion in Flash.

Trigonometry Basics

Trigonometry is based on a circle with a radius of 1 unit (7.1). It doesn't matter if you're talking about inches, meters, pixels, or whatever—the basic principles of trigonometry work no matter which unit of measurement you use. The circle is placed in the center of the x-axis and y-axis.

The center of the circle is at (0, 0). This means that the circle crosses the x-axis at two places: 1 and –1 (7.2). At both points, the y coordinate is 0. Written in pairs (x, y), the coordinates would be (1, 0) and (–1, 0). The circle also crosses the y-axis at 1 and –1. At both of

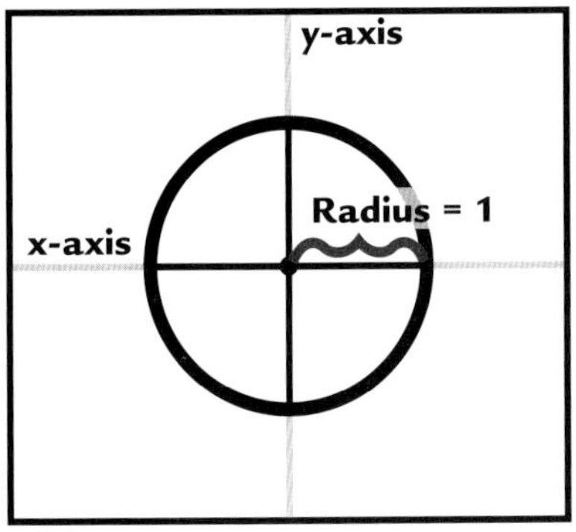

7.1: The distance from the center of the circle to the perimeter of the circle is the radius.

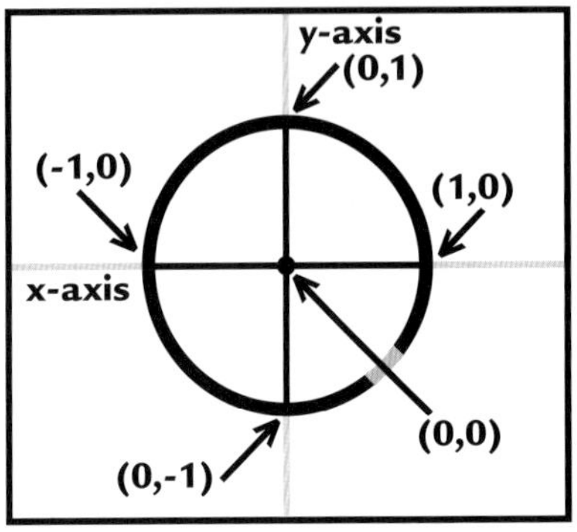

7.2: Where the points of a circle are located in x, y *coordinates*

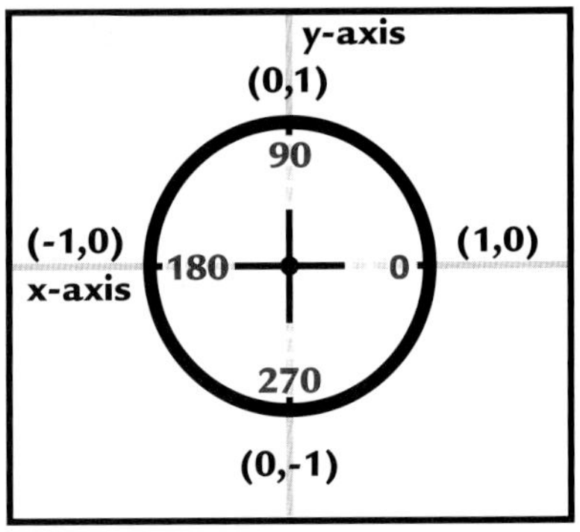

7.3: The x, y *coordinates corresponding to 0, 90, 180, and 270 degrees.*

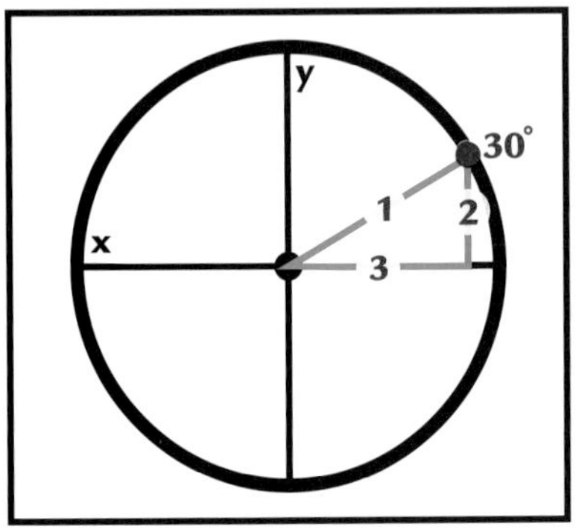

7.4: The distances along the x-*axis and the* y-*axis form a right angle (lines 2 and 3).*

these points, the *x* coordinate is 0, so these would be written as (0, 1) and (0, –1).

The circle is divided into 360 degrees (7.3), and the 0 and 360 degrees are at the point (1, 0). The degrees increase in the counter-clockwise direction: (0, 1) equals 90 degrees, (–1, 0) equals 180 degrees, (0, –1) equals 270 degrees, and (1, 0) equals 360 degrees.

For circular motion, you move along the coordinates of the circle (called the *unit circle*). Let's pick a point on the circle at 30 degrees and draw a line from the center of the circle to this point. Since the radius of the circle is 1, you know that the length of the line is 1, but you want to know how far along the *x*-axis and *y*-axis it is. When you need to know how far along the *x*-axis and *y*-axis a certain point is, you're essentially looking for the *x* and *y* coordinates.

Let's use a right triangle to clarify this concept (7.4). You begin by drawing a straight line from the center of the circle to the 30-degree point. Next draw a line down from the 30-degree point to the *x*-axis line. To complete the triangle, draw a line from the intersection of the previously drawn line to the center of the circle (the 0, 0 point).

The length of the vertical line, line 2, which parallels the *y*-axis, provides you with the *y* coordinate. The vertical line's intersection with the circle at the 30-degree point is the *y* coordinate. That *y* coordinate can be mathematically derived by the sine function. Similarly, the length of the horizontal line, which parallels the *x*-axis, provides you with the *x* coordinate. The line's intersection with the vertical line is the *x* coordinate. That *x* coordinate can be mathematically derived by the cosine function.

Flash Built-in Math Functions

Flash employs the cosine and sine functions to calculate *x* and *y* coordinates. These coordinates are used to reposition an object along progressive points of a circle, which is how a circular type of animation is achieved.

One important difference is the coordinate system Flash uses in the y direction. In the Cartesian coordinate system, which is the coordinate system used in trigonometry, *y* values increase in positive values as you move up from the *x*-axis. However, in Flash (and in all

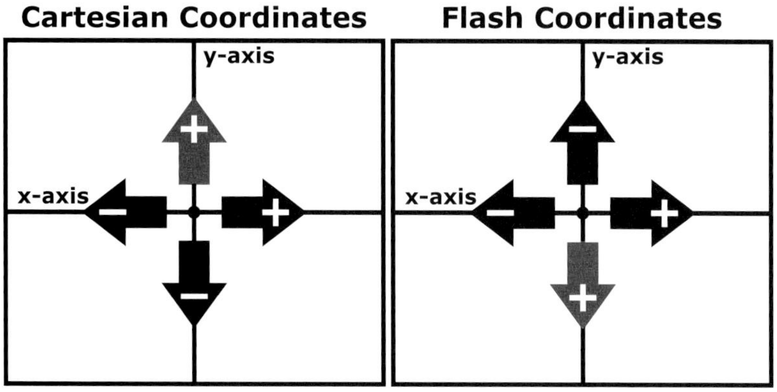

7.5: Flash's coordinate system treats y *values differently than Cartesian coordinates. In Cartesian coordinates, positive* y *values move up. In Flash coordinates, positive* y *values move down.*

computer graphics programs), *y* values increase in positive values as you move *down* from the *x*-axis (7.5).

The cosine (`Math.cos()`) and sine (`Math.sin()`) methods are already built into Flash. This means that you don't need to write any elaborate code to provide the same functionality.

So back to our example of 30 degrees, the cosine of 30 degrees is 0.866 (cos(30) = 0.866), and the sine of 30 degrees is 0.5 (sin(30) = 0.5). This means that at 30 degrees, you are further along the *x*-axis in the positive direction than you are along the *y*-axis (0.866 is greater than 0.5). This is reflected in the right-triangle example (7.4) in the previous section, where the line along the *x*-axis is longer than the line along the *y*-axis. Indeed, it's nearly twice as long (just as 0.866 is nearly twice as much as 0.5).

However, the cosine and sine numbers (0.866 and 0.5) are a bit small to work with in Flash. If you plug those numbers into an equation, you'll get a really tiny circle, which is not very useful. You need to give those numbers a bit of a boost. To do this, you multiply the sine and cosine results by the radius of the circle you wish produce or to move around.

For example, let's work with a radius of 100. If you want to plot a point that's located at 30 degrees along a circle that has a radius of 100, you simply multiply the cosine and sine results by 100. This gives you an *x* coordinate of 86.6 and a *y* coordinate of 50. The only problem with these calculations is that in Flash, the (0, 0) point is the upper-left (7.6), whereas in trigonometry, the (0, 0) point is in the center. So you need to adjust the calculation to account for the difference.

Let's say you're working with a Flash movie that has a stage size of 300×300, and you want the rotation to be around the center of the stage. In this example, the center of the stage is at $x = 150$ and $y = 150$. Since radius is the measurement of the center of the circle out to its perimeter, the largest circle that you can actually display in the 300×300 stage area is a circle with the radius of 150.

Consequently, if the center of the circle were at (0, 0), you would see only one quarter of the circle. Instead, you want the *x* and *y* values to be plotted around the center of the stage, which is $x = 150$, $y = 150$.

Calculating the *x* coordinate is easy to understand. Without the correction, the *x* value is at 86.6 on the stage, so all you need to do is add 150 to it (7.7), which will push it to the right (farther out onto the stage).

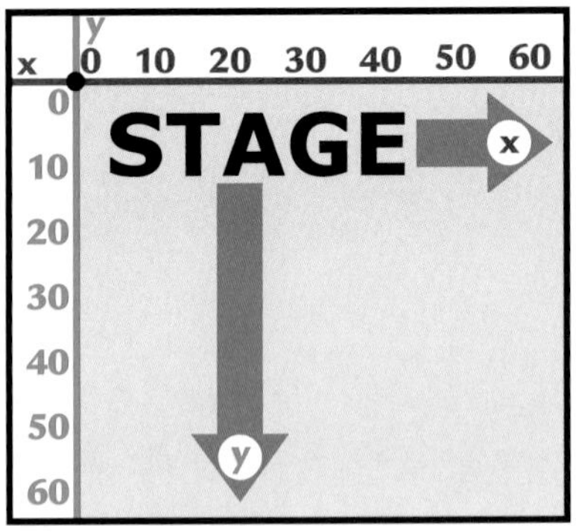

7.6: *Positive* x *values move an object to the right, and positive* y *values move an object down.*

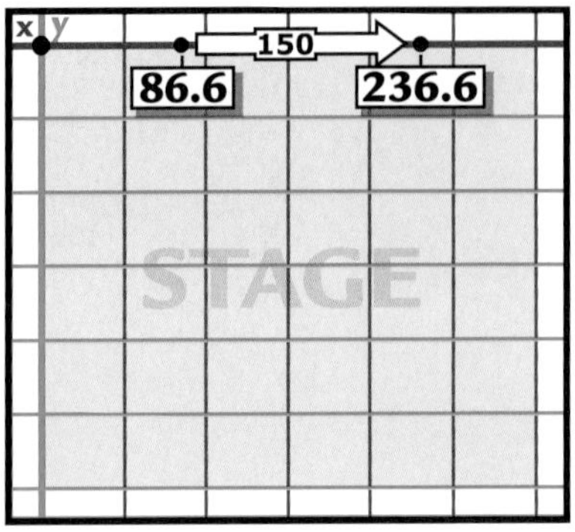

7.7: *Adding a positive value to the* x *value increases the value and moves the object to the right.*

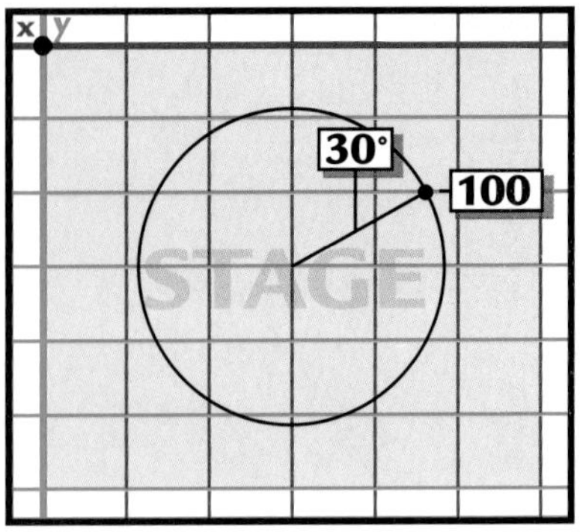

7.8: *An angle of 30 degrees corresponds to a* y *coordinate of 100.*

However, calculating the *y* coordinate is a little trickier. If you add the center of the stage (150) to the *y* value of 50, you get 200. If you plot that, you won't get a 30-degree angle. Instead, it would be a negative 30-degree angle (330 degrees). If you subtract the center of the stage, 150 from 50, you get –100. If you plot that, it would be off the stage (off the top edge). The calculation that works is to subtract the *y* value, 50, from the center of the stage, 150. That results in 100, which does, indeed, give you the 30-degree angle you want (7.8). Remember that the center of the stage is also the center of the circle for this example.

There's one extra step for the calculations, because Flash doesn't use degrees for the `Math.cos()` and `Math.sin()` methods. Instead, Flash uses radians. Radians are a unit based on π (pi). The circumference of the circle is equal to 2π radians, instead of 360 degrees. In your code, you'll need to convert the degrees to radians using the following formula:

radian = *degree* * pi / 180

Now that you have an understanding of how trigonometry is used in Flash to generate circular animation, let's take a look at some code that employs these principles.

Animating Circular Motion

The first example of using ActionScript's trigonometric functions to control circular movement is a simple program that duplicates an object and rotates each copy at various speeds, directions, and radii. You'll see how you can achieve really interesting effects with only a few lines of code.

1. Open the File

WWW.

Open Chapter7_A_Start.fla. Save the file to your local hard drive as Chapter7_A_Modified.fla (7.9). (For the finished version, see Chapter7_A_Final.fla.)

Notice that this file has four layers: Actions, Black Mask, Movement, and BackGround. The Black Mask layer serves as a mask for the Movement layer, so that any circles that fall outside the stage will not be seen.

There are two movie clips in the library: Star Movie and StarHolder Movie. The StarHolder Movie clip has the Star Movie clip inside it. This way, all the action can happen within the StarHolder Movie clip, and it can be layered in any way, without affecting the graphics on the other layers.

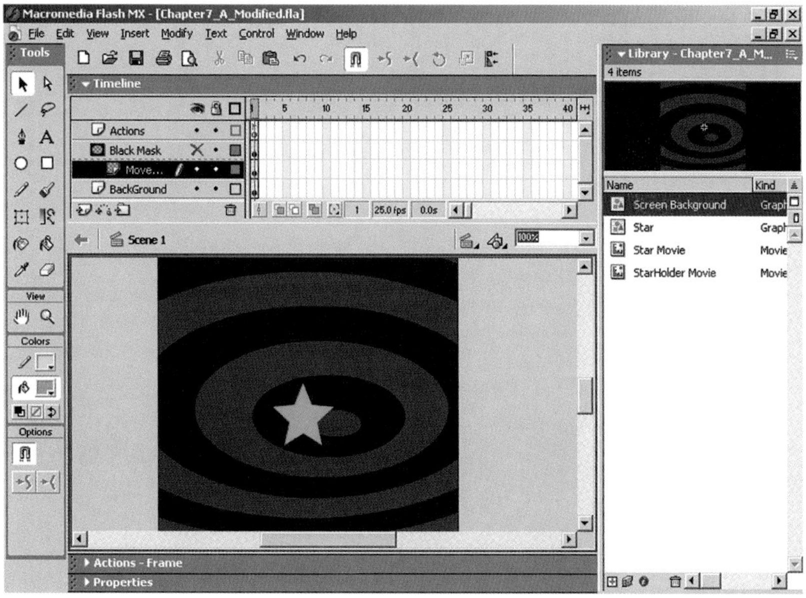

7.9: The Chapter7_A_Modified *file contains a movie clip within a movie clip, which is already set on the stage.*

2. Attach Initialization Code

Add the following ActionScript to frame 1 of the Actions layer (7.10).

```
// Initialization
// maximum radius of circle - half the stage size
var radiusMax = Stage.width / 2;
var radiusMin = 25;
// number of objects - at least  5
var maxObject = Math.random() * 23 + 5;
stop();
```

You begin by setting the variable `radiusMax` to half the width of the stage. This will be the maximum radius that a circle will travel on the stage. It's half the `Stage.width`, so none of the circles will go off the stage.

Next you set the `radiusMin` variable, which is the minimum a circle radius will be. This will prevent circles from bunching up in the center of the stage, by forcing all objects to rotate at least this far away from the center of the stage.

The final variable is `maxObject`, which controls the maximum number of objects on the stage. You want at least 5 objects on the stage, but no more than 28 objects, so the number of objects is randomly computed. This is stored in `maxObject`.

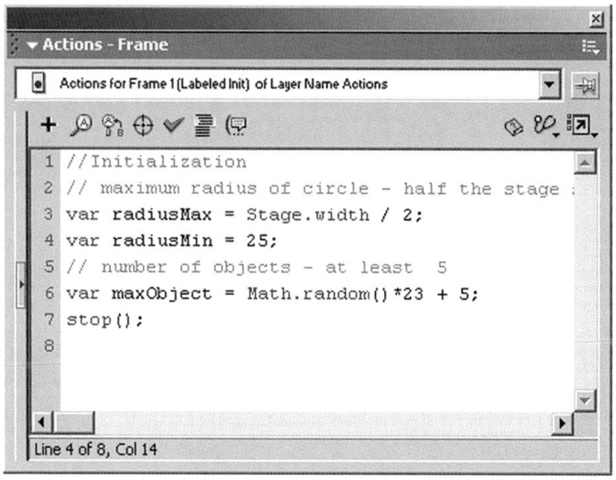

7.10: Add the initialization code to the Actions layer.

3. Duplicate the Star Movie

Attach the following ActionScript to the instance of the StarHolder Movie movie clip that is on the stage (7.11).

```
onClipEvent(load) {
   for (var level = 1; level <= _root.maxObject; level++) {
      var newMovieName = "Star" + level;
      // duplicate the object
      StarBase.duplicateMovieClip(newMovieName, level);
   }
}
```

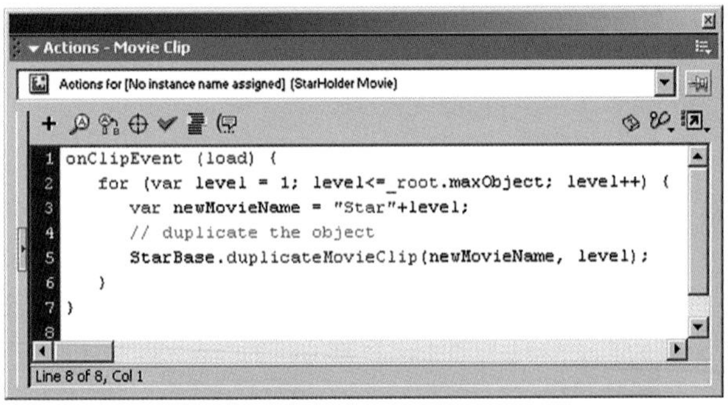

7.11: Add the `onClipEvent(load)` *code to the StarHolder Movie clip.*

This duplicates the Star Movie clip that is within the StarHolder Movie clip. This movie has an instance name of StarBase. The movie clip is duplicated `maxObject` number of times. So in the `for` loop, the code loops through `maxObject` number of times. Within each loop, you create a local variable, `newMovieName`, to hold the name of the new movie. This is a simple concatenation of `"Star"` and `level`. Then the code duplicates the StarBase movie, gives it the `newMovieName` value, and places it on the new level using the `level` variable. This is the same technique you've used in previous examples to duplicate movie clips, except here it's in two stages: separating the new name in a variable, `newMovieName`, and then using the variable to name the duplicated movie.

Finally let's set up the StarBase movie within the StarHolder Movie clip.

4. Initialize Each Duplicate Movie

Edit the StarHolder Movie clip and attach the following ActionScript to the Star Movie clip (7.12).

```
onClipEvent(load) {
   // randomize alpha transparency
   _alpha = Math.random() * 70 + 30;
   // how big is the object
   var scale = Math.random() * 50 + 50;
   _yscale = _xscale = scale;
   // rotation speed about itself
   var selfRotation = Math.random() * 30 - 15;
   // rotation speed around center
   var stageRotation = Math.random() * 5 + 1;
   // direction of rotation around stage
   if (Math.round(Math.random()) == 1) {
      stageRotation *= -1;
   }
}
```

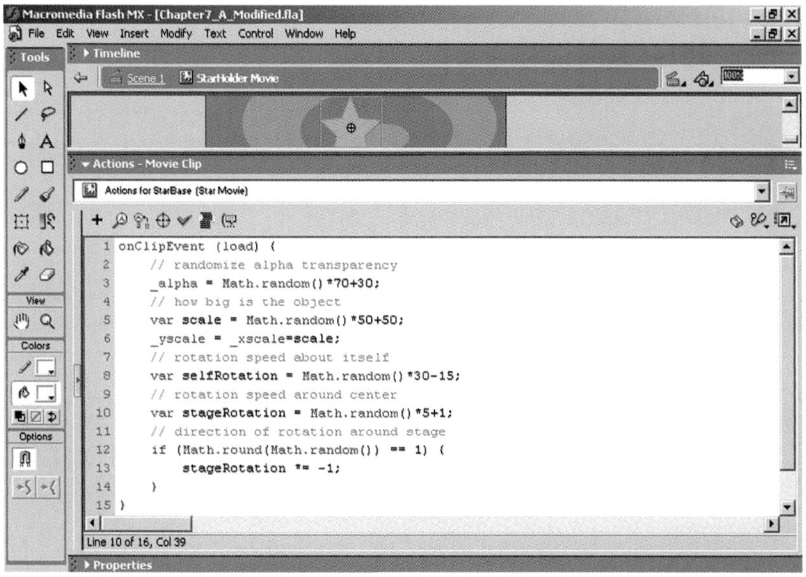

7.12: Add the code to the Star Movie clip within the StarHolder Movie clip.

Because this code is in the `onClipEvent(load)` section, it executes for each star that is duplicated from within StarHolder Movie. This way, each Star Movie clip will look and act differently.

First, you set the `_alpha` property using the `Math.random()` method. You want the alpha transparency to be between 30 and 100, so you take the results from the `Math.random()` method and multiply it 70 and then add 30 to the result. This will make sure the result is between 30 and 100.

Next you want to scale the Star Movie clip to be between 50 and 100 percent. This is computed by taking the result of `Math.random()`, multiplying it by 50 and adding 50 to it. You put the result in the *`scale`* variable. Then you set the `_xscale` and `_yscale` properties to the *`scale`* variable.

After setting up the scaling, you set up the rotation. The *`selfRotation`* variable will cause the Star Movie clip to rotate about itself based on the registration point, which is the center of the Star Movie movie clip. The *`selfRotation`* value is a random number between –15 and 15, based on the following line of code:

```
selfRotation = Math.random() * 30 - 15;
```

If the number is between –15 and –1, the Star Movie clip will rotate counter-clockwise. If the number is between 1 and 15, it will rotate in the clockwise direction. If the *`selfRotation`* variable is equal to 0, the Star Movie clip will not rotate at all.

Next the code determines rotation around the center of the stage. This code is essentially the same as the code that establishes rotation around the object itself. You use the *`stageRotation`* variable to determine which way to rotate the Star Movie clip around on the stage:

```
stageRotation = Math.random() * 5 + 1;
// direction of rotation around stage
if (Math.round(Math.random()) == 1) {
   stageRotation *= -1;
}
```

stageRotation is first calculated using a random number between 1 and 5. Then you want the movie clip to also rotate in both directions, but you don't want there to be a possibility of 0, because then the star would just sit in one place on the stage and rotate about itself. This is not the desired end result. So the *stageRotation* is calculated in two steps. The first `Math.random()` gets the speed of the rotation, and the second `Math.random()` gets the direction. Since there are only two possible directions, you need `Math.random()` to return either a 0 or a 1, so you take the results and round it using `Math.round()`. Then you let the result of 1 mean the Star Movie clip will go backwards, or counter-clockwise. The counter-clockwise rotation is handled in an `if` statement. If the result of the calculation is equal to 1, then multiply the *stageRotation* variable by –1. This will create a negative number for the rotation.

This is the first time you have seen the `*=` operator. This is the same as saying `stageRotation = stageRotation * -1`. It's just as simple as the `+=` and the `-=` operators.

Now let's finish the initialization.

5. Add More Star Movie Initialization Code

Add the following ActionScript to the bottom of the code you entered in the previous section, within the closing brace. This will finish the setup (7.13).

```
// get radius to rotate around
var radius = Math.random()*(_root.radiusMax - _root.radiusMin) + ▶
_root. radiusMin;
// compute where on the circle in degrees and place
var compDegree = Math.random() * 360;
var startRadian = compDegree *(Math.PI / 180);
_x = radius * Math.cos(startRadian);
_y = -radius * Math.sin(startRadian);
```

Now you compute the radius the Star Movie clip will move around within the StarHolder Movie clip. This result goes in the *radius* variable.

For this calculation, you get a random number from *radiusMax* minus *radiusMin*, and then add *radiusMin* to the random result. Remember that the *radiusMax* variable contains the maximum circle to rotate around the stage based on the `Stage.width` property, and the *radiusMin* variable is used to make sure that the Star Movie clip is far enough away from the center of the stage. So you want to adjust the *radius* value so that the clip isn't clustered around the center and is still on the stage. Since these variables were defined on the main timeline, you need to target the variable references by using `_root`. So, the `Math.random()` method takes the number assigned to the *radiusMin* variable (25) and subtracts it from the value of the *radiusMax* variable (150). This gives you a number between 0 and 124. Then you add the value of *radiusMin*, which means that *radius* will be a random number between 25 and 149.

Now you've reached the point in the code that uses the trigonometry discussed at the beginning of the chapter. To begin with, you give the Star Movie movie clip a starting place using this code:

```
compDegree = Math.random() * 360;
```

compDegree is a random number between 0 and 360. The next line converts degrees to radians using the standard formula:

```
startRadian = compDegree *(Math.PI / 180);
```

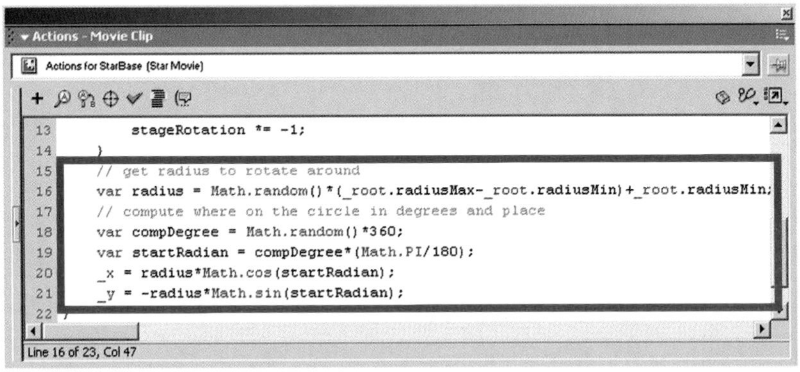

7.13: Add the code to the Star Movie clip within the StarHolder Movie clip.

Finally, the code calculates the *x* and *y* coordinates for the Star Movie clip. It gets the *x* coordinate with the following code:

```
_x = radius * Math.cos(startRadian);
```

To find the *x* coordinate, you take the cosine (`Math.cos()`) of the radian (*`startRadian`*) and multiply it by the radius of the circle (*`radius`*). This is then applied to the `_x` property of the Star Movie clip.

It gets the *y* coordinate with this code:

```
_y = -radius * Math.sin(startRadian);
```

You take the sine of the radian (`Math.sin()`) and multiply the final results by –1. The minus sign (–) in front of the `radius * Math.sin(startRadian)` code works the same as multiplying by –1.

NOTE As explained at the beginning of the chapter, you need to make some adjustments in trigonometry calculations, because the *y*-coordinate system for graphics runs in the opposite direction of the *y*-coordinate system in the Cartesian system. Since the results from the `radius * Math.sin(startRadian)` calculation are based on the Cartesian system, you simply multiply by –1 to make the adjustment into the graphic system.

To understand how the coordinate computations work, let's say that the *`compDegree`* variable is equal to 76 and the *`radius`* is equal to 55. The value for the *`compDegree`* variable, 76, would then be used to calculate the radian, as follows:

```
compDegree *(Math.PI / 180);
```

which is:

```
76 * (3.14 / 180)
```

which is equal to 1.33. So the value of the *`startRadian`* variable in this case would be 1.33.

Next the *x* coordinate is calculated using the following formula:

```
_x = radius * Math.cos(startRadian);
```

Plugging in the numbers, you get:

```
_x = 55 * Math.cos(1.33)
```

The cosine of 1.33 radians is 0.24, so:

```
_x = 55 * 0.24
```

which is 13.2. So the _x property is 13.2.

```
_x = 13.2
```

The *y* coordinate is calculated as follows:

```
_y = -radius*Math.sin(startRadian);
```

Again, plugging in the numbers, you get:

```
_y = -55 * Math.sin(1.33)
```

The sine of 1.33 radians is 0.97, so:

```
_y = -55 * 0.97
```

which is –53.4. So the _y property is –53.4.

```
_y = -53.4
```

Thus, the initial *x* and *y* coordinates are 13.2 and –53.4, respectively.

This coordinate system is not on the main timeline; it's within the StarHolder Movie clip. This makes it a lot easier to do trigonometry, because the center of the StarHolder movie clip is (0, 0), which is where all the duplicates are automatically going to be placed, so you don't need to worry about moving the *x* and *y* coordinates to make sure they stay on the stage. This does mean, however, that the base of the rotation is located wherever you place the StarHolder Movie clip on the main timeline.

Remember that all of this code executes in the `onClipEvent(load)` section, so it runs only once. Therefore, this code simply places the object so that it's ready for movement. Now let's look at the code that actually moves the object.

6. Move the Star

Add the following ActionScript below the code you added in the previous step (7.14).

```
onClipEvent(enterFrame) {
   // rotate about itself
   _rotation += selfRotation;
   // compute new position based on speed of rotation
   //around stage
   compDegree += stageRotation;
   if (compDegree > 360) {
      compDegree -= 360;
   } else if (compDegree < 0) {
      compDegree += 360;
   }
   var newRadian = compDegree * (Math.PI / 180);
   _x = radius * Math.cos(newRadian);
```

```
        _y = -radius*Math.sin(newRadian);
    }
```

The remaining code is contained within an `onClipEvent(enterFrame)` handler. The first line within the `onClipEvent(enterFrame)` handler causes the movie clip to rotate about itself. The `_rotation` property of the Star Movie clip is increased by the value of the *`selfRotation`* variable. Note that the `_rotation` property starts with a value of 0. So if the *`selfRotation`* variable is set to –7, the Star Movie clip will spin counter-clockwise at a rate of 7 degrees per frame. Remember that the `_rotation` property is based on degrees moving clockwise, with 0 being straight up, or north.

The rest of the code is used to move the Star Movie clip within the StarHolder Movie clip, which is sitting on the main timeline. First, the code adds the value of the *`stageRotation`* variable, which was established in the `onClipEvent(load)` section, to the current value of the *`compDegree`* variable. Now you need to check the boundaries for the *`compDegree`* variable to make sure it doesn't become greater than 360 or less than 0. The rotation about a circle will actually work just fine without the boundary checking, but it's always a good idea to keep variables within known boundaries.

Finally, `onClipEvent(enterFrame)` includes the same three lines of code that are in the `onClipEvent(load)` section. The only difference is that this code executes repeatedly, which will cause the movement.

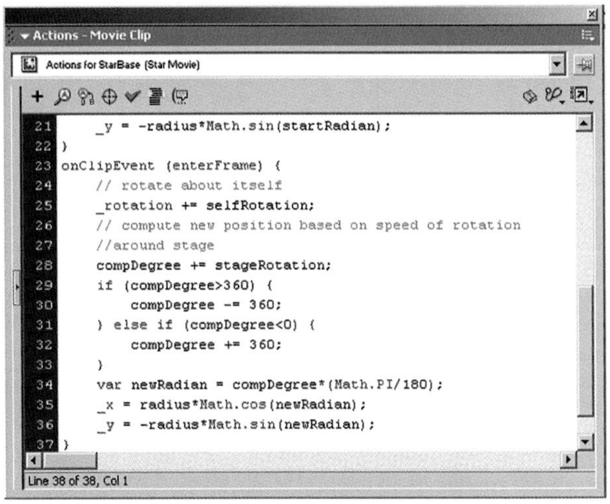

7.14: Add the `onClipEvent(enterFrame)` code to the Star Movie clip within the StarHolder Movie clip.

7. Test the Movie

Test this movie. You'll see that the Star Movie movie clips are different sizes and different transparencies. Also, they rotate about themselves at different rates and directions, and they rotate about the stage differently. Each one is completely separate.

This example demonstrates that it isn't too difficult to produce animated rotation with ActionScript.

Creating Wave Animations

For experienced programmers, creating a wave animation is a classic application of the sine function. In this section, you'll explore how to create different-looking waves, all based on the sine function.

In the previous example of animating circular motion, you used the cosine of the degree for the *x* coordinate and the sine of the degree for the *y* coordinate for the circles. To plot a sine wave, you still take the sine of the degree for the *y* coordinate, but for the *x* coordinate, you simply use the degree, without any further calculations. The examples in this section will clarify how this works.

In the sine wave examples, all of the variance to the motion will occur along the *y*-axis. In other words, the code will generate the wavy motion by varying the position of the movie clip along the *y*-axis, as the movie clip moves along the *x*-axis at a steady, consistent rate.

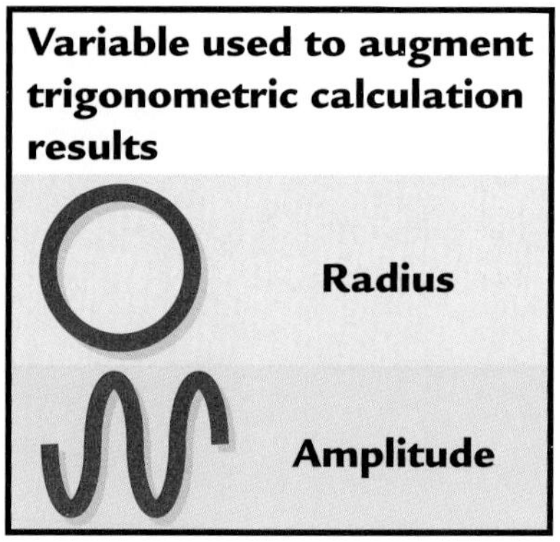

Variable used to augment trigonometric calculation results
Radius
Amplitude

7.15: Just as you use the radius in calculations for circular motion, you use the amplitude in calculations for sine wave motion.

In the previous example, when you were working with a circle, the calculations were essentially based on the value of the degree. For instance, if the degree were equal to 0, the output for the circle would be $x = \cos(0)$, which is equal to 1, and $y = \sin(0)$, which is 0. So the coordinate would be (1, 0).

The calculations for creating sine wave motion are simpler than those for creating circular motion. For the sine wave motion, x is equal to the degree. You already know that $x = 0$, because that is the degree. You only need to calculate the y coordinate. So, completing the example, if the degree is equal to 0, then $y = \sin(0)$, which is 0, so the coordinate would be (0, 0).

Let's look at another value for a degree of a circle. If the degree is 60, the x would be cos(60), which is 0.5, and the y would be sin(60), which is 0.87, so the coordinate would be (0.5, 0.87). Remember that you multiplied this by the radius of the circle to get a decent-sized circle.

You'll do something similar to generate the sine wave animation. So for the sine wave, if the degree is 60, x is 60 and y is sin(60), which is 0.87. Therefore, the coordinate would be (60, 0.87). The value for the y coordinate is very small, so just as with the circle, you need to multiply it by a value to make it big enough to see.

Instead of the radius for the circle, you'll use amplitude for the sine wave (7.15). The amplitude is how high the sine wave will go in the up and down direction. The larger the amplitude value, the bigger the sine wave.

1. Open the File

WWW. Open **Chapter7_B_Start.fla**. Save the file to your local hard drive as **Chapter7_B_Modified.fla**. (To see the finished version, open **Chapter7_B_Final.fla**.)

This file has two layers: Actions and Movie. On the Movie layer is an instance of the SquareHolder movie clip. The SquareHolder movie clip contains an instance of the Square movie clip, named Square.

The Actions layer has two lines of code, with comments:

```
// variables used for calculations
// conversion from degrees to radians
var Deg2Rad = Math.PI / 180;
// alpha change based on 1/2 rotation
var alphaChange = 100 / 180;
```

These are two variables that will be used to create the wave. The first variable, `Deg2Rad`, is what you need to convert degrees to radians, so you can use the `Math.sin()` method in Flash. In the previous example, you simply did the calculation each time. In this case, you use a variable to contain the value, which will make the calculations easier to read.

The second variable, `alphaChange`, will be used to set the `_alpha` property on the wave so that it varies over 180 degrees. The `alphaChange` variable is based on the maximum allowed in the `_alpha` property (100) and the number of degrees in half the circle (180). Dividing 100 by 180 provides the code with the number that it uses to vary the `_alpha` over 180 degrees.

NOTE When you divide 100 by 180, you get a fractional value (0.55). Flash cannot produce an alpha based precisely on a fractional value. However, you don't need to go to the trouble of rounding the value to a whole number, because Flash will round it to a whole number automatically.

Now let's write some code to use these variables and get the SquareHolder movie clip to move along a wave.

2. Create a Wave

Edit the SquareHolder movie clip and apply the following ActionScript to the Square movie clip, which appears as a tiny, white square to the far-left center of the stage (7.16).

```
onClipEvent(load){
   var position = 0;
   var amplitude = 120;
}
onClipEvent(enterFrame){
   position ++;
   _x = position;
   _y = -amplitude * Math.sin(_root.Deg2Rad * position);
}
```

In the `onClipEvent(load)` event handler, you create two variables: *`position`* and *`amplitude`*. The *`position`* variable is essentially the degree to be used in the calculations. It's used to establish the initial *x* position of the movie clip, at 0, and then its value is incremented in every pass through the `onClipEvent(enterFrame)` event handler using the ++ operator. So the code that controls the _x property of the Square movie clip simply starts the movie clip at the 0 position and moves it to the right (along the *x*-axis), 1 pixel per frame (at a rate of 12fps) within the `onClipEvent(enterFrame)`. Then the *`amplitude`* variable is set to 120. As explained at the beginning of this section, the amplitude controls how high the sine wave will go.

Then in the `onClipEvent(enterFrame)` code, the *`position`* variable is incremented, and the *x* coordinate is set to the new *`position`* value. Finally, there is the calculation for the *y* coordinate. In a simplified form, the calculation for the *y* coordinate could be expressed like *amplitude * sin(degree)*, or for Flash, as *amplitude * sin(radian)*. Because Flash uses radians, rather than degrees, in the `Math.sin()` method, you need to convert to radians. This is accomplished with the following code:

```
_root.Deg2Rad * position
```

The value of the *`Deg2Rad`* variable is the result of the calculation 3.14 / 180, which is 0.0174, done on

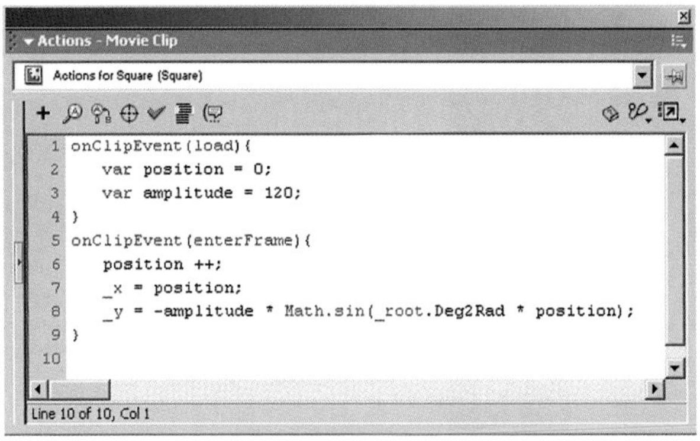
Actions - Movie Clip
Actions for Square (Square)
onClipEvent(load){
var position = 0;
var amplitude = 120;
}
onClipEvent(enterFrame){
position ++;
_x = position;
_y = -amplitude * Math.sin(_root.Deg2Rad * position);
}
Line 10 of 10, Col 1

7.16: Add `onClipEvent(load)` and `onClipEvent(enterFrame)` code to the Square movie clip (the tiny white square to the far-left center of the stage).

the main timeline. For example, if *position* is 60, the calculation is 0.0174 × 60 = 1.046. Then the sine is taken of the results:

```
Math.sin(_root.Deg2Rad * position)
```

Flash calculates the sine of 1.046 (based on radians) to 0.087. Remember that the *position* variable is basically the degree on the circle.

NOTE You might not get 0.087 on your calculator if you tried to calculate the sine of 1.046 (depending on whether your calculator was set for radians or for degrees). If you want to make the same calculation on your computer or calculator using degrees, you could simply calculate the sine of 60. You need to go to the extra lengths of working with radians because that's what Flash requires to work with the `Math.sin()` and `Math.cos()` methods.

This will give you the base *y* coordinate, but once again it's very small, so you multiply it by the amplitude:

```
amplitude * Math.sin(_root.Deg2Rad * position)
```

Earlier, you set the value of the *amplitude* variable to 120. If you apply this to the example, you get 120 × 0.87 = 104.4. Now you almost have the *x* and *y* coordinates. If the value of the *position* variable is 60, then the value of the *y* coordinate is 104.4. Therefore, you have $x = 60$ and $y = 104.4$. But remember that this code is manipulating the instance of the Square movie clip, which is contained within the SquareHolder movie clip. Therefore, when the `_x` and `_y` properties are set within the code, the Square movie clip is repositioned to those coordinates relative to the position of the SquareHolder movie clip, rather than relative to the overall stage, and the SquareHolder movie clip is not moving.

The SquareHolder movie clip is positioned at the middle-left edge of the stage. If you plugged in the values that you calculated ($x = 60$, $y = 104.4$), the Square movie clip would be repositioned 60 pixels to the right of the (0, 0) point of the SquareHolder movie clip and 104.4 pixels down from the (0, 0) point of the SquareHolder movie clip. The (0, 0) point, or registration point, of the SquareHolder movie clip is $x = -2$, $y = 198$. This means that the new position of the Square movie clip inside the SquareHolder movie clip would actually appear to be $x = 58$, $y = 302.4$ on the stage (7.17).

Finally, you need to make sure that the Square movie clip starts out going upward, as sine waves normally do, rather than downward. This is handled by the negative (–) sign in front of the `Math.sin()` code, which makes the result of the calculation negative, rather than positive:

```
_y = -amplitude * Math.sin(_root.Deg2Rad * position);
```

Basically, here you're making the adjustment from Cartesian coordinates to graphic coordinates. So in the example, *y* now equals –104.4. The actual position of the Square movie clip on the stage will be $x = 58$, $y = 93.6$.

You now know how the numbers plug into the calculations, but how does this result in a sine wave animation? Well, it will be easier to understand that by testing this movie and making some observations.

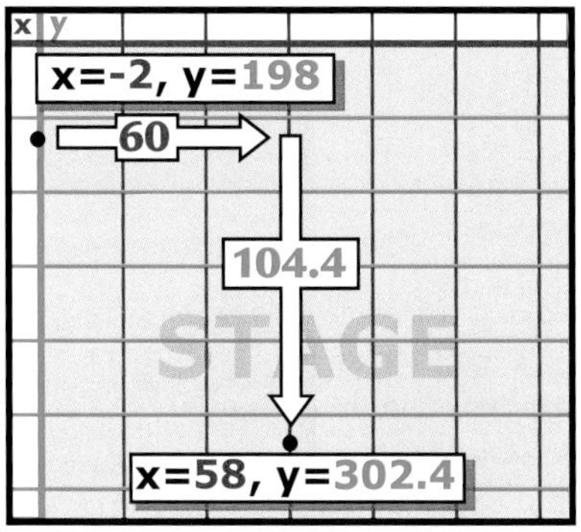

7.17: *The code moves the Square movie clip inside the SquareHolder movie clip.*

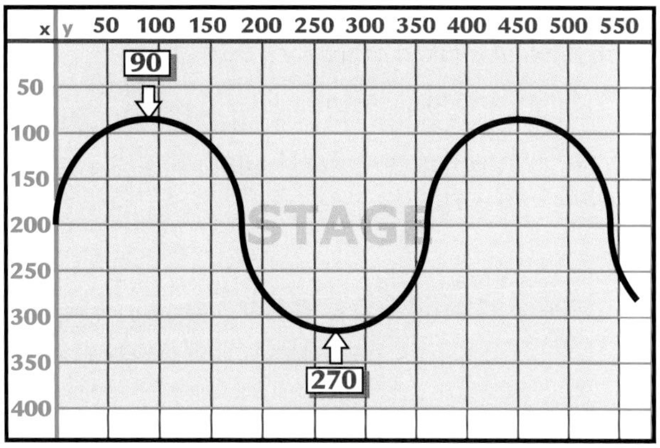

7.18: *The movie clip shifts directions from upward to downward at 90 along the* x-axis, *and then reverses from downward to upward at 270 along the* x-axis.

3. Test the Movie

Test this movie. You'll notice that the SquareHolder movie clip moves slowly up and then down. It's moving only 1 pixel per frame, so you might need a little patience.

The graph on the stage represents pixels, so the 50 is at pixel 50. If you watch closely, you'll see that the little square moves upward until it reaches at 90 along the *x*-axis (7.18). Then it starts moving downward, crossing the horizontal, white line at 180 along the *x*-axis, until it gets to at 270 along the *x*-axis. Then it starts moving upward again. It crosses the horizontal, white line again at 360 along the *x*-axis.

Do the numbers 90, 180, 270, and 360 sound familiar? Those numbers are similar to 360 degrees of a circle, right? In fact, that's exactly what the sine wave code is using. Let's plug in some numbers for the degrees or `position` variable and plot the points:

Degree	Sine
45	0.7
90	1
135	0.7
180	0
225	-0.7
270	-1
315	-0.7
360	0

Notice that between 180 degrees and 359 degrees, the sine values become negative. So the values for the sine fluctuate between 1 and –1, and that's how the movie clip changes directions from going up to going down. After the value of the `position` variable reaches 180, the results of the sine calculations start becoming negative. This is where the sine wave crosses the *x*-axis and goes below it. This gives you a negative value multiplied by a negative value (since you placed a negative sign in front of the `amplititude` variable), resulting in a positive value. When the result of the calculation for the *y* coordinate is positive, the move clip goes downward instead of upward.

Of course, a tiny, moving square isn't very fascinating. Let's make this a little more visually interesting by adding some duplicates. This will also allow you to see the sine wave more clearly.

4. Create a Standing Wave and Test

Edit the SquareHolder move clip. Delete the code attached the Square movie clip. Go back to scene 1 or the main timeline. Assign the following code to the SquareHolder movie clip (7.19).

```
onClipEvent(load) {
   var numberToDuplicate = 360;
   // variables for the sine wave calculation
   var amplitude = 120;
   // duplicate squares
   for (var i = 0; i < numberToDuplicate; i++) {
      Square.duplicateMovieClip("sq" + i, i);
      var clipName = this["sq" + i];
      clipName._x = i;
      clipName._y = -amplitude * Math.sin(_root.Deg2Rad * i);
   }
   Square._visible = false;
}
```

This will create a solid sine wave across the screen. Each Square movie clip duplicate is positioned one degree higher than the previous duplicate. This code works similarly to the code for the moving wave, except that you're creating 360 duplicates of the Square movie clip, and you're not using the `onClipEvent(enterFrame)` event handler in order to generate an animation. This code uses only the `onClipEvent(load)` event handler, so it executes just once and then stops.

First, you set the `numberToDuplicate` variable to 360, which is equivalent to 360 degrees for a full circle. This will give you a complete sine wave. The `amplitude` variable is set to 120, just as in the previous example.

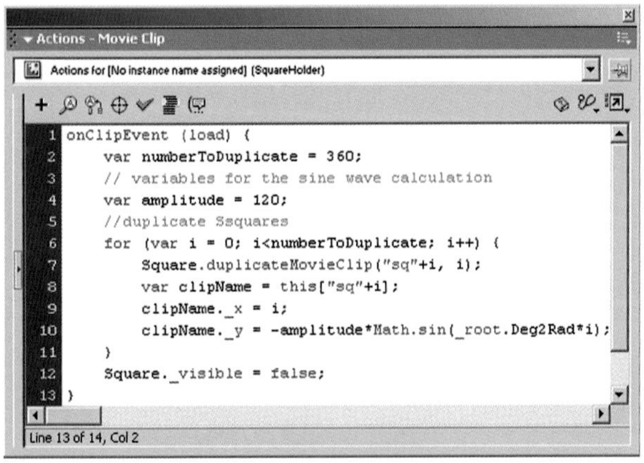
Actions - Movie Clip
Actions for [No instance name assigned] (SquareHolder)
onClipEvent (load) {
var numberToDuplicate = 360;
// variables for the sine wave calculation
var amplitude = 120;
//duplicate Ssquares
for (var i = 0; i<numberToDuplicate; i++) {
Square.duplicateMovieClip("sq"+i, i);
var clipName = this["sq"+i];
clipName._x = i;
clipName._y = -amplitude*Math.sin(_root.Deg2Rad*i);
}
Square._visible = false;
}
Line 13 of 14, Col 2

7.19: Delete the code on the Square movie clip and add this code to the SquareHolder movie clip.

Then you duplicate the Square movie clip using a `for` loop. Each duplicated movie clip is named `"sq"` plus the level number (`i`) and placed on a new level (`i`). Here, you're using the `i` variable from the `for` loop to give each duplicate a different name and different level. Next you create the `clipName` variable to contain the name of the newly created movie clip (you need this because you'll be referring to the duplicated movie clip a couple more times). Then you set the *x* coordinate of this movie clip to the variable `i`, so each new duplicate will be placed 1 pixel to the right of the previous duplicate. Notice that you're also using the `i` variable as the degree to do the positioning. The *y* coordinate is computed

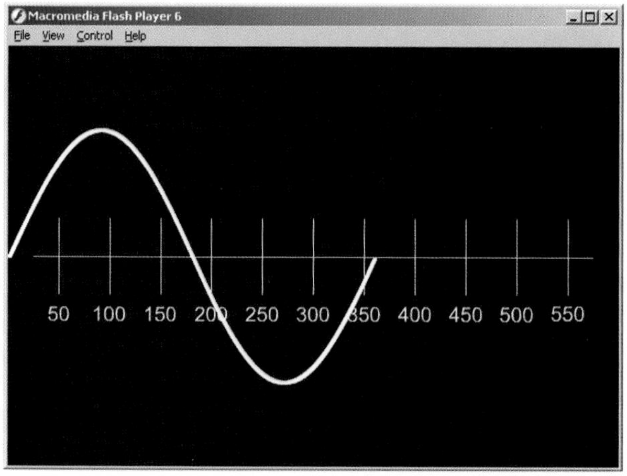

7.20: *The code results in a nonanimated sine wave.*

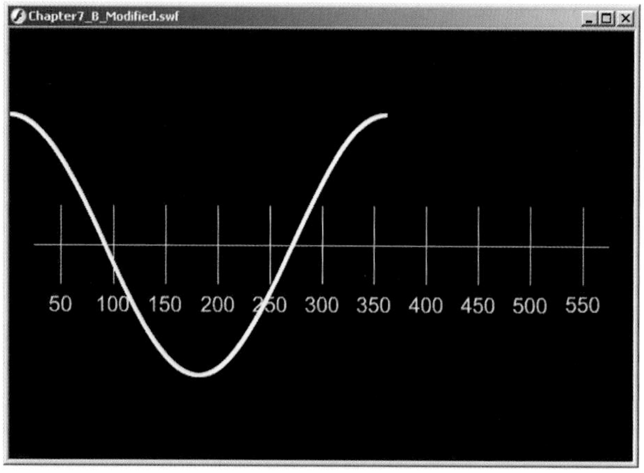

7.21: *Using* `Math.cos()` *results in a cosine wave.*

using the same formula as in step 2 earlier in this section, except *i* is used instead of the *position* variable. Finally, the code makes the original movie clip, Square, invisible. You just used the Square movie clip to duplicate all the other movie clips.

Test this version. Notice that you have a solid, unmoving wave (7.20). This is a sine wave. Notice that you have a complete wave. About the time it starts to repeat itself, it quits.

If you wanted a cosine wave, you would replace the `Math.sin()` with `Math.cos()`. You would see that the cosine wave looks like the sine wave, except for where it starts (7.21). The sine wave starts at a middle point, actually 0; the cosine wave starts at the top.

Now let's make the sine wave move across the stage.

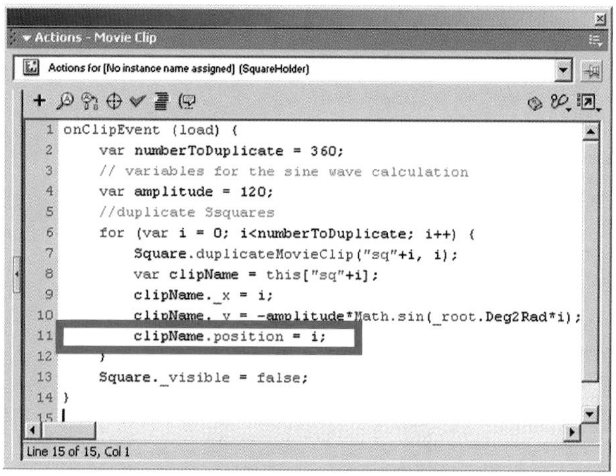

7.22: *Add one line of code to the* `for` *loop.*

5. Add to the SquareHolder Movie Clip Code

Add the following line of code within the `for` loop on the SquareHolder movie clip (7.22), below where the variable *clipName* is defined.

```
clipName.position = i;
```

6. Create a Moving Sine Wave and Test

Edit the SquareHolder movie clip. Then attach the following code to the Square movie clip (7.23).

```
onClipEvent(enterFrame) {
    // increment position on the sine wave
    position++;
    // move object over on x-axis
    _x++;
```

continues

```
        // check if off the stage on right, move clip to far left of stage
        if (_x > Stage.width) {
            _x = 0;
            position = 0;
        }
        // calculate new y position
        _y = -_parent.amplitude * Math.sin(_root.Deg2Rad * (position));
    }
```

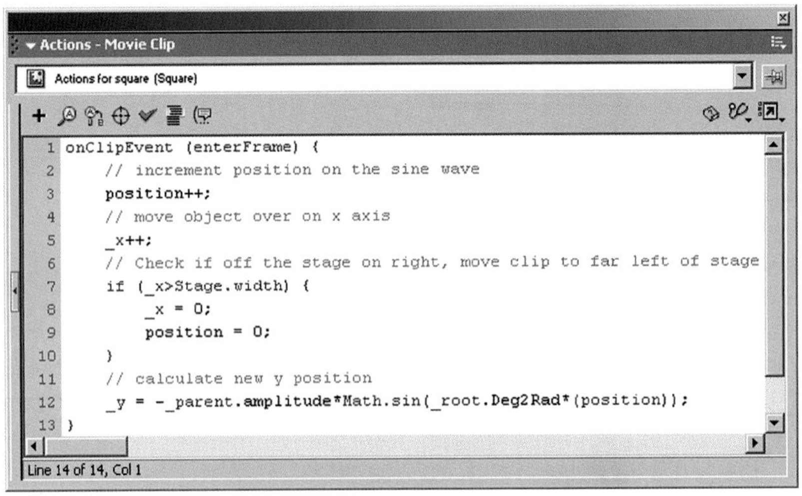
Actions - Movie Clip
Actions for square (Square)
onClipEvent (enterFrame) {
// increment position on the sine wave
position++;
// move object over on x axis
_x++;
// Check if off the stage on right, move clip to far left of stage
if (_x>Stage.width) {
_x = 0;
position = 0;
}
// calculate new y position
_y = -_parent.amplitude*Math.sin(_root.Deg2Rad*(position));
}
Line 14 of 14, Col 1

7.23: Add code to the Square movie clip (within the SquareHolder movie clip) to generate the sine wave motion.

The first line of code that you added in the previous step was to create the variable *position* within the duplicated Square movie clip. You create this variable within the Square movie clip by linking it to the *clipName* variable, so that it will exist within each duplicated movie clip. This is a way to pass information to a movie clip. The *position* variable doesn't exist until this line:

```
clipName.position = i;
```

which is within the SquareHolder movie clip code. Then you treat it just like any other property variable. The *position* variable will be used within each duplicated Square movie clip to move along the sine wave.

The ActionScript attached to the Square movie clip handles the actual movement, so it is within an `onClipEvent(enterFrame)` event handler. First, you increment the *position* variable. The value of the *position* variable will also be used for the degree calculation in the `Math.sin()` calculation. So you're creating the motion simply by incrementing the value of the *position* variable. Then the *x* coordinate is moved over by one. The *x* coordinate changes by only 1 pixel (although the real movement is in the *y*-axis). Then the code checks for boundaries. If the `_x` property has gone off the stage, based on the `Stage.width`, then `_x` is returned to 0 and *position* is reset to 0 also. Finally, you calculate the *y* coordinate in the same manner as for the previous examples.

The SquareHolder code generates only 360 duplicates of the SquareHolder movie clip and arranges them along the sine wave. The code on the Square movie clip (which is within each duplicate) actually generates the motion.

When you test the movie, you'll see that the sine wave moves across the stage to the right in a snake-like fashion. The SquareHolder movie clip duplicates are so close together that they look like a solid line.

NOTE If the movie at this point were the end result you had in mind, there's a better way to achieve the same effect. You could move just one movie clip at a time, instead of having them all march in a row. In other words, the movie clip that is to the far left would move to be the farthest right, then the next clip would move, and so on. This approach would result in the same appearance and be less CPU-intensive.

Now let's make the sine wave a bit fancier.

7. Add More Wave Variables

Add the following ActionScript at the top of the SquareHolder `onClipEvent(load)` section, before the `for` loop and below the `amplitude = 120;` line of code (7.24).

```
var period = 1;
var phaseShift = 0;
// distance to move along the x-axis
var incrementSpace = 1;
```

This code defines some more variables to be used in the sine function, which you'll use by adding some more code in the next step. You'll use the *incrementSpace* variable to determine how close to each other the new duplicated movie clips will be placed across the *x*-axis. Instead of assuming it is every pixel (as you have been by using the ++ operator), this code explicitly sets it to every pixel. If you want to later change the spacing, you can just replace the value of the *incrementSpace* variable.

The *period* and *phaseShift* are standard variables used in wave functions. The *period* variable is used to determine how frequently the sine function cycles, or how fast it goes around

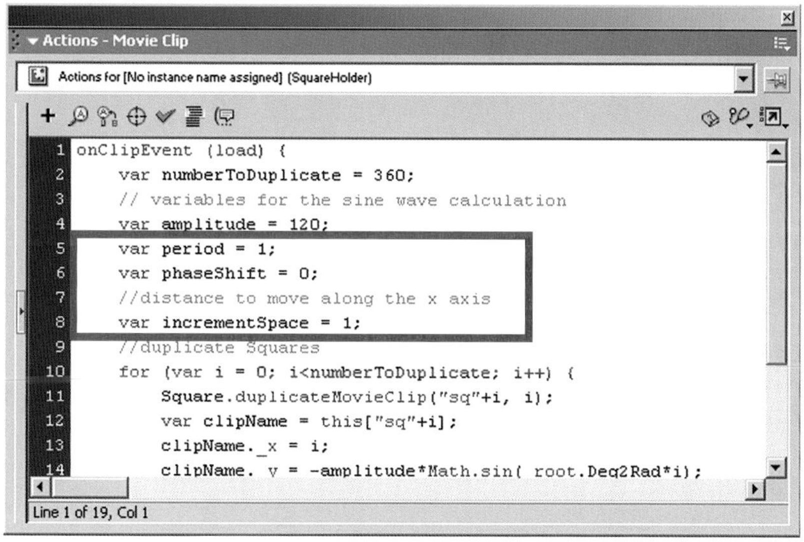
Actions - Movie Clip
Actions for [No instance name assigned] (SquareHolder)
onClipEvent (load) {
var numberToDuplicate = 360;
// variables for the sine wave calculation
var amplitude = 120;
var period = 1;
var phaseShift = 0;
//distance to move along the x axis
var incrementSpace = 1;
//duplicate Squares
for (var i = 0; i<numberToDuplicate; i++) {
Square.duplicateMovieClip("sq"+i, i);
var clipName = this["sq"+i];
clipName._x = i;
clipName._y = -amplitude*Math.sin(_root.Deg2Rad*i);
Line 1 of 19, Col 1

7.24: Add code to the SquareHolder movie.

the circle. The *phaseShift* variable shifts the sine wave over. For example, if *phaseShift* is equal to 90, the sine wave will start using 90 degrees for its base instead of 0. These variables will be easier to understand after you test the movie, but first you need to add more code.

8. Add Code to Use the Wave Variables

Edit the code on the SquareHolder movie clip. Replace these two lines (within the `for` loop):

```
clipName._x = i;
clipName._y = -amplitude * Math.sin(_root.Deg2Rad * i);
```

with the following code (7.25).

```
clipName._x = i * incrementSpace;
// calculate the y position
clipName._y = -amplitude * Math.sin(_root.Deg2Rad * (period * i + ►
phaseShift));
```

This code uses the new variables you added in the previous step. The *x* coordinate uses the *incrementSpace* variable by simply multiplying the *i* variable by the *incrementSpace* variable. This code handles the spacing of the duplicate movie clips on the *x*-axis.

Then the other new variables for the sine wave are used to generate the *y* coordinate, as follows:

```
-amplitude * Math.sin(_root.Deg2Rad * (period * i + phaseShift))
```

Notice that the main difference between this code and the code you used previously is that you will no longer be using a simple value of the *position* variable within the sine function. Now you're making a calculation: You're multiplying the value of the *i* variable by the *period* variable, and then adding the value of the *phaseShift* variable.

If you test the movie now, you won't see any difference from the previous version, because the values for the *period* and *phaseShift* variables are effectively equivalent to those you used before you added this extra code. Now let's change the code that is attached to the Square movie clip.

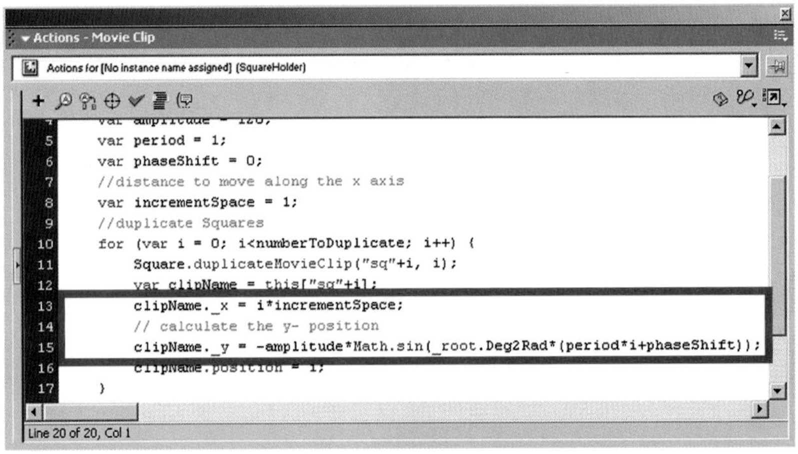

Actions - Movie Clip
Actions for [No instance name assigned] (SquareHolder)
var period = 1;
var phaseShift = 0;
//distance to move along the x axis
var incrementSpace = 1;
//duplicate Squares
for (var i = 0; i<numberToDuplicate; i++) {
Square.duplicateMovieClip("sq"+i, i);
clipName._x = i*incrementSpace;
// calculate the y- position
clipName._y = -amplitude*Math.sin(_root.Deg2Rad*(period*i+phaseShift));
}
Line 20 of 20, Col 1

7.25: Replace the original `clipName._x` *and* `clipName._y` *lines of code within the* `for` *loop on the SquareHolder movie clip.*

9. Create the *enterFrame* Wave Variables

Change the ActionScript that is attached to the Square movie clip within the SquareHolder movie clip to the following (7.26).

```
onClipEvent(enterFrame) {
    // increment position on the sine wave
    position++;
    // move object over on x-axis
    _x += _parent.incrementSpace;
    // check if off the stage on right, move clip to far left of stage
    if (_x > Stage.width) {
        _x -= _parent.numberToDuplicate * _parent.incrementSpace;
        position -= _parent.numberToDuplicate;

    }
    // calculate new y position
    _y = -_parent.amplitude * Math.sin(_root.Deg2Rad * ▶
    (_parent.period * position + _parent.phaseShift));
}
```

Most of this is the same as the original code, with a few exceptions. The first difference is how you're handling a movie clip that goes off the stage.

Now that you can change the space between the movie clips, simply moving the movie clip to 0 won't always work. This is because it's possible to have movie clips piled up on top of each other the first time the movie runs.

In this version, you spread the movie clips out and let it be okay if the movie clips are off the stage to the left as they approach the stage. But as soon as the movie clips get off the stage to the right, they go to the end of the line on the left. You accomplish this by using the `incrementSpace` and `numberToDuplicate` variables. The new `_x` property will be moved according to this computation, and the `position` variable is decremented by the `numberToDuplicate`. This allows you to change any of the variables used to generate this sine wave, and the code will still work.

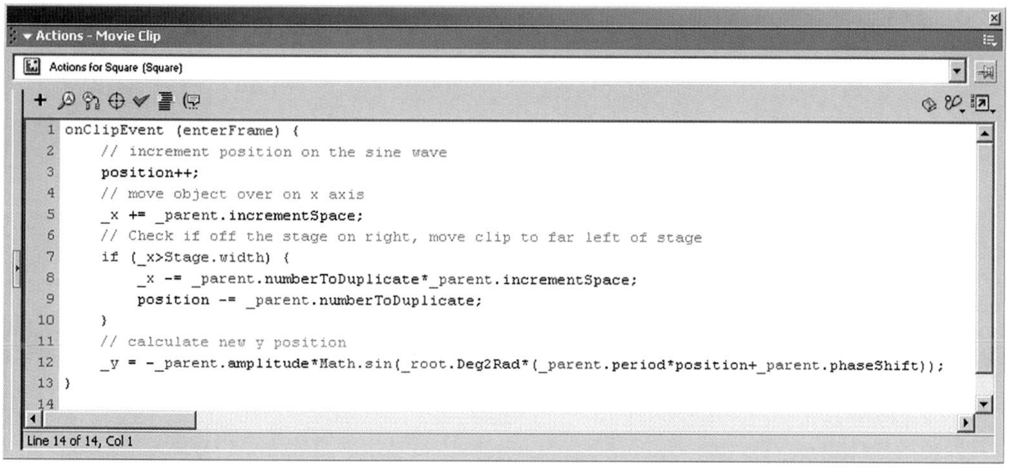
Actions - Movie Clip
Actions for Square (Square)
onClipEvent (enterFrame) {
// increment position on the sine wave
position++;
// move object over on x axis
_x += _parent.incrementSpace;
// Check if off the stage on right, move clip to far left of stage
if (_x>Stage.width) {
_x -= _parent.numberToDuplicate*_parent.incrementSpace;
position -= _parent.numberToDuplicate;
}
// calculate new y position
_y = -_parent.amplitude*Math.sin(_root.Deg2Rad*(_parent.period*position+_parent.phaseShift));
}
Line 14 of 14, Col 1

7.26: Replace the code on the Square movie clip with code that uses the new variables.

Also notice that you increment the _x property using the `incrementSpace` variable from the parent movie clip (which is the SquareHolder movie clip), using the `_parent` reference to access the value of this variable. This code now uses the += operator instead of the ++ operator. Rather than incrementing the value of the _x property by one, the code is now increasing the value of the _x property by the value of the `incrementSpace` variable.

The other difference in this code is that you're computing the _y property using the `period` and `phaseShift` variables. You also access both of these variables from the parent movie clip, using the `_parent` reference.

Now you have all the code in place to take advantage of the new variables. However, once again, if you test the movie clip now, you won't see any change. This is because the variables are still set so that everything is effectively the same as when you started. Now let's adjust some variables and see what happens.

10. Change Variable Values and Test

Return to the SquareHolder movie clip and change the `period` variable's value to 5. Now test the movie (7.27). Notice that there are five complete cycles instead of one. In other words, you now have five sine waves instead of one. Also, the duplicates are spaced out a little more. Since the duplicates are traveling up and down five times more than in the original version, the distance that they are moving in the vertical direction has increased, and they are being arranged across more distance in the *y* direction.

If you change the `phaseShift` variable's value, it's hard to see any difference right now. However, if you look closely, you'll see that the wave starts at a different place in the cycle. When you compare two sine waves with different `phaseShift` settings, you can more easily see the difference. You'll be able to take a better look at the effects of the `phaseShift` variable shortly.

Change the `amplitude` variable's value to 50. Notice that the height of the waves is much smaller (7.28). Also, the duplicates are closer together. This is because the distance that the movie clips are moving in the vertical direction has decreased. Return the `amplitude` value to 120 when you're finished testing.

Finally, change the `incrementSpace` value to 3. This causes the sine wave to stretch out. The `incrementSpace` variable increases the distance between the duplicates along the *x*-axis.

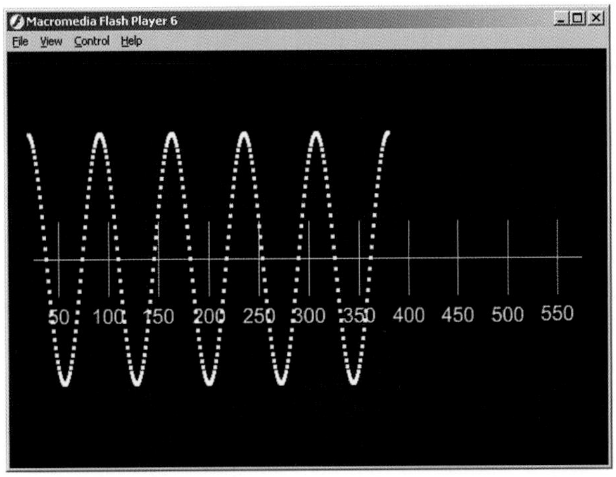

7.27: Changing the `period` variable to 5 creates five sine waves rather than only one.

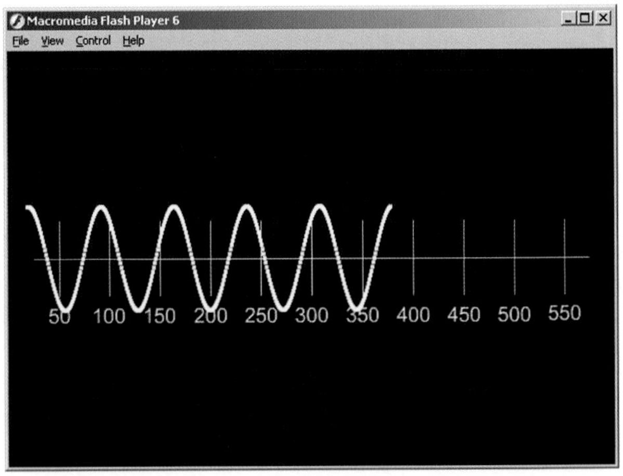

7.28: Changing the `amplitude` variable to 50 results in smaller sine waves.

This gives the appearance of changing the period, but it actually only affects how the wave is displayed. The `amplitude`, `phaseShift`, and `period` variables really do affect the sine wave.

Up to this point, you've been moving tiny, white squares along a sine wave path. You can do a lot of things to make this basic effect more interesting. Let's look at a few possibilities. First, you'll manipulate the `_alpha` property, and then you'll add color.

11. Create a Faded Sine Wave and Test

Edit the SquareHolder movie clip and add the following ActionScript to the Square movie clip (7.29). This is an `onClipEvent(load)` handler, so add it before the `onClipEvent(enterFrame)` code.

```
onClipEvent(load) {
   // calculate shading
   var myDegree = (_parent.period * position + _parent.phaseShift) % 360;
   if (myDegree >= 0 && myDegree < 180) {
      _alpha = myDegree * _root.alphaChange;
   } else {
      _alpha = (360 - myDegree) * _root.alphaChange;
   }
}
```

This sets the `_alpha` property depending on where the Square movie clip starts out in the cycle.

Test the movie to see the effect in action. Notice that the sine wave has a fade that moves across the screen. Now you can see the movement across the stage very distinctly (7.30).

To see what the code in the `onClipEvent(load)` event handler is actually doing, comment out the `onClipEvent(enterFrame)` code on the Square movie clip. Test the movie again (7.31). Without the animation, it is easier to see what's happening in the `onClipEvent(load)` event code.

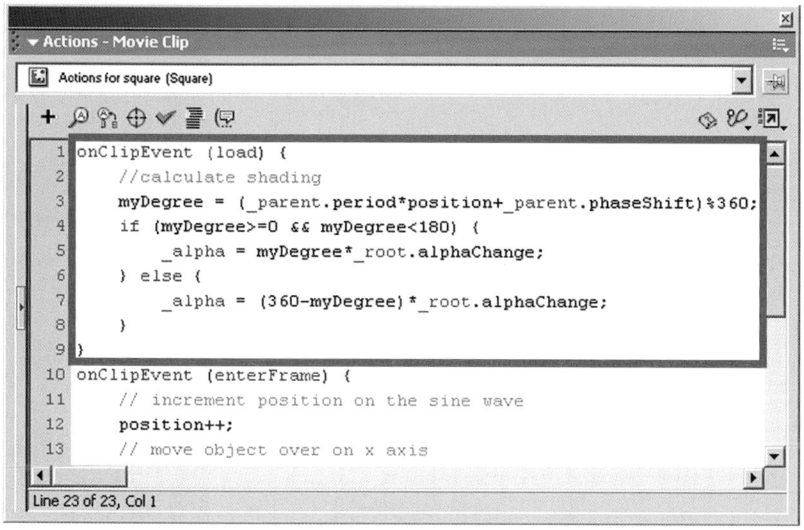

7.29: Add an `onClipEvent(load)` *event handler to create variance in the* `_alpha` *property*

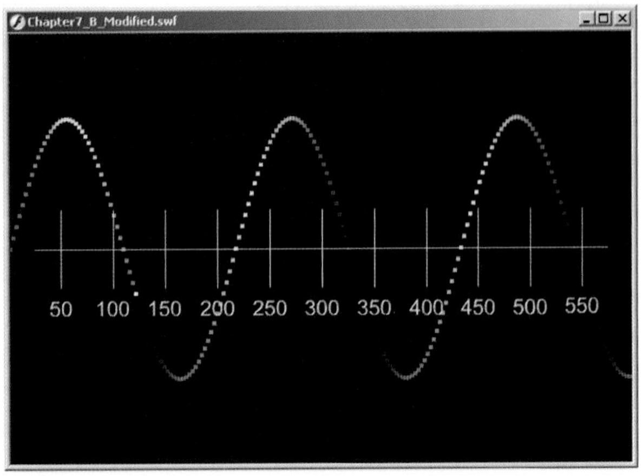

7.30: *The effect makes it very easy to see the motion. The faded and bright movie clips seem to rotate around a center axis.*

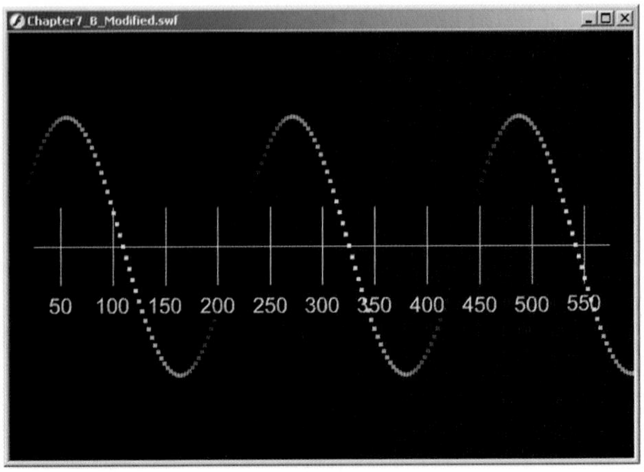

7.31: *Without the* `onClipEvent(enterFrame)` *code, it's easier to see what the code in the* `onClipEvent(load)` *event handler does.*

The sine waves are composed of cycles. A cycle for a sine wave starts at the center of the stage, where the sine wave crosses 0 on the *x*-axis and moves upward. The sine wave reaches an apex, and then moves downward. The sine wave continues downward past the 0 point on the *x*-axis until it reaches its lowest point, and then it continues back up to the 0 point on the *x*-axis. This is one cycle. For the purposes of discussion, you can break the cycle into four parts: phases 1 through 4 (7.32).

The code in the `onClipEvent(load)` event handler uses the *`alphaChange`* variable to set the `_alpha` property of each of the movie clips so that they change as follows during the four phases of the cycle:

- From fully transparent (0%) at the beginning of phase 1 to 50% transparent at the end of phase 1.
- From 50% transparent at the beginning of phase 2 to fully opaque (100%) at the end of phase 2.
- From fully opaque (100%) at the beginning of phase 3 to 50% transparent at the end of phase 3.
- Finally, phase 4 starts at 50% transparent and ends at fully transparent (0%).

The net effect is an illusion. The movie clips in phases 1 and 4 appear to be farther away than the movie clips in phases 2 and 3. When the `onClipEvent(enterFrame)` code is added, the movie clips appear to rotate.

Here, you finally use the *`alphaChange`* variable that you entered in the first step of this example. The `_alpha` property is based on the computed degree, *`myDegree`*, and then the modulus is taken of the computation. The variable *`myDegree`* is the same code that is used within the sine function computation without the conversion to radians. It simply finds the degree being used to place this movie clip at the beginning. But here, you want to make sure that the *`myDegree`* variable contains only true degrees, from 0 to 360, so you use the modulus (`%`) operator. The `%` operator finds the remainder of a division. For example, for the calculation 485 modulo by 360 (485 % 360), the result (remainder) is 125. This is a way to keep the number between 0 and 360. The result is put in the *`myDegree`* variable and used to compute the `_alpha` property.

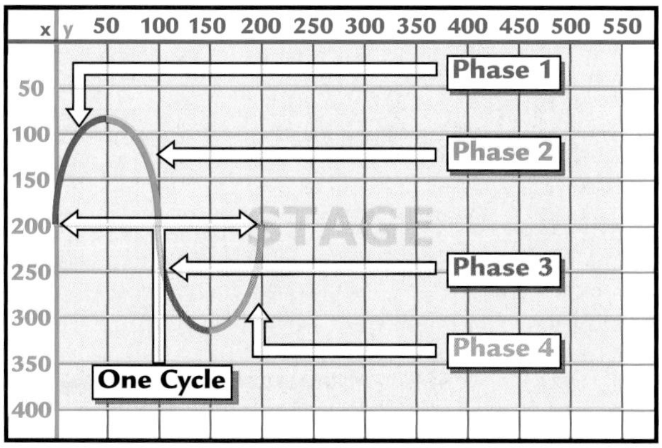

7.32: *Sine waves can be described as cycles with four phases.*

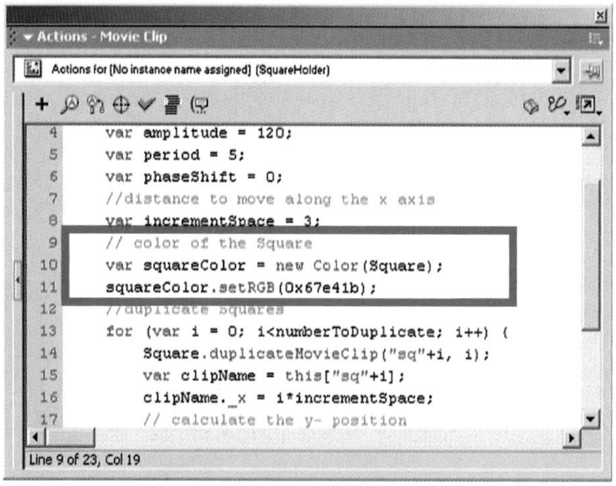

7.33: *Add code to colorize the contents of the Square-Holder movie clip.*

If *myDegree* is between 0 and 180, you want the `_alpha` property to gradually increase, so you multiply *myDegree* by *alphaChange*. This will cause the `_alpha` property to increase as *myDegree* gets closer to 180. If *myDegree* is between 180 and 360, you want the `_alpha` property to gradually fade. So you subtract *myDegree* from 360. This will give you a gradually smaller number, as *myDegree* gets closer to 360, which when multiplied by *alphaChange*, will cause the `_alpha` property to decrease.

Now you've seen the effects you can achieve by manipulating the `_alpha` property. Finally, let's add some color to the sine wave.

12. Add Color to the Sine Wave and Test

Uncomment out the `onClipEvent(enterFrame)` code on the Square movie clip. Then add the following ActionScript to the code attached to the SquareHolder movie clip, directly above the duplicate section (7.33).

```
// color of the square
var squareColor = new Color(Square);
squareColor.setRGB(0x67e41b);
```

This changes the original square to a different color using the `Color` object. This uses the `setRGB()` method of the `Color` object to set the color, as you did in Chapter 5, "Coded Animation Techniques." In the previous examples, you split the color into three variables for red, green, and blue. Here, you just put in the color directly, by simply typing in the hex number for the color. The `0x` in front of the number lets Flash know that this is a hex number.

NOTE The `setRGB()` method will take a decimal number, but it is usually easier to figure out what the hex number is, by using the Color Mixer panel or some other color-selection tool.

You could have simply edited the actual color of the square in the Square movie clip, but using this method give you much more flexibility for future changes. It allows you to change everything in one place.

When you test this version, you'll see that the sine wave looks much better with color.

Now that you've seen some basic sine wave animations, let's look at another variation that you can apply to the sine wave animation effect: rotating images.

Rotating Flowers with the Sine Function

You can also use the sine wave animation effect with a rotated image. In this exercise, you'll use a petal as your graphic to create a flower.

1. Open the File

WWW. Open Chapter7_C_Start.fla. Save the file to your local hard drive as Chapter7_C_Modified.fla. (To see the finished version, open Chapter7_C_Final.fla.)

This movie is the same as the one you ended up with in the previous section, with one exception: It has a new movie clip named Petal. The important thing about the Petal movie clip is that its registration point is off to the right, rather than centered. You'll use this new movie clip instead of the Square movie clip.

2. Replace the Square Movie Clip

Edit the SquareHolder movie clip and swap the Square movie clip out with the Petal movie clip (7.34). Test this and see that the sine wave looks very different with the Petal movie clip.

Now let's add a little rotation to the Petal movie clip.

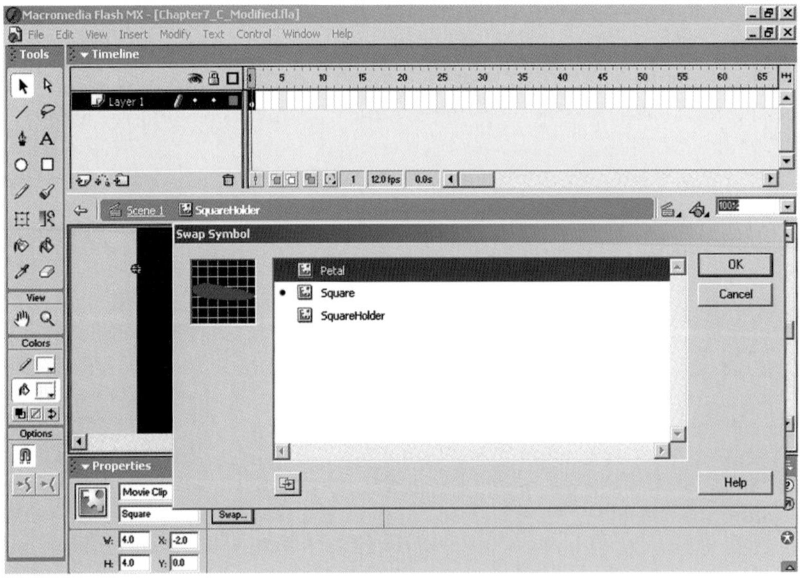

7.34: Swap the Square movie clip with the Petal movie clip.

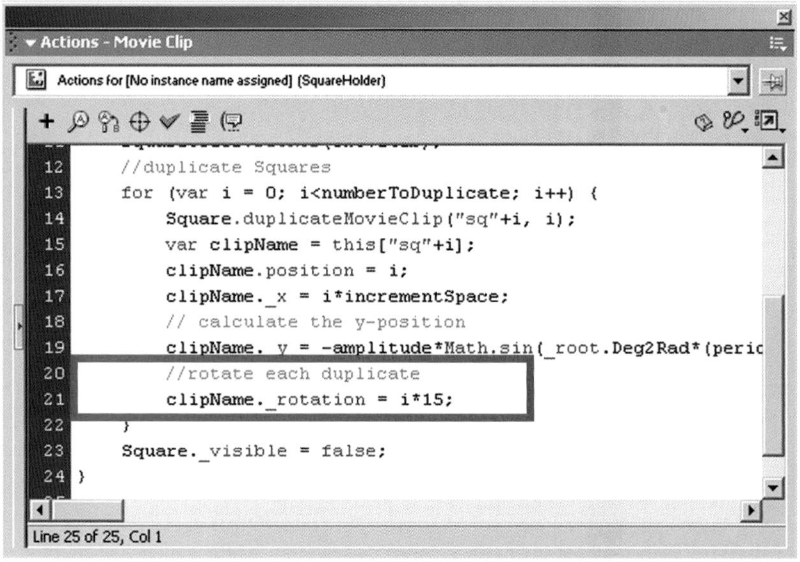

7.35: Add code that rotates the duplicates by 15 degrees to the SquareHolder movie clip.

3. Rotate Petals and Test

Add the following ActionScript to the code attached to the SquareHolder movie clip, within the `for` loop (7.35).

```
// rotate each duplicate
clipName._rotation = i * 15;
```

This rotates each duplicated Petal movie clip by 15 degrees and uses the *i* variable to have the rotation be different for each Petal clip. Test this and see the beautiful results (7.36).

This effect looks better with a smaller amplitude. Set the *amplitude* value to 25. Then test the movie again (7.37).

The movie looks even better with a smaller increment space. Set the *incrementSpace* to 1 and the *numberOfDuplicates* to 720. Test it one more time (7.38).

Let's look at one more variation on the sine wave animation effect. The next example will demonstrate how to add sine waves together.

Joining Two Sine Waves

The sine waves you've created so far are fluid, but many things in nature are not as smooth; they are more jagged and less ordered. When you add together two sine waves that have two different periods, they stack on top of each other and create a very different kind of sine wave that appears much more chaotic.

For example, consider two sine waves, one with a period of 5 and the other with a period of 8 (7.39). Their apexes and the locations where they cross the *x*-axis are different.

When you add the two sine waves together, you get a very interesting pattern (7.40). Compare this to the separate waves (7.39). You can see that at some points, the waves combine

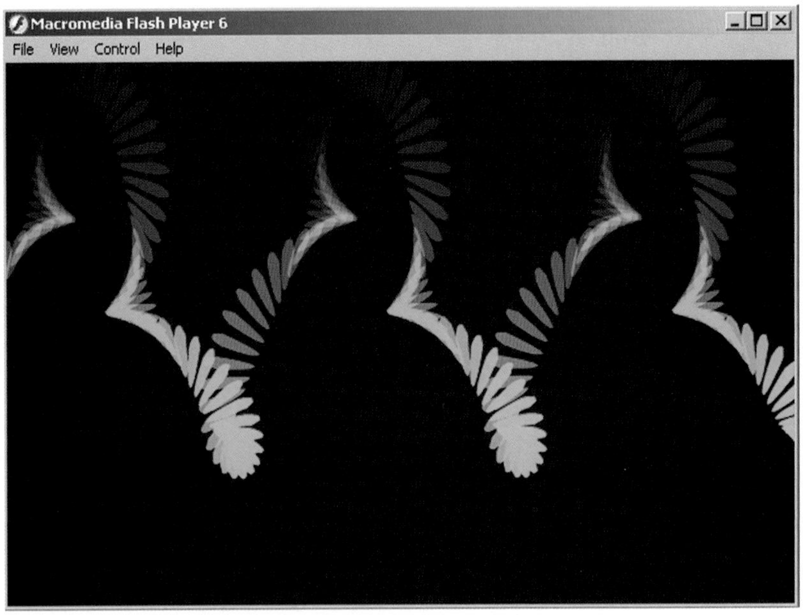

7.36: The sine wave animation with the Petal movie clip set at an amplitude of 120, an increment space of 3, and a period of 5.

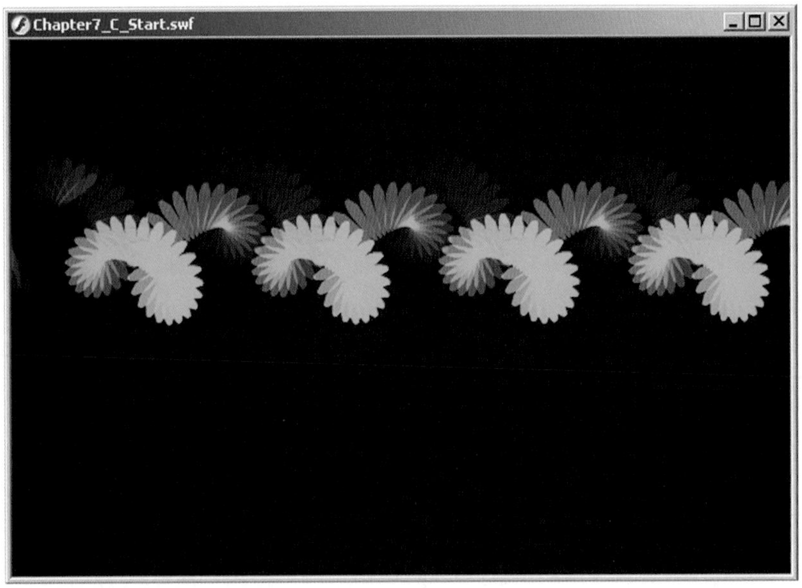

7.37: The sine wave animation with the Petal movie clip set at an amplitude of 25, an increment space of 3, and a period of 5.

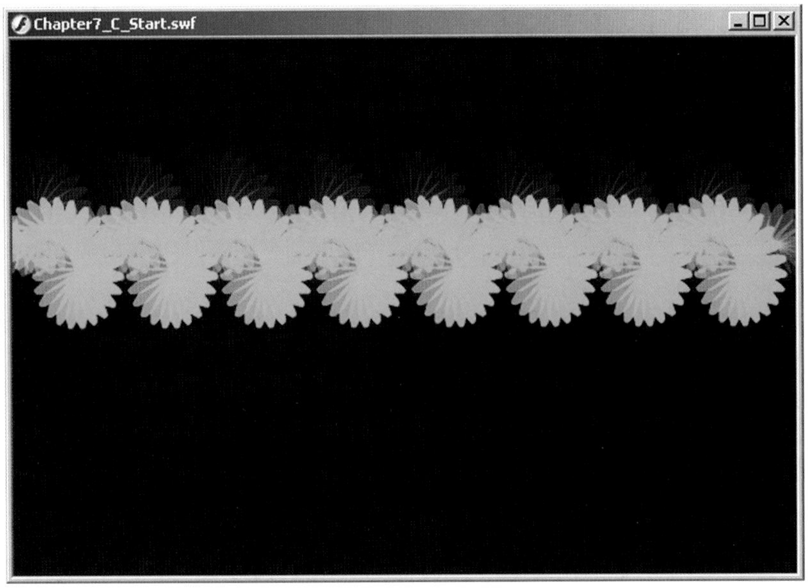

7.38: The sine wave animation with the Petal movie clip set at an amplitude of 25, an increment space of 1, and a period of 5.

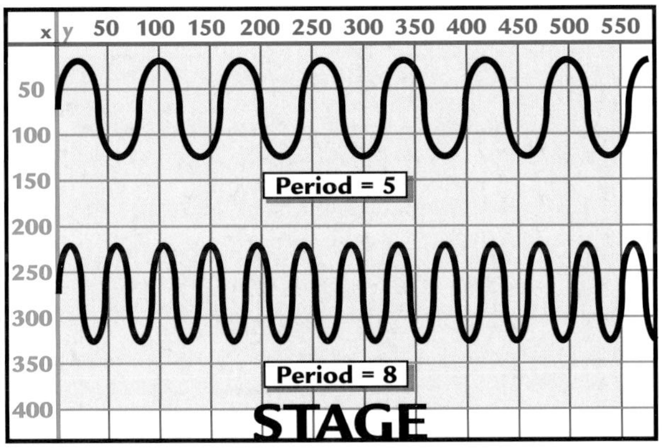

7.39: A sine wave with a period of 5 and a sine wave with a period of 8

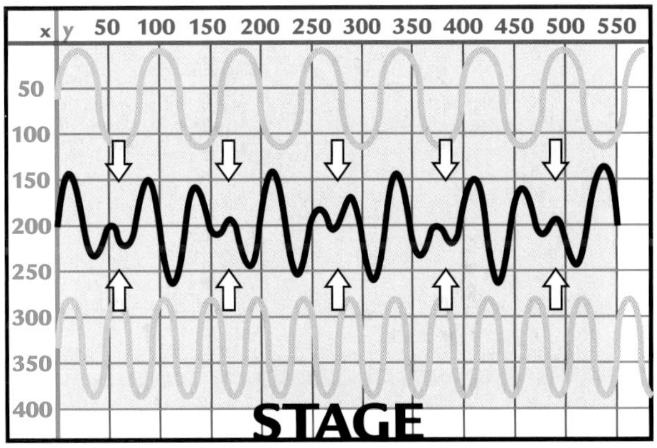

7.40: Sine waves with periods of 5 and 8 added together

to create a taller wave (when both sine waves are on the same side of the *x*-axis). At other points, the waves cancel each other out.

In this example, you'll see how adding sine waves works with both the Square movie clip and the Petal movie clip.

1. Open the File

Open Chapter7_D_Start.fla. Save the file to your local hard drive as Chapter7_D_Modified.fla. (To see the finished version, open Chapter7_D_Final.fla.)

This movie is the same as the start file you used in the previous example. First, let's use the Square movie clip for the animation.

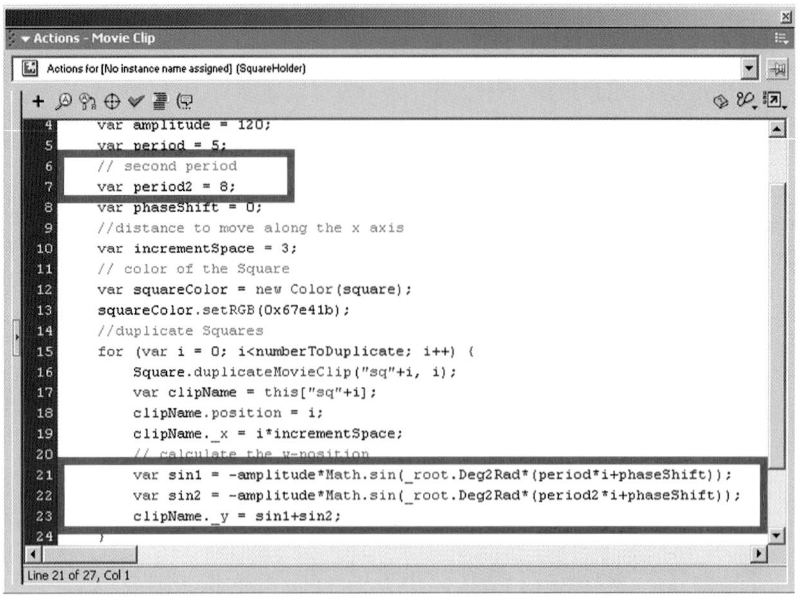

7.41: Add code to calculate adding two `Math.sin()` *calculations including a second period variable.*

2. Add Sine Waves Together

Add the following line of ActionScript to the code attached to the SquareHolder movie clip, directly below the line of code for the *period* variable.

```
// second period
var period2 = 8;
```

Then change the `clipname._y` line of code within the `for` loop to the following (7.41).

```
var sin1 = -amplitude * Math.sin(_root.Deg2Rad * (period * i + ▶
phaseShift));
var sin2 = -amplitude * Math.sin(_root.Deg2Rad * (period2 * i + ▶
phaseShift));
clipName._y = sin1 + sin2;
```

First, you create another variable for the second period, *period2*. For this example to work, it's very important that the two period values are different. Make sure that the *period2* variable's setting is different from the *period* variable's setting.

Next the original sine value using the *period* variable is computed in the variable *sin1*, and the new sine value using the second period, *period2*, is computed in the variable *sin2*. These two values are added together for the value of *_y*.

3. Animate the Added Sine Waves and Test

Edit the SquareHolder movie clip and add the following code to the Square movie clip. Replace the *_y* line of ActionScript with the following (7.42).

```
var sin1 = -_parent.amplitude * Math.sin(_root.Deg2Rad * ▶
(_parent.period * position + _parent.phaseShift));
```

```
var sin2 = -_parent.amplitude * Math.sin(_root.Deg2Rad * ▶
(_parent.period2 * position + _parent.phaseShift));
_y = sin1 + sin2;
```

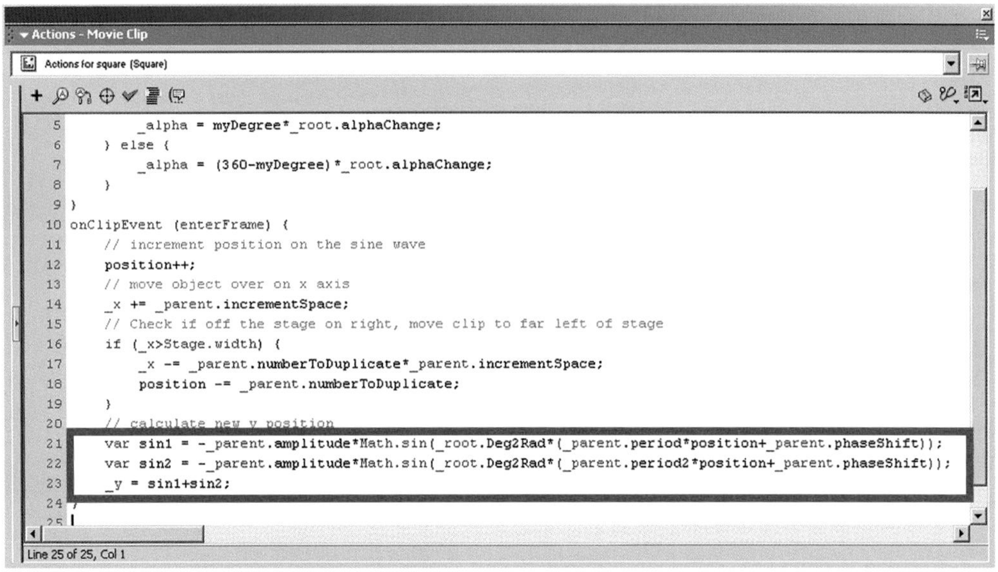

7.42: Add the code that uses the two sine values to move the _y property of the Square movie clip.

This is the same change that was applied to the SquareHolder movie clip code for the initial _y position. However, this code has been added to the `onClipevent(enterFrame)` section, so it will be repeated again and again.

Test the movie. Notice that this sine wave is very different. When two sine waves that have different periods are added together, sometimes one of the sine waves is going up when the other one is going down, and they are moving at different rates. The result is an irregular sine wave (7.43).

The actual result is a little difficult to see because it's spaced out too much. Let's change a few of the settings to better see what's going on.

4. Change Variable Settings and Test

Within the ActionScript attached to the SquareHolder movie clip, change the *`amplitude`* variable to 35 and the *`incrementSpace`* variable to 1. Then delete the current *`numberToDuplicate`* line of code, move it below the *`incrementSpace`* line, and change it to the following (7.44).

```
var numberToDuplicate = Math.ceil(Stage.width / incrementSpace);
```

Notice the *`numberToDuplicate`* variable now uses the *`incrementSpace`* variable to calculate the number of objects to cover the entire width of the screen. You calculate the needed number based on the width of the stage, `Stage.width` divided by the *`incrementSpace`* value. This will return the number of duplicates based on the spacing needed to cover the stage. The *`numberToDuplicate`* value must be an integer, so you use the `Math.ceil()` method to round up the results.

Test this version. You'll be able to see much more clearly what is happening to the two added sine waves (7.45).

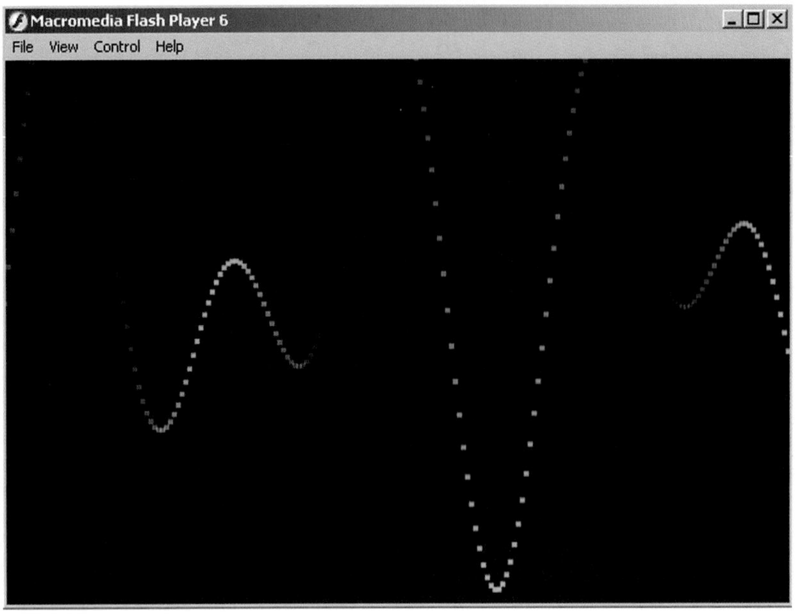

7.43: Now the sine waves are irregular because two different waves have been merged together.

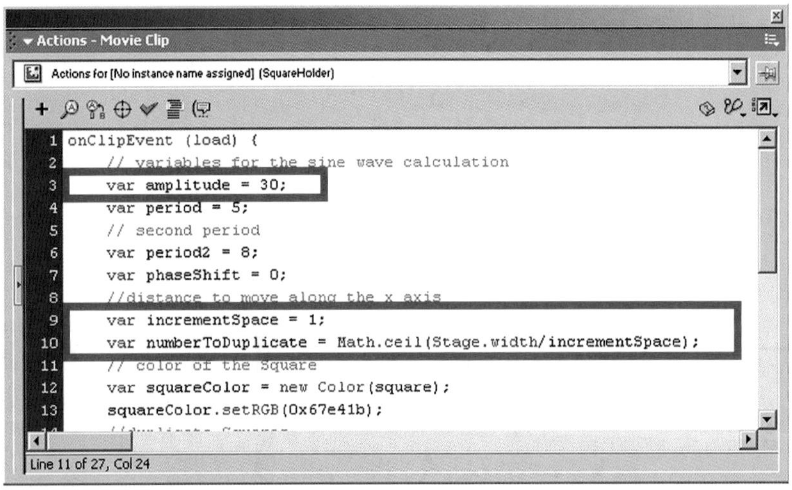

7.44: Change the settings and add code for calculating the number of duplicates.

Now let's use the Petal movie clip instead of the Square movie clip.

5. Replace the Square Movie Clip, Add the Code, and Test

Edit the SquareHolder movie clip and swap the Square movie clip with the Petal movie clip. Then add the rotation code again, within the `for` loop attached to the SquareHolder movie clip.

```
// rotate each duplicate
clipName._rotation = i * 15;
```

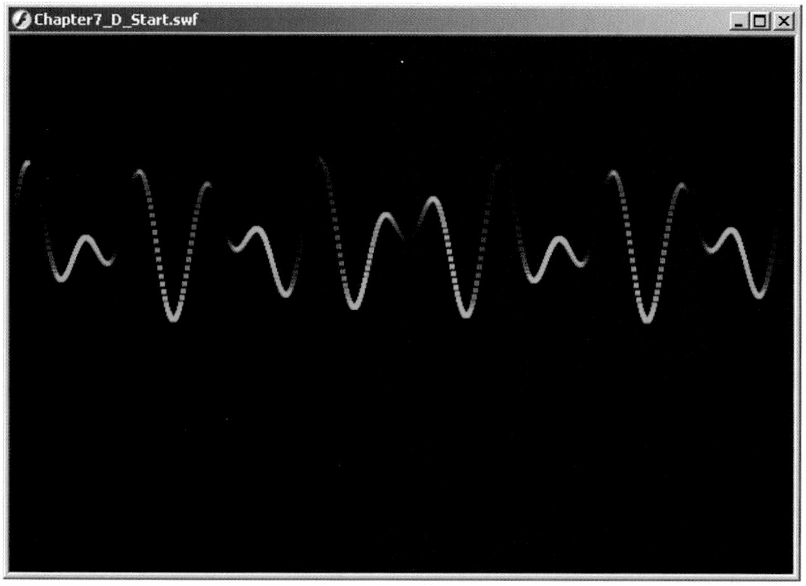

7.45: Clearer view of added sine waves

Test the animation and notice the very interesting result (7.46). This is an ever-changing animation. And all of it's done using ActionScript and math.

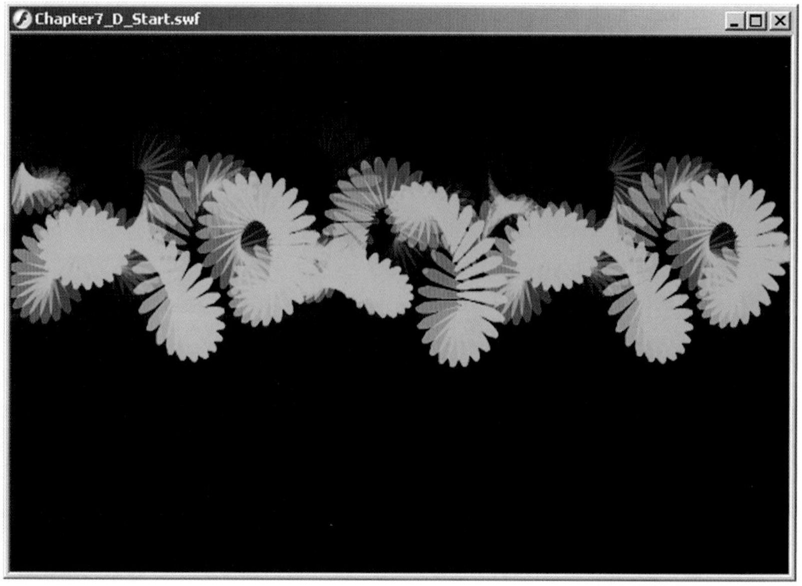

7.46: Swapping in the Petal movie clip makes the animation appear very organic.

Conclusion

Using trigonometry to create animations is relatively simple. Having circles rotate around the stage, as you did in this chapter, is just one application of rotation that you can achieve with ActionScript trigonometry. You also saw that you can use sine wave calculations to produce some stunning animations.

It's true that you could have used graphics to achieve similar effects to those in the examples here. However, you wouldn't get the ever-changing variety each time you run your movie. When you use ActionScript to create these effects, you also have much more flexibility. You can easily change the animation by altering the radius or amplitude and the period, providing a vast number of great animations. The examples in this chapter should give you an idea of some of the effects you can produce with trigonometry, circles, and sine waves.

CHAPTER eight

Games: Responding to Events

In this chapter, *you'll further explore ActionScript's tools for interactivity while you build a simple game. If you expect to build games in your work with Flash MX, topics like detecting collisions and responding to keyboard input are essential. But don't skip this chapter even if you "don't do games." The techniques you'll learn here are important to scripting many kinds of interaction and animation.*

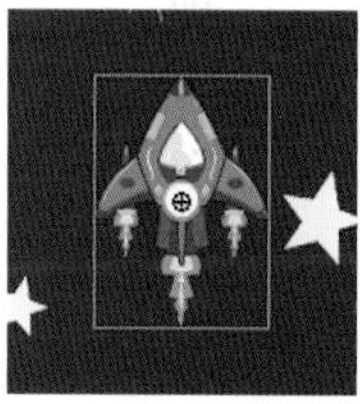

As you create the game in this chapter, you'll continue working with some of the ActionScript techniques you've used in previous chapters, including global and built-in functions and trigonometry. You'll also be introduced to some other Flash features, such as the built-in hit-detection method and the `Key` object, which lets you capture user input from the keyboard.

Detecting Collisions

In previous chapters, you've learned how to write code to handle events, such as the `onRollover()` or `onClipEvent(enterFrame)` event handlers. Another very useful event handler, particularly for games, is the `hitTest()` method of the `MovieClip` object. You can use the `hitTest()` method to discover if two movie clips have overlapped; in other words, this method can detect collisions.

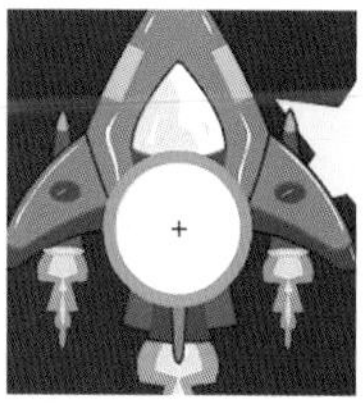

The `hitTest()` method offers three basic approaches for testing for collision detection. Depending on the syntax you employ, `hitTest()` can test for a collision (intersection) between two objects using the following guidelines:

- The two objects' bounding boxes
- The shape of one object and a point within the other object
- The bounding box of one object and a point within the other object

In this chapter, you'll work with each of these approaches for detecting collisions and learn the advantages and disadvantages of each approach. You'll continue with the Flash movie you started in Chapter 4, "Used and Reused ActionScript," which moves satellites around on the screen (**Chapter4_D_Final.fla**). First, you'll write some code to test if the satellites hit the spaceship.

1. Open the File

WWW.

Open **Chapter8_A_Start.fla**. Save the file to your local hard drive as **Chapter8_A_Modified.fla**. (For the finished version, open **Chapter8_A_Final.fla**.)

This file is similar to the file you ended with in Chapter 4, with one exception: There is a new movie clip of a spaceship on the stage called Attacker, which is on the Attacker layer. You'll use this movie clip in the hit detection. If one of the Satellite movie clips overlaps or collides with the Attacker movie clip, the Satellite movie clip will explode.

You want each of the Satellite movie clips to explode upon touching the Attacker movie clip. You have a choice of putting the hit detection in one of two places:

- You can put the hit detection on the Attacker movie clip and detect for each of the Satellite movie clips (all six plus the original).
- You can put the hit detection on all of the Satellite movie clips and detect if each one of them intersects the Attacker movie clip.

If you used the first method, you would need to write code to test for seven collisions. The latter option is easier, even though it sounds like more work. Because the Satellite movie clips are being duplicated, you can attach the hit detection ActionScript to the original Satellite movie clip, and it will be copied when each of the Satellite movie clips is duplicated. Thus, you'll need to write code to test for only one collision, rather than writing code to test for seven collisions.

2. Add the Hit Test

Attach the following ActionScript to the Satellite movie clip. Make sure it is within the `onClipEvent(enterFrame)` code (8.1).

```
// check if hit Attacker
if (this.hitTest(_root.Attacker)){
   play();
}
```

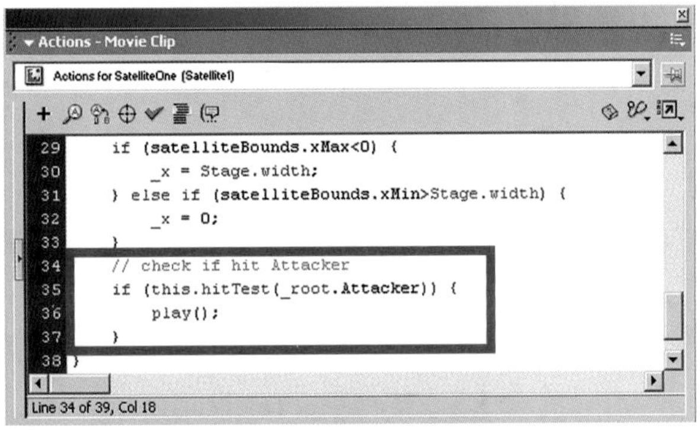

Actions - Movie Clip
Actions for SatelliteOne (Satellite1)
if (satelliteBounds.xMax<0) {
_x = Stage.width;
} else if (satelliteBounds.xMin>Stage.width) {
_x = 0;
}
// check if hit Attacker
if (this.hitTest(_root.Attacker)) {
play();
}
}
Line 34 of 39, Col 18

8.1: Add the `hitTest()` *code to the* `onClipEvent(enterFrame)` *event handler on the Satellite movie clip.*

You want to check to see if the Satellite movie clips (the original and its duplicates) have hit the Attacker movie clip. It's important to put the code within the `onClipEvent(enterFrame)` event handler because you need the code to continuously check for the collision.

The `hitTest()` method is built into the `MovieClip` object. It takes at least one argument. In this case, you give it the name of the object that it needs to check for: `_root.Attacker`. You couldn't just enter `Attacker` as the argument for the `hitTest()` method, because the Attacker movie clip is on the main timeline, not on the timeline within the Satellite movie clip.

If the two movie clips' bounding boxes intersect, the `hitTest()` will be positive and will execute the `play()` command in the `if` statement. The *bounding box* of a movie clip is the smallest rectangle that encompasses all of the movie clip. You'll take a closer look at the bounding box soon, but first let's add some code to make it easier for you to test the movie.

3. Move the Attacker Clip and Test

Attach the following ActionScript to the Attacker instance (8.2).

```
onClipEvent(load){
   this.startDrag(true);
}
```

The `startDrag()` method allows you to drag an object around. This is usually done when you select an object with the mouse and then drag it, but in this case, you want to drag it all the time. This is similar to what you did in Chapter 3, "Cursor Interactions," where you had an object follow the mouse around using the `_xmouse` and `_ymouse` properties (**Chapter3_D_Final.fla** and **Chapter3_E_Final.fla**).

Setting `startDrag()` to `true` for the Attacker instance (`this`) will allow you to move the spaceship around and attack all those poor, helpless satellites, and then watch them explode.

Now test the movie. Move the Attacker movie clip around and notice that the Satellite movie clips explode when the spaceship collides with them (8.3).

Watch carefully as you move the Attacker movie clip around. You'll notice that sometimes you barely touch the Satellite movie clips, but they still explode. In fact, if you move the Attacker movie clip so that the nose of the spaceship is just to the right or the left of a Satellite movie clip, a collision will occur, even though the Attacker movie clip and the Satellite movie clip don't appear to have touched.

This demonstrates a problem with this approach to collision detection: Collisions occur even when objects do not appear to have collided (8.4). This occurs because the hit

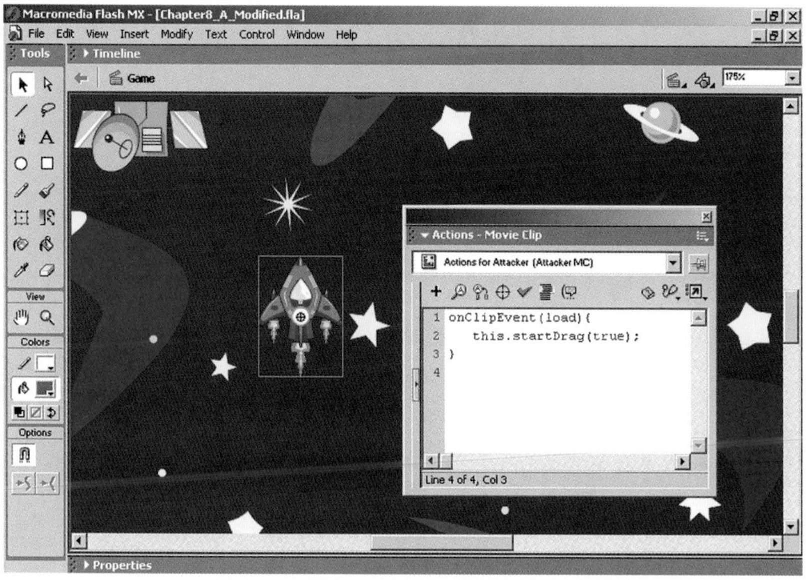

8.2: Select the Attacker movie clip (the spaceship) and apply the `startDrag()` *method within the* `onClipEvent(load)` *event handler.*

8.3: *The satellites explode when the spaceship collides with them.*

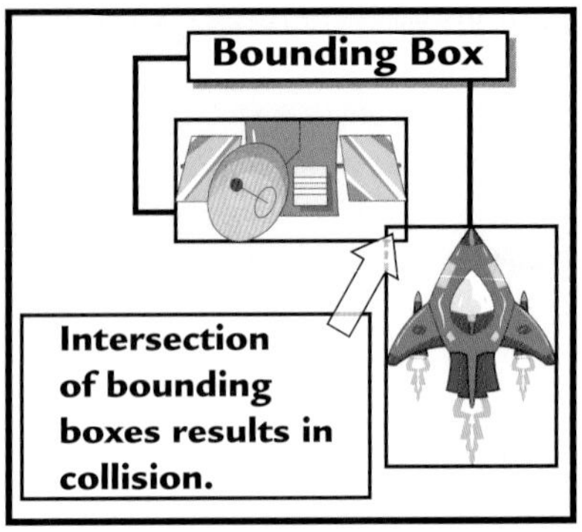

8.4: *A collision occurs, even if the two movie clips aren't actually touching.*

detection is based on the bounding box of the two movie clips. This is the default test, which will be used when the `hitTest()` method has only one argument. The `hitTest()` method will be `true` if the bounding boxes of the two movie clips intersect, even if the actual graphics within the movie clip are not touching.

The `hitTest()` method is fairly sophisticated. If you send the `hitTest()` method one argument, Flash automatically knows that the argument is the name of a movie clip. In step 2, you entered the following statement:

```
if (this.hitTest(_root.Attacker)){
```

This can be translated as, "Test for a collision between `this` (the object to which the code is attached; namely, the Satellite movie clip) and Attacker (the movie clip identified in the method's argument)."

However, the `hitTest()` method behaves differently if you enter three arguments. Flash then automatically assumes that that the first two arguments are *x* and *y* coordinates. The *x* and *y* coordinate represent a spot on the stage for the hit detection. The third argument signals to Flash whether it should use the actual shape of the graphic (when it's set to `true`) or the bounding box (when it's set to `false`). Let's change the code to try another approach to implementing collision detection.

4. Use *hitTest()* Coordinates and Test

Change the `hitTest()` method that is attached to the Satellite movie clip to the following ActionScript (8.5).

```
if (this.hitTest(_root.Attacker._x, _root.Attacker._y, true)){
   play();
}
```

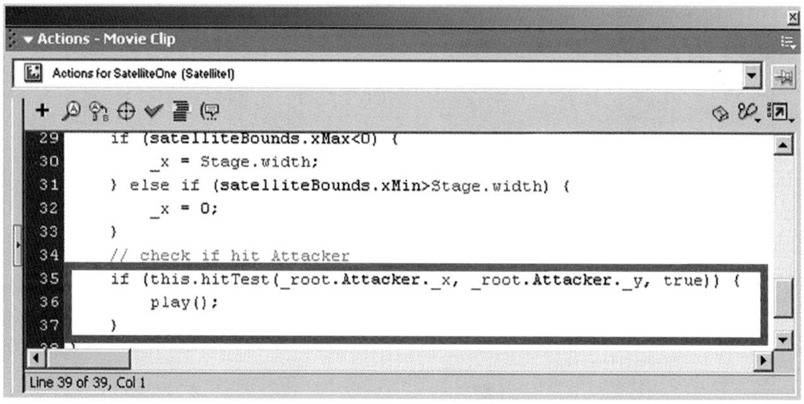

8.5: Replace the `hitTest()` *code attached to the Satellite movie clip.*

This `hitTest()` method is sending three arguments. The first two are the *x* and *y* coordinates of the Attacker movie clip (the spaceship), as you move it around. The third argument is the word `true`, which means you want to use the shape of the Satellite movie clip, not the bounding box (8.6).

This might be a little confusing because the *x* and *y* coordinates used for the `hitTest()` method are coordinates on the stage. How does Flash detect the collision of the Attacker movie clip? Notice that the arguments being passed in are the coordinates of the Attacker movie clip on the stage, and they are changing based on where you move the Attacker movie clip. So even though you're testing for a collision with a spot on the stage, the middle of the Attacker movie clip also happens to be at the same point.

Test the movie. Notice how the spaceship must get within a satellite graphic before the satellite explodes. In fact, the center of the Attacker movie clip must be within the Satellite movie clip before it explodes.

This approach to implementing collision detection has the opposite problem of the first approach: A collision does not occur soon enough. One of the objects must be at least halfway overlapping the other object before the collision occurs.

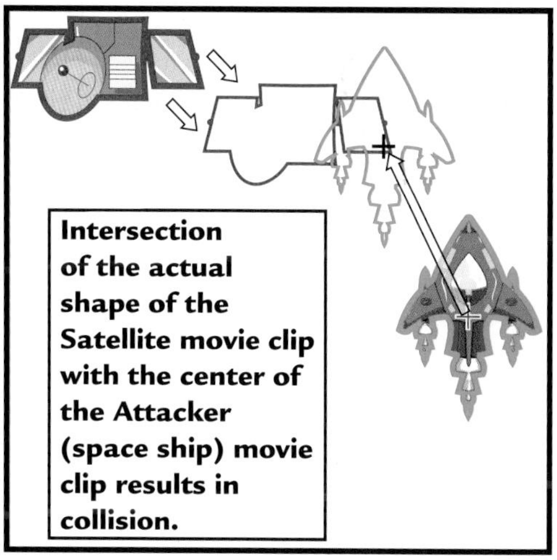

8.6: The actual shape of the movie clip (Satellite) that contains the `hitTest()` *method is used with the centerpoint of the other movie clip (the spaceship) to generate the collision detection.*

So you've looked at two different ways to use the `hitTest()` method. The first technique employs the bounding boxes of two different movie clips. The second technique employs the shape of the host movie clip (the movie clip that has the `hitTest()` method code) with the centerpoint of the other movie clip. There's another way. By setting the third argument to `false`, you tell Flash to use the bounding box of the Satellite movie clip instead of the shape. This implements collision detection with a bounding box and a point.

Unfortunately, all three of these options leave something to be desired. Unless you happen to be using rectangular objects for your graphics, you'll typically want the collision detection to occur somewhere in between the bounding box and the centerpoint. To get around this, there is a simple trick that you can employ. The trick involves placing a second, smaller movie clip within the main movie clip, and then using that smaller movie clip to test for the collision. Let's use that approach now.

5. Use the HitSpot Movie Clip and Test

Change the ActionScript with the `hitTest()` method that is attached to the Satellite movie clip to the following (8.7).

```
if (this.hitTest(_root.Attacker.HitSpot)){
   play();
}
```

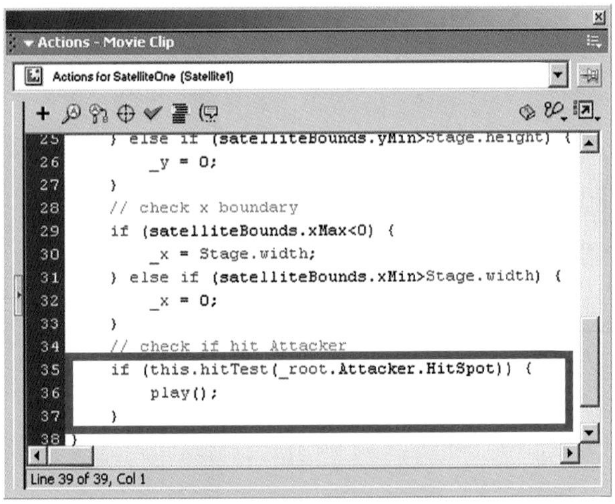

8.7: Replace the `hitTest()` *code attached to the Satellite movie clip.*

This detects if the Satellite movie clip has hit the HitSpot movie clip within the Attacker movie clip.

If you edit the Attacker movie clip, you'll see a layer called HitSpot, which contains a movie clip with the instance name HitSpot MC (8.8). This is the movie clip that is used for the hit detection. Notice that it's smaller than the Attacker movie clip, but it is still bigger than the small point at the center of the movie clip. Also notice that the HitSpot movie clip has ActionScript attached to it to make it invisible upon loading. This way, the HitSpot movie clip is not visible to the user, but it's still visible to the code.

Test this version of the movie. Notice that it does have a smaller hit range than the first version, but a larger hit range than the second version. In many cases, this approach is the best way to go. You can change the size of the hit range simply by changing the size of the HitSpot movie clip.

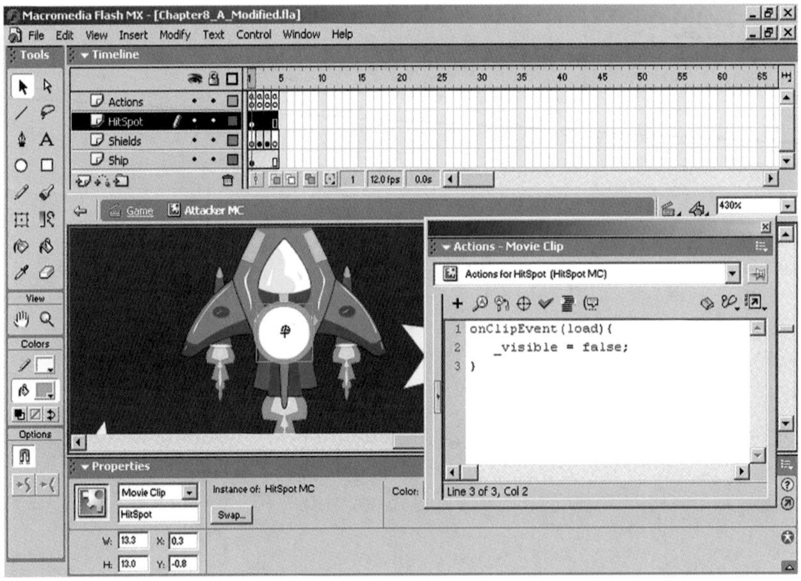

8.8: The HitSpot movie clip has code assigned to it to make it invisible when the movie clip loads.

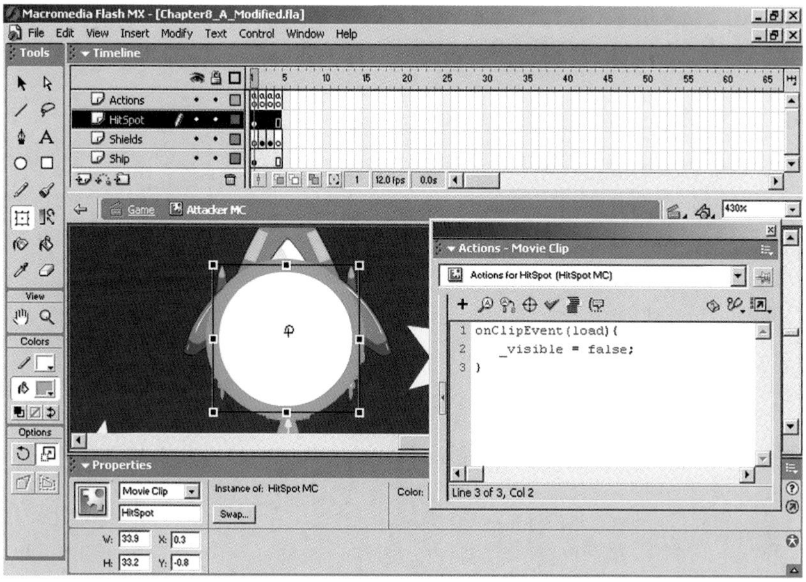

8.9: Use the Free Transform tool to enlarge the HitSpot movie clip and then retest the movie.

Try going back in and editing the HitSpot movie clip. Use the Free Transform tool to enlarge the HitSpot movie clip a little (8.9), and then retest. Notice that the collision detection is a bit better than the previous two examples. It's still not ideal, but typically, the collision does not appear to happen too soon or too late.

Now you've learned the basic techniques for implementing collision detection. Let's put these principles into practice. Dragging the ship around doesn't make for a very fun game. Let's add keyboard controls.

Adding Keyboard Movement Controls

It doesn't take a whole lot of skill to hit the satellites by moving the spaceship around. The game would be a lot more interesting if the arrows on the keyboard controlled the spaceship (the Attacker movie clip).

In this example, you'll write the script so that players can use the arrows on the keyboard to move the spaceship around—not just up and down, but at angles, too. You'll use Flash's `Key` object to capture the keys that are pressed on the keyboard. The `Key` object is very handy for game applications.

1. Open the File

Open Chapter8_B_Start.fla. Save the file to your local hard drive as Chapter8_B_Modified.fla. (For the finished version, open Chapter8_B_Final.fla.) WWW.

The file is similar to the file you ended with in the previous example, except that you cannot move the Attacker movie clip using the mouse. First, you'll add some code that will make the Attacker movie clip move in response to the keyboard arrow keys.

2. Capture Key Movement and Test

Attach the following ActionScript to the Attacker instance (8.10).

```
onClipEvent(load) {
   var xSpeed = 0;
   var ySpeed = 0;
}
onClipEvent(enterFrame) {
   // Detect keypresses = calculate angle thrust
   var keyPressed = Key.getCode();
   switch (keyPressed) {
      case Key.UP:
         // up arrow
         xSpeed--;
         ySpeed--;
         break;
      case Key.DOWN:
         // down arrow
         xSpeed++;
         ySpeed++;
         break;
      case Key.SPACE:
         // space bar stop moving
         xSpeed = 0;
         ySpeed = 0;
         break;
   }
   // check to make sure speed is not too fast
   if (xSpeed > 10) {
      xSpeed = 10;
   } else if (xSpeed <- 10) {
      xSpeed = -10;
   }
   if (ySpeed > 10) {
      ySpeed = 10;
   } else if (ySpeed <- 10) {
      ySpeed = -10;
   }
   // Actual Movement
   _x += xSpeed;
   _y += ySpeed;
}
```

This code will make the Attacker movie clip respond to the left and right arrow keys, but in a very limited way. Also, pressing the spacebar will stop the Attacker movie clip.

In the `onClipEvent(load)` section, the code initializes a couple of variables. The *xSpeed* and *ySpeed* variables are used for the amount of movement in each direction, and they are set to 0 to begin with. Each time the right or left arrow is pressed, the speed in both directions increases.

As usual, the code within the `onClipEvent(enterFrame)` event handler does most of the work. First, you need to find out which key is being pressed. The code uses the `getCode()` method of the `Key` object to obtain what key was last pressed. This information is stored in the variable *`keyPressed`*. The `getCode()` method returns the key code value of the last key pressed, and this code is in the `onClipEvent(enterFrame)` section of the code. This means that if the player presses a key once, and then no other key is pressed, `getCode()` will continue to send the same key, as if the user were pressing the same key many times.

The next section of the code uses the value of *`keyPressed`* to set the *`xSpeed`* and *`ySpeed`* variables depending on which key was pressed. This is in a `switch` statement. A `switch` statement is similar to an `if/else if` statement, except it is faster in execution and easier for programmers to read. The `switch` statement is given a variable to test on, which is *`keyPressed`* in this case. The key code value of the up arrow is `Key.UP` or 38, and the down arrow is `Key.DOWN` or 40.

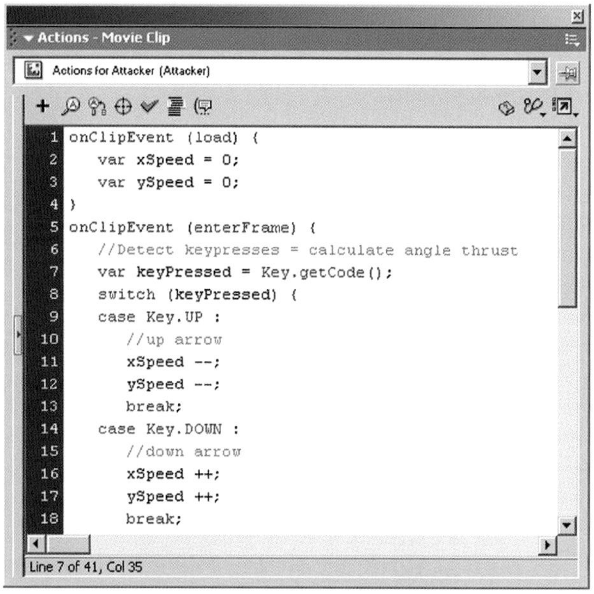

8.10: Enter the code to implement keyboard control for the Attacker movie clip.

NOTE Here, you're using the properties of the `Key` method. There are many properties of the `Key` method that contain the value of special keys. For example, the property `Key.DOWN` has the value of 40 and cannot be changed. This way, you don't need to know the actual value of the down arrow key. See Table A.1 in the Appendix of this book for a complete list of the key codes.

Within the `switch` statement is the keyword `case`, with the `Key` properties after it. This is similar to the checking part of the `if` statement. In other words, it is similar to writing something like `if keyPressed = Key.DOWN`. Also, the keyword `break` is used in the `switch` statement. This is a signal that tells the `switch` statement that you're finished doing whatever you need to do for this `case`. If you didn't include the `break` statement, when the first `case` code was executed, Flash would continue and execute all of the `case` statements until the end of the `switch` statement.

The above `switch` statement would be written as follows using an `if/else if` statement.

```
if (keyPressed == Key.UP){
   // up arrow
   xSpeed--;
   ySpeed--;
} else if (keyPressed == Key.DOWN){
   // down arrow
   xSpeed++;
   ySpeed++;
} else if (keyPressed == Key.SPACE){
   // space bar stop moving
```

continues

```
        xSpeed = 0;
        ySpeed = 0;
    }
```

As you can see, the structure of a `switch` statement and an `if/else if` statement is similar, but it's easier to see what you're testing for in a `switch` statement.

So if the user presses the up arrow, the speed is decreased and even goes in the negative direction. If the user presses the down arrow, the speed is increased. If the user presses the spacebar, the speed is set to 0.

Variations for *switch* Statements

By intentionally omitting a `break` statement in your switch statement, you can execute the same code for multiple `case` statements. In addition to `case` and `break` statements for the `switch` statement, there is a `default` option available. The `default` statement captures all the rest of the `case` statements and does whatever you specify in the code. The following is an example of using multiple `case` statements with one `break` statement and the `default` statement.

```
switch (color){
    case "blue":
    case "red":
        // do something for blue and red
        break;
    case "yellow":
        // do something for yellow
        break;
    default:
        // do something for every other color
}
```

The next section makes sure that the speed is not too fast or too slow. The limits are set from 10 to –10 for both directions of speed.

Finally, the `_x` and `_y` properties of the Attacker movie clip are incremented by the new *xSpeed* and *ySpeed* values.

Test this movie. Notice that the spaceship goes in only two directions—either up and to the left or down and to the right—and the movement along the *x*-axis and *y*-axis is at the same speed. This is because the *xSpeed* and *ySpeed* values increase or decrease at the same rate. For example, when *xSpeed* is equal to 5, *ySpeed* is equal to 5. This is not what you want, so let's fix this using some trigonometry.

3. Add Rotation and Movement

Add the following variable to the end of the `onClipEvent(load)` section of the code on the Attacker movie clip (8.11):

```
var rotateRate = 15;
```

Also, change the `switch` statement to look like the following (8.11):

```
switch (keyPressed) {
   case Key.UP :
```

```
        // up arrow
        xSpeed += Math.sin(Math.PI / 180 * (90 - _rotation));
        ySpeed -= Math.cos(Math.PI / 180 * (90 - _rotation));
        break;
    case Key.DOWN :
        // down arrow
        xSpeed -= Math.sin(Math.PI / 180 * (90 - _rotation));
        ySpeed += Math.cos(Math.PI / 180 * (90 -_rotation));
        break;
    case Key.RIGHT :
        // right arrow
        _rotation += rotateRate;
        break;
    case Key.LEFT :
        // left arrow
        _rotation -= rotateRate;
        break;
    case Key.SPACE :
        // space bar stop moving
        xSpeed = 0;
        ySpeed = 0;
        break;
}
```

This code rotates the Attacker movie clip when you press the left and right arrow keys. The up and down arrow keys still move the Attacker movie clip up and down, but now this movement is relative to the Attacker movie clip's current degree of rotation. This results in a wider range of motion for the spaceship.

The *rotateRate* variable is used to determine how fast the Attacker movie clip will rotate around itself. It will affect the `_rotation` property of the movie clip. The left and right arrow keys affect the `_rotation` property of the movie clip by adding or subtracting the *rotateRate* variable to the `_rotation` property.

The up and down arrow keys are now using trigonometry to define what direction to go and how much. This is based on the `_rotation` property of the movie clip.

As you learned in Chapter 7, "ActionScript Trigonometry," the sine and the cosine can be used to return the *x* and *y* coordinates. To compute the *xSpeed* value, you calculate the cosine of 90 minus the `_rotation` property of the Attacker movie clip and either add it to or subtract it from *xSpeed*. To compute the *ySpeed* value, you calculate the sine of 90 minus the `_rotation` property and add it to or subtract it

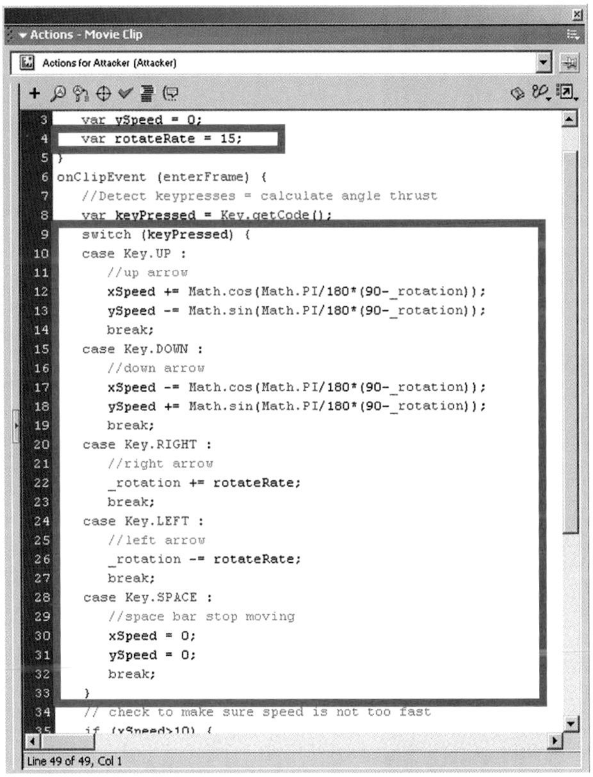

8.11: Edit the code on the Attacker movie clip so that the movie clip rotates when the left and right arrow keys are pressed.

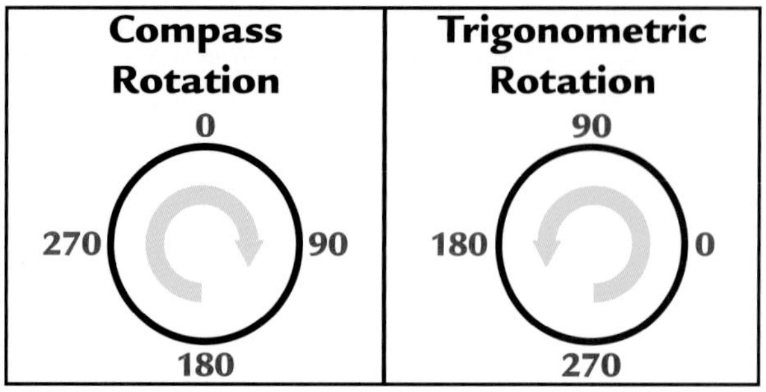

8.12: *Compass rotation versus trigonometric rotation*

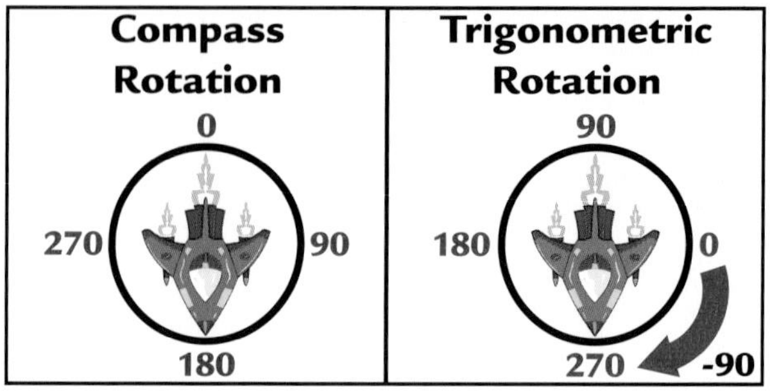

8.13: *Subtracting the* `_rotation` *value from 90 puts the spaceship in the trigonometric system of rotation.*

from *ySpeed*. You need to subtract the `_rotation` from 90 because the `_rotation` property bases its values on a compass rotation, where 0 is at the top and rotation is in the clockwise direction. However, in the trigonometry style of rotation, 0 is to the right and rotation is in the counter-clockwise direction (8.12).

To convert the `_rotation` property into a rotation or degree that the cosine and sine functions can use, you subtract the `_rotation` value from 90. This puts the rotation value of the spaceship into the trigonometric system (8.13).

Now let's make sure that the Attacker movie clip stays on the stage.

4. Add Boundary-Checking Code and Test

Add the following ActionScript to the code on the Attacker movie clip within the `onClipEvent(enterFrame)` event handler section of the code, at the bottom (8.14).

```
// Screen wrap
AttackerBounds = this.getBounds(_root);
if (AttackerBounds.yMax < 0) {
   _y = Stage.height;
} else if (AttackerBounds.yMin > Stage.height) {
   _y = 0;
}
// check x boundary
if (AttackerBounds.xMax < 0) {
   _x = Stage.width;
} else if (AttackerBounds.xMin > Stage.width) {
   _x = 0;
}
```

This is the same boundary-checking code that is attached to the Satellite movie clips (see Chapter4_D_Final.fla). Test the movie. Notice that you can control the direction and speed of the Attacker movie clip with the arrow keys, and you can stop the Attacker movie clip with the spacebar.

But there is still the problem with the keypress handling. You want the Attacker movie clip to speed up only if you repeatedly press a key, not automatically speed up. To accomplish this, you'll use a new feature in Flash MX called a *listener*. A listener is used to wait for a specific user interaction and then let the code know when it happens. This way, you'll be able to tell when there is a new keypress. Let's add the listener code.

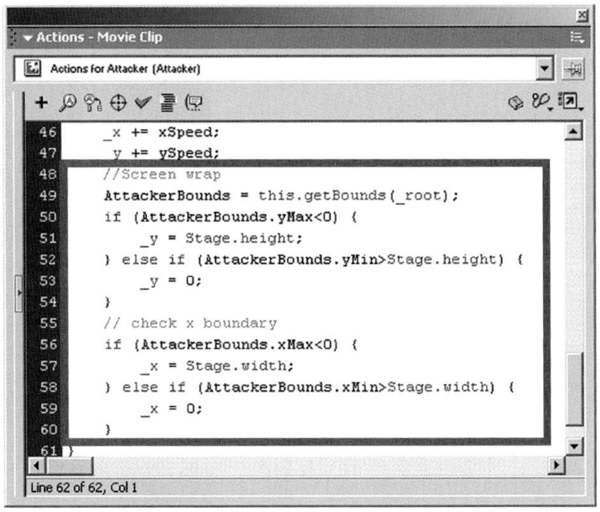

8.14: *Add code to the Attacker movie clip so that the move clip wraps around when it moves off the stage.*

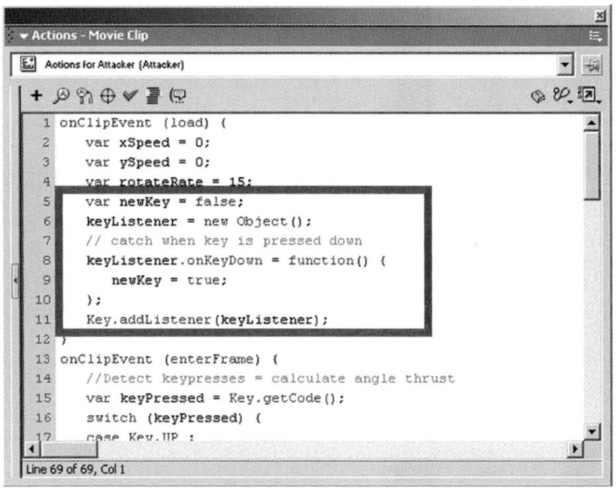

8.15: *Add code to the Attacker movie clip so that it only catches a new keypress.*

5. Add the Key Listener

Add the following code within the `onClipEvent(load)` section, at the bottom (8.15).

```
var newKey = false;
keyListener = new Object();
// catch when key is pressed down
keyListener.onKeyDown = function() {
   newKey = true;
};
Key.addListener(keyListener);
```

This code uses the listener feature of the `Key` object. First, you define a variable, *`newKey`*, that will be `true` when a key is pressed and `false` as long as it is held down or no new key is pressed. The speed increase will be added only if a key is pressed. The *`newKey`* variable starts out as `false`.

Then you add the listener for the key. To use a listener, first you need to create it using the generic `Object` object. The key listener object is called *`keyListener`*.

After you create a listener object, you can use the available listener methods. In the case of the `Key` object, there are two listener methods: `onKeyDown()` and `onKeyUp()`. You next create a method called `onKeyDown()` for the *`keyListener`* object that sets the *`newKey`* variable to `true`. So far, this is simply an object with one method, `onKeyDown()`.

Then you use the `addListener()` method of the `Key` object to specify which listener object to call, which is *`keyListener`* in this case. You use the `Key` object because you want to catch a keystroke. The `addListener()` method needs an argument that is the name of the object that is set up for listening. Each of these methods will be called automatically when a key is pressed and released.

Now you need to use the *`newKey`* variable to make sure that the speed increases only when you press a new key.

6. Use the *newKey* Variable and Test

Add the following `if` statement at the top of the `onClipEvent(enterFrame)` section (8.16).

```
if (newKey) {
   newKey = false;
```

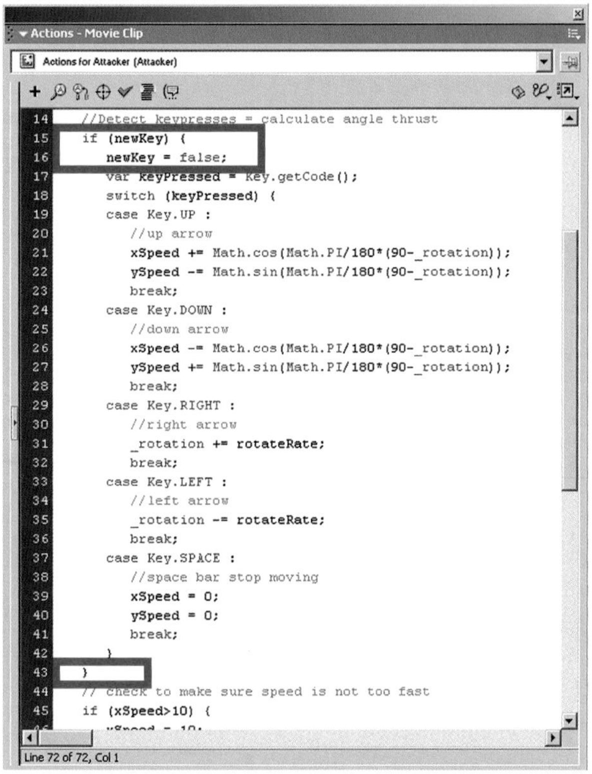

8.16: Add code to the Attacker movie clip so that it catches only a new keypress.

To end the `if` statement, place a closing brace (`}`) below the `switch` statement (8.16).

Here, you've made sure that the only time you actually call the `Key.getCode()` and `switch` statement is when a key has been pressed. As soon as you enter the `if` statement, the variable *`newKey`* is set to `false`, so that the only time the `switch` statement is called is when a key is pressed.

Test this version. You'll see that now when you press one of the arrow keys, the spaceship doesn't just zoom off. The movement is actually a little controlled. Now you need to press the arrow keys multiple times to speed the ship up.

To make the game a little more exciting, you'll add one more element—bullets for the spaceship to shoot at the satellites.

Firing Bullets

Next, you'll set up the game so that the spaceship can fire bullets at the satellites from a distance. The spaceships will explode when they're hit by bullets. The bullets will be activated by a mouse click.

Firing bullets from a stationary object is rather easy. You simply create a movie clip, and in the `onClipEvent(enterFrame)` section, move it in the direction you want. But in this case, you want the bullets to come from a moving object—the rotating spaceship—and from the front of the spaceship at all times. You'll use trigonometry with a twist to get the bullets to fire from the front of the ship.

You also want the bullets to explode the satellites. To accomplish this, you'll need to use arrays and more `hitTest()` methods to detect if the bullets have hit any of the satellites.

1. Open the File

WWW.

Open **Chapter8_C_Start.fla**. Save the file to your local hard drive as **Chapter8_C_Modified.fla**. (For the finished version, open **Chapter8_C_Final.fla**.)

This is almost exactly where you left off in the previous example, except there are two new movie clips called Bullet and Bullet MC. The Bullet MC movie clip contains the Bullet movie clip and has a linkage name of Bullet. One movie clip has been embedded within another so that you can move the Bullet movie clip and check the boundaries within an `onClipEvent(enterFrame)` event handler.

First, you need to create an array to hold the names of the Satellite movie clips for easier referencing.

2. Create a Satellite Array

Change the Satellite `for` loop on frame 1 of the Actions layer to the following (8.17).

```
var SatelliteArray = new Array(numberOfSatellites + 1);
SatelliteArray[0] = SatelliteOne;
for (var level = 1; level <= numberOfSatellites; level++){
   SatelliteOne.duplicateMovieClip("Satellite" + level, level);
   SatelliteArray[level] = _root["Satellite" + level];
}
```

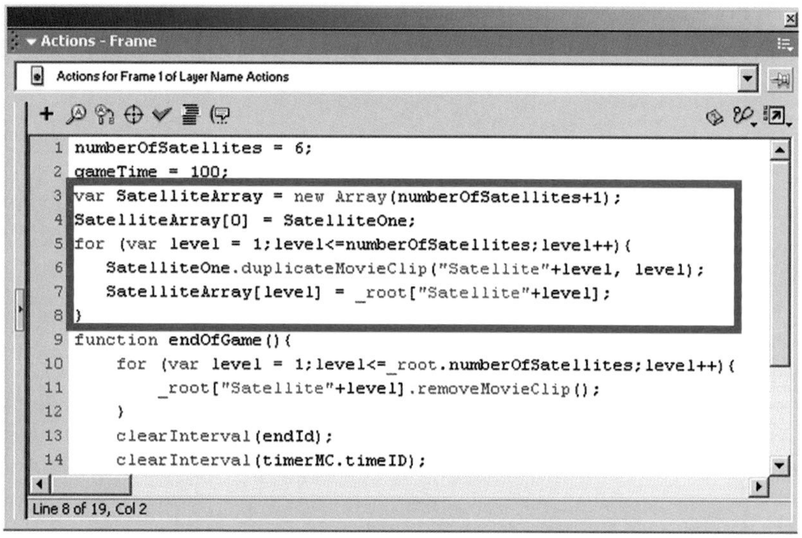
Actions - Frame
Actions for Frame 1 of Layer Name Actions
numberOfSatellites = 6;
gameTime = 100;
var SatelliteArray = new Array(numberOfSatellites+1);
SatelliteArray[0] = SatelliteOne;
for (var level = 1;level<=numberOfSatellites;level++){
SatelliteOne.duplicateMovieClip("Satellite"+level, level);
SatelliteArray[level] = _root["Satellite"+level];
}
function endOfGame(){
for (var level = 1;level<=_root.numberOfSatellites;level++){
_root["Satellite"+level].removeMovieClip();
}
clearInterval(endId);
clearInterval(timerMC.timeID);
Line 8 of 19, Col 2

8.17: Edit the code on the Actions layer to create an array for the Satellite movie clips.

First, you create an array called *SatelliteArray* and make sure it has the correct spaces available for the number of Satellite movie clips with the `numberOfSatellites + 1` argument. Remember that *numberOfSatellites* is the number of duplicate Satellite movie clips on the stage. You need to have the base Satellite, SatelliteOne, in the array also, so the length of the array is one greater than the *numberOfSatellites* value. This array contains the names of all of the Satellite movie clips, so the code puts SatelliteOne into the first place of the array (index 0). Then, as the code loops through the `for` loop and duplicates each Satellite movie clip, it also loads the new Satellite name into the *SatelliteArray* array. This will be used by the Bullet movie clip to detect if it has hit a Satellite movie clip.

Next you need to catch the mouse click and create the function that will attach the Bullet movie clip on the stage.

3. Attach the Bullet Movie Clip

Add the following ActionScript on frame 1 of the Actions layer on the main timeline. It should be near the bottom but before the `stop()` command (8.18).

```
_root.onMouseUp = function(){
   attachMovie("Bullet", "Bullet" + level, level);
   _root["Bullet" + level]._x = Attacker._x;
   _root["Bullet" + level]._y = Attacker._y;
   _root["Bullet" + level]._rotation = Attacker._rotation;
   level++;
};
```

Here, you use the event handler `onMouseUp()` and attach a function to it. This code makes a bullet appear on the stage each time the mouse is clicked. The `onMouseUp()` event is triggered by any mouse click, not just a mouse click that is related to the Attacker movie clip

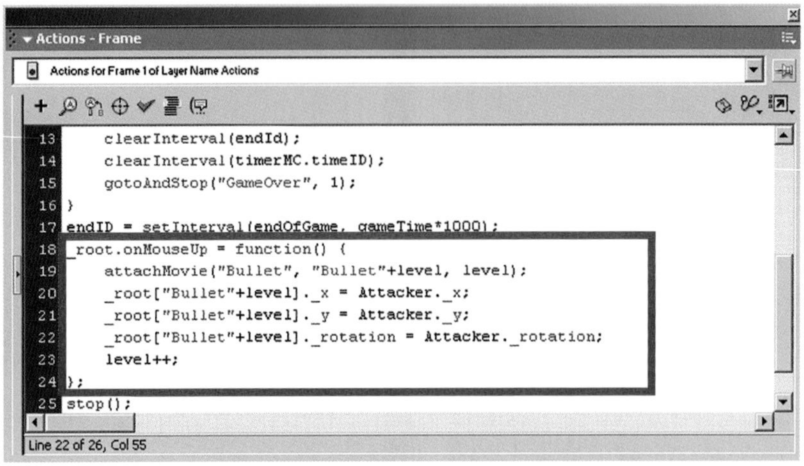
Actions - Frame
Actions for Frame 1 of Layer Name Actions
clearInterval(endId);
clearInterval(timerMC.timeID);
gotoAndStop("GameOver", 1);
}
endID = setInterval(endOfGame, gameTime*1000);
_root.onMouseUp = function() {
attachMovie("Bullet", "Bullet"+level, level);
_root["Bullet"+level]._x = Attacker._x;
_root["Bullet"+level]._y = Attacker._y;
_root["Bullet"+level]._rotation = Attacker._rotation;
level++;
};
stop();
Line 22 of 26, Col 55

8.18: Edit the code on the Actions layer to create a function for the bullets.

(in other words, you don't need to click on the Attacker movie clip to fire a bullet). The function is attached to the `_root` movie clip. First, the *`BulletN`* movie clip is created using `attachMovie()`; this is the Bullet MC movie clip, because it's the one that has the linkage.

The new *`BulletN`* movie clip is placed in the same position as the Attacker movie clip, using `Attacker._x` and `Attacker._y` to set the `_x` and `_y` properties of the *`BulletN`* movie clip. You need the *`BulletN`* movie clip to face the direction it's shooting. To accomplish this, you set the `_rotation` of the *`BulletN`* clip to be the same as that of the Attacker movie clip, so that the bullet will shoot in that direction.

If you test this now, the bullets will appear wherever the spaceship is, but they just sit there. They are more like mines that are waiting to destroy the satellites. Let's make the bullets move.

4. Move the Bullets and Test

Edit the Bullet MC movie clip and attach the following code to the Bullet movie clip within it (8.19).

```
onClipEvent(load){
   var bulletSpeed = 20;
}
onClipEvent(enterFrame) {
   _y -= bulletSpeed;
   for (var i = 0; i < _root.SatelliteArray.length; i++) {
      if (this.hitTest(_root.SatelliteArray[i])) {
         _root.SatelliteArray[i].play();
         _parent.removeMovieClip();
      }
   }
   // Screen wrap
   var bulletBounds = _parent.getBounds(_root);
   if (bulletBounds.yMax < 0 || bulletBounds.yMin > Stage.height) {
      _parent.removeMovieClip();
```

```
        }
        // check x boundary
        if (bulletBounds.xMax < 0 || bulletBounds.xMin > Stage.width) {
            _parent.removeMovieClip();
        }
    }
```

Now you can see why there is a movie clip within a movie clip. The Bullet MC movie clip is the one that is duplicated. Then this code is already attached to all the *BulletN* movie clips, and you use the `onClipEvent(enterFrame)` event handler to create a loop that executes the code repeatedly.

The `onClipEvent(load)` section simply sets a variable named *bulletSpeed*, which is the speed of the bullet.

In the `onClipEvent(enterFrame)` section, you first update the _y properties, so the *BulletN* movie clip will move. You want the *BulletN* movie clip to move only in the *y* direction, because that is the direction it's facing. Actually, it's facing in the negative *y* direction, so you move the Bullet movie clip in the negative *y* direction. This is the wonderful thing about rotating movie clips. The coordinates inside the movie clip also get rotated. Because you're moving the Bullet movie clip inside the Bullet MC movie clip, and the Bullet MC is rotated, all you need to do is tell the Bullet movie clip to go up, or negative *y*.

Then you need to check if the *BulletN* movie clip has hit a Satellite movie clip. The code loops through each of the Satellite movie clips using a `for` loop and performs a `hitTest()` on each Satellite movie clip in the array with this Bullet movie clip. If the *BulletN* movie clip has

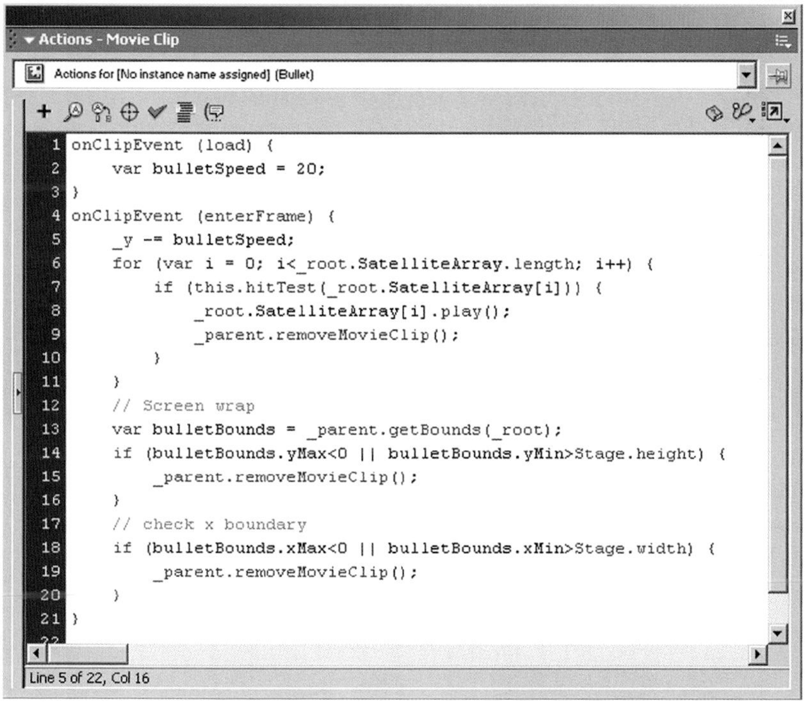

Actions - Movie Clip
Actions for [No instance name assigned] (Bullet)
onClipEvent (load) {
var bulletSpeed = 20;
}
onClipEvent (enterFrame) {
_y -= bulletSpeed;
for (var i = 0; i<_root.SatelliteArray.length; i++) {
if (this.hitTest(_root.SatelliteArray[i])) {
_root.SatelliteArray[i].play();
_parent.removeMovieClip();
}
}
// Screen wrap
var bulletBounds = _parent.getBounds(_root);
if (bulletBounds.yMax<0 || bulletBounds.yMin>Stage.height) {
_parent.removeMovieClip();
}
// check x boundary
if (bulletBounds.xMax<0 || bulletBounds.xMin>Stage.width) {
_parent.removeMovieClip();
}
}
Line 5 of 22, Col 16

8.19: Add code that moves the bullet to the Bullet movie clip within the Bullet MC movie clip.

hit a Satellite movie clip, the code tells the Satellite movie clip to `play()` (explode), and then it deletes the *BulletN* movie clip. Notice that to delete the *BulletN* clip, you must actually delete the `_parent` clip, because it's the `_parent` clip that was created with `attachMovie()`.

If the *BulletN* movie clip doesn't hit anything, then you check for boundaries. In this case, you really don't want the *BulletN* movie clip to wrap around. Therefore, if it goes off the stage, the code simply deletes this instance of the Button MC movie clip.

Test this version. Move the spaceship around and fire bullets using the mouse. Notice that the bullets fire each time you click the mouse. The bullets go off in the direction that the spaceship is facing, not necessarily the direction the spaceship is moving.

Right now, the only way to end this game is to time out. Let's give the spaceship a limited number of lives, which will also end the game.

Ending the Game

Games aren't very interesting when you're invulnerable. As the game is now, you can use the spaceship as a sort of battering ram, with no adverse effects. Let's code the game so that the player loses lives, and the game ends if the player runs out of lives.

1. Open the File

WWW. Open Chapter8_D_Start.fla. Save the file to your local hard drive as Chapter8_D_Modified.fla. (For the finished version, open Chapter8_D_Final.fla.)

This is exactly as you left the movie from the previous section, except that there are shields added to the Attacker movie clip. If you edit the Attacker movie clip, you'll notice that the Actions layer contains four keyframes, with a `stop()` command on each one. There are also four keyframes on the Shields layer. This setup allows the artwork on the Shields layer to change. At each progressive frame, the shields get smaller, until there isn't a shield at all on frame 4. You want to access this artwork by moving the frame of the Attacker movie clip to the next frame each time it hits something (8.20).

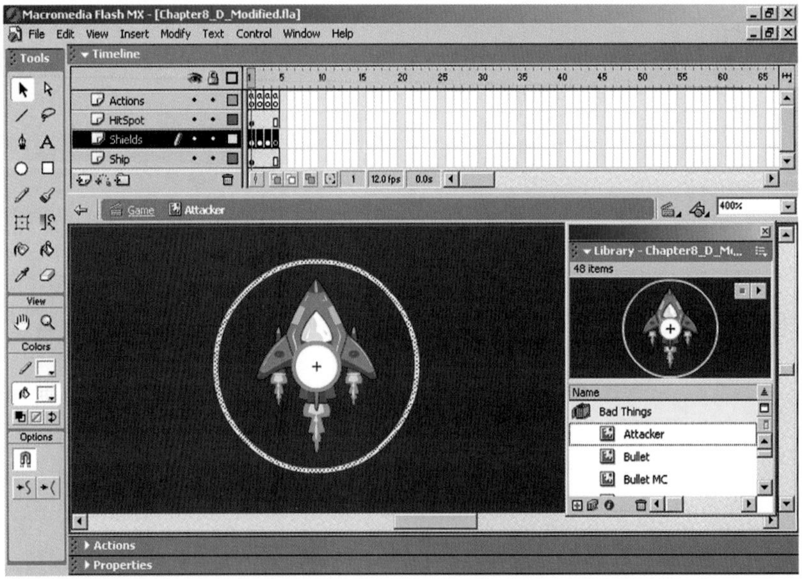

8.20: The Attacker movie clip contains four stages for the shields.

For this version, you're simply going to use a `play()` action to move to the next shield each time the Attacker movie clip hits a Satellite movie clip. When the Attacker movie clip is out of shields, you'll trigger the end-of-game function.

2. Access the Shields

Add the following ActionScript to the Satellite movie clip within the `onClipEvent(load)` section of the code (8.21):

```
// whether satellite hit or not
var satHit = false;
```

Then, within the `onClipEvent(enterFrame)` section of the code, change the `if` statement that contains the `hitTest()` method to the following (8.22):

```
if (satHit == false && this.hitTest(_root.Attacker.HitSpot)) {
   play();
   _root.Attacker.nextFrame();
   satHit = true;
}
```

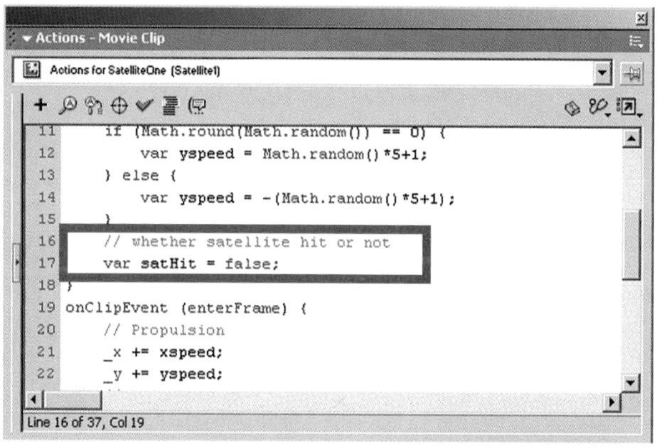

8.21: Add a declaration of the `satHit` variable to the `onClipEvent(load)` event handler on the Satellite movie clip.

Remember that the satellite hit detection was attached to the Satellite movie clip, because you didn't want to loop through all the Satellite movie clips within the Attacker movie clip in order to test for a collision.

The variable *`satHit`* will be used to determine whether this Satellite movie clip has been hit by the Attacker movie clip and to make sure it doesn't register a hit more than once for the same crash. So *`satHit`* is set to `false` in the `onClipEvent(load)` section.

Then, in the `if` statement, you want to check for the hit only if this Satellite clip has not been hit yet. In this case, the *`satHit`* variable is `false`, so you check if it's hit. So only if both the *`satHit`* variable is `false` and the satellite is currently hit by the spaceship do you move into the `if` statement. Within the `if` statement, you still tell the Satellite movie clip to `play()` when hit, but you also tell the Attacker movie clip to move to the next frame, which will reduce the size of the shield. Finally, you set the *`satHit`* variable to `true`, so that a hit won't be triggered again until the *`satHit`* variable is set back to `false`.

Let's reset the *`satHit`* variable so that the Satellite movie clip can take another hit after it explodes.

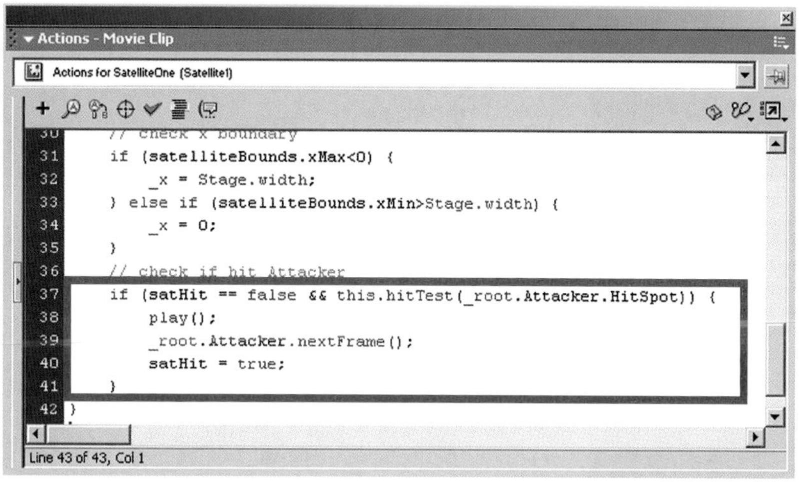

8.22: Replace the `hitTest()` code at the end of the frame with code to support the shields.

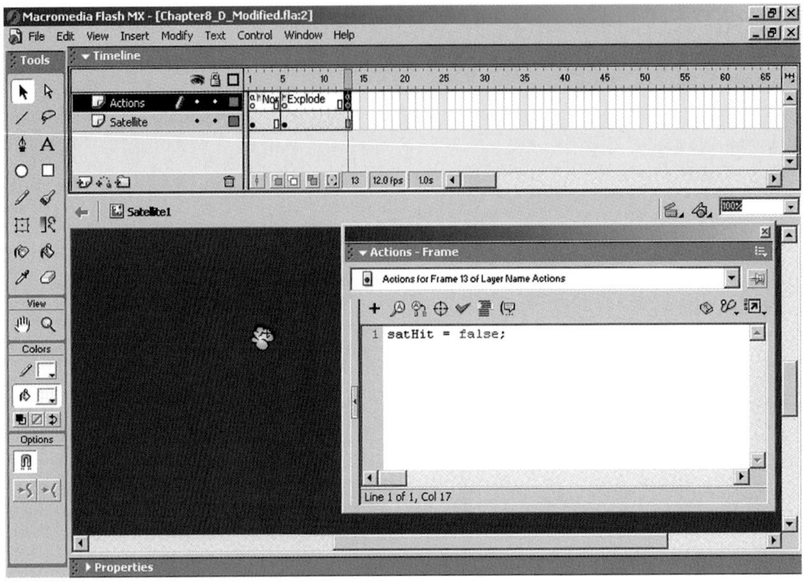

8.23: Add a keyframe on the last frame of the Actions layer on the Satellite movie clip and set the satHit *variable to* `false`.

3. Reset the *satHit* Variable

Edit the Satellite movie clip. Add a keyframe in the Actions layer on the last frame of the Explode section and attach the following ActionScript in this last frame (8.23).

```
satHit = false;
```

This will reset the *`satHit`* variable after the explosion, so now the satellite is ready for action again.

4. Add End-of-Game Code and Test

Edit the Attacker movie clip and add the following ActionScript to the last frame in the Actions layer (8.24).

```
_root.endOfGame();
```

When you reach the last frame of the Attacker movie clip, you're out of shields, and the game is over. This calls the *`endOfGame()`* function when the Attacker movie clip gets to the last frame or is out of shields.

Test the movie. You'll notice that if you run into three satellites, the game is over.

Conclusion

This game is almost complete. There are some ways that you could improve it. For example, you could add some scoring. You could also add a way to make sure the satellites do not pop up exactly where the spaceship is on the stage. Some cleanup would help, too. For example,

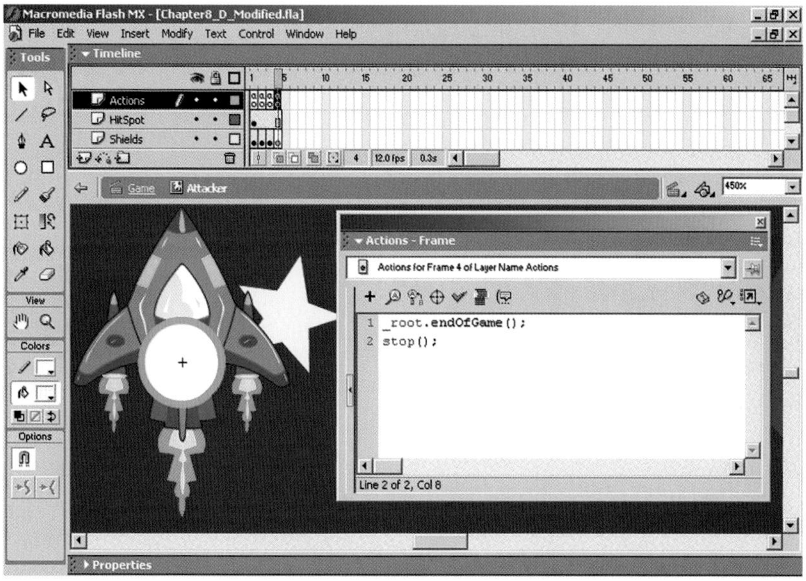

8.24: Add a call to the `endOfGame()` function on the last frame of the Actions layer within the Attacker movie clip.

when you play again, some of the variables, like the speed of the Attacker movie clip, are not reset. The version you have now is a good start, which you can continue to work on to perfect the game.

What you have learned here is how to use trigonometry to help make a game workable and more fun. You used the `hitTest()` method to check for collisions of different objects. You also used the `Key` object for the Attacker movie clip controls, as well as some of the built-in `Key` methods and properties for the properties for specific keys and methods used with the listener to catch when a key is pressed. The rest of the coding in this chapter involved basic `play()` and `goto` statements, with a review of some of the techniques covered in previous chapters.

This chapter demonstrated that you can do a lot with a few core ActionScript tools like functions, `for` loops, and basic property manipulations. There is a lot of strength in just a little bit of ActionScript.

CHAPTER nine

Drawing with ActionScript

File size is *an important issue for web designers, since large files take longer to download. Viewers may lose interest and decide to move on to another website rather than waiting for the content to download.*

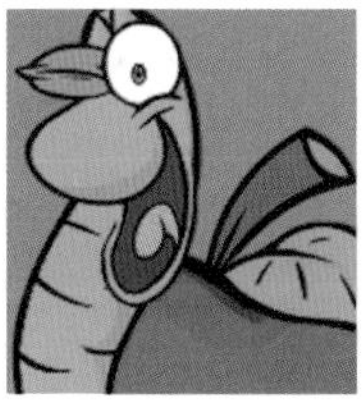

One of the more compelling characteristics of Flash is that the output of Flash—`.swf` *files—can be very small. Now, with the new Flash MX drawing methods, you can make Flash file sizes even smaller. Another benefit of the drawing methods is that they allow graphics to be created dynamically. This means that you can create an* `.swf` *file that takes almost no time to download, because it's essentially empty. All of the imagery can be dynamically generated on the fly on the client side (that is, after the file has been downloaded over the Internet). You can create all of your graphics with the drawing methods.*

The drawing methods are a group of related methods of the `MovieClip` *object. This does not mean that they need to be attached to an existing movie clip, although they can be. The drawing methods include* `beginFill()`, `beginGradientFill()`, `clear()`, `curveTo()`, `endFill()`, `lineStyle()`, `lineTo()`, *and* `moveTo()`. *You can draw any shape using a combination of the* `lineTo()` *and* `curveTo()` *methods. The other six methods are used for setup and filling the shape.*

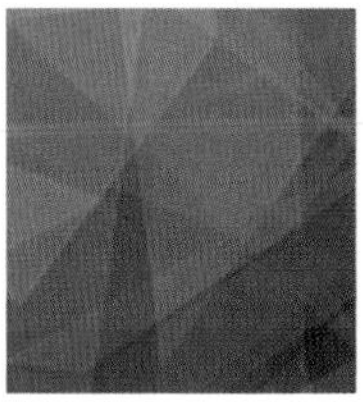

Drawing a Simple Line

As a first example of drawing with ActionScript, you'll create a simple connect-the-dots game. You'll use the `lineTo()` method to draw a line between the dots.

To draw a line, you need a starting point and an ending point. The `lineTo()` method takes two arguments, representing the *x* and *y* coordinates of the endpoint. The starting point is the location of the movie clip to which the drawing method is attached.

1. Open the File

WWW.

Open the **Chapter9_A_Start.fla** file. Save the file to your local hard drive with the name **Chapter9_A_Modified.fla** (9.1). (To see a finished version of this movie, open **Chapter9_A_Final.fla**.)

This file is almost complete. It lacks only the lines that will connect the dots. It consists of five layers:

- The BadApple layer contains the final image.
- The Dots layer contains the dots that the user will be connecting.
- The Numbers layer contains the number for each dot.
- The Replay Button layer contains the Replay button to start the game over.
- The Actions layer contains the ActionScript.

The file is also broken up into two sections: Start and End. The main part of the game is in the Start section. This is where the user will connect the dots. The End section is where all the dots are connected and the final image is shown. The End section is six frames long, with the `stop()` command on the last frame, instead of on the first frame. This will allow the user to see the image with the dots and then the image without the dots.

For now, you'll be working with the Dots layer. The dots are instances of a movie clip named Dot MC. Each instance has already been assigned an instance name: Dot1 for the movie clip next to the number 1, Dot2 for the movie clip next to the number 2, and so on.

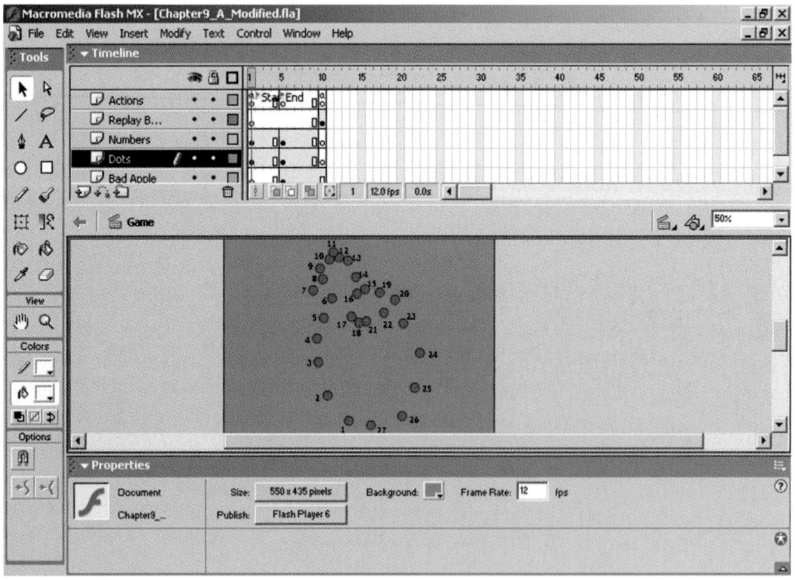

9.1: The layout of the connect-the-dots game

Each dot is actually a button within a movie clip. When the user clicks the dot that's active, a line is drawn from the previous dot to the one clicked. You want only one dot to be active at a time, so you'll need to tell each dot when it can be used, and you'll also need to let the user know that only the one dot is available to choose. The code attached to the button within the Dot MC movie clip handles both of those tasks. But before you begin adding ActionScript, let's see how the Dot MC movie clip is set up.

2. Edit and Inspect the Dot MC

Open the Dot MC for editing (9.2). Notice that it consists of two dot buttons, in two sections (designated by labels on the Actions layer).

The Default section contains the Inactive button, and the Glow section contains the Glow button. This way, each Dot MC movie clip on the stage actually contains two buttons: one button (Inactive) that is usually visible and does not respond to a mouse click and another button (Glow) that becomes visible only when its dot is the next one in the sequence to be connected. The only button that needs any ActionScript attached to it is the Glow button. Exit the Dot MC movie clip.

Now look at the ActionScript attached to frame 1 of the Actions layer (9.3).

```
var numberOfDots = 27;
var dotNumber = 2;
Dot2.gotoAndStop("Glow");
stop();
```

The `numberOfDots` variable is the number of dots on the screen. You'll use this variable to determine when the user has reached the last dot. The `dotNumber` variable will determine which dot is the one that needs to be selected by the user. You want the first available dot to be the second dot, so the `dotNumber` variable is set to 2. Then you need to move the Dot2 movie clip to the Glow section, so that it's available. You do this by sending a command to the Dot2 instance to move to the Glow frame.

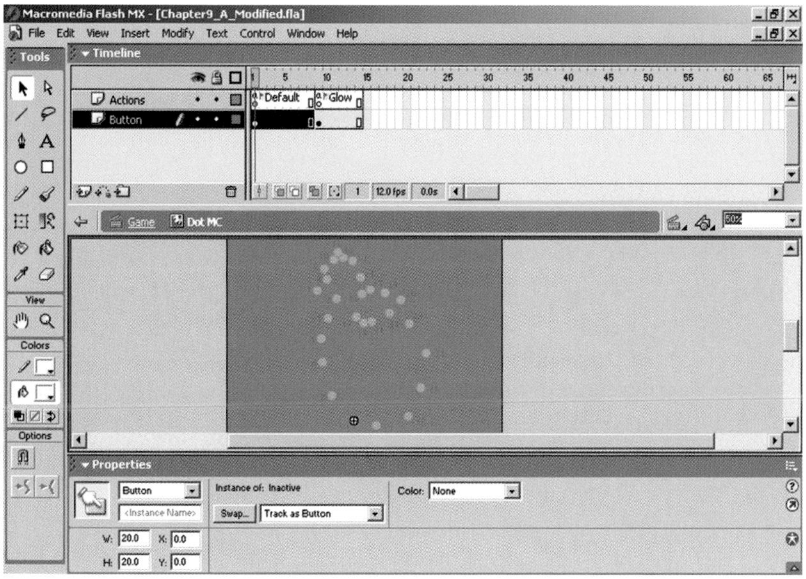

9.2: The Dot MC movie clip

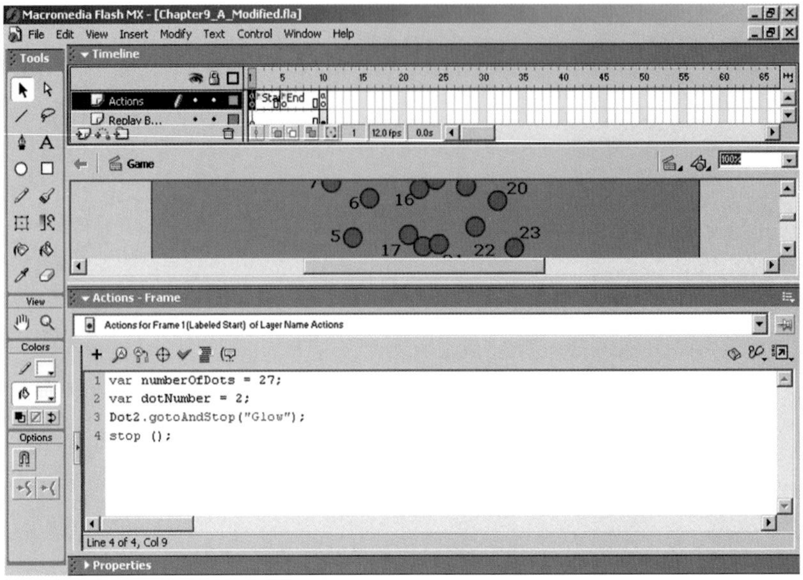

9.3: *The ActionScript assigned to the Actions layer*

That's all you need to do for the setup. Since you don't want to proceed to the next section until the user has selected all the dots in order, you place a `stop()` command at the end of the code.

Now let's start drawing a line.

3. Draw a Line and Test

Add the following ActionScript to frame 1 of the Actions layer, before the `stop()` action (9.4):

```
createEmptyMovieClip("Line", 1);
Line.lineStyle(3, 0x000000, 100);
Line.moveTo(Dot1._x, Dot1._y);
Line.lineTo(0, 0);
```

In order to use the drawing methods, you need a movie clip. This code creates an empty movie clip with the new `createEmptyMovieClip()` method. You'll use this empty movie clip with the drawing methods.

The `createEmptyMovieClip()` is a method of the `MovieClip` object that creates a movie clip within a movie clip. If you don't specify which movie clip to create the new movie clip within when calling this method, as in this case, the default is the movie clip that the method is being called from. Here, you are creating an empty movie clip off the `_root` timeline.

The `createEmptyMovieClip()` method takes two arguments (9.5). The first argument is the name of the new movie clip, and the second argument specifies the level for the newly created movie clip. The ActionScript names the new movie clip Line and places it on level 1. (Notice that the `createEmptyMovieclip()` method is similar to the `attachMovie()` method.)

NOTE Using the `createEmptyMovieClip()` method is the same as creating an empty movie clip graphically and placing it on the stage physically.

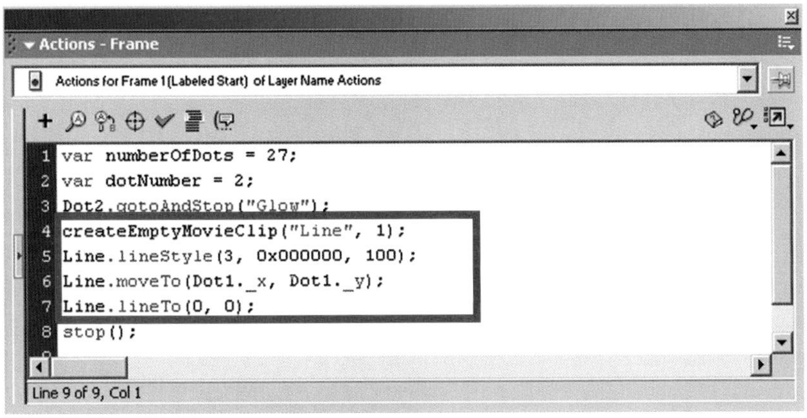

9.4: Add the drawing code to frame 1 of the Actions layer.

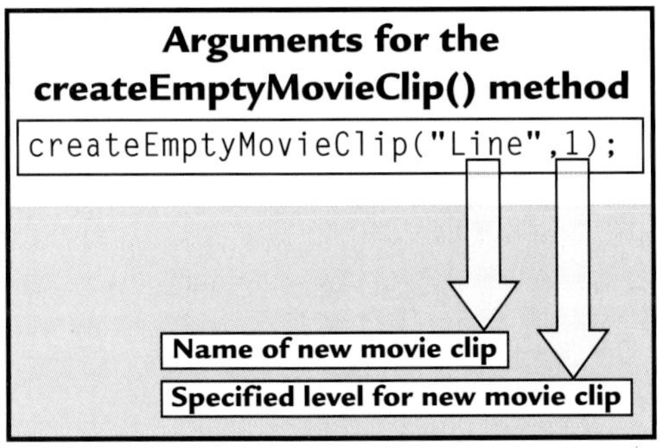

9.5: The `createEmptyMovieClip()` *method takes two arguments.*

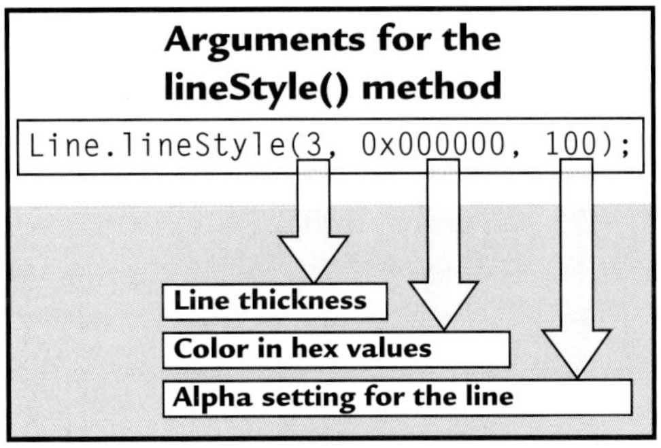

9.6: The new `lineStyle()` *method takes three arguments.*

Next the code specifies the type of line to draw and its color using the `lineStyle()` method. This method takes three arguments (9.6). The first argument is the thickness of the line, which can be from 0 (hairline) to 255. The second argument is the color in hex. The third argument is the alpha value of the line. In this case, the line thickness is 3, the color is black, and the alpha is 100%. This is applied to the Line movie clip, which was created by the previous line of code.

Then the code specifies where the line should start using the `moveTo()` method. This is like picking up a pencil and placing it where you want to start drawing, without actually making any marks. You need to specify the starting position unless you want the drawing to start from (0, 0). Whenever you create a movie clip with `createEmptyMovieClip()`, the default position is (0, 0). You want the line to start at Dot1, so you use the `_x` and `_y` properties of the Dot1 movie clip as the `moveTo()` method's arguments to move the Line movie clip to that position.

Finally, to give the code a test run, you tell Flash to draw a line to point (0, 0) by using the `lineTo()` method: `Line.lineTo(0,0)`.

Test the movie (9.7). You'll see that a line is drawn from Dot1 to the upper-left corner of the stage. This may not be what you want, but at least now you know it works.

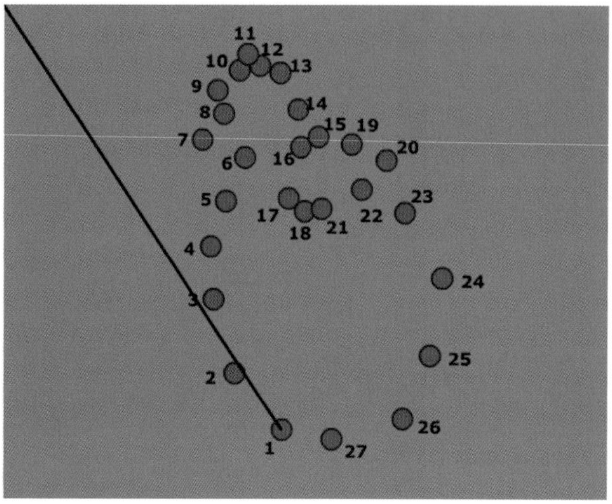

9.7: Flash draws a line from the Dot1 button to the top-left corner of the stage.

NOTE As with all new methods in Flash MX, the drawing methods won't work if you're publishing in Flash 5. However, Flash won't give you a warning if you're using the drawing methods and publishing in Flash 5. It simply won't work when you try to play the movie.

Now let's get each dot to draw the line as the user selects it.

4. Connect the Dots and Test

Delete the following line from the ActionScript on frame 1 of the Actions layer.

```
Line.lineTo(0, 0);
```

Edit the Dot MC movie clip and move to the Glow section. Attach the following ActionScript to the Glow button (9.8).

```
on(release){
   // turn off clicked button
   _root["Dot" + _root.dotNumber].gotoAndStop("Default");
   _root.dotNumber++;
   // turn on next button
   _root["Dot" + _root.dotNumber].gotoAndStop("Glow");
   _root.Line.lineTo(this._x, this._y);
   if (_root.dotNumber > _root.numberOfDots){
      _root.Line.lineTo(_root.Dot1._x, _root.Dot1._y);
      _root.gotoAndPlay("End");
   }
}
```

Notice that since you attached the code to the Glow section of the Dot MC movie clip, the button with this code on it will only be available if the dot is the correct number or in the Glow section. In other words, when you test the movie, the Dot MC movie clip next to the Dot2 movie clip is actually showing the Glow button. All of the other instances of the Dot MC movie clip are displaying the Inactive button. When you click the dot next to the number 2, it switches from the Glow button to the Inactive button, the Dot MC movie clip next to the number 3 switches to display the Glow button, and a line is drawn from dot number 1 to dot number 2.

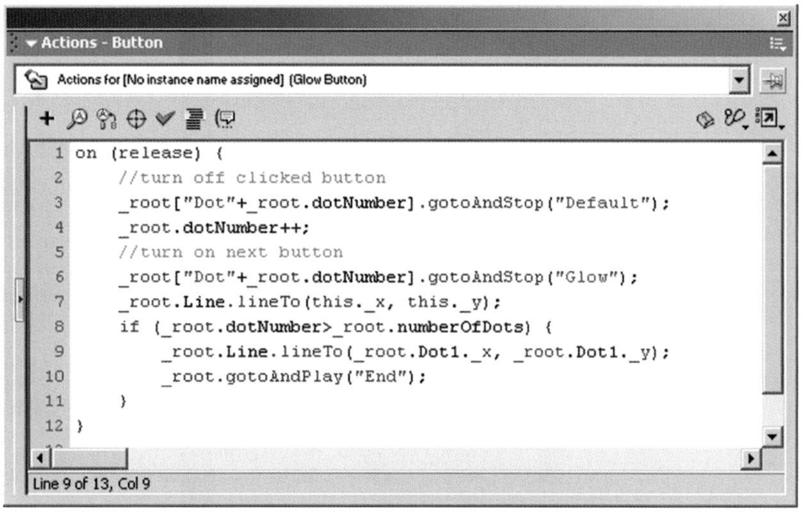

9.8: Edit the Dot MC movie clip, move to the frame labeled Glow, and assign the ActionScript for the `lineTo()` *method to the Glow button.*

This process continues as you click sequentially through the instances of the Dot MC movie clips. The Inactive button and the Glow button look exactly the same until the user rolls over them, so there is no visible change as these transition from the Inactive button to the Glow button and back again.

This code begins by turning off the current dot by using the variable *`dotNumber`* and the `gotoAndStop()` action. The *`dotNumber`* variable contains the number of the current dot, so you need to tell it to move to the Default section. (You could have used the keyword `this` to change to the Default section instead of using the section name, but this format is the same as the one used to move to the Glow section, two lines down, so it makes the code clearer.)

Then the *`dotNumber`* variable is incremented so that it contains the number of the next button, which is the new button to select. Remember that this variable is keeping track of which Dot MC instance should display the Glow button. After the *`dotNumber`* variable is incremented, this new value is used to tell the appropriate dot button to move to the Glow section. This is the next button to be selected.

Next the code moves the line with `lineTo()`, using the `_x` and `_y` properties of the Dot MC movie clip that was just selected:

```
_root.Line.lineTo(this._x, this._y);
```

Finally, the code checks to see if the user has completed the puzzle, which is dot number 27, using the *`numberOfDots`* variable. If dot number 27 is selected, the *`dotNumber`* value is 28, which is greater than *`numberOfDots`*, and the code goes into the `if` statement. This closes the connection by moving the line to the Dot1 button using its `_x` and `_y` properties, back to the start, and then moves the game to the next section—the End section.

Test the movie clip. Click the dot next to the number 2, and then keep clicking sequentially up to the dot next to the number 27 (9.9). The code on the first frame of the Actions layer tells Flash where to start the line, and then the code on the Glow buttons within each of

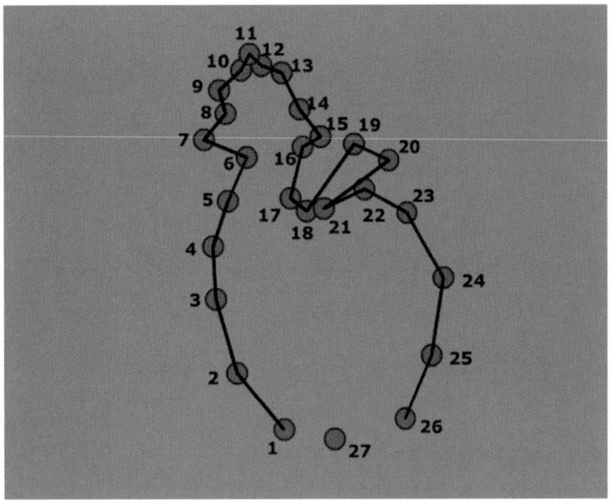

9.9: Flash draws a line between each instance of the Dot MC movie clip as you click sequentially through them.

9.10: After clicking the last Dot MC movie clip, an animation appears.

the Dot MC movie clips tells Flash were to draw the line every time you click one of them. Notice that only one dot is available at any one time.

When you're finished, the connection is closed. You'll see the final picture (9.10).

Lines are very simple. Now let's draw something a little more complicated— curves.

Drawing Curves

Drawing lines with Flash is fairly straightforward (no pun intended). When you want to add curves, you need to use a more roundabout method (okay, pun intended). To draw curved lines and shapes in Flash, you use the new drawing method `curveTo()`. The `curveTo()` method allows you to create all kinds of shapes, with a little bit of math or just plain guesswork. In this example, you'll learn how to draw different types of curves and curved shapes.

1. Open the File

WWW. Open the **Chapter9_B_Start.fla** file. Save the file to your local hard drive with the name **Chapter9_B_Modified.fla.** (To see a finished version of this movie, open **Chapter9_B_Final.fla.**)

This file contains only an Actions layer, which has a variable named *`level`* set to 1 (used to set the movie clips on separate levels) and a call to create an empty movie clip called Curves on this level.

You'll begin by using the `curveTo()` method to draw some curves.

2. Draw a Curve and Test

Add the following ActionScript to the Actions layer (9.11).

```
Curves.lineStyle(5, 0xff0000, 100);
Curves.moveTo(100, 100);
Curves.curveTo(275, 250, 450, 100);
```

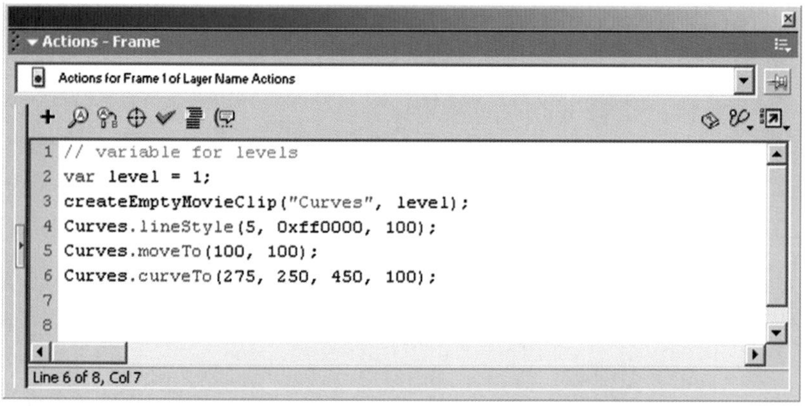

9.11: Add ActionScript to use the `curveTo()` *method.*

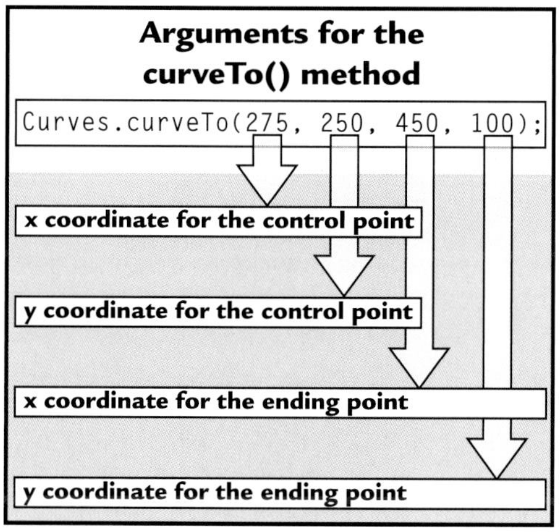

9.12: The arguments for the `curveTo()` *method*

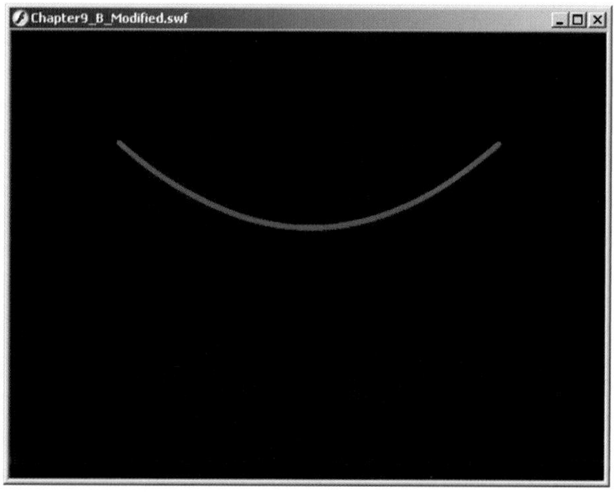

9.13: The code on the Actions layer generates this curved line.

Here, you set up the line type with the `lineStyle()` method and then give it a starting point with the `moveTo()` method. Thus, the first two lines of code are very similar to the code you used in the previous example. The work of drawing the curved line is done by the last line of code: the `curveTo()` method.

To draw a curve, you need a starting point and an ending point, just as with a line, but you also need something to tell Flash how to shape the curve, such as whether it's a sharp curve or a smooth curve with just a bit of an angle. The `curveTo()` method takes four arguments (9.12). The first two arguments are the control points for the curve and are used to define the shape of the curve. The last two arguments are the ending points for the curve (where *x* is the third argument and *y* is the fourth argument).

Figuring out the ending point of the curve it usually fairly easy, since you'll usually have a pretty good idea as to where you want the curve to begin and end. The real trick to drawing the curve is in determining the values for the control points. But before you explore how control points work, test this script (9.13). You'll see a simple curved line.

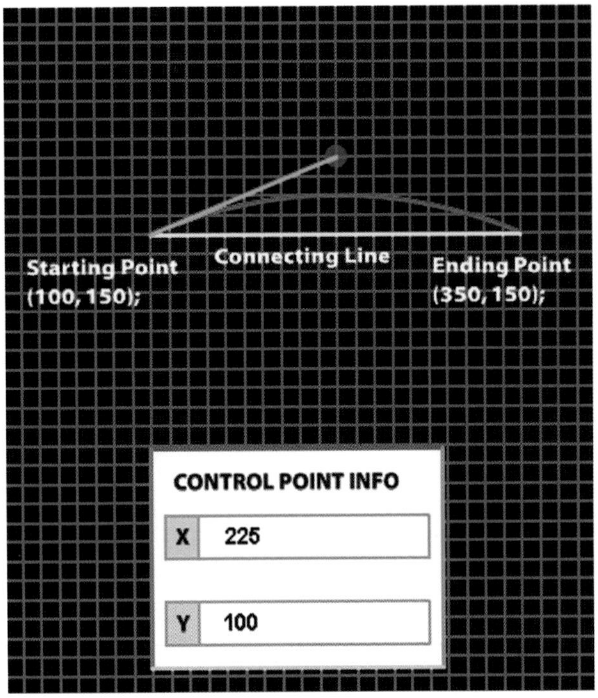

9.14: Open the CurveDemo.swf *file and drag the blue circle around to observe how it affects the curve.*

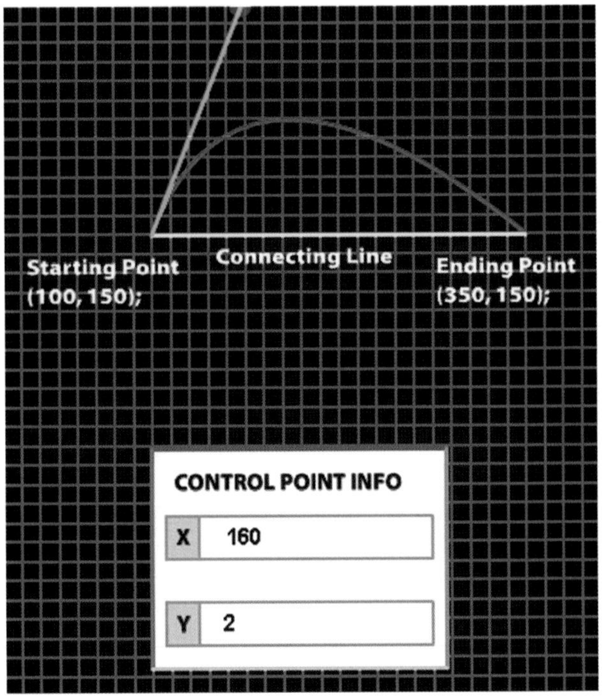

9.15: The upward curve is more pronounced and the apex has moved to the left when the control points are set to x = *160,* y = 2.

4. Examine Control Point Information

The control point for a curve is an *x*, *y* coordinate that affects the curve. It's easier to understand how the control point works with an interactive sample. Run the CurveDemo.swf file (9.14). Drag the blue circle around the stage and watch how the movement of the blue circle affects the curve. Note the values that are dynamically displayed in the Control Point Info box. The blue circle is the control point for the curve.

NOTE The `curveTo()` method's control point is based on the Bézier curve, but most Bézier curves have two control points: one for the starting point and one for the ending point. The `curveTo()` method has a control point for only the starting point.

To understand how the control point affects the curve, visualize a line between the starting point and the ending point. Let's call this line the connecting line. If the control point lies on the connecting line, you'll get a straight line rather than a curve. However, if the control point lies above or below the connecting line, you'll get a curve. In the curve you see when you open CurveDemo.swf (9.14), the connecting line is horizontal, and the control point is above and directly in the middle of the connecting line. This produces a curved line above the connecting line. You can adjust the curve of the line by adjusting the position of the control point.

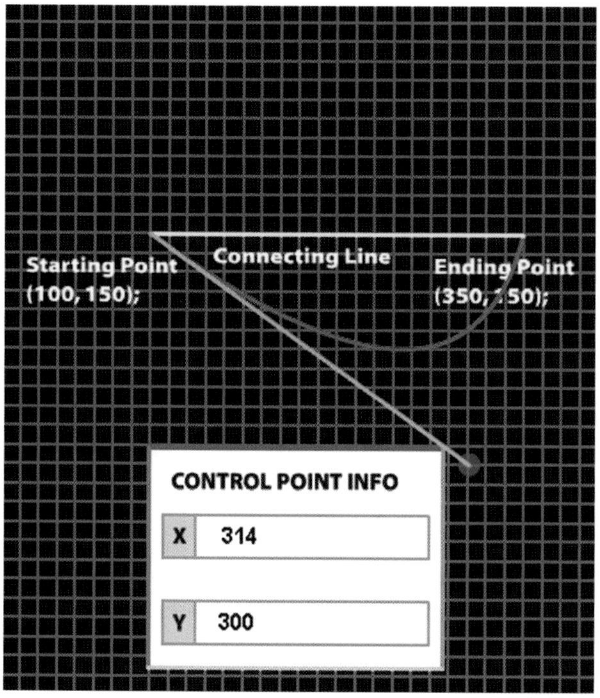

9.16: The line shifts to a downward curve and the apex has moved to the right when the control point is set to x = *314,* y = *300.*

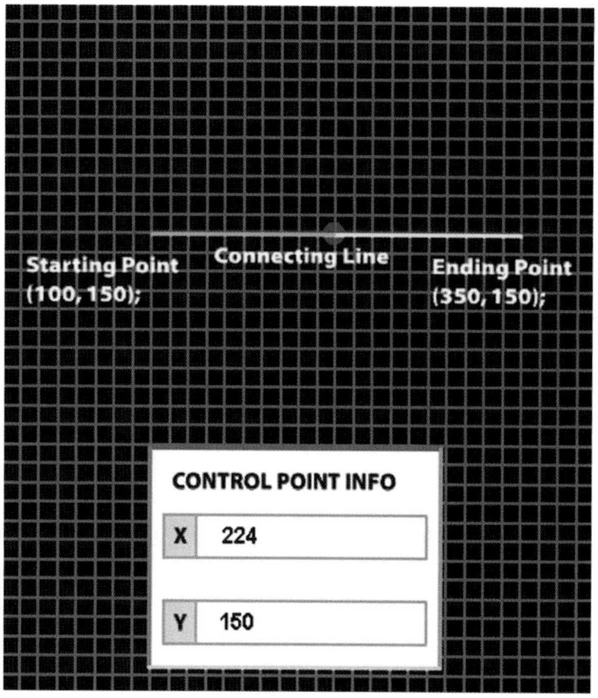

9.17: When the control point is on the connecting line, the tangent overlaps both the curve and the connecting line.

You can also change the apex (the topmost point) of the curve. In the starting curve in CurveDemo.swf (9.14), the apex is directly in the middle of the connecting line. If you move the control point closer to the starting point, the apex will also move toward the starting point. If you move the control point closer to the ending point, the apex will move toward the ending point.

Drag the blue circle up and to the left so that the Control Point Info box shows 160 for the *x* coordinate and 2 for the *y* coordinate (9.15). Notice that the curved line is now more pronounced. The lower *y* value pulls the curve upward; the lower *x* value pulls the apex to the left.

Now drag the blue circle down and to the right so that the Control Point Info box shows 314 for the *x* coordinate and 300 for the *y* coordinate (9.16). The curved line is now dipping below the connecting line. The higher *y* value pulls the curve downward; the higher *x* value pushes the apex to the right.

The curve is based on a line that runs from the starting point to the control point and is tangent to the curve. The light-blue line in CurveDemo.swf represents the tangent line. *Tangent* means the line touches the curve at one point. If the curve is flattened, as when a control point is close to the connecting line, the tangent line may appear to touch the curve. This occurs when the curve is in almost a straight line (9.17).

Suppose that you want to draw a curve that tips all the way down to the bottom of the stage and has its apex over to the right of the stage. How would you do that? To move the curve downward, you increase the value of the *y* control point, and to move the apex to the

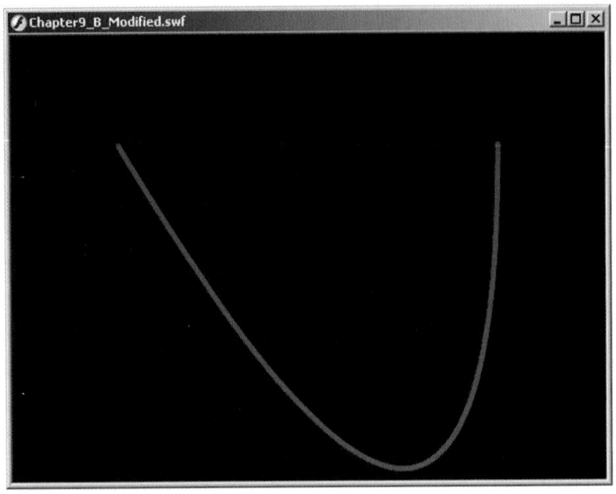

9.18: The curve dips downward much more and the apex has moved to the right.

right, you increase the value of the *x* control point. Try changing the `curveTo()` code on frame 1 of the Actions layer to the following.

```
Curves.curveTo(450, 675, 450, 100);
```

The curve now dips downward much further because you increased the value of the *y* control point from 250 to 675 (9.18). Also, the apex has moved to the right because you increased the value of the *x* control point from 275 to 450.

Now you understand how the control point affects the curve, and how to approximate the location of a control point for the type of curve you want to draw. Let's move on to drawing more curves. You'll use a function to draw a curve with a certain number of points. So the next step is to set up the function.

5. Start the *drawRandomCurve()* Function

Delete the code you added on the Actions layer, but leave the `level` and the `createEmptyMovieClip()` call.

Add the following ActionScript on the Functions layer (9.19).

```
// draw random curve with number of points
function drawRandomCurve(curveName, curvePoints, filled, fillColor, ►
fillAlpha, strokeThickness, strokeColor, strokeAlpha) {
   // maximum size
   var maxX = Stage.width / 4;
   var maxY = Stage.height / 4;
   // start line and fill for circle
   curveName.lineStyle(strokeThickness, strokeColor, strokeAlpha);
   if (filled == true) {
      curveName.beginFill(fillColor, fillAlpha);
   }
}
```

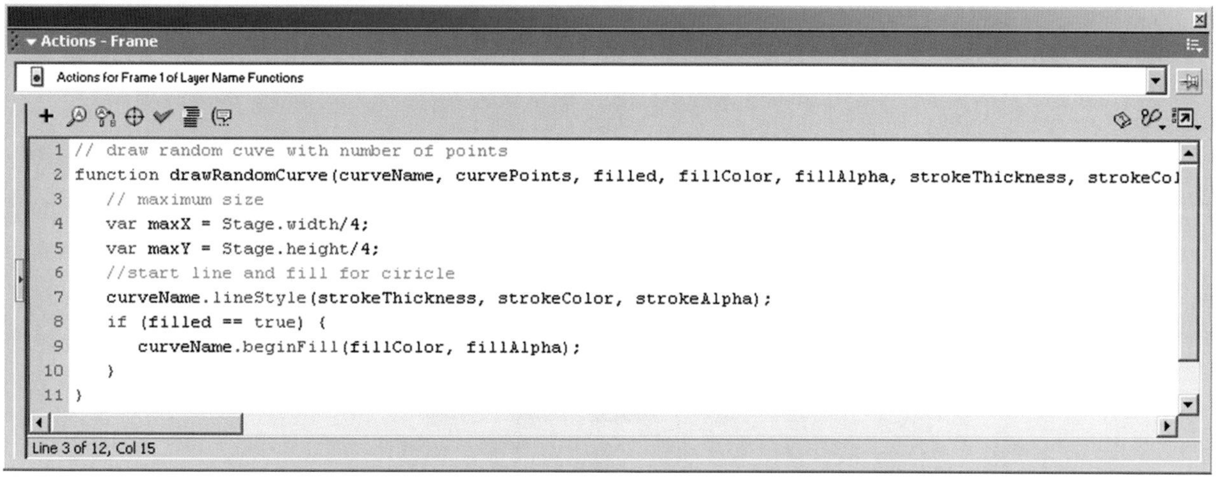


```
// draw random cuve with number of points
function drawRandomCurve(curveName, curvePoints, filled, fillColor, fillAlpha, strokeThickness, strokeCol
   // maximum size
   var maxX = Stage.width/4;
   var maxY = Stage.height/4;
   //start line and fill for ciricle
   curveName.lineStyle(strokeThickness, strokeColor, strokeAlpha);
   if (filled == true) {
      curveName.beginFill(fillColor, fillAlpha);
   }
}
```

9.19: Add code for a function to draw random curves.

This is the initialization of a function that will be used to draw a random set of curves. The function is called `drawRandomCurve()` and has eight arguments:

- The name of the movie to do the drawing with, `curveName`
- The number of points to use in drawing the curve, `curvePoints`
- Whether the curve is filled or not, `filled`
- The color to fill the curve, `fillColor`
- The alpha of the fill, `fillAlpha`
- The thickness of the stroke, `strokeThickness`
- The color of the stroke, `strokeColor`
- The alpha of the stroke, `strokeAlpha`

All of these will be passed in to the `drawRandomCurve()` function.

NOTE It isn't possible to draw a shape without a stroke. A stroke thickness of 0 is a still a hairline stroke. You can hide the stroke by making it the same color as the fill or the background, but you must have a stroke.

First, the code determines the largest curve to draw based on the size of the stage. Here, the code sets the `maxX` variable to be a quarter of the width of the stage and the `maxY` variable to be a quarter of the height of the stage. These represent the largest distance a single curve will travel.

Next you set up the characteristics of the lines the code will draw using the `lineStyle()` method. Here, the code passes the `lineStyle()` method the three variables passed into `drawRandomCurve()` that pertain to the stroke: `strokeThickness`, `strokeColor`, and `strokeAlpha`.

Then if the `filled` variable is true, you start the fill with `beginFill()` and the fill variables `fillColor` and `fillAlpha`.

The `drawRandomCurve()` function doesn't actually draw anything yet. Let's do that next.

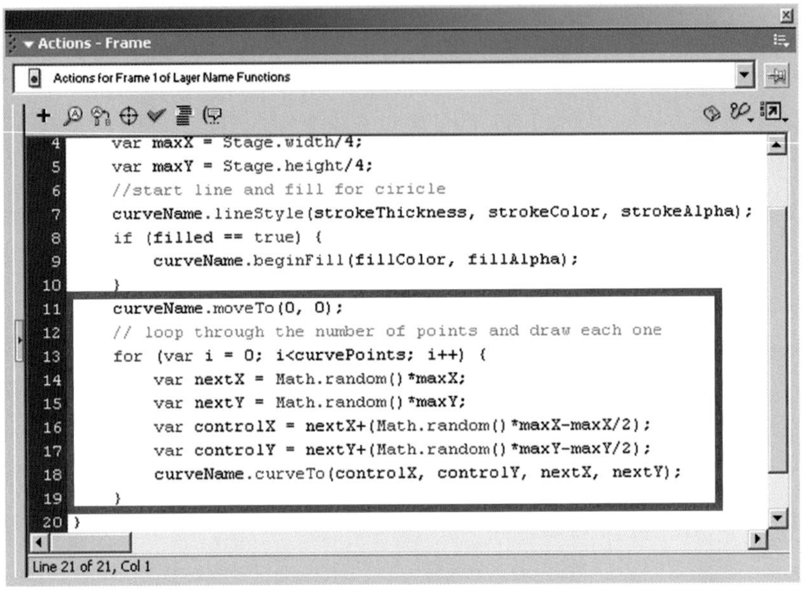

9.20: Add code to the function to draw the random curves.

6. Add to the *drawRandomCurve()* Function

Add the following ActionScript within the `drawRandomCurve()` function, below the existing code (9.20).

```
curveName.moveTo(0, 0);
// loop through the number of points and draw each one
for (var i = 0; i < curvePoints; i++) {
   var nextX = Math.random() * maxX;
   var nextY = Math.random() * maxY;
   var controlX = nextX + (Math.random() * maxX - maxX / 2);
   var controlY = nextY + (Math.random() * maxY - maxY / 2);
   curveName.curveTo(controlX, controlY, nextX, nextY);
}
```

This code does the actual drawing, using as many curved lines as were passed in the argument `curvePoints`. First, you need to make sure the movie clip is in the starting position that you want—in this case, the default starting position of (0, 0). So the code explicitly places it there with the `moveTo(0, 0)` method.

Next the code starts looping the number of `curvePoints` and drawing a curve each time using the `curveTo()` method. The code computes the next point to move to using the `maxX` and `maxY` variables. You want these curves to be random, so you set the `nextX` point to be `Math.random() * maxX` and the `nextY` point to be `Math.random() * maxY`. Each time the code loops through for a curve point, this value will be recalculated.

Then the code determines the control point for the next point. This is based on the `nextX` and the `nextY` values that were calculated and also a random number using the `maxX` and `maxY` values. Here, you want a random number that is sometimes negative, so you use the trick of finding a random number and subtracting half of the number. `maxX` is equal to a quarter of the stage width, so in this case, it's 138. The `Math.random() * 138` calculation

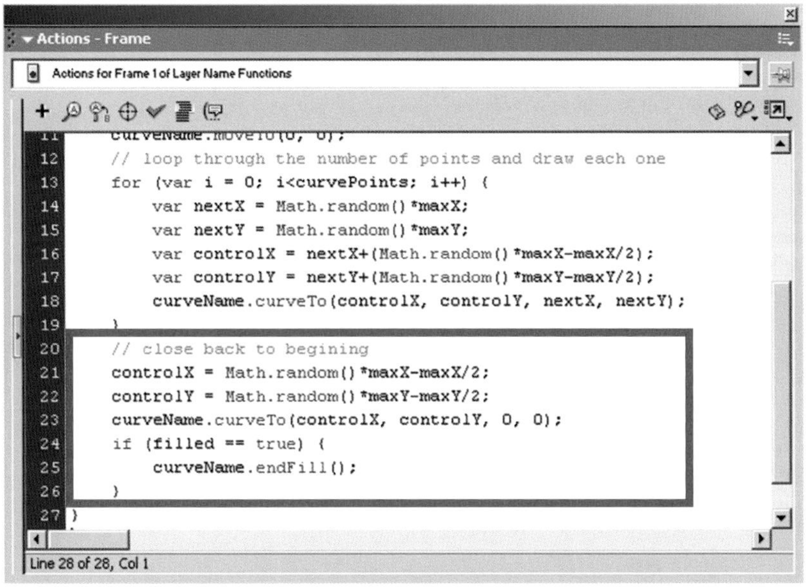

9.21: Add code to the function so that it will close properly.

returns a number between 0 and 137.99. You then subtract `maxX / 2`, which is 69, from each of the results. If the random number returned is 50, when you subtract 69, you get –19. This means that half of the time, the number will resolve to a negative value. In other words, the number will range from –69 to 68.99.

Once the code has the control points and the next points, it calls the `curveTo()` method using these variables. This is done as many times as specified by the *`curvePoints`* variable.

Now you're finished with the main section. Let's add some cleanup.

7. Add Function Cleanup Code

Add the following ActionScript below the code you entered in the previous step and within the *`drawRandomCurve()`* function (9.21).

```
// close back to beginning
controlX = Math.random() * maxX - maxX / 2;
controlY = Math.random() * maxY - maxY / 2;
curveName.curveTo(controlX, controlY, 0, 0);
if (filled == true) {
   curveName.endFill();
}
```

This is the cleanup. You need to make sure that the curve closes properly, which means it returns to its starting point of (0, 0). You compute a random control point and then call the `curveTo()` method using that control point and the point (0, 0). Finally, outside the `for` loop, you check to see if you need to end the fill of the circle using the `endFill()` method.

If you were to test this function, it wouldn't work yet, because you haven't called it. So let's add the call to the function.

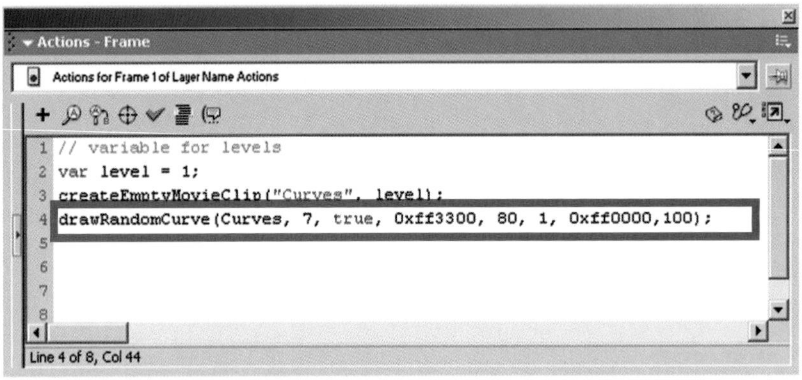
Actions - Frame
Actions for Frame 1 of Layer Name Actions
// variable for levels
var level = 1;
createEmptyMovieClip("Curves", level);
drawRandomCurve(Curves, 7, true, 0xff3300, 80, 1, 0xff0000,100);
Line 4 of 8, Col 44

9.22: Add a call to the `drawRandomCurve()` function on the Actions layer.

8. Call the *drawRandomCurve()* Function and Test

On frame 1 of the Actions layer, add the following ActionScript below the creation of the Curve movie clip (9.22).

```
drawRandomCurve(Curves, 7, true, 0xff3300, 80, 1, 0xff0000, 100);
```

This calls the `drawRandomCurve()` function, passing in the eight arguments:

Movie clip name	`Curves`
Number of points	`7`
Whether to fill	`true`
Fill color	`0xff3300`
Fill alpha	`80`
Stroke thickness	`1`
Stroke color	`0xff0000`
Stroke alpha	`100`

Test the movie. You'll see an orange-red, curved object in the upper-left area of the stage. Now let's complete the code by calling the `drawRandomCurve()` function a number of times, changing the color and location randomly.

9. Call the *drawRandomCurve()* Function Multiple Times and Test

Delete all of the code from the Actions layer and replace it with the following (9.23).

```
// variable for levels
var level = 1;
// loop to produce curved images
for (var i = 1; i < 60; i++) {
   createEmptyMovieClip("Curves" + level, level);
   // random color
   var ranRed = Math.random() * 256;
```

```
        var ranGreen = Math.random() * 256;
        var ranBlue = Math.random() * 256;
        var curveColor = ranRed << 16 | ranGreen << 8 | ranBlue;
        var curveAlpha = Math.random() * 25 + 25;
        // random whether filled or not
        if (Math.round(Math.random()) == 0) {
           drawRandomCurve(_root["Curves" + level], Math.ceil(Math.random() * ▶
        5 + 2), true, curveColor, curveAlpha, 1, curveColor, curveAlpha);
        } else {
           drawRandomCurve(_root["Curves" + level], Math.ceil(Math.random()*▶
        5 + 2), false, curveColor, curveAlpha, 1, curveColor, curveAlpha);
        }
        // placed randomly
        _root["Curves" + level]._x = Math.random() * Stage.width;
        _root["Curves" + level]._y = Math.random() * Stage.height;
        _root["Curves" + level]._rotation = Math.random() * 360;
        level++;
    }
```

This code calls the `drawRandomCurve()` function 60 times within a `for` loop. First, within the `for` loop, you create the empty movie clip with the name `"Curves" + level`. Then you compute a random color, using three variables to hold the three parts of the color and then bit-encoding them in one variable, `curveColor`. (This is the same way that you added

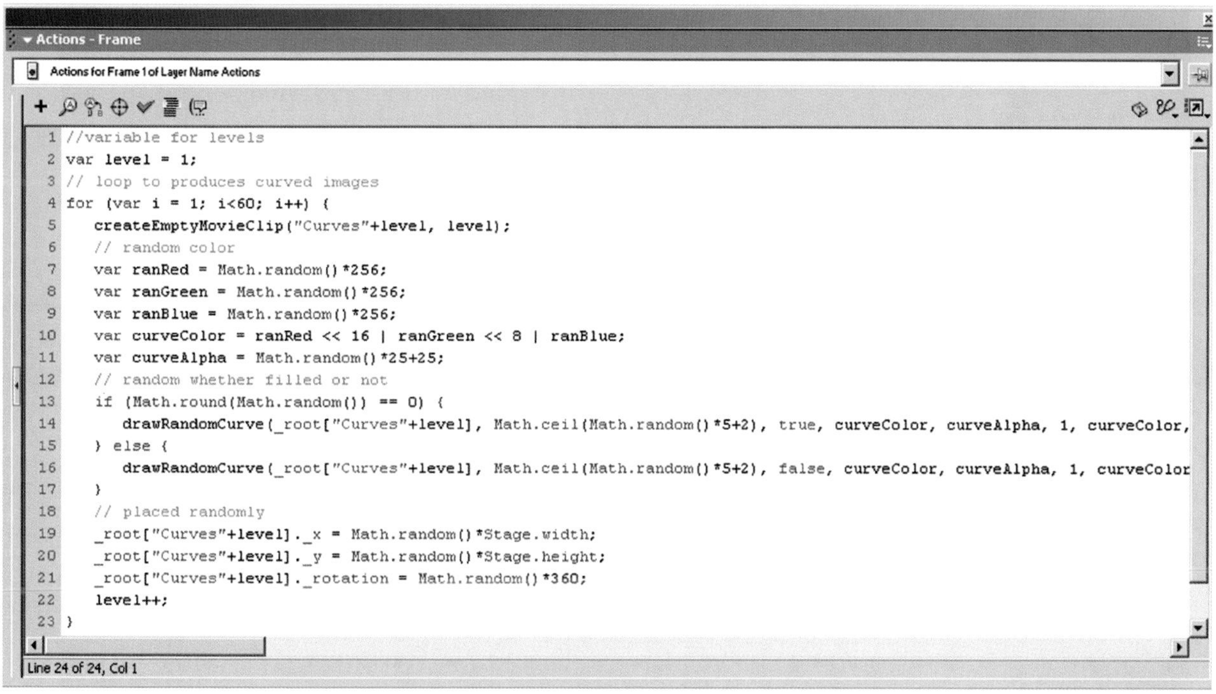
Actions - Frame
Actions for Frame 1 of Layer Name Actions
//variable for levels
var level = 1;
// loop to produces curved images
for (var i = 1; i<60; i++) {
createEmptyMovieClip("Curves"+level, level);
// random color
var ranRed = Math.random()*256;
var ranGreen = Math.random()*256;
var ranBlue = Math.random()*256;
var curveColor = ranRed << 16 | ranGreen << 8 | ranBlue;
var curveAlpha = Math.random()*25+25;
// random whether filled or not
if (Math.round(Math.random()) == 0) {
drawRandomCurve(_root["Curves"+level], Math.ceil(Math.random()*5+2), true, curveColor, curveAlpha, 1, curveColor,
} else {
drawRandomCurve(_root["Curves"+level], Math.ceil(Math.random()*5+2), false, curveColor, curveAlpha, 1, curveColor
}
// placed randomly
_root["Curves"+level]._x = Math.random()*Stage.width;
_root["Curves"+level]._y = Math.random()*Stage.height;
_root["Curves"+level]._rotation = Math.random()*360;
level++;
}
Line 24 of 24, Col 1

9.23: Add a `for` *loop that randomly draws curved shapes on the stage.*

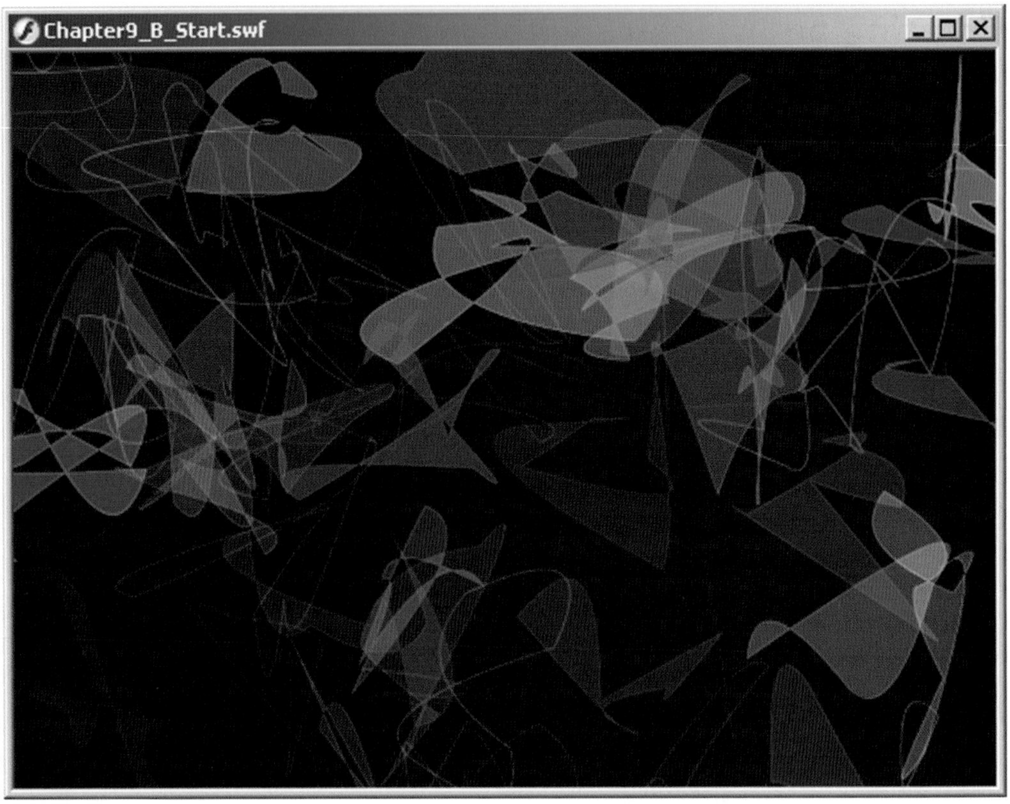

9.24: The code creates a random texture with curved lines, both filled and unfilled.

color in Chapter 5, "Coded Animation Techniques.") Next you randomly compute the alpha and store it in the variable `curveAlpha`.

You want some of the curves to be filled and some of them not to be filled, and you want the number that is filled to be different each time. To accomplish this, you use `Math.round(Math.random())` to decide when to fill or not. `Math.random()` returns numbers between 0 and 0.99, so by rounding this result, you get either a 0 or a 1. If it is a 0, then the `drawRandomCurve()` function is called with the `filled` variable set to `true`. If the result is 1, the `drawRandomCurve()` function is called with the `filled` variable set to `false`. In either case, the code passes in the computed `curveColor` and `curveAlpha` values.

For the number of points, the code specifies a random number from 2 to 7. You want to make sure that at least two points are passed in. This will actually make a three-pointed curve because of the starting point.

Once the curves are drawn, you randomly place them on the stage and rotate them in a random direction.

Test the movie (9.24). You'll see curved shapes scattered across the stage. This is pretty cool, although it isn't particularly useful.

Now let's move onto something a bit fancier and more useful. Since you can draw anything and everything with Flash's drawing methods, let's create a whole user interface with just these methods.

Creating an Interface with Lines

In this example, you'll create an entire graphical interface with ActionScript. Remember that the best thing about the drawing methods is how small the actual `.swf` file is, so the download time for this interface will be minimal.

First, you'll create the background for the interface. Then you'll build a menu system. In most cases, you would create the interface before the background, but here you'll start with the background, since the main point is to demonstrate what you can do with the drawing methods.

Creating a Textured Backdrop

The background will be a texture created from randomly generated, four-sided polygons, and it will change each time it's viewed. This will give you a very nice static background for your interface.

1. Open the File

Open the **Chapter9_C_Start.fla** file. Save the file to your local hard drive with the name **Chapter9_C_Modified.fla.** (To see a finished version of this movie, open **Chapter9_C_Final.fla.**) WWW.

This file contains a movie clip called Empty MC in the Background layer, with the instance name of Background, and two other layers, Actions and Functions, which are empty. In this example, you're essentially starting from scratch. Let's add the code to dynamically generate a rich, textured backdrop for the interface.

2. Start the Background Code and Test

Attach the following ActionScript to the Background movie clip (9.25).

```
onClipEvent(load) {
   // determine size of 4-sided polygon
   var theBiggestX = Stage.width;
   var theBiggestY = Stage.height;
   // loop to create polygons
   for (var i = 1; i < 10; i++) {
      createEmptyMovieClip("Shape" + i, i);
      // set up 1st point
      var startX = Math.random() * theBiggestX;
      var startY = Math.random() * theBiggestY;
      var maxX = Stage.width / 2;
      var maxY = Stage.height / 2;
      this["Shape" + i]._x = startX;
      this["Shape" + i]._y = startY;
      this["Shape" + i].lineStyle(1, 0xffffff, 100);
      this["Shape" + i].moveTo(0, 0);
      // compute 2nd point
      var nextPointX = Math.random()*maxX;
      var nextPointY = Math.random() * maxY;
```

continues

```
            this["Shape" + i].lineTo(nextPointX, nextPointY);
            // compute 3rd point
            nextPointX = Math.random() * maxX;
            nextPointY = Math.random() * maxY;
            this["Shape" + i].lineTo(nextPointX, -nextPointY);
            // compute 4th point
            nextPointX = Math.random() * maxX;
            nextPointY = Math.random() * maxY;
            this["Shape" + i].lineTo(-nextPointX, -nextPointY);
            // back to start
            this["Shape" + i].lineTo(0, 0);
        }
    }
```

This code is attached to the Background movie clip to take advantage of the fact that all movie clips created within a movie clip do not affect the levels on the `_root` timeline. Notice that everything happens in the `onClipEvent(load)` event handler. This code is executed when the movie loads, and then nothing for the background texture changes after that. There is no `onClipEvent(enterFrame)` event handler for generating any sort of continuous movement.

This code draws four-sided polygonal shapes (not squares or rectangles). The code sets the variables *theBiggestX* and *theBiggestY* based on `Stage.width` and `Stage.height`. These values will be used to place each polygon and also to compute the longest any one side can be.

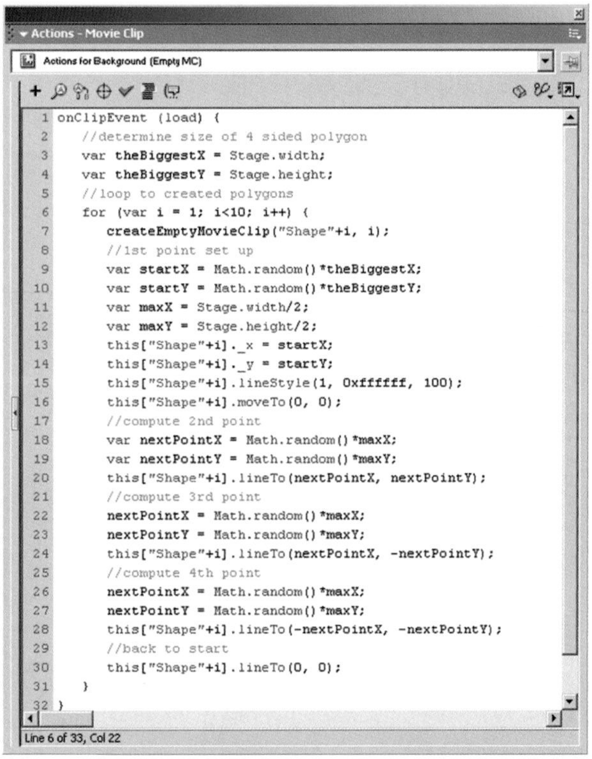

9.25: Add code for creating a textured backdrop to the Empty MC movie clip instance.

Then the code starts the `for` loop. For now, you'll run the `for` loop only ten times, but you'll increase this number later for the final program. The `for` loop will create a new movie clip and draw each polygon each time around. First, within the `for` loop, you create the empty movie clip. This is set on a different level each time, based on the *i* variable from the `for` loop, and given the name `"Shape" + i`.

Next the code computes the starting place on the stage based on the variables *theBiggestX* and *theBiggestY*. The *startX* and *startY* variables are randomly computed, so that each time a user views this program, the background will be different. The maximum sides for the *x* and *y* points are based on half of *theBiggestX* and *theBiggestY*. This means that the largest polygon will be no bigger than half the stage.

The maximum lengths for the sides are loaded into the variables *maxX* and *maxY*. Then you position the actual Shape*NN* movie clip using the *startX* and *startY* variables. Notice that you use the keyword `this` in front of the `"Shape" + i`. Remember that you cannot just say `"Shape" + i`, because you need to evaluate `"Shape" + i`. Since the movie clips are attached to this movie clip, you use the keyword `this[…]` to force the evaluation. (You cannot use `_root`, because the Shape*NN* movie clips do not reside on the `_root` timeline.) This will place the Shape*NN* movie clip on the stage of the Empty MC movie clip.

The `startX` and `startY` values will never be negative numbers. Remember that a value of 0 for *x* is at the left edge of the stage, and positive values for *x* move to the right. Similarly, a value of 0 for *y* is along the top edge of the stage, and positive values for *y* move downward. Therefore, in order to cover the entire stage, the Empty MC movie clip needs to be located at the upper-left corner of the main stage, or the (0, 0) point. In other words, the (0, 0) coordinate from the Empty MC movie clip needs to be located at the (0, 0) point of the main stage.

Then the code starts preparing for the drawing process. First, the code defines the line style. In this case, it's a simple white line of stroke 1 and alpha 100. Next you move to the starting place. The `moveTo(0, 0)` is redundant, because the drawing always starts at (0, 0), unless you say otherwise. This just serves as a reminder of where it's starting, and it doesn't hurt to be explicit. The `moveTo(0, 0)` is different from moving the movie clip with `ShapeNN._x` and `ShapeNN._y`. When you change the movie clip's `_x` and `_y` properties, you actually move the Shape*NN* movie clip within the Background movie clip. When you use the `moveTo(0, 0)` method, you are moving the position to start drawing to a specific place within the Shape*NN* movie clip.

Now you need to determine where to draw to, so you compute the variables `nextPointX` and `nextPointY` based on the `maxX` and `maxY` variables. You get a random number from each for `nextPointX` and `nextPointY`. This is your first point to draw to, so that is the next call. You call the `lineTo()` method using the Shape*NN* movie clip and the `nextPointX` and `nextPointY` variables. Then the code simply computes the `nextPointX` and `nextPointY` values the same way two more times, and it calls the `lineTo()` method to each of the `nextPointX` and `nextPointY` points that are computed. You know that the final line needs to return to the starting place (0, 0), so the last `lineTo()` just goes to (0, 0).

Notice that the `nextPointX` and the `nextPointY` values are never going to be negative. Now notice that in the second and third calls to the `lineTo()` method there are negative signs in front of these variables. In the second call there is a negative sign in front of the `nextPointY` variable, and in the third call there is a negative sign in front of both. This will create a shape in which none of the lines cross over each other.

Let's walk through the `for` loop to see how it works. The code begins by creating an empty movie clip and randomly positioning it on the stage. Since this is the first pass through the `for` loop, this newly created movie clip will be called Shape1. Let's say during the first pass through the `for` loop, the code positions the new Shape1 movie clip and *x* = 100 and *y* = 100. Then the code starts drawing a line at (0, 0). Again, that is (0, 0) *within* the newly created Shape1 movie clip. However, (0, 0) within the newly created movie clip is actually (100, 100) on the overall stage, since that is where the Shape1 movie clip was positioned (9.26).

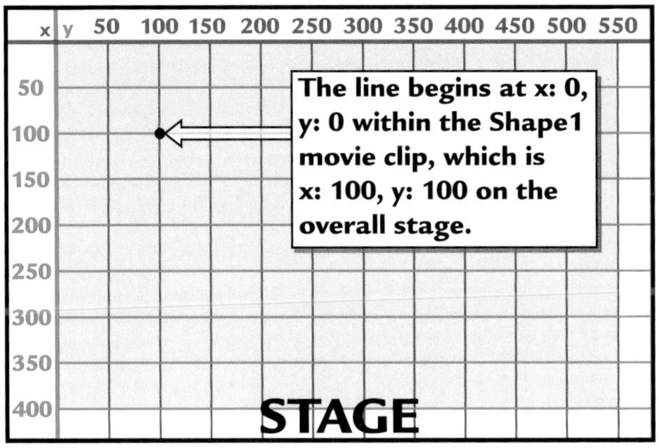

9.26: The Shape1 movie clip is randomly positioned at (100, 100), which is where the line begins.

Continuing through the `for` loop, the code determines the next point in the way as it computed the previous point. When using the `lineTo()` method, both the points are positive. This means that the line is drawn to the right and down. Let's say that the code comes up with random values of 200 for both the `nextPointX` and `nextPointY` variables. This would

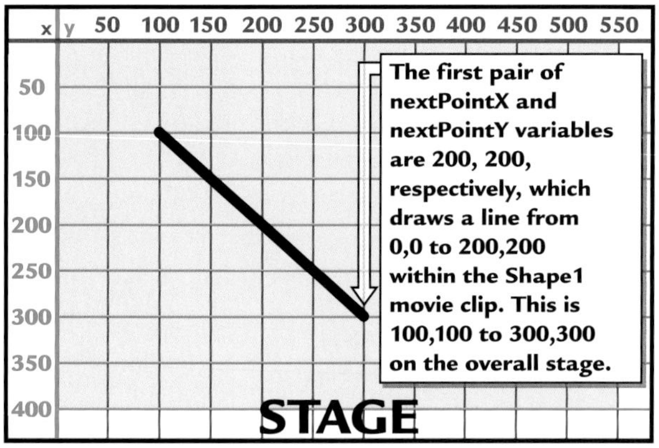

9.27: The code draws a line from the starting point to the first point specified by the `nextPointX` and `nextPointY` variables.

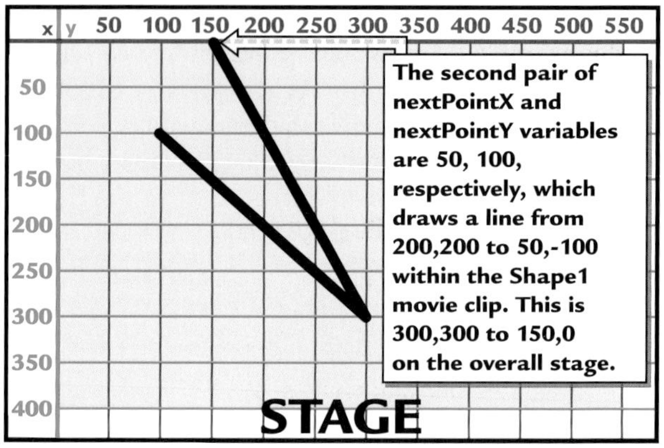

9.28: The code draws a line from the second point to the third point specified by the `nextPointX` and `nextPointY` variables.

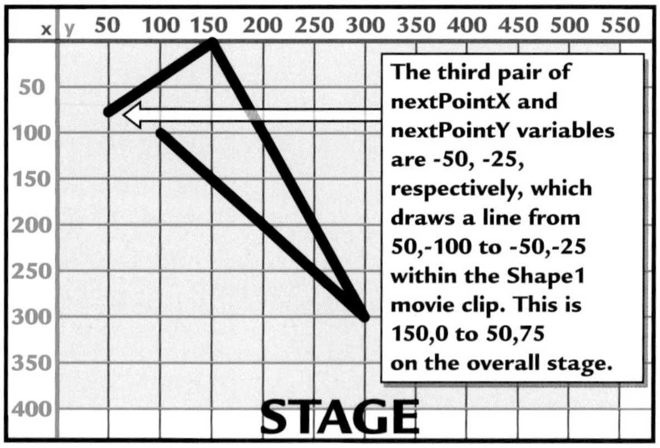

9.29: The code draws a line from the third point to the fourth point specified by the `nextPointX` and `nextPointY` variables.

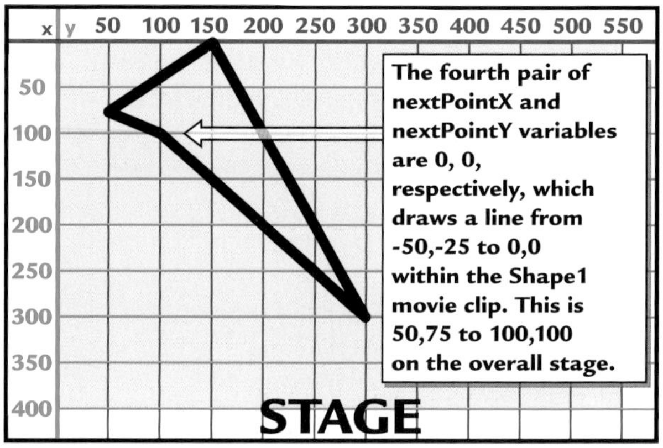

9.30: The code draws a line from the fourth point back to (0, 0), the beginning point, to complete the shape.

mean that a line would be drawn from (0, 0) to (200, 200) within the Shape1 movie clip, which would be from (100, 100) to (300, 300) on the overall stage (9.27).

Then the next point is computed in the same manner, but when used in the `lineTo()` method, the *y* argument, `nextPointY`, has a negative sign in front of it. So the lines ending point would be up and to the right of the original starting point (0, 0). Let's say that the code comes up with random values for the `nextPointX` and `nextPointY` variables of 50 and 100, respectively. A line would be drawn from (200, 200) to (50, –100) within the Shape1 movie clip, which would be from (300, 300) to (150, 0) on the overall stage (9.28).

For the next point, a negative sign is placed in front of both arguments in the `lineTo()` method. Thus, the point is negative in both the *x* and *y* directions, so the ending point for the next line would be up and to the left of the original starting point (0, 0). Let's say that the code comes up with random values for the `nextPointX` and `nextPointY` variables of 50 and 25, which when passed to the `lineTo()` method become –50 and –25, respectively. A line would be drawn from (50, –100) to (–50, –25) within the Shape1 movie clip, which would be from (150, 0) to (50, 75) on the overall stage (9.29).

Finally, the code draws a line back to (0, 0) to complete the four-sided polygon shape. In this example, a line would be drawn from (–50, –25) to (0, 0) within the Shape1 movie clip, which would be from (50, 75) to (100, 100) on the overall stage (9.30).

Test the movie. You'll see that ten polygon shapes are randomly generated for the background. But this really isn't very pretty, so let's add some color and a few other tricks.

3. Add Color to the Background

Replace the following line of code on the Empty MC movie clip:

```
this["Shape" + i].lineStyle(1, 0xffffff, 100);
```

with the following ActionScript (9.31):

```
// rotate polygon
this["Shape" + i]._rotation = Math.random() * 360;
// color polygon
var ranAlpha = Math.random() * 25;
var ranRed = Math.random() * 256;
var ranGreen = Math.random() * 256;
var ranBlue = Math.random() * 256;
var ranColor = ranRed << 16 | ranGreen << 8 | ranBlue;
this["Shape" + i].lineStyle(1, ranColor, ranAlpha);
this["Shape" + i].beginFill(ranColor, ranAlpha);
```

And then add the following line to the end of the `for` loop (9.31):

```
this["Shape" + i].endFill();
```

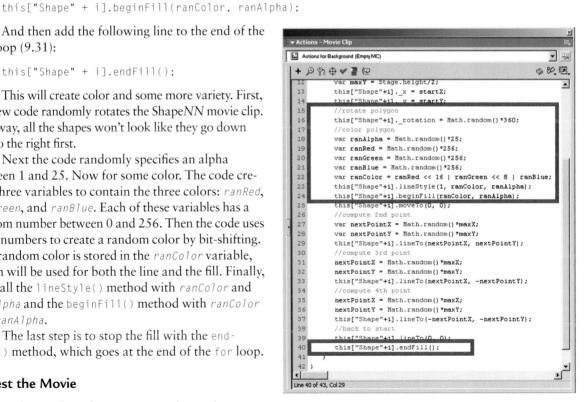

This will create color and some more variety. First, the new code randomly rotates the Shape*NN* movie clip. This way, all the shapes won't look like they go down and to the right first.

Next the code randomly specifies an alpha between 1 and 25. Now for some color. The code creates three variables to contain the three colors: *ranRed*, *ranGreen*, and *ranBlue*. Each of these variables has a random number between 0 and 256. Then the code uses these numbers to create a random color by bit-shifting. This random color is stored in the *ranColor* variable, which will be used for both the line and the fill. Finally, you call the `lineStyle()` method with *ranColor* and *ranAlpha* and the `beginFill()` method with *ranColor* and *ranAlpha*.

The last step is to stop the fill with the `endFill()` method, which goes at the end of the `for` loop.

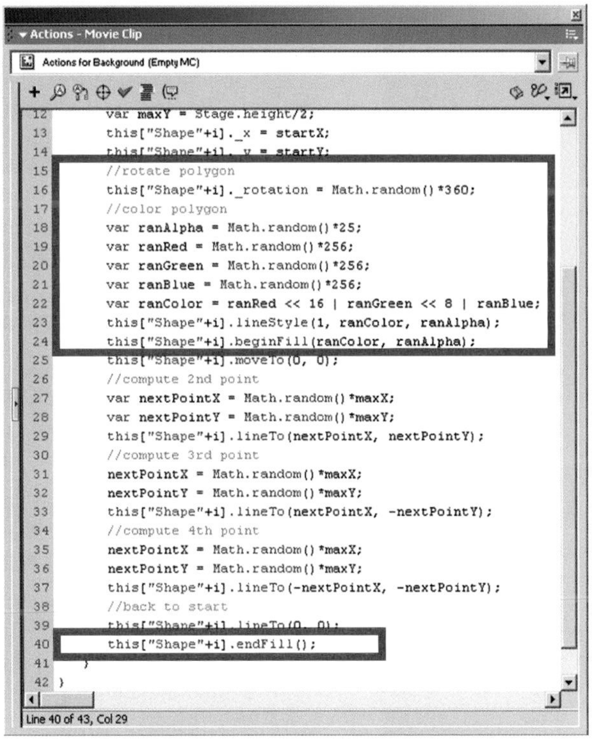

9.31: Add code to the Empty MC movie clip to add color and variation to the four-sided polygon shapes.

4. Test the Movie

Change the number of increments in the `for` loop from 10 to 100 (9.32).

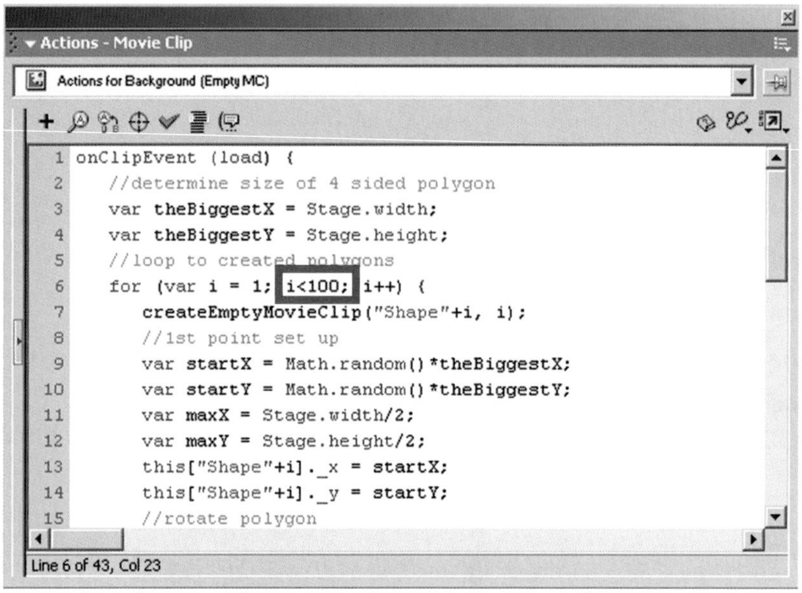

9.32: Change the increments in the `for` *loop to 100.*

Now test the movie. It takes a split second to show up. Then you see a very interesting layer of color on color using 100 four-sided polygons (9.33). Press Cmd+Return (Mac)/ Ctrl+Enter (Win), and you'll get a different background.

You didn't need to draw a single graphic on the stage to create this effect. It's drawn entirely with ActionScript. Furthermore, each time you run it, it's different.

Drawing the Menu System

Next you'll create a menu system using the drawing methods. The menu system will consist of rectangular buttons and lines (9.34). The work will be done by some basic functions.

1. Create a Function to Draw Rectangles

Attach the following ActionScript to frame 1 of the Functions layer (9.35).

```
// function to draw a rectangle - filled or not
function drawRectangle(rectName, filled, rectWidth, rectHeight, ►
rectColor, rectAlpha) {
   _root[rectName].lineStyle(1, rectColor, rectAlpha);
   if (filled == true) {
      _root[rectName].beginFill(rectColor, rectAlpha);
   }
   _root[rectName].moveTo(0, 0);
   _root[rectName].lineTo(rectWidth, 0);
   _root[rectName].lineTo(rectWidth, rectHeight);
   _root[rectName].lineTo(0, rectHeight);
   _root[rectName].lineTo(0, 0);
```

continues

9.33: The code generates a textured background using 100 four-sided polygons.

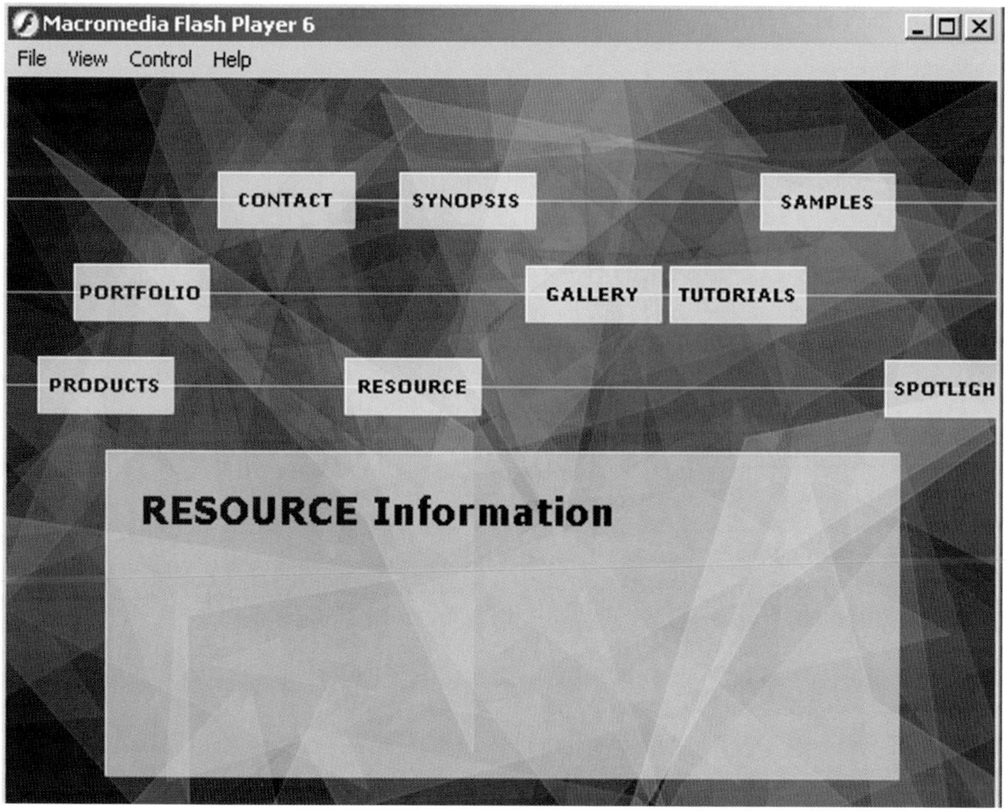

9.34: A user interface created with drawing methods

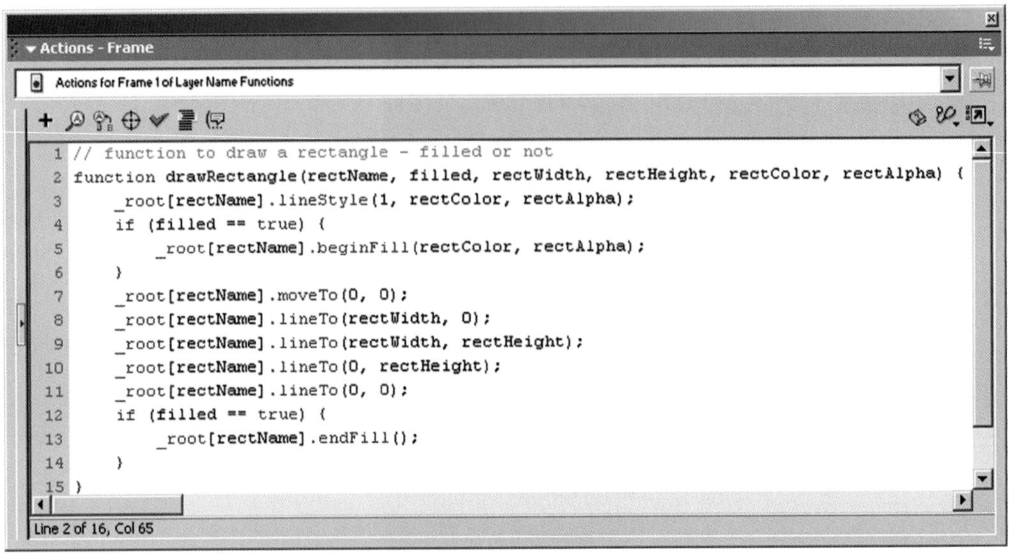

Actions - Frame
Actions for Frame 1 of Layer Name Functions
// function to draw a rectangle - filled or not
function drawRectangle(rectName, filled, rectWidth, rectHeight, rectColor, rectAlpha) {
_root[rectName].lineStyle(1, rectColor, rectAlpha);
if (filled == true) {
_root[rectName].beginFill(rectColor, rectAlpha);
}
_root[rectName].moveTo(0, 0);
_root[rectName].lineTo(rectWidth, 0);
_root[rectName].lineTo(rectWidth, rectHeight);
_root[rectName].lineTo(0, rectHeight);
_root[rectName].lineTo(0, 0);
if (filled == true) {
_root[rectName].endFill();
}
}
Line 2 of 16, Col 65

9.35: Add a function to the Functions layer to draw rectangular shapes.

```
    if (filled == true) {
        _root[rectName].endFill();
    }
}
```

NOTE As in examples in previous chapters, you're putting your functions on a separate layer. Keeping functions separate from the other ActionScript helps you organize your code.

The function is called `drawRectangle()` and has six arguments:

- The name of the movie clip to draw the rectangle in, `rectName`
- Whether the rectangle is filled or not, `filled`
- The width of the rectangle, `rectWidth`
- The height of the rectangle, `rectHeight`
- The color of the rectangle, used for both the fill and the line, `rectColor`
- The alpha of the rectangle, also used for both the fill and the line, `rectAlpha`

At first glance, it might look a little complex, but that's only because of the various references to the arguments in the `drawRectangle()` function. The code within the `drawRectangle()` function is actually fairly basic. Notice there is no call to create the movie clip, so the name passed in the argument, `rectName`, must already be a movie clip.

First, the code defines `lineStyle()` with `rectColor` and `rectAlpha`. Notice there is no argument passed into the `drawRectangle()` function for the rectangle line thickness. You could easily add this, but in this case, all of the rectangles will have a stroke width of 1.

If the `filled` variable is `true`, you call the `beginFill()` with the `rectColor` and `rectAlpha` arguments. Then the code moves to the point (0, 0) and starts drawing the rectangle. First, the code draws the top by going to the right, to the `rectWidth` value. Second, the code draws the right side, but moving straight down, to the `rectHeight` value.

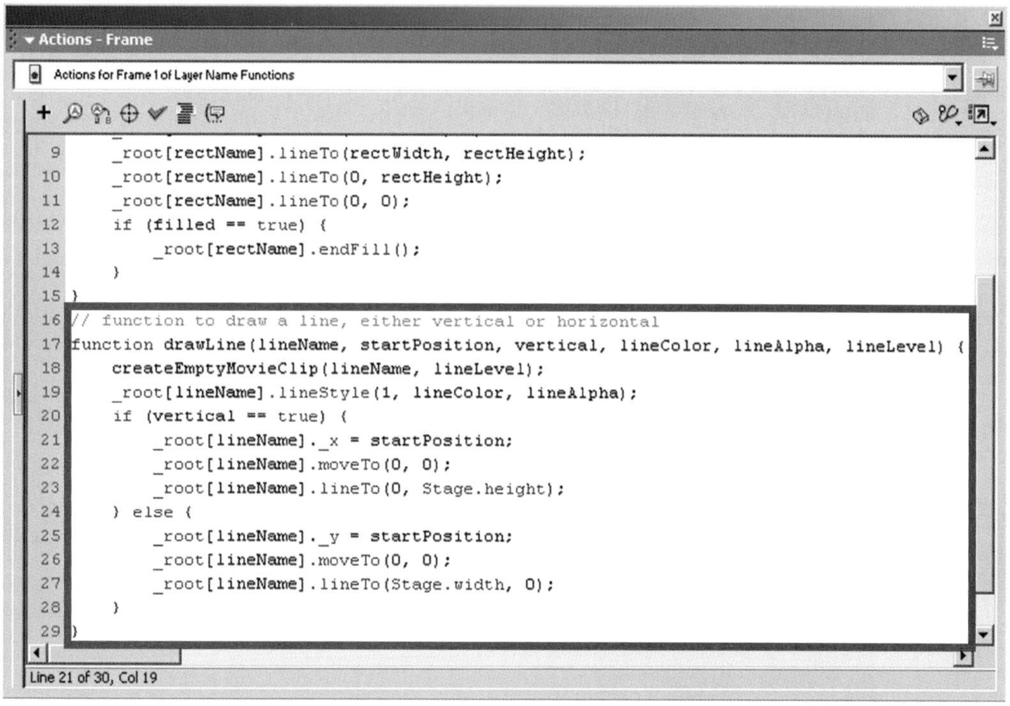

9.36: Add a function to the Functions layer to draw lines.

Third, the code draws the bottom by moving left back to the 0 point. To complete the shape, the code draws the left side by moving straight up to the starting point. Finally, if the *`filled`* variable is true, you end the fill with `endFill()`.

Now let's create the function to draw lines.

2. Create a Function to Draw Lines

Add the following ActionScript below the function from the previous step in the Functions layer (9.36).

```
// function to draw a line, either vertical or horizontal
function drawLine(lineName, startPosition, vertical, lineColor, ▶
lineAlpha, lineLevel) {
   createEmptyMovieClip(lineName, lineLevel);
   _root[lineName].lineStyle(1, lineColor, lineAlpha);
   if (vertical == true) {
      _root[lineName]._x = startPosition;
      _root[lineName].moveTo(0, 0);
      _root[lineName].lineTo(0, Stage.height);
   } else {
      _root[lineName]._y = startPosition;
      _root[lineName].moveTo(0, 0);
      _root[lineName].lineTo(Stage.width, 0);
   }
}
```

This is another simple function that looks a little complex due to the references to the arguments from the function in the code. In the *drawRectangle()* function, you're passing in the name of an already created movie clip and simply drawing the rectangle within it. In the *drawLine()* function, you're actually creating the movie clip.

The *drawLine()* function takes six arguments:

- The name of the movie clip to draw the line in, *lineName*
- The starting place for the line, *startPosition*
- Whether the line is vertical or horizontal, *vertical* (if vertical is `true` then it's vertical; otherwise, it's horizontal)
- The color of the line, *lineColor*
- The alpha of the line, *lineAlpha*
- The level to put the line on, *lineLevel*

Since you are actually creating the movie clip within this function, you need to know on which level to place it. Here, once again the code assumes you always want a line of thickness 1. This would be very easy to change, but it's not necessary for this project.

First the code creates the empty movie clip with `createEmptyMovieClip()` and the *lineName* and *lineLevel* values. Then the code defines the line style with `lineStyle()` and the *lineColor* and *lineAlpha* values.

Next the code prepares to draws the line. If the line is supposed to be vertical (`vertical == true`), you want the starting position to be at the top of the stage, so the code moves the movie clip *lineName* over in the *x*-axis to the *startPosition* value (`_x = startPosition`). If you want the line to be horizontal, the starting position should be along the left side of the stage, so the code moves the movie clip down in the *y*-axis to the *startPosition* value (`_y = startPosition`). Remember the movie clip starts at point (0, 0) so for the vertical direction the y is equal to 0 and for the horizontal direction the x is equal to 0. This moves the actual movie clip.

Then all you need to do is draw the line. The code calls the `moveTo()` method for the point (0, 0) and draws the line along either the height of the stage, for the vertical direction, or the width of the stage, for the horizontal direction.

Now you've created functions for drawing boxes and lines. Next let's create a function that draws buttons for your menu. This function will use the *drawRectangle()* function you've created.

3. Create a Function to Draw Buttons

In the Functions layer, add the following ActionScript below the function you created in the previous step (9.37).

```
// function to create a rectangular button with text
function createRectButton(buttonName, buttonText, buttonWidth, ▶
buttonHeight, buttonX, buttonY, buttonColor, buttonLevel) {
   createEmptyMovieClip(buttonName, buttonLevel);
   _root[buttonName]._x = buttonX;
   _root[buttonName]._y = buttonY;
   drawRectangle(buttonName, true, buttonWidth, buttonHeight, ▶
   buttonColor, 100);
   _root[buttonName]._alpha = 70;
}
```

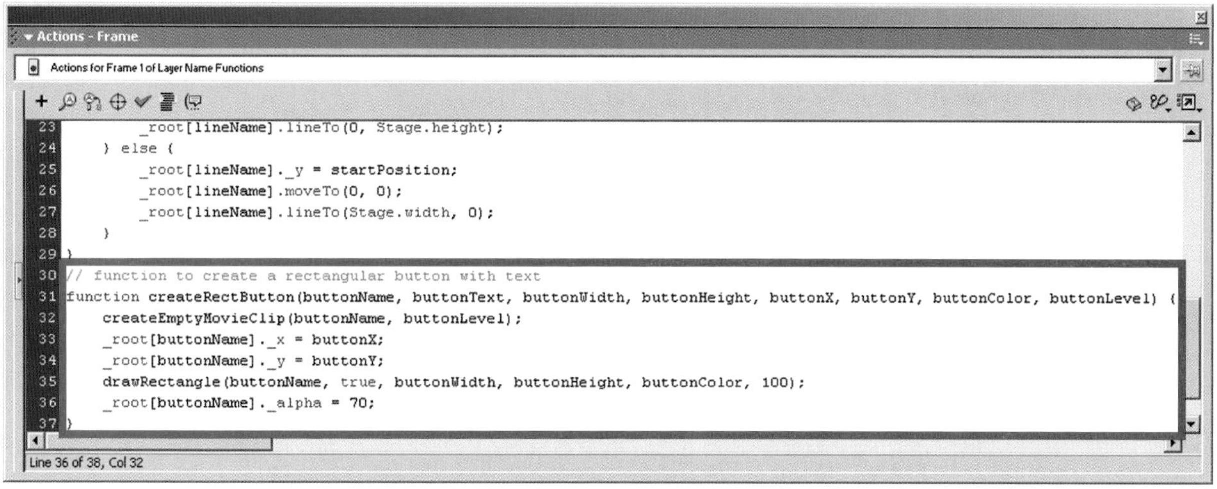

9.37: Add a function for creating buttons to the Functions layer.

The button function is called `createRectButton()`, because it will create a rectangular button. It takes eight arguments:

- The name of the button, `buttonName`
- The text that will go on the button, `buttonText`
- The width of the button, `buttonWidth`
- The height of the button, `buttonHeight`
- The position of the button, `buttonX` and `buttonY`
- The color of the button, `buttonColor`
- The level to create the button on, `buttonLevel`

This function is similar to the `drawLine()` function in that it creates the movie clip to draw on within the function. It begins by using `createEmptyMovieClip()` with the `buttonName` and `buttonLevel` arguments. Then the code positions the button with the `buttonX` and `buttonY` arguments.

Next the code calls the `drawRectangle()` function and passes in the six arguments:

Name of the rectangle	`buttonName`
Whether to fill	`true`
Width of the rectangle	`buttonWidth`
Height of the rectangle	`buttonHeight`
Color of the rectangle	`buttonColor`
Alpha of the button	`100`

Now you can see why the `drawRectangle()` function didn't need to create a movie clip: because one is being passed in.

Finally, you set the `_alpha` property of the button to 70%.

Now let's call the `createButton()` function and see the results of your work.

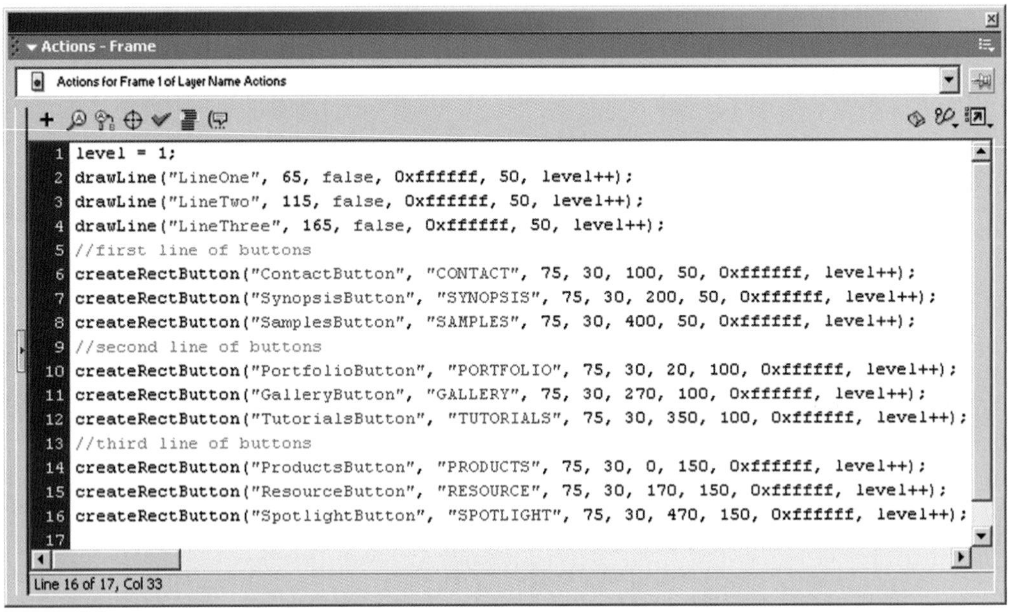
Actions - Frame
Actions for Frame 1 of Layer Name Actions
level = 1;
drawLine("LineOne", 65, false, 0xffffff, 50, level++);
drawLine("LineTwo", 115, false, 0xffffff, 50, level++);
drawLine("LineThree", 165, false, 0xffffff, 50, level++);
//first line of buttons
createRectButton("ContactButton", "CONTACT", 75, 30, 100, 50, 0xffffff, level++);
createRectButton("SynopsisButton", "SYNOPSIS", 75, 30, 200, 50, 0xffffff, level++);
createRectButton("SamplesButton", "SAMPLES", 75, 30, 400, 50, 0xffffff, level++);
//second line of buttons
createRectButton("PortfolioButton", "PORTFOLIO", 75, 30, 20, 100, 0xffffff, level++);
createRectButton("GalleryButton", "GALLERY", 75, 30, 270, 100, 0xffffff, level++);
createRectButton("TutorialsButton", "TUTORIALS", 75, 30, 350, 100, 0xffffff, level++);
//third line of buttons
createRectButton("ProductsButton", "PRODUCTS", 75, 30, 0, 150, 0xffffff, level++);
createRectButton("ResourceButton", "RESOURCE", 75, 30, 170, 150, 0xffffff, level++);
createRectButton("SpotlightButton", "SPOTLIGHT", 75, 30, 470, 150, 0xffffff, level++);
Line 16 of 17, Col 33

9.38: Add code to the Actions layer to draw three lines and call the `createRectButton()` *function.*

4. Draw Lines and Buttons and Test

Attach the following ActionScript to frame 1 of the Actions layer (9.38).

```
level = 1;
drawLine("LineOne", 65, false, 0xffffff, 50, level++);
drawLine("LineTwo", 115, false, 0xffffff, 50, level++);
drawLine("LineThree", 165, false, 0xffffff, 50, level++);
// first line of buttons
createRectButton("ContactButton", "CONTACT", 75, 30, 100, 50, ▶
0xffffff, level++);
createRectButton("SynopsisButton", "SYNOPSIS", 75, 30, 200, 50, ▶
0xffffff, level++);
createRectButton("SamplesButton", "SAMPLES", 75, 30, 400, 50, ▶
0xffffff, level++);
// second line of buttons
createRectButton("PortfolioButton", "PORTFOLIO", 75, 30, 20, 100, ▶
0xffffff, level++);
createRectButton("GalleryButton", "GALLERY", 75, 30, 270, 100, ▶
0xffffff, level++);
createRectButton("TutorialsButton", "TUTORIALS", 75, 30, 350, 100, ▶
0xffffff, level++);
// third line of buttons
createRectButton("ProductsButton", "PRODUCTS", 75, 30, 0, 150, ▶
0xffffff, level++);
```

```
createRectButton("ResourceButton", "RESOURCE", 75, 30, 170, 150, ▶
0xffffff, level++);
createRectButton("SpotlightButton", "SPOTLIGHT", 75, 30, 470, 150, ▶
0xffffff, level++);
```

This code will actually draw the lines and buttons. It creates three lines running horizontally on the stage, with three buttons on each line.

First, you need to define a variable to hold the level number so that nothing will be duplicated on the same level. Here, the variable `level` is set to 1.

Then the code starts drawing three lines, named `LineOne`, `LineTwo`, and `LineThree`. They all run horizontally, are colored white, and have their alpha set to 50. The only difference between the three calls to `drawLine()`, besides the names of the movie clips, is the position. The lines are spaced 50 pixels from each other.

The rest of the code creates the buttons. Here, the code calls the `createRectButton()` function nine times and gives each button a name that is appropriate for the text that will appear on the button. Next come the size variables; all of the buttons are 75 pixels wide by 30 pixels high. Then the code places the buttons. The first three buttons are on the first line, the next three are on the second line, and the last three on the third line, with the *x* position staggered. All of the buttons are white (0xffffff).

Notice that in all of the calls to both the `drawLine()` and `createRectButton()` functions, the last argument is the `level` variable, and it is incremented in the argument. This is something you haven't seen before in this book. This is similar to incrementing a variable in a `for` loop. The `level` variable is incremented *after* the function is finished executing.

Test the movie. You'll see three lines running across the stage and nine boxes sitting on the lines (9.39).

The lines and boxes look nice, but these boxes aren't very good buttons. They don't act like buttons when you roll over them with your mouse, and they don't say anything. Let's fix the missing text problem first. You already have the function set up to catch the text that goes on the button; you just haven't coded it yet.

5. Add Text to Buttons and Test

On the Functions layer, add the following ActionScript to the end of the `createRectButton()` function, but still within the function (9.40).

```
// text
_root[buttonName].createTextField("SquareText", 1, 0, buttonHeight/4, ▶
buttonWidth, buttonHeight);
_root[buttonName].SquareText.textColor = 0x1f1a16;
_root[buttonName].SquareText.text = buttonText;
_root[buttonName].SquareFormat = new TextFormat();
_root[buttonName].SquareFormat.align = "center";
_root[buttonName].SquareFormat.size = 10;
_root[buttonName].SquareFormat.font = "Verdana";
_root[buttonName].SquareFormat.bold = true;
_root[buttonName].SquareText.setTextFormat._root[buttonName].SquareFormat);
```

This will add the text to the button. Because you created this movie clip out of thin air, it doesn't have any place to put text. Fortunately, there is a new movie clip method to take

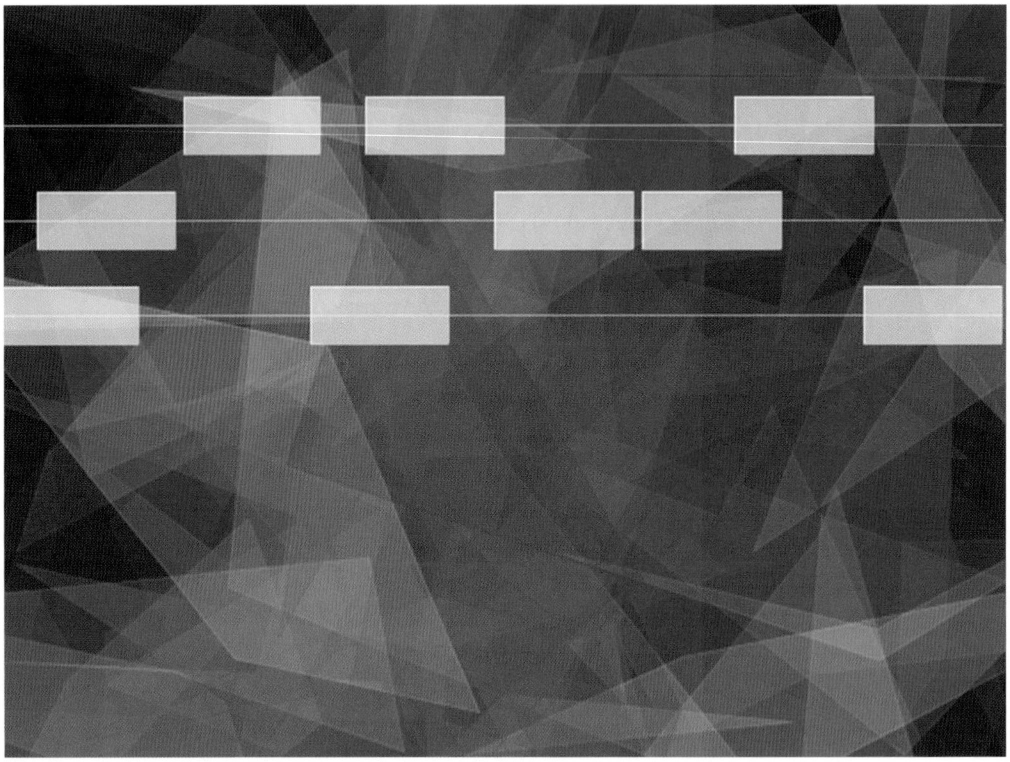

9.39: At this point, you have the shapes for the buttons, but they aren't interactive and there is no text on them.

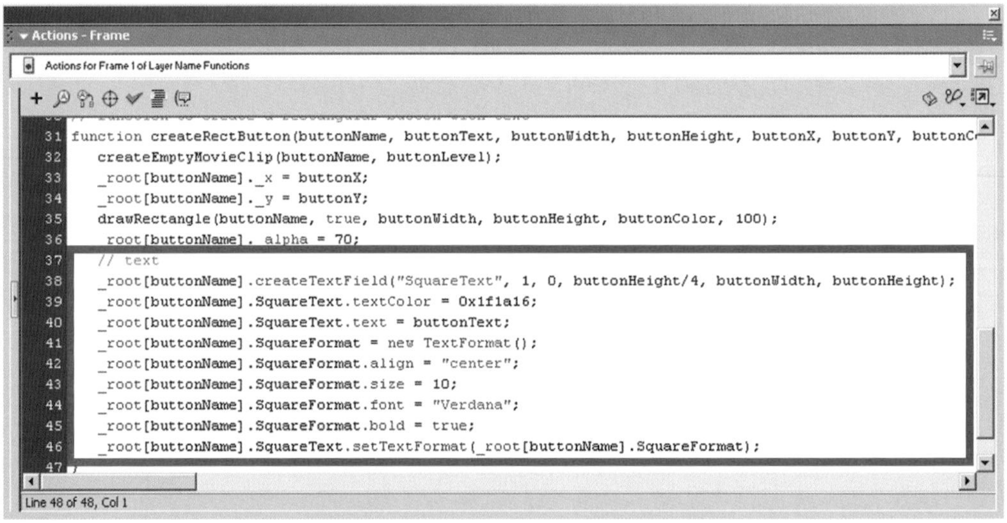

Actions - Frame
Actions for Frame 1 of Layer Name Functions
function createRectButton(buttonName, buttonText, buttonWidth, buttonHeight, buttonX, buttonY, buttonC
createEmptyMovieClip(buttonName, buttonLevel);
_root[buttonName]._x = buttonX;
_root[buttonName]._y = buttonY;
drawRectangle(buttonName, true, buttonWidth, buttonHeight, buttonColor, 100);
_root[buttonName]._alpha = 70;
// text
_root[buttonName].createTextField("SquareText", 1, 0, buttonHeight/4, buttonWidth, buttonHeight);
_root[buttonName].SquareText.textColor = 0x1f1a16;
_root[buttonName].SquareText.text = buttonText;
_root[buttonName].SquareFormat = new TextFormat();
_root[buttonName].SquareFormat.align = "center";
_root[buttonName].SquareFormat.size = 10;
_root[buttonName].SquareFormat.font = "Verdana";
_root[buttonName].SquareFormat.bold = true;
_root[buttonName].SquareText.setTextFormat(_root[buttonName].SquareFormat);
Line 48 of 48, Col 1

9.40: Add code to the `createRectButton()` function on the Functions layer to add text to the buttons.

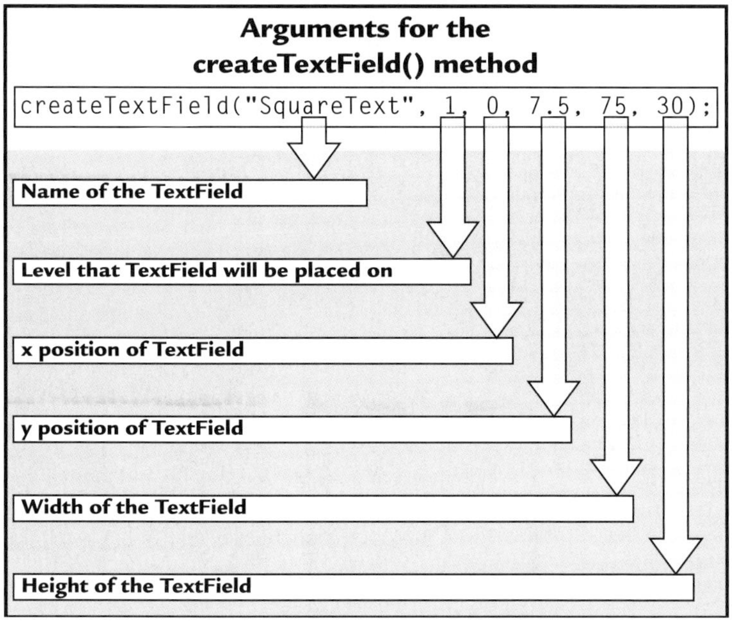

9.41: Arguments for the `createTextField()` *method*

care of this: `createTextField()`. This method allows you to generate a `TextField` object dynamically. The `createTextField()` method takes six arguments (9.41). The first argument is the name of the `TextField`, and then comes the level, the *x* and *y* positions, and the width and height. The *x* and *y* positions are relative to the movie clip that contains it, so they are relative to the buttonName movie clip.

Once you've created the `TextField` object, you're ready to set it up. (You learned about `TextField` object and its properties in Chapter 6, "Working with Text.") First, you set the text color to dark gray (0x1f1a16) using the `textColor` property. Then you set the text with the `text` property, passing it in as the *`buttonText`*.

Now you need to do some formatting. You accomplish this with the new `TextFormat` object, which lets you format the text in `TextField` objects. First you create a new `TextFormat` object using the `new` keyword and attaching it to the *`buttonName`* movie clip. The new `TextFormat` object is called *`SquareFormat`*. Then you set the format of the text as follows:

- Centered, with the `SquareFormat.align` property
- Size 10, with the `SquareFormat.size` property
- Verdana font, with the `SquareFormat.font` property
- Bold font, with the `SquareFormat.bold` property set to `true`

Finally, you set the text that is in the *`SquareText`* object to this format using the `set-TextFormat()` method of the `TextField` object.

Test the movie (9.42). You now have text on your buttons, but they still don't act like buttons. Now let's add the rollover code for this functionality.

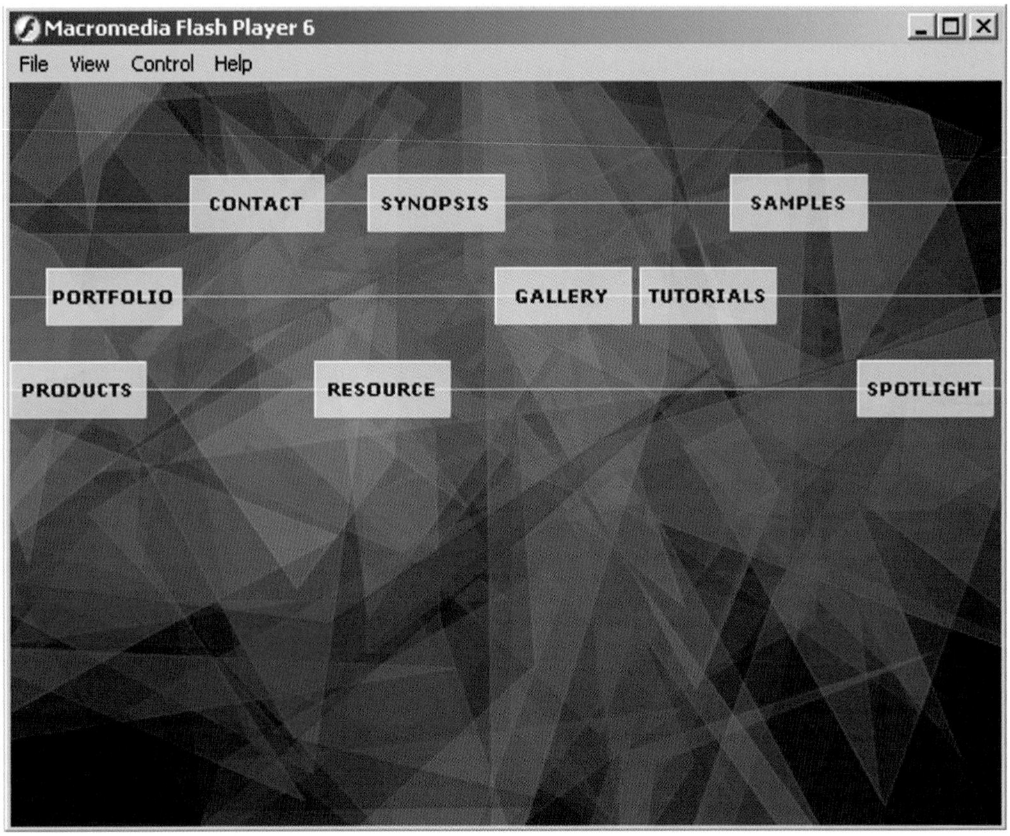

9.42: Now the buttons have text on them.

6. Add Rollover Code to the Buttons and Test

Add the following code to the `createRectButton()` function, at the bottom (9.43).

```
// rollover
_root[buttonName].onRollOver = function() {
   _root[buttonName]._alpha = 100;
};
// rolloff
_root[buttonName].onRollOut = function() {
   _root[buttonName]._alpha = 70;
};
// move button on stage
function moveButton() {
   if (_root[buttonName]._x > Stage.width - 50) {
      _root[buttonName]._x -= Stage.width;
   }
   _root[buttonName]._x++;
}
setInterval(moveButton, 1);
```

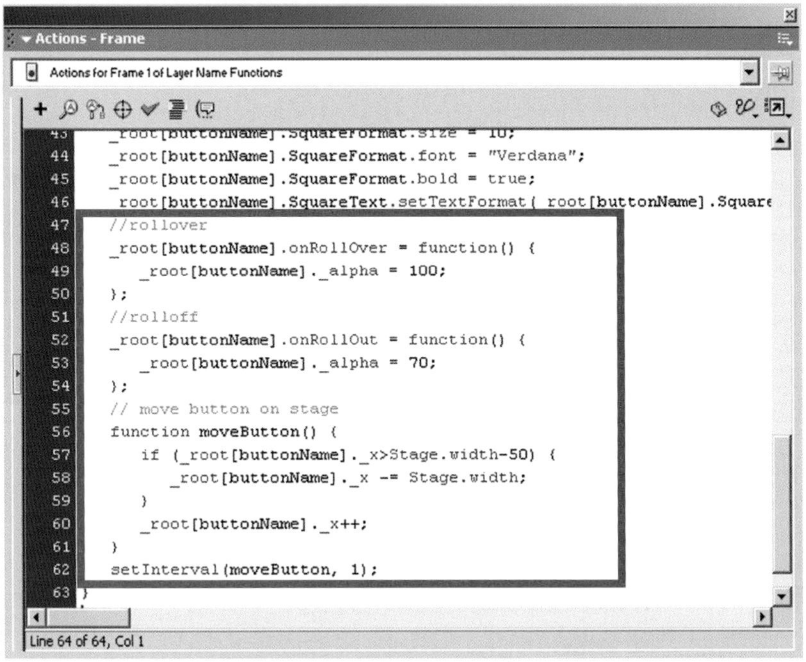

9.43: *Add code to generate rollover and rolloff effects, as well as simple motion.*

First, you want the button to increase its alpha to 100% when it's rolled over and return to its 70% alpha when it's rolled off. Here's where the great `MovieClip` object event handlers come in handy. You're using the `onRollOver()` and `onRollOut()` event handlers to have the buttons do something. These are built-in event handlers, but they have no actions associated with them. To use one of these events, you need to tell Flash which button it is associated with. For the rollover event, you write the following:

```
_root[buttonName].onRollOver = function() {
```

This sets it equal to a function that is defined next but does not get a name. Within the function, the button changes its `_alpha` property to 100. The same technique is used for the `onRollOut()` event handler, except the `_alpha` property is changed to 70.

This code also moves the buttons across the stage. It creates a function called *`moveButton()`* that takes no arguments. All the *`moveButton()`* function does is move the button over to the right by 1 pixel. If the button has gotten close to the end of the stage (`Stage.width - 50`), you move the button over to the left side of the stage by subtracting the stage width from the button's position.

You could have put this code in an `onEnterFrame` event, like this

```
_root[buttonName].onEnterFrame = function() {
   if (_root[buttonName]._x > Stage.width - 50) {
      _root[buttonName]._x -= Stage.width;
   }
   _root[buttonName]._x++;
};
```

However, this would only trigger the move based on the frame rate, and it's best to have the button move independently of the frame rate. Here, you use a `setInterval()` function and call the *moveButton()* function every millisecond.

Test the movie. Now the buttons work when you roll over them, and they move across the screen to the right. They are not really moving as fast as 1 pixel per millisecond, because there is so much on the screen that the Flash processor really cannot keep up with all that needs to be processed (the 100 polygons in the background plus moving the buttons).

Although the buttons behave as they should, they still don't really serve any purpose. Let's code a function that will create an information box. Then will add more code to have the information box pop up when the user clicks a button.

7. Create a Function to Draw an Information Box

On the Functions layer, add the following ActionScript, at the bottom (9.44).

```
function createInfoBox(infoBoxName, infoText, infoBoxWidth, ▶
infoBoxHeight, infoBoxX, infoBoxY, infoBoxColor, infoBoxLevel) {
   createEmptyMovieClip(infoBoxName, infoBoxLevel);
   _root[infoBoxName]._x = infoBoxX;
   _root[infoBoxName]._y = infoBoxY;
   drawRectangle(infoBoxName, true, infoBoxWidth, infoBoxHeight, ▶
   infoBoxColor, 55);
   // text
   _root[infoBoxName].createTextField("InfoTextField", 1, ▶
   infoBoxHeight / 10, infoBoxHeight / 10, infoBoxWidth, infoBoxHeight);
   _root[infoBoxName].InfoTextField.textColor = 0x1f1a16;
   _root[infoBoxName].InfoTextField.text = infoText;
   _root[infoBoxName].InfoFormat = new TextFormat();
   _root[infoBoxName].InfoFormat.align = "left";
   _root[infoBoxName].InfoFormat.size = 20;
   _root[infoBoxName].InfoFormat.font = "Verdana";
   _root[infoBoxName].InfoFormat.bold = true;
   _root[infoBoxName].InfoTextField.setTextFormat(_root▶
   [infoBoxName].InfoFormat);
}
```

This function will draw a large rectangle in the lower part of the screen and place text in it, depending on which button was pressed. The function is called *createInfoBox()* and takes eight arguments:

- The name of the movie clip to create, *infoBoxName*
- The text to place in the information box, *infoText*
- The width and height of the information box, *infoBoxWidth* and *infoBoxHeight*
- The position for the information box, *infoBoxX* and *infoBoxY*
- The color of the box, *infoBoxColor*
- The level to create the movie clip on, *infoLevel*

The *createInfoBox()* function is almost identical to the *createRectButton()* function. It has the same arguments and does the same setup; it just doesn't do the button rollover action.

Actions - Frame
Actions for Frame 1 of Layer Name Functions
}
_root[buttonName]._x++;
}
setInterval(moveButton, 1);
}
function createInfoBox(infoBoxName, infoText, infoBoxWidth, infoBoxHeight, infoBoxX, infoBoxY, infoBoxColor, infoBoxLe
createEmptyMovieClip(infoBoxName, infoBoxLevel);
_root[infoBoxName]._x = infoBoxX;
_root[infoBoxName]._y = infoBoxY;
drawRectangle(infoBoxName, true, infoBoxWidth, infoBoxHeight, infoBoxColor, 55);
// text
_root[infoBoxName].createTextField("InfoTextField", 1, infoBoxHeight/10, infoBoxHeight/10, infoBoxWidth, infoBoxHei
_root[infoBoxName].InfoTextField.textColor = 0x1f1a16;
_root[infoBoxName].InfoTextField.text = infoText;
_root[infoBoxName].InfoFormat = new TextFormat();
_root[infoBoxName].InfoFormat.align = "left";
_root[infoBoxName].InfoFormat.size = 20;
_root[infoBoxName].InfoFormat.font = "Verdana";
_root[infoBoxName].InfoFormat.bold = true;
_root[infoBoxName].InfoTextField.setTextFormat(_root[infoBoxName].InfoFormat);
}
Line 84 of 86, Col 1

9.44: Add another function to the Functions layer for creating an information box.

First, the function creates the empty movie clip to draw in. Then it positions the movie clip based on the `infoBoxX` and `infoBoxY` arguments. Next you call `drawRectangle()` and pass in the arguments:

- The name of the movie clip, `infoBoxName`
- Whether it's filled, `true`
- The width and the height of the rectangle to draw, `infoBoxWidth` and `infoBoxHeight`
- The color of the rectangle, `infoBoxColor`
- The alpha of the rectangle, 55

This will draw the rectangle.

Now you need to add some text to the information box. As you did for the button text, you create a text field using `createTextField()`. Here, you want the text to start in the upper-left corner, so you place the text based on the width and height of the rectangle divided by 10. This will place it up in the upper left, but with some padding around it. Then you set up the text field in the same way as you did the text for the buttons. In this case, the size is 20 and the text is left-justified.

Now let's call this function when the user clicks the button.

8. Create a Function for the *onPress()* Event and Test

Add the following ActionScript within the `createRectButton()` function, at the bottom (9.45).

```
// pressed
_root[buttonName].onPress = function() {
   createInfoBox("InfoBox", buttonText + " Information", ►
Stage.width * 8 / 10, 175, Stage.width / 10, 200, 0xffffff, level);
};
```

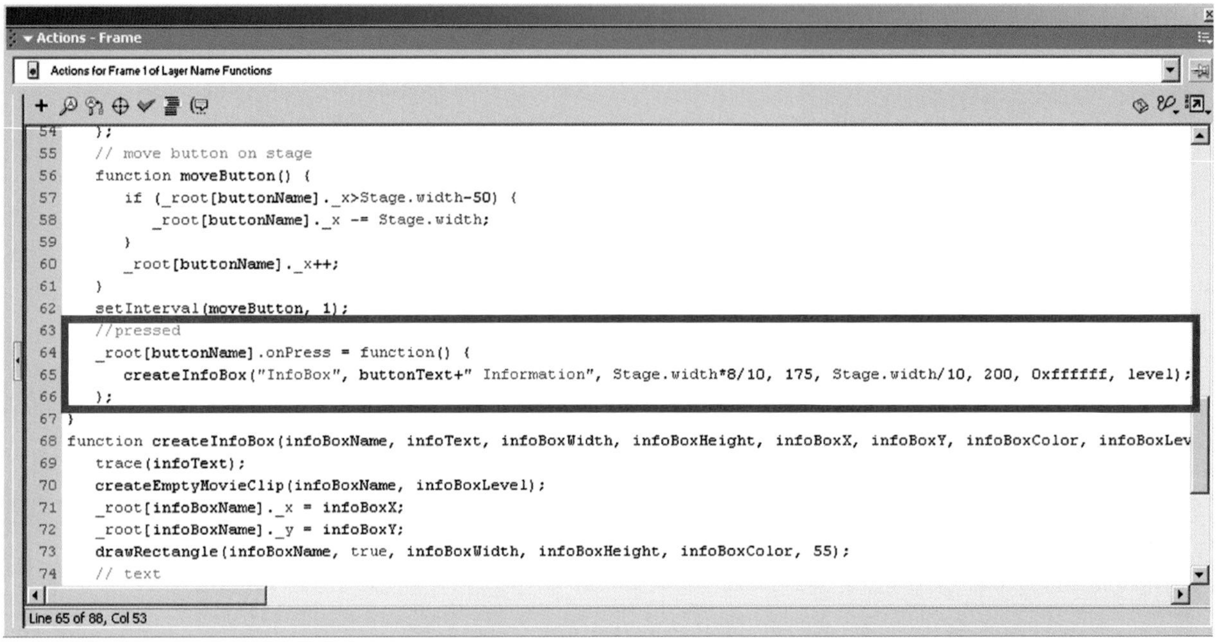
Actions - Frame
Actions for Frame 1 of Layer Name Functions
};
// move button on stage
function moveButton() {
if (_root[buttonName]._x>Stage.width-50) {
_root[buttonName]._x -= Stage.width;
}
_root[buttonName]._x++;
}
setInterval(moveButton, 1);
//pressed
_root[buttonName].onPress = function() {
createInfoBox("InfoBox", buttonText+" Information", Stage.width*8/10, 175, Stage.width/10, 200, 0xffffff, level);
};
}
function createInfoBox(infoBoxName, infoText, infoBoxWidth, infoBoxHeight, infoBoxX, infoBoxY, infoBoxColor, infoBoxLev
trace(infoText);
createEmptyMovieClip(infoBoxName, infoBoxLevel);
_root[infoBoxName]._x = infoBoxX;
_root[infoBoxName]._y = infoBoxY;
drawRectangle(infoBoxName, true, infoBoxWidth, infoBoxHeight, infoBoxColor, 55);
// text
Line 65 of 88, Col 53

9.45: Add a catch for the user press and call the `createInfoBox()` *function*

This will create a function for the `onPress()` event. This function will call the `createInfoBox()` function and pass in the name InfoBox, which is what the new movie clip will be called. The text that will be written in the box is simply the same as the `buttonText`, with the word *Information* added to it. You also pass in the width and height, position, color, and level of the information box.

The `level` variable is the same `level` variable that you used in the Actions layer to create all the rest of the movie clips for drawing. This ensures that the information box will be placed on top of everything. Notice that you did not increment the `level` variable, as you did in the previous calls to the functions. This is because you want the information boxes to replace each other, so you put them on the same level. (Remember that only one movie clip can exist on a level at one time.) If one information box is up for one of the buttons and you click another button, the information box will be replaced with the new one, not stacked on top.

Test this version (9.46). Click the buttons. Notice that as you select each different button, the information text changes. You are actually creating a new movie clip each time. For a final product, you would add more text in the information box.

Conclusion

The drawing methods are very useful tools that can help you reduce the size of your Flash files so they load faster. They also can create a randomness to the look and feel of your final product that would be very difficult to create with graphics and would take a lot of overhead.

In this chapter, you learned how to work with almost all of the drawing methods, with the exception of `beginGradientFill()` and `clear()`. The `beginGradientFill()` method fills

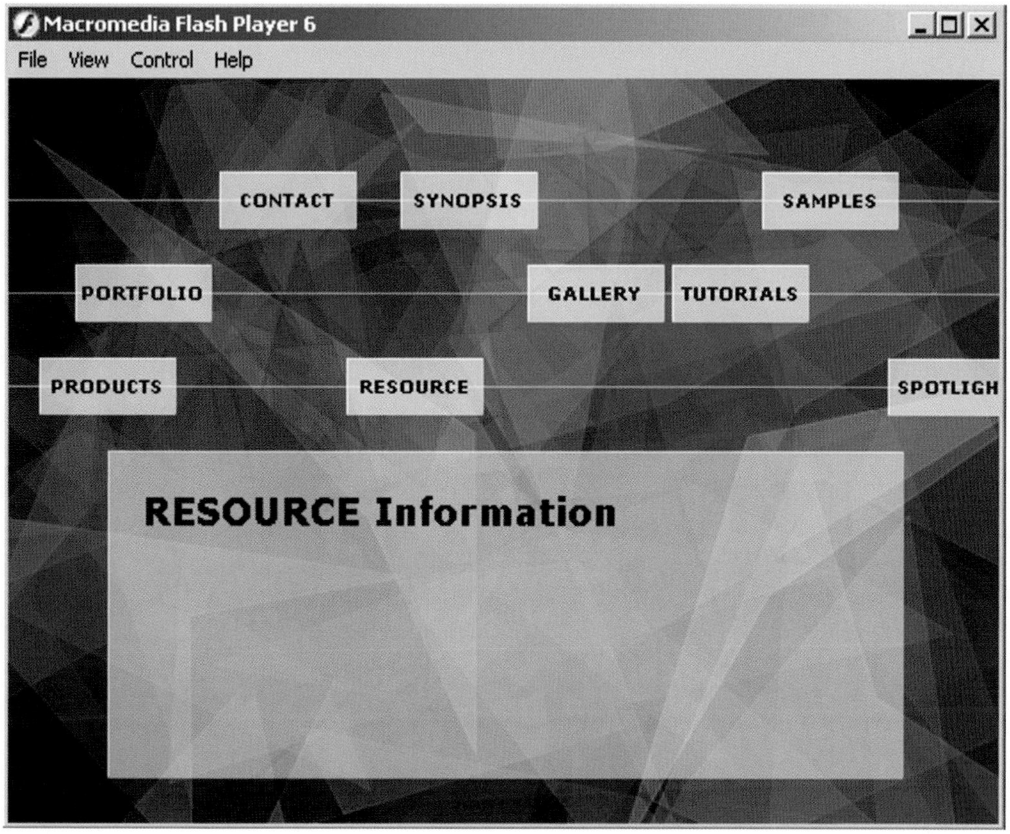

9.46: The final interface with an information box

a shape with a gradient instead of a solid color. The `clear()` method clears all of the drawing that was done with a specific movie clip.

Using the drawing methods, you could create all of your graphics dynamically. Sometimes this will be the best way to build your Flash movie; other times, it will be easier to create standard graphics. In most cases, you'll use both techniques together.

ten

CHAPTER

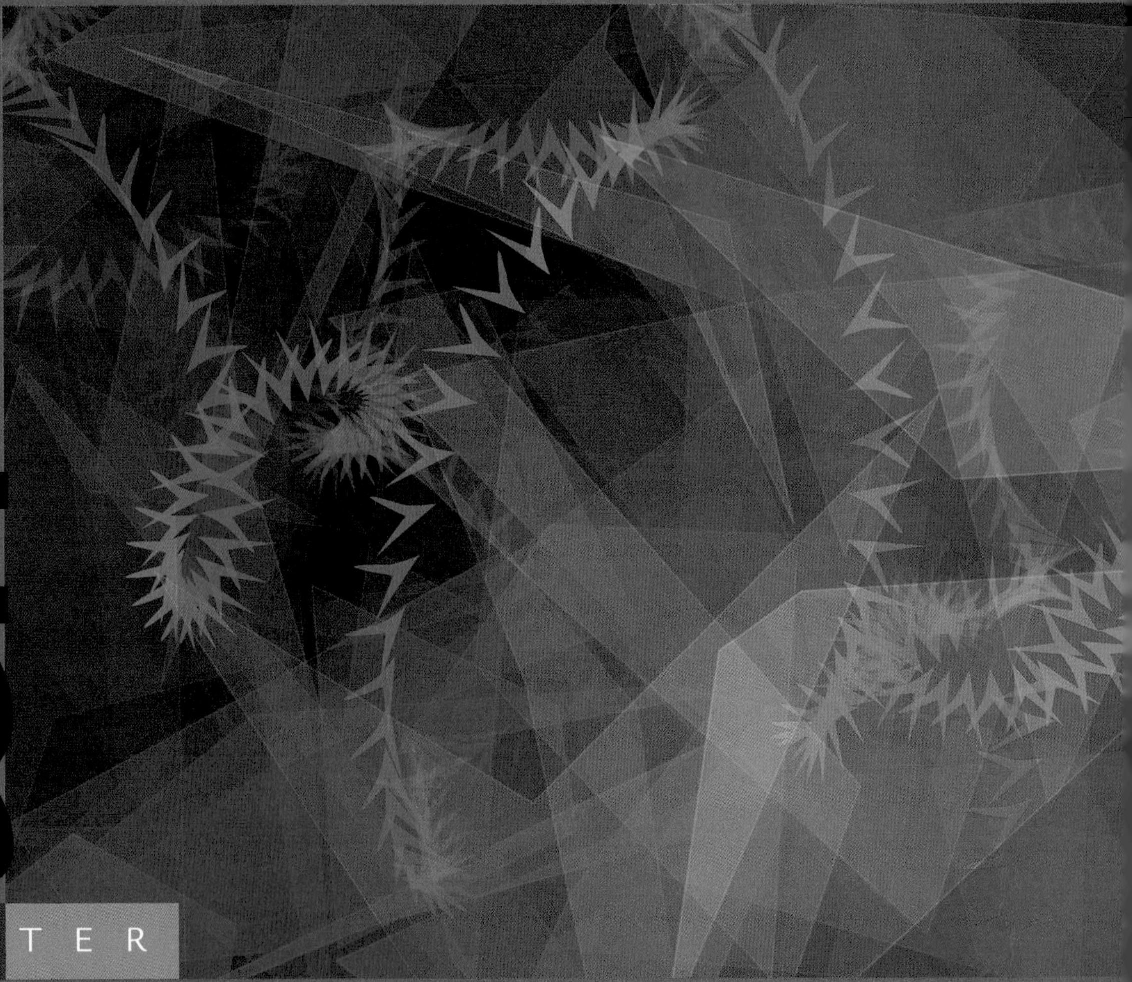

Flash Components

Flash 5 introduced *a coding tool called* components *(or* smart clips*). Components are a tool for encapsulating reusable code, something like a cross between macros found in programs like Microsoft Word and plug-ins for programs such as Adobe Photoshop. Thanks to this encapsulation, you don't need to work directly with the code when you use the component.*

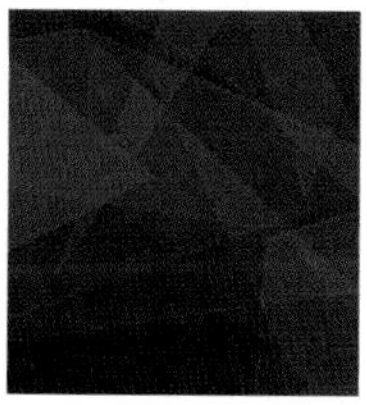

The code that many Flash developers are likely to reuse most often are the basic elements of a user interface, such as the standard types of buttons, radio buttons, check boxes, and so on. Flash MX ships with built-in components for these common elements: the CheckBox, ComboBox, ListBox, PushButton, RadioButton, ScrollBar, and ScrollPane components.

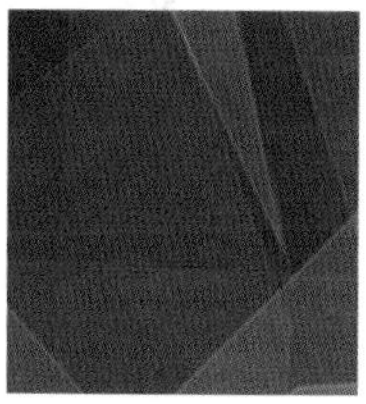

In this chapter, you'll dabble with the built-in components only long enough to get acquainted with how components work. Then you'll move onto discover the real potential of components: You can build your own components to create whole web interfaces, games, and other more advanced applications. In this chapter, you'll create two of your own components: one that uses Flash's built-in interface for entering the parameters and one that uses a custom user interface.

Understanding Components

Although the components that come with Flash can be handy, they aren't very exciting. However, they will serve nicely as a means to get acquainted with how to use a component, change the settings of a component, and interface a component with ActionScript.

NOTE In this book, the focus is on how to interface with components in ActionScript. For information about how each of the built-in components works, please see the Macromedia documentation.

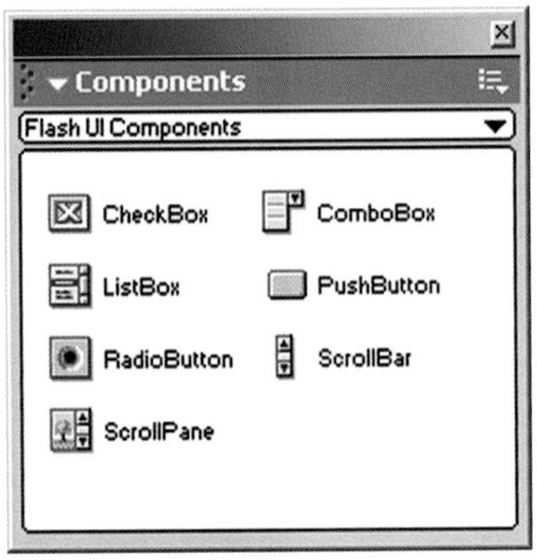

10.1: Flash MX ships with a small collection of built-in components.

1. Open a New Flash File

Open a new flash file and save it as **Chapter10_Comp.fla**. That's right—you don't need to download anything for this example, and there is no final file. In the previous examples, you've used Flash files that have already been created for you. In a sense, that's exactly what a component is.

If the Components panel is not already nested on the right side of your screen, press Cmd/Ctrl+F7 to open it. The Components panel contains the built-in components that come with Flash MX (10.1).

2. Add the CheckBox Component

Drag the CheckBox component from the Components panel onto the stage, name the layer **Component**, and run the movie. The CheckBox component is a toggle on or off button, and it uses a check to show when it's on.

Notice that you now have a folder in your library called Flash UI Components, which contains the CheckBox component, as well as all of the graphics and symbols for the CheckBox component (10.2). The CheckBox component needs all of these items to work.

Once the component is in your movie, you can view all of its ActionScript and graphics. You can change anything and everything associated with this component, without affecting the original component in the Components panel. Any modifications you make apply only to the local copy.

3. View the CheckBox Component's Parameters

Stop testing the movie. Select the CheckBox component on the stage and open the Properties panel. When you have a component selected, the Properties panel looks a little different than it does for other objects. On the far right are two buttons: Properties and Parameters. If you select the Properties button, you'll see the standard Properties panel. When you select the Parameters button, you'll see the Parameters panel, showing the parameters attached to the CheckBox component (10.3).

In the center box of the Parameters panel, the left column shows the names of the parameters and the right column shows their values. You can change the value in the right column, but you cannot change the parameter name in the left column. The CheckBox component has four parameters listed:

Label This is the actual string or text that will be displayed next to the check box. For example, if you change the value of the Label parameter to Check Me, the component will display the words "Check Me" next to the check box.

Initial Value This parameter is set to `false`, so the box will not have a check mark when the movie is first played. If you change the value of the Initial Value parameter to `true`, a check mark will be in the check box when the movie first plays.

Label Placement This parameter determines if the label should be placed to the left or right of the check box.

Change Handler This parameter value is blank by default. It provides a place where you can add a function call. If you add a function call, it will occur each time the check box changes state (each time it's checked and each time it's unchecked).

Now let's create a function that you can call with the Change Handler parameter.

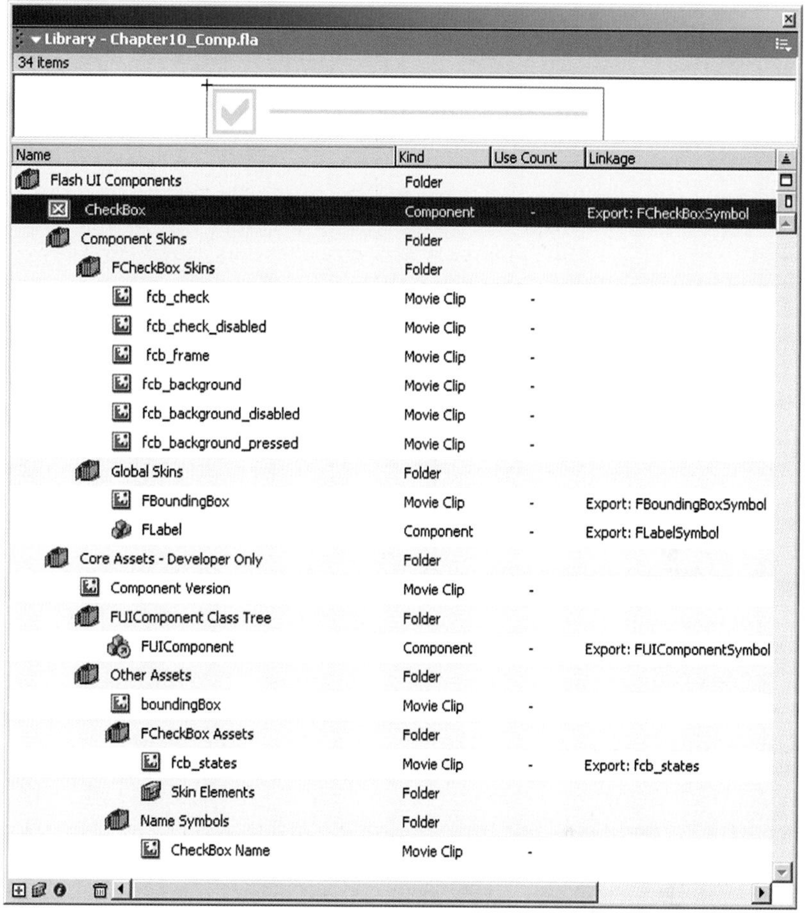

10.2: A lot of resources are imported into your Flash file when you drag the CheckBox component onto the stage.

4. Create the *checkBoxChange()* Function

Add a layer named **Functions**. Then add the following ActionScript (10.4) to the Functions layer.

```
function checkBoxChange(){
   trace("in checkBoxChange");
}
```

This function will cause Flash to write the words "in checkBoxChange" in the Output panel, but it won't work until you add a call to the function from the CheckBox component.

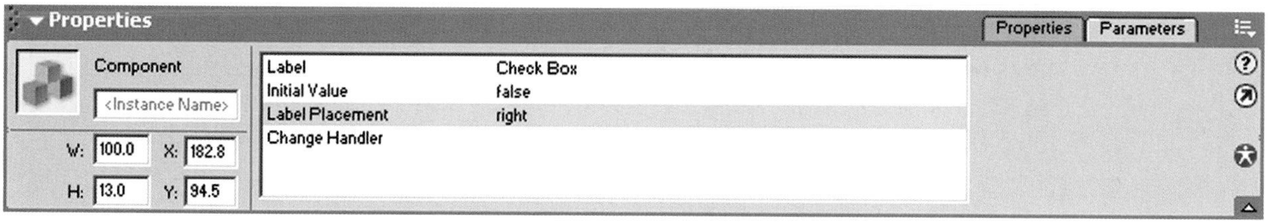

10.3: The Parameters panel displays the parameters for the CheckBox component.

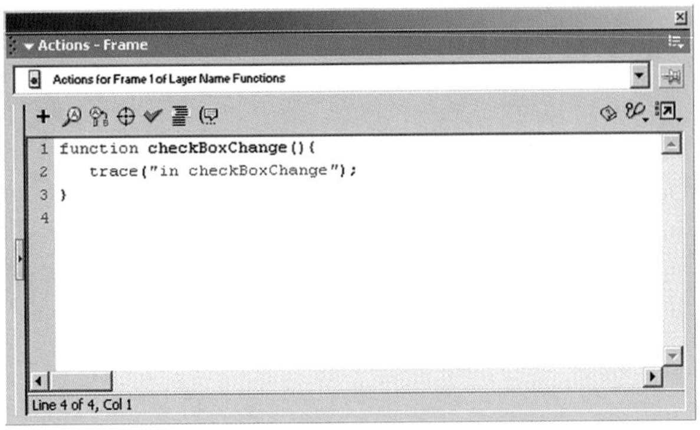

10.4: Add a layer named Functions and write a simple function to test the CheckBox component.

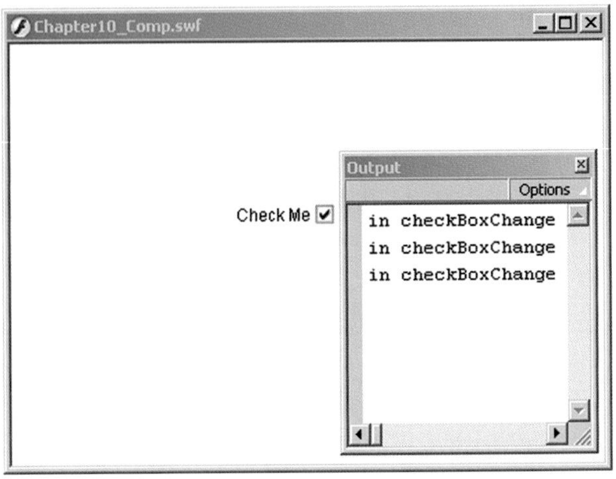

10.5: The Output panel displays the text from the `checkBoxChange()` *function when you click the check box.*

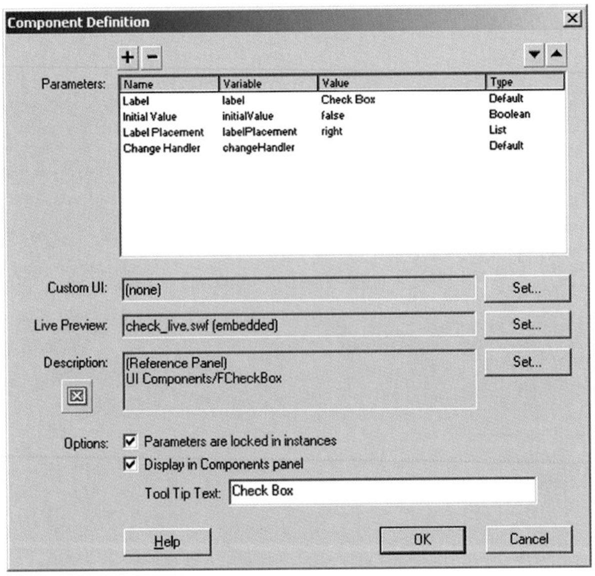

10.6: The Component Definition dialog box for the CheckBox component

5. Call the *checkBoxChange()* Function and Test

In the CheckBox Parameters panel, enter **checkBoxChange** as the value of Change Handler parameter.

Now test the movie. Click the component to toggle the check on and off. Notice that each time you change the check box, the words "in checkBoxChange" appear in the Output panel (10.5).

That was easy enough. Now let's see how you can add code that checks if the check box has been checked.

In order to write the code to determine whether the check box is checked, you need to know the variable name of the Initial Value parameter. The variable name for the Initial Value parameter is not information that you can retrieve from the Parameters panel. However, you can get this information from the Component Definition dialog box.

6. View the Component Definition Dialog Box

Select the CheckBox component that is in the **Chapter10_Comp.fla** library. Open the library options pull-down menu and select Component Definitions. to open the Component Definition dialog box (10.6).

This is the interface that you use to create or modify a component. Once you drag a component from the Components panel onto the stage, you can change it any way you want. The changes you make in the Component Definition dialog box will not affect the original component in the Components panel.

Let's take a look at what the Component Definition dialog box has to offer:

Parameters The Parameters section contains a list of parameters available for the component. This section has four columns. The Name column shows the same parameter

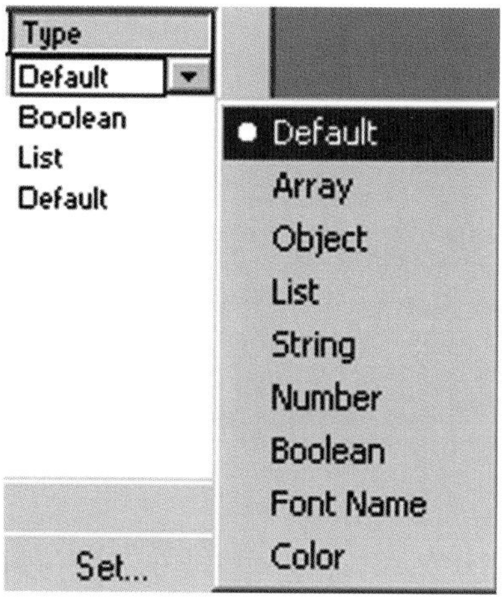

name that you see in the Parameters panel. The Variable column contains the variable name used to access a particular parameter. The Value column shows the default parameter value. The Type column shows the parameter type. There are several choices for type, including Array, Object, Boolean, and Color.

Add and Remove Parameters Above the Parameters section are + and – buttons, which allow you to add or remove a parameter. Adding parameters is one way that you can add some extra functionality to this component. Again, any changes you make here will not affect the original component in the Components panel.

Custom UI Below the Parameters section is the Custom UI field. Flash provides a user interface (UI) for components. You have already seen this in the Properties panel. However, you can also create your own UI by creating a Flash movie that acts as an interface for the component. The Custom UI field is where you enter the name of the movie to be used as the custom UI. You'll be creating a custom UI later in this chapter.

Live Preview The Live Preview field enables you to see the changes on the screen as the parameters are changed in the Parameters panel without running the movie in test mode.

Description The Description field is used to display information in the Reference panel.

Icon The Icon button allows you to choose an icon from a list of available built-in icons. You can also create your own icon and use it. You'll specify a custom icon in the last example of this chapter.

Parameters Are Locked in Instances When this option is checked, the only changes that you can make from the Parameters panel are to the Value setting. All other changes must be made from the Component Definition box. When this option is unchecked, you can make additions and changes from the Parameters panel, but those changes apply to only that instance of the component.

Display in Components Panel This option allows you to have this component show up in the Components panel, with a tool tip containing the text you enter in the text box below. You'll use this option in the last example in this chapter.

For now, you're just interested in the Initial Value variable. The Initial Value parameter is associated with the *`initialValue`* variable. That's really all you need to know, so go ahead and close the Component Definition dialog box.

Now you need to use the *`initialValue`* variable to access whether the CheckBox component is on or off.

7. Name the Component

In the Properties panel, give the CheckBox component an instance name of **myCheck**. In order to access the *`initialValue`* variable in the CheckBox component, you need to have an instance name for that component. Using the instance name, you can refer to the *`initialValue`* variable of the CheckBox component like this: `myCheck.initialValue`.

Now let's add to the *`checkBoxChange()`* function. You'll use a `trace()` statement to track the *`initialValue`* variable.

8. Add a `trace()` Statement to the Function and Test

On the Functions layer, insert the following line of code in the *`checkBoxChange()`* function (10.7).

```
trace(myCheck.initialValue);
```

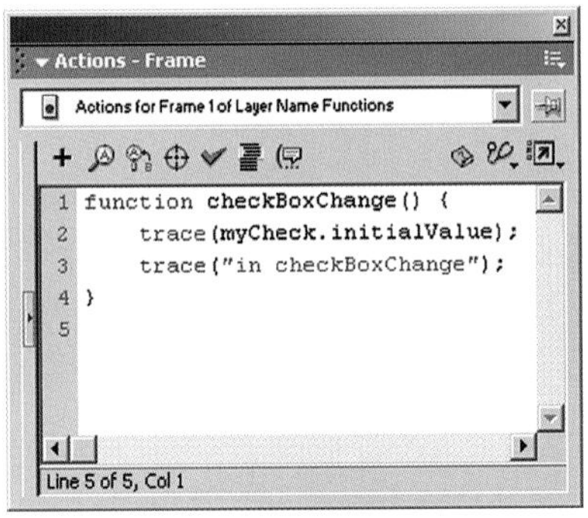

10.7: Add a `trace()` statement to the function on the Functions layer.

Test the movie. You'll see the results of the `trace()` statement in the Output panel. The *`initialValue`* variable is always false.

Knowing the *`initialValue`* value may not seem very useful, but it is. This variable tells you the value that the check box starts out as. You could have a variable, say *`currentValue`*, that was initialized to the *`initialValue`* value. Then each time the check box was changed, you would change the *`currentValue`* variable and do something based on the *`currentValue`* value.

In this example, you used the built-in CheckBox component. The other built-in components work in a similar manner. You've been introduced to the main aspects of components, how to access their variables with ActionScript, and how to change their parameter values. Now let's move onto creating you own component from scratch.

Creating a Basic Component

Many times, you'll find that you use a particular functionality over and over again. Just as the built-in components provide reusable code for common elements, custom components can provide reusable code for the functionality you need. As an example of how to create a custom component, you'll build a component that works as an interface.

1. Open the Files

Open Chapter10_A_Start.fla. Save it to your local hard drive as Chapter10_A_Modified.fla. (For the final version, see Chapter10_A_Final.fla.) You'll also need to save the text file named Chapter10_A.txt in the same place as your Chapter10_A_Modified.fla file.

This is the same file that you finished in Chapter 9, "Drawing with ActionScript" (Chapter9_C_Final.fla), with one small exception. This file contains a button named Customize Button in the library.

In this example, you'll create a component that will allow a Flash programmer to quickly and easily specify aspects of a dynamically generated menu. You'll provide options to specify the button color, the size, the text, and the location. You'll also provide parameters that will adjust the number of background polygons. When you're finished, you'll have a component that will allow Flash programmers to easily change all the look of the menu without requiring that they edit the actual ActionScript.

A component is basically a movie clip with some extra added capability, but you must start out with a movie clip to make a component. You need to create a movie clip that you can, in turn, transform into a component. You'll convert the Customize Button into a movie clip, and then make it a component.

2. Create a Movie Clip

Add a layer above the Background layer named **Component**. Drag the Customize Button on to the stage into the Component layer. Place it so that it's not actually on the stage, because

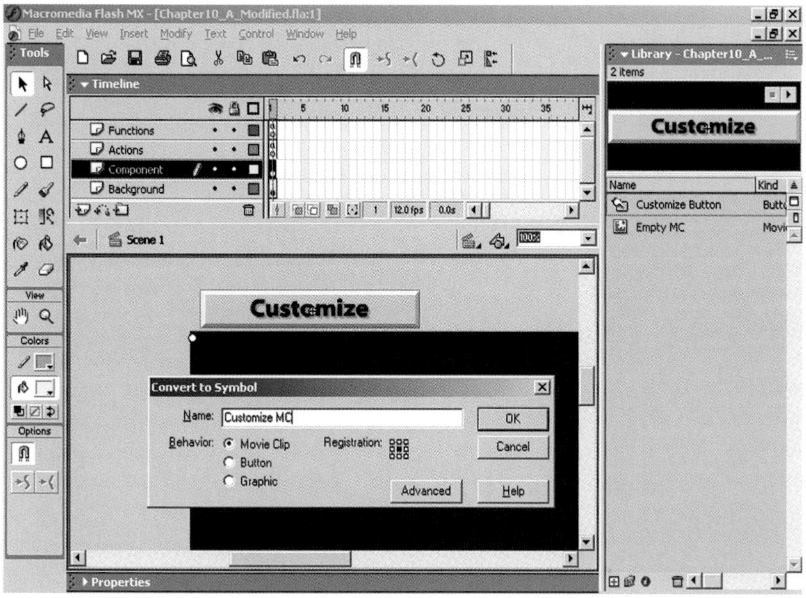

10.8: *Drag an instance of Customize Button on the Stage and make it a movie clip named Customize MC.*

you don't want it to be visible when the movie is running. With the Customize Button selected, press F8 to convert it to a symbol. Choose Movie Clip for its behavior and name it **Customize MC** (10.8).

3. Create a Component

Customize MC will appear in the library. Select it in the library, open the library options pull down menu, and select Component Definitions. In the Component Definition dialog box, click the + button to add a parameter (10.9).

Initially, you don't need to name the parameter or worry about any of the other settings. If you don't add a parameter, the movie clip stays a movie clip. For now, you're just adding a temporary parameter. Make sure that the Parameters Are Locked in Instances option is selected, and then close the Component Definition dialog box.

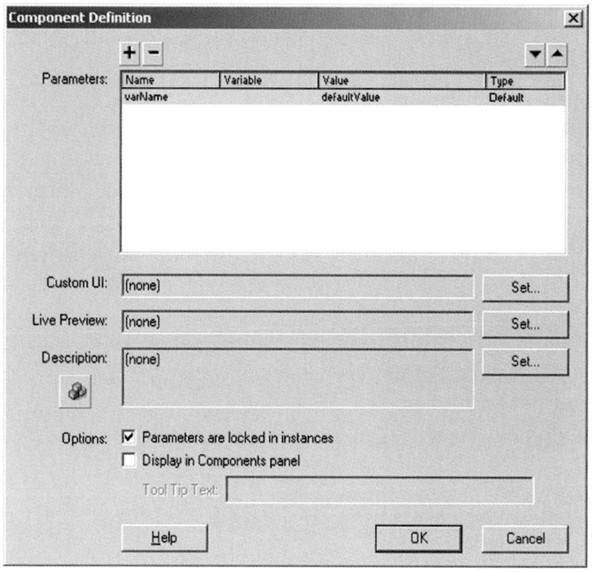

10.9: *Open the Component Definition dialog box and click the + button to add a parameter.*

Notice that now Customize MC has a different symbol attached to it in the library (10.10). This is the default component icon. That's how easy it is to create a component.

You've created a component, and it's already on the stage. If you select the Customize MC component on the stage and open the Properties panel, you'll have the Parameters panel available, with a parameter already there. This is the parameter that you added earlier as a placeholder. Let's replace it with a parameter to select how many background polygons show up.

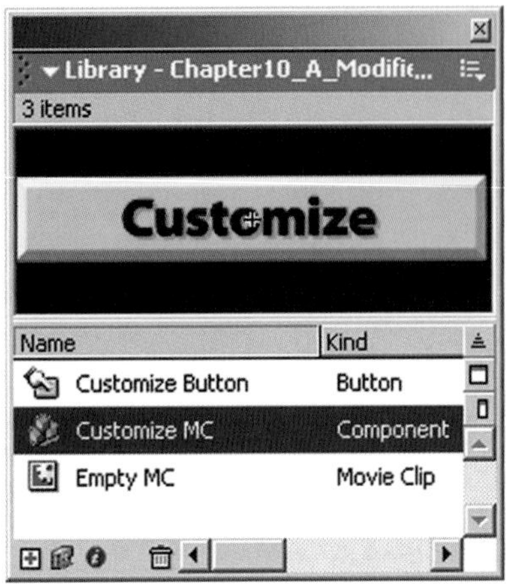

10.10: The default component icon is displayed next to Customize MC, signaling that it is now a component.

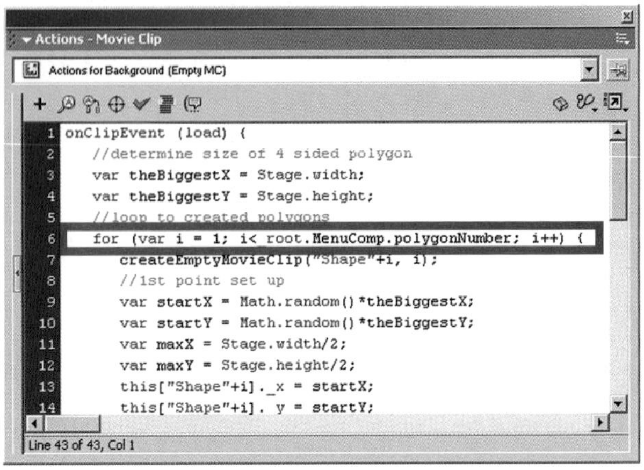

10.11: Add the reference to the `_root.MenuComp` *instance name for the component to the code on the Empty MC movie clip.*

4. Add a Parameter to the Component

Select the Customize MC component in the library and open the Component Definition dialog box. Remove the temporary parameter that is there. Then add the following parameter:

Name	Variable	Value	Type
Number of Polygons	PolygonNumber	40	Number

NOTE When you add a parameter, it's best to specify the type first, and then set the value. If you enter a value, like 40, and then change the type to Number, Flash will change the value to 0. You can avoid this by specifying the type first, and then entering the numeric value.

The name you enter in the Name column is what will appear in the Parameters panel to prompt the user for entry. The variable you enter in the Variable column is the variable name that your ActionScript will use to access the information that is entered in the Parameters panel. After you've added the Number of Polygons parameter, close the Component Definition dialog box.

Now let's use this new parameter.

5. Name the Component, Use the *polygonNumber* Variable, and Test

Select the Customize MC component on the stage and give it the instance name **MenuComp**. Next, in the ActionScript attached to the Empty MC movie clip (in the upper-left area on the stage), change the following line:

```
for (var i = 1; i < 100; i++) {
```

to use the `polygonNumber` variable of the MenuComp component (10.11):

```
for (var i = 1; i < _root.MenuComp.polygonNumber; i++) {
```

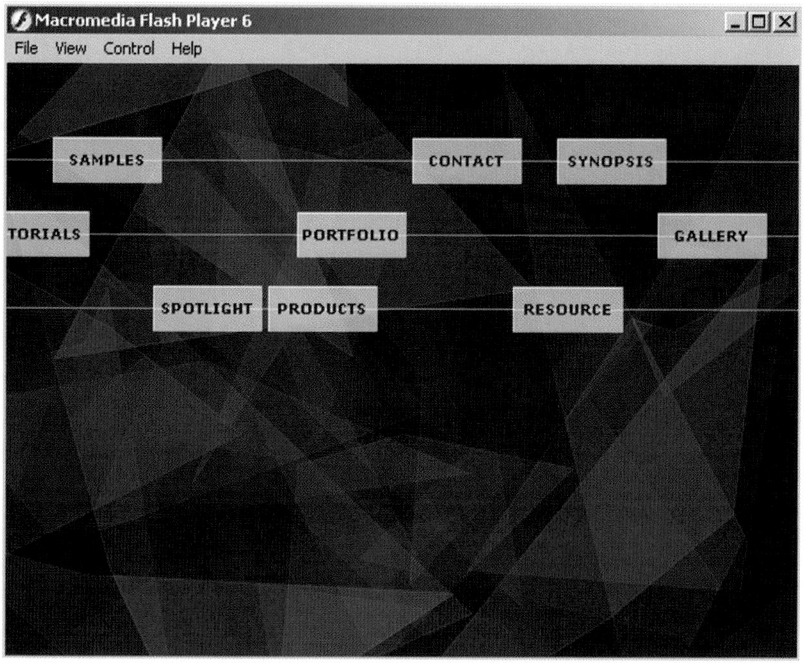

10.12: The values from the Customize MC component are used to generate polygons.

Now the code will access the variables that are within the MenuComp instance of the Customize MC component.

Test the movie. Notice that you now have 40 polygons in the background (10.12). This is really easy to change. You simply select the Customize MC component on the stage, open the Parameters panel, and change the number associated with the Number of Polygons parameter. Then you can test the movie again. This is a lot easier than finding the references in the code and changing each one, just for a simple test of what looks better.

Now let's add another parameter for changing the color of the buttons.

6. Add a Button Color Parameter

Return to the library and open the Component Definition dialog box (10.13). Add the following parameter:

Name	Variable	Value	Type
Color of Button	buttonColor	#FFFFFF	Color

Notice that as soon as you choose the type to be Color, you see a rectangle with the color. If you click the color rectangle, Flash will display a color chooser (10.13). This way, you can just click a color, rather than typing in the hex number for the color. Close the Component Definition dialog box after you've added the Color of Button parameter.

Open the Parameters panel with the instance of the Customize MC component selected. You'll see that you have two parameters, including one that allows you to choose a color for the buttons. Select a bright red from the color picker in the Parameters panel.

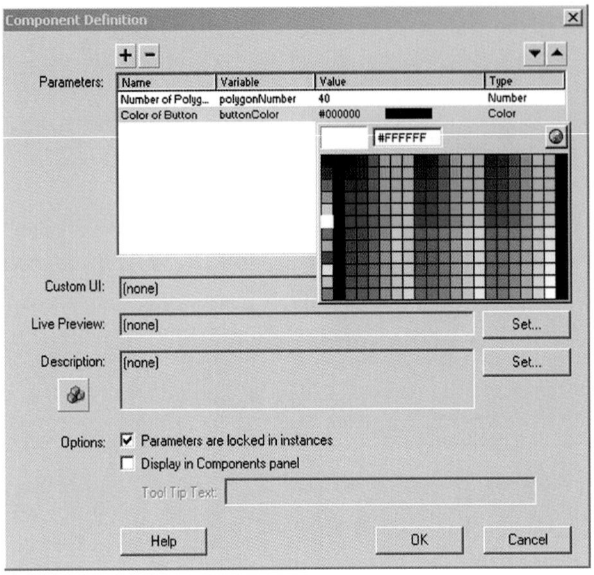

10.13: Flash provides a built-in palette for color variables in the Component Definition dialog box.

If you tested the movie now, you wouldn't see any change. Once again, you need to add a reference to the `buttonColor` variable in the code.

7. Use the *buttonColor* Variable and Test

On the Actions layer, change the color sent into the `createRectButton()` function to use the variable `MenuComp.buttonColor` in all instances of the `createRectButton()` function calls (10.14). The first instance should look like this:

```
createRectButton("ContactButton", "CONTACT", 75, 30, 100, 50, ►
MenuComp.buttonColor, level++);
```

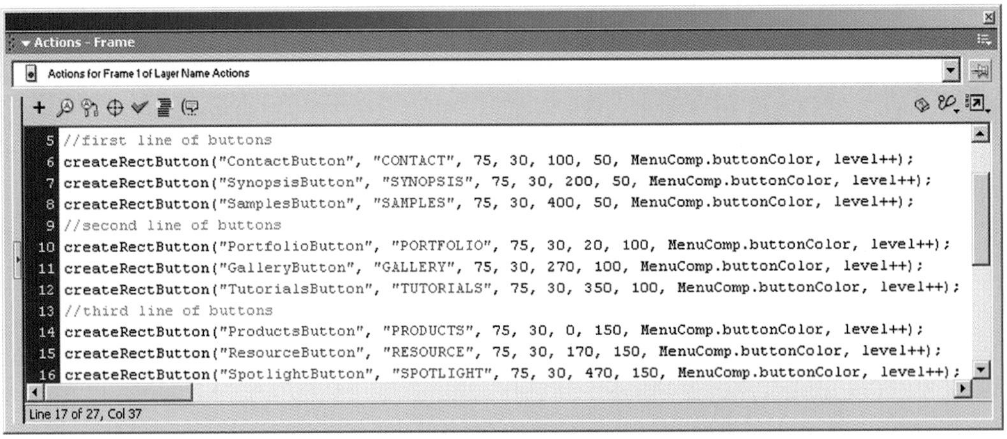

Actions - Frame
Actions for Frame 1 of Layer Name Actions
//first line of buttons
createRectButton("ContactButton", "CONTACT", 75, 30, 100, 50, MenuComp.buttonColor, level++);
createRectButton("SynopsisButton", "SYNOPSIS", 75, 30, 200, 50, MenuComp.buttonColor, level++);
createRectButton("SamplesButton", "SAMPLES", 75, 30, 400, 50, MenuComp.buttonColor, level++);
//second line of buttons
createRectButton("PortfolioButton", "PORTFOLIO", 75, 30, 20, 100, MenuComp.buttonColor, level++);
createRectButton("GalleryButton", "GALLERY", 75, 30, 270, 100, MenuComp.buttonColor, level++);
createRectButton("TutorialsButton", "TUTORIALS", 75, 30, 350, 100, MenuComp.buttonColor, level++);
//third line of buttons
createRectButton("ProductsButton", "PRODUCTS", 75, 30, 0, 150, MenuComp.buttonColor, level++);
createRectButton("ResourceButton", "RESOURCE", 75, 30, 170, 150, MenuComp.buttonColor, level++);
createRectButton("SpotlightButton", "SPOTLIGHT", 75, 30, 470, 150, MenuComp.buttonColor, level++);
Line 17 of 27, Col 37

10.14: Add references to the `buttonColor` variable to the code on the Actions layer.

Test the movie. You'll see that the buttons are now red. Now that you've added this new parameter to the component, you can easily change the colors of the buttons without needing to edit the code.

Next let's add component parameters for the height and width of the buttons.

8. Create and Use Button Height and Width Parameters, and Test

Select the Customize MC component in the library and open the Component Definition dialog box. Add the following parameters to the Customize MC component in the Component Definition dialog box (10.15):

Name	Variable	Value	Type
Height of Button	buttonHeight	30	Number
Width of Button	buttonWidth	75	Number

Then change all the `createRectButton()` function calls to use the `buttonHeight` and the `buttonWidth` variables (10.16). The first line should look like this:

```
createRectButton("ContactButton", "CONTACT", MenuComp.buttonWidth, ►
MenuComp.buttonHeight, 100, 50, MenuComp.buttonColor, level++);
```

Test the movie. If you change the Height of Button parameter or the Width of Button parameter in the Parameters panel, you'll see the change to the button on the stage.

Finally, let's make it easy to change the text label for the button. You'll modify the script so that the label for each button is read from a text file. Then all you'll need to do to make changes to the text is change the text file.

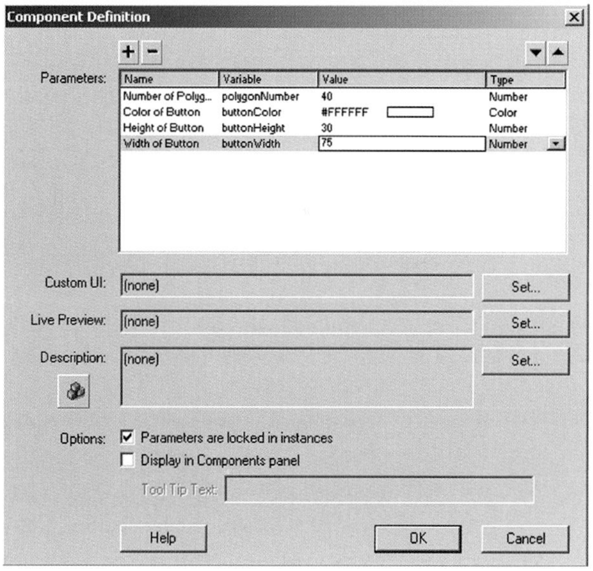

10.15: Add parameters for the width and height of the buttons.

9. Add Code to Read from an External File and Test

Add a layer called **File** and drag a copy of the Empty MC movie clip on the stage. Name this instance **FileHandler**. Attach the following ActionScript to the FileHandler instance (10.17):

```
onClipEvent(load) {
   this.loadVariables("Chapter10_A.txt");
}
onClipEvent(data) {
   trace("Finished loading Data");
   trace(button1);
}
```

This is your first look at the movie clip method `loadVariables()`. This method loads variables from an external file (or from another program or script) that will produce output in the form of variables. The variables are loaded into this movie clip. In this case, you're reading

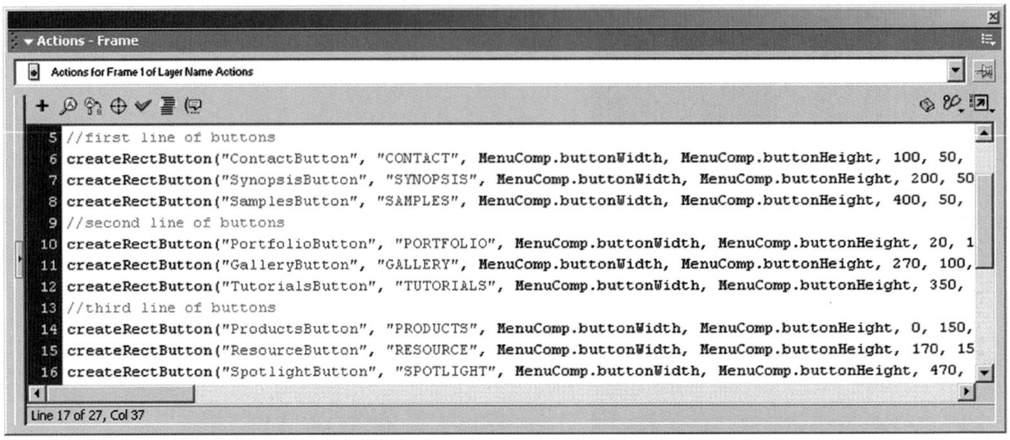

10.16: Edit the code on the Actions layer to reference the `buttonHeight` *and* `buttonWidth` *variables.*

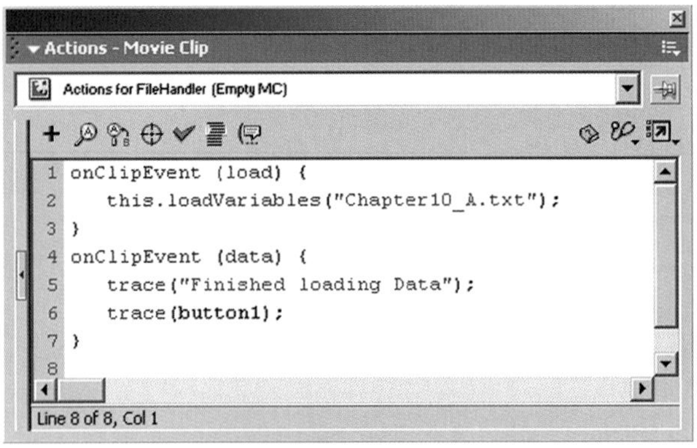

10.17: Add ActionScript to another instance of the Empty MC movie clip.

from an external file called **Chapter10_A.txt** (which you stored in the same place as your **Chapter10_A_Modified.fla** file in step 1 of this example).

Notice that the `loadVariables()` method uses the keyword `this` in front of it. This is because there is also a `loadVariables()` global function that does the same thing but does not have the same format.

NOTE If you wrote `loadVariables("Chapter10_A.txt");`, Flash would think you wanted to use the global function and would display an error message telling you that `loadVariables` requires between two and three parameters. You could use the global function, but you would need to pass as an argument the movie clip in which to load the variables. The code would look like this: `loadVariables ("Chapter10_A.txt", this);`. There is also a `loadVariablesNum()` global function, which loads the variables based on a level number rather than a timeline. Be sure to use the function that is the most appropriate for your purpose.

The main reason to load the variables into a movie clip is so that you can take advantage of the `onClipEvent(data)` event handler. The `data` event handler is called as soon as

Flash is finished reading the text file and loading all of the variables. Otherwise, you would need to do some looping and testing to keep Flash from moving onto the rest of the movie before all the variables were read in. In the `onClipEvent(data)` handler code, there are two `trace()` statements, just so you can see that it works.

The **Chapter10_A.txt** text file that you're loading has the following format (10.18):

```
&button1=JENNIFER&
&button2=FLASH&
&button3=GODDESS&
&button4=CLIMBER&
```

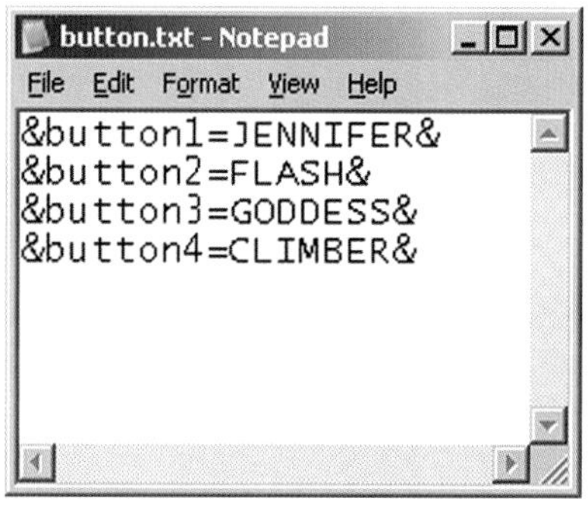

10.18: The text file contains several button variables.

The ampersand (`&`) character tells Flash that this is a new variable. The first variable name is *`button1`*, and it has the value `JENNIFER`. Notice there are no spaces in the lines.

This text file has each variable on its own line, with an ampersand at the beginning and the end of the line. This format makes it easier to read and edit the text file. Placing an ampersand at the end of the line effectively tricks Flash. Flash looks for a variable after the second ampersand on the line, loads a variable with no name and no value, and then goes to the next line.

You could have written the text file like this:

```
&button1=JENNIFER&button2=FLASH&button3=GODDESS&button4=CLIMBER&
```

Flash will load the same variables, but it's not as easy to read and edit, even with just four variables. Imagine how difficult it would be to work with this format if you needed 100 variables.

When Flash loads **Chapter10_A.txt**, it loads the values directly into the variables. For example, as soon as the text file is loaded, you can access the *`button1`* variable, and it will have the value `JENNIFER`.

Test the movie clip. You'll see the message "Finished loading Data" in the Output panel, along with the value of the *`button1`* variable. This lets you know that the data from the text file has been loaded.

Now you need to access the variables that are loaded in with the `loadVariables()` method to label the buttons. Here, you run into a problem, because of the order in which Flash executes ActionScript code. It executes all of the ActionScript on frame 1 of the timeline first, and then it executes the code within a movie clip's `onClipEvent(load)` handler. In our example, the variables are loaded into the FileHandler movie clip. Let's add some `trace()` statements to see how this works.

10. Add *trace()* Statements and Test

Add the following at the top of the ActionScript in the Functions layer (10.19).

```
trace("executing Function Layer");
```

Add the following at the top of the ActionScript in the Actions layer (10.20).

```
trace("executing Actions Layer");
```

Add the following at the top of the ActionScript attached to the FileHandler movie clip within the `onClipEvent(load)` event handler (10.21):

```
trace("Loading variables");
```

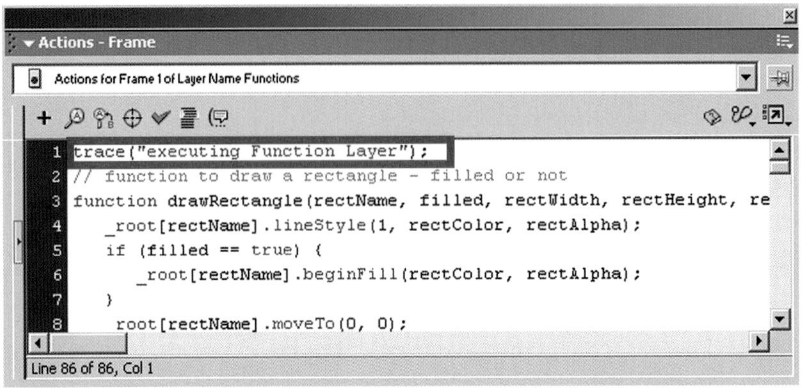
Actions - Frame
Actions for Frame 1 of Layer Name Functions
trace("executing Function Layer");
// function to draw a rectangle - filled or not
function drawRectangle(rectName, filled, rectWidth, rectHeight, re
_root[rectName].lineStyle(1, rectColor, rectAlpha);
if (filled == true) {
_root[rectName].beginFill(rectColor, rectAlpha);
}
root[rectName].moveTo(0, 0);
Line 86 of 86, Col 1

10.19: Add a `trace()` *statement to the code on the Functions layer.*

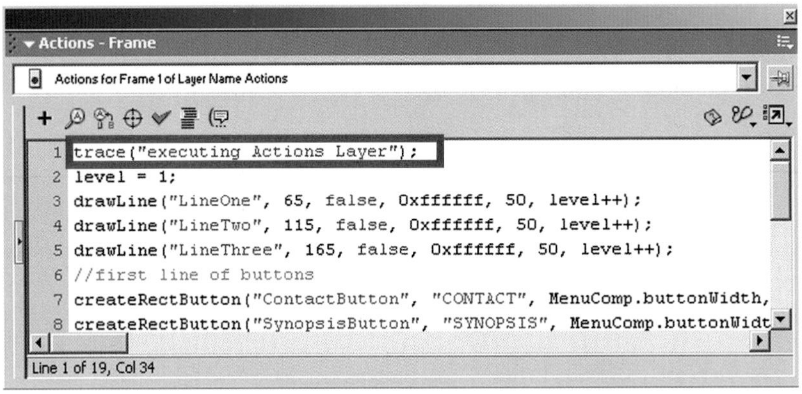
Actions - Frame
Actions for Frame 1 of Layer Name Actions
trace("executing Actions Layer");
level = 1;
drawLine("LineOne", 65, false, 0xffffff, 50, level++);
drawLine("LineTwo", 115, false, 0xffffff, 50, level++);
drawLine("LineThree", 165, false, 0xffffff, 50, level++);
//first line of buttons
createRectButton("ContactButton", "CONTACT", MenuComp.buttonWidth,
createRectButton("SynopsisButton", "SYNOPSIS", MenuComp.buttonWidt
Line 1 of 19, Col 34

10.20: Add a `trace()` *statement to the code on the Actions layer.*

Now test the movie clip. Watch the order in which the `trace()` statements appear in the Output panel (10.22):

```
executing Function Layer
executing Actions Layer
Loading variables
Finished loading Data
JENNIFER
```

You can see that the "Loading variables" statement comes after the "executing Actions Layer" statement. Even if you move the layers around and put the File layer on top of the Functions layer, you'll still get the same result. This means that the ActionScript that is creating the buttons (`createRectButton()`), which is located in the Actions layer, cannot possibly use the information from the text file to add the text to the buttons. There are two ways to solve this problem:

- Create a function that produces the buttons and then call this function from the `onClipEvent(data)` event section of the FileHandler movie clip.
- Move all of the code that creates the buttons into the FileHandler movie clip.

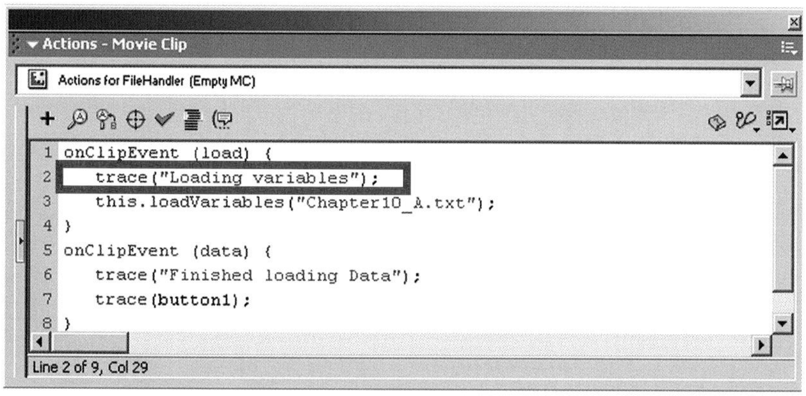

10.21: Add a `trace()` *statement to the* `onClipEvent(load)` *event handler on the FileHandler movie clip.*

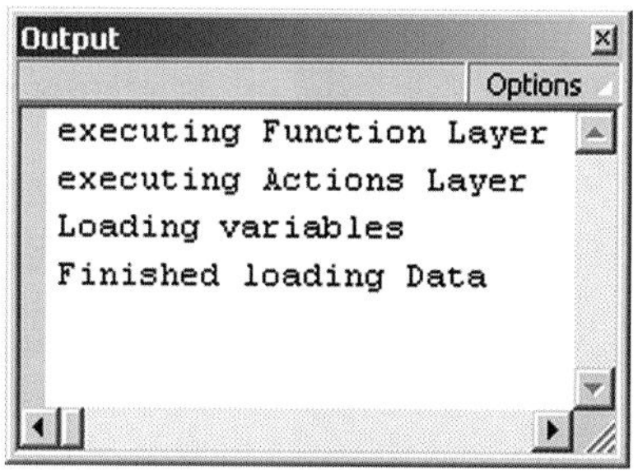

10.22: The `trace()` *statements on the timeline execute before the* `trace()` *statements on the movie clips.*

Let's take the first approach. It keeps all of the main code located on the layers, and it doesn't hide the code that creates the graphics and buttons in the movie clip. First, define a function for creating the buttons.

11. Create a Function to Produce the Buttons

First, remove all of the `trace()` calls. Then delete all the *`createRectButton()`* ActionScript from the Actions layer. Add the following ActionScript to the Functions layer, at the bottom (10.23).

```
function createAllButtons() {
   // first line of buttons
   createRectButton("Button1", FileHandler.button1, MenuComp.buttonWidth, ▶
   MenuComp.buttonHeight, 100, 50, MenuComp.buttonColor, level++);
   createRectButton("Button2", FileHandler.button2, MenuComp.buttonWidth, ▶
   MenuComp.buttonHeight, 200, 50, MenuComp.buttonColor, level++);
   createRectButton("Button3", FileHandler.button3, MenuComp.buttonWidth, ▶
   MenuComp.buttonHeight, 400, 50, MenuComp.buttonColor, level++);
   // second line of buttons
   createRectButton("Button4", FileHandler.button4, MenuComp.buttonWidth, ▶
   MenuComp.buttonHeight, 20, 100, MenuComp.buttonColor, level++);
   createRectButton("Button5", FileHandler.button5, MenuComp.buttonWidth, ▶
   MenuComp.buttonHeight, 270, 100, MenuComp.buttonColor, level++);
   createRectButton("Button6", FileHandler.button6, MenuComp.buttonWidth, ▶
   MenuComp.buttonHeight, 350, 100, MenuComp.buttonColor, level++);
   // third line of buttons
   createRectButton("Button7", FileHandler.button7, MenuComp.buttonWidth, ▶
   MenuComp.buttonHeight, 0, 150, MenuComp.buttonColor, level++);
   createRectButton("Button8", FileHandler.button8, MenuComp.buttonWidth, ▶
   MenuComp.buttonHeight, 170, 150, MenuComp.buttonColor, level++);
   createRectButton("Button9", FileHandler.button9, MenuComp.buttonWidth, ▶
   MenuComp.buttonHeight, 470, 150, MenuComp.buttonColor, level++);
}
```

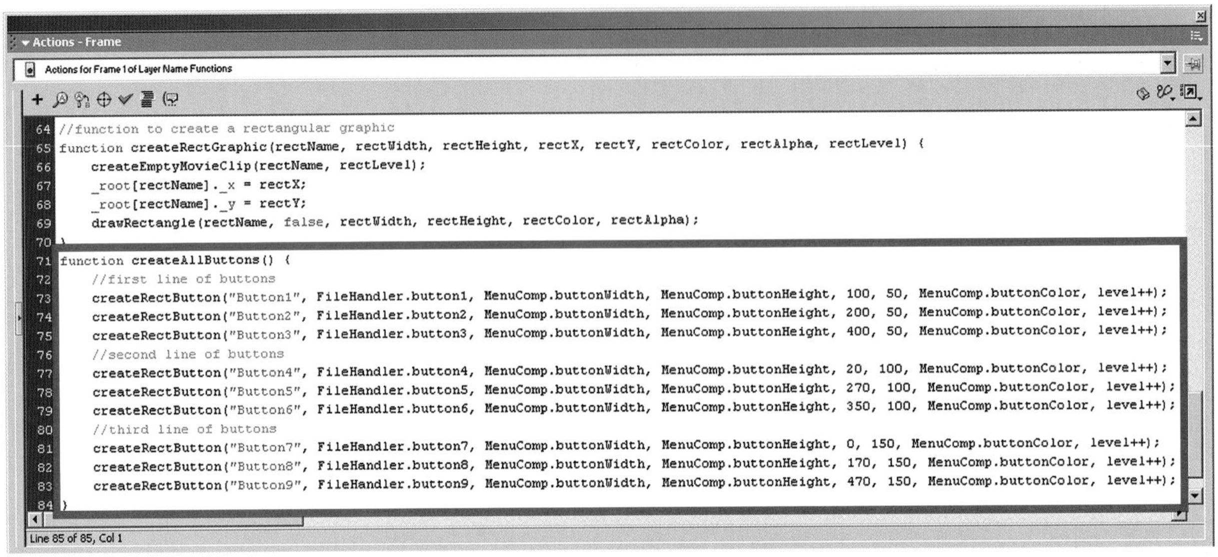
Actions - Frame
Actions for Frame 1 of Layer Name Functions
//function to create a rectangular graphic
function createRectGraphic(rectName, rectWidth, rectHeight, rectX, rectY, rectColor, rectAlpha, rectLevel) {
createEmptyMovieClip(rectName, rectLevel);
_root[rectName]._x = rectX;
_root[rectName]._y = rectY;
drawRectangle(rectName, false, rectWidth, rectHeight, rectColor, rectAlpha);
}
function createAllButtons() {
//first line of buttons
createRectButton("Button1", FileHandler.button1, MenuComp.buttonWidth, MenuComp.buttonHeight, 100, 50, MenuComp.buttonColor, level++);
createRectButton("Button2", FileHandler.button2, MenuComp.buttonWidth, MenuComp.buttonHeight, 200, 50, MenuComp.buttonColor, level++);
createRectButton("Button3", FileHandler.button3, MenuComp.buttonWidth, MenuComp.buttonHeight, 400, 50, MenuComp.buttonColor, level++);
//second line of buttons
createRectButton("Button4", FileHandler.button4, MenuComp.buttonWidth, MenuComp.buttonHeight, 20, 100, MenuComp.buttonColor, level++);
createRectButton("Button5", FileHandler.button5, MenuComp.buttonWidth, MenuComp.buttonHeight, 270, 100, MenuComp.buttonColor, level++);
createRectButton("Button6", FileHandler.button6, MenuComp.buttonWidth, MenuComp.buttonHeight, 350, 100, MenuComp.buttonColor, level++);
//third line of buttons
createRectButton("Button7", FileHandler.button7, MenuComp.buttonWidth, MenuComp.buttonHeight, 0, 150, MenuComp.buttonColor, level++);
createRectButton("Button8", FileHandler.button8, MenuComp.buttonWidth, MenuComp.buttonHeight, 170, 150, MenuComp.buttonColor, level++);
createRectButton("Button9", FileHandler.button9, MenuComp.buttonWidth, MenuComp.buttonHeight, 470, 150, MenuComp.buttonColor, level++);
}
Line 85 of 85, Col 1

10.23: Place all the calls to the `createRectButton()` function on the Functions layer within a function.

This function contains all of the `createRectButton()` calls in one function, but you've changed the names of the buttons to be more generic. Now the button text that will be passed into the `createRectButton()` function can come from the variables in the **Chapter10_A.txt** file. Each of the button text variables needs to be referenced through the FileHandler movie clip, and a different button variable is used for each button created.

Now you just need to call the `createAllButtons()` function from the FileHandler movie clip.

12. Call the *createAllButtons()* Function from FileHandler and Test

Select the FileHandler move clip and add the following ActionScript within the `onClipEvent(data)` event handler (10.24).

```
_root.createAllButtons();
```

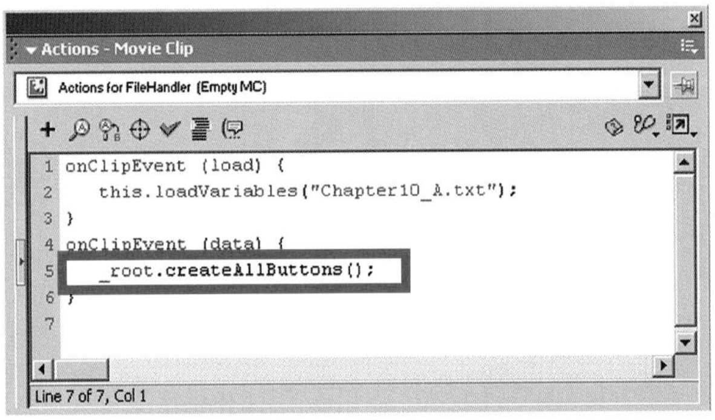

10.24: Add a call to the `onClipEvent(data)` event handler on the FileHandler movie clip.

This will call the function that you just created, which will, in turn, create all of the buttons. Because the function call is in the `onClipEvent(data)` event handler, it won't be triggered until all of the variables are loaded from the file. So there won't be a problem with trying to execute something that is not ready.

Change the variables for all nine buttons in the text file. Test the movie. You'll see that you've changed the appearance of the buttons in many ways, including their color, width, height, and text labels.

You've created a much easier way to tweak the look of this interface using a component. This is not the standard way people think of using a component. Rather than creating a macro-like object like the check box, you've built something closer to a mini-application.

You've created an interface for making changes in Flash that can be used by just about anyone, no matter what level of experience they have with Flash.

Next you'll create a more standard type of component, and you'll also create a custom UI for managing this component.

Create a Sine Wave Component

This chapter's last exercise returns to the sine wave example from Chapter 7, "ActionScript Trigonometry." This time, you'll produce the wave by creating a component. Also, rather than using the standard Flash interface for components—the Components panel—to specify the parameters, you'll use a custom UI. Using a custom UI allows you to create the complete package of the component and to configure the information the user enters.

1. Open the Files

Open Chapter10_B_Start.fla. Save it to your local hard drive as Chapter10_B_Modified.fla. (For the final version, see Chapter10_B_Final.fla.) You'll also need the file Chapter10_Icon.gif for the icon and the file Chapter10_B_StartUI.fla for the UI. WWW.

This is the same file that you created in the second example in Chapter 7 (Chapter7_B_Final.fla), except it doesn't include the background. If you test the movie, you'll see a green sine wave snaking across the screen.

The file contains the Square movie clip and the SquareHolder movie clip, which contains an instance of the Square movie clip. Also, the code attached to the SquareHolder movie clip duplicates and places the Square movie clip. The code that is attached to the Square movie clip moves the square along the sine wave.

Remember that the sine wave is created using the `amplitude`, `phaseShift`, and `period` variables. Also, the code uses the `numberToDuplicate` variable to determine how many copies of the Square movie clip to create and the `incrementSpace` variable to space them across the screen. The Square movie clip is just a basic white, square graphic. The color is added using the `setRGB()` method so that each square is the same color. You'll enter all of these variables as the parameters for your new component. Let's start by creating the component.

2. Create the Sine Component

Select the SquareHolder movie clip on the stage and press F8 to convert it to a symbol. Select Movie Clip as the behavior and name it **Sine Component**. Select the new Sine Component movie clip from the library and open up the Component Definition dialog box. Click the + button to add one parameter for a placeholder. Make sure that the Parameters Are Locked in Instances option is selected, and then close the dialog box. The Sine Component now appears in the library as a component (10.25).

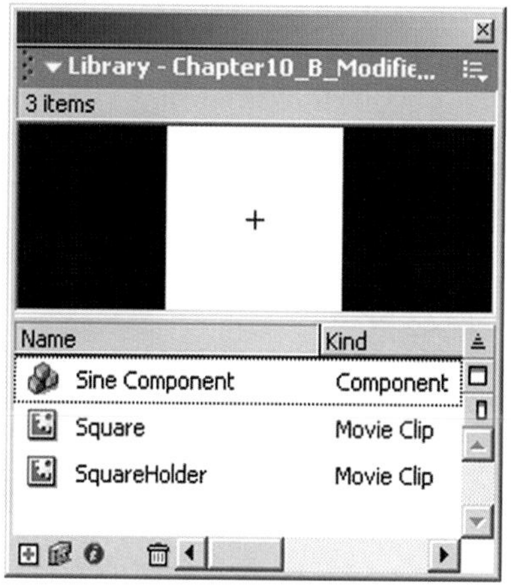

10.25: Make the SquareHolder movie clip on the stage into a component named Sine Component.

You could have just created a component of the SquareHolder movie clip, but then you would have lost all of the code that duplicates the Square movie clip. Creating the component by first embedding the movie clip on the stage into another movie clip ensures that all of that code is within the component. However, there is still some necessary code missing.

Some ActionScript in the Actions layer will not be attached to the component, and this is very important ActionScript. The missing code sets two variables: the `Deg2Rad` for the degree to radian conversion and

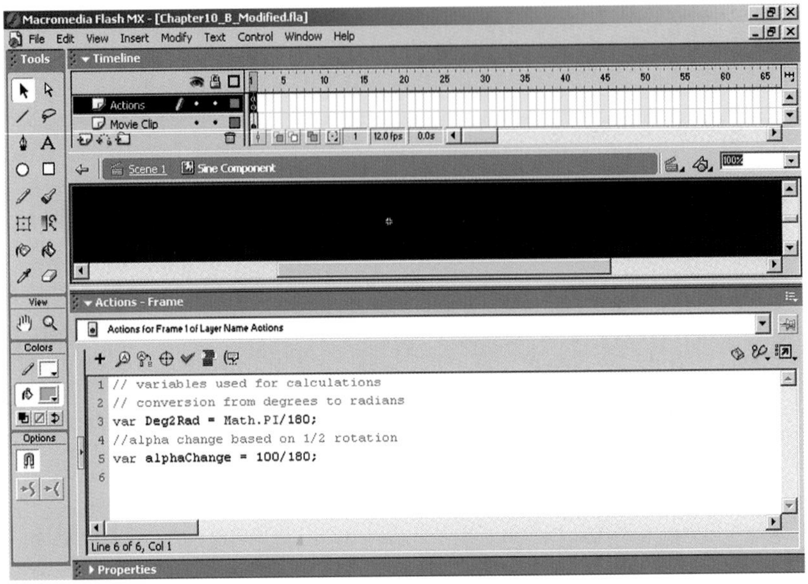

10.26: Move the code on the Actions layer on the main timeline to a layer named Actions within the Sine Component.

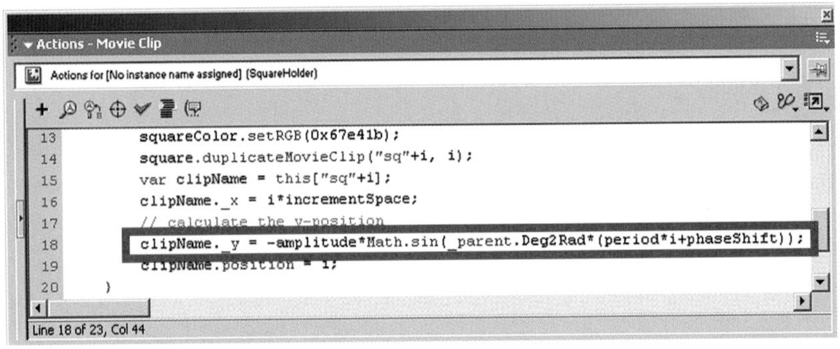

10.27: Change the code for `clipName._y` *to reference the* `Deg2Rad` *variable using* `_parent` *instead of* `_root`.

the `alphaChange` to vary the alpha. You need to put both of these variables within the component and reference them so that everything you need is embedded within the component.

3. Embed *Deg2Rad* and *alphaChange* within the Sine Component and Test

Cut all of the ActionScript on the Actions layer. Edit the Sine Component, add a layer named **Actions**, and paste the ActionScript on this layer in frame 1 (10.26). Name the other layer **Movie Clip.**

Now you need to reference the location of these new variables. Within the ActionScript attached to the SquareHolder movie clip within the Sine Component, change the line that sets `clipName._y` to the following (10.27).

```
clipName._y = -amplitude * Math.sin( _parent.Deg2Rad * (period * i + ▶
phaseShift));
```

Within the ActionScript attached to the Square movie clip within the SquareHolder movie clip, change the lines that set the `_alpha` in the `onClipEvent(load)` section to the following (10.28).

```
if (myDegree >= 0 && myDegree < 180) {
   _alpha = myDegree * _parent._parent.alphaChange;
} else {
   _alpha = (360 - myDegree) * _parent._parent.alphaChange;
}
```

Also, change the line that sets the `_y` property in the `onClipEvent(enterFrame)` section to the following (10.29).

```
_y = -_parent.amplitude * Math.sin( _parent._parent.Deg2Rad * ▶
(_parent.period * position + _parent.phaseShift));
```

Test the movie. It should look exactly as it did before you moved the variables. Delete the Actions layer on the main timeline.

You've moved the necessary variables into the Sine Component, and then referenced the variables in their new place. You don't know what the Sine Component is going to be named or on what level it will be placed, so you referenced the variables using the `_parent` keyword.

In the code that is attached to the SquareHolder movie clip, you needed to use `_parent`. Even though the SquareHolder movie clip and the variables are on the same level, the code attached to the SquareHolder movie clip is actually within the SquareHolder movie clip, so you need to use `_parent` in order to get to the variables that are on the timeline. Then for the Square movie clip, you needed to use `_parent._parent` because the variables are two levels up.

Now let's look at the custom UI for the Sine Component.

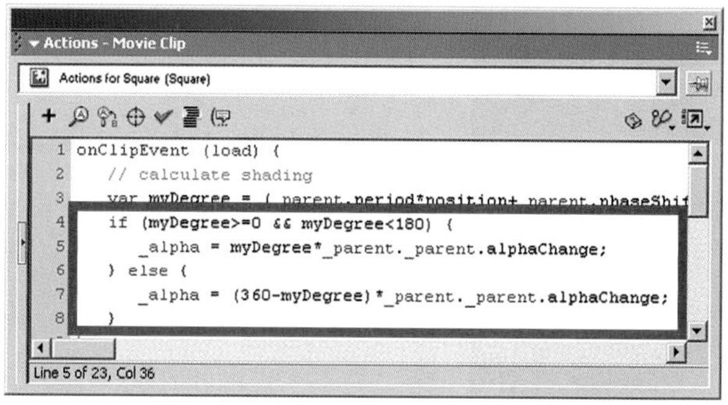

10.28: Change the `if/else` *conditional on the Square movie clip to reference the* `alphaChange` *variable using* `_parent._parent` *instead of* `_root`.

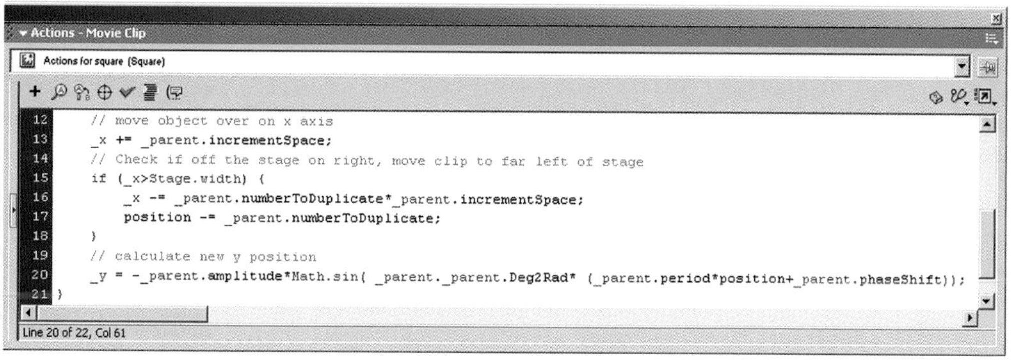

10.29: Change the `_y` *property code on the Square movie clip to reference the* `Deg2Rad` *variable using* `_parent._parent.` *instead of* `_root`.

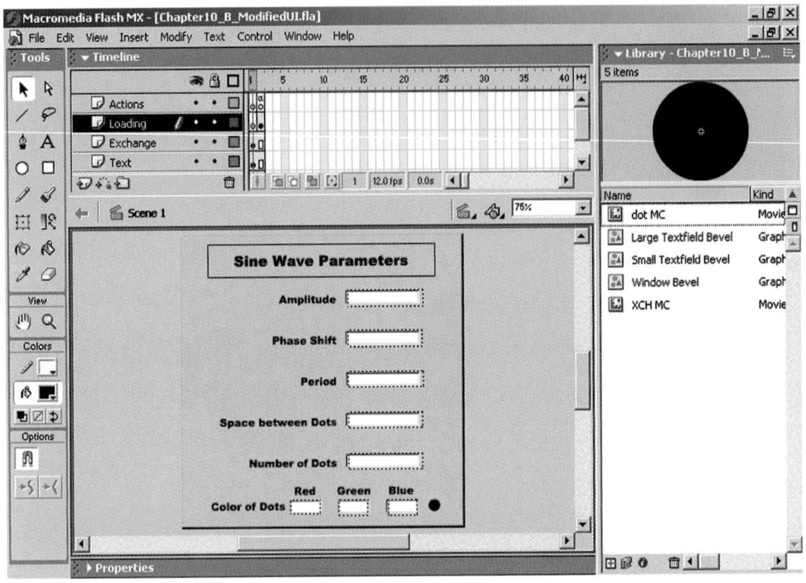

10.30: The custom UI file is a Flash file that will replace the Components panel as a means for users to edit the component.

4. Open the User Interface for the Sine Component

Open **Chapter10_B_StartUI.fla**. Save it to your local hard drive as **Chapter10_B_ModifiedUI.fla** (10.30). (For the final version, see **Chapter10_B_FinalUI.fla.**)

This is the UI for the Sine Component. The file has four layers. The top is the Actions layer with two keyframes. The second keyframe has a `stop()` action in it. The second layer is the Loading layer, which contains a movie clip named Loader on frame 2. The third layer is the Exchange layer, which contains a movie clip named xch. The final layer, Text, holds all of the input text boxes for the interface. These input boxes are labeled Amplitude, Phase Shift, Period, Space between Dots, Number of Dots, and Color of Dots (with Red, Green, and Blue boxes for color numbers and a sample dot to show you the color). Each of the input text boxes has an instance name, which is used to get the information to the Sine Component.

The only code that exists in the file right now is the ActionScript to change the sample color dot based on the numbers entered into the three color input boxes. This is the standard color code you've used in previous exercises, and it's attached to the dot that is to the right of the color boxes. The color code is within a `onClipEvent(enterFrame)` event handler, so that the color sample immediately changes when the user makes an entry in the color boxes.

The xch movie clip is crucial to this example. It's the tool that allows you to create a custom UI for the component. Specifically, it allows you to transfer information between the UI and the component. Flash is programmed to look for a file named xch in order to transfer this information. The xch movie clip must be on the stage at all times, and its instance must be named xch.

As the user enters information, the code needs to pass this information to the xch movie clip, so that the movie using this UI can access the information. Also, if you want Flash to remember your user-entered information—so that it isn't lost each time you open and close the Parameters panel—you need to get the variables from the xch movie clip each time you run this UI movie. Passing the information to the xch movie clip is easy, so let's do that first.

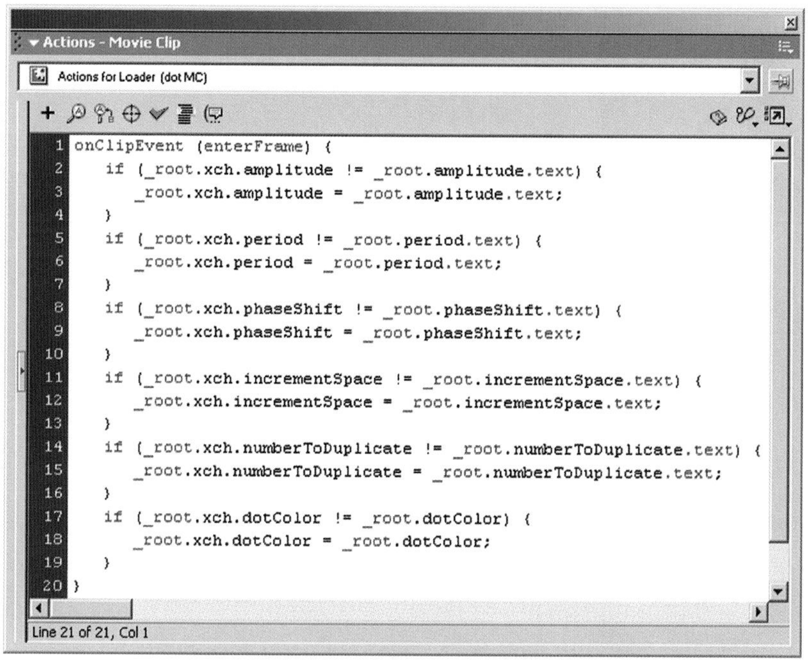

10.31: Add code to the Loader movie clip, on the second frame of the Loading layer, that checks for input values and passes them to the xch movie clip.

5. Pass User Input to the xch Movie Clip

Select the Loader movie clip (the black dot above the stage), which is in frame 2 of the Loading layer, and attach the following ActionScript to it (10.31).

```
onClipEvent(enterFrame) {
   if (_root.xch.amplitude != _root.amplitude.text) {
      _root.xch.amplitude = _root.amplitude.text;
   }
   if (_root.xch.period != _root.period.text) {
      _root.xch.period = _root.period.text;
   }
   if (_root.xch.phaseShift != _root.phaseShift.text) {
      _root.xch.phaseShift = _root.phaseShift.text;
   }
   if (_root.xch.incrementSpace != _root.incrementSpace.text) {
      _root.xch.incrementSpace = _root.incrementSpace.text;
   }
   if (_root.xch.numberToDuplicate != _root.numberToDuplicate.text) {
      _root.xch.numberToDuplicate = _root.numberToDuplicate.text;
   }
   if (_root.xch.dotColor != _root.dotColor) {
      _root.xch.dotColor = _root.dotColor;
   }
}
```

This code is continuously checking to see if any of the input values have changed from the values that are in the xch movie clip. In other words, it discovers if the user has entered anything or changed anything in the input fields. If any values are different, it sends the information from the input text field to the xch movie clip. For example, if the `amplitude.text` value changed from what is stored in `_root.xch.amplitude`, the information in the Amplitude input field is loaded into the variable `_root.xch.amplitude`.

It's important to remember that all this information must pass through the xch movie clip. This movie clip needs to be continuously updated because the user could close the UI window at any time. You could put a close button in the UI and pass information to the xch movie clip only when the user clicked that button, but what if the user closed the UI using the window close button? Then the changes wouldn't be loaded. The continuous check that you coded is the most foolproof method for ensuring that the values are transferred to the xch movie clip.

Even though you aren't finished with the UI, let's attach it to the Sine Component.

6. Attach the User Interface to the Sine Component and Test

Test the UI movie to create an `.swf` file. You need an `.swf` file to attach to the component.

Open the **Chapter10_B_Modified.fla** again and select the Sine Component from the library.

Open the Component Definition dialog box and click the Set button next to the Custom UI option. The Custom UI dialog box appears. For Type, select the Custom UI with .swf File Embedded in .fla File option. For Display, select the Display in Component Parameters Panel option. Then click the Browse button at the bottom of the dialog box, find the **Chapter10_B_ModifiedUI.swf** file, and click the Open button. The file path and name will appear in the Custom UI .swf File box (10.32). Close the Custom UI dialog box.

Make sure that the proper file was embedded. In the Component Definition dialog box, the Custom UI box should now show **Chapter10_B_ModifiedUI.swf** (embedded) (10.33).

Next delete the placeholder parameter in the Parameters section of the Component Definition dialog box, since you no longer need it. Then close the Component Definition dialog box.

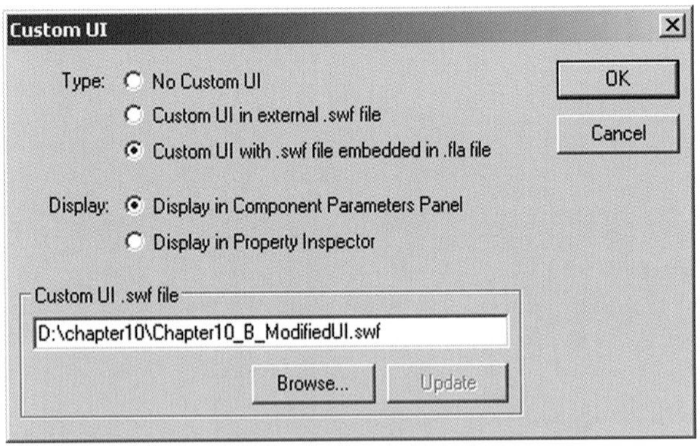

10.32: Select **Chapter10_B_ModifiedUI.swf** *in the Custom UI dialog box as the custom UI for the Sine Component.*

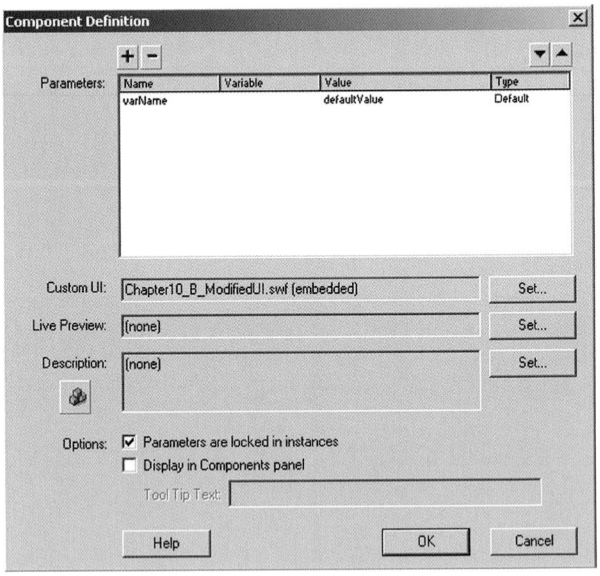

10.33: The **Chapter10_B_ModifiedUI.swf** *file should be listed as embedded.*

Now select the Sine Component on the stage, open the Parameters panel, and click the Launch Component Parameters Panel button. This will open the custom UI that you created. When it first shows up, it might be small. If necessary, expand the window to make it larger. Enter the following information in the input boxes (10.34):

Amplitude	100
Phase Shift	0
Period	3
Space between Dots	3
Number of Dots	360
Red	255
Green	0
Blue	0

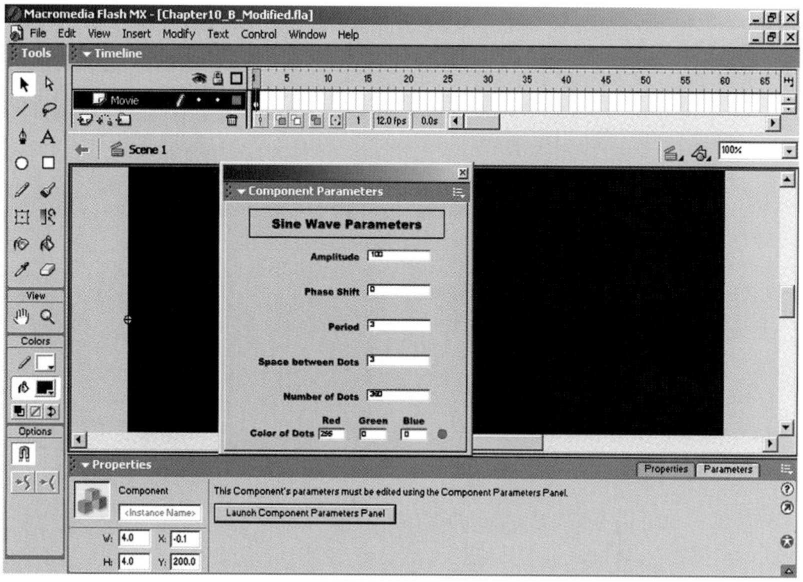

10.34: Use the custom UI to enter values for the Sine Component.

Then close the custom UI.

Test the movie. You'll see that although the interface seemed to work when you entered values, nothing has changed. This is because you're still using the hard-coded (written literally into the code) input that is in the ActionScript. The input for the variables from the UI is not being used by the component. You'll fix that next, but first let's talk about what you just did.

Flash requires an `.swf` file to use for a custom UI. In the Custom UI dialog box, you can choose to not use a custom UI, to embed it in the `.fla` file, or to use a custom UI from an `.swf` file that is not embedded in the `.fla` file.

NOTE In Flash 5, you did not have the option of embedding the `.fla` file for your custom UI. You needed to make sure that the `.fla` file with the component in it also had the `.swf` file for the custom UI in the same directory. If the custom UI's `.swf` file was not in the correct place, you would not see the custom UI when you attempted to edit the parameters for the smart clip (the name for components in Flash 5). In Flash MX, you can embed the file, so you don't need to worry about keeping track of the custom UI's `.swf` file.

As your display choices in the Custom UI dialog box, you can place the UI in the Parameters panel or have it as a popup. This UI is too big to fit in the Parameters panel, so you chose to display it in the Components Parameters panel.

Then you selected the appropriate `.swf` file. Recall that when you created the `.swf` file, you didn't do anything special (except set up the xch movie clip) to let it know it was going to be used in this way. You could select any `.swf` file, and it would show up. It might not work as a UI, but it would show up.

Now that you understand your choices for a custom UI, let's fix the code so that it will use the information from your UI.

7. Use the Custom UI Information and Test

Edit the Sine Component and change the following ActionScript that is attached to the SquareHolder movie clip:

```
var numberToDuplicate = 360;
// variables for the sine wave calculation
var amplitude = 120;
var period = 5;
var phaseShift = 0;
// distance to move along the x axis
var incrementSpace = 3;
```

to the following (10.35):

```
var numberToDuplicate = _parent.numberToDuplicate;
// variables for the sine wave calculation
var amplitude = _parent.amplitude;
var period = _parent.period;
var phaseShift = parent.phaseShift;
// distance to move along the x axis
var incrementSpace = parent.incrementSpace;
```

And change the line of code that sets the color:

```
squareColor.setRGB(0x67e41b);
```

to the following (10.36):

```
squareColor.setRGB(_parent.dotColor);
```

You've changed the code so that the variables' values are no longer hard-coded. They are now read from the custom UI. To accomplish this, you replaced all of the numbers with equivalent variables, referencing `_parent`. You also set the color based on the variable *dotColor* from `_parent`. Remember that the parent movie clip is the actual component, and the SquareHolder movie clip is just embedded within the component. In order to access the variables entered in the custom UI, you need to reference `_parent`, which is the Sine Component.

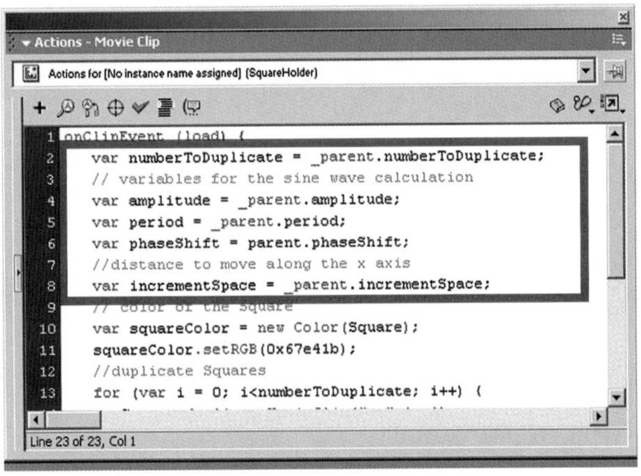

10.35: Update the code on the SquareHolder movie clip to reference the variables from the custom UI.

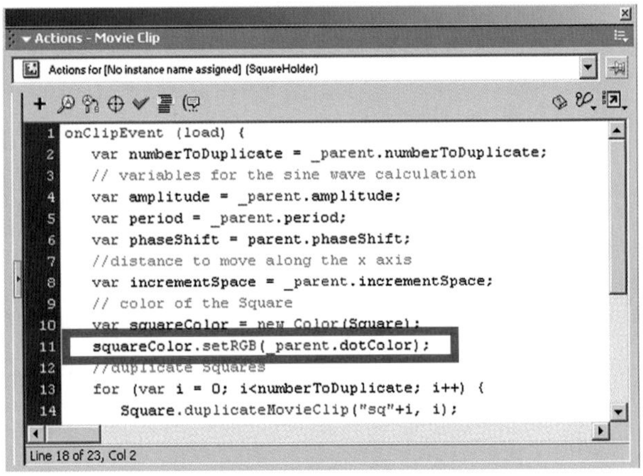

10.36: Update the code that sets the color to reference the variable from the custom UI.

Test the movie. You'll notice that the sine wave is red. Although you might not be able to tell, it's also using the amplitude and other values you entered in the UI. You didn't need to reenter the values in the custom UI. Flash remembered the values you set earlier, even though you entered those values before you fixed the code to access those values. That is the magic of the xch movie clip. Even though the xch movie clip isn't running in this movie, the component, it still did its work from the UI `.swf` file.

Now open the custom UI again by opening the Component Parameters panel. Notice that all of the fields are blank; the values you entered earlier are not there. If you tested the movie again now, all the parameters would be set to 0. You could reenter the values—after all, there are only a few—but it's still frustrating. Fortunately, you can fix this with a bit of code, as you'll do in the next step.

8. Retain User Input

Open **Chapter10_B_ModifiedUI.fla** again and add the following code to the Loader movie clip, above the `onClipEvent(enterFrame)` section (10.37).

```
onClipEvent(load) {
   // check if first time in and set to defaults
   // otherwise use previously entered values retrieved from the
   // xch movie clip
   // if first time in for amplitude
   if (_root.xch.amplitude == undefined) {
      _root.amplitude.text = 130;
   } else {
      _root.amplitude.text = _root.xch.amplitude;
   }
   // if first time for phaseshift
   if (_root.xch.phaseShift == undefined) {
      _root.phaseShift.text = 0;
   } else {
      _root.phaseShift.text = _root.xch.phaseShift;
   }
   // if first time for period
   if (_root.xch.period == undefined) {
      _root.period.text = 1;
   } else {
      _root.period.text = _root.xch.period;
   }
   // if first time for number to duplicate
   if (_root.xch.numberToDuplicate == undefined) {
      _root.numberToDuplicate.text = 360;
   } else {
      _root.numberToDuplicate.text = _root.xch.numberToDuplicate;
   }
   // if first time for dot increment
   if (_root.xch.incrementSpace == undefined) {
      _root.incrementSpace.text = 1;
   } else {
      _root.incrementSpace.text = _root.xch.incrementSpace;
```

continues

```
        }
        // if first time in for color
        if (_root.xch.dotColor == undefined) {
            _root.dotColor = 0xffffff;
        } else {
            _root.dotColor = _root.xch.dotColor;
        }
        // set dot color and text colors on stage
        _root.dotColSample.myColor.setRGB(_root.dotColor);
        _root.DotColR.text = _root.dotColor >> 16;
        _root.DotColG.text = (_root.dotColor & 0x0000ff00) >> 8;
        _root.DotColB.text = _root.dotColor & 0x000000ff;
    }
```

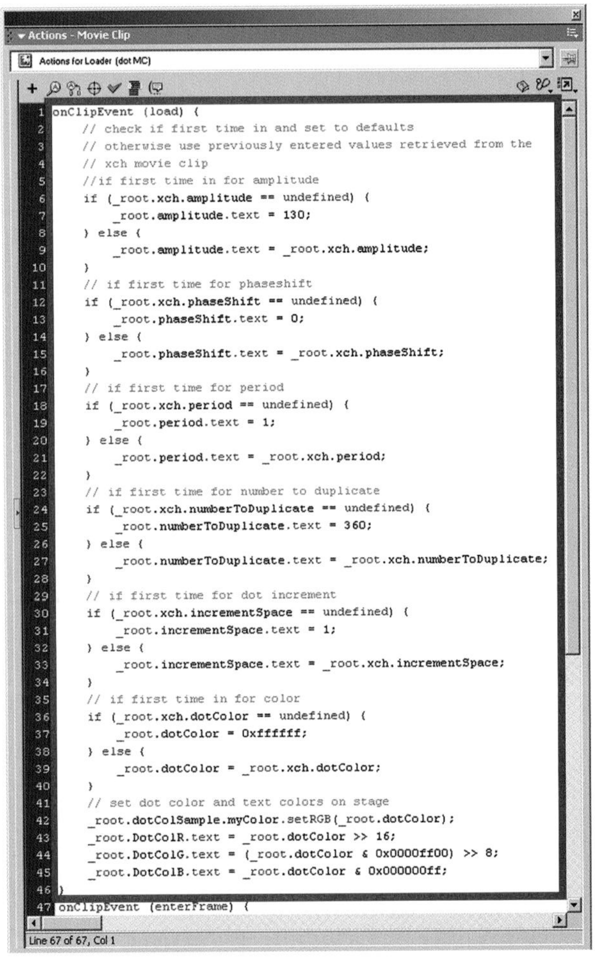

10.37: Add code to the `onClipEvent(load)` *section of the Loader movie clip to force Flash to maintain the values entered in the custom UI.*

The purpose of this code is to retain the information entered in your custom UI. To access that information, you need to get it from the xch movie clip. Also, rather than opening with blank input boxes the first time the custom UI is used, you want default values to appear for the parameters.

For each variable, the code first checks to see if there is a value from the xch movie clip. If it doesn't exist or there is no value, the variable is equal to the keyword `undefined`. Flash sets variables to `undefined` if a value for the variable does not exist. If the variable doesn't exist within the xch movie clip, the code sets the main timeline version of the variable (not the xch variable) to a default. The main timeline version of the variable is what shows up in the input text boxes. If the variable does exist within the xch movie clip, the code uses that to set the main timeline version. After the code checks each variable this way, in the last four lines, it sets the starting values for the Red, Green, and Blue values, so the color sample will be remembered also.

Remember that this code is attached to the Loader movie clip, which is attached to frame 2, not frame 1. You need to construct the custom UI file in this way to accommodate how Flash retrieves previously entered information. You can load the variables to the xch movie clip on frame 1 without any problems. However, if you try to get the previously entered values on frame 1, they don't exist—there has not been enough time for Flash to process them. Even if you attach this code to the xch movie clip, which loads after the frame ActionScript, it still won't work. To have the UI remember the values each time the user opens the UI, you need to perform this operation on frame 2 to give the UI some startup time.

Now make sure that the Sine Component is using this new UI file.

9. Update the Embedded User Interface File

Test the Chapter10_ModifiedUI file to create a new `.swf` file.

Open the Chapter10_Modified.fla and select the Sine Component from the library. Open the Component Definition dialog box and click the Set button next to the Custom UI setting. In the Custom UI dialog box, click the Update button (at the bottom of the dialog box, next to the Browse button). Close the Custom UI dialog box, and then close the Component Definition dialog box.

Open the custom UI. You'll see that all of the fields are populated with the information that you entered previously. (If your values aren't there, enter them again.) Change the period to 5 and close the UI.

Test the movie, and then reopen the custom UI. All of the values you entered will still be there, because they were saved.

You've created a very useful component. You're finished with its functionality, but let's finish up by making it appear more professional. You'll add a custom icon for the Sine Component.

10. Attach a Special Icon to the Sine Component

Select the Sine Component from the library and open the Component Definition dialog box. Click the Icon button and make sure that Default Icon is selected in the drop-down list (10.38). Then close the Component Definition dialog box.

Select Import to Library from the File menu and import the file Chapter10_Icon.gif. Create a folder in the library called FCustomIcons, move the Chapter10_Icon.gif into this folder, and rename the icon **Sine Component**. The component and the icon must have the same name. Save the file so that it's current. Close the library and reopen it. You should see the new icon graphic attached to the Sine Component (10.39). (If you don't, close the Chapter10_B_Modified.fla movie and reopen it.)

In order to use your own icon, the following requirements must be met:

- The Component Definition dialog box is set to use the default icon.
- The icon is a 22×20 bitmap image. Although other sizes show up, they don't fill the icon space.
- The icon file resides in the FCustomIcons folder within the library.
- The icon file has the same name as the component.

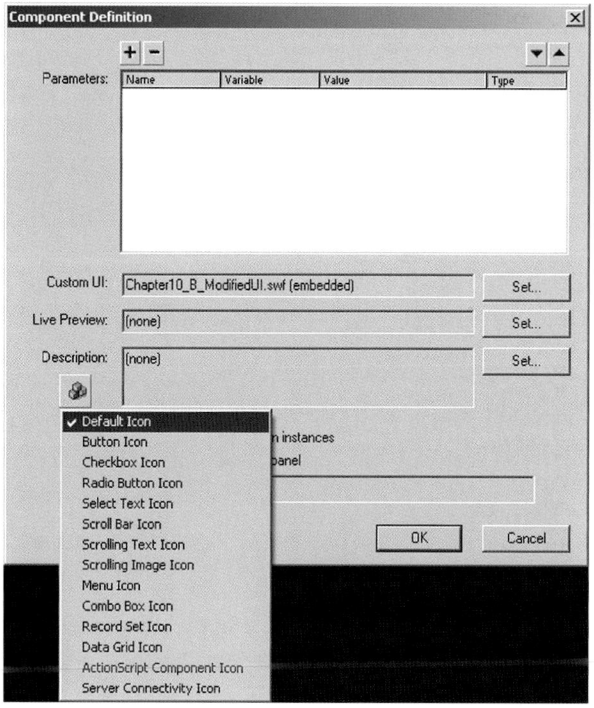

10.38: Set the icon to Default Icon in the Component Definition dialog box.

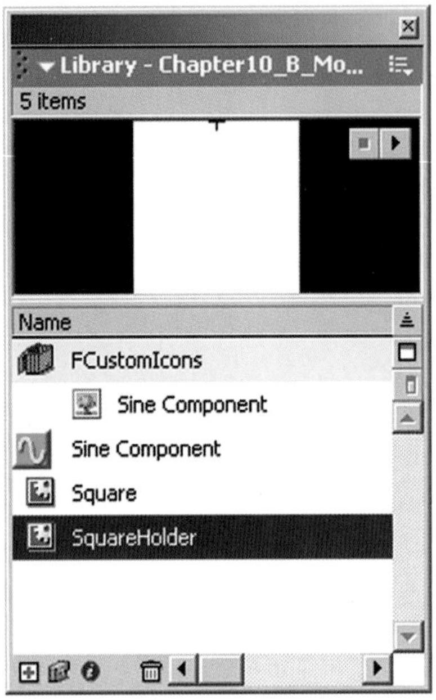

10.39: The component has a new custom icon.

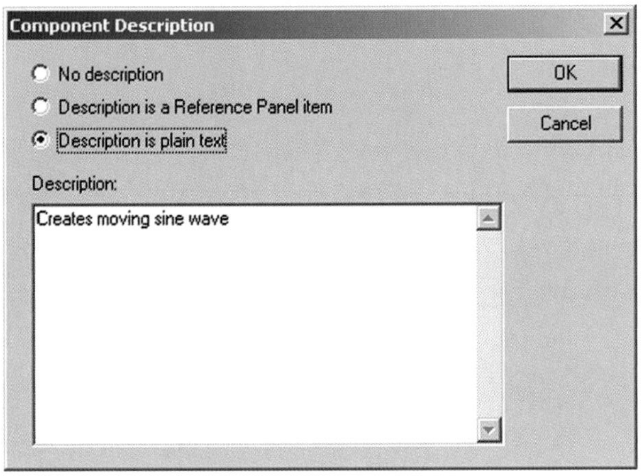

10.40: Set the description to plain text and enter a short description.

As you saw in this example, it's fairly simple to set up a custom icon.

As a final enhancement, you'll add the Sine Component to the Components panel. That way, it will be available to all of your Flash movies.

11. Add the Sine Component to the Components Panel

Select the Sine Component from the library and open the Component Definition dialog box. Click the Set button under Description to open the Component Description dialog box. Select the Description Is Plain Text option. In the text box, enter **Creates moving sine wave** (10.40). Click OK to close the Component Description dialog box.

In the Component Definition dialog box, select the Display in Components Panel option. In the Tool Tip Text box, enter **Sine Wave** (10.41). Close the Component Definition dialog box.

Save the Chapter10_B_Modified.fla file as SineComponent.fla. Find the Components folder, under the Flash MX/FirstRun on your computer. Copy the SineComponent.fla file to this Components folder. Close Flash and reopen it.

Open the Components panel. You'll now see a drop-down list on the right side. Open the drop-down list and select SineComponent from the drop-down list (10.42). You'll see your Sine Component with its special icon. If you place this component on your stage and open the Parameters panel, you'll see the custom UI that you created.

To add a component to the Components panel, you must select the Display in Components Panel option in the Component Definition dialog box. The description that you entered in the Component Description dialog box is the description that will appear in the Reference panel. The tool tip text that you entered will show up when you roll your mouse over the Sine Component (assuming you have tool tips turned on in the Preferences dialog box).

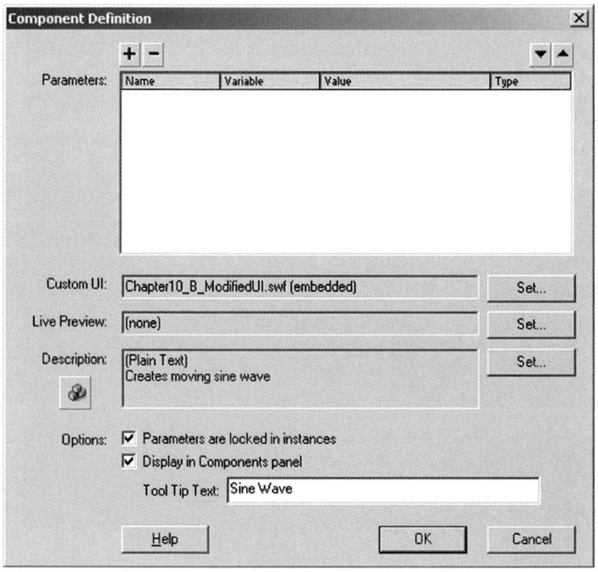

10.41: *Select the Display in Components Panel option and add some text for the tool tip.*

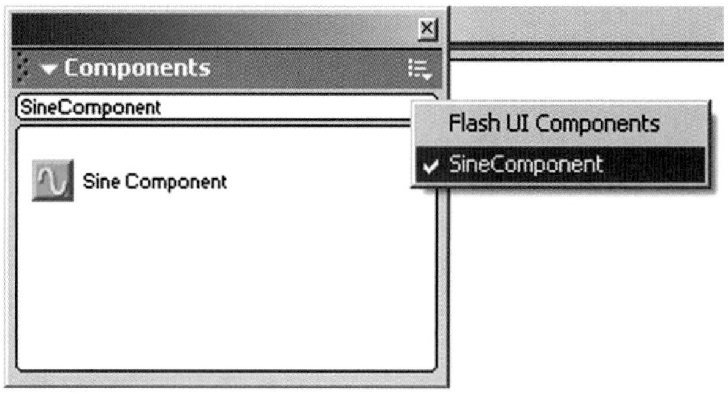

10.42: *Now the Sine Component is accessible directly from the Components panel.*

You didn't need to change the name of the component file, but it's the name of the file, not the component, that shows up in the Components panel drop-down list. You probably wouldn't want to see Chapter10_B_Modified as a component choice.

If you hadn't embedded the custom UI into the `.fla` file, there would be one more requirement for this example: The `.swf` file for the custom UI would need to go in the same Flash MX/FirstRun/Components folder, so that the component could access it.

Conclusion

In this chapter, you learned about components as well as how to read from an external file. You used one of Flash's built-in components to become familiar with how to set up component parameters and use them in code. Then you created a custom component that allows Flash programmers to change the look of a menu without editing ActionScript. This example demonstrated that a component does not need to be just an object that you drop on the stage; it can provide the functionality of a "mini-application." In the final exercise, you created another component, which produces sine waves, and gave it a custom UI.

Even though you need to do a little extra coding to get components to work, they are worth it. This is particularly true when you're going to reuse an object. Creating components is another way to build up your collection of reusable ActionScript.

CHAPTER eleven

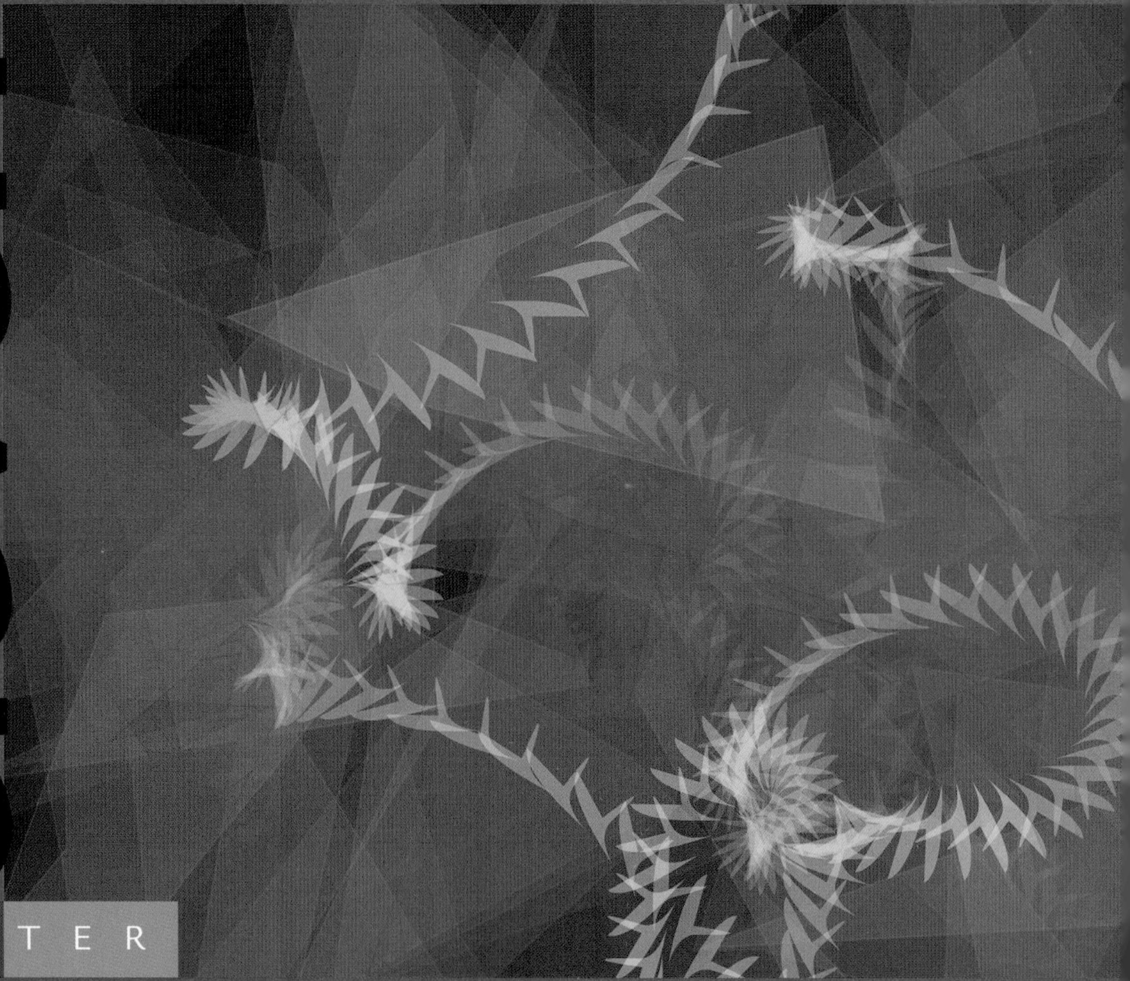

Debugging and Troubleshooting

Debugging and troubleshooting *code—discovering why something isn't working and fixing it—isn't hard to do, but it is an acquired skill. At this point, with your experience from the previous examples under your belt, you should have a good grasp of how ActionScript works in general, and that's an important first step.*

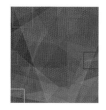

Beyond understanding ActionScript in general, it takes practice to learn to debug and troubleshoot quickly and with minimal frustration. It's a matter of knowing what to look for, and that does come with experience. Once you've already identified an issue that has caused a problem, you should be able to identify (and often avoid) that issue in the future.

In this chapter, you'll get some tips on writing code that will be less prone to errors, as well as easier to troubleshoot when problems do occur. Then you'll review the main debugging tools. Finally, you'll look at some ActionScript examples that have problems, and with some guidance, you'll figure out what's wrong and fix it.

Tips for Writing (Mostly) Bug-Free Code

There is no surefire way to avoid all coding problems. Even experienced programmers need to debug some of their code. However, if you follow all of the tips presented here, you'll have fewer bugs. Also, it will be easier to find the bugs you do have because you can eliminate many other potential problems.

Be consistent with your variable names. Make sure your variable names are spelled correctly and the capitalization is consistent. In the examples in this book, you've given the variables names that start with a lowercase letter and have uppercase letters for the subsequent words in the name, such as `xSpeed`, `ySpeed`, and `rotateRate`.

Organize your code. Put your ActionScript, including functions, in a consistent place. For instance, in the examples in this book, you've put your functions on a separate Functions layer. This way, you can easily find the various elements of your code.

Document your code. Include comments like the ones you've seen throughout this book. Descriptive comments let you quickly understand what a section of code is doing. This will prevent you from adding or changing something in it that will cause an error. Another form of documentation is simply naming your variables, functions, and other user-defined elements descriptively, so you can see at a glance what value a variable represents or what operation a function should perform.

Add code in increments. Add your ActionScript in small increments. This way, you have fewer lines of code to look through if you do have a bug. Also, when you write code in small increments, you also think in small increments. This approach tends to slow down your thinking, which alleviates errors.

Test your code frequently. Testing your movie often will help minimize your problems, especially if you have added your code in small increments.

Following these tips does not guarantee you won't have any problems, but you will reduce your frustration level and the amount of rewriting you'll need to do.

Now let's look at the main Flash debugging tools.

Debugging Tools

Each of the tools discussed in this section is used for debugging. Some of them are used together; some are used separately. They are presented in the order that we recommend you use them to test and debug each movie. While you often need to resort to a certain amount of guesswork when you debug and troubleshoot code, using the tools described here in the recommended order can help you to narrow down the possibilities of where problems lie.

Test Movie

Test Movie is not commonly regarded as a debugging tool. Because it's used to test the movie, people just assume that's all it does. But it does the first check for bugs in your code, and it's the means by which many programmers find the lion's share of their code errors. Many programmers use Test Movie in combination with `trace()` calls to do most of their debugging.

If you attempt to test a movie that contains any syntax errors that affect the running of your code, the Flash Player won't play the movie. Instead, Flash will provide you with a description of the syntax error, along with the location of the error (the line number), in the Output panel. Therefore, by using Test Movie, you can often get Flash to do your bug hunting for you. Of course, you'll still need to fix the problems it finds.

The Flash Player will often still play a movie if there are errors that don't affect the running of your code. In that case, it's up to you to notice whether or not the movie performs as expected. An example of code that would not keep Flash from playing the movie with Test Movie might be the following:

```
myName = ;
```

where `myName` is never used anywhere in the code, or where you use `myName` but misspell it. Neither of these mistakes will cause Flash to display an error in the Output panel, but they are bugs that need to be fixed.

The Output panel lists all of the bugs it finds in order. Sometimes the bugs have a trickle-down effect—you might see one error that effectively causes 20 bugs. You should always fix the first bug in the list and then test again, until there are no more bugs. If you're lucky, fixing the first bug might effectively fix all of the bugs listed in the Output panel.

When the movie runs, sometimes you have an infinite loop. The movie appears to hang, and then a message pops up on the screen that says:

```
A script in this movie is causing Flash Player to run slowly. If
it continues to run, your computer may become unresponsive.
Do you want to abort the script?
```

You will want to click the Yes button if this message appears. If you click the No button, the movie will continue to try to run, and Flash will display this error message again after a short time. Again, this message appears when you have an infinite loop. When you get this message, it's time to use the debugging tools to ferret out the problem.

Auto Format

The Auto Format button is available in the Expert mode of the Actions panel. Like Test Movie, Auto Format may not seem like a debugging tool, but it's very useful for finding errors.

As you enter your code, use the Auto Format button whenever you are finished with a section. This keeps the code neat (and it will also add missing semicolons if you forgot them at the end of a line), which helps when you are debugging. Using Auto Format also makes it easier to edit your code in general.

When you click the Auto Format button, Flash lets you know quickly if you have syntax errors. You'll see this message:

```
This script contains syntax errors, so it cannot be Auto Formatted.
Fix the errors and try again.
```

While this doesn't tell you where your problem is, it at least lets you know that you have a syntax error.

If you click the Auto Format button often while you're entering your code, you'll know that the syntax error was introduced after the last time you clicked the button. If it's not readily apparent to you where the syntax error is, you can run Test Movie to get Flash to show you its location (it will appear in the Output panel). You can also try clicking the Check Syntax button.

Check Syntax

The Check Syntax button is what you might consider an honest-to-goodness debugging tool. Check Syntax actually checks the syntax in all of the ActionScript in your movie. If you have an error, you'll see a message like this:

```
This script contains errors. The errors encountered are listed in the
Output Window.
```

Although its message is similar to Test Movie's message, using the Check Syntax button is actually better than using Test Movie, because Test Movie displays only the syntax errors that affect the running of the movie; Check Syntax lists all syntax errors.

As with the syntax errors listed when you use Test Movie, it's always a good idea to start with the bugs listed at the top of the Output panel. Fix the first problem, and then click the Check Syntax button again. Often, fixing the first bug will fix several other bugs.

Publish Settings

If you have fixed all of the syntax problems and the program is still not doing what you want it to do, the next place to check is the Publish Settings dialog box. Choose Publish Settings from the File menu and click the Flash tab to see the settings of interest. You need to make sure you're publishing to the right version of the Flash Player. If you're writing code that uses methods or functions introduced in Flash MX, such as the drawing methods covered in Chapter 9, "Drawing with ActionScript," it won't work if your publishing settings are set to Flash 5. You need to make sure you're publishing to Flash 6 (11.1). This problem is most likely to occur when you open a Flash file that was created with an earlier version, because the Publish Setting option will be set to that earlier version.

For some ActionScript problems, you'll see this warning message:

```
This movie uses features that are not supported in Flash Player version 5.
View the Output windows for details.
```

However, Flash MX does not display this error message in all cases.

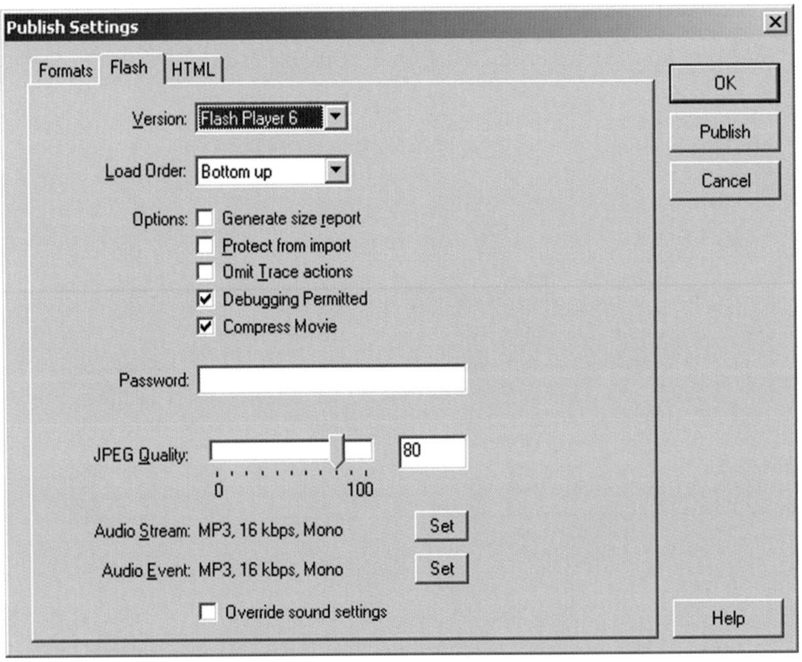

11.1: In the Publish Settings dialog box, check that you're publishing to the correct version.

NOTE There is a Warn on Save for Macromedia Flash 5 Compatibility setting on the Warnings tab of the Preferences dialog box. If this setting is unchecked, you won't see a warning message when you attempt to publish Flash MX code to Flash 5.

You need to check the Publish Settings dialog box only once per movie. After you set your Publish Settings options for a movie, they don't change.

trace()

If you've tried all the easier troubleshooting techniques described in the previous sections (using Test Movie, Auto Format, and so on) and haven't found the problem, it's time to start the bug hunt. This is usually a job for the `trace()` function.

The `trace()` function is very useful for helping you to hunt down pesky little problems in your code that are causing unexpected or undesired results. You typically will resort to using the `trace()` function when your program works but it isn't doing what you want it to do.

NOTE Before using `trace()`, make sure you don't have the Omit Trace Actions option selected in the Publish Settings dialog box (11.1). It's the third check box in the Options section.

The `trace()` function displays information in the Output panel. In the function's simplest form, this information can be just the literal text you enclose within quotation marks.

Generally, you'll add `trace()` function calls at places in a script where you suspect there may be problems. If you don't have the faintest idea where your problem lies, start at the beginning of your code and add short `trace()` statements, like these:

```
trace( "in function that draws box" );
trace( "in function for counting" );
trace( "creating movie" );
```

You would put these `trace()` statements in separate places throughout your code. They would help you to determine if the program is running through all of the functions, frames, and movie clips that you think it should and in the order you think it should.

You might also want to check some variables to make sure that their current values at specific points in the program execution are as you would expect. For example, you might write ActionScript like this:

```
trace( "x position = " + _x);
trace( "name of movie clip  " + this._name);
trace( "what level are you on " + level);
```

These statements will give you a hint as to what's going on in the variables.

The nice thing about the `trace()` function is that it's quick and easy to implement. You can put in a few `trace()` function calls, run the code, and see the output. For example, consider tracing the *x* position of a moving movie clip, as in the first example above. Using the Debugger (the more powerful but cumbersome tool you'll look at soon), you would need to restart execution each time it paused to report the new *x* position. But you could put the `trace()` in the same place where the *x* position is being changed, and you would see a stream of information in the Output panel.

Another time it's much easier to use the `trace()` function rather than the Debugger is when your script catches user interaction, such as when the user is dragging an object or typing in information. It's sometimes difficult to see this in the Debugger panel, because once the Debugger panel is open, it captures all your mouse and keyboard interactions until you tell the Debugger to run your movie.

The `trace()` function is often the simplest and quickest debugging tool. In fact, sometimes it's the only tool you can use.

List Objects and List Variables

Sometimes it is helpful to get a snapshot of what is loaded in Flash at a specific moment while the movie is running. You can do this within the Flash Player by selecting List Objects and/or List Variables from the Debug menu (11.2). Both of these lists appear in the Output panel. Note that you must select these options while the movie is playing in the Flash Player.

The List Objects option shows all of the objects that are loaded (11.3). The List Objects list is especially helpful if you think you've loaded a movie clip with code and it doesn't show up. You can see in the list of objects if it's really there. You can also see where it is and what it's named.

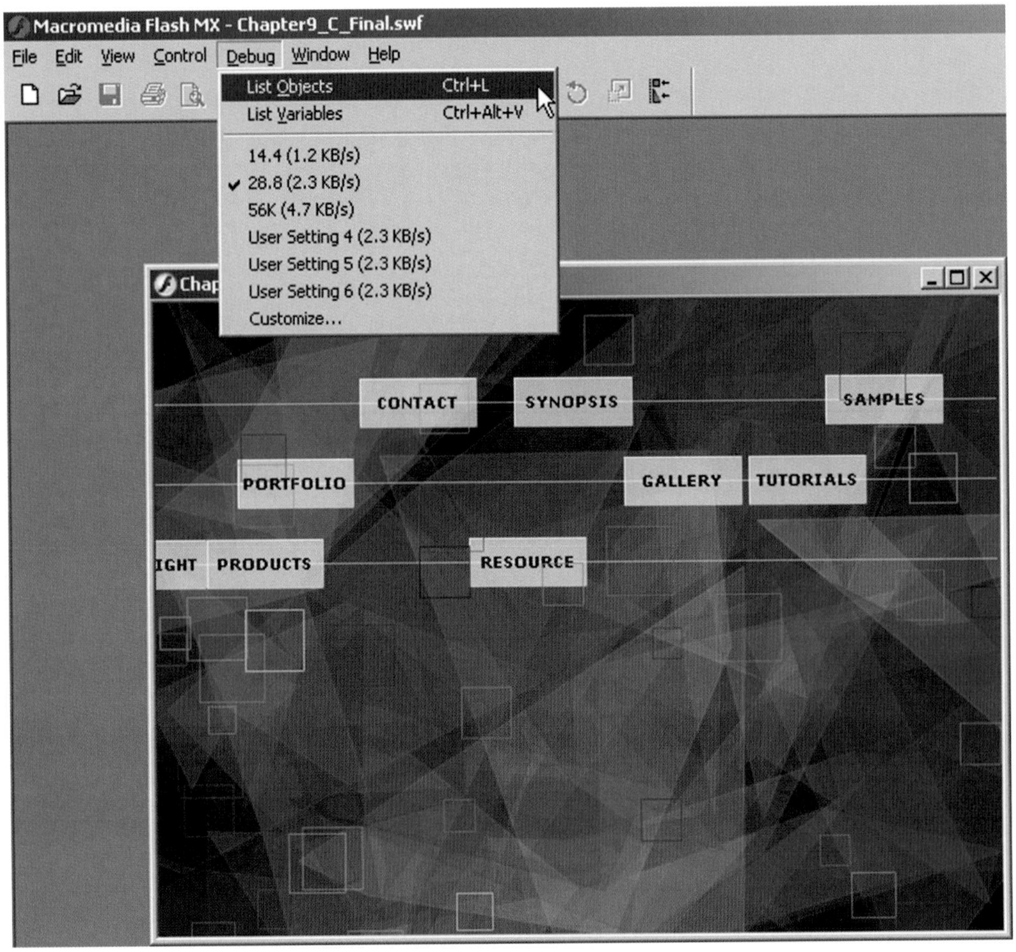

11.2: When you use Test Movie, the Debug menu appears on the menu bar. From this menu, you can select List Variables or List Objects.

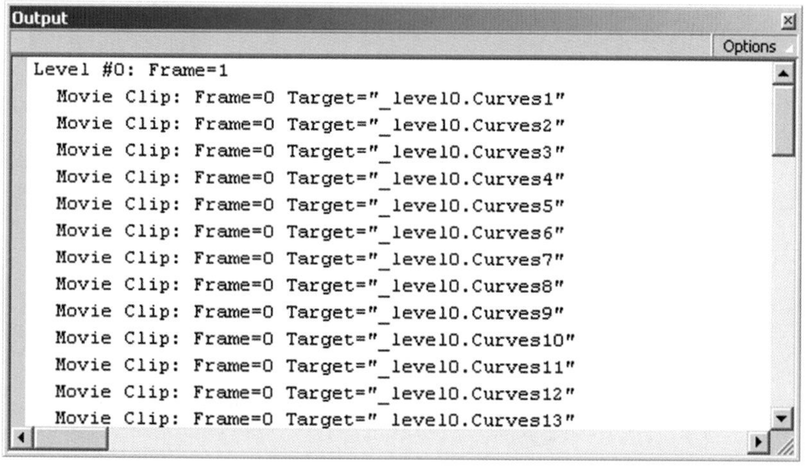
Output
Options
Level #0: Frame=1
Movie Clip: Frame=0 Target="_level0.Curves1"
Movie Clip: Frame=0 Target="_level0.Curves2"
Movie Clip: Frame=0 Target="_level0.Curves3"
Movie Clip: Frame=0 Target="_level0.Curves4"
Movie Clip: Frame=0 Target="_level0.Curves5"
Movie Clip: Frame=0 Target="_level0.Curves6"
Movie Clip: Frame=0 Target="_level0.Curves7"
Movie Clip: Frame=0 Target="_level0.Curves8"
Movie Clip: Frame=0 Target="_level0.Curves9"
Movie Clip: Frame=0 Target="_level0.Curves10"
Movie Clip: Frame=0 Target="_level0.Curves11"
Movie Clip: Frame=0 Target="_level0.Curves12"
Movie Clip: Frame=0 Target="_level0.Curves13"

11.3: When you select Debug ➢ List Objects, the Output panel lists all of the objects that are loaded.

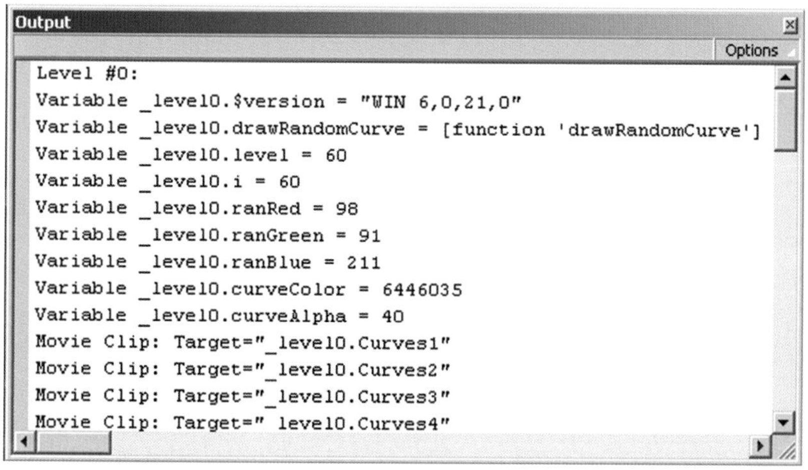
Output
Options
Level #0:
Variable _level0.$version = "WIN 6,0,21,0"
Variable _level0.drawRandomCurve = [function 'drawRandomCurve']
Variable _level0.level = 60
Variable _level0.i = 60
Variable _level0.ranRed = 98
Variable _level0.ranGreen = 91
Variable _level0.ranBlue = 211
Variable _level0.curveColor = 6446035
Variable _level0.curveAlpha = 40
Movie Clip: Target="_level0.Curves1"
Movie Clip: Target="_level0.Curves2"
Movie Clip: Target="_level0.Curves3"
Movie Clip: Target="_level0.Curves4"

11.4: When you select Debug ➢ List Variables, the Output panel lists all of the variables that are loaded.

The List Variables option shows all of the variables that are loaded and their values (11.4). Using this option, you can find out all of the variables Flash has loaded at a specific time and see how they are related to each other. Sometimes you want to see all of the variables, but you don't want to put a `trace()` in for each one, so you simply select List Variables.

The only downside to using these two features is that they clear the Output panel each time, so you can't do a comparison in real time very easily. For example, you couldn't easily compare all the variables and their values at the start of the movie to the variables and their values in the middle of the movie. The Output panel only shows one list at a time.

The Debugger

The Flash MX Debugger is the most powerful and all-encompassing debugging tool available to Flash. You might wonder why we didn't suggest that you use it first. The short answer is that it takes more time to use the Debugger than it does to use the other tools. You don't want to resort to using the Debugger if you can easily and more quickly root out the problem with the other debugging tools. The Debugger is most useful when you have no idea what is wrong with your script.

Setting Breakpoints

To use the Debugger, you simply add a breakpoint or a couple of breakpoints in the code and then run the movie using the Debugger. A *breakpoint* simply stops the code at the exact place you tell it to. You can place as many breakpoints as you need. When the Debugger gets to a breakpoint as it executes your code, it will pause to display the current values of variables or other information you request. Be sure to look at all of the variables, not just the ones you suspect are causing problems.

Here are the steps for running the Debugger and setting a breakpoint:

WWW.

1. Open the **Chapter11_A.fla** file. This will be used to inspect the Debugger.
2. Make sure you have the Debugging Permitted option selected in the Publish Settings dialog box. Choose File ➢ Publish Settings and click the Flash tab. The Debugging Permitted option is the fourth check box in the Options section (see 11.1 earlier in this chapter).
3. Open the ActionScript on the Actions layer. Place the cursor within line 4 of code, the third `DrawLine()` function call. Click the Debug Options button (it looks like a stethoscope) on the right side of the Actions panel toolbar, and select Set Breakpoint (11.5).
4. Flash places a red dot next to the line you've selected (11.6). Now run the movie in Debug mode by choosing Control ➢ Debug Movie. This will start your movie and open the Debugger panel.

   The first thing you'll see is the Debugger panel with a text message at the top, giving you an opportunity to change the placement of the breakpoints (11.7). You'll

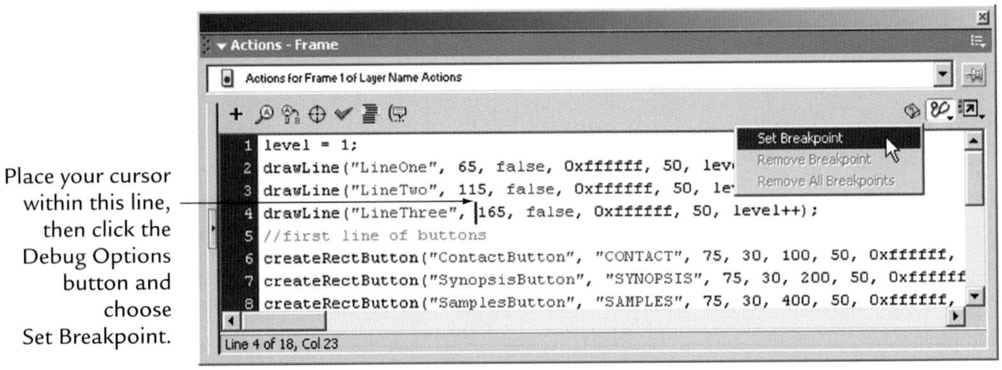
Place your cursor within this line, then click the Debug Options button and choose Set Breakpoint.
Actions - Frame
Actions for Frame 1 of Layer Name Actions
Set Breakpoint
Remove Breakpoint
Remove All Breakpoints
1 level = 1;
2 drawLine("LineOne", 65, false, 0xffffff, 50, lev
3 drawLine("LineTwo", 115, false, 0xffffff, 50, le
4 drawLine("LineThree", 165, false, 0xffffff, 50, level++);
5 //first line of buttons
6 createRectButton("ContactButton", "CONTACT", 75, 30, 100, 50, 0xffffff,
7 createRectButton("SynopsisButton", "SYNOPSIS", 75, 30, 200, 50, 0xffffff
8 createRectButton("SamplesButton", "SAMPLES", 75, 30, 400, 50, 0xffffff,
Line 4 of 18, Col 23

11.5: Setting a breakpoint

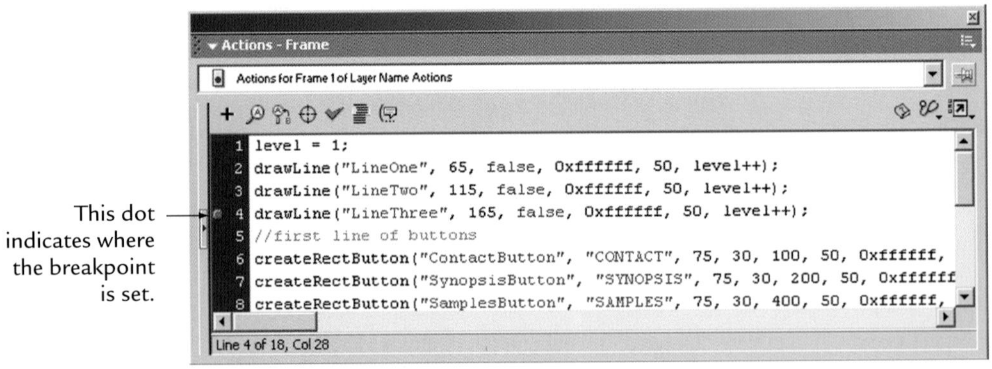
This dot indicates where the breakpoint is set.
Actions - Frame
Actions for Frame 1 of Layer Name Actions
1 level = 1;
2 drawLine("LineOne", 65, false, 0xffffff, 50, level++);
3 drawLine("LineTwo", 115, false, 0xffffff, 50, level++);
4 drawLine("LineThree", 165, false, 0xffffff, 50, level++);
5 //first line of buttons
6 createRectButton("ContactButton", "CONTACT", 75, 30, 100, 50, 0xffffff,
7 createRectButton("SynopsisButton", "SYNOPSIS", 75, 30, 200, 50, 0xffffff
8 createRectButton("SamplesButton", "SAMPLES", 75, 30, 400, 50, 0xffffff,
Line 4 of 18, Col 28

11.6: Flash adds a red dot to the left of the line of code to indicate that a breakpoint has been set.

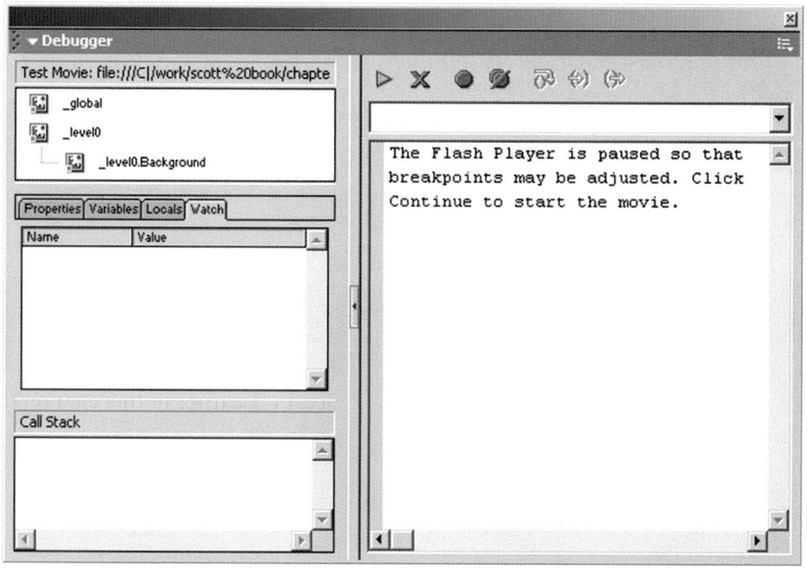

11.7: The Flash Debugger panel

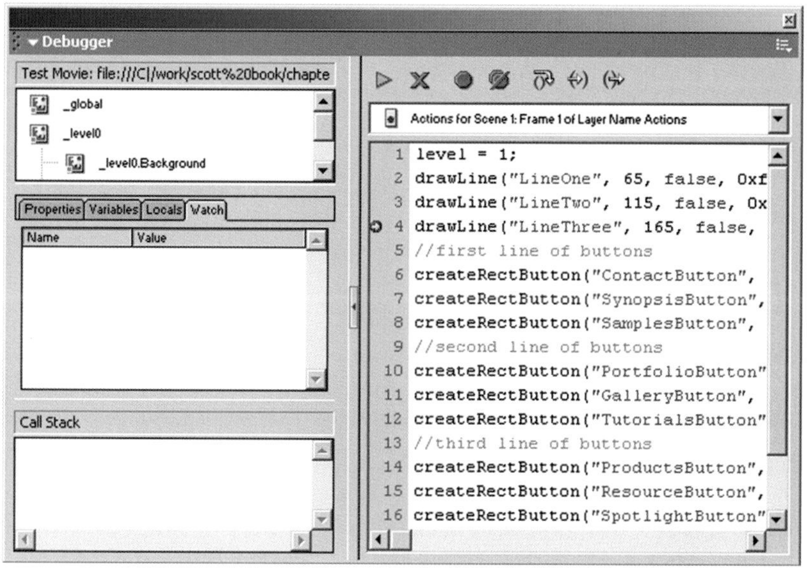

11.8: The Debugger paused at the breakpoint.

get this message whenever you debug a movie for the first time. The movie is actually waiting for the Debugger to signal it to start.

5. Click the Continue button (the green arrow) on the left side of the Debug panel toolbar to proceed. This will start the movie. The movie will run until it hits the breakpoint (11.8).

Take a look at the Debugger panel. On the right side are the lines of code in the Actions layer displayed in the code view pane. Notice the red dot and a yellow arrow at the

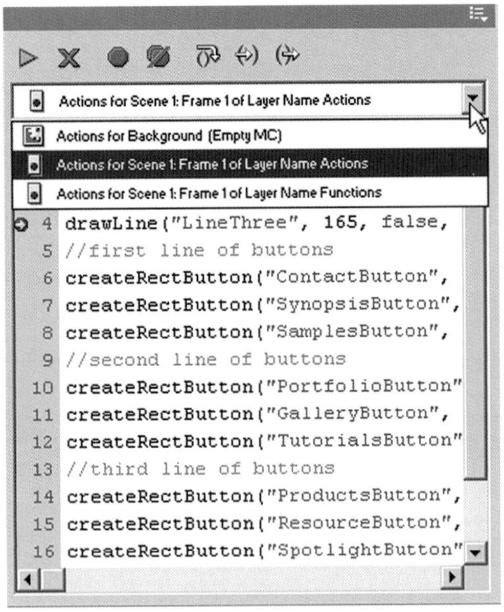
Actions for Scene 1: Frame 1 of Layer Name Actions
Actions for Background (Empty MC)
Actions for Scene 1: Frame 1 of Layer Name Actions
Actions for Scene 1: Frame 1 of Layer Name Functions
4 drawLine("LineThree", 165, false,
5 //first line of buttons
6 createRectButton("ContactButton",
7 createRectButton("SynopsisButton",
8 createRectButton("SamplesButton",
9 //second line of buttons
10 createRectButton("PortfolioButton"
11 createRectButton("GalleryButton",
12 createRectButton("TutorialsButton"
13 //third line of buttons
14 createRectButton("ProductsButton",
15 createRectButton("ResourceButton",
16 createRectButton("SpotlightButton"

11.9: The Debugger panel drop-down list of available ActionScript

line on which you put your breakpoint. Let's explore the other Debugger panel tools.

Using the Debugger Panel

At the top of the right side of the Debugger panel is a drop-down list that shows you where all your ActionScript is and allows you display any of your ActionScript in the code view pane (11.9). Choosing another section of code from this list does not execute the code; it just displays it.

On the top-left side of the Debugger panel is the status bar. This shows you what file you are currently debugging.

Below the status bar is the display list. This shows you all the available movie clips and objects that you've created at this point in time of the movie. Currently, this window shows two main movie clips: `_global` and `_level0`. All of your movies will have these two movie clips. The `_level0` movie clip represents anything—variables or objects—on the `_root` or main timeline. The `_global` movie clip is almost the same thing, except it represents anything that you have specifically assigned as `_global`. You can specifically assign variables and functions as global. In this book, we have effectively done the same thing by placing variables and functions on the main timeline and referring to them using the `_root` keyword. Under the `_level0` movie clip are three more movie clips. These are the movie clips that have been created by the ActionScript.

Under the display list is a window with four tabs:

Properties The Properties tab displays all of the properties affiliated with the selected movie clip (11.10). Click the Properties tab and notice that there is a list of properties and the values. You can inspect and change the values of any property that is not grayed out.

Variables The Variables tab also applies to the selected movie clip. It displays all the variables available. If you select the `_global` movie clip, you'll see that there are no variables that have been made global; all the variables are in the `_level0` movie clip.

Locals The Locals tab shows only variables that are local to the particular place you have stopped. In this case, you stopped on the main timeline, so all the variables are the same as for the Variables tab. If you stop within a movie clip, the Locals tab would show only those variables defined within the movie clip.

Watch The Watch tab is where you can pay special attention to certain variables of your choosing. Sometimes there is a long list of variables within a movie clip. To make it easier to see what is happening, you can track one or more variables in the Watch window. To add a variable to the Watch window, click the Watch tab and select Add from the pop-up menu.

Within each of these tabs, you cannot only see what the value is, but you can also change it. This will affect the code as it's running. For example, you could change the value of `level` to be 100, and whatever code was executed after the change would have `level` starting with the value of 100.

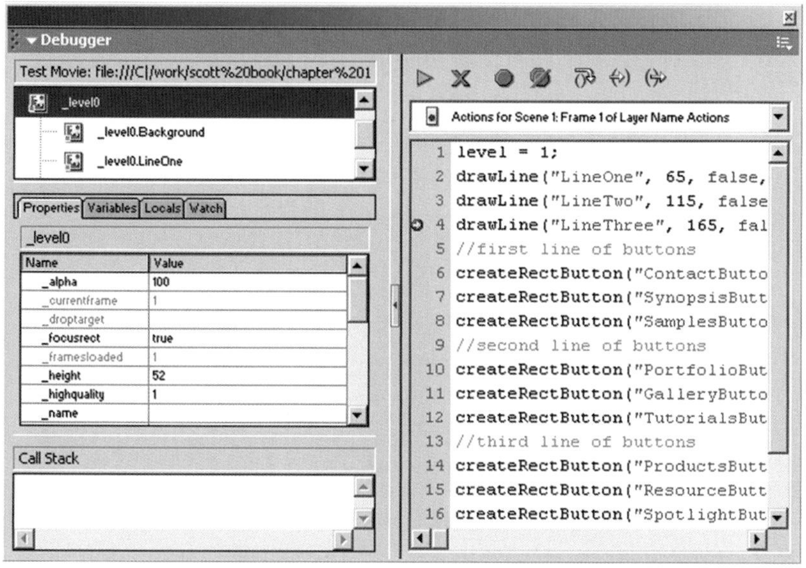

11.10: *The Debugger panel's Properties tab displays a list of the available properties for the selected movie clip.*

Finally, beneath the tabbed window on the left is the Call Stack. The Call Stack displays which function is currently being executed and all nested functions. It's very useful to see the order in which functions are called. If a movie clip calls a function that then calls a function, in the Call Stack, you'll see the order that these functions are called and where the functions are being called. Right now, there is nothing on the Call Stack because you are looking at the main timeline.

Stepping through Your Code

After you reach a breakpoint, you may want to step through one line of code at a time as it executes. This allows you to see exactly what is happening in your code and discover where there are problems.

The three Step buttons (arrows) on the right side of the Debugger panel toolbar allow you to step through your code. Each does something slightly different. The first button, Step Over, executes the line of code that you are currently on and goes to the line of code that is directly below it. The second button, Step In, executes this line of code, and if it is a function, you move into the first line of the function. The third button, Step Out, is valid only if you are in a function. This button executes all of the code within the function and takes you back to where the function was called.

To step through the code, click the Step In button (the middle arrow) on the Debugger panel toolbar.

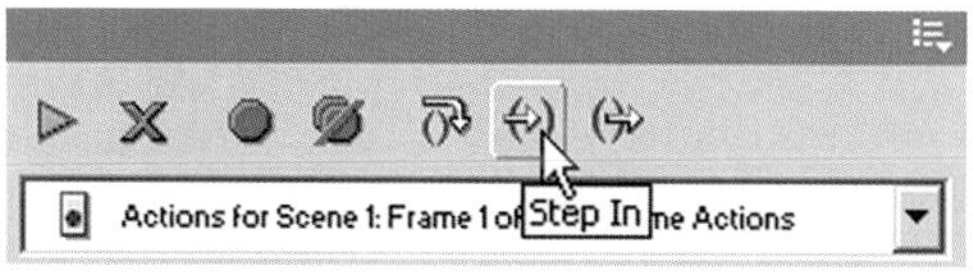

You are now within the `drawLine()` function, about to execute the first line of code. Notice the yellow arrow, which shows you the line of code you are about to execute. Also notice that the Call Stack shows that you are within the `drawLine()` function (11.11).

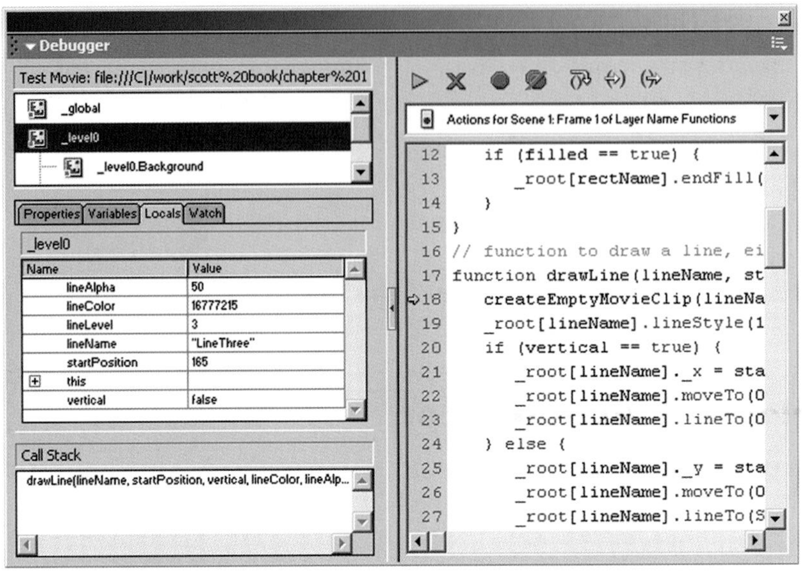

11.11: Stepping into the `drawLine()` *function*

Click the Step In button again. This does not take you into the `createEmptyMovieClip()` function, because it's a built-in function. The yellow arrow moves to the next line. If you look at the display list, you'll see that there is now another movie clip called LineThree.

You can continue using the Step In button to move through the function and all the rest of the ActionScript. Watch how the movie clips appear in the display list and how the variable values change as you move through the code. When you're ready to continue, close the Debugger panel. This will immediately execute the rest of the code and take you back to the Flash Player.

The purpose of setting and monitoring breakpoints is so that you can see what is going on at any given step as the movie progresses. You would usually want to add breakpoints at places in the code where you suspect the problem is occurring. As you step through the ActionScript using the Debugger, you can see exactly what is happening as Flash plays the movie. When you see something that is not occurring as expected or desired, you will have a clue to what the problem is.

NOTE Using the Debugger is an excellent way to get a feel for how ActionScript works. However, the Debugger only shows you what is happening in the code. If you don't know what is supposed to be happening, you can use the Debugger all day long, and you're not going to be able to find the problem. So it's a good exercise to get familiar with the Debugger and the way ActionScript works on code that does not have any problems. This way, when it's time to fix a problem, you'll actually know what to look for and how the Debugger works.

Although the Debugger is time-consuming compared to the other debugging tools, this can actually be an advantage. The time it takes to run the Debugger slows you down, forcing you to look at the code and the values. It might slow you down enough to stop assuming you know what is going on and actually see what is happening.

A Second Set of Eyes (and Ears)

If you've spent hours trying to figure out what's going on (and you shouldn't wait that long), you have one last recourse for debugging help: Get someone else to look at your code. It's best if they stand over your shoulder while you explain it. If they can't physically be there, send them the code so they can look at it while you're talking.

Explaining your code to someone else forces you to think about everything it's doing. Often, the other person won't even need to say anything. Typically, you'll figure out what is wrong just by talking about your code. If this happens, you'll say, "Thanks a lot." The other person will say, "But I didn't do anything," but they did. Just by listening, they were the catalyst for finding the problem.

Fixing Problematic ActionScript

Now that you have reviewed all of the debugging tools available, let's see them in action. You'll look at some examples of problematic ActionScript and use the debugging tools to fix them.

You'll open a few different Flash files that have bugs in them and walk through how to find the problem. All of the examples are based on the movie you created in the last example in Chapter 9, which created a user interface completely with the drawing methods (Chapter9_C_Final).

Problem 1: Nothing Happens When You Test the Movie

Open the Chapter11_B_Start.fla file. Save the file to your local hard drive with the name Chapter11_B_Modified.fla. (To see a fixed version of this movie, open Chapter11_B_Final.fla.)

WWW.

1. Test the movie. Nothing appears, but there is no warning box. You should be seeing the menu. What could be happening? You need to use the debugging tools to find out what's wrong. You've already used Test Movie and gotten as much information as you can from this tool. So you move onto your next debugging tools, in order.
2. In the Actions panel, click the Auto Format button (11.12). Open the different sections of code and use the Auto Format button for each section. There is code attached to the Functions layer, the Actions layer, and the invisible movie clip in the upper-left corner of the stage. You're looking for an "unable to Auto Format" warning box, but you won't see one.

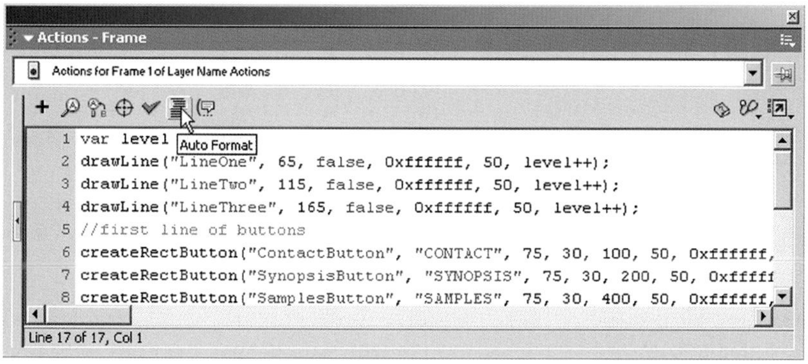
Actions - Frame
Actions for Frame 1 of Layer Name Actions
Auto Format
1 var level
2 drawLine("LineOne", 65, false, 0xffffff, 50, level++);
3 drawLine("LineTwo", 115, false, 0xffffff, 50, level++);
4 drawLine("LineThree", 165, false, 0xffffff, 50, level++);
5 //first line of buttons
6 createRectButton("ContactButton", "CONTACT", 75, 30, 100, 50, 0xffffff,
7 createRectButton("SynopsisButton", "SYNOPSIS", 75, 30, 200, 50, 0xfffff
8 createRectButton("SamplesButton", "SAMPLES", 75, 30, 400, 50, 0xffffff,
Line 17 of 17, Col 1

11.12: View the various elements of the movie that have code and click the Auto Format button to see if an error message will appear.

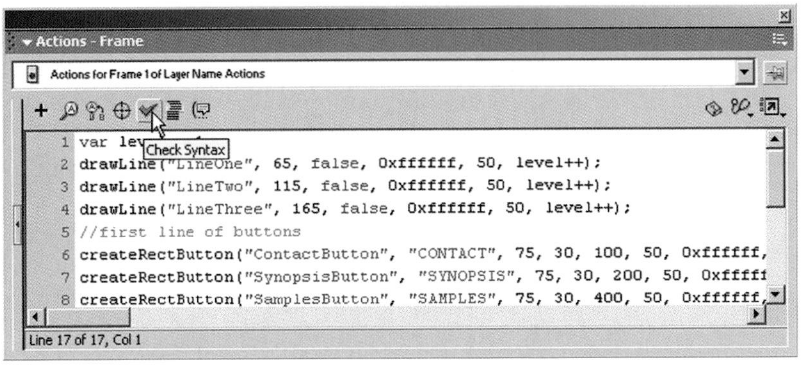
Actions - Frame
Actions for Frame 1 of Layer Name Actions
Check Syntax
var lev
drawLine("LineOne", 65, false, 0xffffff, 50, level++);
drawLine("LineTwo", 115, false, 0xffffff, 50, level++);
drawLine("LineThree", 165, false, 0xffffff, 50, level++);
//first line of buttons
createRectButton("ContactButton", "CONTACT", 75, 30, 100, 50, 0xffffff,
createRectButton("SynopsisButton", "SYNOPSIS", 75, 30, 200, 50, 0xfffff
createRectButton("SamplesButton", "SAMPLES", 75, 30, 400, 50, 0xffffff,
Line 17 of 17, Col 1

11.13: View the various elements of the movie that have code and click the Check Syntax button to see if an error message will appear.

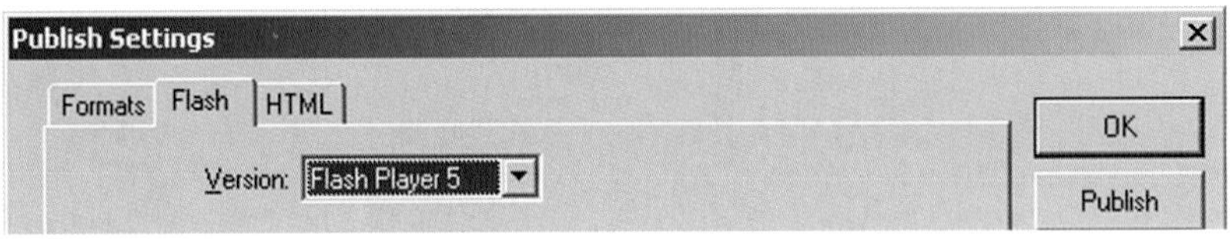
Publish Settings
Formats
Flash
HTML
Version:
Flash Player 5
OK
Publish

11.14: The version is set to Flash 5 in the Publish Settings dialog box, and that version doesn't work with the drawing methods in the script.

Using the Auto Format button will not produce an error message in this example. This hasn't given you much information about the problem, but now you know that it's not in the formatting. So move on to the next tool.

3. Click the Check Syntax button (11.13). Look for warning boxes with information in the Output panel. Note that in troubleshooting a real-world problem, you would not need to do this extra step now; any syntax error would have been flagged when you clicked the Auto Format button.
4. It's pretty clear that the problem is not in the code syntax anywhere, so next check the Publish Settings dialog box. Select File ➢ Publish Settings and click the Flash tab to see what version of Flash you are set to publish to. Here is where the problem lies. The settings are set to Flash 5 (11.14), and the drawing method is not supported in Flash 5. Notice you did not get any type of error message that warned you that the drawing methods are not supported in Flash 5.
5. In the Publish Settings dialog box, change the Version setting to Flash 6 and click OK.
6. Test the movie again. It should run without any problems.

Problem 2: The Movie Loads Slowly and Aborts

WWW.

Open the Chapter11_C_Start.fla file. Save the file to your local hard drive with the name Chapter11_C_Modified.fla. (To see a fixed version of this movie, open Chapter11_C_Final.fla.)

1. Test the movie. Notice that it takes a long time to load. Then you get the message asking if you want to abort the script (11.15). Click the Yes button.

   After you click the Yes button, Flash displays what it was able to accomplish before it ran into the infinite loop (11.16). This gives you a hint about what might be the

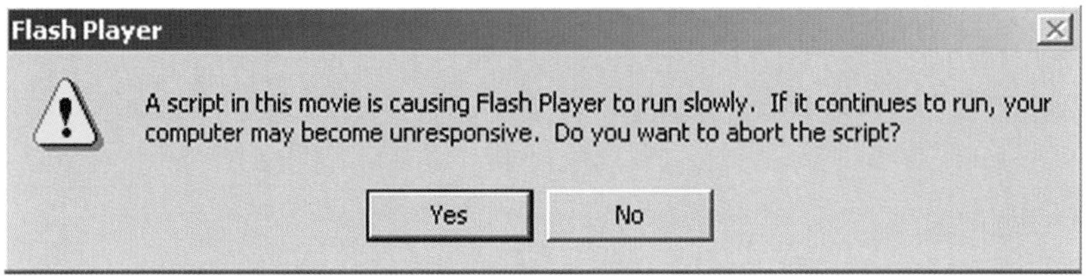

11.15: The example contains an infinite loop.

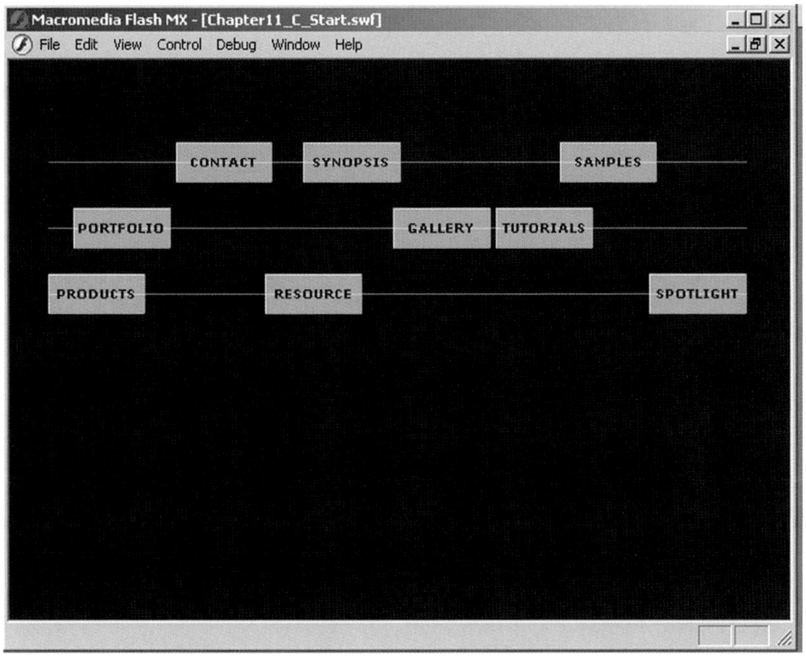

11.16: Flash displays what it can, which provides you with a clue to where the problem lies.

problem. Usually, you'll have a good idea of what the movie should look like, so you can see what's missing. You can assume that the problematic code has something to do with what Flash couldn't produce. In this case, you can see that the script got as far as drawing the buttons but not the colored background. What does that suggest? Since the background is not working, it's likely that the problem is in the code attached to the Background movie clip.

At this point, you have gotten some information from Test Movie, and you might consider skipping some of the debugging options, but if you get in the habit of going over each possible problem in the same order each time, you will be less likely to miss something.

2. Click the Auto Format button. No messages appear.
3. Click the Check Syntax button. Again, there are no messages about syntax errors.
4. Check the Publish Settings dialog box. Actually, you already know this is not the problem because the drawing methods worked (well, at least some of them).

5. It's time to dig in and try the `trace()` function. Add a `trace()` statement in the code that you think has the problem. Since the background is not being drawn, this is where to put a `trace()` statement. The background code is attached to the Background movie clip. Add one `trace()` statement within the `onClipEvent(load)` event handler code, at the top, to make sure that the code is getting loaded:

   ```
   trace( "in load" );
   ```

   Also add a `trace()` statement within the `for` loop section to make sure it's looping. It should look something like this:

   ```
   trace( "in for loop" + i);
   ```

   Again, each `trace()` statement should say something that pertains to where it's placed. Also notice that the `trace()` statement within the loop is returning the `i` variable, which is the counter. This way, you can see how many times it's looping—if it's looping at all.

NOTE It's not a bad idea to hit the Auto Format button after you enter your debugging `trace()` statements to make sure you didn't inadvertently introduce syntax errors with your `trace()` statements.

---

6. Test this and see what appears in the Output panel. Since you haven't fixed the problem yet, it will still stall and give you the abort message. After you click the Yes button, you'll see information in the Output panel (11.17).

   In the Output panel, you don't see the `"in load"` statement, but you do see a bunch of `"in for loop 1"` statements. These wouldn't be displayed if the movie hadn't loaded. There are so many `"in for loop 1"` statements that the `"in load"` statement has been removed. (There is only so much the Output panel can handle.) You would expect to see the number after the `"in for loop"` to increment one each time. It should not be always equal to 1. This means that somewhere the variable `i` is either not getting incremented or is being reset to 1 after it is incremented.
7. Look at the code and see that the problem is in the `for` loop itself, the line that reads:

   ```
   for (var i = 1; i < 100; i) {
   ```

   But it needs to increment the `i` in the last section.
8. Fix the code by adding the ++ operator, so that it reads as follows (11.18):

   ```
   for (var i = 1; i < 100; i++) {
   ```
9. Test the movie to see if you've fixed the problem.

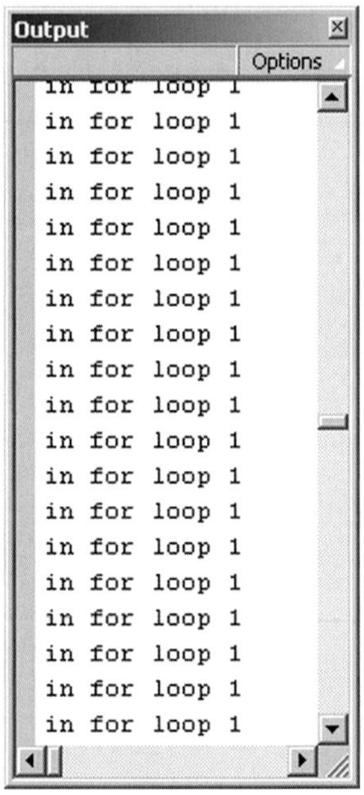

11.17: The Output panel displays the results of the `trace()` statement.

In this example, the `trace()` statement was helpful in letting you know where to look. Since the value of the `i` variable was not incrementing, it provided the necessary clue for you to look in the `for` loop to make sure it was written properly.

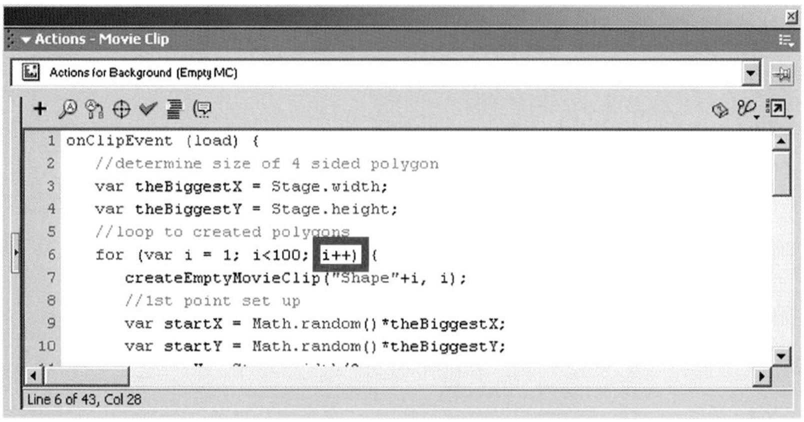

11.18: Fix the `for` *loop so that it increments the* `i` *variable.*

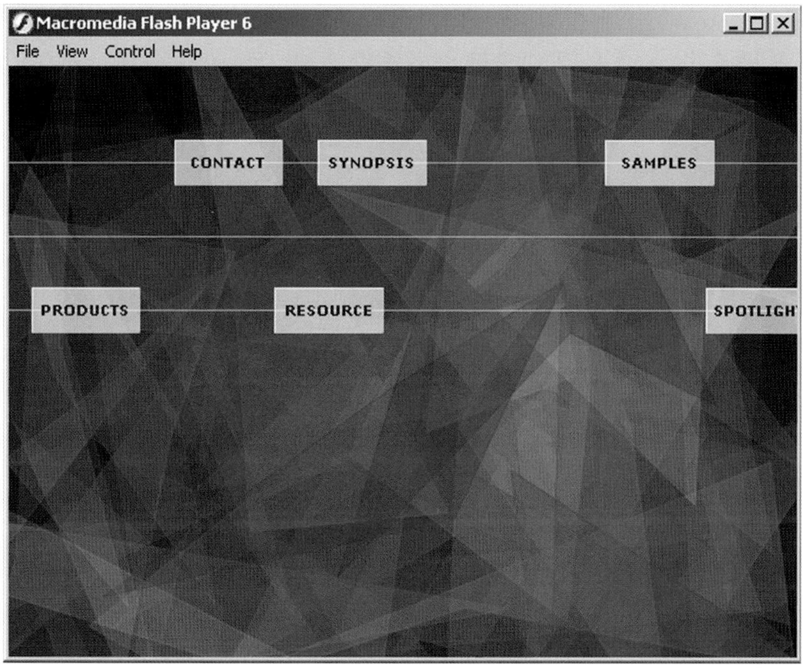

11.19: The buttons on the second line went AWOL.

Problem 3: Some of the Movie's Buttons Don't Appear

Open the Chapter11_D_Start.fla file. Save the file to your local hard drive with the name Chapter11_D_Modified.fla. (To see a fixed version of this movie, open Chapter11_D_Final.fla.)

1. Test the movie and observe the results. It loads fast enough, but there are supposed to be buttons on all three of the lines, and they aren't there (11.19). Once again, you can easily jump to the debugging tool you think is the most obvious choice, but in some cases, you'll spend more time because you overlooked something. Let's go ahead and use each debugging tool.

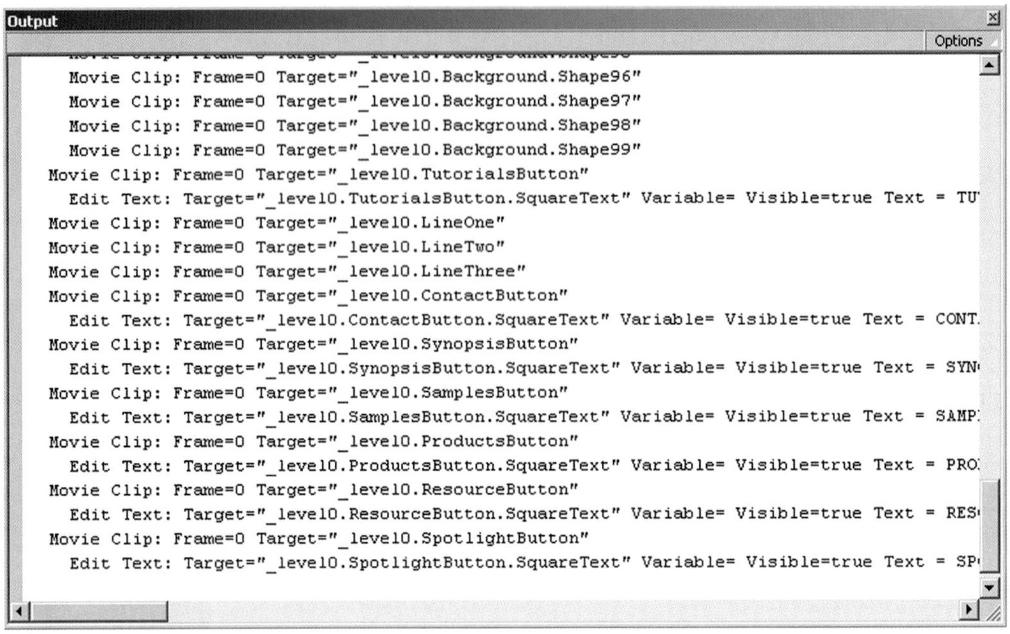
Output
Options
Movie Clip: Frame=0 Target="_level0.Background.Shape96"
Movie Clip: Frame=0 Target="_level0.Background.Shape97"
Movie Clip: Frame=0 Target="_level0.Background.Shape98"
Movie Clip: Frame=0 Target="_level0.Background.Shape99"
Movie Clip: Frame=0 Target="_level0.TutorialsButton"
Edit Text: Target="_level0.TutorialsButton.SquareText" Variable= Visible=true Text = TU
Movie Clip: Frame=0 Target="_level0.LineOne"
Movie Clip: Frame=0 Target="_level0.LineTwo"
Movie Clip: Frame=0 Target="_level0.LineThree"
Movie Clip: Frame=0 Target="_level0.ContactButton"
Edit Text: Target="_level0.ContactButton.SquareText" Variable= Visible=true Text = CONT.
Movie Clip: Frame=0 Target="_level0.SynopsisButton"
Edit Text: Target="_level0.SynopsisButton.SquareText" Variable= Visible=true Text = SYN
Movie Clip: Frame=0 Target="_level0.SamplesButton"
Edit Text: Target="_level0.SamplesButton.SquareText" Variable= Visible=true Text = SAMP
Movie Clip: Frame=0 Target="_level0.ProductsButton"
Edit Text: Target="_level0.ProductsButton.SquareText" Variable= Visible=true Text = PRO
Movie Clip: Frame=0 Target="_level0.ResourceButton"
Edit Text: Target="_level0.ResourceButton.SquareText" Variable= Visible=true Text = RES
Movie Clip: Frame=0 Target="_level0.SpotlightButton"
Edit Text: Target="_level0.SpotlightButton.SquareText" Variable= Visible=true Text = SP

11.20: The Output panel displays the objects.

2. Click the Auto Format button. Open the different sections of code and use the Auto Format button for each section. Look for the "unable to Auto Format" warning box. It doesn't appear.
3. Click the Check Syntax button. Look for warning boxes and information in the Output panel. Again, no syntax errors are found.
4. Check the Flash tab of the Publish Settings dialog box (even though you know that some of the drawing methods work, so the Publish Version setting is not the problem).
5. You could put a `trace()` statement in the code that you think has the problem, but first let's see if the objects even exist. Test the movie and select Debug ➢ List Objects. The Output panel lists quite a lot of information (11.20). The objects are listed in the order they are created: first all the background polygons, then the three lines, and then the buttons. Notice that there are only six buttons listed in the Output panel.

   The three buttons that are missing on the stage are not actually created. This provides you with a clue: There is a problem with the creation of these three buttons. Let's put a breakpoint at the first problematic button and see what happens. Also, let's put a breakpoint on the button before it. Sometimes it's helpful to see what the correct behavior is so you can tell what's broken.
6. Open the Actions panel and look at the code assigned to the Actions layer. Add two breakpoints in the Actions panel for following lines (11.21):

   ```
   createRectButton("SamplesButton", "SAMPLES", 75, 30, 400, 50, ▶
   0xffffff, level++);
   ```

   and

   ```
   createRectButton("PortfolioButton", "PORTFOLIO", 30, 20, 100, ▶
   0xffffff, level++);
   ```

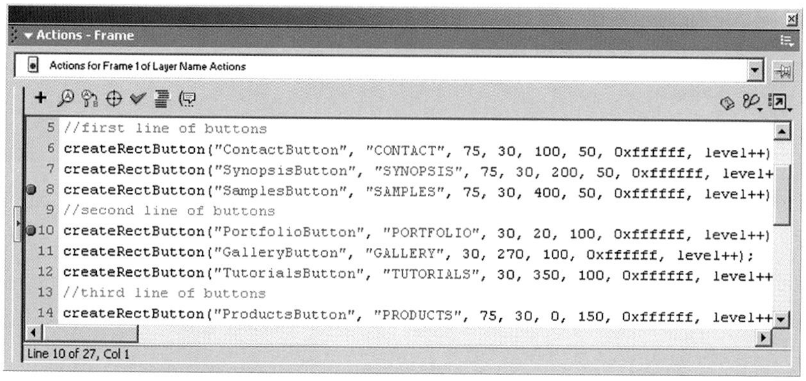
Actions - Frame
Actions for Frame 1 of Layer Name Actions
5 //first line of buttons
6 createRectButton("ContactButton", "CONTACT", 75, 30, 100, 50, 0xffffff, level++)
7 createRectButton("SynopsisButton", "SYNOPSIS", 75, 30, 200, 50, 0xffffff, level+
8 createRectButton("SamplesButton", "SAMPLES", 75, 30, 400, 50, 0xffffff, level++)
9 //second line of buttons
10 createRectButton("PortfolioButton", "PORTFOLIO", 30, 20, 100, 0xffffff, level++)
11 createRectButton("GalleryButton", "GALLERY", 30, 270, 100, 0xffffff, level++);
12 createRectButton("TutorialsButton", "TUTORIALS", 30, 350, 100, 0xffffff, level++
13 //third line of buttons
14 createRectButton("ProductsButton", "PRODUCTS", 75, 30, 0, 150, 0xffffff, level++
Line 10 of 27, Col 1

11.21: Add two breakpoints.

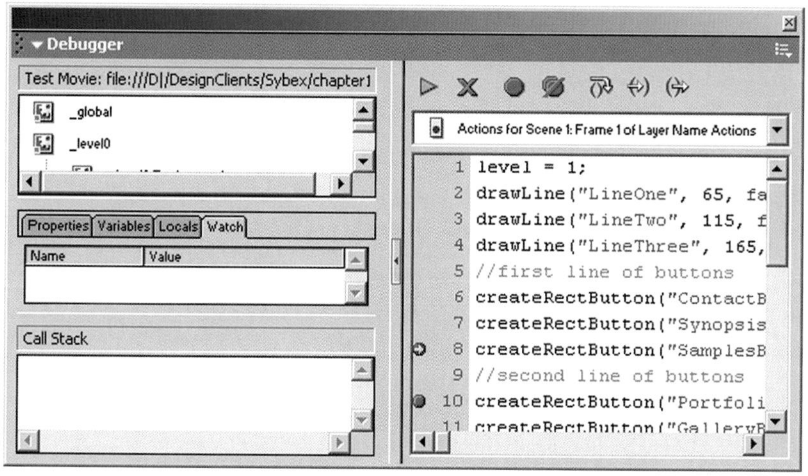
Debugger
Test Movie: file:///D|/DesignClients/Sybex/chapter1
_global
_level0
Properties
Variables
Locals
Watch
Name
Value
Call Stack
Actions for Scene 1: Frame 1 of Layer Name Actions
1 level = 1;
2 drawLine("LineOne", 65, fa
3 drawLine("LineTwo", 115, f
4 drawLine("LineThree", 165,
5 //first line of buttons
6 createRectButton("ContactB
7 createRectButton("Synopsis
8 createRectButton("SamplesB
9 //second line of buttons
10 createRectButton("Portfoli

11.22: Click the Continue button to progress to the first breakpoint.

7. Select Debug Movie from the Control menu. This will open the Debugger, ready to run the movie. Click the Continue button (the green arrow), and the Debugger will jump to the first breakpoint, which is for the correctly created button (11.22).
8. You want to step into the function `createRectButton()` to see what is happening for a correctly created button. Click the Step In button (the middle arrow). The Debugger takes you to the function call (11.23).
9. Make sure the Locals tab is selected in the middle left section of the Debugger panel so you can see the variables that are in this function. Step through this function using the Step Over button (the first arrow) and watch the local variables.

   Notice that the `buttonColor` value is a fairly large number, there is a value for the `buttonLevel` variable, and the value of the `buttonY` variable is 50. When you get to the last line of the function, the `setInterval()` line, and you click the Step Over button, you'll be back to the code in the Actions layer and getting ready to execute the line that creates the problem button.

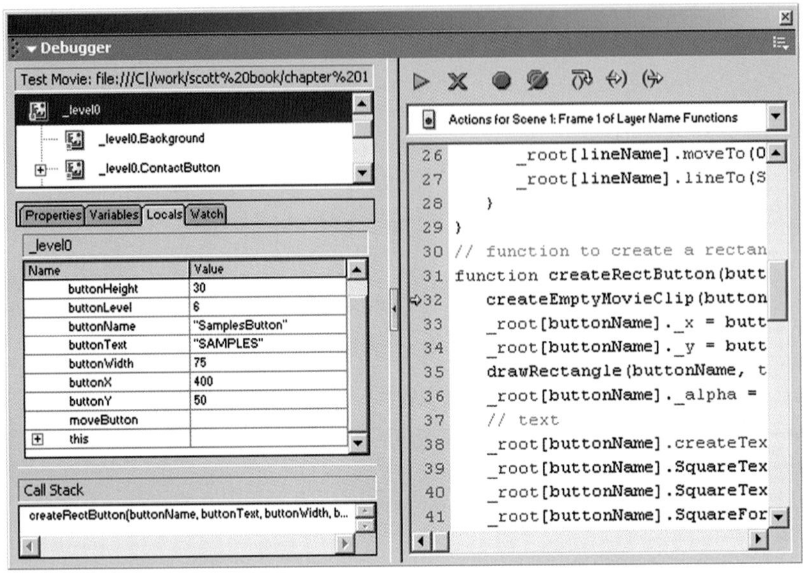

11.23: Click the Step In button to move into the `createRectButton()` function call.

10. Here, once again, you want to step into the `createRectButton()` function to see what's going wrong. Click the Step In button again. Before you go any further, check the variables in the Locals tab (11.24).

    There are a couple of variables that look odd. The `buttonColor` variable is equal to 7; it should be a bigger number, because you want it to be white, and white is definitely not equal to 7. The `buttonLevel` variable is undefined; that's obviously a problem. The `buttonY` variable is a huge number; it looks more like what should be in

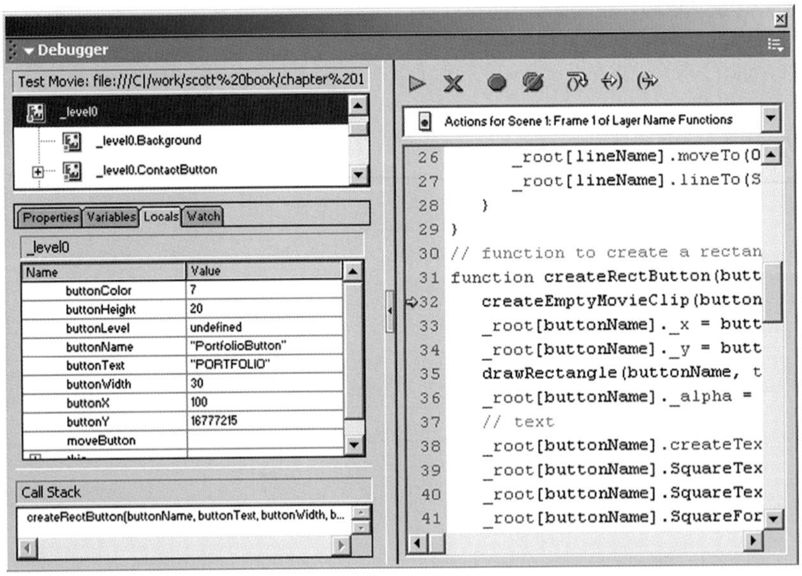

11.24: Several of the variables have odd values.

the `buttonColor` variable. So it looks like there is a problem with the arguments that are being passed into the function.

11. Quit the Debugger, quit testing, and go back to the code on the Actions layer. Look at the call to this function and see what might be the problem. Compare the properly created button with the bad button:

```
createRectButton("SamplesButton", "SAMPLES", 75, 30, 400, 50, ▶
0xffffff, level++);
```

and

```
createRectButton("PortfolioButton", "PORTFOLIO", 30, 20, 100, ▶
0xffffff, level++);
```

It's a little hard to see because the length of the lines seems okay, but there is a number missing between the name of the button and the color of the button. The correctly created button has a total of eight arguments passed in, and the broken button has only seven. If you compare it to the other buttons, you will see that this button is missing the width argument.

12. Add the number `75` before the `30` to all three of the middle buttons that didn't appear when you tested the movie.
13. Test the movie. That was it. You fixed the problem.

Conclusion

This chapter covered Flash MX's debugging tools and gave you some hands-on experience using them. When you first start out, debugging can be a frustrating experience. Of course, the best way to avoid debugging is to write bug-free code. Unfortunately, very few programmers can write perfect code; humans make mistakes.

Finding problems in your code and fixing them will be less painful if you start with the basic guidelines for debugging your code presented in this chapter. As you become more experienced and familiar with your own mistakes, you'll learn to avoid some of them. You'll also know which are the best debugging tools to use when you need them. In the examples in this chapter, we suggested that you walk through all of the debugging tools in sequence. As you become more experienced, however, you'll begin to get a sense of which tools will be most helpful in which situations.

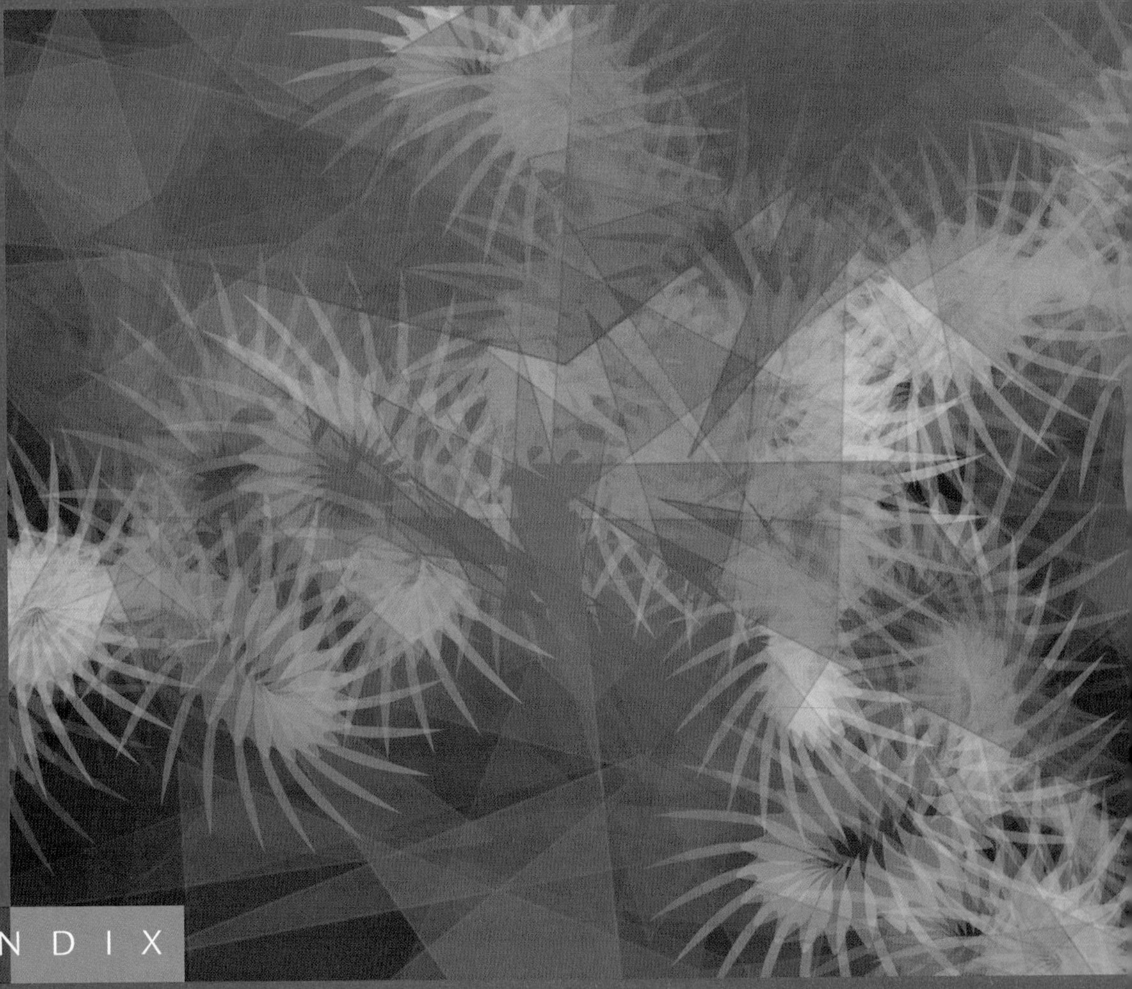

APPENDIX

Appendix

The reference material *in this appendix includes a quick introduction to server-side communications and a handy table of keycodes and ASCII values.*

Exchanging Data with Servers

An important theme throughout this book has been the need to build interaction into your scripts. Flash movies often need to interact not only with human users, but also with other software. For example, consider a site for a ticket or reservation service: The user enters dates and other relevant information and hits the Send button in her browser. Back on the server hosting the site, ActionScript reads this input data and forwards it to a database application, which looks up the availability and sends ActionScript new values to update the display.

ActionScript provides many ways to send data to and from Flash, including the following methods, functions, and objects:

```
getURL()               LoadVars.send()
loadMovie()            LoadVars.sendAndLoad()
loadMovieNum()         XML.load()
loadVariables(         XML.send()
loadVariablesNum()     XML.sendAndLoad()
LoadVars.load()        XMLSocket.send()
```

Each of these tools has a specific use, which you can generally tell from its name. Except for the `XMLSocket` object, each of these tools works in the same way: When sending and retrieving data, it opens a connection to the server just long enough for the data to be transmitted, and then it closes the connection. The connection is established from the Flash movie; the server cannot open the connection.

Using these methods and functions, you can read from a file or exchange data with any server that is set up to pass information. Exchanging data in Flash is not hard, but it can take a little time to master and to decide which method or function works best for your particular application. Of course, it will also help to have some familiarity with data-exchange programming and server-side scripting languages.

Leaving a Connection Open with XMLSocket

The `XMLSocket` object allows for a continuous information stream that stays open until you close it. With the other data-exchange tools, if you need to get the data every second, you must initiate the connection from the Flash side for each time data is exchanged. It takes time to actually open a connection, which means that real-time communication is not possible with any method other than `XMLSocket`.

You can use the `XMLSocket` object and just leave the connection open continuously. This alleviates the need to establish a connection each time you want to send or receive data. This also gives the server a way of contacting Flash and sending updated information.

However, there is one caveat to using `XMLSocket`: it works only with data in the XML format. Using the `XML` object, you have very specific control over the data you wish to send and receive—more control that you have using the other ways of working with external data.

Sending and Receiving Variables

When sending data, you have little control over which variables to send. All the variables that are within the scope are sent. This means that all global variables, as well as any other variables that are within the scope of your call, are sent. For example, if you use one of the `MovieClip` object's methods to load variables, the variables within the scope of the movie clip will include all of your global variables and the variables that are within the movie clip.

A new object, `LoadVars`, allows you to gain more control over which variables to send. The `LoadVars` object sends only the data that is associated with that specific object. For example, to send just the variables *`myName`* and *`myBirth`*, you would first create an instance of the `LoadVars` object, like this:

```
myLoadVars = new LoadVars();
```

Then you would attach the variables to the *`myLoadVars`* object and send it:

```
myLoadVars.myName = "Scott";
myLoadVars.myBirth = "April";
myLoadVars.load(url);
```

There are now two variables named *`myName`* and *`myBirth`* attached to the *`myLoadVars`* object. When you send the *`myLoadVars`* object, it sends only these two variables. You use the `load()` method to pass just these variables.

NOTE The `LoadVars` object offers a great new way to tighten your control of variables. In earlier versions, Flash just spewed all of its information, and the catcher program needed to parse out what it didn't need.

When receiving variables, you can determine when all of the variables are loaded using the `onClipEvent(data)` event handler. This will trigger only when all of the variables are loaded into the movie clip, so you can start processing them. For an example of loading variables with the `onClipEvent(data)` event handler, see the "Creating a Basic Component" section in Chapter 10, "Flash Components" (**Chapter10_A_Final.fla**).

Getting ASCII and Keycode Values

As a tool for reading keyboard input, ActionScript provides the `Key` object. Two of its most important methods are `Key.getAscii()`, which returns the ASCII value of a keystroke, and `Key.getCode()`, which returns the keycode.

Keycodes are proprietary, mapping all keystrokes to specific instructions to Flash. These represent not only alphanumeric characters, but also tasks like cursor movement. In Table A.1, notice that some keys—the function keys, Num Lock, and other keys for controlling computer operations rather than representing data—have only a keycode value. For an example of using the `Key.getCode` method, see the "Adding Keyboard Movement Controls section in Chapter 8, "Games: Responding to Events" (**Chapter8_B_Final.fla**).

ASCII (American Standard Code for Information Interchange) is the standard set of numeric keystroke codes underlying all character sets using the Roman alphabet. It includes only a limited set of control operations.

The ASCII value for a numeral is the same for a number, no matter which key you pressed to type it—a key in the row at the top of the keyboard or a key in the numeric keypad. If you want to know whether a standard keyboard of numeric keypad key was pressed, use the `getCode()` method. With alphabetic keys, uppercase and lowercase letters have different ASCII values, but they have the same keycode values. Use the `getAscii()` method when you need to know the case.

Table A.1: The ASCII Character Set and Keycode Values

Key	ASCII	Keycode
Backspace	8	8
Tab	9	9
Enter (keyboard)	13	13
Enter (number pad)	13	108 (not trappable)
Escape	27	27
Space	32	32
!	33	49
"	34	222
#	35	51
$	36	52
%	37	53
&	38	55
'	39	222
(	40	57

continues

Table A.1: The ASCII Character Set and Keycode Values (continued)

Key	ASCII	Keycode
)	41	48
* (keyboard)	42	56
* (number pad)	42	106
+ (keyboard)	43	187
+ (number pad)	43	107
- (keyboard)	45	189
- (number pad)	45	109
. (keyboard)	46	190
. (number pad)	46	110
/ (keyboard)	47	191
/ (number pad)	47	111
0 (keyboard)	48	48
0 (number pad)	48	96
1 (keyboard)	49	49
1 (number pad)	49	97
2 (keyboard)	50	50
2 (number pad)	50	98
3 (keyboard)	51	51
3 (number pad)	51	99
4 (keyboard)	52	52
4 (number pad)	52	100
5 (keyboard)	53	53
5 (number pad)	53	101
6 (keyboard)	54	54
6 (number pad)	54	102
7 (keyboard)	55	55
7 (number pad)	55	103
8 (keyboard)	56	56
8 (number pad)	56	104
9 (keyboard)	57	57
9 (number pad)	57	105
:	58	186
;	59	186
<	60	188
=	61	187
>	62	190
?	63	191
@	64	50
A	65	65
B	66	66

Table A.1: The ASCII Character Set and Keycode Values (continued)

Key	ASCII	Keycode
C	67	67
D	68	68
E	69	69
F	70	70
G	71	71
H	72	72
I	73	73
J	74	74
K	75	75
L	76	76
M	77	77
N	78	78
O	79	79
P	80	80
Q	81	81
R	82	82
S	83	83
T	84	84
U	85	85
V	86	86
W	87	87
X	88	88
Y	89	89
Z	90	90
[	91	219
\	92	220
]	93	221
^	94	54
_	95	189
`	96	192
a	97	65
b	98	66
c	99	67
d	100	68
e	101	69
f	102	70
g	103	71
h	104	72
I	105	73
j	106	74

continues

Table A.1: The ASCII Character Set and Keycode Values (continued)

Key	ASCII	Keycode
k	107	75
l	108	76
m	109	77
n	110	78
o	111	79
p	112	80
q	113	81
r	114	82
s	115	83
t	116	84
u	117	85
v	118	86
w	119	87
x	120	88
y	121	89
z	122	90
{	123	219
|	124	220
}	125	221
~	126	192
Delete	127	46
Shift		16
Control		17
Alt		18 (not trappable)
Pause/Break		19
Caps Lock		20
Page Up		33
Page Down		34
End		35
Home		36
Left arrow		37
Up arrow		38
Right arrow		39
Down arrow		40
Print Screen		44
Insert		45
F1		112
F2		113
F3		114
F4		115

Table A.1: The ASCII Character Set and Keycode Values (continued)

Key	ASCII	Keycode
F5		116
F6		117
F7		118
F8		119
F9		120
F10		121 (not trappable)
F11		122
F12		123
Num Lock		144
Scroll Lock		145

Index

Note to reader: **Bolded** page references indicate definitions and main discussions of a topic. *Italicized* page references indicate illustrations.

Symbols

A

B

E

F

G

H

L

M

N

O

S

T

U

V

W

X

Y

Z

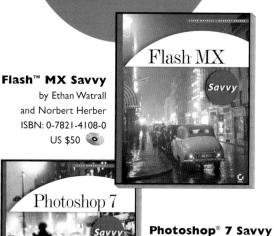

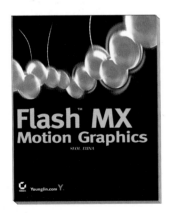